Worlds of Music

AN INTRODUCTION TO THE
MUSIC OF THE WORLD'S PEOPLES

MW01000256

FIFTH EDITION

Jeff Todd Titon
GENERAL EDITOR

WITH

Timothy J. Cooley

David Locke

David P. McAllester

Anne K. Rasmussen

David B. Reck

John M. Schechter

Jonathan P. J. Stock

R. Anderson Sutton

 SCHIRMER

CENGAGE Learning

Australia • Brazil • Japan • Korea • Mexico • Singapore • Spain • United Kingdom • United States

...o the Music
...Peoples
...on

...odd Titon, General Editor, with
...mothy J. Cooley, David Locke,
David P. McAllester, Anne K.
Rasmussen, David B. Reck, John
M. Schechter, Jonathan P. J. Stock,
and R. Anderson Sutton

Publisher: Clark Baxter

Senior Development Editor: Sue Gleason

Senior Assistant Editor: Emily A. Ryan

Editorial Assistant: Nell Pepper

Associate Technology Project Manager:
Morgen Murphy

Marketing Manager: Christina Shea

Marketing Communications Manager:
Heather Baxley

Content Project Manager: Georgia
Young

Creative Director: Rob Hugel

Art Director: Maria Epes

Manufacturing Buyer: Rebecca Cross

Permissions Editor: Bob Kauser

Production Service: Antima Gupta,
Macmillan Publishing Solutions

Text and Cover Designer: Marsha
Cohen, Parallelogram Graphics

Photo Researcher: Bryan Rinnert

Copy Editor: Molly Roth

Cover Image: R. Anderson Sutton

Compositor: Macmillan Publishing
Solutions

© 2009, 2002 Schirmer Cengage Learning

ALL RIGHTS RESERVED. No part of this work covered by the copyright herein may be reproduced, transmitted, stored, or used in any form or by any means graphic, electronic, or mechanical, including but not limited to photocopying, recording, scanning, digitizing, taping, Web distribution, information networks, or information storage and retrieval systems, except as permitted under Section 107 or 108 of the 1976 United States Copyright Act, without the prior written permission of the publisher.

For product information and technology assistance, contact us at
Cengage Learning Customer & Sales Support, 1-800-423-0563

For permission to use material from this text or product, submit all requests online at **www.cengage.com/permissions**
Further permissions questions can be e-mailed to
permissionrequest@cengage.com

Library of Congress Control Number: 2007939783

Student Edition:
ISBN-13: 978-0-534-59539-5

ISBN-10: 0-534-59539-1

Schirmer Cengage Learning
10 Davis Drive
Belmont, CA 94002-3098
USA

Cengage Learning products are represented in Canada by Nelson Education, Ltd.

For your course and learning solutions, visit **academic.cengage.com.**

Purchase any of our products at your local college store or at our preferred online store **www.ichapters.com.**

Printed in Canada
1 2 3 4 5 6 7 8 12 11 10 09

Contents

Recorded Selections   viii

Preface   xvi

The Authors   xxiv

1 The Music-Culture as a World of Music | 1

JEFF TODD TITON

THE SOUNDSCAPE · 1

THE MUSIC-CULTURE · 2

WHAT IS MUSIC? · 4

STRUCTURE IN MUSIC · 8

    Rhythm and Meter 8 / Melody 10 / Harmony 12 / Form 13

A MUSIC-CULTURE PERFORMANCE MODEL · 14

THE FOUR COMPONENTS OF A MUSIC-CULTURE · 18

    Ideas About Music 18 / Activities Involving Music 23 /
    Repertories of Music 26 / Material Culture of Music 29

ECOLOGICAL AND SUSTAINABLE WORLDS OF MUSIC · 30

2 North America/Native America | 33

DAVID P. McALLESTER

THREE DIFFERENT STYLES · 33

    Sioux Grass Dance 33 / Zuni Lullaby 39 /
    Iroquois Quiver Dance 41 / Making a "Cow-Horn" Rattle 41

MUSIC OF THE NAVAJOS · 45

    A Yeibichai Song from the Nightway Ceremony 45 / "Folsom Prison
    Blues" 49 / The Navajo Way of Life 49 / Traditional Popular Music 53 /
    The Circle Dance Song "Shizhané'é" 53 / The Enemyway Ceremony 56 /
    The "Classical" Music of the Navajos 59 / The Life Story of a Navajo
    Ceremonial Practitioner 62 / The Native American Church 68 /
    The Water Drum 71 / The Sun Dance 72 / Navajo Hymn Music 72 /
    New Composers in Traditional Modes 75 / Music with Newly Created Navajo
    Texts and Melodies 77 / New Navajo Music with English Texts
    and Orchestral Accompaniment 77

THE NATIVE AMERICAN FLUTE REVIVAL · 80

3 Africa/Ewe, Mande, Dagbamba, Shona, BaAka | 83

DAVID LOCKE

POSTAL WORKERS CANCELING STAMPS · 84
Generalizations About African Music-Culture 85 / Musical Analysis: Toward Participation 87

AGBEKOR: MUSIC AND DANCE OF THE EWE PEOPLE · 89
The Ewe People 89 / Agbekor: History and Contemporary Performance 91 /
Music of the Percussion Ensemble 96 / Songs 102

MANDE JALIYA, "LAMBANGO" · 110
Historical and Social Background 110 / Music-Culture 112 /
Elements of Performance 113 / A Hearing of "Lambango" 115

A DRUMMER OF DAGBON · 119
The Drums 119 / A Praise Name Dance 119 / Life Story: Abubakari Lunna 121 /

SHONA MBIRA MUSIC · 123
Cultural Context 123 / The Mbira 124 / "Nhemamusasa" 127 /
Thomas Mapfumo and Chimurenga Music 131

THE BAAKA PEOPLE SINGING "MAKALA" · 134
Three Images of the Forest People 135 / "Makala," a Mabo Song 136 /
Music-Culture as an Adaptive Resource 142

CONCLUSION · 143

4 North America/Black America | 145

JEFF TODD TITON

MUSIC OF WORSHIP · 145
MUSIC OF WORK · 156
MUSIC OF PLAY · 164
BLUES · 165
Blues and the Truth 165 / Response to the Lyrics of "Poor Boy Blues" 166 /
Autobiography and the Blues 169 / Learning the Blues 174 / The Blues Scale 176 /
Composing the Blues 177 / A Blues Song in the Making 178 /
How to Make and Play a One-Stringed Diddly-Bow 180 / Social Context and the
Meaning of the Blues 185 / The Blues Yesterday 189 / The Blues Today 199
A FEW FINAL WORDS · 202

5 Europe/Central and Southeastern Regions | 205

TIMOTHY J. COOLEY

EUROPE: AN OVERVIEW · 210
SOCIAL AND POLITICAL ORGANIZATION · 210
Religion and Society 211 / Nationalism and Nation-States 214

THE SOUNDS OF EUROPEAN MUSIC · 215

Rhythm and Meter 215 / Pitches, Scales, and Melody 224 /
Harmony 225 / Summary 229

CASE STUDY: PODHALE, POLISH TATRA REGION · 230

People and Music in Podhale 232 / Genres of *Muzyka Podhala* 232 /
Music for Dancing 238 / Life Story: Krzysztof Trebunia-Tutka 246 /
European Village Music on Stage and in Your Neighborhood 250

EUROPEAN REGIONAL MUSICS ON THE GLOBAL STAGE:
THREE CASE STUDIES · 251

Muzyka Podhala and Reggae 252 / *Balkanski Dzhaz* (Balkan Jazz), Yuri Yunakov,
and Ivo Papasov 256 / Riffing on Music from the "Southern Slavs" 259

REINTERPRETING EUROPE · 262

6 India/South India | 265

DAVID B. RECK

HISTORY, CULTURE, AND MUSIC · 267

The Indus Valley Civilization (c. 2500–c. 1700 B.C.E.) 267 /
The Aryans (c. 1700–c. 500 B.C.E.) 268 / Kingdoms Through the Classic
and Medieval Periods (500 B.C.E.–c. 1400 C.E.) 268 /
The Moghuls (1527–c. 1867) 269 / The Period of British
Colonization (1600s–1947) 270 / Independence and the Modern
Period (1947–Present) 271

MANY MUSICS · 273

Pop Music 273 / Religious Music 276

CLASSICAL MUSIC · 277

The Sound World 279 / Concerts 281 / The Ensemble:
Musical Texture 282 / *Raga:* The Melodic System 284 /
The *Melakarta* System 284 / *Tala:* The Time Cycle 286 /
The Drummer's Art 287

A CARNATIC MUSIC PERFORMANCE · 288

Alapana 292 / *Tanam* 293 / *Kriti* "Sarasiruha" 293 /
Kalpana Svaras 294 / The Drum Solo: *Tani Avartanam* 295

INDIAN MUSIC AND THE WEST · 295

7 Asia/Music of Indonesia | 299

R. ANDERSON SUTTON

CENTRAL JAVA · 301

Gamelan 302 / *Gamelan* Instrumentation 303 /
Gamelan Construction 308 / *Gamelan* Identity 308 /
Gamelan Performance Contexts 308 / *Gamelan* Music: A Javanese *Gendhing*
in Performance 312 / *Irama* Level 321 / Performing Your Own
Gamelan Music 321 / A Javanese *Gendhing* in Soft-Playing Style 322 /
Pathet 322 / A Close Examination of *Ladrang* "Wilujeng" 324 /
Biography of Ki Nartosabdho—A *Gamelan* Musician, Composer, and Puppeteer 330 /
Gamelan Music and Shadow Puppetry 334

BALI · 338
NORTH SUMATRA · 341
INDONESIAN POPULAR MUSIC · 345 /
    Rhoma Irama, *Dangdut* 345 / Responses to Globalization 347

8 *East Asia/China, Taiwan, Singapore, Overseas Chinese* | 353

JONATHAN P. J. STOCK

A MUSICIAN BETWEEN TRADITIONAL AND MODERN WORLDS · 358
A CROSS-SECTION OF CHINESE MUSIC · 364
FOLK SONG · 366
    The Marriage Lament Tradition 366 / Lady Mengjiang 367 /
    Shan'ge (Songs of Agricultural Work, Flirting, and Courting) 369
INSTRUMENTAL ENSEMBLE TRADITIONS · 374
    Jiangnan *Sizhu* 376 / *Beiguan* 379
OPERA AND BALLAD TRADITIONS · 384
    Jingju (Beijing Opera) 384 / Suzhou *Tanci* (Suzhou Ballad Singing) 390
SOLO INSTRUMENTAL TRADITIONS · 393
    Zither (Qin) Solos 393 / *Erhu* Solos 399 / Piano Solos 401
RELIGIOUS TRADITIONS · 403
POPULAR MUSIC · 408
CHINESE MUSIC/WORLD MUSIC? · 414

9 *Latin America/Chile, Bolivia, Ecuador, Peru* | 415

JOHN M. SCHECHTER

CHILEAN *NUEVA CANCIÓN* · 417
    Víctor Jara and Inti Illimani 417 / Violeta Parra 421 /
    The Front Lines of Social Change 423
BOLIVIAN *K'ANTU* · 424
THE QUICHUA OF THE NORTHERN ANDES OF ECUADOR · 431
    The Musical Tradition: *Sanjuán* 433 / A Classic *Sanjuán* 439 /
    African Ecuadorian Music of the Chota River Valley 443
THE ANDEAN ENSEMBLE PHENOMENON: GOING ABROAD · 447
WAWA VELORIO · 453
THE CAREER DILEMMA OF DON CÉSAR MUQUINCHE · 459
AFRO-PERUVIAN MUSIC: A *LANDÓ* · 466
DESPEDIDA, OR FAREWELL · 470

10 *The Arab World* | 473

ANNE K. RASMUSSEN

"ARABIA" · 474

THE *TAKHT* ENSEMBLE · 475

> The Performers and Their Instruments 475 / Musical Texture 476
> Rhythm 477 / Form, Melody, and Improvisation 478 / Tarab 482

CATEGORIES AND TERMINOLOGY: *MIDDLE EAST, ARAB WORLD, MUSLIM WORLD* · 483

RELIGION AND MUSIC IN THE ARAB WORLD · 484

> A Chance Meeting with Sabri Mudallal 485 / The Call to Prayer: *Azan* 485 /
> Music and Islam 490

MUSIC IN HISTORY/MUSIC AS HISTORY · 491

> Musical Life in Medieval Mesopotamia 491 / Interview with Rahim Alhaj,
> Musician from Baghdad 492 / The Ottoman Empire and the Colonial Era 499 /
> Music Theory in the Colonial Era 500 / The Twentieth Century 502

THE MAGHRIB · 502

> The Andalusian Legacy 503 / Independent Morocco 509

THE MUSIC OF CELEBRATION: COMMUNAL MUSIC MAKING AT A WEDDING IN MOROCCO · 510

> The Public Baths 510 / The Wedding Celebration 511 / The *Zaffah*
> Wedding Procession 512 / Wedding Traditions of the Eastern Mediterranean
> Arab World (the Levant) 514

POETRY AND CORE VALUES OF BEDOUIN CULTURE · 516

> *Sirat Bani Hilal* 516 / Theory of Formulaic Composition 517 / Formulaic
> Composition and the Solo *Taqasim* 523

HOMELAND AND DIASPORA: AN UNEXPECTED REACTION · 527

FROM DIASPORA TO GLOBALIZATION: OFRA HAZA AND WORLD BEAT · 529

CONCLUDING REMARKS · 530

11 *Discovering and Documenting a World of Music* | 533

JEFF TODD TITON AND DAVID B. RECK

MUSIC IN OUR OWN BACKYARDS · 533

> Family 534 / Generation and Gender 535 / Leisure 535 /
> Religion 536 / Ethnicity 537 / Regionalism 539 /
> Nationalism 540 / Commodified Music 540

DOING MUSICAL ETHNOGRAPHY · 542

> Selecting a Subject: Some Practical Suggestions 542 / Collecting Information 545 /
> Gaining Entry 545 / Participation and Observation 545 /
> Selecting a Topic 546 / Library and Internet Research 549 / Ethics 551 /
> Field Gear: Notebook, Recorder, Camera 552 / Interviewing 554 /
> Other Means of Collecting Information 557 / Finishing the Project 558

References 560
Credits 589
Index 591

Recorded Selections

CD 1

CHAPTER 1

1. Postal workers canceling stamps at the University of Ghana post office (2:59). The whistled tune is the hymn "Bompata," by the Ghanaian composer W. J. Akyeampong (b. 1900). Field recording by James Koetting. Legon, Ghana, 1975. Used by permission of the artists.
2. Songs of hermit thrushes (0:44). Field recording by Jeff Todd Titon. Little Deer Isle, Maine, 1999.

CHAPTER 2

3. Grass Dance (1:51). Traditional Sioux War Dance. Field recording by Ray Boley, n.d. *Sioux Favorites.* Canyon Records Productions CR-6054. Phoenix, Arizona.
4. Lullaby (0:58). Traditional Zuni song. Performed by Lanaiditsa. Field recording by David McAllester. White Water, New Mexico, 1950.
5. "Gadasjot" (0:47). Iroquois Quiver Dance or Warrior's Stomp Dance song. Twenty Jacobs of Quaker Ridge. Performed by Joshua Billy Buck and Simeon Gibson. Field recording by William Fenton, c. 1942. *Songs from the Iroquois Longhouse.* Archive of Folk Song of the Library of Congress AFS L6. LP. Washington, D.C. Used by permission of collector.
6. Yeibichai (2:15). Navajo dance song from Nightway. Led by Sandoval Begay. Field recording by Willard Rhodes, n.d. Archive of Folk Song of the Library of Congress AFS L41. LP. Washington, D.C. Used by permission of collector.
7. "Folsom Prison Blues" (2:50). Johnny Cash. Published by Hi-Lo Music. Performed by the Fenders on The Fenders, *Second Time Roun'.* LP. Thoreau, New Mexico, 1966. Used by permission The Harry Fox Agency, Inc.
8. "Shizhané'é" ("I'm in Luck") (1:20). Navajo Circle Dance song from Enemyway. Performed by Albert G. Sandoval, Jr., and Ray Winnie. Field recording by David P. McAllester. Sedona, Arizona, 1957. Used by permission of Albert G. Sandoval and Ray Winnie.
9. Navajo Sacred Prayer (0:59). Episode from Navajo Shootingway ceremony. Led by Dinet Tsosie. Field recording by David P. McAllester. Lukachukai, Arizona, 1958. Used by permission of Dinet Tsosie.
10. Hymn of the Native American Church. (1:14). Navajo Peyote song. Performed by George Mitchell and Kaya David. Field recording by Willard Rhodes, n.d. Archive of Folk Song of the Library of Congress AFS 14. LP. Washington, D.C. Used by permission of Willard Rhodes.

11. "Clinging to a Saving Hand" (3:42). Traditional Christian hymn. Performed by the Chinle Galileans. *Navajo Country Gospel* LPS 909. LP. Chinle, Arizona, n.d. Used by permission of Roland Dixon.

12. "Mother Earth" (2:57). Sharon Burch. Performed by Sharon Burch. *Yazzie Girl.* Canyon Records CR-534. © 1989 Sharon Burch. Courtesy Canyon Records Productions, Phoenix, Arizona.

13. "Proud Earth" (3:32). Arliene Nofchissey Williams. Performed by Arliene Nofchissey Williams and Chief Dan George. *Proud Earth.* Salt City Records SC-80. LP. Provo, Utah, n.d. © Arlienne Nofchissey Williams. Used by permission.

14. "Origins" (4:00). R. Carlos Nakai. *Cycles: Native American Flute Music.* Canyon Records Productions CR614-C 1985. Used by permission Canyon Records Productions, Phoenix, Arizona.

Chapter 3

15. *Agbekor* (5:32). Traditional music of the Ewe people. Field recording by David Locke. Anlo-Afiadenyigba, Ghana, 1976. Used by permission of the artists.
    a. Three slow-paced songs (0:00–2:52)
    b. One song in free rhythm (3:02–4:20)
    c. One fast-paced song (4:27–5:32)

16. Demonstration: *Agbekor* (3:54). Performed by David Locke. You will hear the bell by itself, followed by each instrument with the bell (*axatse, kaganu, kidi, kloboto, and totodzi*), and finally, the polyrhythm of all the parts.

17. "Lambango" (3:02). Mande song. Mariatu Kuyateh. Performed by Mariatu Kuyateh, Kekuta Suso, and Seni Jobateh. Field recording by Roderic Knight. The Gambia, 1970. Used by permission of Roderic Knight.

18. "Nag Biegu" ("Ferocious Wild Bull") (2:08). Traditional Praise Name Dance song of Dagbon. Performed by *lunsi* drummers of the Dagbamba people. Field recording by David Locke. Ghana, 1984. Used by permission of the artists.

19. "Nhemamusasa" (lit. "Cutting Branches for Shelter"), *kushaura* section (2:39). Traditional Shona. Field recording by Paul Berliner. Zimbabwe, 1971. Used by permission of Paul Berliner.

20. "Nyarai" ("Be Ashamed"), excerpt (2:29). Thomas Mapfumo. Performed by Thomas Mapfumo and Blacks Unlimited. *Thomas Mapfumo: The Chimurenga Singles, 1976–1980.* Gramma Records Zimbabwe. Shanachie CD 43066.

21. "Makala" (name of unknown person) (2:20). Traditional BaAka song. Field recording by Michelle Kisliuk. Central African Republic, 1988. Used by permission of Michelle Kisliuk.

Chapter 4

22. "Amazing Grace" (2:36). Traditional. Performed by deacon and congregation of the New Bethel Baptist Church. Field recording by Jeff Todd Titon. Detroit, Michigan, 1977. Used by permission of Rev. C. L. Franklin.

23. "Amazing Grace" (2:52). Traditional. Performed by the congregation of the Fellowship Independent Baptist Church, led by Rev. John Sherfey. Field recording by Jeff Todd Titon. Stanley, Virginia, 1977. Used by permission of John Sherfey.

24. Field Holler (0:43). Traditional solo work song. Performed by Leonard "Baby Doo" Caston. Field recording by Jeff Todd Titon. Minneapolis, Minnesota, 1971. (Background noise from the apartment is audible.) Used by permission of Leonard Caston.

25. "Rosie" (2:50). Traditional work song. Performed by prisoners at Mississippi State Penitentiary. Field recording by Alan Lomax. Parchman, Mississippi, 1947. © Alan Lomax. Used by permission of Alan Lomax.

26. "Poor Boy Blues" (3:16). Performed by Lazy Bill Lucas Trio. Field recording by Jeff Todd Titon, Minneapolis, Minnesota, 1970. Used by permission of the artists.

27. "She Got Me Walkin'" (3:01). William "Lazy Bill" Lucas. Performed by Lazy Bill and His Blue Rhythm: Lazy Bill Lucas, piano and vocal; Louis Myers, guitar; Elga Edmonds, drums. Chance 10" 78-rpm record. Chicago, Illinois, 1954. Used by permission of William Lucas.

CD 2

CHAPTER 4 (CONTINUED)

1. "I Need $100" (2:59). Performed by One-String Sam, c. 1956. Detroit, Michigan. Reissued on *Detroit Blues: The Early 1950s.* Blues Classics LP, BC-12.

2. "Kokomo Blues" (2:40). Fred McDowell. Performed by Fred McDowell, vocal and guitar; Jeff Todd Titon, guitar; Mitchell Genova, drums. Field recording by Michael Justen. Minneapolis, Minnesota, July 1970. © Tradition Music, BMI; administered by BUG. Used by permission of the copyright holder.

3. "From Dark Till Dawn" (3:27). John Ned "Johnny" Shines. Performed by Johnny Shines, vocal and guitar. Field recording by Jeff Todd Titon. Beloit, Wisconsin, March 1970. (Background noise from the audience is audible.) Used by permission of the artist and the copyright holder, Uncle Doris Music, ASCAP.

4. "You Don't Love Me" (3:35). Lyrics by Willie Cobbs. Performed by Magic Sam (Sam Maghett), vocal and guitar; Sam Lay, drums; unknown bass player. Field recording by Jeff Todd Titon. Ann Arbor, Michigan, August, 1969. Used by permission of the artists and the copyright holder, Embassy Music Corp., BMI.

5. "Ain't Enough Comin' In" (5:53). Otis Rush. Performed by Otis Rush on *Otis Rush: Ain't Enough Comin' In.* Mercury CD 314518769-2. 1994. © 1994 OTIS RUSH MUSIC, administered by BUG. Used by permission of the copyright holder.

CHAPTER 5

6. Wedding procession (1:33). Singers (*pytace*) Stanisław Krupa and Jan Krzeptowski-Sabała, and a string band consisting of Stanisław Styrczula-Maśniak, lead violin; Sebastian Karpiel-Bułecka, lead violin; Jurek Niton, second violin; Andrzej Frączysty, second violin; Henryk Krzyptowski-Bochać, second violin; and Tadeusz Styrczula-Maśniak, *basy.* Field recording by Timothy J. Cooley. Olcza, Poland, 1995. Used by permission of Stanisław Styrczula-Maśniak.

7. "Oifn Pripetshik" (3:49). Mark Warshawsky. Katherine Meizel, voice; Lillie Gordon, violin; and Ralph Lowi, guitar. Arranged by Meizel, Gordon, and Lowi. Studio recording by Kevin Kelly at the University of California, Santa Barbara, 2006. Used by permission of the artists.

8. *Ruchenitsa* (2:14). Performed by Yanko Atanasov Kumitov, *gaida;* Georgi Mitov Uchkov, *kaval;* Vladi Dimitrov, *gudulka;* and Panyo Georgiev Gurgov, *tupan.* Field recording by Timothy Rice. Tenevo, Yambol region, Bulgaria, 1969. Used by permission of Timothy Rice.

9. "Sister, Hold Your Chastity" (0:38). Traditional women's *ganga* song. Performed by Azra Bandić, Mevla Luckin, and Emsija Tatarović. Field recording by Mirjana Laušević. Umoljani village, Bosnia, 1990. Used by permission of Mirjana Laušević.

10. *Pasterska* (pastoral) (0:29). Performed by the troupe Skalni at a festival in Zakopane, Poland. Field recording by Timothy J. Cooley, 1992. Used by permission of troupe directors and performers Krzysztof Trebunia-Tutka, Stanisława Trebunia-Staszel, and Ryszard Gąska.

11. *Wierchowa* (0:52). Performed by Góralska Kapala, from Chicago: Bogusława Łowisz, voice; Jan Rózalowski, lead violin; Stanisław Zatłoka, second violin; and Andrzej

Tokarz, *basy*. Field recording by Diana Lantz. University of California, Santa Barbara, 2003. Used by permission of the collector and artists.

12. *Ozwodna* (1:05). Performed by the troupe Skalni at a festival in Zakopane, Poland. Field recording by Timothy J. Cooley, 1992. Used by permission of troupe directors and performers Krzysztof Trebunia-Tutka, Stanisława Trebunia-Staszel, and Ryszard Gąska.

13. *Góralski* suite part 1: *Ozwodna* (0:57). Performed by Krzysztof Trebunia-Tutka, lead violin; Jan Trebunia-Tutka, second violin and voice; Paweł Trebunia-Tutka, *basy;* with Anna, Marcin, and Aniela Styrczula-Maśniak dancing. Field recording by Timothy J. Cooley. Kościelisko, Poland, 2005. Used by permission of the artists.

14. *Góralski* suite part 2: *Ozwodna* (1:07). Same musicians and dancers as Track 13.

15. *Góralski* suite part 3: *Krzesana* "trzy a ros" (1:26). Same musicians and dancers as Track 13.

16. *Góralski* suite part 4: *Krzesana* "po dwa" (0:54). Same musicians and dancers as Track 13.

17. *Góralski* suite part 5: *Krzesana* "ze stary" and "zielona" (2:07). Same musicians and dancers as Track 13.

18. "Krzesany Po Dwa" ("Going to the Village") (5:04). Music and words adapted by Władysław Trebunia and Norman Grant from traditional songs. Performed by the Twinkle Brothers band and the Trebunia-Tutka family band. Produced by Norman Grant and Włodzimierz Kleszcz. Released by Kamahuk (www.kamahuk.net), Tutki (www.trebunie.pl), and Twinkle Music (www.twinklemusic.com) in 1992 on *Twinkle Inna Polish Stylee: Higher Heights* and rereleased on *Twinkle Brothers, Trebunia-Tutki Greatest Hits* on CD in 1997. Used with permission of the producers and artists.

19. "Kurdzhaliiska Ruchenica" (7:10). Music and arrangement by Ivo Papasov. *Yuri Yunakov & Ivo Papasov: Together Again.* Ivo Papasov, clarinet; Yuri Yunakov, saxophone; Neshko Neshev, accordion; Salif Ali, drum set; Kalin Kirilov, guitar, bass; and Seido Salifoski, *tarabuka.* Traditional Crossroads (BMI), CD 4330, 2005. Used with permission of Traditional Crossroads.

20. "Žuta Baba" (2:59). Traditional words and music, arranged by Mirjana Laušević, Tim Eriksen, and Peter Irvine. Performed by Bosnian/American fusion band *Žabe i Babe.* Tim Eriksen (electric guitar), Peter Irvine (drums), Donna Kwon (voice), Mirjana Laušević (voice, keyboards), and Tristra Newyear (voice). Bison Publishing, BP 110857, 1997.

CHAPTER 7

21. *Bubaran* "Kembang Pacar" ("Red Flower"), *pélog pathet nem* (3:04). Central Javanese *gamelan* music in loud-playing style, performed by musicians affiliated with the royal palace in Yogyakarta. Field recording by R. Anderson Sutton. Yogyakarta, Java, Indonesia, 1980. Used by permission of the artists.

22. Demonstration: *Bubaran* "Kembang Pacar," *pélog pathet nem* (3:55). Balungan melody alone, followed by addition of other instruments one by one. Performed by University of Wisconsin–Madison Javanese *gamelan* ensemble, directed by R. Anderson Sutton. Recorded at the University of Wisconsin, Madison, December 2000.

23. *Ladrang* "Wilujeng" ("safe, secure"), *pélog pathet barang* (8:47). Central Javanese *gamelan* music in "soft-playing" style. Performed by musicians of Ngudya Wirama *gamelan* group under the direction of Ki Suhardi. Field recording by René Lysloff. Yogyakarta, Java, Indonesia, 1980.

CD 3

CHAPTER 7 (CONTINUED)

1. *Playon* "Lasem," *sléndro pathet nem,* Rendition 1 (1:20). Central Javanese *gamelan* music for shadow puppetry. Performed by *gamelan* group under the direction of Ki Suparman. Field recording by R. Anderson Sutton. Yogyakarta, Java, Indonesia, 1974. Used by permission of the artists.

2. *Playon* "Lasem," *sléndro pathet nem,* Rendition 2 (0:33). Central Javanese *gamelan* music for shadow puppetry. Performed by *gamelan* group under the direction of Ki Suparman. Field recording by R. Anderson Sutton. Yogyakarta, Java, Indonesia, 1974. Used by permission of the artists.

3. "Kosalia Arini" (10:48). *Gamelan gong kebyar.* Composed by Wayan Beratha. Performed by STSI (Sekolah Tinggi Seni Indonesia) *gamelan* musicians, directed by Nyoman Windha and Pande Gde Mustika. Recorded by Michael Tenzer and Ketut Gde Asnawa, with Yong Sagita. STSI campus, Denpasar, Bali, August 1998.

4. *Gendang keteng-keteng,* two excerpts (1:58). Traditional Batak music. Performed by ensemble led by Tukang Ginting on *kulcapi.* Field recording by R. Anderson Sutton. Karo Batak highlands of North Sumatra, 1979. Used by permission of the artists.

5. "Begadang II" ("Staying up All Night") (3:33). Popular *dangdut* music. Performed by Rhoma Irama and his Soneta Group. *Begadang II.* Yukawi Indomusic. 1978. Used by permission.

6. "Shufflendang-Shufflending" (4:11). Ethno-jazz fusion, Sundanese. Performed by Krakatau: Dwiki Dharmawan, keyboard; Pra Budidharma, fretless bass; Budhy Haryono, Western drum set ("traps"); joined by Yoyon Darsono, *rebab* and flute; Adhe Rudiana, *kendang;* Elfik Zulfiqar and Tudi Rahayu, *saron;* Zainal Arifin, *bonang.* *Magical Match.* Kita Music. 2000.

7. "Distorsi" ("Distortion") (5:19). Indonesian rock music. Performed by Ahmad Band: Dhani Ahmad Manaf, vocal; Andra Ramadhan, guitar; Bimo, drum; Bongky, bass; Pay, guitar. *Ideologi Sikap Otak.* Aquarius P 9173. 1998.

CHAPTER 6

8. "Engal Kalyanam" ("Our Wedding"), cine song (3:25). Music by M. S. Viswanathan, lyrics by Vali. Performed by P. Susheela, T. M. Soundararajan, P. B. Sreenivos, and L. R. Eswari. From *Hits from Tamil Films,* Vol. 6. EMI Odeon (India) 3AECS 5519. LP. Calcutta, India, 1969. Published and copyrighted to The Gramophone Company of India, Ltd. Used by permission.

9. "Devi Niye Tunai" ("O Devi! with Fish-Shaped Eyes") (4:37). Papanasan Sivan. Performed by Shobha Vasudevan, vocal, and David P. Nelson, *mridangam.* Recorded for author by recording engineer Owen Muir. Amherst, Massachusetts, January, 2001. Used by permission of the artists.

10. "Sarasiruha" ("To the Goddess Saraswati") (22:32). *Kriti* in Natai *raga, Adi tala,* by Pulaiyur Doraismy Ayyar. Performed by Ranganayaki Rajagopalan, *veena;* Raja Rao, *mridangam.* Recorded for author by recording engineer Rahul K. Raveendran. Chennai, India, 2001. Used by permission of the artists.

CHAPTER 8

11. "Da lang tao sha" ("Great Waves Washing the Sands"), excerpt (1:06). Abing [Hua Yanjun]. Performed by Abing, *pipa.* Field recording by members of the Music Research Institute. Wuxi, China, 1950. Used by permission.

12. "Yundao ge" ("Weeding song") (1:33). Traditional Jiangsu folksong. Performed by Jin Wenyin. Field recording by Antoinet Schimmelpenninck and Frank Kouwenhoven. Qiandai, China, 1987. *Chinese Folk Songs and Folk Singers: Shan'ge Traditions in Southern*

Jiangsu. Leiden, 1997. Copyright © 1997 by China Foundation. Used by permission of the copyright holder.

13. "Fang ma shan'ge" ("Releasing the Horse into Pasture") (0:58). Traditional Yunnan folksong. Performed by Zhao Yue. Field recording by Zhao Yue. Sheffield, UK, 2007. Used by permission of the artist.

14. Jiangnan *sizhu* (0:28). Performed by musicians at the Huxin Tea Shop. Field recording by Jonathan Stock. Shanghai, China, 1990. Used by permission of the collector.

15. "Huanle ge" ("Song of Happiness") (1:24). Jiangnan *sizhu. Musique de la region du fleuve Yangtse.* Playasound PS65048.

16. "Qi cun lian" ("Seven-Inch Lotus") (0:25). Performed by Wu Wanyi. Field recording by Jonathan Stock. Jilong, Taiwan, 1999. Used by permission of the collector.

17. "Qi cun lian" ("Seven-Inch Lotus") (1:47). Performed by Baifushequ Juleshe Beiguan Troupe. Field recording by Jonathan Stock. Jilong, Taiwan, 2001. Used by permission of the collector.

CD 4

CHAPTER 8 (CONTINUED)

1. *Sanniang jiao zi* (*Third Wife Teaches Her Son*), excerpt (4:33). Performed by Li Shiji and the Beijing Jingju Troupe. *Sanniang jiao zi.* Copyright © 1962. China Record Company HD-128.

2. "Qian xiucai: Yanda zhao jing" ("Scholar Qian: Yanda Looks in the Mirror"), excerpt (1:25). Performed by Zhang Jianting. *Pingtan: Zhang Jianting changduan jing pin.* 1962. Copyright © by Shanghai Audio Book Company X-4012.

3. "Yangguan san die" ("Three Variations on Yang Pass"), third variation and coda (1:55). Performed by Wang Tingting, *qin.* Field recording by Jonathan Stock. Sheffield, UK, 2005. Used by permission of the collector.

4. "Li chun: Xinnian jiajie" ("The Joyous Festival of Lunar New Year's Day") (1:24). Liao Shengjing. Performed by Hsu Shuo-Wen, piano. Field recording by Jonathan Stock. Sheffield, UK, 2005. Used by permission of the collector.

5. *Pasibutbut* (*Prayer for a Rich Millet Harvest*), excerpt (1:15). Traditional Bunun chant. Performed by villagers from Mingde, Taiwan. Field recording by Wu Rung-Shun. *Bunong zhi ge.* Copyright © 1993 by Wind Records Co. Ltd. TCD1501. Used by permission of the copyright holder.

6. "Tindei jaan mei" ("Praise from Heaven and Earth") (1:16). Music by Joseph Chi. Lyrics by Chorping Chang. Performed by Cherith Baptist Church. Field recording by Hera Tang. Hong Kong, China, 2005. Used by permission of the collector.

7. "Weidao" ("Scent") (1:42). Music by Huang Guolun, lyrics by Yao Qian. Performed by Winnie Hsin, voice; Ni Fanglai, guitar; and Tu Ying, keyboards. *Xin Xiaoqi: Weidao.* Copyright 1994 by Rock Records (Taiwan) Co. Ltd. RD1296.

CHAPTER 9

8. "El aparecido" ("The Apparition") (3:33). Chilean *cueca.* Víctor Jara. Inti Illimani ensemble: Max Berrú, Horacio Durán, Jorge Coulon, José Miguel Camus, José Seves, Horacio Salinas. Monitor Presents *Inti-Illimani 2: La Nueva Cancion Chilena.* 1991. Used by permission.

9. "Kutirimunapaq" ("So That We Can Return") (3:50). *K'antu* of Bolivia. Performed by Ruphay. *Jach'a Marka.* 1982. Ruphay, Discos Heriba SLP 2212. Heriba Ltda. La Paz, Bolivia. Used by permission.

10. "Muyu muyari warmigu" ("Please Return, Dear Woman") (4:19). Performed by Efraín, harp; Rafael, voice and *golpe.* Field recording by John M. Schechter, inside a schoolhouse in a *comuna* on the slopes of Mount Cotacachi, October 13, 1990. Used by permission of the artists.

11. "Ilumán tiyu" ("Man of Ilumán") (3:17). Segundo "Galo" Maigua Pillajo. *Sanjuán* of Ecuador. Performed by "Galo," guitar and vocal, with the Quichua ensemble Conjunto Ilumán. Field recording by John Schechter. Ilumán, Ecuador. October 1990. Used by permission of the artists.

12. "Me gusta la leche" ("I Like Milk") (2:31). Performed by Germán Congo, lead guitar (*requinto*); Fabián Congo and Milton Tadeo, vocals and guitars; Eleuterio Congo, *bomba;* Ermundo Mendes León, *güiro.* Field Recording by John M. Schechter, outside Ibarra, Imbabura, Ecuador, October 21, 1990.

13. "Amor imposible" ("Impossible Love") (2:31). Traditional Peruvian *wayno.* Performed by Chaskinakuy. Edmond Badoux, harp; Francy Vidal, vocal and *golpe. Chaskinakuy, Music of the Andes: Cosecha.* CD engineered and mixed by Joe Hoffmann and remastered by Brian Walder at Hoffmann Studios. Occidental, California, 1993. Used by permission.

14. *Vacación* (1:23). Performed by Quichua harpist Sergio, at a child's wake. Field recording by John Schechter, outside Cotacachi, Ecuador, February 1980. Used by permission of the artist.

15. Ecuadorian Quichua mother's lament to her deceased two-year-old girl, the morning after the child's wake (preceded by 15 seconds of Sergio's *Vacación*) (3:07). Field recording by John Schechter, outside Cotacachi, Ecuador, January 1980. Used by permission.

16. "Toro barroso" ("Reddish Bull") (3:32). *Albazo* of Ecuador. Performed by Don César Muquinche. Field recording by John Schechter, outside Ambato, Ecuador, 1980. Used by permission of the artist.

17. "Azúcar de caña" ("Sugar cane") (4:20). Performed by Eva Ayllón and ensemble. *The Soul of Black Peru/El Alma Del Perú Negro/Afro-Peruvian Classics.* 1995. Used by permission.

CHAPTER 10

18. "Al-Shaghal" ("Obsession"), excerpt (2:48). Performed by A. J. Racy, Simon Shaheen, and the Arabic Music Retreat Ensemble. Field recording by Anne Rasmussen. South Hadley, Massachusetts, August 2001. Used by permission of the artists.

19. Call to Prayer (*Azan*) (2:24). Performed by Sabri Mudallal. Field recording by Anne Rasmussen. Aleppo, Syria, 1994. Used by permission.

20. "The Horses" (1:42). Rahim Alhaj. Performed by Rahim Alhaj. *Rahim Alhaj: Iraqi Music in a Time of War.* Live in concert, New York City, April 5, 2003. Voxlox 103. Copyright by Rahim AlHaj. Used by permission of the artist.

21. "Abenamar" (2:04). Performed by Ramon Tasat, vocal and guitar, with Tina Chauncy, viol, and Scott Reiss, flute and percussion. English translation by Ramón Tasat and Dwight F. Reynolds. From *Como la Rosa en la Güerta.* Recording produced by Roman Tasat. No date. Used by permission of the artist.

22. *Zaffah* procession at a Casablanca wedding (1:39). Field recording by Anne Rasmussen. Casablanca, Morocco, June 1997. Used by permission of the family.

23. *El-Funoun,* "Initiation of Ecstasy" (2:08). Performed by *El-Funoun* (The Arts). From *Zaghareed: Music from the Palestinian Holy Land.* Sounds True STA M109D. 1999. Copyright by Sounds True. Used by permission.

24. *Sirat Bani Hilal,* excerpt (3:44). Performed by Sheikh Taha. Field recording, transliteration, and translation by Dwight Reynolds. Al-Bakatush, Kafr al-Shaykh Province, Egypt, June 1–2, 1987. Used by permission.

25. *'Ud Taqasim* in *Maqam Rast* (3:45). Performed by Ayad al-Asadi, *'ud.* Field recording by Anne Rasmussen. Nazareth, Israel, July 2000. Used by permission of the artist.

26. "Lamma Ya Albi" ("When, O Heart of Mine"), excerpt (1:55). Sana Khadaj, vocal; Amer Khadaj, Jalil Azzouz, and Naim Karakand, violin; and Muhammad al-Aqqad, *qanun.* New York, New York. Alamphon 2096-1 and 2, c. 1949. Rereleased on *The Music of Arab Americans: A Retrospective Collection.* Produced by Anne Rasmussen. Rounder 1122. 1997. Used by permission of the Khadaj family.

27. "Im Nin'alu" (2:24). Ofra Haza, vocal, with instrumentalists Iki Levy, Chaim Gispan, Eli Magen, Yigal Tuneh, Rima Kaminkowski, Yuval Kaminkowski, Israel Berkowitch, Yitchak Markowetzki, Israela Wisser, Abraham Rosenblatt, Elchanan Bregman, Abigail Erenheim, Meril Grinberg, Lesli Lishinski, and Ilan School Shlomo Shochat. From *Fifty Gates of Wisdom: Yemenite Songs.* Shanachie 64002. 1988. Track 1. Recorded at Triton Studios, Tel Aviv, Israel. Copyright by Shanachie Records Corp. Used by permission.

Preface

Why study music? There are many reasons, but perhaps the most important are pleasure and understanding. We have designed this book and its accompanying CD set to introduce undergraduates to the study of music the world over. The only prerequisites are a curious ear and an inquisitive mind.

Worlds of Music offers a textbook aimed squarely at students who want an authoritative and pleasurable introduction to the music of the world's peoples. It comes in two versions: this full version, in its fifth edition; and a shorter version, now in its second edition. This fifth edition differs markedly from the fourth in several ways. First, timed listening guides keyed to the musical examples on the accompanying CD set have been added to the transcriptions in musical notation, making discussions of musical form and structure accessible to beginning students who do not read music as well as those who do. Second, two new chapters introduce music-cultures new to this book, those of China and the Arab World. Third, a new chapter on Europe replaces the corresponding chapter from the fourth edition. The chapter on Japan from the fourth edition, including the musical selections, has been moved to the *Worlds of Music* companion website, where it will be accessible to teachers and students who use the book: academic.cengage.com/music/titon/worlds_5. Fourth, the addition of color photographs in most of the chapters portrays people, musical instruments, performances, places and contexts more vividly. Finally, key terms are now boldfaced for ease of identification and referenced in the Index; as before, in-text pronunciation guides smooth readers' way through potentially difficult terminology.

All features that were new in the fourth edition have been retained. The first chapter introduces the elements of world music. Using as illustrations the popular Ghanaian postal workers' stamp-canceling music and the song of the hermit thrush, Chapter 1 asks students how one draws the line between music and nonmusic. Using everyday ideas of rhythm, meter, melody, and harmony, it sharpens these rudimentary concepts and shows how they can help one understand the various musics presented in this book. In an ethnomusicological context, rudiments include not only the familiar elements of musical organization but also a basic approach to music's place in human life. For that reason we introduce a performance model showing how music relates to communities and their history; we also introduce a component model that includes musical sound and structure as well as other elements of a music-culture, including ideas, social behavior, and material culture. In this fifth edition the first chapter sharpens the discussion of musical worlds as ecological, sustainable human systems, a theme that is picked up in many of the succeeding chapters. Finally, two much-appreciated features from the fourth edition remain in the fifth. The CD set includes a Javanese *gamelan* demonstration in which the orchestral layers are gradually incorporated, thereby showing how the ensemble's parts relate to the whole. We also include the same kind of demonstration featuring the component parts of the drum ensemble that performs *Agbekor*. Such demonstrations help students to understand the way these complex ensembles function.

College and university courses in music of the world's peoples have increased dramatically in recent years, and the reasons why are easy to comprehend. Students who love music are alive to all music. So are composers, and many use the world's musical resources in their newest works. This is an important feature of today's music, and the people who listen to it—now and in the future—will want to keep their musical horizons broad.

Another reason for the interest in all kinds of music is the upsurge in ethnic awareness. As modern people try to locate themselves in a world that is changing with bewildering speed, they find music especially rewarding, for music is among the most tenacious of cultural elements. Music symbolizes a people's way of life; it represents a distillation of cultural style. For many, music *is* a way of life.

The authors of this book are ethnomusicologists; our field, *ethnomusicology,* is often defined as the study of music in culture. Some ethnomusicologists define the field as the study of music *as* culture, underlining the fact that music is a way of organizing human activity. By *culture* we do not mean "the elite arts," as it is sometimes used. Rather, we use the term as anthropologists do: Culture is a people's way of life, learned and transmitted through centuries of adapting to the natural and human world. Ethnomusicology is the study of music in the context of human life.

I like to define ethnomusicology as *the study of people making music.* People "make" music in two ways: They make or construct the *idea* of music—what music is (and is not) and what it does—and they make or produce the *sounds* that they call music. Although we experience music as something "out there" in the world, our response to music depends on the ideas we associate with that music, and those ideas come from the people (ourselves included) who carry our culture. In that way, music also makes (affects) people; the relationship is reciprocal. To use academic language, people make music into a cultural domain, with associated sets of ideas and activities. We could not even pick out musical form and structure, how the parts of a piece of music work with one another, if we did not depend on the idea that music must be organized rather than random, and if we had not learned to make music that way. (Analyzing form and structure is characteristic of some cultures, including Western ones, but in other areas of the world people do not habitually break a thing down into parts to analyze it.)

As students of music in culture, then, ethnomusicologists investigate *all* music. From the outset, therefore, *Worlds of Music* has presented case studies of Western folk, popular, and ethnic musics along with those from non-Western cultures. It may be that a future edition will include an ethnomusicological case study on Western art music.

Further, because ethnomusicologists believe there is no such reality as "the music itself"—that is, music apart from cultural considerations—we are not satisfied merely to analyze and compare musical forms, structures, melodies, rhythms, compositions, and genres. Instead, we borrow insights and methods from anthropology, sociology, literary criticism, linguistics, and history to understand music as human expression. In fact, until the 1950s ethnomusicology courses in U.S. universities were more likely to be found in anthropology departments than music departments, and some nineteenth-century founders of ethnomusicology were psychologists. Ethnomusicology is therefore interdisciplinary, combining elements of the arts, humanities, and social sciences. Because of its eclectic methods and worldwide scope, ethnomusicology is well suited to students seeking a liberal arts education.

When the first edition of this textbook appeared in 1984, formal study of music of the world's peoples emphasized the musics of indigenous (formerly termed tribal or native) peoples, classical musics of Asia and the Middle East, and the folk, ethnic, and immigrant musics of the Western continents. The integrity of any curriculum in ethnomusicology today requires that a historical, geographic, cultural, and genre-based emphasis continue, and yet in the past twenty years ethnomusicologists have moved toward a more complex and nuanced picture. The older map of a world divided into markedly different human groups, each with its own distinct music, is no longer accurate, and perhaps never was. Transnationalism, which connects individuals and institutions without much regard for national boundaries, has been facilitated by the increasingly globalized world economy and by worldwide information systems such as the Internet. This phenomenon has made many twenty-first-century people into musical cosmopolitans, participating in more than one music-culture.

Musical transnationalism is the result of at least four major changes in the previous century. First, the enormous influence of media on contemporary musical life, not only in the largest cities but also in the remotest villages, has enabled people to hear many different kinds of music, including music that they have never heard before. Second, the increasing migrations of peoples have engendered musical exchange and interchange. In the nineteenth and the first half of the twentieth century, these migrations were chiefly one-way trips, forming diasporic settlements linked to a homeland mainly by memory; but today, with globalized information systems and easier travel, migrations are transnational and more fluid, the migrants moving back and forth between different geographic and cultural spaces. Third, modernization and Westernization throughout the world has brought Western music and musical institutions to non-Western cultures, where they have been variously resisted, adapted, and transformed. Finally, "world music," a new category of popular, mass-mediated music based on a mix or fusion of elements associated with one or more musical cultures, a music with a market niche of its own, has become an intriguing path for musicians and a significant commodity of the media industry. Globalization today characterizes virtually all commerce, and many people regard music primarily as a commodity.

Indeed, some musical consumers equate "world music" with the music of world's peoples. Of course, as most music-making throughout the world falls outside of that marketing category, no responsible introduction to the music of the world's peoples should focus on "world music"; yet the rise of world music and a global economy challenges ethnomusicologists' categories, whether they be categories of genre or geography. It presents new challenges to fundamental concepts such as ethnicity and culture as well.

Not only is "world music" important in the mass media marketplace, but the ideal of multicultural diversity has also encouraged ethnic festivals, always featuring music. Musicians from all over the globe now appear on college and university campuses and in city auditoriums. Many younger people searching for musical roots have looked into their ethnic pasts and chosen to learn the music of their foreparents, while others view the variety of musics in the world as a vast resource to be drawn on in creating their own sounds.

Comprehensive coverage of the great variety of musics all over the globe is properly the subject of a multivolume encyclopedia, not an introductory textbook. The best introduction to the music of the world's peoples, we think, is not a musical world tour, inevitably superficial, but an approach that explores in some depth the music of representative human groups. This approach is not new; it adapts to ethnomusicology the case method in anthropology, the touchstone approach in literature, and the problems approach in history. The object is not primarily to pile up factual knowledge about various musical worlds, though certainly many facts will be learned. Rather, the point is to experience something of what it is like to be an ethnomusicologist puzzling out an understanding of an unfamiliar music. This process, we believe, is the best foundation for either future coursework (including surveys and seminars) or self-directed study and enjoyment of music after college.

We decided on a small number of case studies because that is how we teach the introductory-level world-music course at our colleges and universities. We thought also that by writing about music in societies we know firsthand, we could write an authoritative book. Each chapter, then, reflects an individual choice of subject. It also reflects our different ways of approaching music, for we agree that music cannot be "caught" by one method only.

We organized the chapters following six guiding principles. First, we think a textbook in world music should go beyond merely avoiding elitism and ethnocentrism. From the start, students need to understand an unfamiliar music on its own terms—that is, as the people who make the music understand it. Second, in order to know music as a human activity, not just a sequence of organized sound, we need to ask what the life of a musician is like in different societies and find answers in life histories and autobiographies. Third, we single out the words of songs for special attention because they often convey the meaning and purposes of musical performances as the music makers comprehend them. Fourth, we have made certain that the musical examples discussed in the book can be heard on the CDs accompanying this book. Fifth, student music-making projects—singing, building, and playing instruments—should, if properly directed and seriously approached, greatly increase appreciation of a musical style. Sixth, and most important, an introduction to world music should provide pleasure as well as knowledge.

We suggest that students begin with Chapter 1. The case studies, Chapters 2 through 10, may be taken in any order. In our experience, about two weeks per case study is about right; we encourage instructors to add or substitute a case study based on their own research. Because any fieldwork project should begin well before the end of the term, we suggest that Chapter 11 be read just after the first case study and that students begin fieldwork immediately afterward, based on a proposal in which they present both a subject and preliminary topic, discuss their projected role and access to the musical culture, and present a tentative work plan. In most cases the proposals will need to be revised in consultation with the instructor as the students proceed. Many students say the field projects are the most valuable experiences they take away from this course, particularly when they must make sense of what they document in the field. The field project encourages original research. Students find it attractive and meaningful to make an original contribution to knowledge. For instructors who find the fifth edition of *Worlds of Music* more than they need, a shorter version is also available from the publisher and can be ordered from academic.cengage.com/music/titon/worlds_5. Supporting materials for students and instructors are also available at academic.cengage.com/music/titon/worlds_5.

Worlds of Music has had a pretty long run, going through five major editions, two shorter editions, and translations into Italian and Chinese. On its first publication in 1984 it became the best-selling textbook in its field, a position it has never relinquished. Neither I nor any of the other authors imagined that we would be working on this book for so long or that it would become such a phenomenon. Over the years it has attracted attention from historians of ethnomusicology and of music education. The book has been the subject of reviews, of papers and panels presented at music conferences, and of at least one Ph.D. dissertation. One of the comments frequently directed toward the book concerns the alleged canonization of certain music cultures; that is, the book has appeared to favor certain music cultures by their inclusion while neglecting others. I would like to enter this dialogue here, responding to the canonization question by telling a little bit of the book's early history.

Worlds of Music came about in response to a request in 1977 from the publisher of Schirmer Books, Ken Stuart, that I write a textbook for the introductory course in the music of the world's peoples. The Society for Ethnomusicology, which in 2005 celebrated its fiftieth anniversary, was then only twenty years old and had but one-quarter of the membership it now enjoys. Similarly, the number of colleges and universities offering courses in the musics of the world's peoples was a fraction of what it is now. In 1977 there were two textbooks available, one surveying folk and traditional music on the Western continents, and the other providing an overview of the art musics of Asia. Small in size yet broad in coverage, they offered glimpses of the great variety of music on the planet.

I had been invited to propose a textbook—but I disliked textbooks. Most of those I had encountered as a high school student had been deeply unsatisfying; like most teenagers I knew, I was skeptical of their representations and claims to authority. In my first two years of college I had seldom been assigned a textbook. Rather, the professors asked us to work intensively with original documents, then write essays in answer to carefully posed questions or problems that were raised by our encounter with those documents.

I told Stuart that I could not write a good ethnomusicology textbook alone. Further, I thought that no single ethnomusicologist was qualified to write a good textbook. I believed that one could only write authoritatively based on one's own in-depth fieldwork. The only kind of introductory textbook that would have integrity would be coauthored, would concentrate on the musical cultures of a few representative human groups, and would attempt to integrate our understanding of those musical cultures through common features built into the textbook. I proposed to invite a small group of ethnomusicologists to collaborate with me on a textbook that would consist of case studies of various music-cultures, one that would present musical documents on recordings and discuss them in detail, and one that would present verbal documents such as autobiographies and approach meaning in music and culture through these. Over thirty years later, not only this case method but also our rationale for it has become common in coauthored textbooks introducing the musics of the world.

The primary reason that certain music-cultures may seem to constitute an ethnomusicological canon lies not in *Worlds of Music* but, rather, in the opportunities for study available and the choices that the first generation of North American ethnomusicologists made, beginning in the 1940s and 1950s, concerning which music cultures to study. Indonesia, India, Japan, Ghana, Native America—these were among those most studied. Further, ethnomusicology ensembles (often with native teachers) were established at a few colleges and universities, reflecting these choices: the *gamelan* musics of Indonesia, Ghanaian drumming and dancing, the Hindustani and Carnatic musics of India, and some others, many of which are represented in the case studies in *Worlds of Music*. These emphases and ensembles were already in place when I gathered the coauthors. If *Worlds of Music* has appeared to privilege certain music cultures by virtue of their inclusion, any privileging was inadvertent; like most ethno-musicologists, we believe that all music in all cultures is worthy of documentation and interpretation.

For the first edition I did not select music cultures first and then try to find authors; quite the opposite: I chose the authors first. I chose to work face-to-face with a community of coauthors who were close to one another in both spirit and location. These were ethnomusicologists I had gotten to know in New England and who shared my some of my views about what this textbook could be, and who would (and did) contribute many concepts of their own. The case studies followed from our areas of research; if we had done fieldwork in different music cultures, then those would have been the ones represented in *Worlds of Music*. Because we lived close to one another we were able to get together in person to discuss what would make a good textbook and how we would write our chapters. In short, the music cultures that appeared in the first edition of *Worlds of Music* grew out of my decision to have a small community of like-minded scholars work together, and not because I thought particular geographic areas should be included and canonized. The scholars I had invited were David McAllester, David

Reck, Jim Koetting, and Mark Slobin. All were happy to join in the project and we started at once.

In addition to determining that each of us would write a case-study chapter, one which would begin with an overview of or introduction to the musical cultures in the broad geographic area and then concentrate on the case study on a particular musical culture, we decided that we needed an introductory chapter to provide an overview and a concluding chapter that would teach students how to conduct a field research documentation project. After several pleasurable and exciting meetings as well as many phone calls and letters (this was before e-mail), we embarked on the manuscript, circulating chapter drafts to one another for comments and suggestions. We finished the manuscript in 1979. Schirmer Books published the first edition with the original five case studies, accompanied by a set of cassettes with the musical examples.

As *Worlds of Music* went through a succession of editions, adding music-cultures (the current, fifth edition has nine), we maintained a community of coauthors and our belief that in-depth case studies of particular music-cultures is the best introduction to the music of the world's peoples. The genius of *Worlds of Music*, one of my other colleagues told me in the early days, was that it was complete in itself: It not only encouraged students to learn the subject but it taught the professors how to teach it. While no such book could ever be complete, perhaps its combination of depth and user-friendliness has accounted for its success over the years. If *Worlds of Music* has been canonical, perhaps it has been so in other ways: It has taught generations of students to consider not just the world's musical sounds but also musical cultures in some depth; to think not only about musical structures and genres and instruments, but also about the ways in which people within musical cultures experience music; to think about lyrics and their meaning; to learn by doing—by singing, building instruments, and playing; and to accomplish a fieldwork project and experience what it is like to be an ethno-musicologist. That is, it has promoted an in-depth, experiential, hands-on, ears-open, and thoughtful introductory approach to the study of people making music.

We have appreciated the assistance, over the years, of several editors at Schirmer Books (now Schirmer/Cengage Learning)—Richard Carlin, Robert Axelrod, Jonathan Wiener, Clark Baxter, Abbie Baxter, Sue Gleason, and Molly Roth—in seeing this project through production. We offer special thanks to editors Maribeth Anderson Payne and Ken Stuart. We are pleased to acknowledge Martin Sherry's fine work on the instructor's manual. We are grateful for the contributions of Mark Slobin, who has departed for other projects; not only did he write the chapter on Europe and see it through four editions but, along with David Reck, he also helped me write the first and last chapters for the first edition. We remember the late James T. Koetting, my predecessor at Brown, who authored the chapter on Africa through the first two editions of this book and whose field recording of the Ghanaian postal workers will always remain in it. We are grateful to Henrietta Mckee Carter who was in Ghana when Jim made that recording and who supplied us with additional information about it. We remember the contributions of the late Linda Fujie, who authored the chapter on Japan that appeared in the second, third, and fourth editions, and which has been moved to the website for *Worlds of Music*. We mourn the recent passing of David McAllester, one of the original coauthors, and one of the cofounders of the Society for Ethnomusicology, whose chapter on Native American music stands as a monument to a great teaching career. We would be pleased to hear from our readers; you can reach us by writing the publisher or any of us directly at our respective colleges and universities.

—Jeff Todd Titon
Brown University

The Authors

Timothy J. Cooley

is an associate professor of Ethnomusicology at the University of California–Santa Barbara, where he teaches courses in Polish and in American vernacular, folk and popular musics, among other things, in the Department of Music. He is also Affiliated Faculty with the university's Global and International Studies Program. He earned a Master's in Music History at Northwestern University and received his Ph.D. in Ethnomusicology at Brown University, where he studied with Jeff Todd Titon. His book, *Making Music in the Polish Tatras: Tourists, Ethnographers, and Mountain Musicians,* won the 2006 Orbis Prize for Polish Studies, awarded by the American Association for the Advancement of Slavic Studies. He enjoys playing Polish mountain fiddle music, playing American old-time banjo, and singing in choirs. A revised second edition of his book *Shadows in the Field: New Perspectives for Fieldwork in Ethnomusicology,* edited with Gregory F. Barz, is being prepared for publication in 2008. Cooley is currently the editor of *Ethnomusicology,* the journal of the Society for Ethnomusicology, and is the president of the Society for Ethnomuscology, Southern California Chapter. His recent research considers how surfers, especially in California, musically express their ideas about surfing and the surfing community, and how surfing as a sport and lifestyle is represented in popular culture.

David Locke

received the Ph.D. in ethnomusicology from Wesleyan University in 1978, where he studied with David McAllester, Mark Slobin, and Gen'ichi Tsuge. At Wesleyan his teachers of traditional African music included Abraham Adzinyah and Freeman Donkor. He conducted doctoral dissertation fieldwork in Ghana from 1975 to 1977 under the supervision of Professor J. H. K. Nketia. In Ghana his teachers and research associates included Godwin Agbeli, Midawo Gideon Foli Alorwoyie, and Abubakari Lunna. He has published numerous books and articles on African music and regularly performs the repertories of music and dance about which he writes. He teaches at Tufts University, where he currently serves as the director of the Master's degree program in ethnomusicology and as a faculty advisor in the Tufts-in-Ghana

Foreign Study Program. His current projects include an oral history and musical documentation of dance-drumming from the Dagbamba people and an in-depth musical documentation of *Agbadza,* an idiom of Ewe music, in collaboration with Professor Gideon Foli Alorwoyie. He is active in the Society for Ethnomusicology and has served as the president of its Northeast Chapter.

David P. McAllester

received the Ph.D. in anthropology from Columbia University, where he studied with George Herzog. A student of American Indian music since 1938, he undertook fieldwork among the Comanches, Hopis, Apaches, Navajos, Penobscots, and Passamaquoddies. He was the author of such classic works in ethnomusicology as *Peyote Music, Enemy Way Music, Myth of the Great Star Chant,* and *Navajo Blessingway Singer* (with coauthor Charlotte Frisbie). He was one of the founders of the Society for Ethnomusicology, and he served as its president and the editor of its journal, *Ethnomusicology.* Professor emeritus of anthropology and music at Wesleyan University, he passed away in 2006.

Anne K. Rasmussen

is an associate professor of ethnomusicology at the College of William and Mary, where she also directs a Middle Eastern Music Ensemble. In 1991 she received the Ph.D. in ethnomusicology from the University of California–Los Angeles, where she studied with A. J. Racy, Timothy Rice, and Nazir Jairazbhoy. Gerard Béhague and Scott Marcus are also among her influential teachers. Her first area of research is Arab music and culture in diasporic enclaves of North America. Her current project, based on two years of ethnographic research in Indonesia, concerns Islamic ritual and performance. Her book *Women's Voices, the Recited Qur'ân, and Islamic Musical Arts in Indonesia* is forthcoming with University of California Press. Rasmussen is a contributing coeditor of the book *Musics of Multicultural America* (Schirmer 1997), and she has written articles that have appeared in the journals *Ethnomusicology, Asian Music, Popular Music, American Music,* and *The World of Music,* as well as in *The Garland Encyclopedia of World Music* and *The Harvard Dictionary of Music.* She has also produced four compact disc recordings documenting immigrant and community music in the United States. A former Fulbright senior scholar, she has served as First Vice President of the *Society for Ethnomusicology* and is the recipient of a Phi Beta Kappa award for excellence in teaching as well as the Jaap Kunst Prize for the best article published annually in the field of ethnomusicology.

David B. Reck

professor emeritus in Asian Languages and Civilizations, and Music, Amherst College, received his Ph.D. in ethnomusicology from Wesleyan University, where he studied under Mark Slobin, David P. McAllester, and Gen'ichi Tsuge. He has traveled extensively in India, Mexico, and Southeast and East Asia under grants from the Guggenheim Foundation, the Rockefeller Arts Foundation, the American Institute of Indian Studies, and others. A senior disciple of the legendary master musician, Mme. Ranganayaki Rajagopalan, he is an accomplished *veena* player and has concertized widely in India, Europe, and the Americas. As a composer in the 1960s and 1970s, he saw his works performed at Carnegie Hall,

Town Hall, Tanglewood, and numerous international new music festivals. His publications include *Music of the Whole Earth*, chapters in *It Was Twenty Years Ago Today* and *The Garland Encyclopedia of World Music*, and articles on aspects of India's music, the Beatles, J. S. Bach, and cross-influences between the West and the Orient. He and his wife, the photographer Carol Reck, live in Chennai.

John M. Schechter

is Professor of Music (ethnomusicology and music theory) at the University of California, Santa Cruz. He received the Ph.D. in ethnomusicology from the University of Texas at Austin, where he studied ethnomusicology with Gerard Béhague, folklore with Américo Paredes, Andean anthropology with Richard Schaedel, and Quechua with Louisa Stark and Guillermo Delgado-P. From 1986 to 2000 he directed the U.C. Santa Cruz Taki Ñan and Voces Latin American Ensembles. With Guillermo Delgado-P., Schechter is coeditor of *Quechua Verbal Artistry: The Inscription of Andean Voices/Arte Expresivo Quechua: La Inscripción de Voces Andinas* (2004), a volume dedicated to Quechua song text, narrative, poetry, dialogue, myth, and riddle. Coauthored with Enrique Andrade Albuja, his article in this anthology examines the Quichua-language rhetorical style of this gifted northern Ecuadorian highland raconteur. Schechter is general editor of, and a contributing author to, *Music in Latin American Culture: Regional Traditions* (1999), a volume examining music-culture traditions in distinct regions of Latin America, with chapters by ethno-musicologists specializing in those regions. He authored *The Indispensable Harp: Historical Development, Modern Roles, Configurations, and Performance Practices in Ecuador and Latin America* (1992). In 2005 he penned a tribute to Gerard Béhague, at this major scholar's untimely passing on June 13 of that year. Schechter's other publications have explored, among other topics, formulaic expression in Ecuadorian Quichua *sanjuán* and the ethnography, cultural history, and artistic depictions of the Latin American/Iberian child's wake music-ritual. In January 2007 he was interviewed by John Summa and John Travers, the codirectors of the planned documentary film *The Power of Their Song: The Untold Story of Latin America's New Song Movement;* he addressed the songs of Víctor Jara and general characteristics of the *Nueva Canción* Movement. The film is scheduled for airing and distribution in fall 2007.

Jonathan P. J. Stock

received the Ph.D. in ethnomusicology at the Queen's University of Belfast, where he studied with Rembrandt Wolpert, Martin Stokes, and John Blacking. His field research has been funded by the British Council, China State Education Commission, the United Kingdom's Arts and Humanities Research Council, the British Academy, and Taiwan's National Endowment for the Arts. It has been carried out in several parts of China, Taiwan, and England, and centered primarily on understanding the transformation of folk traditions in the modern and contemporary worlds. He is the author of two academic books on Chinese music, as well as a multivolume text for use in schools called *World Sound Matters: An Anthology of Music from Around the World*. He is also active as an editor, currently coediting the journal *The World of Music,* published three times a year in Berlin. Aiming to spend at least one month of each year on fieldwork, his current focus is the music of the Bunun people in Taiwan, but he has also written recently on the use of recordings in fieldwork, on the analysis of Chinese traditional opera, on the mechanics of sessions in English traditional music, and on musical biography. Formerly the chair of the British Forum for Ethnomusicology and now an executive board member of the International Council for Traditional Music, he founded the ethnomusicology program at the University of Sheffield in 1998 and now serves there as Professor of Ethnomusicology, Research Director of the White Rose East Asia Centre, and Director of the Centre for Applied and Interdisciplinary Research in Music.

R. Anderson Sutton

received the Ph.D. in musicology from the University of Michigan, where he studied with Judith Becker and William Malm. He was introduced to Javanese music while an undergraduate at Wesleyan University, and he made it the focus of his Master's study at the University of Hawaii, where he studied *gamelan* with Hardja Susilo. On numerous occasions since 1973 he has conducted field research in Indonesia, with grants from the East-West Center, Fulbright-Hays, Social Science Research Council, National Endowment for the Humanities, Wenner-Gren Foundation, and American Philosophical Society. He is the author of *Traditions of Gamelan Music in Java, Variation in Central Javanese Gamelan Music, Calling Back the Spirit: Music, Dance, and Cultural Politics in Lowland South Sulawesi,* and numerous articles on Javanese music. His current research concerns music and media in Indonesian and South Korea. Active as a *gamelan* musician since 1971, he has performed with several professional groups in Indonesia and directed numerous performances in the United States. He has served as the first vice president and book review editor for the Society for Ethnomusicology, as well as a member of the Working Committee on Performing Arts for the Festival of Indonesia (1990–1992). He has taught at the University of Hawaii and the University of Wisconsin–Madison, where he is Professor of Music and Director of the Center for Southeast Asian Studies.

Jeff Todd Titon

received the Ph.D. in American Studies from the University of Minnesota, where he studied ethnomusicology with Alan Kagan and musicology with Johannes Riedel. He has done fieldwork in North America on religious folk music, blues music, and old-time fiddling, with support from the National Endowment for the Arts and the National Endowment for the Humanities. For two years he was the guitarist in the Lazy Bill Lucas Blues Band, a group that appeared in the 1970 Ann Arbor Blues Festival. The author or editor of seven books, including *Early Downhome Blues,* which won the ASCAP–Deems Taylor Award, and the five-volume *American Musical Traditions,* named by *Library Journal* as one of the outstanding reference works of 2003, he is also a documentary photographer and filmmaker. In 1991 he wrote a hypertext multimedia computer program about the old-time fiddler Clyde Davenport that is regarded as a model for interactive representations of people making music. He founded the ethnomusicology program at Tufts University, where he taught from 1971 to 1986. From 1990 to 1995 he served as the editor of *Ethnomusicology,* the journal of the Society for Ethnomusicology. A Fellow of the American Folklore Society, since 1986 he has been Professor of Music and the director of the Ph.D. program in ethnomusicology at Brown University.

The Music-Culture as a World of Music

JEFF TODD TITON

CHAPTER

1

The Soundscape

The world around us is full of sounds. All of them are meaningful in some way. Some are sounds you make. You might sing in the shower, talk to yourself, shout to a friend, whistle a tune, sing along with a song on your mp3 player, practice a piece on your instrument, play in a band or orchestra, or sing in a chorus or an informal group on a street corner. Some are sounds from sources outside yourself. If you live in the city, you hear a lot of sounds made by people. You might be startled by the sound of a truck beeping as it backs up, or by a car alarm. The noise of the garbage and recycling trucks on an early morning pickup or the drone of a diesel engine in a parked truck nearby might irritate you. In the country you can more easily hear the sounds of nature. In the spring and summer you might hear birds singing and calling to each other, the snorting of deer in the woods, or the excited barks of a distant dog. By a river or the ocean you might hear the sounds of surf or boats loading and unloading or the deep bass of foghorns. Stop for a moment and listen to the sounds around you. What do you hear? A computer hard drive? A refrigerator motor? Wind outside? Footsteps in the hallway? A car going by? Why didn't you hear those sounds a moment ago? We usually filter out "background noise" for good reason, but in doing so we deaden our sense of hearing. For a moment, stop reading and become alive to the soundscape. What do you hear? Try doing that at different times of the day, in various places: Listen to the soundscape and pick out all the different sounds you may have taken for granted until now.

Just as landscape refers to land, **soundscape** refers to sound: the characteristic sounds of a particular place, both human and nonhuman. (The Canadian composer R. Murray Schafer developed this term; see Schafer 1980.) The examples so far offer present-day soundscapes, but what were they like in the past? What kinds of sounds might dinosaurs have made? With our wristwatches we can always find out what time it is, but in medieval Europe people told time by listening to the bells of the local clock tower. Today we take the sounds of a passing railroad train for granted, but people found its sounds arresting when first heard.

The American naturalist Henry David Thoreau was alive to the soundscape when he lived by himself in a cabin in the woods at Walden Pond 160 years ago. As

1

he wrote in *Walden,* "The whistle of the steam engine penetrated my woods summer and winter—sounding like the scream of a hawk sailing over some farmer's yard." After this ominous comparison—the hawk is a bird of prey—Thoreau describes the train as an iron horse (a common comparison at the time) and then a dragon, a threatening symbol of chaos rather than industrial progress: "When I hear the iron horse make the hills echo with his snort like thunder—shaking the earth with his feet, and breathing fire and smoke from his nostrils, what kind of winged horse or fiery dragon they will put into the new mythology I don't know." Writing about his wilderness soundscape, Thoreau first made sure his readers knew what he did *not* hear: the crowing of the rooster, the sounds of animals—dogs, cats, cows, pigs—the butter churn, the spinning wheel, children crying, the "singing of the kettle, the hissing of the urn": This was the soundscape of a farm in 1850, quite familiar to Thoreau's readers. (We might stop to notice which of these sounds have disappeared from the soundscape altogether, for who today hears a butter churn or spinning wheel?) What Thoreau heard instead in his wilderness soundscape were "squirrels on the roof and under the floor; a whippoorwill on the ridge-pole, a blue jay screaming in the yard, a hare or woodchuck under the house, a screech-owl or a cat-owl behind it, a flock of wild geese or a laughing loon in the pond, a fox to bark in the night"; but no rooster "to crow nor hens to cackle in the yard—no yard!" In Thoreau's America you could tell, blindfolded, just by hearing, whether you were in the wilderness, on a farm, or in a town or city. How have those soundscapes changed since 1850? What might Thoreau have written about automobiles in the countryside, tractors on the farms, trucks on the interstate highways, and jet planes everywhere?

In Thoreau's "wild soundscape" at Walden in 1850 each living thing that made a sound had its own niche in what we might think of as an acoustic **ecology** or what the aural environmentalist Bernie Krause calls a *biophony,* the combined voices of living things. Krause points out that "non-industrial cultures," particularly those that live in the more-remote regions of the planet, like the BaAka of central Africa we will learn about in Chapter 3, "depend on the integrity of undisturbed natural sound for a sense of place," of where they are as well as who they are (Krause 2002:25). Every nonhuman species has its own acoustic niche in the soundscape, whether it is a bird singing or an insect making noise by rubbing its legs together. Dolphins, whales, and bats navigate largely by means of sound. But as we have learned, humans make their own acoustic niches and interact sonically with nonhuman sounds in whatever soundscape they encounter, whatever place they happen to be.

Listen now to CD 1, Track 1. The soundscape is a post office, but it is unlike any post office you will likely encounter in North America. You are hearing men canceling stamps at the University of Accra, in Ghana, Africa. Two of the men whistle a tune while three make percussive sounds. A stamp gets canceled several times for the sake of the rhythm. You will learn more about this example shortly. For now, think of it as yet another example of a soundscape: the acoustic environment where sounds, including music, occur.

CD 1:1

Postal workers canceling stamps at the University of Ghana post office (2:59). The whistled tune is the hymn "Bompata," by the Ghanaian composer W. J. Akyeampong (b. 1900). Field recording by James Koetting. Legon, Ghana, 1975.

The Music-Culture

Every human society has music. Although music is universal, its meaning is not. For example, a famous musician from Asia attended a European symphony concert approximately 150 years ago. He had never heard Western music

before. The story goes that after the concert, his hosts asked him how he had
liked it. "Very well," he replied. Not satisfied with this answer, his hosts asked
(through an interpreter) what part he liked best. "The first part," he said. "Oh,
you enjoyed the first movement?" "No, before that." To the stranger, the best
part of the performance was the tuning-up period. His hosts had a different
opinion. Who was right? They both were. Music is not a universal language in
the sense that everyone understands what music means. People in different
cultures give music different meanings. Recall from the Preface that **culture**
means the way of life of a people, learned and transmitted from one generation
to the next. The word *learned* is stressed to differentiate a people's cultural
inheritance from what is passed along biologically in their genes: nurture,
rather than nature. From birth, people all over the world absorb the cultural
inheritance of family, community, schoolmates, and other larger social
institutions such as the mass media—books, newspapers, video games,
movies, television, and computers. This cultural inheritance tells people
how to understand the situations they are in (what the situations mean) and
how they might behave in those situations. It works so automatically that they
are aware of it only when it breaks down, as it does on occasion when people
misunderstand a particular situation. Like the people who carry them, cultures
do not function perfectly all the time.

Musical situations and the very concept of music mean different things and
involve different activities around the globe. Because music and all the beliefs and
activities associated with it are a part of culture, we use the term **music-culture** to
mean a group's total involvement with music: ideas, actions, institutions, material
objects—everything that has to do with music. A music-culture can be as small as
a single human's personal music-culture, or as large as one carried by a
transnational group. We can speak of the music-culture of a family, a community,
a region, a nation. We can identify music-cultures with musical genres: there is a
hip-hop music-culture, a classical music-culture, a jazz music-culture. We can
identify subcultures within music-cultures: Atlanta hip-hop, for example, within
the hip-hop music culture, or early music within classical music, or progressive
bluegrass within bluegrass. In our example of concert music, the European
American music-culture dictates that the sound made by symphony musicians
tuning up is not music. But to the listener from Asia, it was music. That we can say
so shows our ability to understand (and empathize with) each music-culture
context from the inside, and then to move to an intellectual position outside of
them. We can then compare them and arrive at the conclusion that, considered
from their points of view, both the stranger and his hosts were correct.
Contrasting the music of one culture with the music of another after stepping
outside of both is a good way to learn about how music is made and what music is
thought to be and do.

People may be perplexed by music outside their own music-culture. They
may grant that it is music but find it difficult to hear and enjoy. In Victorian
England, for example, people said they had a hard time listening to the strange
music of the native peoples within the British Colonial Empire. The expansive and
exciting improvisations of India's classical music were ridiculed because the music
was not written down "as proper music should be." The subtle tuning of Indian
raga scales was considered "indicative of a bad ear" because it did not match the
tuning of a piano (see Chapter 6). What the British were really saying was that
they did not know how to understand Indian music on its own cultural terms. Any

music sounds "out of tune" when its tuning system is judged by the standards of another.

A person who had grown up listening only to Armenian music in his family and community wrote about hearing European classical music for the first time:

> I found that most European music sounds either like "mush" or "foamy," without a solid base. The classical music seemed to make the least sense, with a kind of schizophrenic melody—one moment it's calm, then the next moment it's crazy. Of course there always seemed to be "mush" (harmony) which made all the songs seem kind of similar. (posted to SEM-L public listserver July 9, 1998)

Because this listener had learned what makes a good melody in the Armenian music-culture, he found European classical melodies lacking because they changed mood too quickly. Unused to harmony in his own music, the listener responded negatively to it in Western classical music. Further, popular music in the United States lacked interesting rhythms and melodies:

> The rock and other pop styles then and now sound like music produced by machinery, and rarely have I heard a melody worth repeating. The same with "country" and "folk" and other more traditional styles. These musics, while making more sense with their melody (of the most undeveloped type), have killed off any sense of gracefulness with their monotonous droning and machine-like sense of rhythm. (Ibid.)

You might find these remarks offensive or amusing—or you might agree with them. Like the other examples, they illustrate that listeners throughout the world have prejudices based on the music they know and like. Listening to music all over the planet, though, fosters an open ear and an open mind. Learning to hear a strange music from the viewpoint of the people who make that music enlarges our understanding and increases our pleasure.

What Is Music?

Sound is anything that can be heard, but what is music? In the Preface I emphasized that music isn't something found in the natural world, like air or sand; rather, music is something that people make. And they make it in two ways: They make or produce the sounds they call music, and they also make music into a cultural domain, forming the ideas and activities they consider music. As we have seen, not all music-cultures have the same idea of music; some music-cultures have no word for it, while others have a word that roughly translates into English as "music-dance" because to them music is inconceivable without movement. Writing about Rosa, the Macedonian village she lived in, Nahoma Sachs points out that "traditional Rosans have no general equivalent to the English 'music.' They divide the range of sound which might be termed music into two categories: *pesni,* songs, and *muzika,* instrumental music" (Sachs 1975:27). Of course, this distinction between songs and music is found in many parts of the world. Anne Rasmussen, when chatting with her taxi driver on the way to a conference at the Opera House in Cairo, Egypt, was told by her taxi driver that he liked "*both* kinds of music:

singing (*ghina*) *and* music with instruments (*musiqa*)." We also find it in North America. Old-time Baptists in the southern Appalachian Mountains (see Figure 1.1) sometimes say, "We don't have music in our service," meaning they do not have instrumental music accompanying their singing. Nor do they want it.

Some music-cultures have words for song types (lullaby, epic, historical song, and so on) but no overall word for music. Nor do they have words or concepts that directly correspond to what Euro-Americans consider the elements of musical structure: melody, rhythm, harmony, and so forth. Many of the readers of this book (and all of its authors) have grown up within the cultures of Europe and North America. In Chapter 5, the sections "Europe: An Overview" and "The Sounds of European Music" consider specific qualities of European and, by association, North American musical practices that Euro-Americans consider "normal." Consciously and unconsciously, our approaches and viewpoints reflect this background. But no matter what our musical backgrounds are, we must try to "get out of our cultural skins" as much as possible in order to view music through cultural windows other than our own. We may even learn to view our own music-culture from a new perspective. Today, because of the global distribution of music on radio, television, film, digital video, sound recordings, and the Internet, people in just about every music-culture are likely to have heard some of the same music. Although the local is emphasized throughout this book, music-cultures should not be understood as isolated, now or even in the past. In particular, thinking about the interaction between the local and the global can help us appreciate music-cultures, including our own.

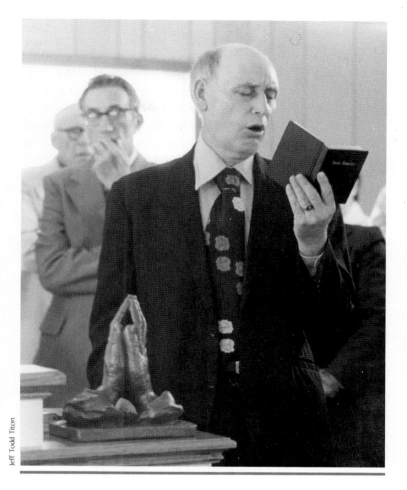

Jeff Todd Titon

FIGURE 1.1

Russell Jacobs leading the singing at the Left Beaver Old Regular Baptist Church in eastern Kentucky, 1979.

If we want to understand the different musics of the world, then, we need first to understand them on their own terms—that is, as the various music-cultures themselves do. But beyond understanding each on its own terms, we want to be able to compare and contrast the various musics of the world. To do that we need a way to think about music as a whole.

To begin to discover what all musics might have in common, so that we may think about music as a general human phenomenon, we ask about how people perceive differences between music and nonmusic. The answer does not involve simple disagreements over whether something people call "music" is truly music. For example, some people say that rap is not music, but what they mean is that they think rap is not good or meaningful music. Rather, there are difficult cases that test the boundaries of what differentiates sound from music, such as the songs of birds or dolphins or whales—are these music?

Consider bird songs. Everyone has heard birds sing, but not everyone has paid attention to them. Try it for a moment: Listen to the songs of a hermit thrush at dusk in a spruce forest (CD 1, Track 2). At Walden Pond, Thoreau heard hermit thrushes that sounded like these.

Many think that the hermit thrush has the most beautiful song of all the birds native to North America. Most bird songs consist of a single phrase, repeated, but the hermit thrush's melody is more complicated. You hear a vocalization (phrase) and then a pause, then another vocalization and pause, and so on. Some people hear them in pairs, the second a response to the first. Do you hear them that way, or as separate vocalizations? Each vocalization has a similar rhythm and is composed of five to eight tones. The phrase is a little higher or lower each time. If you listen closely, you also hear that the thrush can produce more than one tone at once, a kind of two-tone harmony. This is the result of the way his syrinx (voice box) is constructed.

Is bird song music? The thrush's song has some of the characteristics of music. It has rhythm, melody, repetition, and variation. It also has a function: Scientists believe that birds sing to announce their presence in a particular territory to other birds of the same kind, and that they sing to attract a mate. In some species one bird's song can tell another bird which bird is singing and how that bird is feeling. Bird song has inspired Western classical music composers. Some composers have taken down bird songs in musical notation, and some have incorporated, imitated, or transformed bird song phrases in their compositions. Bird song is also found in Chinese classical music. In Chinese compositions such as "The Court of the Phoenix," for *suona* (oboe) and ensemble, extended passages are a virtual catalog of bird calls and songs imitated by instruments.

Yet people in the Euro-American music-culture hesitate to call bird songs music. Because each bird in a species sings the same song over and over, bird songs appear to lack the creativity of human expression. Euro-American culture regards music as a human expression, and bird songs do not seem to belong to the human world. By contrast, people in some other music-cultures think bird songs do have human meaning. For the Kaluli people of Papua New Guinea, bird songs are the voices of their human ancestors who have died and changed into birds. These songs cause humans grief, which expresses itself in weeping (Feld 1990). The Kaluli give a different meaning to bird songs than Euro-Americans do. Does this mean it is impossible to find a single idea of what music is? Not really. Euro-Americans may disagree with the Kaluli over whether bird songs have human meaning, but they both agree that music has human meaning. Our thought experiment with bird song and its meanings in different music-cultures suggests that music has something to do with the human world. We can go further and say that music is sound that is humanly patterned or organized (Blacking 1973).

For another example of a sound that tests the boundary between music and nonmusic, listen again to CD 1, Track 1. Throughout the life of *Worlds of Music,* listeners have found the Ghanaian postal workers' sounds especially intriguing. Not long ago we learned a little more about the circumstances of the recording.

CD 1:2

Songs of hermit thrushes (0:44). Field recording by Jeff Todd Titon. Little Deer Isle, Maine, 1999.

Henrietta Mckee Carter (personal communication to Jeff Todd Titon, July 2000) wrote as follows:

> Sometime in 1975, Bill Carter and I were sitting in Jim and Ernestina Koetting's quarters at the University of Ghana chatting with Ernestina, while awaiting dinner. Jim came in excitedly, picked up his recording equipment and disappeared, saying on his way out that he had just heard something he wanted to record. He came back a while later and described the scene.

These postal workers hand-canceling stamps at the post office of the University of Ghana are making drumming sounds, and two are whistling; but there are no drums, and the workers are just passing the time. How, exactly? Koetting (Titon 1992:98–99) wrote as follows:

> Twice a day the letters that must be canceled are laid out in two files, one on either side of a divided table. Two men sit across from one another at the table, and each has a hand-canceling machine (like the price markers you may have seen in supermarkets), an ink pad, and a stack of letters. The work part of the process is simple: a letter is slipped from the stack with the left hand, and the right hand inks the marker and stamps the letter. . . .
>
> This is what you are hearing: the two men seated at the table slap a letter rhythmically several times to bring it from the file to the position on the table where it is to be canceled. (This act makes a light-sounding thud.) The marker is inked one or more times (the lowest, most resonant sound you hear) and then stamped on the letter (the high-pitched mechanized sound you hear). . . . The rhythm produced is not a simple one-two-three (bring forward the letter—ink the marker—stamp the letter). Rather, musical sensitivities take over. Several slaps on the letter to bring it down, repeated thuds of the marker in the ink pad and multiple cancellations of single letters are done for rhythmic interest. Such repetition slows down the work, but also makes it much more interesting.
>
> The other sounds you hear have nothing to do with the work itself. A third man has a pair of scissors that he clicks—not cutting anything, but adding to the rhythm. The scissors go "click, click, click, rest," a basic rhythm used in [Ghanaian] popular dance music. The fourth worker simply whistles along. He and any of the other three workers who care to join him whistle popular tunes or church music that fits the rhythm.

Work song, found in music-cultures all over the world, is a kind of music whose function ranges from coordinating complex tasks to making boring and repetitive work more interesting. In this instance the workers have turned life into art. Writing further about the postal workers' recording, Koetting says,

> It sounds like music and, of course it is; but the men performing it do not quite think of it that way. These men are working, not putting on a musical show; people pass by the workplace paying little attention to the "music." (Titon 1992:98)

Even though the postal workers do not think of this activity as a musical performance, Koetting is willing to say, "It sounds like music and, of course it is." He can say so because he connects it with other music-cultures' work-song activities (see for example, the work songs in Chapter 4). He has found a common pattern in their musical performance that transcends the specificity of any single music-culture, in the sense that he hears people whistling a melody and accompanying it with interesting percussive rhythms: The music affected him, and not only did he feel himself moved, he was moved to record it. At the same time he respects the postal workers' idea that, in their way of thinking, it is "not quite" music. In other words, the workers are doing this as a part of their work, to pass the time; it is their way of being in the world as workers canceling stamps, not as singers and musicians intent on a musical performance.

People in music-cultures organize sounds into musical patterns. Although the patterns vary across cultures, all music-cultures pattern sounds into something we call music. How can we think comparatively about the kinds of musical organization that we find throughout the world? Koetting understood the postal workers' activities as music in comparison with other musics he knew. He recognized a familiar pattern of melody and harmony that he heard, as you probably did too. Although this hymn-tune was composed by a Ghanaian, the melody is European, a legacy of Christian missionary music in Ghana. As a student of Ghanaian drumming, he recognized the cross-rhythms of the percussion as native Ghanaian. He thought in terms of melody, harmony, meter, and rhythm.

Indeed, the European American music-culture recognizes these four characteristics and talks about them in ordinary language. The ideas themselves are already familiar to many readers of this book. These terms describe patterns or structure (form) in sound. It will be interesting to see what happens to these Western (but not exclusively Western) ideas when, for better or worse, they are applied to every music-culture throughout this book. In the next section, on musical structure, we briefly review these ideas. Then in the following section we turn our attention to a music-culture model and show how music becomes meaningful in performance. In the next section we consider the four components of a music culture, which in music textbooks are not usually considered rudiments but are no less a part of humanly organized sound: ideas, activities, repertories, and the material culture of music. In the last section of this chapter, we return to the idea of acoustic ecology with which we began. We do this not only in terms of the interactions of sounds in a soundscape but also in terms of the interconnections of music cultures throughout human history on planet Earth, as well as the sustainability of music in the future.

Structure in Music

RHYTHM AND METER

In ordinary language we say **rhythm** when we refer to the patterned recurrence of events, as in "the rhythm of the seasons," or "the rhythm of the raindrops." As Hewitt Pantaleoni writes, "Rhythm concerns time felt as a succession of events rather than as a single span" (1985:211). In music, we hear rhythm when we hear a time-relation between sounds. In a classroom you might hear a pen drop from a desk and a little later a student coughing. You do not hear any rhythm, because you hear no relation between the sounds. But when you hear a person walking in the hall outside, or when you hear a heartbeat, you hear rhythm.

If we measure the time-relations between the sounds and find a pattern of regular recurrence, we have **metrical rhythm.** Think of the soldiers' marching rhythm: HUP-two-three-four, HUP-two-three-four. This is a metered, regularly recurring sound pattern. The recurring accents fall on HUP. Most popular, classical, and folk music heard in North America today has metered rhythm. Of course, most of those rhythms are more complex than the march rhythm. If you are familiar with Gregorian chant, of the Roman Catholic Church, you know musical rhythm without meter. Although not music, ordinary speech provides an example of nonmetrical rhythm, whereas poetic verse is metrical (unless it is free verse). Think of the iambic pentameter in Shakespeare's plays, for example. Most of the musical examples in this book, including the postal workers' canceling stamps (CD 1, Track 1), are examples of metrical rhythm. In a metrical rhythm you feel the beat and move to it. The song of the hermit thrush is both metrically rhythmic and not (CD 1, Track 2). You can find a beat while the thrush sings a phrase, but after he stops you cannot predict exactly when the bird will start again.

"Sister, Hold Your Chastity," the Bosnian *ganga* song (CD 2, Track 9), lacks any sense of a beat. You can't tap your foot to it. Although we hear rhythm in the relationship between successive sounds, this rhythm is highly flexible. Yet it is not arbitrary. The singers, who have spent years performing this music together, know how to coordinate the melody and harmony by signals other than a pulse. But the lack of a beat makes it difficult for someone to learn *ganga* (see Chapter 5). Try singing along with the recording and see for yourself. Similarly, the rhythm in the Chinese weeding song (CD 3, Track 12) flows in a flexible way as the singer aims to produce a musical effect by lengthening the duration of certain syllables.

On the other hand, the rhythm of *karnataka sangeeta* (CD 3, Track 10) is intricate in another way. The opening *alapana* section has a flexible, nonmetered rhythm, but the following sections are metrically organized. This classical music of South India divides a metrical rhythm into long, complex, improvised accent patterns based on various combinations of rhythmic figures. The *mridangam* drummer's art (see Figure 1.2) is based on fifteen or more distinct types of finger and hand strokes on different parts of the drumheads. Each stroke has its own *sollukattu,* or spoken syllable that imitates the sound of the drum stroke. Spoken one after another, they duplicate the rhythmic patterns and are used in learning and practice.

Although most North Americans and Europeans may not be aware of it, the popular music they listen to usually has more than one rhythm. The singer's melody falls into one pattern, the guitarist's into another; the drummer usually plays more than one pattern at once. Even though these rhythms usually relate to the same overall accent pattern, the way they interact with each other sets our bodies in motion as we move to the beat. Still, to the native Armenian who grew up on a diet of more-intricate rhythms, this monometer is dull. Rhythm in the postal workers' canceling stamps (CD 1, Track 1) emphasizes the tugs of different rhythmic patterns. (For a detailed analysis, see Chapter 3.) This simultaneous occurrence of several rhythms with what we can perceive as a shifting downbeat is called **polyrhythm.** Polyrhythm is characteristic of the music of Africa and wherever Africans have carried their music. In Arab music, nonmetrical music—that is, singing and instrumental improvisation in **free rhythm**—is juxtaposed with metered music and sometimes, as we will hear in Chapter 10, metrical and nonmetrical

FIGURE 1.2

T. Viswanathan, flute, Ramnad V. Raghavan, *mridangam.*

Courtesy T. Viswanathan.

playing are combined in the same moment. In Chapter 3 you will learn to feel yet a further layer of complexity—**polymeter,** or the simultaneous presence of two different metrical systems—as you "construct musical reality in two ways at once" while playing an Ewe (pronounced *eh*-way) bell pattern in *Agbekor* (see Chapter 3).

MELODY

In ordinary language we say **melody** when we want to refer to the tune—the part of a piece of music that goes up and down, the part that most people hear and sing along with. It is hard to argue that melody and rhythm are truly different qualities of music, but it helps our understanding if we consider them separately. When we say that someone has either a shrill or a deep voice, we are calling attention to a musical quality called **pitch,** which refers to how high or low a sound is. When a sound is made, it sets the air in motion, vibrating at so many cycles per second. This vibrating air strikes the eardrum, and we hear how high or low pitched it is depending on the speed of the vibrations. You can experience this yourself if you sing a tone that is comfortable for your voice and then slide the tone down gradually as low as you can go. As your voice goes down to a growl, you can feel the vibrations slow down in your throat. Pitch, then, depends on the frequency of these sound vibrations. The faster the vibrations, the higher the pitch.

Another important aspect of melody is **timbre,** or tone quality. Timbre is caused by the characteristic ways different voices and musical instruments vibrate. Timbre tells us why a violin sounds different from a trumpet when they are playing a tone of the same pitch. We take the timbre of our musical instrument palette for granted, but when we encounter an instrument with a timbre that we may never have heard before, such as the Australian didgeridoo, we sit up and take notice. Some music-cultures, like the European, favor timbres that we may describe as smooth or liquid; others, like the African, favor timbres that are buzzy; others, like the Asian, favor timbres that we might describe as focused in sound. The construction of instruments in various cultures often reflects the preference for various timbres or a combination of them, as we see with the Moroccan *bendir* in Chapter 10, an instrument that reflects both Arab and African techniques of construction and aesthetic preferences with regard to timbre. Other important aspects of melody, besides pitch and timbre, include volume—that is, how melodies increase and decrease in loudness. The Navajo Yeibichai song (CD 1, Track 6) begins at the loudest possible volume, while the solo for the Chinese *qin* (pronounced "chin") (CD 4, Track 3) is performed softly.

Another critical aspect of melody to pay attention to in world music is *emphasis:* for example, the way the major tones of the melody are approached (by sliding up or down to them in pitch, as some singers do; by playing them dead on, as a piano does; by "bending" the pitch, as a blues guitarist (Figure 1.3) does when pushing the string to the side and back (CD 2, Tracks 4 and 5). Figure 6.7 contrasts notes and melodies on the piano with their counterparts in Indian music.

Yet another way to emphasize a point in a melody is to add **decorative tones** or what in classical music are called **ornaments.** These, too, occur in many of the musics of the world. See if you can find them as you listen to the CD set. Concentrate on the way the singers and musicians do not simply sing or play tones, but play *with* tones.

Finding how different music-cultures organize sounds into melodies is one of the most fascinating pursuits for the student of music. If we sing the melody of the Christmas carol "Joy to the World," we hear how Westerners like to organize a melody. Try it:

Joy to the world, the Lord has come!
(do ti la   so, fa mi re do!)

This is the familiar do-re-mi (solfège) **scale,** in descending order. Try singing "Joy to the World" backwards, going up the do-re-mi scale and using the syllables in this order: "come has Lord the world the to joy." You might find it difficult! But if you first sing the do-re-mi scale using the solfège syllables, and then replace do-re-me with "come has Lord," and so forth, you will be able to do it more easily.

Jeff Todd Titon

FIGURE 1.3

Blues guitarists Johnny Winter (left) and Luther Allison, Ann Arbor (Michigan) Blues Festival, August 1970.

The white keys of the piano show how most melodies in European and Euro-American music have been organized since the eighteenth century. Do-re-mi (and so forth) represent a **major scale.** Notice that these pitches are not equally spaced. Try singing "Joy to the World" starting on "re" instead of "do." You will see that it throws off the melody. If you are near a keyboard, try playing it by going down the white keys, one at a time. Only one starting key (C) gives the correct melody. This indicates that the **intervals,** or distances between pitches, are not the same.

The Euro-American culture prefers the major scale. As such, Euro-Americans set up many instruments, such as the piano or the flute, so that they can easily produce the pitch intervals of this scale. Timothy Cooley writes more fully about Euro-American scales and melodic organization in Chapter 5, using the same "Joy to the World" tune. But other music-cultures set up their instruments and their scales differently. For example, Javanese musical gongs organize the **octave** (the solfège interval between one "do" and another) into five nearly equidistant intervals in their *sléndro* (*slayn*-dro) scale. The Javanese have a second scale, *pélog* (*pay*-log), which divides the octave into seven tones, but the intervals are not the same as those in any Western scales (see Transcription 7.1). The sounds of their *gamelan,* or percussion ensemble, reflect these different tunings (for example, CD 2, Track 22, is in the *pélog* scale). In the classical music of South India, known as Carnatic music, each melody conforms to a set of organizing principles called a *raga*. Although each *raga* has its own scale (based on one of seventy-two basic scale patterns), it also has its own characteristic melodic phrases, intonation patterns, and ornaments as well as a mood or feeling. A *raga* is an organized melodic matrix inside of which the South Indian singer or musician improvises melodically in performance (see Chapter 6). The modal system of Arab music, *maqam,* is like the Indian *raga,* in that characteristic phrases and ornamental patterns are as much a part of the composition of a musical mode as are the notes

Russell Lee. Courtesy of the Library of Congress.

FIGURE 1.4

Teenagers harmonizing gospel music. Bristow, Oklahoma, 1938.

of its scale, which, in Arab music, can incorporate nontempered "quarter tones" (see Chapter 10).

HARMONY

Most readers of this book use the word *harmony* to describe something that can happen to a melody: It can be harmonized. You sing a melody and someone else sings a **harmony,** a part different from the melody, at the same time (see Figure 1.4). You hear the intervals between the tones not only in a sequence, as in a melody, but also simultaneously. These simultaneously sounding tones are called **chords.** Although Western music theory is not always useful in describing music outside the Euro-American traditions, in this case **texture,** a word taken by analogy from the world of textiles to describe the interweaving of fibers, helps describe how melody and harmony interact in various musics throughout the world. Just as threads weave together to make cloth, so melodies can intertwine to make a multimelodic musical whole. Texture refers to the nature of these melodic interrelationships.

When the musical texture consists of a single melody only—for example, when you sing by yourself, or when several people sing the same melody in unison—we call the texture **monophonic** ("mono" meaning "single," "phono" meaning "voice"). If you add one or more voices doing different things, the melodic texture changes, and we describe the way the voices relate. The classical music of India commonly includes a *drone,* an unchanging tone or group of tones sounding continuously, against which the melody moves (see Chapter 6). European bagpipes also include drones. When two or more voices elaborate the same melody in different ways at roughly the same time, the texture is **heterophonic.** Heterophony may be heard in the voices of the African American congregation singing lined-out hymnody (CD 1, Track 22) and among the musicians performing "Ilumán tiyu" (CD 4, Track 11). Heterophony is the desired texture in much ensemble playing in Arab music, in which each musician performs the same melody, but with their own additions and omissions, nuances and ornaments, as we hear in several of the musical examples from Chapter 10.

When two or more distinct melodies are combined, the texture is **polyphonic.** Polyphony can also be heard in New Orleans–style jazz from the first few decades of the twentieth century: Louis Armstrong's earliest recordings offer good examples in which several melodic lines interweave. Javanese *gamelan* and other ensemble music of Southeast Asia (Chapter 7) consist of many layers of melodic activity that some scholars have described as polyphony. Polyphony is characteristic of European classical music in the Renaissance period (roughly 1450 to 1600) and the late Baroque (Bach was a master of polyphony).

When two or more voices are combined in a such way that one dominates and any others seem to be accompanying the dominant voice—or what most people mean when they say they hear a harmony (accompaniment)—the texture is **homophonic.** Homophony is typical of folk and popular music throughout the world (Figure 1.5).

A homophonic texture characterizes country music in the United States, such as the Fenders' Navajo rendition of "Folsom Prison Blues" (CD 1, Track 7) and Efraín's performance of the Quichua *sanjuán* "Muyu muyari warmigu" on the harp, which is an example of an instrument that can play a melody and an accompaniment simultaneously (CD 4, Track 10). Piano playing in jazz, rock, and other popular music is homophonic. The pianist usually gives the melody to the right hand and an accompaniment to the left. Sometimes the pianist plays only accompaniment, as when "comping" behind a jazz soloist. Blues guitarists such as Blind Blake and Mississippi John Hurt developed a homophonic style in the 1920s in which the fingers of the right hand played melody on the treble strings while the right-hand thumb simultaneously played an accompaniment on the bass strings.

FIGURE 1.5

Ladies' String Band, c. 1910. Family photos can be a useful source of musical history, even when identifying information is unknown. Photographer unknown.

FORM

The word *form* has many meanings. From your writing assignments you know what an outline is. You might say that you are putting your ideas in "outline form." By using the word *form* here, you call attention to the way the structure of your thoughts is arranged. Similarly, in music, painting, architecture, and the other arts, *form* means structural arrangement. To understand form in music, we look for patterns of organization in rhythm, melody, and harmony. Patterns of musical organization involve, among other things, the arrangement of small- to medium-sized musical units of rhythm, melody, and/or harmony that show repetition or variation. Just as a sentence (a complete thought) is made up of smaller units such as phrases, which in turn are made up of individual words, so a musical thought is made up of **phrases** that result from combinations of sounds. Form can also refer to the arrangement of the instruments, as in the order of solos in a jazz or bluegrass performance, or the way a symphonic piece is orchestrated. **Form** refers to the structure of a musical performance: the principles by which it is put together and how it works.

Consider the pattern of blues texts (lyrics). The form often consists of three-line stanzas: A line is sung ("Woke up this morning, blues all around my bed"), the line is repeated, and then the stanza closes with a different line ("Went to eat my breakfast and the blues were in my bread"). Blues melodies also have a particular form, as do the chord changes (harmony) in blues (see Chapter 4). In the Jiangnan *sizhu* music of China (Chapter 8), the same music may be played twice as fast in a second section. The form of traditional Native American melodies (Chapter 2) involves the creative use of small units and variation. This form is not apparent to someone listening to the music for the first time or even the second, which is one of the reasons we pay careful attention to it.

Structural arrangement is an important aspect of the way music is organized. It operates on many levels, and it is key to understanding not only how music-cultures organize music but also how various cultures and subcultures think about time and space in general. For these reasons musical form is an important consideration in all the chapters that follow.

Our understanding of rhythm, meter, melody, and harmony is greatly enriched when we consider how music-cultures throughout the world practice these organizing principles of human sound. But there is more to music than the structure of sounds. When people make music, they do not merely produce sounds—they also involve themselves in various social activities and express their ideas about music. To ethnomusicologists considering music as a human phenomenon, these activities and ideas are just as important as the music's structure. In fact, the activities and ideas are also part of the human organization of the sound. In other words, ethnomusicologists strive for a way to talk about all the aspects of music, not just its sound. Where, for example, is there room to talk about whether musicians are true to an ideal or whether they have "sold out" to commercial opportunity? This book presents music in relation to individual experience, to history, to the economy and the music industry, and to each music-culture's view of the world, which includes ideas about how human beings ought to behave. To help think about music in those ways, we next consider music as it exists in performance.

A Music-Culture Performance Model

Even when we are curious about the music of the world's peoples and want to understand more about it, confronting a new music can be daunting. When watching a live performance, for example, our first impulse might be simply to listen to it, to absorb it, to see whether we like it or whether it moves us. Our next impulse may be to let our bodies respond by moving to the music. But soon we will ask questions about it: What is that instrument that sounds so lovely? How does one play it? Why are the people dancing? (Or are they dancing?) Why is someone crying? Why are the musicians in costume? What do the words mean? What kind of a life does the head musician lead? To formulate and begin to answer these questions in a comprehensive way, we need some kind of systematic outline, or model, of any music-culture or subculture that tells us how it might work and what its components might be.

In this book we propose a music-culture model that is grounded in music as it is performed (Titon 1988:7–10). To see how this model works, think back to a musical event that has moved you. At the center of the event is your experience of the music, sung and played by performers (perhaps you are one of them). The performers are surrounded by their audience (in some instances, performers and audience are one and the same), and the whole event takes place in its setting in time and space. We can represent this by a diagram of concentric circles (Figure 1.6).

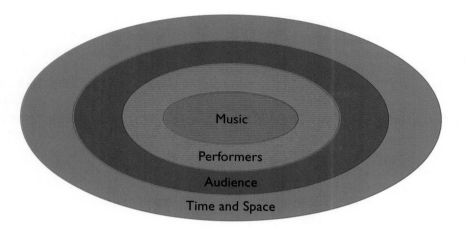

FIGURE 1.6

Elements of a musical
performance.

Now we transpose this diagram into four circles representing a music-culture model (Figure 1.7).

FIGURE 1.7

A music-culture model
(after Titon 1988:11).

At the center of the music (as you experience it) is its radiating power, its emotional impact—whatever makes you give assent, smile, nod your head, sway your shoulders, dance. We call that music's **affect,** its power to move, and place affective experience at the center of the model. Performance brings music's power to move into being, and so we move from performers in Figure 1.6 to performance in Figure 1.7. **Performance** involves many things. First, people mark performances, musical or otherwise, as separate from the flow of ordinary life: "Have you heard the story about..." or "Now we're going to do a new song that one of the members of the band wrote while thinking about...." When performance takes place, people recognize it as performance. Sammy Davis, Jr., told an interviewer, "Once I get outside my house in the morning, I'm *on.*" We often mark endings of performances with applause. Second, performance has purpose. The performers intend to move (or not move) the audience, to sing and play well (or not well), to make money, to have fun, to learn, to advance a certain rite or ceremony. The performance is evaluated partly on how well those intentions have been fulfilled. Third, a performance is interpreted, as it goes along, by the audience, who may cry out, applaud, or hiss, and by the performers, who may smile when things are going well or wince when they make a mistake.

The most important thing to understand about performance is that it moves along on the basis of agreed-on rules and procedures. These rules enable the musicians to play together and make sense to each other and to the audience. The performers usually do not discuss most of the rules; they have absorbed them and agreed to them. Starting at the same time, playing in the same key, playing in the same rhythmic framework, repeating the melody at the proper point—these are a few of the many rules that govern most of the musical performances that Westerners experience. Even improvisation is governed by rules. In a rock concert, for example, guitarists improvise melodic "breaks," but they usually do not use all twelve tones of the chromatic scale; instead they almost always choose from the smaller number of tones represented by the blues scale (see Chapter 4). Instrumental improvisation in Arab music, or *taqasim,* is also governed by rules, in that a performer is expected to know how to combine the characteristic riffs and phrases of a particular *maqam,* while at the same time making his of her improvisation sound fresh and original. Audiences, too, often respond to improvisations with shouts of approval and encouragement for the musician, during pauses and after closing phrases called *qafla* (see Chapter 10). In Chapter 5 we will see how rules govern improvisation in music and dance in Poland. Rules or accepted procedures govern the audience, too. In some situations shouting is not only permitted but expected. What to wear, what to say—these, too, are determined by spoken or unspoken rules at any musical performance. Sometimes musicians try to break these rules or expectations, as in a ritual destruction of their instruments at the close of the concert, which in turn can become an expectation.

The music-culture model presented here defines music in performance as meaningfully organized sound that proceeds by rules. (Does bird song conform to this model? How and why?) Finding out those rules or principles becomes the task of analysis. These rules include (but are not limited to) what is usually covered under **musical analysis:** breaking music down into its component parts of mode, motif, melody, rhythm, meter, section, and so forth, and determining how the parts operate together to make the whole. Beyond that, the task in exploring music-cultures is to discover the rules covering ideas about music and behavior in relation to music, as well as the links between these rules or principles and the sound that a group of people calls "music."

You may resist the notion that music, which you think should be free to express emotion, is best thought of as rule-governed behavior. But rules govern all meaningful human cultural behavior in just this way. The point is not that musical performance is predetermined by rules, but that it proceeds according to them. In this view, music is like a game or a conversation: Without rules we could not have a game, and without agreement about what words are, what they mean, and how they are used, we could not hold a meaningful conversation. Nonetheless, just as meaningful conversations can express emotion, so meaningful music can express it as well, though not, of course, in exactly the same way. Further, if a listener does not understand the rules, he or she can understand neither the intention of the composer or musician nor the music's structure.

The circle corresponding to audience in Figure 1.6 becomes community in the music-culture model (Figure 1.7). The **community** is the group (including the performers) that carries on the traditions and norms, the social processes and activities, and the ideas of performance. By community we do not always mean a group of people living close to one another. For our purposes, a community in a music-culture forms when they participate in a performance in some way—as performer, audience, composer, and so forth. We call these communities where people come together over common interests *affinity groups*. People in an affinity group may not know each other very well and may not even be in each other's physical presence, as for example in an Internet community. Today some websites allow a person to lay down a bass line, and later someone else from a different part of the world can lay down a guitar track on top of that, while another person can insert a drum track, and another provide a vocal, and yet another add vocal harmony, and so on, until eventually all of it adds up to a song that can be played from the website or downloaded. These "musicians" may never meet in person, yet they form a community.

Performance, then, is situated in community and is part of a people's music-culture. The community pays for and supports the music, whether directly with money or indirectly by allowing the performers to live as musicians. Community support usually influences the future direction of a particular kind of music. In a complex society such as the United States, various communities support different kinds of music—classical, rock, jazz, gospel—and they do so in different ways. When music becomes a mass-media commodity for sale, then packaging, marketing, and advertising are as crucial to the success of musicians as they are to the popularity of a brand of perfume.

How the community relates to the music makers also has a profound effect on the music. Among the folk music-cultures of nonindustrial village societies, the performers are drawn from the community; everyone knows them well, and communication takes place face-to-face. At the other end of the spectrum is the postindustrial music-culture celebrity who guards his or her private life, performs from a raised platform, offers a disembodied voice coming through a machine, and remains enigmatic to the audience. How the community relates to itself is another important aspect of performance. This is the place to consider music in relation to age, gender, identity, region, and class. For example, do men, women, old people, and young people experience music differently? We will consider this issue later in this chapter.

Time and space, the fourth circle in Figure 1.6, become memory and history in our music-culture model (Figure 1.7). The community is situated in history and borne by memory, official and unofficial, whether remembered or recorded or written down. Musical experiences, performances, and communities change over time and space; they have a history, and that history reflects changes in the rules governing music as well as the effect of music on human relationships. For example, the development of radio, recordings, and television meant that music did not need to be heard in the performer's presence. This took the performer out of the community's face-to-face relationships and allowed people to listen to music without making it themselves. Today music is an almost constant background to many people's lives, with the musicians largely absent.

Music critics and historians also alter the effect of music by influencing the stock of ideas about music. The critic who writes for newspapers, magazines, or the Internet helps listeners and music makers understand the impact of performances. When white America became interested in blues music in the 1960s and began presenting blues concerts and festivals (see Chapter 4), magazine and newspaper writers began asking blues singers questions about their music and its history. Knowing they would be asked these questions, blues singers prepared their answers, sometimes reading and then repeating what writers had already said about blues, sometimes having fun with their questioners and deliberately misleading them, and sometimes answering truthfully based on their experiences. This pattern is repeating itself today with hip-hop. Many times the subject of music is history itself. The Homeric poets sang about Odysseus; Serbian *guslars* sang about the deeds of their heroes; European ballads tell stories of nobles and commoners; African *griots* sing tribal genealogies and history, and the Arab *sha'ir*, or poet-singers, recount the travels and definitive battles of their tribal ancestors.

Today, digital recorders, computers, and multimedia programs are revolutionizing community music history in the West, for they empower musicians and audience alike to record what they want to hear, represent it as they wish, and listen to it again and again; in this way they gain a kind of control over their history never before experienced. In studying the history of a music-culture, or some aspect of it, you need to know not only what that history is but also who tells or writes that history and what stake the historian has in it.

As you read through each of the case studies in the following chapters, bear this underlying music-culture **performance model** in mind. Because each of the case studies focuses on music and performance, you can use this model to understand how each chapter moves among experience, performance, community, memory, and history. Musical analysis is an important part of this procedure. Unlike the analyst who investigates Western classical music by looking at the composer's written score, ethnomusicologists must usually deal with music that exists only in performance, without notation or instructions from a composer. The ethnomusicologist usually transcribes the music—that is, notates it—and then analyzes its structure. But it is impossible to understand structure fully without knowing the cultural "why" along with the musical "what."

The Four Components of a Music-Culture

A music-culture ultimately rests in the people themselves—their ideas, their actions, and the sound they produce (Merriam 1964:32–33). For that reason, we now introduce another way of talking about all these aspects of music—a component model of a music-culture. This model, which complements the performance model we have just discussed, is divided into four parts: ideas about music, activities involving music, repertories of music, and the material culture of music (Table 1.1).

IDEAS ABOUT MUSIC

Music and the Belief System

What is music, and what is not? Is music human, divine, or both? Is music good and useful for humankind or is it potentially harmful? Does music belong to individuals, to groups, as if it were private property? Or is music a public resource that should be treated as common property? (We will have more to say about who owns music in the section "Activities Involving Music.") These questions reach

TABLE 1.1 The Four Components of a Music Culture.

I. Ideas about music
    A. Music and the belief system
    B. Aesthetics of music
    C. Contexts for music
    D. History of music
II. Activities involving music
III. Repertories of music
    A. Style
    B. Genres
    C. Texts
    D. Composition
    E. Transmission
    F. Movement
IV. Material culture of music

into a music-culture's basic ideas concerning the nature of human society, art, and the universe. Cultures vary enormously in their answers to these questions, and the answers often are subtle, even paradoxical; they are embodied in rituals that try to reconcile love and hate, life and death, the natural and the cultural. In Chapter 8 we will see how the Chinese concept of complementarity, yin and yang, often symbolized by ☯, is an integration of divergence and accord that applies to music as it does to history, language, geography, and religion. Further, the answers may change over time even within a single music-culture. For example, a medieval Christian would have trouble understanding one of today's folk masses.

Throughout the book you will see many examples of how belief systems and music-cultures interact. You will see in Chapter 2 that music is a major part of Navajo ceremonies to cure disease. Navajos understand the medical theories of the Euro-American world, and they use Western medicine. But they also believe that certain kinds of illness, such as depression, indicate that the person's relationship to the natural and the human world is out of balance. Further, Navajos view nature as a powerful force capable of speaking directly to humans and teaching them the songs and prayers for the curing rituals that restore harmony. Music is so important to Native Americans that their stories of the creation of the universe are expressed traditionally in ceremonial chants (see Figure 1.8).

In Chapter 3 you will see that among the Ewe of Ghana, funerals feature singing, dancing, and drumming because the ancestral spirits, as well as their living descendants, love music and dance. Similarly, in Chapter 9 you will find that among the Quichua of Ecuador, as well as other Roman Catholic cultures of Latin America, music and dance are integral to the child's wake, a ceremony that takes place when a baptized infant dies. Joyous singing and dancing in the presence of death is understood as an affirmation of life. The *ragas* of India, considered in Chapter 6, are thought to have musical personalities, to express particular moods. In Chapter 5 you will learn why music is essential for weddings in Poland and Bulgaria, as well as how major world religions impacted musical practices in many parts of Europe. As you read through the chapters in this book, see how each music-culture relates music to its worldview.

FIGURE 1.8

Mr. and Mrs. Walker Calhoun, holding eagle feathers. Big Cove, near Cherokee, North Carolina, 1989. The Calhouns are leaders in preserving traditional songs and dances among the east coast Cherokee.

Aesthetics of Music

When is a song beautiful? When is it beautifully sung? What voice quality is pleasing, and what grates on the ear? How should a musician dress? How long should a performance last? Not all cultures agree on these questions about what is proper and what is beautiful. Some people in the United States find Chinese opera singing strained and artificial, but some Chinese find the European bel canto opera style imprecise and unpleasant. Harmonic intervals considered "ugly" in some parts of Europe are desirable in others (CD 2, Track 9). Some jazz saxophone players (and listeners) favor a "hot," buzzy, honking sound while others prefer the "cool," smooth, saxophone timbre found in classical music. Music-cultures can be characterized by preferences in sound quality and performance practice, all of which are **aesthetic** discriminations; that is, they are concerned with ideas of beauty, pleasure, enjoyment, form, and affect.

Javanese *gamelan* music (Chapter 7) is not featured in concert the way we hear classical music in the West; rather, it is usually performed to accompany dance or theater. *Gamelan* music also accompanies a family's celebration of a birth, wedding, or other event; people are expected to mingle and talk while the music takes place in the background. The music for the Chinese *qin* (Chapter 8) was associated many centuries ago with amateur musicians, scholars for whom music was a pastime, not a profession. It was felt that a *qin* musician need not strive for virtuosity in performance nor learn more than a few pieces of music. The story goes that, nearly two thousand years ago, a young scholar went to visit a renowned older Chinese scholar. On seeing that the elder's *qin*, hanging on the wall of his study, was dilapidated and missing three of its seven strings, the young scholar inquired as to how it might make music. "Ah," replied the older scholar, "the unplayed melodies are the sweetest to contemplate of all."

Contexts for Music

When should music be performed? How often? On what occasions? Again, every music-culture answers these questions about musical surroundings differently (see Figure 1.9).

In the modern world, where context can depend on the mere flip of an on-off switch and a portable mp3 player, it is hard to imagine the days when all music came from face-to-face performances. Our great-grandparents had to sing or play music or hear it from someone nearby; they could not produce it on demand from the disembodied voice of a radio, television, CD player, iPod, or computer. How attentively you would have listened to a singer or a band 125 years ago if you had thought that the performance might be the only time in your life you would hear that music!

Jeff Todd Titon

FIGURE 1.9

Gospel singers at a Pentecostal revival in the Southeastern United States. Guitars, banjos, and camp-meeting songs that would be out place in some U.S. churches, such as the one in Figure 1.1, are appropriate in this context.

Even though much of the music around the globe today comes through mass media, people in music-cultures still associate particular musics with particular contexts. Navajo ceremonial music is appropriate in certain ceremonial contexts but not others. As we will see in Chapter 2, these ceremonies have names such as Enemyway and Blessingway, and each has a specific music that must be performed properly for the ceremony to be effective. *Vacación* is a special symbolic composition for the harp that is performed at the start of the Quichuan child's wake, at the late-evening adorning of the corpse, and at the closing of the casket at dawn (Chapter 9). The usual context for blues is a bar, juke joint, dance hall, or blues club (Chapter 4). This is a far cry from the concert halls that provide the context for symphony orchestra performances. For many centuries in India the courts and upper classes supported the classical music that we will consider in Chapter 6. But concerts of classical music in India are more relaxed and informal than those in Europe, where the patronage of the courts and the aristocracy, as well as the Church, traditionally supported classical music. Today in Europe and North America the government, the wealthy classes, and the universities supply this patronage. Classical music in various parts of the world, then, is usually associated with patronage from the elite classes, and it is performed in refined contexts that speak of its supporters' wealth and leisure.

Sometimes governments intervene to support other kinds of music. For example, during the twentieth century the Soviet Union and other Communist states encouraged a certain kind of folk music, or workers' music, thought to inspire solidarity. Typically, under government management what had been a loose and informal village musical aesthetic was transformed into a disciplined, almost mechanized, urban expression of the modern industrial nation-state (see Chapter 5). Folk festivals, supported by Communist governments, showcased this music. In the United States, the last few decades have also witnessed the rise of government-supported folk festivals (Figure 1.10). Here, though, the diversity of

FIGURE 1.10

Folk festivals in the United States often feature traditional music from ethnic communities. Here Jae Sook Park plays the *komungo*, a six-stringed Korean plucked lute, at the National Folk Festival, Bangor, Maine, 2003.

Jeff Todd Titon

ethnic musics is celebrated, and the government encourages the most traditional expressions within the music-cultures that are represented. Folk festivals provide an artificial context for traditional music, but the hope is that in a world where young people are powerfully attracted to new, mass-mediated, transnational popular music, folk festivals will encourage this local music in its home context. When nations modernize and traditional ideas and practices become old-fashioned, as for example in present-day China (Chapter 8), various individuals and institutions (schools, clubs, societies) get involved in efforts to preserve and revive traditional music for contemporary life; in doing so, they also transform it (see the section on musical sustainability, later in this chapter).

History of Music

Why is music so different among the world's peoples? What happens to music over time and space? Does it stay the same or change, and why? What did the music of the past sound like? Should music be preserved? What will the music of the future be? Some cultures institutionalize the past in museums and the future in world's fairs; they support specialists who earn their living by talking and writing about music. Other cultures transmit knowledge of music history mainly by word of mouth through the generations. Recordings, films, videotapes, CDs, DVDs, and now the Internet allow us to preserve musical performances much more exactly than our ancestors could—but only when we choose to do so. For example, one ethnomusicologist was making tapes as he learned to sing Native American music. His teacher advised him to erase the tapes and reuse them once he learned his lessons, but he decided to preserve them.

Musical history responds to changes in human cultures. The work songs that facilitated human labor gave way to the whine of machines with the industrial revolution (Chapter 4), but today the hum of the computer provides a background to individual musical composition and arranging as well as listening over the Internet.

European and Asian rural wedding and funeral ceremonies that involved important music making to celebrate these passage rites have become far less elaborate. The Chinese wedding laments discussed in Chapter 8 represent a survival of this tradition, while the wedding music presented in Chapter 5 represents an ongoing revival of music and ceremony that the Polish mountain peoples wish to preserve.

Questions about music history may arise both inside and outside a particular music-culture. Most music-cultures have their own community scholars who are historians or music authorities, formally trained or not, whose curiosity about music leads them to think and talk about music in their own culture, ask questions, and remember or write down answers. In some music-cultures, authority goes along with being a good musician; in others, one need not be a good musician to be a respected historian of music. Such historians usually are curious about music outside their own cultures as well, and they often develop theories to account for musical differences.

The four categories of ideas about music that we have just discussed—music and the belief system, aesthetics, contexts, and history—overlap. Though we separate them here for convenience, we do not want to suggest that music-cultures present a united front in their ideas about music or that a music-culture prescribes a single aesthetic. People within a music-culture often differ in their ideas about music. Ragtime, jazz, rock and roll, and hip-hop were revolutionary when they were introduced in the United States. They met (and still meet) opposition from some within the U.S. music-culture. This opposition is based on aesthetics (the music is thought to be loud and obscene, while some question whether it is music at all) and context (the music's associated lifestyles are thought to involve narcotics, violence, free love, radical politics, and so forth).

When organized divisions exist within a music-culture, we recognize music-subcultures, worlds within worlds of music. In fact, as we have seen, most music-cultures in the modern world can be divided into several subcultures, some opposed to each other: classical versus rock, for example, or (from an earlier era) sacred hymns versus dance music and drinking songs. Many Native American music-cultures in the northeastern United States have a subculture of traditionalists interested in older musics that are marked as Native American, while other subcultures are involved more with the music of the Catholic Church, and yet others with forms of contemporary popular music (rock, jazz, country) that they have adapted to their needs and desires. Sometimes the subcultures overlap: The performance of a hymn in a Minnesota church may involve region (the upper Midwest), ethnicity (German), and religion (Lutheranism)—all bases for musical subcultures. Which musical subcultures do you identify with most strongly? Which do you dislike? Are your preferences based on contexts, aesthetics, the belief system—or a combination of these?

ACTIVITIES INVOLVING MUSIC

People in a music culture do not just have ideas about music, of course; they put those ideas into practice in a variety of activities—everything from making the sounds to putting music up on the Internet, from rehearsing in their rooms alone to playing in a band to managing a concert to making recordings and marketing them. More and more people are becoming active consumers of music, carefully selecting the music they want to experience from the great variety available.

Human activities involving music also include the way people divide, arrange, or rank themselves in relation to music. Musical ideas and performances are unevenly divided among the people in any music-culture. For example, some perform often, others hardly at all. Some musicians perform for a living, while others play for the love of it. People sing different songs and experience music differently because of age and gender. Racial, ethnic, and work groups also sing their own songs, and each group may develop or be assigned its own musical role. All of these differences have to do with the social organization of the music-culture, and they are based on the music-culture's ideas about music. We may ask, "What is it like in a given music-culture to experience music as a teenage girl in a West Coast suburb, a young male urban professional, or a rural grandmother of Swedish ethnic heritage who lives on a farm?"

Sometimes the division of musical behavior resembles the social divisions within the group and reinforces the usual activities of the culture. Until 1997 the Vienna Symphony had no women in its orchestra. Throughout most of the nineteenth century men acted the female roles in *jingju* opera (see Chapter 8) as the Chinese government felt it was improper for men and women to appear onstage together. In many traditional ceremonies throughout the world, men and women congregate in separate areas; some ceremonies center exclusively on men and others on women. On the other hand, music sometimes goes against the broad cultural grain, often at carnival time or at important moments in the life cycle (initiations, weddings, funerals, and so forth). People on the cultural fringe become important when they play music for these occasions. In fact, many music-cultures assign a low social status to musicians but also acknowledge their power and sometimes even see magic in their work. The most important features of music's social organization are status and role: the prestige of the music makers and the different roles assigned to people in the music-culture. In the interview with the Iraqi refugee musician Rahim al-Haj in Chapter 10 we read of the familiar reaction of his father, who disapproves of his son's ambitions to be a musician, a sentiment that resonates with the historical accounts of the tenth century written in his native city, Baghdad. In contrast, Don César Muquinche (Chapter 9) decided to become a hatmaker rather than follow the career of his father, a harpist; but gradually as an adult he took up the harp, chiefly because the public expected him to follow in his father's footsteps—and in responding to the challenge, he discovered his own talent.

Many of the musical situations in this book depend on these basic aspects of social organization. When blues arose early in the twentieth century, most middle-class African Americans associated it with the black underclass and tried to keep their children away from it. Blues musicians were assigned a low social status (Chapter 4). Neither the Argentine tango nor the Trinidadian steelband were considered respectable when they arose. Only after they gained popularity abroad and returned to their home countries did they become respectable to the point of becoming national symbols of music in their respective countries.

Increasingly, ethnomusicologists have turned to the ways in which race, ethnicity, class, gender, region, and identity are embedded in musical activities. When people in a music-culture migrate out of their region, they often use music as a marker of ethnic identity. Throughout North America, ethnic groups perform and sometimes revive music that they consider to be their own, whether Jewish klezmer music, Andean panpipe music, central European polka, Portuguese fado (Figure 1.11), or Peking Opera.

In the twentieth century, the music industry has played an especially important role in various music-cultures. Music is packaged, bought, and sold. How does a song commodity become popular? When is popularity the result of industry hype and when does it come from a groundswell of consumer interest? How do new kinds of music break into the media? Why do certain kinds of music gain (or fall) in popularity? What makes a hit song? Fortunes are gained and lost based on music producers' abilities to predict what will sell—yet most of the music released commercially does not sell. How should a group of musicians deal with the industry? How can they support themselves while remaining true to their musical vision? What constitutes "selling out"? In the last few decades, markets have expanded and musicians from all over the globe now take part. Computer software-assisted music making and the rise of a market on the Internet have empowered consumers to become musicians and have empowered musicians to become producers and marketers.

Jeff Todd Titon

FIGURE 1.11

Ana Vinagre of New Bedford, Massachusetts, sings Portuguese fado. National Folk Festival, Bangor, Maine, 2002.

Music has become an enormously important aspect of the global economy. The current struggles over the future of music delivery on the Internet alone involve profits and losses in the billions of dollars.

A generation ago, people were taking music out of the hands of the corporations by making and trading concert tapes of jam bands. People put together their own "mixes" of already-made popular songs on cassette tapes for themselves and their friends. Today, with software such as GarageBand, the computer has turned tens of thousands of people into serious amateurs, who make *beats,* or background tracks for hip-hop, and who make and mix all kinds of tracks in their spare time and place their own songs on the Internet. Professionals can be hired to compose and add tracks to a mix, while certain websites such as jamglue encourage other amateurs to do this for free. As more people are participate in music by making it, not just listening to it, the line between professional and amateur is blurring. For many, the primary experience of listening to music as a commodity is giving way to the experience of making music with the computer and bypassing traditional commercial channels.

As a great deal of money remains at stake in the distribution of music—new as well as old, along with "world music" that is packaged and distributed globally, debates rage over who owns music. Should music be treated as private property or should it be regarded as common property for the public good? Or, as copyright law in the United States once provided, should it be private property for a given number of years, after which time it would become common property and pass into the "public domain"? Here, as elsewhere, ideas about music generate activities involved with music. People in traditional music-cultures often have regarded music as common property, but as outsiders and multinational corporations profit from their music, their concern to protect their musical resources has grown. International agencies such as World Intellectual Property Organization (WIPO) and United Nations Educational, Scientific and Cultural Organization (UNESCO) have formulated cultural policy to protect what they call "intangible heritage" or traditional arts from commercial exploitation.

REPERTORIES OF MUSIC

A **repertory** is a stock of music that is ready to be performed. It consists of six basic parts: style, genres, texts, composition, transmission, and movement. Think of a music that you are familiar with and see if you can understand it using the following terms.

Style

Style includes everything related to the organization of musical sound itself: pitch elements (scale, melody, harmony, tuning systems), time elements (rhythm, meter), timbre elements (voice quality, instrumental tone color), and sound intensity (loudness/softness). All depend on a music-culture's aesthetics.

Together, style and aesthetics create a recognizable sound that a group understands as its own. For example, the fiddle was the most popular dance instrument in Europe and North America from about the eighteenth century until the turn of the twentieth century. In many areas it is still popular; in others, such as Ireland, it is undergoing a revival. Old-time fiddlers in Missouri prefer their regional dance and contest tunes to the bluegrass tunes of the upper South. Old-time fiddlers in the upper South, on the other hand, prefer their own repertory of breakdown tunes. People new to these repertories do not hear significant differences between them. Are they alike? Not entirely, because each group can distinguish its own music. People learning fiddle tunes know they are getting somewhere when they can recognize the differences in national and regional styles and put those differences into words—or music.

Genres

Genres are the named, standard units of the repertory, such as "song" and its various subdivisions (for example, lullaby, Christmas carol, wedding song) or the many types of instrumental music and dances (jig, reel, waltz, schottische, polka, *hambo,* and so forth). Genres come with built-in rules or expectations regarding performance style and setting, with the result that the "same" song, dance, or piece can be classified into different genres depending on how, when, or by whom it is performed or played back. An Irish jig might be played as an instrumental tune in a pub session, used in a film score, or danced professionally as part of an international show such as *Riverdance.*

Most music-cultures have a great many genres, but their terms do not always correspond to terms in other music-cultures. Among the Yoruba in the African nation of Nigeria, for example, powerful kings, chiefs, and nobles retained praise singers to sing to them (Olajubu 1978:685). The praise songs are called *oriki*. Although we can approximate an English name to describe them (praise songs), no equivalent genre exists today in Europe or America. In Japan, the labels identifying popular music include *gunka* (military songs), *fōku songu* (contemporary folk songs, distinguished from *minyō*, or the traditional folk songs of the countryside), *nyū myūshiku* (new music), and *pops*. In North America, blues is one genre, country music another. Subdivisions of country music include rockabilly and bluegrass. If you listen to country music stations on the radio, you will see that some identify themselves as "real country" (along with the latest hits, more of a mix of oldies and southern-oriented country music) and others as "hard country" (more of a mix of rock-oriented country music). Consider electronica and some of its subdivisions; the website allmusic.com lists more than fifty subgenres including techno, house, trance, trip-hop, happy hardcore, goa trance, and ambient. Subgenres have proliferated as composition and marketing have grown more sophisticated. How many subgenres can you name in your favorite kind of music?

Texts

The words (or lyrics) to a song are known as its **text.** Any song with words is an intersection of two very different and profound human communication systems: language and music. A song with words is a temporary weld of these two systems, and for convenience we can look at each by itself.

Every text has its own history; sometimes a single text is associated with several melodies. On the other hand, a single melody can go with various texts. In blues music, for example, texts and melodies lead independent lives, coupling as the singer desires (Chapter 4). *Pop berat* ("heavy pop") compositions fuse Indonesian patriotic texts, traditional Indonesian musical instruments, and electric guitars and synthesizers (see Chapter 7). Navajo ritual song and prayer texts often conclude by saying that beauty and harmony prevail (see Chapter 2).

Composition

How does music enter the repertory of a music-culture? Is music composed individually or by a group? Is it fixed, varied within certain limits, or improvised spontaneously in performance? Improvisation fascinates most ethnomusicologists: Chapters 3, 4, and 6 consider improvisation in African, African American, and South Indian music. Perhaps at some deep level we prize improvisation not just because of the skills involved but because we think it exemplifies human freedom.

The composition of music, whether planned or spontaneous, is bound up with social organization. Does the music-culture have a special class of composers, or can anyone compose music? Composition is related as well to ideas about music: Some music-cultures divide songs into those composed by people and those "given" to people from deities, animals, and other nonhuman composers.

Transmission

How is music learned and transmitted from one person to the next, from one generation to the next? Does the music-culture rely on formal instruction, as in

FIGURE 1.12

Family photo of a father and son playing music at home, on violin and piccolo, c. 1910. Photographer and place unknown.

South India (Chapter 6)? Or is music learned chiefly through imitation (Chapter 4)? Does music theory underlie the process of formal instruction? Does music change over time? How and why? Is there a system of musical notation? Cipher (number) notation in Indonesia did not appear until the twentieth century (Chapter 7). In the ancient musical notation for the *qin* (Chapter 8), the Chinese writing indicates more than what note is to be played, because many of the Chinese pictograms (picture writing) suggest something in nature. For example, the notation may suggest a duck landing on water, telling the player to imitate the duck's landing with the finger when touching the string. Such notation can also evoke the feeling intended by the composer.

Some music-cultures transmit music through apprenticeships lasting a lifetime (as in the disciple's relation to a guru, Chapter 6). The instructor becomes like a parent, teaching values and ethics as well as music. In these situations, music truly becomes a way of life and the apprentice is devoted to the music and the teacher. Other music-cultures have no formal instruction, and the aspiring musician learns by watching and listening, often over many years. In these circumstances, growing up in a musical family is helpful (Figure 1.12). When a repertory is transmitted chiefly by example and imitation rather than notation, we say the music exists in *oral tradition* rather than written. Blues (Chapter 4) is an example of music in oral tradition; so is the *sanjuán* dance genre of highland Ecuadorian Quichua (Chapter 9). Music in oral tradition varies more over time and space than does music tied to a printed musical score. Sometimes the same music exists both in oral and written traditions. At gatherings called singing conventions, people belonging to Primitive Baptist denominations in the upper South sing hymn tunes from notation in tune books such as *The Sacred Harp.* Variants of these hymn tunes also exist in oral tradition among the Old Regular Baptists (see Figure 1.1), who do not use musical notation but who rely instead on learning the tunes from their elders and remembering them.

Movement

A whole range of physical activity accompanies music. Playing a musical instrument, alone or in a group, not only creates sound but also literally moves people—that is, they sway, dance, walk, work in response. Even if we cannot see them move very much, their brains and bodies are responding as they hear and process the music. How odd it would be for a rock band to perform without moving in response to their music, in ways that let the audience know they were feeling it. This was demonstrated many years ago by the new-wave rock band Devo when its members acted like robots. In one way or another movement and music connect in the repertory of every culture. Sometimes the movement is quite loose, suggesting freedom and abandon, and at other times, as in Balinese dance, it is highly controlled, suggesting that in this culture controlling oneself is beautiful and admirable.

MATERIAL CULTURE OF MUSIC

Material culture refers to the material objects that people in a culture produce—objects that can be seen, held, felt, and used. This book is an example of material culture. So are dinner plates, gravestones, airplanes, hamburgers, cell phones, and school buildings. Examining a culture's tools and technology can tell us about the group's history and way of life. Similarly, research into the material culture of music can help us to understand music-cultures. The most important objects in a music-culture, of course, are musical instruments (see Figure 1.13). We cannot hear the actual sound of any musical performances before the 1870s, when the phonograph was invented, so we rely on instruments for information about music-cultures in the remote past. Here we have two kinds of evidence: instruments preserved more or less intact, such as Sumerian harps over forty-five hundred years old, or the Chinese relics from the tomb of Marquis Yi (see Chapter 8) and instruments pictured in art. Through the study of instruments, as well as paintings, written documents, and other sources, we can explore the movement of music from the Near East to China over a thousand years ago, we can trace the Guatemalan marimba to its African roots, or we can outline the spread of Near Eastern musical influences to Europe. The influence of Near Eastern music on Europe occurred mainly before the Spanish inquisition of 1515, through exchange between a multicultural and multireligious population in Andalusia, the region of southern Europe that we now know as Spain and Portugal; this resulted in the development of most of the instruments in the Euro-American symphony orchestra.

We can also ask questions of today's music-cultures: Who makes instruments, and how are they distributed? What is the relation between instrument makers and musicians? How do this generation's musical instruments reflect its musical tastes and styles, compared with those of the previous generation? In the late 1940s and early 1950s, electric instruments transformed the sound of popular music in the United States, and in the 1960s this electronic musical revolution spread elsewhere in the world. Taken for granted today, electric instruments—guitars, basses, pianos, pedal steel guitars—ushered in a musical revolution. The computer is the most revolutionary musical instrument

FIGURE 1.13

Young man playing a one-stringed diddly-bow. Missouri, 1938. (Instructions for making and playing a similar instrument are given in Chapter 4.)

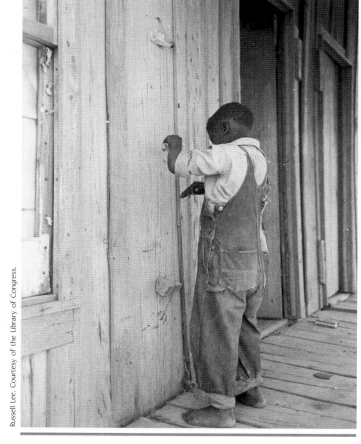

Russell Lee. Courtesy of the Library of Congress.

today. Computer-assisted composition, incorporating sound sampling and other innovations, empowers a new generation of composers to do things they had otherwise been unable to accomplish.

Musical scores, instruction books, sheet music, instructional DVDs, websites devoted to music—these too are part of the material culture. Scholars once defined folk music-cultures as those in which people learn to sing music by ear rather than from print, but research shows mutual influence among oral and written sources during the past few centuries in Europe and America. Because they tend to standardize songs, printed versions limit variety, but paradoxically they stimulate people to create original songs. Also, the ability to read music notation has a far-reaching effect on musicians and, when it becomes widespread, on a music-culture as a whole.

One more important part of a music's material culture should be singled out: the impact of electronic media. This technology has facilitated the information revolution, a twentieth-century phenomenon as important as the industrial revolution was in the nineteenth. Electronic media have affected music-cultures all over the world. People listen to mass-mediated music more than any other kind. Such media are one of the main reasons many now call our planet a global village.

Ecological and Sustainable Worlds of Music

In the eighteenth century, when Europeans began collecting music from the countryside and from faraway places outside their homelands, they thought that "real," traditional music was dying out. From then on, each time a new music-culture was discovered, European and American collectors took the music of its oldest generation to be the most authentic, conferring on it a timeless quality and usually deploring anything new. This neither reflected the way music-cultures actually work nor gave people enough credit for creative choice. At any given moment, three kinds of music circulate within most communities: (1) music so old and accepted as "ours" that no one questions (or sometimes even knows) where it comes from, (2) music of an earlier generation understood to be old-fashioned or perhaps classic, and (3) the most recent or current types of music, marketed and recognized as the latest development. These recent musics may be local, imported, or both. The last is most likely, because today the world is linked electronically; musics travel much more quickly than they did a hundred years ago.

Music-cultures, in other words, are dynamic rather than static. They constantly change in response to inside and outside pressures. It is wrong to think of a music-culture as something isolated, stable, smoothly operating, impenetrable, and uninfluenced by the outside world. Indeed, as we will see in Chapter 4, the people in a music-culture need not share the same language, nationality, or ethnic origin. In the twenty-first century, blues is popular with performers worldwide. People in a music-culture need not even share all of the same ideas about music—as we have seen, they in fact do not. As music-cultures change (and they are always changing) they undergo friction, and the "rules" of musical performance, aesthetics, interpretation, and meaning are negotiated, not fixed. Music history is reconceived by each generation.

In this book we usually describe the older musical layers in a given region first. Then we discuss increasingly more-contemporary musical styles, forms, and attitudes. We wish to leave you with the impression that the world is not a set of untouched, authentic musical villages, but rather a fluid, interactive, interlocking, overlapping soundscape in which people listen to their ancestors, parents, neighbors, and personal CD and cassette machines all in the same day. We think of people as musical "activists," choosing what they like best, remembering what resonates best, forgetting what seems irrelevant, and keeping their ears open for exciting new musical opportunities. This happens everywhere, and it unites the farthest settlement and the largest city.

Music is a fluid, dynamic element of culture, and it changes to suit the expressive and emotional desires of humankind, perhaps the most changeable of the animals. Like all of culture, music is a peculiarly human adaptation to life on this earth. Seen globally, music operates as an ecological system. Each music-culture is a particular adaptation to particular circumstances. Ideas about music, social organization, repertories, and material culture vary from one music-culture to the next. It would be unwise to call one music-culture's music "primitive," because doing so imposes one's own standards on a group that does not recognize them. Such ethnocentrism has no place in the study of world musics.

Music may be viewed ecologically as a human resource that is produced and consumed. Unlike oil, a finite natural resource that decreases as it is used, music is an infinite human resource that is kept alive in use. Although at times considered an economic resource, as a human resource music has an emotion-based dimension that fosters human relationships outside and apart from the economic realm. But, like natural resources, in most cultures music is experienced as a source of energy, and as something whose qualities can be good or bad, improved or polluted, used wisely or wasted. People are responsible for its wise uses and sustainability, its conservation, management, and continuation as a human resource wisely used. Although this stewardship has usually centered on preserving endangered musics, it seems more helpful to think of it as encouraging the people who make music, as well as the conditions (ideas and cultural practices, whether traditional or modern) under which human beings remain free to create all music, including new music. In other words, sustainability stewardship is not just about music; it is about the people who make music.

In the chapters that follow, we explore the acoustic ecologies of several worlds, and worlds within worlds, of music. Although each world may seem strange to you at first, all are organized and purposeful. Considered as an ecological system, the forces that make up a music-culture maintain a dynamic equilibrium. A change in any part of the acoustic ecology, such as the invention of the electric guitar or the latest computer-music technology, may have a far-reaching impact. Viewing music this way leads to the conclusion that music represents a great human force that transcending narrow political, social, and temporal boundaries. Music offers an arena where people can talk and sing and play and reach each other in ways not allowed by the barriers of wealth, status, location, and difference. This book and CD set can present only a tiny sample of the richness of the world's music. We hope you will continue your exploration after you have finished this book.

Book Companion Website

You will find tutorial quizzes, Internet links, and much more at the Book Companion Website for *Worlds of Music,* 5th Edition, at **academic.cengage.com/music/titon/worlds_5**

North America/Native America

DAVID P. McALLESTER

American Indian music is unfamiliar to most non-Indian Americans. Accordingly, this chapter first presents an overall perspective by contrasting three of the numerous different Native American musical styles. Then we look in detail at some of the many types of music being performed today in just one tribe, the Navajos. Their musical life will be studied in relation to their traditional culture and their present history. Learning about the Navajos' cultural setting will greatly enhance your understanding of their music.

CHAPTER

2

Three Different Styles

SIOUX GRASS DANCE

The essence of music is participation, either by listening or, better still, by performing. We will start with the sound likely to be the most "Indian" to the non-Indian American—a Sioux War Dance (Figure 2.1, on page 35). This is also called a Grass Dance, from the braids of grass the dancing warriors used to wear at their waists to symbolize slain enemies. It is also called the Omaha Dance, after the Indians of the western plains, who originated it.

Listen for a moment to the recording of a Sioux Grass Dance (CD 1, Track 3). When European scholars first heard this kind of sound on wax cylinder **field recordings** (recordings made with portable gear on location rather than in a recording studio) brought back to Berlin in the early 1900s, they exclaimed, "Now, at last, we can hear the music of the true savages!" For four hundred years European social philosophers had thought of Americans Indians as noble wild men unspoiled by civilization, and here was music that fit the image.

Nothing known to Europeans sounded like this piercing **falsetto,** swooping down for more than an octave in a "tumbling strain" that seemed to come straight from the emotions. The pulsating voices with their sharp emphases, the driving drumbeat with its complex relation to the vocal part, the heavy slides at the ends of phrases—what could better portray the warlike horsemen of the limitless American plains? Another feature that intrigued Europeans was the use of **vocables**

CD 1:3

Grass Dance (1:51). Traditional Sioux War Dance. Field recording by Ray Boley, n.d. *Sioux Favorites.* Canyon Records Productions CR-6054. Phoenix, Arizona.

33

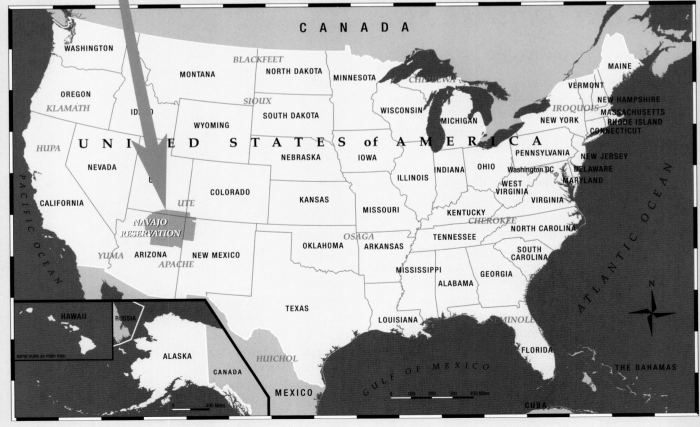

(nonlexical or "meaningless" syllables) for entire texts of songs, as in this Grass Dance. Curt Sachs cited this as another reason for labeling this music pathogenic (arising from the emotions), as contrasted with logogenic music, in which translatable words are the basis of the song (Sachs 1962:51–58). Sachs theorized that one would find pathogenic music in the early stages of a culture's evolution. He may have wondered when listening to Native-American music whether his own Paleolithic ancestors sang like that when they were hunting wild horses across the plains of Europe and had not yet discovered agriculture.

Another supposed proof that American Indians belonged to an early stage of musical evolution was the relatively few kinds of musical instruments they used. From north of Mexico to the Arctic the music was almost entirely vocal and the instruments were chiefly rattles and drums used to accompany the voice. However, the varieties of rattles and drums invented by North American Indians are legion. To name a few, there are rattles made from gourds, tree bark, carved wood, deer hooves, turtle shells, spider nests, and, recently, tin cans. There are frame drums and barrel drums of many sizes and shapes, and the water drum (described in detail later in this chapter), with its wet membrane, is unique. There are a few flutes and **flageolets** (end-blown wind instruments like the recorder except that two of the holes are in the back and closed with the thumbs), and one-stringed fiddles played without the voice, but these are rare. Instrumental ensembles such as Western classical orchestras are unknown in traditional North American Indian music.

In Central and South America, on the other hand, the native high civilizations did have orchestras before the Europeans came. They readily added European instruments to their ensembles and blended their music with new ideas from Portugal and Spain. Only in the last fifty or sixty years has this mingling of musics begun to happen on any large scale in native North American music. The vast majority of traditional songs are still accompanied by only drum or rattle or both.

Clearly, the once-popular Euro-American theories just described did not take into account the actual diversity within Native American cultures. Few scholars today find that a notion of "delayed evolution" explains the so-called simpler cultures of the world. In fact, they turn out not to be simple at all. Survival, whatever the climate, requires encyclopedic knowledge. A language never expressed in writing may contain the most complex grammatical structures known to linguists. Folk music with no harmonies may contain melodic, modal, and rhythmic sophistication unattainable in harmonic music.

Douglas Fulton. Courtesy of Gertrude Kurath.

FIGURE 2.1

War dancers at a Michigan powwow.

Close Listening

GRASS DANCE

CD 1:3

COUNTER NUMBER		COMMENTARY	FORM
0:00	Driving drum beat	Leader sings phrase in *vocables* (meaningless syllables) and piercing *falsetto* (artificially high pitch).	A
0:04		Male voices repeat leader's phrase.	
0:11		Leader and male voices drop to lower pitch.	B
0:19–0:22		Female voices enter at pitch above male voices and end section with *portamento* (slide).	
0:34		Leader repeats opening falsetto phrase.	A
0:37		Male voices repeat leader's phrase.	
0:43		Leader and male voices drop to lower pitch.	B
0:50–0:54		Female voices enter at pitch above men and end section with *portamento* (slide).	
1:04		Leader repeats opening falsetto phrase.	A
1:07		Male voices repeat leader's phrase.	
1:14		Leader and male voices drop to lower pitch.	B
1:19–1:24		Female voices enter at pitch above male voices and end section with *portamento* (slide).	
1:29–1:33		Drum stops then resumes at faster tempo.	
		TAIL OR CODA	
1:37		Leader and male voices repeat opening falsetto phrase and drop to lower pitch.	A
1:42–1:48		Female voices enter at pitch above male voices and end dance with obvious *portamento* (slide).	B

Listen again to the Sioux Grass Dance song and see if you can sing along with it. You may think it is impossible, especially if you are a man and have never tried to sing in falsetto before. You might find it easier at first to try singing the song an octave lower. The Close Listening guide and Transcription 2.1 will help you with the timing, words and melody.

TRANSCRIPTION 2.1
Sioux Grass Dance song.
(All musical transcriptions in this chapter are by David P. McAllester.)

With permission of Canyon Records.

If you cannot read musical notes, think of the transcription as a kind of graph tracing the line of the melody. Even with no musical training you can see patterns of movement from high to low and back up again. The sections of the song that sound alike have been labeled with the same letter of the alphabet to help you see where similar musical ideas are repeated. The overall structure of phrases in this song may be represented as shown here (minus the coda).

½ A A B B
½ A A B B
½ A A B B B

The song starts with an A phrase, sung by a leader, but before he can finish it the other male singers break in with the same phrase, repeated, and he joins them to sing it all the way through. The leader's first, uncompleted phrase is represented here as ½ A. Most of the melodic movement takes place in the B phrase. Here is where the melody drops a full octave below the tonal center established in the A phrase. In fact, the lower part of B is almost an exact repeat of A, performed twice and an octave lower. In Transcription 2.1, the points where this transposition begins and repeats are marked by (A₈). After three repeats of the whole melody, there is a pause; then B is repeated one last time to end the song. Indian singers often call that last brief section the **tail** of the song, which is also what the European musical term coda means.

Although the song's overall structure is easy to understand, you will probably find it difficult to sing. It goes fast and does not have a regular meter. Most of it follows 3-beat patterns, but every now and then the singers introduce a 4-beat phrase (marked by horizontal brackets in the transcription). Notice that the melody makes the same downward dip wherever the meter breaks into four. Another difficulty is that the song's meter (about 200 beats per minute) does not seem to coincide with that of the drum (about 192 beats per minute). "C = BH" means that I have transposed the melody level up a whole step so that it will be easier to read.

The best way to sing this is to relax and not try to count it out mechanically. Concentrate on the excitement that has made this kind of music the most popular Native-American style all over the country where there are Indian fairs, rodeos, and **powwows** (contemporary ceremonial and spiritual gatherings featuring food, singing, and dancing). Like the Plains Indians' eagle-feather war bonnet and their stately, beautifully decorated tepees, the War Dance symbolizes "American Indian" throughout the world. Though Indian singing styles differ from region to region, many non-Plains Indians, especially young people, have learned this style so well that they have been able to compete with Plains singers in song contests. There are non-Indians, also, who have risen to the challenge of this music and have won prizes for their singing, costumes, and dancing at powwows. In singing this song, pay particular attention to the sharp emphases, the pulsations, and the glides. These are not mere "ornamentation" but an important part of the special art of Plains singing.

The dancing that goes with this song style is based on a toe-heel movement first with one foot and then with the other, as follows:

Foot	left	right	right	left	left	right
Movement	step	toe-heel,	change	toe-heel,	change	toe-heel, . . .

Each male dancer creates many personal variations and provides a solo display of his virtuosity. His body dips and bends, but his head is quite erect, sometimes nodding in time to the drumbeat and turning this way and that. His eyes are fixed on space, and the expression is rapt and remote. Often he carries a decorated stick or other object in one hand; during the dance he may manipulate it with all the subtlety of a Japanese dancer using a fan. Every dancer must stop precisely on the last beat at the rhythmic break before the "tail." Then the dancing resumes with all its intensity for the last few moments and must stop exactly on the last beat of the song. One extra step disqualifies a dancer from the competition.

The movement and sound of the costume is an essential part of the Grass Dance and its music. Bells are often tied around the legs; today they are sleigh bells, often quite large, mounted on a leather strap. These resound with every step. Ribbons sway, feathers and porcupine-hair roaches quiver (see the heads of the dancers in Figure 2.1), beads and small mirrors gleam and flash. The costume is as elaborate as the vocal style.

Women participate by either using a subdued version of the dance step or simply walking around the edge of the dance area. They wear shawls with long fringes that sway in time to their movements. In recent years women's "jingle dancing" has become a competitive event. Wearing a dress decorated with scores of cone-shaped metal jingles, younger women leap and step, filling the air with glitter and tintinnabulation. Some women stand behind the male singers, who are seated around a bass drum, and enter the song an octave higher than the men, often on the B phrase when it starts down. In the recording heard here, their voices do not come in until the first point marked A$_8$ in the transcription.

ZUNI LULLABY

The next song (CD 1, Track 4) provides a contrast with Plains singing and helps demonstrate that there is no single "Indian" musical style. It is a lullaby recorded in 1950 by a grandmother, Lanaiditsa, on the Zuni Reservation in western New Mexico. You will have little difficulty joining in with the song. The meter is rather free, and the whole gentle song has only two pitches.

In this case the text is in translatable words instead of vocables (see Transcription 2.2 and the Close Listening guide). The singer's affection for the child is expressed in the repetition of the word *little* and pet names, which seem to be interchangeable in the first half of the song but then settle into the same sequence.

CD 1:4

Lullaby (0:58). Traditional Zuni song. Performed by Lanaiditsa. Field recording by David McAllester. White Water, New Mexico, 1950.

Hm atseki	my boy	**Text, Zuni Lullaby.**
okshits'ana	cottontail little	
pokets'ana	jackrabbit little	
kochits'ana	rat little	

TRANSCRIPTION 2.2
Zuni lullaby.

Close Listening

LULLABY

CD 1:4

COUNTER NUMBER	COMMENTARY	ZUNI LYRICS	ENGLISH TRANSLATION
0:00	The first two pitches you hear—*Hm atseki*—are the only pitches in the entire lullaby. The higher pitch is sung on "Hm atse" and the lower is sung on "ki."	1. Hm atseki, okshits'ana, pokets'ana, pokets'ana.	1. My boy, little cottontail, little jackrabbit, little jackrabbit.
0:08	The singer shows her affection for the child by repeating the word *ana* ("little") and interchangeable pet names.	2. Hm atseki, okshits'ana, kochits'ana, atset s'ana, atset s'ana.	2. My boy, little cottontail, little rat, little boy, little boy.
0:18	Throughout the lullaby, words and rhythms repeat. Repetition is a prominent feature in most North American tribal music.	3. Hm atseki pokets'ana okshits'ana okshits'ana.	3. My boy, little jackrabbit, little cottontail, little cottontail.
0:25	Notice the way the singer emphasizes certain parts of each word every time she repeats the word.	4. Hm atseki pokets'ana okshits'ana kochits'ana, kochits'ana.	4. My boy, little jackrabbit, little cottontail, little rat, little rat.
0:34	Stanza 4 repeats.		
0:44	Stanza 4 repeats and closes the lullaby.		

FIGURE 2.2

Zuni mother and child, showing the costume and hairstyle of the early twentieth century.

Courtesy of the American Museum of Natural History. (Photo: Coles/Bierwert) Neg. no. 121630.

Repetition is a prominent feature in most North American Indian music: in the vocables, in the lexical texts (where they occur), and in the melodic and rhythmic patterns. This is not because Indians cannot create text and music with a "fuller" content, in a Western sense, but because their aesthetic taste delights in repetitions with slight variations that are sometimes too subtle for the ears of outsiders to detect. In Lanaiditsa's song each textual phrase can be used with either of the two musical phrases except for "my boy," which is always on an A. She settles on "my little rat" for the ending of verse 4 and the three repeats of verse 5, which suggests that she finds it the most endearing of the diminutives. (See Figure 2.2.)

This love of repetition shows in Indian folk tales and other narratives and is very much a part of the way the Navajo singer or "medicine man," Frank Mitchell, tells the story of his life (see pp. 63–68).

IROQUOIS QUIVER DANCE

The Quiver Dance song, "Gadasjot," illustrates still another of the many different musical styles in North American Indian singing (CD 1, Track 5). Another name for it is Warrior's Stomp Dance song. This was recorded in 1942 by Joshua Buck and Simeon Gibson at the Six Nations Reserve in Ohsweken, Ontario, but the song was made up years before that by Twenty Jacobs of Quaker Bridge, on the Allegheny Reservation in western New York. Note the difference between the lyrics as they would be spoken and as they appear in the song.

CD 1:5

"Gadasjot" (0:47). Iroquois Quiver Dance or Warrior's Stomp Dance song. Twenty Jacobs of Quaker Ridge. Performed by Joshua Billy Buck and Simeon Gibson. Field recording by William Fenton, c. 1942. *Songs from the Iroquois Longhouse.* Archive of Folk Song of the Library of Congress AFS L6. LP. Washington, DC.

As you listen to the song, follow the Close Listening guide and Transcription 2.3. The first thing that strikes the ear is the **call-and-response** form. One singer utters a phrase of lexical text (the "call") and the other answers him with a vocable pattern: *yowe hi ye ye!* This alternation continues through the song. Although quite common in the Eastern Woodlands, this pattern is rare elsewhere in North American traditional Indian singing. (Call-and-response singing can be heard in many world music cultures, as we will see in later chapters.)

Compared with Plains singing, the singing in this Iroquois song is relaxed. A characteristic of Iroquois singing style is a pulsation of the voice at the ends of phrases, indicated in the transcription by ♫ and ♩♩. In Plains singing, by contrast, pulsations occur all through the song.

The Stomp Dance is a favorite recreational dance among Woodland Indians in the eastern United States and Canada. Among the Iroquois it usually takes place in the **longhouse,** a meetinghouse with a stove at each end of the hall and benches along the sides. The participants form a line behind the leader. They imitate his "short jog step" (Fenton 1942:31) and any other turns and gyrations he may invent as they sing the responses to his calls. More and more of the audience joins the dance until the line is winding exuberantly all over the longhouse floor. Woodland tribes other than the Iroquois may not have longhouses and often do the Stomp Dance outdoors. The singers accompany themselves with a cow-horn rattle.

MAKING A "COW-HORN" RATTLE

The adventure of Native American music involves not only singing but also making instruments to accompany the voice. Here are the steps for creating a serviceable imitation of a cow-horn rattle (Figure 2.3). A section of cow's horn is not easy for most of us to obtain; a small fruit juice can, open at one end, makes a good substitute.

1. Any small metal can, two or three inches tall and two to two and one-half inches in diameter, will do. Make a plug for the open end of the can out of a

Close Listening

"GADASJOT"

CD 1:5

COUNTER NUMBER	LEADER: THE CALL		MALE VOICES: THE RESPONSE (VOCABLES)
A Section			
0:00	Leader sings the call.	*Tga-na ho-n swe-ge** Filled is Ohsweken (Ontario)	
0:03	Leader models response.	*yo-we-hi yeye*	
0:04	Call	*di-jod-di yak-on* With divorced women	
0:06			*yo-we-hi ye ye* (response)
A Section repeats, call and response			
0:07–0:16	*Tga-na ho-n swe-ge* *di-jod-di yak-on* *we-ya ha-no hi yo*	Filled is Ohsweken (Ontario) With divorced women With good looking ones	*yo-we-hi ye ye* *yo-we-hi ye ye* *yo-we-hi ye ye*
0:17	Exclamation at group's response. Call at higher pitch.	*hi-yo* *wi-go hi-no hi-yo* Fine looking ones!	
0:19			*yo-we-hi ye ye* (higher pitch)
0:21	Call	*wi-go no hi yo* Fine looking ones!	
0:22			*yo-we-hi ye ye*
Leader and male voices repeat original call and response many times.			
0:42	Leader sings *portamento*.		
0:43			Response with *portamento*.

*Translation courtesy of William N. Fenton

disk of soft wood slightly wider than the diameter of the can. With a sharp knife or a file, bevel one edge of the disc just enough so that it can be tightly wedged into the can.

2. Find a stick of hard wood, such as a straight tree branch, about three-fourths of an inch in diameter; cut a one-foot length. A piece of birch dowel will do.

TRANSCRIPTION 2.3
Iroquois Quiver Dance song ("Gadasjot").

With permission of William N. Fenton.

Whittle away one end of the stick to make a tapering spindle about an inch longer than the height of the can. At the base of the spindle, leave a shelf as shown in the drawing.

3. Drill a hole in the wooden plug so that it will fit snugly over the spindle and seat itself, beveled side up, on the shelf. Punch a smaller hole in the bottom of the can and slide it, open end down, over the spindle until the rim of the can fits over the beveled edge of the plug. The end of the spindle should project an inch beyond the bottom of the can. Mark the spindle at the point where it emerges from the hole in the can. The mark should be as close to the bottom of the can as possible.

4. Remove the can and plug and fasten the plug in the open end of the can with furniture tacks with shiny brass heads. Drop fifteen or twenty BBs or small pebbles into the can to produce the rattling sound.

5. Drill a small hole in the spindle at the marked place and find a nail or peg that will fit tightly in the hole and project on both sides of the spindle. Fit the can back into place, plug-end down, and wedge the nail or peg through the hole in the spindle. This should hold the can firmly, supported by the shelf at the bottom end.

Extra Niceties

You could remove both ends of the can and have a wooden plug in each end. This would give you two rows of ornamental tacks, holding in the plugs. If you are good at woodworking you could turn the plug for the upper end on a lathe so that it is rounded instead of flat.

FIGURE 2.3

Steps in making a
cow-horn rattle.

Shelf

Wooden plug to close
open end of can

Peg to fasten
rattle together

Upper end (flat)

Upper end (rounded)

Shelf to
hold can

To make the can look like a cow horn you could paint it dark brown with
cream-colored streaks or cream with brown streaks. Figure 2.4 shows several
cow-horn rattles. Notice the different ways the handle can be carved to break the
monotony of a straight stick. You can express your own creativity in how you do it.

FIGURE 2.4

Iroquois cow-horn rattles,
showing a variety of
shapes and handles.

Susan W. McAllester

How to Play the Rattle

A cow-horn rattle may be struck against the user's thigh or palm to produce a sharp impact. At the beginning of a song a tremolo effect is often produced by rapidly shaking the rattle, held high in the air.

Music of the Navajos

Now that we have had a brief look at three of the many different North American Indian musical styles, we will look more deeply into the musical life of still another Indian group, the Navajos of the Southwestern desert. By studying their music in some detail we can see how many different kinds of music exist in just one Indian community. Examining the cultural context of the music will show us how closely music is integrated with Indian life. The autobiographical sketch of Frank Mitchell provides a firsthand account by a professional Navajo singer of how he learned his music and what it meant to him.

A YEIBICHAI SONG FROM THE NIGHTWAY CEREMONY

To begin again with sound, we go first to one of the most exciting kinds of Navajo music, Yeibichai songs. *Yé'ii-bi-cháí* (gods-their-grandfathers) refers to ancestor deities who come to dance at the major ceremonial known as Nightway. The masked dancers who impersonate the gods bring supernatural power and blessing to help cure a sick person.

Listen now to CD 1, Track 6. With its shouts, ornamentation, and falsetto voices, this song makes one think of the Plains Indians. The tense energy of the singing also resembles that of the Plains style. However, the long introduction (phrases X, Y, and Z), sung almost entirely on the basic note (the **tonic**) of the song, differs strikingly from the Indian songs we have heard before (see Transcription 2.4). Then the melody leaps *up* an octave. In the first phrase, A, after the introduction, the song comes swooping briskly down to the tonic again to an ending I have labeled "e^1." This ending appears again later on in the song in two variations, "e^2" and "e^3." (Capital letters denote main phrases and small letters denote motifs within the phrases.) The same descent is repeated (the second A and e^1) and then another acrobatic plunge takes place in B after two "false starts" (labeled $\frac{1}{2}$a) that each closely resemble the first half of A. The song then hovers on the tonic e^2 and e^3 and the phrase *hi ye, hi ye*, which also appears in Y and Z. I call it "z" because it has the weighty function of ending the introduction and, eventually, the song itself, in the Z phrase. After B, another interesting variation in the use of previous motifs occurs: the *second* half of A is sung twice, $a^{\frac{1}{2}}$ and $a^{\frac{1}{2}}$, followed by the first half of A, also repeated, $\frac{1}{2}$a and $\frac{1}{2}$a.

The Navajos are noted for their bold experiments in artistic form. This is true in their silversmithing, weaving, sandpainting, and contemporary commercial painting. It is also true of their music, as the play of melodic and rhythmic motifs in the passage just heard suggests. Listen again, following the pattern of this complex and intriguing song (see Transcription 2.4 and the Close Listening guide), and try to sing it yourself along with Sandoval Begay and his group of Yeibichai singers.

CD 1:6

Yeibichai (2:15). Navajo dance song from Nightway. Led by Sandoval Begay. Field recording by Willard Rhodes, n.d. Archive of Folk Song of the Library of Congress AFS L41. LP. Washington, DC.

TRANSCRIPTION 2.4
Navajo Yeibichai song.

* Repeat from A twice. High yell replaces 1st 2 notes of A on the first repeat; second repeat ends at "Fine".

Transcription by David P. McAllester from a field recording by Willard Rhodes.

Entirely in vocables, this song illustrates how far from "meaningless" vocables can be. Almost any Navajo would know from the first calls that this is a Yeibichai song; these and the other vocables identify what kind of song it is. Moreover, this song includes the call of the gods themselves:

Call of the Yei

Hi   ye,   hi   ye,   ho - ho   ho   ho!

Close Listening

YEIBICHAI

CD 1:6

COUNTER NUMBER	COMMENTARY	VOCABLES	FORM	RATTLE
0:00	Two high shouts.	*wu-wu-o-o-ho*		Shakes
Introduction				
0:04	Sung almost entirely on the basic pitch (*tonic*).	*hi ye hi ye hi ye, ho ho ho ho, hi hi hi*		Quick, insistent rhythm
	Ending phrase or bridge.	*hi ye hi ye*		
Song				
0:10	A phrase begins an octave higher then descends.	*hui yi hui-hu'i ho-e*	A	Constant rhythm
0:14	Repeat First half of A phrase sung twice.	*hui yi hui hu'i ho-e* *yi'au*	A ½A	
0:19	B phrase opens high and slowly descends.	*hui hui hui hui*	B	
0:23	Melodic phrase from introduction.	*ho ho hi ye, hi ye hi ye hi-i hi ho-e*	C	
	Second half of A phrase sung twice.	*hi-i hi ho-e hi-i hi ho-e*	²⁄₂A	
	First half of A phrase sung twice.	*yi'u*	½A	
0:35	B phrase in melody returns.	*hui hui hui hu-i ho ho*	B	
0:39	C phrase returns.	*hi ye, hi ye hi ye ho ho ho ho hi hi hi hi ye hi ye*	C	
	Bridge ends section.	*ho ho ho ho hi hi hi hi ye hi ye*		
0:50–1:30	Shout begins song's repeat.		A	
1:48–2:00	Shout begins song's repeat. Closes with repeat of introduction.	*hi ye, hi ye hi ye ho ho ho ho hi hi hi hi ye hi ye*	A	Rattle shakes as singing ends

Although there are hundreds of different Yeibichai songs, they usually contain some variation of this call of the Yei.

Yeibichai singers are organized in teams, often made up of men from one particular region or another. They create new songs or sing old favorites, each team singing several songs before the nightlong singing and dancing end. The teams prepare costumes and masks and practice a dance of the gods that proceeds in two parallel lines with reel-like figures. They also have a clown, who follows the dancers and makes everyone laugh with his antics: getting lost, bumbling into the audience, imitating the other dancers. The teams compete, and the best combination of costumes, clowns, singing, and dancing receives a gift from the family giving the ceremony. The representation of the presence of the gods at the Nightway brings god power to the ceremony and helps the sick person get well.

This dance takes place on the last night of a nine-night ritual that includes such ceremonial practices as purification by sweating and vomiting, making prayer offerings for deities whose presence is thus invoked, and sandpainting rituals in which the one-sung-over sits on elaborate designs in colored sands and other dry pigments. The designs depict the deities; contact with these figures identifies the one-sung-over with the forces of nature they represent and provides their protective power (see Figure 2.5). In the course of the ceremony hundreds of people may attend as spectators, whose presence supports the reenactment of the myth on which the ceremony is based.

FIGURE 2.5

Ceremonial practitioner making a sandpainting of a Lightning Deity in flint armor.

Courtesy of the American Museum of Natural History. (Photo: Boltin) Neg. no. 2A 3634.

The one-sung-over takes the role of the mythic hero, and the songs, sandpaintings, prayers, and other ritual acts recount the story of how this protagonist's trials and adventures brought the Nightway ceremony from the supernatural world for the use of humankind (Faris 1990). Besides the Yeibichai songs there are hundreds of long chanted songs with elaborate texts of translatable ritual poetry, as discussed in the section on Navajo "classical" music.

Such a ritual drama as Nightway is as complex as "the whole of a Wagnerian opera" (Kluckhohn and Leighton 1938:163). The organization and performance of the entire event is directed by the singer or ceremonial practitioner, who must memorize every detail. Such men and women are among the intellectual leaders of the Navajo communities. The life story later in this chapter offers a rare glimpse into the mind of such a person.

Most readers find the Yeibichai song difficult to learn. The shifts in emphasis, the many variations, and the difficult vocal style demand hours of training before one can do it well. But there are many other kinds of Navajo music.

"FOLSOM PRISON BLUES"

You should be able to join in with the next song (CD 1, Track 7) right away, especially if you already listen to country music. This version of Johnny Cash's "Folsom Prison Blues" is played and sung by the Fenders, an all-Navajo country band from Thoreau, New Mexico, who were popular in the 1960s and 1970s (Figure 2.6). Follow the Close Listening guide as you listen.

Country music has long been a great favorite with Indian people, especially in the west. There are several country and western bands on the Navajo reservation. Some, such as the Sundowners and Borderline, have issued records that sell well in Indian country. Even more popular are non-Indian country singers such as Tim McGraw. The cowboy and trucker images appeal to most people in the western states, including Indians, who identify with the open life and the excitement of the roundup and the rodeo. The Fenders' liner notes begin as follows:

> The five Fenders are genuine cowboys ... as much at home on the back of a bucking rodeo bronc as behind the wild guitar at a good old rodeo dance. These boys believe that to be a No. 1, all-around cowboy, you must be able to play the guitar and sing just as well as you ride, rope and bull-dog.

CD 1:7

"Folsom Prison Blues" (2:50). Johnny Cash. Published by Hi-Lo Music. Performed by the Fenders on The Fenders, *Second Time Roun'*. LP. Thoreau, New Mexico, 1966.

THE NAVAJO WAY OF LIFE

Who are these Navajos we have been listening to? Where and how do they live? At more than 290,000, they are our largest Indian tribe. Descended from Athabascan-speaking nomadic hunters who came into the Southwest as recently as six or seven hundred years ago, they now live in scattered communities ranging from extended family groups to small towns on a reservation of 25,000 square miles (larger than West Virginia) spread over parts of New Mexico, Arizona, and Utah (see Figure 2.7). The exact census of the Navajos is uncertain, because thousands live off the reservation in border towns such as Farmington, Gallup, and Flagstaff and cities such as Chicago, Los Angeles, and San Diego. The reason for their move is largely economic: Their population has outgrown the support afforded by the reservation.

On the reservation the Navajos' livelihood is based, to a small but culturally significant degree, on farming, raising stock, weaving, and silversmithing (see Figure 2.8). The main part of their $110 million annual income, however, comes from coal, uranium, oil, natural gas, and lumber. Much of their educational and health care funds

FIGURE 2.6

Album cover of the Fenders, an early Navajo country-and-western group.

"FOLSOM PRISON BLUES"

CD 1:7

COUNTER NUMBER	COMMENTARY	LYRICS
Introduction		
0:00	Electric guitar, bass guitar, rhythm guitar, and drums	
1st stanza		
0:09	Soloist enters. Drums and bass guitar keep the beat.	*I hear the train a comin'* *It's rolling round the bend.* *I ain't seen the sunshine since I don't know when,* *but I'm stuck in Folsom prison, that's where I long to stay.* *When I hear that whistle blow, I hang my head and I cry.*
2nd stanza		
0:35	Soloist occasionally sings against the meter.	*When I was just a baby my mama told me. Son,* *always be a good boy, don't ever play with guns.* *But I shot a man in Reno just to watch him die.* *When I hear that whistle blowin', I hang my head and I cry.*
Break		
1:00	Electric guitar solo. Drums, rhythm and bass guitars accompany. Homophonic texture.	
3rd stanza		
1:25	Soloist occasionally sings against the meter.	*I bet there's rich folks eating in a fancy dining car* *I bet they're drinkin' coffee, smoking big cigars.* *Well I know I had it coming, I just can't be wrong.* *When I hear that whistle blow, I hang my head and I cry.*
Break		
1:50	Electric guitar solo. Drums, rhythm and bass guitars accompany.	
4th stanza		
2:16	Soloist occasionally sings against the meter.	*Well if they'd free me from this prison,* *If this railroad train was mine,* *I'd move just a little further down the line,* *far away from Folsom prison, that's where I long to stay.* *When I hear that whistle blow, I hang my head and I cry.*
2:42	Electric guitar closes. Drums, rhythm and bass guitars accompany.	

FIGURE 2.7

Map of the Navajo Reservation and points of interest.

derive from the Department of the Interior, some of it in fulfillment of the 1868 treaty that marked the end of hostilities between the Navajos and the United States Army. Personal incomes range from the comfortable salaries of tribal administrative and service jobs to the precarious subsistence of marginal farmers. Many Navajos are supported on various kinds of tribal or government relief.

Although much of traditional Navajo culture remains intact, the People (Diné), as the Navajos call themselves, also welcome new ideas and change. Their scholarship funds enable hundreds of young people to attend colleges and universities around the country, including their own Navajo Community College on the

FIGURE 2.8

Navajos still travel on horseback in many parts of the reservation.

Courtesy of the American Museum of Natural History. (Photo: M. Raney) Neg. no. 335258.

reservation. A battery of attorneys and a Natural Resources Committee keep watch on the mining leases and lumber operations. The Navajos also operate motels, restaurants, banks, and shopping centers, and they encourage small industries to establish themselves on the reservation. Some Navajos jet to administrative and development conferences in Washington, D.C.; others speak no English and herd sheep on horseback or on foot miles from the nearest paved road.

The men dress in western style, and some of the women still wear skirts and blouses copied from the dresses worn by United States Army officers' wives in the 1860s, during the imprisonment of the Navajos at Fort Sumner, New Mexico. The skirts have shortened in recent years, and Navajo taste has always demanded the addition of buttons, rings, bracelets, necklaces, and heavy belts of silver set with turquoise. The men wear this jewelry, too, sometimes with the added panache of silver hatbands on big cowboy hats. Young people, male and female, are now usually seen wearing blue jeans like other young people anywhere in the country. Bright blankets from the Pendleton mills in Oregon used to be worn as an overcoat in cold weather. This garment is now so identified with traditional Navajo costume that the protagonist in ceremonials often wears it. The Navajos' own famous rugs are woven for cash income; most of them go to the local store, sometimes still called a trading post, to pay for food and other supplies. Some of these rugs are so finely designed and woven that they have each brought $20,000 or more in the world market for fine arts (see Figure 2.9).

FIGURE 2.9

Hand-weaving is a source of income for many Navajo women. This scene, from the 1920s, is still common today.

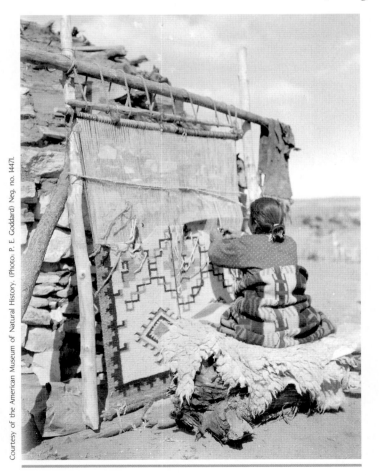

Courtesy of the American Museum of Natural History. (Photo: P. E. Goddard) Neg. no. 1447.

Navajo houses range from the modern stucco ranch houses and large trailer homes of tribal officials, administrative staff, and school personnel to smaller one-room houses of every description. One can still see some of the old-style circular log hogans (Navajo hooghan, "place home"). Navajo ceremony requires a circular floor plan, and many adaptations of this well-loved and ceremonially important shape are designed into new kinds of structures. For example, the Tribal Council Building in Window Rock, Arizona, is a round sandstone structure with Navajo murals inside. It can accommodate the seventy-four council members, who gather there from all parts of the reservation. The Cultural Center at the Navajo Community College at Tsaile, Arizona, is six stories of concrete, steel, and glass, but it is octagonal, with a domed roof. Inside, at the heart of the building, stands a replica of a traditional log hogan with a dirt floor and a smoke hole that goes up four stories through a shaft to the open sky. It serves as a religious symbol and a meditation room. School buildings, chapter houses, information centers, and arts and crafts outlets exhibit other variations in size and design on the circular shape, which symbolizes the earth, and on the domed roof, which symbolizes both mountaintops and the vault of the sky.

TRADITIONAL POPULAR MUSIC

Until the 1940s the most popular musics on the reservation were the different kinds of dance songs from the ceremonials. We have already studied a Yeibichai dance song from Nightway. Corral dance songs from several ceremonies were also popular, but the several different kinds of *Ndáá'* (War Dance) **songs** from Enemyway made up the largest body of traditional popular music. These include Circle Dance, Sway, Two-step, Skip Dance, and Gift songs. Although country and western eclipsed them in the 1960s and 1970s, the traditional songs have found a renewed popularity on the reservation today.

In the 1990s a new recreational pastime called Song and Dance emerged. It makes use of Skip Dance and Two-step songs, and it can take place in any large hall. Couples of all ages, in traditional costumes, participate. Singers or tapes provide the music, and the dancers, identified by large numbered tags, circle the hall while judges note their costumes and dancing skill. Winners receive trophies, and entry fees and donations solicited during the dancing go toward the expenses of the Song and Dance Association hosting the event or for specified benefits such as school programs.

Some traditionalists have objected to *Ndáá'* songs being used in this new, secular context; however, this is only the latest in several new uses. Radio broadcasts have featured *Ndáá'* songs since the 1930s, and they found a new wave of radio popularity in the 1990s.

Also know as Squaw Dance songs. Many Native Americans regard the word squaw *as derogatory, so we use the Novajo term* Ndáá'.

THE CIRCLE DANCE SONG "SHIZHANÉ'É"

Ndáá' songs are the hit tunes of traditional Navajo life. Compared with the Yeibichai songs, *Ndáá'* songs are easy to sing, though for an outsider they can contain some surprises. Many of them are sung entirely with vocables, but the Circle Dance song "Shizhané'é" (CD 1, Track 8) contains words that can be translated as well.

If you play this song a few times and follow the Close Listening guide and then the words and music provided in Transcription 2.5, you should be able to get into the swing of this lively melody. Since you do not have to worry about producing the high falsetto sounds of the Yeibichai songs, you can concentrate on other fine points. Pay attention to the emphases marked with >. See if you can reproduce the nasal tone the Navajos enjoy in their singing. Every phrase ends with

This and the triple meter are characteristic of Circle Dance songs (McAllester 1954:52). Notice how the A phrases introduce the melodic elements that are more fully developed in B and then even more so in C. The whole structure is too long to include on the sound recording.

The translatable portion of the text, in the C phrases, is like a nugget in the middle of the song, framed by a vocable chorus before and after it. This is a favorite principle of design in other Navajo arts as well as music. It is the dynamic

CD 1:8

"Shizhané'é" ("I'm in Luck") (1:20). Navajo Circle Dance song from Enemyway. Performed by Albert G. Sandoval, Jr., and Ray Winnie. Field recording by David P. McAllester. Sedona, Arizona, 1957.

Close Listening

"SHIZHANÉ'É"

CD 1:8

COUNTER NUMBER	COMMENTARY	VOCABLES	FORM
Introduction			
0:00	Begins on tonic then leaps an octave. Vocables sung throughout.	*He ne ya na*	
A and B sections			
0:03	Phrase melody starts on a high pitch, descends, rises, and descends again at end of phrase. Notice the nasal quality of the singers' voices.	*Yo wo yo'o we ya he nai ya he*	A
0:08	Repeat.	*Yo wo yo'o we ya he nai ya he*	A
0:14	New phrase melody starts at a lower pitch and descends.	*A'ha ne ya 'a ha ne yo 'a we ya he, nai ya*	B
0:19–0:42	Repeat.	*A' ha ne ya 'a ha ne yo 'a we ya he, nai ya*	B
C section			
0:43	Longer phrase with limited melodic movement	*Shi zha ne'e shi zha ne'e ki yah si-zi-ni shi-ka no tal/'a we ya he nai ya*	C
0:51–1:15	Repeat		C
Coda or tail			
1:16	Phrase returns to opening note	*he, nai ya*	D

With the permission of Albert Sandoval Jr. and Ray Winnie.

symmetry discussed by Witherspoon (1977:170–74) and illustrated in weaving and silver jewelry designs. The brief, humorous text is, like many another in Navajo song, intended to make the girls laugh and pay attention to the (male) singers. Although the dance is part of a ceremony, it also offers courtship opportunities and serves as a social dance.

With permission of Albert Sandoval, Jr. and Ray Winnie.

TRANSCRIPTION 2.5
"Shizhané'é." Navajo
Circle Dance song.

As the Navajo is spoken, with literal translation:

shizhané	me-good luck
kíyah	house-under/against
sizíní	standing-the one who
shiká	me-for/after (as in running after one)
nóotááł	searching for (3rd person)

Linger for a moment on the choices of expression that make the words so witty. The song begins with fatuous self-congratulation. But then we learn both from the form *yah* after "house" and from the neuter static form of *sizíní*, "the one who is standing," that the girl is really propped against the house. The suggestion is that she has had too much to drink and therefore is unable to be actively searching for ("running after") the singer at all, even though he claims she is. The irony of the situation combines with a jesting implication that women drink too much and chase after young men. Because it is actually the men who do most of the drinking and chasing after the opposite sex, the song is all the funnier. *Kiyah sizíní* also carries the meaning "prostitute." As in all clever poetry, the zest comes from the subtle shades of meaning.

The ´ indicates a glottal stop, as in "oh-oh!" (ó-ó)

ł is like the Welsh ll in Flloyd, unvoiced with the breath coming out on either side of the tongue.

aa indicates a long "a"   likewise: oo and other vowels

á̧ indicates a nasal "a"   likewise o and other vowels

é indicates a high "e:"   Navajo has speech tones like Chinese.

ée indicates a long "e" falling from high to low in tone

Vowels have "Continental values."

Notes on Pronunciation in Navajo

Courtesy of Andy Tsihnahjinnie.

FIGURE 2.10

This scene by the Navaho painter Andy Tsihnahjinnie shows drumming, singing, and dancing at the public part of an Enemyway ceremony.

THE ENEMYWAY CEREMONY

Religion is one of the keys to understanding culture. We can know the Navajos better if we take a closer look at the **Enemyway ceremony** in which "Shizhané'é" is used. Enemyway is one of the most frequently performed rites in traditional Navajo religion. Like Nightway, it is a curing ritual. In this case the sickness is brought on by the ghosts of outsiders who have died. Enemyway is often performed for a returned Navajo member of the United States Armed Forces or for others who have been away from home among strangers for a long time. A Navajo who has been in a hospital and returns home cured, in our sense, may have an Enemyway performed because of the inevitable exposure to the spirits of the many non-Navajos who have died in such a place (see Figure 2.10).

The ceremony involves two groups of participants, the "home camp" and the "stick receiver's camp." Members of the latter represent the enemy and are custodians of a stick decorated with symbols of the warrior deity, Enemy Slayer, and of his mother, Changing Woman, who is the principal Navajo deity. The decorated stick is brought from the home camp along with gifts of many yards of brightly colored yarn. The first night of the ceremony consists of singing and dancing at the stick receiver's camp. This event offers the only time in traditional Navajo life that men and women dance together—a time for fun and courtship. Before the dancing starts a concert of Sway songs takes place. Although these may express the courtship theme, the majority of the Sway songs have texts entirely of vocables.

After an hour or so, the singing shifts to dance songs and the women appear, looking for partners. That the women always choose perhaps reflects the powerful position of women in Navajo society. They own the household; the children belong to the mother's clan, not the father's; and when a couple marry, the husband traditionally moves in with his wife's family.

Heye yeye ya,
Lonesome as I am,
Lonesome as I am, *ha-i na,*
Lonesome as I am,
Lonesome as I am, *ha,*
Lonesome as I am, *na'a- ne hana. . . .*

Text,
Navajo Enemyway
Sway Song

Text, Navajo Sway song. David P. McAllester, Enemy Way Music, pp. 29, 37. Papers of the Peabody Museum of Archaeology and Ethnology, vol. 41, no. 3. Copyright © 1954 by the President and Fellows of Harvard College.

In the dance the women tend to act bashfully, but they find partners and the couples dance along together following other couples in a large circle. The dance is simply a light stepping along with a bounce on each step. When a woman wants to change partners, she lets the man know by demanding a token payment. This is a symbol of the war booty brought back by Enemy Slayer from a mythical war and given away to Navajo women in the story in celebration of the victory. The song texts of the dance songs often poke fun at the women and sometimes refer to these payments.

He-ne, yane, yana-,
Yala'e-le- yado'eya 'ana he,
Yala'e-le- yado'eya ne. . . .

Your daughter, at night,
Walking around, *yado'eya yana hana,*
Tomorrow, money,
Lots of it, there will be, *yana hana,*

Yala'e-le- yado'eya na'ana,
Yala'e-le- yado'eya na'ana he. . . .

Text,
Navajo
Enemyway
Dance Song

Text, Navajo Enemyway Dance song. David P. McAllester, Enemy Way Music, p. 45. Papers of the Peabody Museum of Archaeology and Ethnology, vol. 41, no. 3. Copyright © 1954 by the President and Fellows of Harvard College.

After a few hours of dancing, a Signal song indicates that the singing is to go back to Sway songs (McAllester 1954:27). The dancing stops, but the Sway songs may go on for the rest of the night. Again, the ceremony symbolizes war: The group of singers is divided into two halves, representing the home camp and the enemy, and the singers compete in vigor, repertory, and highness of pitch.

They stop at dawn, but after a rest and breakfast a new kind of singing, a serenade of Gift songs, takes place. The home camp people sing outside the main hogan of the stick receiver's camp; in exchange, small gifts such as oranges and boxes of Cracker Jack are thrown to the singers through the smoke hole. Larger gifts such as expensive blankets are brought out and handed to responsible members of the singing group; these presents will be reciprocated later in the ceremony. Most of the Gift songs are old and have text entirely in vocables, but a few of the newer ones have words concerning the hoped-for gifts.

Text, Navajo Enemyway Gift Song	*Heye yeye yana,*
	Your skirts, how many? *yi-na.*
	To the store I'm going, *'e hyana heye yeye ya.*
	To Los Nores I'm going, *'e hya 'ena hya na. . . .*
	'e-ye yeye yana.
	Goats, I came for them, *yo'o'o 'ene hanena,*
	Goats, I came for them, *yo'o'o 'ene hahe,*
	Yo'o'o 'ena heye yeye yana. . . .

Text, Navajo Enemyway Gift song. David P. McAllester, Enemy Way Music, p. 48, songs 52, 53. Papers of the Peabody Museum of Archaeology and Ethnology, vol. 41, no. 3. Copyright © 1954 by the President and Fellows of Harvard College.

The gifts, like the payments during the dancing, represent war booty: The trip of the home party can be seen as a raid into enemy country and the gifts as the booty they take home with them. But reconciliation is symbolized at the same time, because the stick receiver's camp provides supper and camping facilities and because the meal and gifts will be returned in a similar exchange on the third morning.

After the breakfast and gift singing on the second day, the stick receiver's party prepares to move toward the home camp. Most of the home camp people leave early, but one of them remains as an official guide to lead the stick receiver to a good camping place a few miles from the home camp. They time their arrival to take place at about sundown, and another night of singing and dancing follows at this new camp.

Early the next morning the war symbolism of the ceremony is sharply emphasized with a sham battle. The stick receiver's people ride into the home camp with yells and rifle shots, raising a lot of dust and committing small depredations such as pulling down clotheslines. After four such charges they retire to a new campsite a few hundred yards away, where a procession from the home camp brings them a sumptuous breakfast. After the meal, the return gift singing takes place at the hogan of the one-sung-over.

Now comes further, heavy war drama. In a secret indoor ritual the afflicted person is given power and protection by sacred chanting and is dressed for battle. At the climax of the ceremony he goes forth and shoots at a trophy of the enemy, thus ritually killing the ghost. The songs used to prepare the warrior include long derisive descriptions of the enemy and praise of Navajo warriors (Haile 1938:276–84). If the person being sung over is a woman, a male proxy takes her place in shooting the enemy ghost.

In the late afternoon a Circle Dance is performed at the stick receiver's new camp. Men join hands in a circle, the two halves of which represent the two camps. At this point they compete with songs like "Shizhané'é." The two sides of the circle take turns singing to see who can sing the best songs most beautifully. As the songs alternate, so does the direction in which the Circle Dance moves. Most of the songs have no translatable words, and those that do are not overtly about war; however, the presence of the two competing sides is a reminder of conflict, and it is thought that every drumbeat accompanying the songs drives the enemy ghosts farther into the ground. After a while a girl carrying the stick and several other women may enter the circle and walk around, following the direction of the dancing men. The symbols of Changing Woman and her warrior son incised on the sacred stick remind participants further of the dance's meaning.

After the Circle Dance, another dramatic event takes place: The secret war name of the afflicted person is revealed. Members of the stick receiver's camp walk over to the home camp, singing as they go. Four times on the way, they stop and shout out the identity of the enemy. Then the stick receiver sits down in front of the ceremonial hogan and sings four songs that mention the name of the enemy and that of the one-sung-over. In traditional Navajo life it is impolite to address anyone by name and, in particular, by his or her war name. Polite address uses a kinship term, real or fictitious. Examples of war names are "She Went Among War Parties" and "He Ran Through Warriors" (Reichard 1928:98–99).

The songs describe battle with the enemy and refer to the anguish of the enemy survivors. The death of the enemy ghost is mentioned. Then, after a serenade of Sway songs, the stick receiver's party move back to the dance ground at their camp, and the last night of the ceremony begins with a further selection of Sway songs. After an hour or so the singing changes to dance songs and dancing, which, as on the previous two nights, may go on for several hours. Again the Signal song indicates the end of dancing, and the rest of the night is spent in Sway song competition between the two camps.

At dawn the ceremony ends with a brief blessing ritual conducted while participants face the rising sun. The stick receiver's party departs, and the afflicted person, now protected by the many symbolic ways in which the ghost has been eliminated, spends four days in rest and quiet while the effect of the ceremony settles into the entire household.

THE "CLASSICAL" MUSIC OF THE NAVAJOS

We have listened so far to examples of the public or popular music in two Navajo ceremonials, as well as a relatively new kind of popular music, Navajo country and western. Next we consider the music at the core of Navajo traditional religious philosophy, the great ceremonial chants. These long series of songs accompany ritual procedures such as those for Nightway (purifications, prayer offerings, and sandpainting rituals) and Enemyway (preparation of the drum and decorated stick, dressing the one-sung-over, and giving him or her power and protection). Figure 2.11 shows yet another ceremonial chant, the Mountainway.

These chants are "classic" for several reasons. They represent a tradition generations old (no one knows how many). They also have enormous scope—one chant may contain over five hundred songs, and the texts comprise many thousands of lines of religious poetry. Finally, they contain in their prayers and songs, and in the related myths they present, the meaning the Navajos find in the natural and supernatural worlds.

The performance of the chants may be brief or extended depending on the needs of the one-sung-over, the person to be cured. Excerpts of a few hours may suffice, but an extended version lasting as many as nine nights may be needed. To understand why, we need to consider the Navajo conception of illness.

The Navajos recognize the disease theory of the Euro-American world, and they gladly take advantage of hospitals, surgery, and antibiotics. In addition, however, they see bad dreams, poor appetite, depression, and injuries from

FIGURE 2.11

Navajo fire dance from the Mountainway ceremony. The dancers represent fire deities who have come to help a sick person recover.

Courtesy of the American Museum of Natural History. Neg. no. 127657.

accidents as results of disharmony with the world of nature. Although this view resembles Western psychiatry and psychosomatic medicine in many ways, the Navajos go still further. They see animals, birds, insects, and the elements of earth, water, wind, and sky as active potencies that directly influence human life. Each of these forces may speak directly to human beings and may teach them the songs, prayers, and ritual acts that make up the ceremonials. At the center of this relationship with the natural world is the concept of *hózhǫ́ǫ́* (beauty, blessedness, harmony), which must be maintained and which, if lost, can be restored by means of ritual. The prayers invoke this state over and over at their conclusions.

Text, Concluding Phrase of Navajo Prayer	*Hózhǫ́ǫ́ nahasdlį́į́'.* *Hózhǫ́ǫ́ nahasdlį́į́'.* *Hózhǫ́ǫ́ nahasdlį́į́'.* *Hózhǫ́ǫ́ nahasdlį́į́'!* Conditions of harmony have been restored. Conditions of harmony have been restored. Conditions of harmony have been restored. Conditions of harmony have been restored!

The ceremonial chants, some fifty of them, dramatize the Navajo creation story, an interlocking network of myths as long and complex as Greek mythology or the Vedas of India. No one person knows the entire story, but the tradition lives in the remarkable memories of several hundred ceremonial practitioners, men and women called "singers" (*hatááłí*) in Navajo. They direct the dance, art, and theater; chant the music; and recite the prayers that constitute these extraordinary achievements of the human spirit. They learn in the oral tradition as apprentices over many years. Some of these practitioners teach religion at such culturally oriented schools as the Rough Rock Demonstration School, near Chinle, Arizona, and the Navajo Community College at Tsaile, Arizona. One practitioner has dictated his life story, a narrative of over three hundred pages. Excerpts from this remarkable account will be presented later.

No complete recording of a ceremonial is available on commercial discs or tapes, and there are very few commercial recordings of even one of the thousands of songs that make up this great literature of religious music. The main reason for the scarcity is that most singers feel that these matters are too sacred to be made public. Some feel that that an uninitiated person might use one of these songs improperly, through ignorance, and cause great harm to the community or, worse yet, rob the song of its potency. Although the singers who recorded the next song (CD 1, Track 9) did not share this belief, out of respect for the feelings of those who do I present only a fragment of the song and give the text only in translation here, without a musical transcription or Close Listening guide.

CD 1:9

Navajo Sacred Prayer (0:59). Episode from Navajo Shootingway ceremony. Led by Dinet Tsosie. Field recording by David P. McAllester. Lukachukai, Arizona, 1958.

I have been searching everywhere,
  Over the earth,
  That is what I was told to do,
I have been searching everywhere,
  Over the earth.
I have been searching everywhere,
  Over the mountains,
  That is what I was told to do,
I have been searching everywhere,
  Over the mountains.
I have been searching everywhere,
  Under the sun,
  That is what I was told to do,
I have been searching everywhere,
  Under the sun.
I have been searching everywhere,
  For the fire,
  That is what I was told to do,
I have been searching everywhere,
  For the fire.
I have been searching everywhere,
  With water,
  That is what I was told to do,
I have been searching everywhere,
  With water.

Text, Navajo
Shootingway
Song

The song form is characteristic of ceremonial music. There is an introduction on the tonic, after which a chorus in vocables begins. The melody may be restricted, as in this case, to only three or four notes, or it may move about with a range of an octave or more. In any case, the interest of the music centers on the many subtle variations of a highly repetitive form. A section of the chorus is usually repeated at the end of each verse in a kind of refrain, adding still further to the feeling of repetition.

Shootingway is a ceremonial that reenacts that part of the creation myth in which a hero, Holy Young Man, goes in search of supernatural power. Before his adventures end he has lived among snake people, fish people, and buffalo people and has been carried up into the sky by thunder people. In the sky he is taught the Shootingway ceremonial by the Sun so that this knowledge might be brought back to earth for the protection of humankind. The ceremony has many purposes, such as the restoration of harmony between people and snakes, water, or lightning. A person suffering from snakebite might go to the hospital for treatment and later undergo Shootingway in order to end the bad relations with the snake people that led to the snakebite in the first place.

The Shootingway song tells about Holy Young Man's journey to the snake country. He is singing to the Sun, whom he met when he was in the mountains, and he tells about a fire that he saw glimmering in the distance at night when he was camping. Each day he tried to find the fire and this is what led him at last into the snake country. He married four beautiful snake wives and thus became related to these powerful creatures. During his stay among them he was given their power to take back to earth. Today, when someone is having trouble with the snake people, the restoration of harmony can be achieved by the ceremonial reenactment of this episode in Shootingway.

Before the song begins, a fire is kindled in the ceremonial hogan and a symbolic representation of the snake country prepared. To the east, south, west, and north of the fire, images of snakes are laid out in colored pigments on the ground. A black, zigzag snake about three feet long faces the fire from the east, and a blue one of the same shape faces the fire from the south. On the west is a straight white snake and on the north a straight pink one sprinkled with bits of glittering mica. As the song goes on, the one-sung-over, in the role of Holy Young Man, walks around the fire stepping over the snakes, thus acting out the journey into the snake country. The heat of the fire causes all the participants in the ceremony to sweat profusely in a rite of purification, and a series of other acts also drives out evil and further identifies the one-sung-over with the protagonist of the myth. To conclude this part of the ritual the singer cools off the people in the hogan by sprinkling them liberally with water shaken from a bundle of eagle feathers. This is the water mentioned in the last verse of the song.

Even this brief account of a fraction of one of the great ceremonials suggests how the music functions in support of an impressive drama. Shootingway is one of the ways the Navajos remind themselves of the sources of their means of dealing with the supernatural. The ceremony depicts the Navajos' view of themselves in relation to the natural world about them.

The beauty of the music, the poetry, the sandpaintings, and the myths that lie behind all of these has attracted the attention of scholars worldwide since the 1890s. Some representative examples of the many books written about Navajo myths and ceremonies are listed in the reference list at the end of the book: Matthews 1894, Kluckhohn and Wyman 1940, Haile 1947, Reichard 1950, Witherspoon 1977, McNeley, 1981, Wyman 1983, and Griffin-Pierce, 1992.

THE LIFE STORY OF A NAVAJO CEREMONIAL PRACTITIONER

Frank Mitchell (Ólta'í Tsoh: "Big Schoolboy") was born near Wheatfields, Arizona, in 1881 (see Figure 2.12). Over the course of his eventful life he was a sheepherder, railroad worker, cook, handyman-interpreter, wagon freighter, headman, tribal council member, and tribal judge. In his early maturity he learned Blessingway, one of the most important Navajo ceremonies, from his father-in-law. How this affected his whole life is told in his autobiography.

There is no other full autobiography of a Navajo singer. The excerpts presented here illustrate the following aspects of Navajo life and music:

- *Repetitive narrative style.* Repetition has already been mentioned as a significant element in the form of Navajo music, narrative, and the other arts.
- *Importance of women.* In the opening we receive a glimpse of a matrilocal, matrilineal family. Traditional Navajo families live in the mother's household, and the children belong to the mother's clan. Women own their own property. It is not surprising that the principal deity is Changing Woman.
- *Traveling about.* The old nomadic lifestyle of the Navajos has not entirely disappeared. Mitchell's childhood memories show what it was like to follow the livestock a hundred years ago.
- *Navajo practicality.* Mitchell became a singer for practical as well as spiritual reasons. The spiritual dimension of his calling can be seen only between the lines.
- *The value of Navajo songs.* This is stated not in aesthetic terms but in terms of healing the sick, bringing prosperity, and enabling the possessor of certain songs to become a leader in the community.
- *Speech and leadership.* The word for "chief" in Navajo means "one who speaks." The voices of humans and all other creatures are the culminating point of sacred descriptions in prayers and songs. In Navajo thought, wind is the ultimate power and the voice is the wind made articulate.
- *Navajo humor.* The beloved jokester of his large family, Mitchell was known for his ability to keep up the spirits of the participants in a long ceremonial with his ready supply of jokes and funny comments.

Frank Mitchell died in the hospital at Ganado, Arizona, in 1968, a few weeks after he dictated his last paragraphs of the life story that he wanted to leave as a legacy to his children and grandchildren. (All excerpts reprinted with permission from Frisbie and McAllester 1978.)

> I was just a small boy when I began to remember things. We happened to be living at a place called Tsaile; that is where I first began to remember things. I remember that I had a grandmother and my mother had some sisters besides herself. In those days a family like that used to stay close together. We moved around together; when we moved from one place to another, we always went in groups.

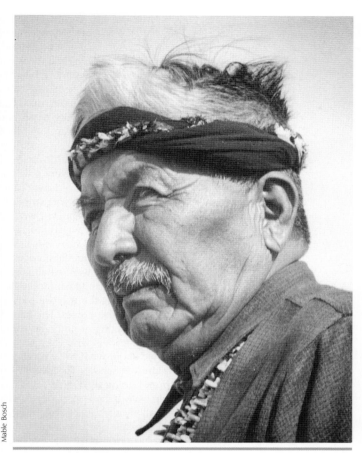

Mabie Bosch

FIGURE 2.12

Frank Mitchell, Navajo Blessingway singer. Chinle, Arizona, 1957.

In those days the men who were singers and performed ceremonies were the only ones who went around and treated the sick. That is what they were occupied with. I had an uncle on my father's side who was very harsh. He would scold us all of the time. One time there was someone sick in the family and they were performing a ceremony. While that was going on we were told not to sleep. Whenever we fell asleep, they would wake us and make us stay awake. Finally I got so sleepy that I could not stay awake any more. I was sitting next to this uncle of mine who was pretty harsh, and I guess that I fell asleep and just rolled over right beside him. My uncle jumped up, grabbed me by the hair on the side of my head, and yanked me up, putting me back down in a sitting position. I could see he was pretty angry. Of course I did not look straight at him; I just glanced sideways over there every now and then to watch him. After that I did not go to sleep again; I just stayed awake for the rest of the ceremony until it was over. Then we were told, "Now you can go to sleep." That was something I remember very plainly because of course I was old enough to remember things then....

The People traveled mostly on horseback; when we moved with the sheep we used horses to carry our belongings. We, being children, of course had to go along. Whenever the family started moving like that we children would sit in back of the rider. We were small and fell asleep sometimes, so they used to take anything they could find and tie us around the waist to the rider so we would not fall off. That is the way we moved around, tied to the riders so we could sleep sitting on those horses. The main reason for moving around like that was to look for new grazing ground and water for the sheep and horses. [pp. 29–30]

The leaders who went around recruiting children for school talked to the People about what the advantages would be in the future if they would put their children in school. The People would get angry and say, "No, absolutely not! I'm not going to give up my child; while I'm still alive I'm not going to turn my child over to those foreigners. Outsiders are not going to take my child away while I am still living." That's what they used to say. They would sometimes get out a butcher knife and toss it in front of those doing the recruiting and say, "Well, go ahead, cut my throat first; you'll have to do that before you can take my child." [p. 57]

At school we just went by the bell. It was a big bell like the one they have there by the cattleguard at the Franciscan church here in Chinle. At a certain hour we would go to bed. Every time that bell rang, it meant that we had to get in line, or go to bed, or get up and get ready for breakfast, or dinner, or supper.... [p. 63]

After awhile I thought I had had enough of school life so I took the first chance I got when I heard of some work that was available down on the railroad. The reason that I did not stay at school was because another boy, a schoolmate of mine, and I planned together to work on the railroad in the west somewhere. We planned this secretly, skipped out from school and went down on the railroad. The Navajos were already working on the railroad then, the railroad that was coming out of California, around Needles, and all down this way. So without telling my folks or his where we were going, we sneaked off.... [pp. 68–69]

Everybody at home started to get suspicious about where we were and my late uncle, my mother's brother whom we called Old Man Short Hair, inquired around and learned that it was likely we were with the railroad crew somewhere in the west. So he went in to Gallup and asked to work on the railroad. Of course he really did not want a job; he just wanted to look for us.... After my uncle overtook us and worked with us for a while, the railroad moved our crew back toward Flagstaff to a place called Seligman, Arizona, at the other side of Ash Fork. They had a railroad camp there where we all worked for a while. Then we were told, "You'll have to move now, go back to your country. There is no more work here...." [pp. 80–81]

[Editor's note: Because Mitchell knows a little English he finds various jobs at trading posts, a mission, and a sawmill. He marries, obtains a wagon from the government, and becomes a freighter, hauling supplies from Gallup, New Mexico, to Chinle.]

Later on I came back over here because my wife's parents were getting pretty old and sick. I gave up hauling freight and started tending their farm and livestock. My father-in-law was a well-to-do man: he had cattle and sheep and horses and I just started taking care of them for him. Also, I knew that he was a Blessingway singer and I went out with him whenever he performed this ceremony. I noticed that the songs I learned from He Who Seeks War were the same as the ones my father-in-law was singing.

Before I began to learn these things, way back before that, I did not even think about life as being an important thing. I did not try to remember things or keep track of what happened at certain times. Nothing seemed to matter to me, I just didn't care about anything, so long as I kept on living. But then when I began to learn the Blessingway it changed my whole life. I began really thinking about ceremonies. I had heard singing before that but now I began to take it more seriously because I began to realize what life was and the kind of hardships we have to go through. Before I started learning Blessingway, the older people used to tell me that I should think about life more seriously. "If you don't know any songs you have nothing to go by. If a child grows up in a family like that he doesn't know where he is going or what he is doing." That is what the older people told me, that I should have something to live by. . . . I used to go out with my father-in-law, Man Who Shouts, whenever he was asked to perform the Blessingway. I went wherever he did. At first I just watched and then finally I had learned practically everything he was doing and before I knew it I was helping him with the ceremony. Finally I reached the point where I had learned it well enough so that I had a ceremony of my own. . . . [pp. 192–93]

[My father-in-law said to me,] "If you are a singer, if you remember your ceremonies really well even if you get old, even if you get blind and deaf, you'll still remember everything by heart, how each part of the ceremony is performed." He said to me, "Even though you are so old you can't ride a horse or you can't even see anymore, people will still have a use for you until old age finally finishes you off."

So that is why I chose that way of life. And I believe it now: it is true that even as old as I am now, unable to get around too much, people still come to have my ceremony done over them. I have it inside my head so well that I remember everything and even though I can't get around they come in a wagon or a car for me and take me over to where the ceremony is needed and then bring me back. So I think my father-in-law was right. If I had decided to be a farmer at that time I probably wouldn't have lasted very long. [pp. 193–94]

It is a custom with the People that, for instance, some family, even though everything may be going all right and nothing is wrong, still may say, "Well, let's have a Blessingway to freshen things up, to renew ourselves again." So they do. Or sometimes they might have acquired some valuable goods, if they have been off trading or something, and have brought them home. Then the things that they brought in from other places, well, it is on their minds that, "That's what we're blessed with in this family." They might feel they need the Blessingway because you do not wait until some misfortune happens before you have it. That is the reason it is called the peaceful way, the healing way, the blessing way. There is no specific time . . . it depends on the family. If they feel they should have it, then they do it, just an ordinary Blessingway.

Of course if you are able to have that ceremony, if you have the means to put it on, well, then you should do it. But if you have not, then in that case you just keep putting it off until you are able to bear the cost. . . .

Blessingway is used for everything that is good for a person, or for the people. It has no use other than that. For instance, when a woman is pregnant she has the Blessingway in order to have a good delivery with no trouble. It is also done so that she and her child may have a happy life. In case of bad dreams it is a kind of warning that there are some misfortunes ahead of you; in order to avoid that you have Blessingway so that you will have happiness instead. Or if you are worried about something, your family will want to get you back, to get that out of your mind, out of your system, so that you may have a good life. It is the same for any other things that could cause you to worry, to feel uneasy about yourself. That is the sort of thing it is used for. As for the prayers, you say, "Beauty shall be in front of me, beauty shall be in the back, beauty shall be below me, above me, all around me." On top of that you say about yourself, "I am everlasting, I may have an everlasting life with beauty." You end your prayers that way.... [pp. 218–19]

I remember all that I know about the Blessingway because I had those years of study to get it all in my head. And from my experience of learning I understand that it is not just my ability that makes it possible. I believe that there is a spirit that really is answering my prayers, because all these years I would not have been able to learn so much if I did not have such help. I could not do it by myself, so there must be something beyond human power helping me.... [pp. 237–38]

In Navajo religion there are prayers for certain purposes. I found out from my own father that in Blessingway there was a song for headman, and I learned that from him. I think that this is another reason why things came easily for me when I was talking to the People. It may be one reason that I was recognized for being a talker and a leader among the People, why I became well known as a headman and even eventually ended up in the Tribal Council.... [p. 241]

There are lots of songs that go with being a headman or leader. They start out from the beginning, way back with the first people. The story starts with how it was planned at first and how the first people decided who were to be the chiefs. After these chiefs were elected, the songs go along describing how they were dressed. They tell about all of the things they were wearing, their shoes, leggings, sash and skirts, belts, wristlets and beads, their head plumes and everything up to the last thing, that which is put in their mouths from which their speeches are known. That last thing is like the power to speak; it was put into their mouths so they could have the wisdom to say wise things and so the People could understand them. There are enough of those songs to sing them all night without sleeping. The songs are used in a series, but they are not just to be sung any place. You can only use them when someone is going to be a chief, a good leader; they can have the songs done for them. There are so many songs in that series that you could almost have a Blessingway done with them; there are just about as many songs involved in that as there are in the Blessingway itself. From the start to the end of that, the whole thing is like a Blessingway. The story of the songs are just like Blessingway right from the beginning: how the earth was first formed, how the mountains came up. The songs go on like that. It would probably take a little longer to do than the regular Blessingway; it is just like Blessingway when you do that except that the ceremony is mostly just singing. Almost all of what takes place is the singing of the Chief songs.... [p. 244]

Once I was placed there as one of the councilmen, I began to be asked to do different things. One of the things that there was a lot of talk about during this time was education and the need for building schools on the reservation. We also talked about hospitals and preventing outsiders from moving in with different things like industrial plants. We did a lot of work and I concerned myself with all those things.... [p. 256] We talked about that a lot on the Council, and we decided to ask for the schools and also hospitals and all of those things from Washington.

Several of us were then appointed to go to Washington to ask that these things be granted. I went over there with several other men. We went before those people and asked for a school and a hospital and other things. Henry Taliman, the tribal chairman, Howard Gorman, the vice-chairman, and Red Moustache's brother were some of the others who went over there, too. We were asked to fly there but most of the delegates were afraid of going in an airplane, so we went on the train. While we were there we were given sight-seeing tours around Washington. I got to see the White House, Arlington Cemetery, the Unknown Soldier's Tomb, and other places. One of the delegates got tired when we were near the Washington Monument. He wanted to rest but he could not find a place to sit down. So he took off his moccasins and laid down on the grass in front of the

Monument. He was wearing half-socks like the ones I used to knit for myself. This man went to sleep and while he was sleeping a crowd gathered around looking at him. When he woke up he asked me, "What are all of these people standing around here looking at me for?" I said, "My younger brother, they are waiting for you to get up to see what kind of a creature you are. They are wondering whether or not when you get up you will crawl on all fours, like a bear." He replied, "You bear, you would say that." [pp. 257–58]

While I, myself, stand for the good of the People, right now I am just watching these things. I cannot step in there and try to do some of the things I used to do because I am getting pretty well along in years. So I just sit by and watch. I think about the future; of course I may never get to see it, but I just wonder how things will be in so many years, what improvements there will be for the benefit of the People. I wish I were young again, so I could see more of these things as time goes on. But those are just wishes and of course I do not expect to see those things.... [pp. 310–11]

In the early days, the old people were our teachers. They said that as long as we observed the rules laid down for us by the Holy People, everything was going to go along smoothly. But they said it would not last forever. Sooner or later we were going to start breaking the rules. Then that would lead us to ruin. It is like a seed of any kind, like corn, or beans, or anything that you put in the ground. You plant it, and it sprouts and bears fruit and grows to a certain extent. When it matures you harvest what it has produced; the stalks and leaves wither because their use is past. But you still have the seeds to continue planting and arriving at a new life. That is what the older people taught us. If you did not observe these things you are bound to ruin yourself.... [p. 311]

When you get put into a position of leadership, that teaches you to have some respect. Even if you have been irresponsible in the past, you now have to behave and lead a good life as an example to your people. [p. 315]

There are still lots of people coming around here wanting me to do Blessingway for them, but sometimes now because of my physical condition I have to refuse. When they come to ask, it just depends on how I feel. If I think that I can stand it, then I accept.... But a lot of the time now I'm not able to sing Blessingway. I can't stand the strain of being in a sitting position for that long, and my voice also gets tired. I especially feel the strain in the wintertime. The nights are long then, and performing that Blessingway is very strenuous even though we wait to start the all-night singing until pretty well on into the night. Of course in the summertime the nights are short. I will do Blessingway again when I get well and when I think that I am able to do it.

As you know, last fall I had my sacred bundle renewed and, of course, a Blessingway was used for that. But even though I had that and all of the other ceremonials I've been telling you about, right now my ailments are still hanging on. I still think we have not done the complete cure. The doctors do not seem to be able to tell me what the matter is, either. I went over to the Ganado hospital and they thoroughly examined my body. They could not find anything anywhere that could be causing my troubles. Finally they decided to take some tissue out of my stomach, just a small piece. I was not really operated on then. The doctor just said that there was no equipment there at Ganado to analyze what they had taken out of me, and that he would send it to Denver to find out what it was. They gave me some medicine and told me to go home.... [pp. 321–22]

While I was over at the Ganado hospital, and even before I went there, I had a lot of dreams and most of them were about dead people, those who had already passed away, even women. Those things were beginning to bother me; I was worrying about them. So I decided to have another ceremony. I also wanted to see if I could get some relief from the pains that I was feeling a lot of time. So I went and asked Black Sheep from Black Mountain to come over here and perform some of his small ceremonies for me to see if those could straighten out my dreams and give me some relief from those pains. He came down here and did some Ghostway rituals for me. He said prayers, cut prayersticks, bathed me and painted me with the blackening and reddening ceremonies. You can do those things to find out what effect they will have. If you feel a bit better after those, then you can go ahead and have the big ceremonial. After he did that I don't remember having any more dreams. I just forgot all about them. Before those things were done, as soon as I woke up, I would begin to think about what I had been dreaming about, but since then I do not do that any more. I still dream, but I do not remember what those dreams are about. I have felt a little better since Black Sheep performed all of those things for me, and right now I am thinking about calling him back again for a big, regular five-night Ghostway. Then, maybe I will go back to the hospital again.... [p. 323]

THE NATIVE AMERICAN CHURCH

In their comparatively recent history the Navajos have felt the call of two highly organized religious movements from outside their traditional culture. One is evangelical Christianity. The other is the **Native American Church,** an Indian movement with roots in ancient Mexico and recent development in Oklahoma. This religion established itself firmly in the United States in the nineteenth century and thereafter developed different perspectives and music from that which can still be seen among the Tarahumare and Huichol Indians of Mexico. It found its way into the Navajo country in the 1930s. By the 1950s it had grown in this one tribe to a membership estimated to be twenty thousand.

This music differs strikingly from traditional Navajo music. Let us listen to a hymn from the Native American Church (CD 1, Track 10) and then consider the role of this music in contemporary Navajo life.

What may strike you first is the quiet, introspective quality of the singing in this simple melody. Members of the Native American Church speak of their music as prayer. Although the text has no translatable words, the repetitive simplicity of vocables and music expresses a rapt, inward feeling (see Transcription 2.6 and the Close Listening guide). According to one theory, Native American Church hymns are derived from Christian hymnody. The quiet, slow movement and the unadorned voice, so unlike the usual boisterous, emphatic, out-of-doors delivery in American Indian singing, support this interpretation. On the other hand, the music shows many more features that are all Indian: the rhythmic limitation to only two note values, ♪ ♩ (a specialty of Navajo and Apache music), the descending melodic direction, the rattle and drum accompaniment, the pure melody without harmony, the use of vocables. These features are present in Native American Church music in many different tribes all across the continent to such a marked extent that one can identify a distinct, pantribal "Peyote style" (McAllester 1949:12, 80–82). In the present song, every phrase ends on *he ne yo,* anticipating the *he ne yo we* of the last phrase. This ending, always sung entirely on the tonic, is as characteristic of Native American Church music as "Amen" is to Christian hymns and prayers.

True to its Oklahoma origin, the Native American Church ideally holds its meetings in a large Plains Indian tepee. This is often erected on Saturday evening for the all-night meeting and then taken away to be stored until the next weekend. Such mobility enables the meeting to move to wherever members want a service. Meetings are sometimes held in hogans because they, too, are circular and have an earth floor where the sacred fire and altar can be built.

The members of the Native American Church use a water drum and a rattle to accompany their singing. The drum is made of a small, three-legged iron pot

CD 1:10

Hymn of the Native American Church (1:14). Navajo Peyote song. Performed by George Mitchell and Kaya David. Field recording by Willard Rhodes, n.d. Archive of Folk Song of the Library of Congress AFS 14. LP. Washington, DC.

Close Listening

HYMN, NATIVE AMERICAN CHURCH

CD 1:10

COUNTER NUMBER	COMMENTARY	VOCABLES	FORM	PEYOTE RATTLE
0:03	Soloist sings two cycles of phrase A, a descending melody, without harmony. All A phrases end with *he ne yo.*	*He yo-we no-we yu-na wu-na he ne yo we yo-we no-we yu-na wu-na he ne yo*	A	*Shaken throughout song*
0:11	Second phrase, B, begins on lower pitch and descends.	*'e yo-we no-we yu-na wu-na he ne yo he yo-we do yu-na wu-na he ne yo we*	B	
0:20	Phrase A repeats twice.	*he yo-we no-we yu-na wu-na he ne yo we yo-we no-we yu-na wu-na he ne yo*	A	
0:27	Phrase B repeats.	*'e yo-we no-we yu-na wu-na he ne yo he yo-we do yu-na wu-na he ne yo we*	B	
0:36	Phrase A repeats twice.	*he yo-we no-we yu-na wu-na he ne yo we yo-we no-we yu-na wu-na he ne yo*	A	
0:45	Phrase B repeats.	*'e yo-we no-we yu-na wu-na he ne yo he yo-we do yu-na wu-na he ne yo we*	B	
0:53	Phrase A repeats twice.	*he yo-we no-we yu-na wu-na he ne yo we yo-we no-we yu-na wu-na he ne yo*	A	
1:03	Phrase B repeats. This last section is always sung on the tonic and is characteristic of the Native American Church.	*'e yo-we no-we yu-na wu-na he ne yo he yo-we do yu-na wu-na he ne yo we*	B	

Transcription by David P. McAllester from field recording by Willard Rhodes. With permission of Willard Rhodes.

TRANSCRIPTION 2.6

Hymn, Native American Church (Navajo Peyote song).

He __ yo - we no - we yu - na wu - na he ne yo

we __ yo - we no - we yu - na wu - na he ne yo,

'e __ yo - we no - we yu - na wu - na he __ ne __ yo

Repeat 4 times

he   yo - we do   yu - na wu - na he   ne   yo   we

Transcription by David P. McAllester from field recording by Willard Rhodes. With permission of Willard Rhodes.

with a wet, almost rubbery, buckskin drumhead stretched over the opening (see Figure 2.13). The pot is half full of water, which is splashed over the inside of the drumhead from time to time by giving the drum a tossing motion. This keeps the drumhead moist and flexible while in use. The player kneels, holding the drum on the ground tipped toward his drumming hand. He controls the tone with pressure on the drumhead from the thumb of his holding hand. He strikes the membrane rapidly and rather heavily with a smooth, hard, slightly decorated drumstick. The water inside the pot most likely contributes to the strong resonance of this and other kinds of water drums, but no physical studies have yet been made to test the theory.

The peyote rattle is made with a small gourd mounted on a handle stick in much the same way as the cow-horn rattle of the Iroquois, discussed earlier. There is no carved shelf on the handle, however; instead, the stick is merely

FIGURE 2.13

Two kinds of water drum. On the left is an Iroquois drum made from a short section of hollowed-out log. On the right is a Navajo pottery water drum, used only in the Enemyway ceremony.

Susan W. McAllester

wedged tightly into the gourd plug. The far end of the stick protrudes two or three inches beyond the gourd, and a tuft of dyed horsehair is attached to it. This is often red to symbolize the red flower of the peyote cactus. Many Native American Church members hold a beautifully decorated feather fan during the service and use it to waft toward themselves the fragrant incense of cedar needles when these are put into the fire. The feathers of the fan are mounted in separate movable leather sleeves, like the feathers of the Plains war bonnet. This allows the user to manipulate the fan so that each feather seems to have a quivering life of its own.

The ritual consists of long prayers, many groups of four songs each (sung in turn by members of the meetings), a special water break at midnight, and a fellowship breakfast in the morning. At intervals, under the direction of the leader of the meetings, a Cedar Chief builds up the fire, puts cedar incense on the coals, and passes the cigarettes to make the sacred smoke that accompanies the prayers. He also passes small pieces of a cactus called peyote (from the Aztec *peyotl*, "wooly," describing the fine white hairs that grow in tufts on the cactus). When eaten, peyote produces a sense of well-being and, sometimes, visions in vivid color. The peyote is eaten as a sacrament, because Father Peyote is one of the deities of the religion. The Native American Church is sometimes called the Peyote Church.

A crescent-shaped earthen altar six or seven feet long lies west of the fire, and a large peyote cactus, symbolic of Father Peyote, is placed at the midpoint of the crescent. Prayers may be directed to Father Peyote, and some members can hear him responding to their pleas for help in meeting the difficulties of life. The intense feeling of dedication and piety at Peyote Meetings is expressed through prayers and testimonies, often with tears running down the cheeks of the speaker. Prayers include appeals to Jesus and God, as well as to Father Peyote. Peyotists consider the Native American Church to be hospitable to all other religions and include their ideas in its philosophy and beliefs. Members pray for friends and family members who are ill or otherwise in need of help. They also include leaders of the church, of the Navajo tribe, and of the country at large in their prayers.

In the past the more tradition-minded Navajos bitterly opposed by the Native American Church; in the late 1940s meetings were raided by the police and church leaders were jailed. But the church constituency grew so large that the new religion had to be accepted, and today the tepees for peyote meetings can be seen in many Navajo communities. One of these tepees stands near the Cultural Center of the Navajo Community College, where participation in the Native American Church's meetings is a recognized student activity.

THE WATER DRUM

Widespread in North and South America, the water drum is the only drum used in traditional Navajo and Apache music. The Navajos make theirs on a clay pot eight or ten inches high and use an unusual drumstick made of a twig bent around and tied in a loop at the far end. The Apaches use the same kind of drumstick but make the drum out of a large iron pot. The buckskin drumhead is stretched over an opening two or two-and-a-half feet across, and several of the singers beat the drum at the same time. A deep booming sound is produced, in contrast to the softer thump of the Navajo drum (see Figure 2.13).

The Iroquois and the Chippewas in the Eastern Woodlands make water drums using a hollowed-out log or a wooden keg. They do not have the looped drumstick but use a straight stick somewhat carved or, as in the case of the medicine drum of the Menomini, a somewhat elaborate curved stick. Eastern Woodland water drums range from five or six inches to two feet or more in height and from five or six inches across the drumhead to as many as fourteen inches or more.

The peyote drum seems to be an elaboration on the pot drum of the Navajos and Apaches. Nowadays the old-fashioned pot is hard to find, and members of the Native American Church can buy a specially manufactured aluminum replica that is much lighter to handle and gives the same sound. The church has also developed its own kinds of jewelry and costume and a genre of Indian painting depicting peyote meetings and peyote visions.

Because the water drum is so widespread in North and South America, students of Native American music may find insight in making one. The peyote drum is difficult to assemble. It is also so intensely symbolic to members of the Native American Church that it might be in questionable taste for a nonmember to attempt to make this particular kind of water drum. However, the traditional Iroquois, Navajo, and Apache water drums are used for social dancing and so do not have the same religious feelings associated with them.

Figure 2.14 contains the instructions for making a simple water drum. Iron pots or wooden kegs are hard to find, but a number ten tin can makes a good substitute. Buckskin is also difficult to obtain, but a piece of chamois from an auto supply store or a piece of rubber from an inner tube will work. Indians themselves sometimes use such materials if they cannot obtain the traditional ones.

THE SUN DANCE

The Plains Sun Dance, another Native American religion, was imported to the Navajo reservation in the last quarter of the twentieth century. This world renewal ceremony has undergone a revival on the Plains, and Sun Dance priests were invited to Navajo communities to perform the ceremony and teach it to Navajo participants. It is now an important part of the spiritual lives of certain Navajo who practice it.

NAVAJO HYMN MUSIC

Christian hymns share the popularity of peyote hymns, as evidenced by the requests that come in at the rate of several hundred a week at such radio stations as WGLF in Gallup, New Mexico. The Navajos who have joined the many Christian missions on the reservation appreciate them especially for their ministry. The hospitals, schools, and other services associated with the missions are a boon not only to church members but also to hundreds of other Navajos.

Navajo listeners make requests for particular hymns on the occasion of a birthday in the family, the anniversary of a death, or some other signal family event. When the request and the hymn are broadcast, the occasion is made known to hundreds of listeners. The hymns may be performed by nationally known gospel singers, but Navajo gospel singers as well have made records, and requests tend to favor these. One such group is the Chinle Galileans, a Navajo country gospel group

#10 can with one end open.

Inner tubing or chamois skin cut to size.

Water added and drumhead stretched in place. This takes two people to give the four pulling points needed (indicated by arrows).

Drumhead tied in place with cord, or better yet with something stretchy like wet rawhide or a long, thin rubber strip cut from an inner tube.

Hard, smooth wooden drumstick, slightly carved or incised.

FIGURE 2.14

Steps in making a water drum.

(CD 1, Track 11). Their lyrics are in English, and their music is the familiar country combination of electric guitar and percussion (see Transcription 2.7 and the Close Listening guide).

Interestingly, this music has few features that could be called traditionally Indian. Like the Fenders (discussed earlier), the Galileans have adopted a new style of music wholeheartedly. The clues that the performers are Navajos are the singers' Navajo accent and, in the case of the Fenders' CD selection, certain melodic and rhythmic shortcuts, compared with the Anglo original. This is what appeals to Navajo listeners and makes them feel that the performing groups are some of "their own."

CD 1:11

"Clinging to a Saving Hand" (3:42). Traditional Christian hymn. Performed by the Chinle Galileans. *Navajo Country Gospel* LPS 909. LP. Chinle, Arizona, n.d.

Close Listening

"CLINGING TO A SAVING HAND"

CD 1:11

COUNTER NUMBER	COMMENTARY AND LYRICS
Introduction	
0:00	Electric pedal steel guitar, piano, and drums.
Chorus—Lyric	
0:18	*Sing me a song of grace and glory* *Help this wondering child to understand* *So when I close my eyes in sleep eternal* *I'll be clinging to a saving hand.*
1st verse—Lyric	
0:51	*Sing to me about the rock of ages* *Sing about eternity so sweet* *So that when I take my last breath of life* *I'll awaken at my savior's feet.*
1:21	Chorus.
Break	
1:52	Electric pedal steel guitar solo. Piano and drums accompany.
2nd verse—Lyric	
2:24	*Tell me about Paul and Matthew* *Sing about my dear savior's birth* *Tell about his trials and tribulations* *While he walked upon this heathen earth.*
2:55	Chorus.
Coda—Last line of chorus repeats	
3:25	*I'll be clingin' to a savin' hand.*

Reprinted by permission of Roland Dixon.

With permission of Roland Dixon.

TRANSCRIPTION 2.7
"Clinging to a Saving Hand."

NEW COMPOSERS IN TRADITIONAL MODES

A recent genre of Navajo music comprises songs based musically on Enemyway style (usually Sway songs or Dance songs) but not intended for use in that ceremony. The texts are in Navajo, because the songs are intended for Navajo listeners, but they contain a different sort of social commentary from that in the popular songs of Enemyway. The new message is one of protest. For example, we can contrast the treatment of the use of alcohol in the old songs and the new. First we have a Skip Dance song from Enemyway, probably dating from the 1920s.

'E- ne- ya.
My younger brother,
My whiskey, have some! *Nana, he, ne-ye.*

My younger brother,
My whiskey, have some! *Nana, he, ne-ye.*

Your whiskey is all gone, *ne.*
My whiskey, there's still some, *wo.*

He yo-o-wo-wo, he yo-o-wo-wo,
Heya, we, heyana, he, nai-ya.

Text,
Enemyway Skip
Dance Song

In contrast, "Navajo Inn" speaks of the damaging effects of drinking. It is a recent song by Lena Tsoisdia, who is a social service worker at Window Rock, the headquarters of the Navajo tribal government. The title takes its name from a drive-in liquor store that used to do a thriving business a few miles from Window Rock. The store was just across the reservation boundary and was thus outside the jurisdiction of the tribal prohibition laws. The lyrics refer to the inn and speak despairingly of women finding their husbands, unconscious, behind "the tall fence."

Such protests cover many topics, based on modern problems as well as historical injustice. Ruth Roessel, a prominent Navajo educator, has composed a song about the "Long Walk," when the Navajos were rounded up by Kit Carson and his troops in 1864 and forcibly removed to a large concentration camp at Fort Sumner, New Mexico (see map, Figure 2.7). The hardships of the march, which preceded four years of captivity, and the Navajo love for their land are recounted here.

Text, "The Long Walk"	Long, long ago, our people, Our grandfathers, our grandmothers, Walking that long distance, There was no food, there was no water, But they were walking a long distance, But they were walking a long distance! At Fort Sumner, it was when they got there They were treated badly, They were treated badly. "I wish I were still back in my own home, I wish I were still back in my own home! We shall never forget this, The walk that we are taking now. We shall never forget this, The walk that we are taking now. Even then, we still like our own land, Even then, we still like our own land!" With permission of Ruth Roessel. Translation by Ruth Roessel for David McAllester.

The two examples here have not been recorded commercially, but several Navajo composers of new songs in styles based on Enemyway popular songs have recorded their work on popular discs. Kay Bennett (Kaibah) has produced three records on her own label. Danny Whitefeather Begay, Cindy Yazzie, and Roger McCabe have released My Beautiful Land on the Canyon Records label with fifteen popular songs in this new genre. "Los Angeles Sweetheart" by Danny Whitefeather Begay gives an idea of how those songs go. It is in the Skip Dance style as indicated by the formula

he   ye,   ya - na

Text, "Los Angeles Sweetheart"	*Heye, yana, heye, yana,* *Awe 'a-no 'aweya'a heye, yana,* *Awe 'a-no 'aweya'a heye, yana,* *Hene ya'o wowo 'awe ya'a heye, yana,* *Hene ya'o wowo 'awe ya'a heye, yana,*

ideas and technology from the Euro-American culture around them. This fact is clearly reflected in the many different kinds of music that coexist on the Navajo reservation and in thousands of Navajo homes in Chicago, Los Angeles, San Francisco, and many other locations away from the reservation.

To varying degrees this picture of Navajo music exemplifies what is happening to other Indian communities around the country. The different Indian cultures have embarked on an adventure that the larger population around them must inevitably share. Many Indian elements have already become part of the culture that is called "American." Some of these are relatively superficial: an Indian word such as *squash* or *moose* or a bit of local legend. Other contributions have had an enormous economic effect, such as the corn and potatoes that feed much of the world. There is now evidence that some of the music and the other Indian arts, and the religious and philosophical ideas that lie beneath them, are becoming accessible to an increasingly sympathetic American public. No culture remains static, and the Indians will continue to contribute to other world cultures, which are themselves in the process of change.

Book Companion Website

You will find tutorial quizzes, Internet links, and much more at the Book Companion Website for *Worlds of Music,* Fifth Edition, at **academic.cengage.com/music/titon/worlds_5**

Africa/Ewe, Mande, Dagbamba, Shona, BaAka

DAVID LOCKE

Consider a misleadingly simple question: Where is Africa's beginning and end? At first you might say that they lie at the borders that mark the continent. But musically, Africa spills over its geographic boundaries. Calling to mind the narrow Strait of Gibraltar, the recently dug Suez Canal, the often-crossed Red and Mediterranean Seas, and the vast Atlantic Ocean, we realize that people from Africa have always shaped world history. If we invoke images—Egypt, Ethiopia, the Moors, Swahili civilization, commerce in humans and precious metals—we know that Africa is not separate from Europe, Asia, and America. As pointed out in Chapter 1, music is humanly made sound; it moves with humankind on our explorations, conquests, migrations, and enslavements. This chapter, therefore, refers us not only to the African continent but also to the many other places we can find African music-culture.

Another question: What music is African music? We could be poetic and say, "Where its people are, there is Africa's music—on the continent and in its diaspora." The truth, however, is messier. Music is never pure; music-cultures are always changing and being shaped by many outside influences. From Benin and Luanda to Bahia, Havana, London, and Harlem, music-cultures blend along a subtle continuum. African-influenced music now circulates the planet by means of electronic media. After people learn new things about music, their own personal music-cultures adjust.

The African continent has two broad zones: (1) the **Maghrib,** north of the Sahara Desert, and (2) **sub-Saharan Africa.** North Africa and the Horn of Africa have much in common with the Mediterranean and western Asia; Africa south of the Sahara in many ways is a unique cultural area. Even so, history records significant contacts up and down the Nile, across the Sahara, and along the African coasts. Just as civilizations from the north (Greece, Rome) and east (Arabia, Turkey) have made an indelible impact on northern Africa, the south has influenced the Maghrib as well. Similarly, Africa south of the Sahara has never been isolated from the Old World civilizations of Europe and Asia. As this chapter will show, the history and cultural geography of sub-Saharan Africa vary tremendously (Bohannan and Curtin 1995).

Permit an ungrammatical question: When is an African? In everyday circumstances, people in Africa do not usually think of themselves as "African" (Mphahlele 1962). Identity arises from local connections of gender, age, kinship, place, language, religion, and work. Ethnicity comes into play only in the presence of people from a different group. One "becomes" a Serer, so to speak, in the presence of a Wolof, an African when among the French, a White in the company of a Black, a Yellow, a Red (Senghor 1967). These terms suggest relationships among people more than they mark essential characteristics of individuals. Although physical appearance and genetic inheritance do not determine culture, the bogus concept of "race" persists, feeding the ignorance that spawns prejudice and the bigotry that fosters injustice (Appiah 1992). Such labels should therefore be marked: USE WITH CARE.

"Africa" serves as a resonant symbol for many people. People of African descent, wherever they are in the world, may regard Africa as the ancestral homeland, the place of empowerment and belonging (Asante 1987). Industrialized citizens of "information societies" may envision Africa as either a pastoral Eden or the impoverished Third World. Historically regarded as a land of "heathens" by Muslims and Christians, Africa is a fount of ancient wisdom for those who practice religions such as *santería* or *vodun.* Famine relief and foreign aid, wilderness safari and Tarzan, savage or sage—Africa is a psychic space, not just a physical place.

The sections that follow introduce six African music-cultures. They show Africa's diversity and some of its widely shared characteristics. Information for two of the sections comes from my own field research; other sections are based on the ethnomusicological scholarship of colleagues—Roderic Knight, Paul Berliner, Michelle Kisliuk, and the late James Koetting. The cooperative effort that underlies this chapter seems fitting, because one vital function of African music is to mold separate individuals into a group.

Postal Workers Canceling Stamps

CD 1:1

Postal workers canceling stamps at the University of Accra, Ghana, post office (2:59). The whistled tune is the hymn "Bompata," by the Ghanaian composer W. J. Akyeampong (b. 1900). Field recording by James Koetting. Legon, Ghana, 1975.

In Chapter 1, you first heard the sounds of African postal workers canceling stamps (CD 1, Track 1). As promised, we will revisit this intriguing recording, this time examining how it reflects some of the general characteristics of African music-culture. To start, recall Koetting's description (1992:98–99):

This is what you are hearing: the two men seated at the table slap a letter rhythmically several times to bring it from the file to the position on the table where it is to be canceled. (This act makes a light-sounding thud). The marker is inked one or more times (the lowest, most resonant sound you hear) and then stamped on the letter (the high-pitched mechanized sound you hear).... The rhythm produced is not a simple one-two-three (bring forward the letter—ink the marker—stamp the letter). Rather, musical sensitivities take over. Several slaps on the letter to bring it down, repeated thuds of the marker in the ink pad and multiple cancellations...are done for rhythmic interest....

The other sounds you hear have nothing to do with the work itself. A third man has a pair of scissors that he clicks—not cutting anything, but adding to the rhythm.... The fourth worker simply whistles along. He and any of the other three workers who care to join him whistle popular tunes or church music that fits the rhythm.

How does this musical event exemplify widely shared characteristics of African music-culture?

GENERALIZATIONS ABOUT AFRICAN MUSIC-CULTURE

Music-Making Events

A compelling feature of this recording is its setting. Canceling stamps can sound like this? How marvelous! Obviously, the event was not a concert, and this most definitely is not art for art's sake. Like **work music** everywhere, this performance undoubtedly lifted the workers' spirits and enabled them to coordinate their efforts. The music probably helped the workers maintain a positive attitude toward their job. Music often helps workers control the mood of the workplace (Jackson 1972). (See "Music of Work" in Chapter 4.)

African music often happens in social situations where people's primary goals are not artistic. Instead, music is for ceremonies (life cycle rituals, festivals), work (subsistence, child care, domestic chores, wage labor), or play (games, parties, lovemaking). Music making contributes to an event's success by focusing attention, communicating information, encouraging social solidarity, and transforming consciousness.

Expression in Many Media

Just as Africans set music in a social context, they associate it with other **expressive media** (drama, dance, poetry, costuming, sculpture). Indeed, this example is unusual because it is a wordless instrumental. Although music making is usually not the exclusive purpose of an event, people do value its aesthetic qualities. Music closely associated with a life event is also enjoyed at other times for its own sake.

Musical Style

The whistled tune probably seems familiar to many listeners. The melody has European musical qualities such as duple meter, a major scale, and harmony (see Transcription 3.1). On the other hand, the percussion exhibits widespread African stylistic features such as polyrhythm, repetition, and improvisation (see Transcription 3.2).

History

These observations about genre and style lead to an important point about the history of music in Africa: The music-cultures of Europe, Asia, and the Americas have strongly affected those in Africa. Foreigners—Christians and Muslims, sailors and soldiers, traders and travelers—have brought to Africa their instruments, musical repertories, and ideas. Modern media technologies such as radio and audio recording have merely increased the intensity of a very old pattern of border crossing. Like people everywhere, Africans have imitated, rejected, transformed, and adapted external influences in a complex process of culture change.

Although the concert music repertory of Europe has held little attraction for most Africans, many other musical traditions have affected African music making.

TRANSCRIPTION 3.1
Postal workers' melody.

Note: $\frac{4}{}$ means four quarter notes per measure without implication of stress patterns.

TRANSCRIPTION 3.2
Postal workers' percussion "voices." (In this chapter, I refer to the musical "parts" that I hear on sound recordings as "voices.")

Throughout Africa, Christian hymns and Muslim **cantillation** (chanting religious texts) have exerted a profound influence on musical style. West Asian civilization has influenced African musical instruments, such as the plucked lutes, double reeds, and goblet-shaped drums of the Sahel area. Euro-American influence shows up in the electric guitar and drum set, although East Asians manufacture many of these instruments. We hear the American influence of Cuban *rumba* on pop music from central Africa, and African American spirituals on southern African religious music. From praise singers to pop bands, musical professionalism is an idea about music that developed in Africa by means of the intercultural exchange of ideas.

Participation

The postal workers join simple musical parts together to make remarkably sophisticated and satisfying music. This kind of musical design welcomes social engagement. Others could participate by adding a new phrase to the polyrhythm or cutting a few dance moves. Undoubtedly, Jim Koetting "got down" while picking up his mail! Much African music shares this generous, open-hearted quality that welcomes participation.

Training

We admire the postal workers because their music seems effortlessly beautiful. The genius we sense in this recording lies in the way the workers are musical together, in their sensitivity to a culturally conditioned musical style. Here, a musical education depends on a societywide process of **enculturation,** that is, the process of learning one's culture gradually during childhood. Babies move on the backs of their dancing mothers, youngsters play children's games and then join adults in worship and mourning, teenagers groove to pop tunes. Raised in this manner, Africans learn a way-of-being in response to music; intuitively, they know how to participate effectively. Genetic and sacred forces may shape musicality, but culture is the indispensable element in musical training.

Beliefs and Values

Often, Africans conceive of music as a necessary and normal part of life. Neither exalted nor denigrated as "art," music fuses with other life processes. Traditional songs and musical instruments are not commodities separable from the flux of life. In his book *African Music: A People's Art,* Francis Bebey quotes a musician who was asked to sell his instrument:

> He replied rather dryly that he had come to town to play his drum for the dancing and not to deliver a slave into bondage. He looked upon his instrument as a person, a colleague who spoke the same language and helped him create his music. (1975:120)

Intercultural Misunderstanding

These beliefs and attitudes about music make intercultural understanding a challenge, especially for scientifically minded people from what might be called concert-music-cultures. What a non-African listener assumes is an item of music may be the voice of an ancestor to an African. When he recorded this example, Koetting found himself in this type of cross-cultural conundrum:

> It sounds like music and, of course it is; but the men performing do not quite think of it that way. These men are working, not putting on a musical show; people pass by the workplace paying little attention to the "music" (I used to go often to watch and listen to them, and they gave the impression that they thought I was somewhat odd for doing so). (1992:98)

MUSICAL ANALYSIS: TOWARD PARTICIPATION

I too think this recording sounds like music, but I hesitate to say that it is music, because that would imply that the postal workers share my ideas about music. However, even though they do not "quite" regard this as music, what they are doing sounds great to me. I want to participate. In my music-culture, analysis can be an effective path toward active involvement, a bridge into the musical style of another culture. I use tools of musical analysis with caution, however, because we can never pin music to cardboard like a lifeless butterfly. For many Africans, music is "a living thing ensouled by the spiritual energy that travels through it" (Amoaku 1985:37).

Melody: Tonality, Texture, Form, Rhythm

The postal workers' melody uses a seven-note scale in a major mode (transcribed for convenience with the tonal center on G). (See Transcriptions 3.1 and 3.2 and the Close Listening guide.) The tune contains two melodic ideas: phrase A, which involves two shorter motives (Aa, Ab), and phrase B, which has three shorter motives (Ba, Bb, Bc). If there were no improvisation, we could mark the musical form as AABA, but because the performers never repeat phrase A in exactly the same way, a more careful marking is $A^1 A^2 B A^3$. The recording fades in at the end of A^3; then we hear four complete choruses of the tune before it fades out at the beginning of phrase A^2. As the recording ends, the homophonic texture fractures into a polyphonic interplay of independent melodies. I have set the rhythm within a meter of 4 quarter-note beats. The melody accentuates beats 1 and 3. Beats 2 and 4 play off beats 1 and 3, giving the music a sense of lift.

Close Listening

POSTAL WORKERS CANCELING STAMPS

CD 1:1

COUNTER NUMBER	COMMENTARY
0:00	Fade in during last phrase of the tune (phrase A^3).
0:07	First complete rendition of tune (phrases A^1, A^2, B, A^3; see Transcription 3.1); two-part harmony; restrained percussion.
0:44	Second time through the tune solo whistle; brief interlude without whistling.
2:04	Tune repeats a fourth time with more melodic and harmonic invention in whistling and rhythmic variety in percussive accompaniment.
2:36	Bass part (voice C in Transcription 3.2) in percussion "takes a solo" as tune finishes.
2:44	Fade-out as next repetition begins.

Percussion

It is hard to reconstruct exactly who played what on the recording; only by slowing the tape speed could I "get inside" the percussion texture. Guided by timbre and rhythm, I hear three percussive "voices," as shown in Transcription 3.2:

- A high-pitched, loud, dry sound (A) plays an ostinato (repeated phrase) on the upbeat of counts 2, 3, and 4. This part (the scissors) shapes musical time, giving a distinctive rhythmic character to the tune and other percussive voices.
- The middle voice in the ensemble (B) may be the sound of moving the letters into position, augmented with tapping on the table just for fun. This part is probably a composite of separate actions by several people. With much less silence than the other two parts, this part increases the density of the music's texture. The workers occasionally break the bubbling flow, allowing brief moments of silence that greatly enhance the music's rhythmic design.
- The lowest-pitched, resonant bass sound (C) plays occasional fills. This must be inking the stamp. Often it responds to the tune like an accompaniment, but at other times its interjections seem disconnected to the tune's progress. The prominent rhythmic figure shown in Transcription 3.2 answers the scissors' part in call-and-response.

Each layer in the texture has a different rhythmic character. Through a clever balance of action and silence, the players generate a forward motion in musical time while remaining within a repeating circle of percussion.

This example gives us a feeling for African music in general. The next example affords a more detailed look at a type of music with profound connections to the history of a specific African ethnic group, the Ewe people.

Agbekor: Music and Dance of the Ewe People

Drawing on my field research in West Africa during the 1970s, we will now consider a type of singing and drumming, originating as a war dance, called *Agbekor* (ah-*gbeh*-kaw; literally, "clear life"). As we will hear on CD 1, Tracks 15 and 16, *Agbekor*'s music features a percussion ensemble and a chorus of singers. A complex lead drumming part rides on a rich polyrhythmic texture established by an ensemble of bells, rattles, and drums of different sizes. Songs are clear examples of call-and-response. *Agbekor* is a creation of Ewe-speaking people who live on the Atlantic coast of western Africa in the nation-states of Ghana and Togo.

THE EWE PEOPLE
Ewe History

Triumph over adversity is an important theme in Ewe (*eh*-way) oral history. Until they came to their present territory, the Ewe people had lived precariously as a minority within kingdoms of more populous and powerful peoples such as the Yoruba and the Fon. One prominent story in their oral traditions recounts their exodus in the late 1600s from Agokoli, the tyrannical king of Notsie, a walled city-state located in what is now southern Togo. Intimidating Agokoli's warriors with fierce drumming, the Ewes escaped under cover of darkness. Moving toward the southwest, they founded many settlements along a large lagoon near the mouth of the Volta River. At last Wenya, their elderly leader, declared that he was too tired to continue. Thus, this Ewe group became known as the **Anlo** (*ahng*-law), which means "cramped." Other families of Ewe-speakers settled nearby along the coast and in the upland hills.

In these new lands, the Ewe communities grew and multiplied. Eventually the small Ewe settlements expanded into territorial divisions whose inhabitants could all trace male ancestors to the original villages. Family heads or distinguished war leaders became chiefs. Despite bonds of common culture and history, each division zealously cherished its independence. The Ewe people have never supported a hierarchical concentration of power within a large state (compare them with the Mande and Dagbamba kingdoms, discussed later in this chapter).

Ever since those early days, the important unit of Ewe social life has been the extended family. Members of a lineage—that is, people who can trace their genealogy to a common ancestor—share rights and obligations. Lineage elders hold positions of secular and sacred authority. The ever-present spirits of lineage ancestors help their offspring, especially if the living perform the necessary customary rituals. The eighteenth and nineteenth centuries saw the Ewes in frequent military conflict with neighboring ethnic groups, with European traders, and even among themselves. The Anlo-Ewe gained a fearsome reputation as warriors.

Ewe Religious Philosophy

An Ewe scholar has commented on the sacred worldview of his people:

> A traveler in Anlo is struck by the predominating, all-pervasive influence of religion in the intimate life of the family and community.... The sea, the lagoon, the river, streams, animals, birds and reptiles as well as the earth with its natural and artificial protuberances are worshipped as divine or as the abode of divinities. (Fiawo 1959:35, in Locke 1978:32)

The Ewe supreme being, **Mawu,** is remote from the affairs of humanity. Other divinities, such as Se (pronounced seh), interact with things in this world. Se embodies God's attributes of law, order, and harmony; Se is the maker and keeper of human souls; Se is destiny. Many Ewes believe that before a spirit enters the fetus, it tells Se how its life on earth will be and how its body will die. If you ask Ewe musicians the source of their talent, they will most likely identify the ancestor whose spirit they have inherited. Ask why they are so involved in music making, and they will say it is their destiny.

> Ancestral spirits are an important force in the lives of Ewe people. The Ewe believe that part of a person's soul lives on in the spirit world after his [or her]

death and must be cared for by the living. This care is essential, for the ancestors can either provide for and guard the living or punish them. . . . The doctrine of reincarnation, whereby some ancestors are reborn into their earthly kin-groups, is also given credence. The dead are believed to live somewhere in the world of spirits, *Tsiefe,* from where they watch their living descendants in the earthly world, *Kodzogbe.* They are believed to possess supernatural powers of one sort or another, coupled with a kindly interest in their descendants as well as the ability to do harm if the latter neglect them. (Nukunya 1969:27, in Locke 1978:35)

Funerals are significant social institutions, because without ritual action by the living a soul cannot become an ancestral spirit. A funeral is an affirmation of life, a cause for celebration because another ancestor can now watch over the living. Because spirits of ancestors love music and dance, funeral memorial services feature drumming, singing, and dancing. Full of the passions aroused by death, funerals have replaced war as an appropriate occasion for war drumming such as *Agbekor.*

Knowledge of Ewe history and culture helps explain the great energy found in performance pieces like *Agbekor.* Vital energy, life force, strength—these lie at the heart of the Ewe outlook:

In the traditional . . . Anlo society where the natural resources are relatively meager, where the inexplicable natural environment poses a threat to life and where the people are flanked by warlike tribes and neighbors, we find the clue to their philosophy of life: it is aimed at life. (Fiawo 1959:41, in Locke 1978:36)

AGBEKOR: HISTORY AND CONTEMPORARY PERFORMANCE

Legends of Origin

During my field research, I interviewed elders about how *Agbekor* began.[*] Many people said it was inspired by hunters' observations of monkeys in the forest. According to some elders, the monkeys changed into human form, played drums, and danced; others say that the monkeys kept their animal form as they beat with sticks and danced. Significantly, hunters, like warriors, had access to esoteric power.

In the olden days hunters were the repository of knowledge given to men by God. Hunters had special herbs. . . . Having used such herbs, the hunter could meet and talk with leopards and other animals which eat human beings. . . . As for *Agbekor,* it was in such a way that they saw it and brought it home. But having seen such a thing, they could not reveal it to others just like that. Hunters have certain customs during which they drum, beat the double bell, and perform such activities that are connected with the worship of things we believe. It was during such a traditional hunting custom that they exhibited the monkey's dance. Spectators who went to the performance decided to found it as a proper dance. There were hunters among them because once they had revealed the dance in the hunting customary performance they could later repeat it again publicly. But if a hunter saw something and came home to reveal it, he would surely become insane. That was how *Agbekor* became known as a dance of the monkeys. (Kwaku Denu, quoted in Locke 1978:38–39)

---

[*]I conducted these interviews with the assistance of a language specialist, Bernard Akpeleasi, who subsequently translated the spoken Ewe into written English.

Although many Ewes consider them legend rather than history, stories like this signify the high respect accorded to *Agbekor*. Hunters were spiritually forceful leaders, and the forest was the zone of dangerously potent supernatural forces. We feel this power in a performance of *Agbekor*.

Agbekor as War Drumming

The original occasion for a performance of *Agbekor* was war. Elders explained that their ancestors performed it before combat, as a means to attain the required frame of mind, or after battle, as a means of communicating what had happened.

> They would play the introductory part before they were about to go to war. When the warriors heard the rhythms, they would be completely filled with bravery. They would not think that they might be going, never to return, for their minds were filled only with thoughts of fighting. (Elders of the Agbogbome *Agbekor* Society, quoted in Locke 1978:44)
>
> Yes, it is a war dance. It is a dance that was played when they returned from an expedition. They would exhibit the things that happened during the war, especially the death of an elder or a chief. (Alfred Awunyo, quoted in Locke 1978:43)
>
> If they were fighting, brave acts were done. When they were relaxing after the battle, they would play the drums and during the dance a warrior could display what he had done during the battle for the others to see. (Kpogo Ladzekpo, quoted in Locke 1978:43)

The Meaning of the Name *Agbekor*

I asked whether the name *Agbekor* has meaning. One elder told me this:

> I can say it signifies enjoying life: we make ourselves happy in life. The suffering that our elders underwent was brought out in the dance, and it could be that when they became settled, they gave the dance this name, which shows that the dance expresses the enjoyment of life. (Kwaku Denu, quoted in Locke 1978:47)

Another elder told me that when people played *Agbekor* during times of war, they called it **atamuga** (ah-*tam*-gah), which means "the great oath." Before going to battle, warriors would gather with their war leaders at shrines that housed spiritually powerful objects. They would swear on a sacred sword an oath to their ancestors to obey their leaders' commands and fight bravely for their community. When the Anlo no longer went to war, the name changed to *Agbekor* (Kpogo Ladzekpo, quoted in Locke 1978:45–46).

The word *Agbekor* is a compound of two short words: *agbe* ("life") and *kor* ("clear"). The professional performer Midao Gideon Foli Alorwoyie translates *Agbekor* as "clear life": The battle is over, the danger is past, and our lives are now in the clear (Locke 1978:47). Many people add the prefix *atsia* (plural *atsiawo*), calling the piece *atsiagbekor* (ah-chah-*gbeh*-kaw). The word **atsia** has two meanings: (1) stylish self-display, looking good, or bluffing and (2) a preset figure of music and dance. As presented shortly, the form of the lead drumming and the dance consists of a sequence of *atsiawo*.

Learning

In Ewe music-culture, most music and dance is learned through enculturation. *Agbekor*, on the other hand, requires special training. The eminent African ethnomusicologist J. H. K. Nketia describes learning through slow absorption without formal teaching:

> The very organization of traditional music in social life enables the individual to acquire his musical knowledge in slow stages, to widen his experience of the music of his culture through the social groups into which he is progressively incorporated and the activities in which he takes part.... The young have to rely largely on their imitative ability and on correction by others when this is volunteered. They must rely on their own eyes, ears and memory. They must acquire their own technique of learning. (1964:4)

Gideon Alorwoyie explains how one learns from the performance of an expert:

> All you have to do is know when he is going to play.... You have to go and pay attention to what you hear... to how the drums are coordinated and to the drum language, to what the responses are to the calls, and so on. You have to use your common sense right there to make sure that you get the patterns clear. Up to today, if you want to be a drummer, you go to the place where people are playing and then pay attention and listen. That's it. (Davis 1994:27)

Because of its complexity, *Agbekor* is hard to learn in this informal way. Members of an *Agbekor* group practice in a secluded area for up to a year before they appear in public. Instruction entails demonstration and emulation. With adept dancers in front, the whole group performs together. No one breaks it down and analyzes it. People learn sequences of movement and music not through exercises but in a simulated performance context. (Compare this with the teaching of *karnataka sangeeta,* described in Chapter 6.)

This style of learning depends on gifted students who can learn long rhythmic compositions merely by listening to them several times. For certain people, drumming comes as easily and naturally as spoken language. Ewes know that drumming talent often comes from one's ancestors. A precocious youngster may be the reincarnation of an ancestor who was a renowned musician. One village drummer told me of a special drummer's ritual:

> My father was a drummer and he taught me. It was when he was old and could no longer play that he gave me the curved sticks. A ceremony has to be performed before the curved sticks are handed over to you.... If the custom is not done the drum language will escape your mind. (Dogbevi Abaglo, quoted in Locke 1978:53)

Gideon Alorwoyie explains the effects of this ritual:

> Once the custom has been made, you can't sleep soundly. The rhythms you want to learn will come into your head while you sleep.... The ceremony protects the person in many ways. It protects your hands when you play and protects you from the evil intentions of other people who may envy you.... Whenever you see a master drummer in Africa, I'm telling you, he has got to have some sort of backbone. (Locke 1978:54–55)

Performing Organizations

Times have changed since Ewe hunters created *Agbekor*. Britain, Germany, and France administered Ewe territory during a brief colonial period (1880s to 1950s); now the Ewe people live in the nation-states of Ghana and Togo. Today, relatively few villages have preserved their heritage of *Agbekor*. But the tradition vigorously

FIGURE 3.1

The Anya Agbekor Society (with the author) in performance.

Godwin Agbeli

continues within drum and dance societies of several types: mutual aid organizations, school and civic youth groups, and theatrical performing companies. Throughout Africa, voluntary mutual aid societies are an important type of performing group (Ladzekpo 1971). *Agbekor* groups of this kind are formal organizations with a group identity, institutionalized procedures, recognized leaders, and so forth. Many members are poor and cannot afford funeral expenses. People solve this financial problem by pooling resources. When a member dies, individuals contribute a small amount so the group can give money to the family. The society's performance of music and dance makes the funeral grand.

In the mid-1970s I studied *Agbekor* with members of this type of cooperative society, the Anya Agbekor Society of Accra (see Figure 3.1). One of their leaders recounted how the group came into existence:

> The first Anya Agbekor group in Accra was formed by our elder brothers and uncles. They all scattered in the mid-sixties and that group died away. We, the younger ones, decided to revive it in 1970. Three or four people sat down and said, "How can we let this thing just go away? Agbekor originated in our place, among our family, so it is not good to let it go." We felt that it was something we had to do to remember the old family members. We formed the group to help ourselves. (Evans Amenumey, quoted in Locke 1978:63)

I also studied with school groups trained by my teacher Godwin Agbeli. In colonial times, missionaries whipped students for attending traditional performance events. These days, most Ewes value their traditional repertory of music and dance as a cultural resource. Since Ghana achieved statehood in 1957, the national government has held competitions for amateur **cultural groups** from the country's many ethnic regions. Young people often join these groups because rehearsals and performances provide social opportunities. Like many African nations, Ghana sponsors professional performing-arts troupes. With its spectacular, crowd-pleasing music and dance, *Agbekor* is a staple of their repertory.

A Performance

On Sunday, March 6, 1977, in a crowded working-class section of Accra, the Anya Society performed in honor of the late chief patron of the group. The evening before, the group had held a wake during which they drummed *Kpegisu*, another prestigious war drumming of the Ewe (Locke 1992). Early Sunday morning they played *Agbekor* briefly to announce the afternoon's performance. Had the event occurred in Anyako, the group would have made a procession through the ward. People went home to rest and returned to the open lot near the patron's family house by 3:30 in the afternoon for the main event.

The performance area was arranged like a rectangle within a circle. Ten drummers sat at one end, fifteen dancers formed three columns facing the drummers, ten singers stood in a semicircle behind the dancers, and about three hundred onlookers encircled the entire performance area. All drummers and most dancers were male. Most singers were female; several younger women danced with the men. Group elders, bereaved family members, and invited dignitaries sat behind the drummers. With the account book laid out on a table, the group's secretary accepted the members' contributions.

The action began with an introductory section called *adzo* (ah-*dzo*), that is, short section. Dancers sang songs in free rhythm. After the *adzo,* the main section, *vutsotsoe* (voo-*tsaw*-tso-eh), that is, fast drumming, started. The first sequence of figures honored the ancestors. Following this ritually charged passage, the dancers performed approximately ten more *atsiawo.* The lead drummer spontaneously selected these "styles" from the many drum and dance sequences known to the group. The singers were also busy. Their song leader raised up each song; the chorus received it and answered. One song was repeated five to ten times before another was begun.

After about twenty minutes the **adzokpi** (ah-*dzoh*-kpee) or "solos" section of the performance began. Group members came forward in pairs or small groups to dance in front of the lead drummer. The dance movement differed for men and women. As in genres of Ewe social dancing, friends invited each other to move into the center of the dance space. When everyone had their fill of this more individualistic display, the lead drummer returned to the group styles. Soon, he signaled for a break in the action by playing the special ending figure.

During the break, the group's leaders went to the center of the dance area to pour a **libation.** Calling on the ancestors to drink, elders ceremonially poured water and liquor onto the earth. An elder explained later:

> We pour libation to call upon the deceased members of the dance [group] to send us their blessings [so we can] play the dance the same way we did when they were alive. How the Christians call Jesus, call God, though Jesus is dead—they do not see him and yet they call him—it is in the same manner that we call upon the members of the dance [group] who are no more so that their blessings come down upon us during the dancing. (Kpogo Ladzekpo, quoted in Locke 1978:82–83)

The performance resumed with **vulolo** (voo-*law*-law), that is, slow drumming, the processional section of *Agbekor.* After about fifteen minutes, they went straight to *vutsotsoe,* the up-tempo section, and then *adzokpi,* the "solos" section. After a brief rest they did another sequence of group figures at slow and fast pace, followed by individual display.

Perhaps because the word *atsia* means "stylishness," many English-speaking Ewe musicians refer to the preformed drum and dance compositions as "styles."

At the peak of the final *adzokpi* section elders, patrons, and invited guests came out onto the dance area. While they danced, singers and dancers knelt on one knee as a mark of respect. After dancing back and forth in front of the drummers, they returned to their position on the benches in back of the drummers.

By 6:00, with the equatorial sun falling quickly, the performance had ended. As the group members contentedly carried the equipment back to the Anya house, the audience dispersed, talking excitedly about the performance.

Although a performance of *Agbekor* follows a definite pattern, it is not rigidly formalized. A. M. Jones, a pioneering scholar of African music, comments on the elasticity of African musical performance: "Within the prescribed limits of custom, no one quite knows what is going to happen: It depends quite a lot on the inspiration of the leading performers. These men [and women] are not making music which is crystallized on a music score. They are moved by the spirit of the occasion" (Jones 1959:108).

CD 1:15

Agbekor (5:32). Traditional music of the Ewe people. Field recording by David Locke. Anlo-Afiadenyigba, Ghana, 1976.

CD 1:16

Demonstration: *Agbekor* (3:54). Performed by David Locke. You will hear the bell by itself, followed by each instrument with the bell (*axatse, kaganu, kidi, kloboto, and totodzi*), and finally, the polyrhythm of all the parts.

MUSIC OF THE PERCUSSION ENSEMBLE

We now turn to music of the percussion ensemble for the slow-paced section of *Agbekor* (see Transcription 3.12, later in the chapter). Instruments in the *Agbekor* ensemble include a double bell, a gourd rattle, and four single-headed drums (see Figure 3.2). Listen to CD 1, Track 15, for the entire ensemble, then listen to CD 1, Track 16, to hear the bell (*gankogui*) by itself, followed by each instrument with the bell (*axatse, kaganu, kidi, kloboto,* and *totodzi*), and finally the polyrhythm of all the parts. We will discuss each instrument shortly, but for now you can follow the demonstration in the Close Listening guide. You can also refer back to the guide in the discussion that follows, seeing where each instrument comes as you refer to the corresponding transcription. Note that I have decided not to present the music of the lead drum here. Not only is the material quite complicated, but I believe it best that students approach lead drumming only after a significant period of study, preferably with an Ewe teacher.

One by one the phrases are not too difficult, but playing them in an ensemble is surprisingly hard. The challenge is to hear them within a polyphonic texture that seems to change depending on one's point of musical reference. The reward in learning to play these parts is an experience of African musical time.

FIGURE 3.2

Agkebor ensemble. (Drawing by Emmanuel Agbeli)

atsimevu   kidi   totodzi   kloboto   kaganu   gankogui   axatse

Close Listening

DEMONSTRATION: AGBEKOR

CD 1:16

COUNTER NUMBER	COMMENTARY
0:00	*Gankogui* phrase by itself; phrase occurs twelve times; each phrase starts on high-pitched stroke 2 and ends on low-pitched stroke 1 (see Transcriptions 3.3 to 3.6)
0:34	*Gankogui* and *axatse* phrases in duet (see Transcription 3.7)
1:07	*Gankogui* and *kaganu* phrases in duet (see Transcription 3.8)
1:40	*Gankogui* and *kidi* phrases in duet (see Transcription 3.9)
2:13	*Gankogui* and *kloboto* phrases in duet (see Transcription 3.10)
2:48	*Gankogui* and *totodzi* phrases in duet (see Transcription 3.11)
3:20	Full ensemble made up of composite of all phrases (see Transcription 3.12)

The Bell

"Listen to the bell"—that is the continual advice of Ewe teachers. Every act of drumming, singing, and dancing is timed in accordance with the recurring musical phrase played on an iron bell or gong called **gankogui** (gahng-*koh*-gu-ee). On first impression, the part may seem simple, but when set in the rhythmic context of Ewe drumming, it becomes a musical force of great potency. Repetition is key. As the phrase repeats over and over, participants join together in a circling, spiraling world of time.

Seven strokes with a wooden stick on the bell make one pass through the phrase. Transcription 3.3 represents the bell part as a sequence of long and short

TRANSCRIPTION 3.3
Gankogui (bell) phrase.

notes. As the part repeats in polyrhythmic context, the musical ear groups the bell tones into a variety of patterns. Although the sonic phenomena never change, the part appears different. We experience an aural illusion.

Despite the chameleonlike nature of the bell part, two phrase shapes matter more than the others (Transcription 3.4).

TRANSCRIPTION 3.4
Two shapes of the bell phrase.

The note marked with the asterisk may be struck on the lower pitched of the *gankogui*'s two bells, a helpful landmark if one becomes rhythmically disoriented. For clarity, I have numbered the bell tones.

Tempo, Pulsation, and Time-Feels

Although many contrasting rhythmic phrases occur simultaneously in the percussion ensemble, competent Ewe musicians unerringly maintain a steady tempo. Rather than confusing the players, the musical relations among parts help them maintain a consistent time flow.

In this chapter I use an unconventional version of time signatures. A number in the numerator shows the number of beats per measure, and a musical note in the denominator shows the time-value of these beats. All beats in the measure have equal "weight" or metric stress.

The time-feel (meter) most significant to Ewe performers is the **four-feel.** Together with the explicit bell phrase, these four beats provide a constant, implicit foundation for musical perception (see Transcription 3.5). Each is a **ternary beat,** meaning that each has three quicker units within it. When my students first learn a dance step, a drum part, or a song melody, I advise them to lock into the bell phrase and the four-feel beats. Interestingly, this type of groove—often marked by a $\frac{12}{8}$ time signature—is widespread in African American music (see Chapter 4).

TRANSCRIPTION 3.5
The chant "*Matikpo matikpo kple ku dza*" with bell and four-feel beats.

Godwin Agbeli uses an Ewe children's game to teach the polyrhythm of bell and the four-feel beats (Transcription 3.5). The chant "*Matikpo matikpo kple ku dza*" means "I will jump, I will jump [to the sound of] '*kple ku dza*'"; children leap upward as they say "*kple*" and land with a hand clap on "*dza*." Practice the bell and four-beat combination by striking your thighs with open palms. When this is flowing easily, bring out the contrast between the parts by changing the weak hand to a fist.

To an Ewe musician, these four-feel beats automatically imply a **six-feel** (six quarter notes, or $\frac{6}{4}$ meter). The four- and six-feels are inseparable; they construct musical reality in two ways at once. Using both hands as shown in

TRANSCRIPTION 3.6
Bell and six-feel beats.

Transcription 3.6, try playing the bell phrase and the six-feel. The bell part feels different. This is the power of 3:2. After mastering the bell and four-feel hand pattern, add a foot tap on the six-feel. Now you have more fully entered the rhythmic world of Ewe music.

How does this analytic perspective relate to an Ewe point of view? How do they hear it? These questions are hard to answer. First, we cannot assume that there is just one pervasive Ewe perspective. Second, until recently Ewe musicians had no reason to think about musical structure in terms suited to intercultural education of the kind attempted in this book. After many years of research, performance, and teaching, I believe that my approach here accurately conveys the perspective of my Ewe teachers (see Locke 1982). However, the discovery of ethnographic truth is not my only intent. I also ask practical questions: Does this approach help one hear the music with insight? Does it help people play? Students must answer this question for themselves. I hope the answer is yes!

The *axatse* (ah-*ha*-tseh) is a dried gourd, about the size of a cantaloupe, covered with a net strung with seeds. In some *Agbekor* groups its role is to sound out the four-feel beats. In another frequently heard phrase, downward strokes on the player's thigh match the *gankogui* while upward strokes against the palm fill in between bell tones (see Transcription 3.7). The longer duration of the tone that matches bell stroke 1 gives definition to the shape of the bell phrase; it suggests to the musical ear that the bell phrase begins on stroke 2 and ends on stroke 1.

TRANSCRIPTION 3.7
Axatse phrase.

As the only instrument played by many people at once, the *axatse* "section" provides a loud, indefinite-pitched sound vital to the ensemble's energy.

The high pitch and dry timbre of the slender *kaganu* (kah-gahng) drum cuts through the more mellow, midrange sounds of the other drums. The *kaganu* part articulates offbeats, that is, moments between the four-feel beats (see Transcription 3.8).

TRANSCRIPTION 3.8
Kaganu phrase.

Although not every *Agbekor* group uses the same phrase (Locke 1983:23–27), a good one for newcomers to learn marks the second and third pulses within each four-feel beat. Many Ewe teachers advise students to focus on the synchrony between *kaganu* and bell tones 3 and 4; remember—listen to the bell! The late Freeman Donkor, one of my first teachers of Ewe music, said that the rhythm of *kaganu* brings out the flavor of the other parts, like salt in a stew.

The *gankogui, axatse,* and *kaganu* parts create a distinctive quality of musical temporal experience (Locke 1988). The long and short tones in the bell phrase sculpt time into asymmetrical proportions. Symmetrical units also are important: the duration of the bell phrase is a literal measure of time; the tones of *axatse* and *kaganu* mark that measure into four equal ternary units. All four beats are strong, but the moments when bell and beat fall together—beats 4 and 1, bell tones 6 and 1—are specially marked in musical awareness; beat 3 is distinctive because it marks the midpoint in the bell phrase. These stable qualities of musical time provide the solid rhythmic foundation for the shifting offbeats found in the songs and lead drumming.

In descending order of relative pitch, the three other drums in the ensemble are **kidi, kloboto,** and **totodzi** (kee-dee, kloh-boh-toh, and toh-toh-*dzee*). Each drum adds its own phrase to *Agbekor*'s unique polyphony. There are two ways of striking a drum skin. In bounce strokes the stick bounces off the drum skin, producing an open ringing sound; in press strokes the stick presses into the drum skin, producing a closed muted sound. Bounces contribute the most to the group's music; presses keep each player in a groove. The parts discussed as follows are widespread, but some *Agbekor* groups use slightly different versions.

- In the *kidi* part, three bounces and three presses move at the twelve-unit pulsation rate; the phrase occurs twice within the span of one bell phrase (see Transcription 3.9). Polyrhythmic relationships to the time parts help in learning the *kidi:* (1) in each group of bounces and presses the third stroke is on a beat, (2) bell tones 5 and 6 match open *kidi* tones, and (3) *kidi* closely coincides with *kaganu*.

TRANSCRIPTION 3.9
Kidi phrase.

- The *kloboto* phrase has the same duration as the bell phrase (see Transcription 3.10). As if inspired by bell tones 7–1, the part's main idea is a brief bounce-press, offbeat-onbeat figure. The *kloboto*'s insistent accentuation of offbeat moments can reorient a listener into perceiving them as onbeats. This type of implied beat shift (displacement) adds to the multidimensional quality of the music. For example, a person concentrating on *kloboto* may hear the second stroke in each pair of *kaganu* tones to be on the beat. Competent Ewe musicians, however, never lose orientation—they always know the *kloboto* presses are right on the four-feel time.

TRANSCRIPTION 3.10
Kloboto phrase.

- The *totodzi* part begins and ends with the *kloboto* (see Transcription 3.11). Its two bounce strokes match bell tones 2 and 3, its three press strokes match four-feel beats 3, 4, and 1. Notice the impact of sound quality and body movement on rhythmic shape: The phrase is felt as two strong-hand bounces followed by three weak-hand presses, not according to a three-then-two timing structure.

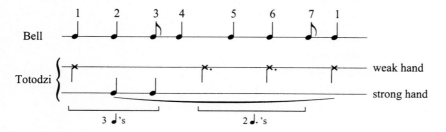

TRANSCRIPTION 3.11
Totodzi phrase.

   To get into the drumming, begin by hearing each phrase "in four" and in duet with the bell. Then, stay "in four" but hear ever-larger combinations with other parts. Next, switch to the six-feel. The point is to explore the potency of these phrases, not to create new ones. Stretch your way of hearing, rather than what you are playing. Strive for a cool focus on ensemble relationships, not a hot individual display (Thompson 1973).

Drum Language

As happens in the instrumental music of many African peoples, Ewe drum phrases often have vernacular texts, called **drum language.** Usually only drummers know the texts. Even Ewe speakers cannot understand drum language just by hearing the music—they must be told. Secrecy makes restricted information valuable and powerful. In many parts of Africa, "speech must be controlled and contained if silence is to exercise its powers of truth, authenticity, seriousness and healing" (Miller 1990:95). During my field research, I asked many experts whether they knew drum language for *Agbekor*. Saying he learned them from elders in his hometown of Afiadenyigba, Gideon Alorwoyie shared the following with me. *Agbekor*'s themes of courage and service are apparent (see Transcription 3.12 and text). His word-for-word and free translations appear beneath the Ewe texts.

TRANSCRIPTION 3.12
Agbekor drum language.

Ewe Text and Translation of *Agbekor* Drum Language

Totodzi   Dzogbe dzi dzi dzi.
            battlefield/on/on/on
            We will be on the battlefield.

Kloboto   Gbe dzi ko mado mado mado.
            Battlefield/on/only/I will sleep/I will sleep/I will sleep
            I will die on the battlefield.

Kidi   Kpo afe godzi.
            Look/home/side-on.
            Look back at home.

Kaganu   Miava yi afia.
            We will come/go/will show
            We are going to show our bravery.

SONGS

Texts

Agbekor songs engage the subject of war. Many songs celebrate the invincibility of Ewe warriors; others urge courage and loyalty; some reflect on death and express grief. Songs memorialize heroes but do not provide detailed historical information. Unlike the freshly composed songs found in contemporary idioms of Ewe traditional music, *Agbekor* songs come from the past. A song's affective power derives, in part, from its association with the ancestors.

Structural Features

In performance, a song leader and a singing group share the text and melody. As illustrated in the songs presented shortly, this **call-and-response** idea supports a variety of subtly different musical forms. The tonal system of *Agbekor* songs has evolved entirely in response to the human singing voice, without being influenced by musical instruments. An ethnomusicologist can identify scales, but in comparison to tuning in South Indian music-culture, for example, an Ewe singers' intonation seems aimed at pitch areas rather than precise pitch points. Melodic motion usually conforms to the rise and fall of speech tones, but Ewe speakers easily understand song lyrics even if the melodic contour contradicts the tonal pattern of the spoken language. Songs add another layer to the rhythm of *Agbekor*. Not surprisingly, a song's polyrhythmic duet with the bell phrase is all-important.

On CD 1, Track 15, listen again to excerpts from my recording of a performance by an *Agbekor* group from the town of Anlo-Afiadenyigba on August 14, 1976. There are three slow-paced songs, one song in free rhythm, and one fast-paced song, which will be discussed in turn.

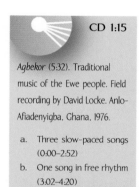

CD 1:15

Agbekor (5:32). Traditional music of the Ewe people. Field recording by David Locke. Anlo-Afiadenyigba. Ghana, 1976.

a. Three slow-paced songs (0:00–2:52)

b. One song in free rhythm (3:02–4:20)

c. One fast-paced song (4:27–5:32)

Slow-Paced Songs

We begin with the slow-paced songs (see the Close Listening guide). Song 1 announces that people should prepare for the arrival of the *Agbekor* procession. It has a rounded ABA musical form: $\|: A^1 \; A^2 :\| B \; B \; A^2$. In the A section, the group repeats the leader's text but with a different tune. In the B section, the melodic phrases are shorter, the rhythm of call-and-response more percussive. The song ends with leader and group joining to sing the group's first response.

Leader: ‖:	*Emiawo miegbona 'feawo me.*		Text,
	Afegametowo/viwo. midzra nuawo do.	A¹	SONG 1
Group:	Repeat lines 1 and 2 :‖	A²	
Leader: ‖:	*Oo!*		
Group:	*Midzra nuawo do.* :‖	B	
All:	Repeat lines 1 and 2	A²	
Leader: ‖:	We are coming into the homesteads.		
	People/Children of the noble homes. get the things ready.		
Group:	Repeat lines 1 and 2 :‖		
Leader:	*Oh!*		
Group:	Get the things ready.		

Close Listening

AGBEKOR VULOLO (SLOW-PACED SECTION)

CD 1:15

COUNTER NUMBER	COMMENTARY
0:00	Fade-in on Song 1.
0:05	One time through Song 1 (see Text, Song 1, and Transcription 3.13).
0:38	Song leader begins Song 1 again, but group raises Song 2 so song leader joins them.
0:42	Song leader continues Song 2 from line B^2 (see Text, Song 2, and Transcription 3.14).
0:48	Song 2 repeated seven times, each time taking about 10 seconds.
2:02	Song 3 (see Text, Song 3, and Transcription 3.15).
2:21	Song 3 repeated.
2:40	Fade-out during next repetition of Song 3.

TRANSCRIPTION 3.13
Agbekor Song 1.

The song's rhythm moves in the three-then-two groove (see Transcription 3.13). I hear the song's final pitch as its tonal center (here set on E). The intonation of the second scale degree is variable—sometimes natural, sometimes flat, often somewhere in between. When the song's transcribed pitches are ordered into a scale, we see five pitches with two half steps—1 ♭2 or ♯2 ♭3 5 ♭6. (Compare with the *pélog* scale in Chapter 7.)

Song 2, set at sunrise on the day of battle, urges Manyo and his warriors to "be cunning." Leader and group divide the text: the leader identifies the actors and the action, then the group evokes the scene. Unlike the rounded form of Song 1, this song has a linear AB musical form: A^1 B^1 A^2 B^2.

Leader:	*Agbekoviawo, midze aye.*	A^1	Text,
Group:	*Ada do ee.*	B^1	SONG 2
	Kpo nedze ga nu.		
	Ada do!		
Leader:	*Manyo hawo, midze aye ee*	A^2	
Group:	Repeat lines 2–4	B^2	
Leader:	*Agbekor* group, be cunning.		
Group:	The day has come.		
	Beat the double bell.		
	The day has come.		
Leader:	Manyo's group, be cunning.		
Group:	Repeat lines 2–4.		

This song has five pitches with no half steps (see Transcription 3.14). As I hear it, the melody moves between two tonal centers: the phrases in A^1 B^1 strongly cadence on A; A^2 shifts the tonal center to G; B^2 begins there, but then it ends back on A. Form, melody, and tonality combine in creating a circular musical effect.

TRANSCRIPTION 3.14
Agbekor Song 2.

Song 3 expresses an important sentiment in *Agbekor* songs: celebrating the singers' power and denigrating the opponent (see Transcription 3.15). Here, the enemy is a "hornless dog," that is, an impotent person, and "we" are incomparably great. Ewe composers often make this point by means of rhetorical questions: "Who can trace the footprints of an ant?" that is, Who can defeat us? "Can the pigeon scratch where the fowl scratches?" that is, Can the enemy fight as strongly as we can? "Can a bird cry like the sea?" that is, How can the enemy compare to us? In these playful self-assertions and witty put-downs, we see a parallel with the genres of African American expressive culture called **signifying** (Gates 1988; see Chapter 4 of this book for examples).

Text, SONG 3			
Leader:	‖:	*Avu matodzo.*	A¹
		Dewoe lawuma?	
Group:		Repeat lines 1 and 2 :‖	A²
Leader:	‖:	*Dewoe?*	B¹
Group:		*Dewoe lawuma?* :‖	B²
All:		*Avu matodzo*	A²
		Dewoe lawuma?	
Leader:		A hornless dog.	
		Are there any greater than we?	
Group:		Repeat lines 1 and 2.	
Leader:		Any?	
Group:		Greater than we	
All:		Repeat lines 1 and 2	

TRANSCRIPTION 3.15
Agbekor Song 3.

Close Listening

AGBEKOR ADZO (FREE-RHYTHM INTERLUDE)

CD 1:15

COUNTER NUMBER	COMMENTARY
2:50	Break in recorded selection.
3:02	Song 4: Leader calls A and group responds B; sung twice (see Text, Song 4, for all references to sections).
3:18	Song 4: Leader calls C^1 and group responds D.
3:23	Song 4: All sing section E.
3:37	Song 4: All sing section B.
3:39	Exhortation from lead drum and song leader.
3:43	Song 4: Leader calls A and group responds B; sung twice.
3:56	Song 4: Leader calls C^2 and group responds D.
4:01	Song 4: All sing section E.
4:14	Song 4: All sing section B.

Free-Rhythm Songs

Rhythmically free songs make up the *adzo* section here. They have longer texts than do songs from the slow- and fast-paced portions of an *Agbekor* performance. Like Songs 1 and 3, Song 4 (see the Close Listening guide) begins with two sections of leader-group alternation but has a noticeably longer third section sung by the whole group. The issues raised in Song 4 are not new to us: The song compares the *Agbekor* group's strength with the power of the ocean and derides the potency of the enemy's weapons. This song makes a factual historical reference to Avusu Kpo, an enemy war leader.

Leader:	‖:	'Gbekoviwo, xe de ado ahoyo gbe.	A	**Text,**
		Be tsawoyo?		**SONG 4**
Group:		Xe ke lado gbe.	B	
		Gavi tsawoyo? :‖		
Leader:		Tu nedi!	C^1	

Group:	Miahee de alada me.	D
Leader:	Hewo nu,	C^2
Group:	Miahee de alada me.	D
All:	Be la bada fo soshi	E
	Ko de alada me.	
	Tu la kaka,	
	Mietsoe da de agboawo dzi	
	Xe de mado ahoyo gbe ee?	
	Avusu Kpowoe mado lo na xe	
	Be xe nedo dika na alado me.	
	Tsawoyo	
	Repeat lines 3 and 4	B
Leader: ‖:	Members of the *Agbekor* group, Can a bird cry like the sea? "Tsawoyo?"	
Group:	Which bird can cry like the sea? "Gavi Tsawoyo?" :‖	
Leader:	Fire the gun!	
Group:	We will turn it aside!	
Leader:	The tips of knives,	
Group:	We will brush them aside!	
All:	A wild animal has found a horsetail switch	
	And put it at his side.	
	The gun broke,	
	We put it on the barricade.	
	Can a bird cry like the sea?	
	Avusu Kpo and his people cannot talk in proverbs to the bird.	
	[unknown]	
	"Tsawoyo."	
	Repeat lines 3 and 4	

Fast-Paced Songs

Like many songs from the fast-paced section, song 5 celebrates heroic passion. For example, another song says simply, "Sweet, to put on the war belt is very sweet." Song 5 (see the Close Listening guide) opens with the vivid image of a confrontation between two war gods (So). The Fon from Dahomey and the Anlo are about to fight; the beautiful warriors are preparing; will they have the courage to enter the fray?

Text, SONG 5	Leader: ‖:	So kpli So, ne ava va gbedzia	A
		Tsyo miado.	
	Group:	Woyawoya	B
		Ava va gbedzia.	
		Tsyo miado. :‖	
	Leader:	Oo,	C

Group:	*Fowo do gbea,*	C
	Miayia?	
	Anlowo do gbe.	
Leader:	*Oo.*	D
Group:	*Anawo do gbea*	
	Tsyo miado.	
All:	Repeat lines 3–5	B
Leader: ‖:	So and So—if war breaks out on the battlefield	
	We will have to dress gorgeously.	
Group:	*"Woyowoya"*	
	War breaks out on the battlefield.	
	We have to dress gorgeously. :‖	
Leader:	Oh,	
Group:	The Fon are out on the battlefield,	
	Should we go?	
	The Anlo are out on the battlefield.	
Leader:	Oh,	
Group:	The cowards are out on the battlefield.	
	Should we go?	
	The Anlo are out on the battlefield.	
	Repeat lines 3–5.	

Close Listening

AGBEKOR VUTSOTSOE (FAST-PACED SECTION)

CD 1:15

COUNTER NUMBER	COMMENTARY
4:19	Break in recorded selection.
4:28	Fade in on Song 5 leader call A and group response B sung twice (see Text, Song 5).
4:39	Song 5 leader-group call and response C and D (see Text, Song 5).
4:44	Song 4 all sing section B (see Text, Song 4).
4:47	Song 5 repeated.
5:05	Song 5 repeated.
5:24	Fade-out as new song is raised.

As we have seen, *Agbekor* is a group effort. Music and dance help cement social feeling among members of an *Agbekor* society. Others types of African music depend more on the virtuosity and special knowledge of individuals. We turn now to an example of such a solo tradition. Information for the next section of the chapter draws primarily on the research of the ethnomusicologist Roderic Knight.

Mande Jaliya, "Lambango"

On CD 1, Track 17, we hear the artistry of Mariatu Kuyateh (vocal), her husband, Kekuta Suso (stringed instrument), and Seni Jobateh (speech and percussion) as they perform the piece "Lambango." You may be drawn toward Kuyateh's wordy solo song and Suso's virtuosity on the *kora* (bridge-harp, discussed later). These experts in speech, song, and the playing of instruments are often called **griots** (*gree*-oh). Not only musicians, they are counselors to royalty, entertainers for the public, and guardians of history (see Figure 3.3). Before closely listening to the work, we will look its context in some detail.

The performers, who call themselves *jalolu* (singular *jali*), are professional "sound artisans" of the Mande ethnic tradition (see Charry 2000). *Jaliya,* that is, what *jalolu* do, has played many important roles in Mande civilization since the thirteenth century, when Sunjata Keita founded the empire of Mali. At its apogee (fourteenth to sixteenth centuries), Mali exerted authority over a vast territory of river and grassland stretching west from the Upper Niger to the Atlantic coast. Age-old patterns of Mande culture remain influential today.

FIGURE 3.3

Mariatu Kuyateh and Kekuta Suso (with *kora*). Boraba, Gambia, 1970.

HISTORICAL AND SOCIAL BACKGROUND

Cultural Crossroads

Distinct civilizations meet in the West African savanna south of the desert and north of the forest—Sudanic African, Tuareg, Berber, Arab, European. The routes of intercultural communication run between north and south as well as east and west. For Arabic speakers on trading caravans between the Mediterranean and the Sudan (*Bilad es Sudan,* "Land of the Blacks"), the Sahara was a sand sea. The semiarid Sahel was its southern "coast." East–west travel followed rivers such as the Gambia, the Senegal, and most importantly the Niger, whose seasonal floods fostered an agricultural base for empire.

Mali

A succession of great states arose in this broad cultural crossroads: first Ghana, then Mali, Songhai, Kanem-Bornu, Hausa, Mossi, and others. Mali was fabulously wealthy. It was a centralized, hierarchically organized empire with distinct social classes. Islamic libraries and universities of world renown flourished in great cosmopolitan cities. A class of literati (writing in Arabic) operated the empire's systems of commerce and law.

> The duty of Mande *jalolu* was to serve this array of wealthy patrons. The jali held the only records of genealogy and history and was the only one who knew and could perform the music called for on important occasions. The people who most often employed the services of these people were in a position to provide ample recompense in the form of lodging, cattle, clothing and other manifestations of wealth. For the jali ... this meant that he was virtually assured of permanent patronage. ... As one jali has put it, "The jali was king." (Knight 1984:62)

Learning helped determine one's status in such cities as Timbuktu. Some intellectuals became **praise singers** (*muddah*) who received alms for lauding the Prophet Muhammad (Saad 1983:86). Such refined professionals included erudite *jalolu*. In the Islamic Sudan, the formal exchange of praise for wealth remains a respected institution. In this music-culture, gifts to a *jali* are not commercial payments for products sold but rather are respectful offerings that mark the interdependence of praiser and praised.

Although the political leaders were nominally Muslim, the bulk of the population kept faith with pre-Islamic religion. Some Mande peoples still retain a mythic consciousness that links natural landmarks to the primordial, creative feats of superhuman ancestors (Dieterlen 1957, in Skinner 1973). In addition to serving their elite patrons, the *jalolu* transmit these ancient, secret mysteries to every member of society (Laye 1983).

After 1600, the history of these Sudanic empires is a story of fracture and gradual decline. Forces of change included internal rebellion, invasion by a Moroccan expeditionary force (1591), the Atlantic slave trade (1700s), Islamic jihads (1800s), and finally British and French colonialism (1900s). All the while, in songs like "Lambango," the Mande bards told legends of the empire's founder, Sunjata Keita, and news of more recent heroes.

Kingdoms Along the Gambia

At the western edge of the Mande heartland, many small kingdoms formed along the Gambia River. Modeled on the much larger empires of the Upper Niger, each state had its hierarchy of royals, courtiers, warriors, state officials, merchants, clerics, and so on. Prospering through trade with Europe—notably, slaves for manufactured goods—the elite were remarkably cosmopolitan.

> French traders in the eighteenth century reported that the *mansas* of Niumi [kings of a state on the north bank of the Gambia] lived in European-style houses and dressed in elaborate costumes. ... [One] mansa's daughter, who was said to read and write French, Portuguese and English, had established herself as the chief intermediary between the traders and her father. At one time married to a Portuguese, she lived in a large square European house and held soirees for the commercial community in a style that boasted fine table linen and other imported luxuries. (Quinn 1972:41)

A distinctive music-culture of *jali* with *kora* developed in these kingdoms along the Gambia.

MUSIC-CULTURE
Social Organization

Where do the *jalolu* fit within the Mande system of social rank and its associated roles? Slavery existed in this African society; even today, descendants of the freeborn (*horon*) are distinguished from people of slave descent (*jong*), especially in the matter of marriage. Among the freeborn, **nyamalo**—craft specialists including *jalolu*—occupy a separate niche from **sula**—nonspecialists, including royals, Islamic literates, merchants, and farmers—who are a *jali*'s prospective patrons. Among *nyamalo*, boys inherit their fathers' craft as a lifelong profession; young women marry within their fathers' occupational group (see Knight 1984:60–66).

Duties to Patrons

In former times when kings were rich, *jali* and patron shared a mutually beneficial relationship. Playmates as children, they retained their intimacy as adults.

> Griots woke the king each morning by singing his praises outside his quarters, they accompanied him wherever he traveled, singing and playing behind him and especially when he met another king, they were in attendance singing their patron's praises. From time to time a court griot would entertain the king and members of his court by reciting accounts of the careers of some of the king's forebears, perhaps of some deeds of the king himself.... The whole narration glorified the king, often bathing him in the reflected glory of his mighty ancestors.... [The griot] would take real pride in [this] history and would want to present it in the best possible light, for he would surely feel able to share in the glory of his patron's family. (Innes 1976:5)

Before our era, the *jali* received the wholehearted respect merited by a learned artist with significant duties in the affairs of state. A *jali*'s performance bridged time and space, bringing the historical and mythic past into the lives of the living.

> When the jali sings the name of a past hero, he views what he is doing as waking him up, bringing him back to life (*Mb'a wulindila*).... If in the end the listener can say of the music, *Wo le dunta n na* (It has entered me), then the desired effect will have been achieved. (Knight 1984:73)

This music-culture changed after the Gambia became a British protectorate in 1894. Since the wealth of the royals was much reduced, their patronage alone could not sustain a *jali.* Thus today, *jalolu* must serve a broader clientele by freelancing at social occasions such as weddings and naming ceremonies where people value their knowledge and artistry. Yet even in our cash-oriented, dislocated world, where an African royal may hold a menial job in Europe, the *jalolu* retain warm relations with their patrons and provide a vital link to profound dimensions of Mande culture.

Transmission

A *jali* learns the craft of playing a musical instrument through a formal apprenticeship with a single master. During adolescence and young adulthood, fathers send their sons to a relative who enforces a strict training regimen. Some *jalolu* specialize in the *kora*, others play xylophone (*balo*) or one of several kinds of plucked, long-neck lute (**konting, ngoni,** or **guitar**). Young women, whose primary duty is to sing, participate in a more informal apprenticeship. While they serve their elders, young *jalolu* gradually learn an impressive body of knowledge. *Jalolu* keep elaborate genealogies and stories of their patrons' forebears. More than dry objective historical accounts, their performances entail rousing artistry designed to elicit the respect and gratitude of an audience.

The *Jali's* Knowledge

A key element in *jaliya* is speech (**kuma**). Narratives in the Gambian tradition refer to two historical periods: (1) the times of Sunjata and the formation of Mali (1200s) and (2) the times of the last **mansas** (kings; 1800s). The stories are told in the vernacular with few poetic devices; the *jali* enlivens the characters by recreating their words. Songs contain wise sayings about people and situations that are always relevant to the living. Here are some examples (Knight 1984:78–80):

Islamic fatalism:	"Before God created life, he created death."
Moral judgments:	"The talkative kings are plentiful, but men of great deeds are few."
	"Misery is hard on a woman, shame is hard on a man."
Advice:	"The world is ever-changing. If someone doesn't know your past, don't tell him your present affairs."
Observations:	"Life is nothing without conversation."
On wealth:	"Wealth is not a tonic for life; wealth is to save you from disgrace."
	"The wealthy inherit the wealth."
On *jaliya:*	"For the person who puts one hundred in my hand, I will give him a hundred-worth praise with my mouth."
	"The great carrier of loads has put me on his back—the elephant never tires of carrying his trunk."

ELEMENTS OF PERFORMANCE

Kora

The *kora* is an indigenous African instrument with a unique array of parts (Figure 3.4). Scholars of musical instruments (organologists) classify the instrument as a **bridge harp,** a variety of spike harp. **Spike harps** have a long neck that passes entirely through the resonator, usually a large skin-covered half-calabash. The bridge harp variety, of which the *kora* is the best example, has a high bridge with notches on the sides through which the strings pass; the harp designation refers to the plane of the strings, perpendicular to the soundboard (see Charry 1994, 2000; DeVale 1989; Knight 1971, 1972).

The *kora* has left and right sides, just like the human body. Plucking in left-right alternation, the player takes full advantage of this bilateral symmetry. Sometimes a flat metal rattle attached to the bridge enhances the flavor of the rhythm and timbre. As in "Lambango," pieces may call for *konkong,* an ostinato (repeated phrase) rapped on the resonator. By adjusting the tuning rings along its neck, the *jali* tunes his *kora*'s twenty-one strings in patterns of seven pitches per octave. Just as the tonality of each Javanese gamelan is a unique variant of a

FIGURE 3.4

The *kora.*

general standard, the intervals between pitches on a *kora* are not precisely reckoned against an invariant abstract standard. "Lambango" is in the *sauta* tuning (see Figure 3.5).

As in most music-cultures, Mande musicians metaphorically link musical pitch to physical space through the words like *high-low* and *ascend-descend.* English speakers and Mande speakers, however, use these terms in opposite ways (Charry 2000:325). For instance, *kora* players call the bass strings "high" and the treble strings "low." This is because the longer, thicker strings are physically above the shorter, thinner strings when a *jali* holds the instrument. An ascending passage in Western terms "goes down" for the *kora* player.

During performance, when the emphasis is on text, the *kora* player accompanies the singer with **kumbengo,** an instrumental ostinato. Played over and over with subtle variation, the *kumbengo* establishes the tonal and metric framework of a piece. Virtuosic instrumental passages (***birimintingo***) provide interludes between vocal sections. On CD 1, Track 17, Suso accompanies Kuyateh by playing *kumbengo* with occasional *birimintingo*-like passages. Unlike full-fledged *birimintingo,* which forcefully suspend the *kumbengo*'s framework, these fills always remain within its time span.

FIGURE 3.5

Bridge of the *kora,* with strings shown as pitches in *sauta* tuning. (Drawing by Roderick Knight)

During apprenticeship, lessons focus on the *kumbengo.* Talented youngsters pick up *birimintingo* riffs as they listen to their master's playing. Interestingly, a master does not teach tuning until an apprentice is ready to leave. "Giving him an actual lesson on how to tune the instrument is regarded as the final key to his independence. This lesson is therefore withheld from him until his master feels he is fully qualified to embark on his own career" (Knight 1984:77).

Verbal Art

The "Lambango" recording shows that singers can mix several styles of verbal presentation in one performance. At different points in a performance *jalolu* may tell stories in everyday speech, sing tunefully, or declaim highly formulaic praises, proverbs, and references to specific heroes in narrative songs. The preferred timbral quality, a forceful chest resonance sung with a tensed throat, evokes the strength of the Mande heroes in sound itself.

The vocalist works with two building blocks of form: ***donkilo,*** a tune with several phrases of text, and ***sataro,*** an open-ended, extemporaneous passage of spoken or chanted text. After a section of *sataro,* a singer may return to the *donkilo,* or give way for an instrumental break. In her performance of "Lambango," Kuyateh begins by ever so briefly singing the tuneful *donkilo;* the rest of the performance is *sataro.* As Jobateh taps the *konkong* part, he interjects comments and praises with stylized speech.

Women (***jali musolu***) set the standard for all singers. As the *jali* Nyulo Jebateh told Roderic Knight:

> A ***ngara*** [superior singer] is a woman who is not afraid of crowds, not afraid of anything, except God. She can stand before a crowd with all eyes upon her and not become confused (*kijo fara*). She can shout (*feteng*), literally "split" the air with her voice, but do it with feeling (*wasu*) and sentiment (*balafa*), so that people will sympathize with her. She sticks to her forte (*taburango*) in performing, never jumbling the words together (*faranfansandi*) so that they are unintelligible, but choosing words which contain the essences of her message (*sigirango*), words which all listeners will agree are true (*sahata*). (Knight 1984:74)

A HEARING OF "LAMBANGO"

I have never studied *jaliya* with experts. The following section is an interpretation of "Lambango" based on my careful listening to the sound recording (CD 1, Track 17). For this piece, the Close Listening guide offers a broad overview, while the discussion of the text more closely follows the CD. I urge you to apply this type of close hearing to all the sound recordings in *Worlds of Music.*

The repeating phrases of the *kora* and *konkong* establish the tonal and rhythmic context for the song. The slowly moving knocks in the *konkong* part mark three moments within a cycle of eight beats: 5 6 7 8 1 2 3 4. During beats 5–1 the texture sounds multilayered and polyrhythmic; during beats 1–5, however, we hear only the *kora*'s treble voice.

CD 1:17

"Lambango" (3:02). Mande song. Mariatu Kuyateh. Performed by Mariatu Kuyateh, Kekuta Suso, and Seni Jobateh. Field recording by Roderic Knight. The Gambia, 1970.

Song

Kuyateh's song works within the restrained melodic range of a fifth or sixth. Her pitches conform to the tuning system of the *kora,* and her melody helps establish the tonal center of the piece. A Western analyst could describe the contour of her

Close Listening

"LAMBANGO"

CD 1:17

**COUNTER
NUMBER**   **TEXT AND TRANSLATION***

Praises for Musa Molo (lines 1–10)

0:00   1 [spoken]
Nte Kekuta Suso, ning Seni Jobate, ning Mariatu Kuyate. Ntelu be rekotola jang bi.
I am Kekuta Suso, with Seni Jobateh and Mariatu Kuyateh. We are recording here today.

0:14   2 [sung]
Ye, mba jaja, Jaba Sirimang ning Jaba Tarawari. Fulo ning kelo be mang kanyang.
[*Jamundiro* for Musa Molo.] The Fulas and war are not one and the same.
[Note: *Jamundiro* means stylized praise lyrics for Musa Molo, a king of the Fula people, neighbors to the Mande.]

0:26   3 [spoken]
Bande banna. Fulo Sirimang jang.
Wealthy Fula. Sirimang, the Fula here.

0:34   4 [sung]
Wo Bala. Jigi-o Bala banta, Nya-naani Musa.
Oh, Bala. Bala is gone, Four-eyed Musa.
[Note: Bala is a nickname for Musa. "Four-eyed" means "all-seeing."]

0:43   5 [sung]
Aniya na Bala. Parumba kumbengo diyata Bala la, Nya-naani Musa.
Aniya's Bala. The events at Parumba went in Bala's favor, Four-eyed Musa.
[Note: "Went in Bala's favor"—literally, "were sweet for Bala."]

0:47   6 [spoken]
Bala Mafaro. Surabali janjungo diyata a la.
Bala the Great. The campaign at Surabali was successful for him.
[Note: Parumba and Surabali were strongholds of the Soninke people, a Mande subgroup; the text alludes to battle between Fula and Soninke.]

0:52   7 [sung]
Aniya la Bala. Surabali kumbengo diyata Bala la, Nya-naani Musa.
Aniya's Bala. The events at Surabali were sweet for Bala, Four-eyed Musa.

0:59   8 [sung]
Bala mfa Musa me do go jameng to (?) Bala mfa Musa aning bulu si simba (?)
Bala mfa Musa aning ke domoda (?). Jigo-o Bala, Bala sumayata.
[*Jamundiro*.] Bala has grown cold [is dead].
[Note: *Jamundiro* means praise to the effect that Bala was a man who did not enter a battle if he knew he might die in it.]

1:11 9 [spoken]
A fele laring Keserekunda. A ning malo mang ta Yomali Kiyama.
He is buried in Keserekunda. He went without shame to the next world.

1:18 10 [sung]
Wo ka mansaya ke, duniya; wolu bee, i jamano banta.
Those people made kingship in this world; all of them, their days are gone.

Praises for Dembo Danso (lines 11–21)

1:26 11 [sung]
Wo ka mansaya di, Kibili-o Demba; E, Yasin Baro la Demba sumayata.
Those people gave us kingship, Kibili-o Demba; Eh, Yasin Barrow's Demba has grown cold.

1:31 12 [spoken]
Salimata Bunja Fara. Demba Damudu aning Demba Tegelema (?). Wo fanang be Kanjelebeti.
[*Jamundiro* for Dembo Danso.] He too lies at Kanjelebeti.

1:36 13 [sung]
Kibili-o Demba. Bu Majila na Demba sumayata (?). Demba . . . Kanjelebeti.
Kibili-o Demba. Yasin Baro la Demba sumayata.
[*Jamundiro* for Demba.] Demba has died and lies at Kanjelebeti. Yasin Barrow's Demba has grown cold.

1:51 14 [spoken]
Wo fanang mu ninsi dimba le ti. A ka a dingolu balundi, aning wandi dingolu balundi. Salimata Bunja Fara. Wo le mu Dembo Danso ti.
He was like a mother cow. He could feed his own young and those of others too. Salimata Bunja Fara. That was Dembo Danso.

1:58 15 [sung]
Wo lungolu bee mang di. Lungolu bee mang di mogo fanang na lungolu bee mang di (?).
Every day is not a holiday (?).

2:03 16 [sung]
Nte Musa fele lota Dembo da la lung do la. A ko, "Mansa jong si kemo di n na?" Dembo kamfata.
I saw Musa standing at Dembo's door one day. He said, "What king can give me a hundred?" This made Dembo angry.
[Note: To be asked for only a hundred was demeaning to Dembo, famous for his largesse in giving cows or slaves.]

2:12 17 [sung]
Nying ne mang na keme di . . . Musa Fili. Konte la Demba mang tumbung ke (?).
Did he not give a hundred to Musa Fili? Konte's Demba did not make ruins of the village (?).

2:18   18 [sung]
            Keme ni mansolu banta; jali mara mansolu dogoyata.
            The hundred-giving kings are gone; the *jali*-patron kings are few.

2:23   19 [sung]
            Ntelu keta konoba ti. M be yaarana; sita yoro te n na. I salam aleka.
            We [*jalis*] have become like vultures. We are soaring; we have no place to sit down. My
            peace be upon you.[Note: "Sit down"—that is, searching for patrons.]

2:28   20 [spoken]
            Salimata Bunja Fara, Dembo Damudu aning Dembo Tegelema (?). A ye
            Kosemari ke, a ye Jakaling ke.
            [*Jamundiro* for Dembo Danso.] He did well for the villages of Kosemari and Jakaling.

2:35   21 [sung]
            Siba-o, wolu bee tambirinna ko (?). Sarakata Bunja Fara, Bunja Mamadi.
            Siba-o, those are all in the past. [*Jamundiro* for Bunja, an associate of Dembo and son of
            Mamadi.]

Praises for Jewunu Kurubali (lines 22–23)

2:42   22 [sung]
            Ko, ni i be na 'waye' folo la, i sa folo Ma Biraima Konate. Yamaru jang, siba-o.
            [Praise for Sunjata Keita.] Say, when you begin your "waye" [singing], you should begin
            with praise for Ma Biraima Konateh.

2:51   23 [sung]
            Sibo banta. I salam aleka.
            The great one is gone. Peace be upon you.

*The *kora* player Alhaji Papa Susso and the ethnomusicologist Roderic Knight have provided the transcription and translation in this Close Listening guide.

melodies as terraced descent with some undulation. She phrases the rhythms freely, giving the impression that her voice floats elusively over the tightly interlocked instrumental parts. The text comes in a rapid explosion of syllables; occasionally, however, she sings several pitches to one syllable of text (**melisma**). Like members of an African American church (see Chapter 4), Jobateh responds to Kuyateh's "sermon" with affirmation and elaboration.

Text

This rendition of "Lambango" celebrates three twentieth-century Gambian leaders: Musa Molo (lines 1–10), Dembo Dansa (lines 11–21), and Jewuru Kurubali (lines 22–23). The text cites places where significant events in their lives occurred, praises their generosity, and honors them through recitation of stylized praise lyrics (*jamundiro*). The text is not a continuous narrative but rather a series of praises and a commemoration of events.

A Drummer of Dagbon

Musicians have had important functions in the political affairs of many African traditional states. We turn now to the life story of one such person.

On CD 1, Track 18, we will hear singing and drumming of the Dagbamba people (also known as Dagomba) from the southern savanna of western Africa (Ghana). I recorded the music in 1984. The performers are **lunsi** (*loon*-see; singular *lunga*, *loong*-ah), members of a hereditary clan of drummers. Like a Mande *jali,* a *lunga* fulfills many vital duties in the life of the Dagbamba—verbal artist, genealogist, counselor to royalty, cultural expert, entertainer. The *lunsi* tradition developed in Dagbon, the hierarchical, centralized kingdom of the Dagbamba (Chernoff 1979; Djedje 1978; Locke 1990).

THE DRUMS

Lunsi play two kinds of drums—*gung-gong* and *lunga* (see Figure 3.6). For both types, a shoulder strap holds the drum in position to receive strokes from a curved wooden stick. The **gung-gong** (goong-*gawng*) is a cylindrical, carved drum with a snare on each of its two heads. The cedarwood of a **lunga** is carved into an hourglass shape. By squeezing the leather cords strung between its two drumheads, a player can change the tension of the drum skins, which changes the pitch of the drum tones. In the hands of an expert, the drum's sound closely imitates Dagbanli, the spoken language of the Dagbamba. *Lunsi* "talk" and "sing" on their instruments. These musicians are storytellers, chroniclers of the history of their people and their nation.

A PRAISE NAME DANCE

"Nag Biegu" (*nah*-oh bee-*ah*-oo) is one of the many Praise Name Dances (*salima*) of Dagbon. Its title means "ferocious wild bull," referring to an enemy leader whom Naa Abudu defeated in a dramatic man-to-man fight. This *salima* praises Naa Abudu, a king of Dagbon in the late 1800s who is remembered for his courage and firm leadership. Scoffing at the challenge of a war leader from a neighboring nation, Naa Abudu said, "I am dangerous wild bull. Kill me if you can." As they dance to the drumming, people recall the bravery of the king.

The music has a verse-chorus form (see Transcription 3.16 and the Close Listening guide). In the verse, the vocalist and leading *lunga* drummers praise Naa Abudu and allude to events of his chieftaincy; the answering *lunsi* and two *gung-gong* drummers punctuate the verses with booming, single strokes. The

CD 1:18

"Nag Biegu" ("Ferocious Wild Bull") (2:08). Traditional Praise Name Dance song of Dagbon. Performed by *lunsi* drummers of the Dagbamba people. Field recording by David Locke. Ghana, 1984.

FIGURE 3.6

Lunsi in performance.

Patsy Marshall

drummed chorus phrase works like a "hook" in a pop song, that is, a catchy, memorable phrase. In this piece, we can hear another case of music built from the temporal duality of 3:2. The notation in Transcription 3.16 only sketches the musical artistry of these masterful players.

TRANSCRIPTION 3.16
"Nag Biegu" chorus phrases and verse answer. (The rhythm in measures 5–7 is a standard, if simpler, version of the more exciting phrases heard on the recording.)

Chorus

Nag Biegu la to to to   Nag Biegu la to to to   Nag Biegu la to   n nyeo

Verse   D. C.

Nag Biegu la to   Nag Biegu la to   Nag Biegu la to   kumo

repeat ad lib.

Close Listening

"NAG BIEGU" ("FEROCIOUS WILD BULL")

CD 1:18

COUNTER NUMBER	COMMENTARY
0:00	Call by leading *lunga* drum
0:08	Chorus by answer *lunga* and *gung-gong* drums
0:21	Verse by vocalist and leading *lunga* drum
0:59	Chorus by answer *lunga* and *gung-gong* drums
1:09	Verse by vocalist and leading *lunga* drum
1:45	Chorus by answer *lunga* and *gung-gong* drums
1:55	Fade-out during verse

Text,
"NAG BIEGU"

The Dagbanli text and an English translation of the chorus phrase are as follows:

Nag Biegu la to to to,	It is Nag Biegu,
Nag Biegu la to to to,	*It is Nag Biegu.*
Nag Biegu la to—n nyeo!	It is Nag Biegu—that's him!
Nag Biegu la to,	It is Nag Biegu,
Nag Biegu la to,	It is Nag Biegu,
Nag Biegu la to—kumo!	It is Nag Biegu—kill him!

LIFE STORY: ABUBAKARI LUNNA

I have tape-recorded many interviews with my teacher from Dagbon, Abubakari Lunna (see Figure 3.7). When I met Mr. Lunna in 1975, he was working as a professional with the Ghana Folkloric Company, a government-sponsored performing arts company based in Accra, the capital of Ghana. In 1988 he retired from government service and returned to northern Ghana, where he served his father, Lun-Naa Wombie, until Mr. Wombie's death. Presently, Mr. Lunna supports his large family as a drummer, farmer, and teacher. The following excerpt of his life story focuses on his teachers.

My Education in Drumming

My father's grandfather's name is Abubakari. It is Abubakari who gave birth to Azima and Alidu; Azima was the father of [my teacher] Ngolba and Alidu was father of Wombie, my father. Their old grandfather's name is the one I am carrying, Abubakari. My father never called me "son" until he died; he always called me "grandfather." I acted like their grandfather; we always played like grandson and grandfather.

When I was a young child, my father was not in Dagbon. My father was working as a security guard in the South at Bibiani, the gold town. I was living with one of my father's teachers, his uncle Lun-Naa Neindoo, the drum chief at Woriboggo, a village near Tolon. When I was six or seven, my mother's father, Tali-Naa Alaasani [a chief of Tolon], took me to his senior brother, a chief of Woriboggo at that time. I was going to be his "shared child." In my drumming tradition, when you give your daughter in marriage and luckily she brings forth children, the husband has to give one to the mother's family. So, I was living in the chief's house.

I was with my mother's uncle for four or five years when he enrolled me in school. They took four of us to Tolon, my mother's home. I lived with my mother's father. We started going to the school. Luckily, in several weeks' time my father came from the South. He called my name, but his uncle told him, "Sorry. The boy's grandfather came and took him to be with the chiefs. Now he is in school." My father said, "What?! Is there any teacher above me? I am also a teacher. How can a teacher give his child to another teacher for training in a different language?" Early in the morning, he walked to Tolon. He held my hand. I was happy because my father had come to take me [see Figure 3.8].

My father spent one month. When he went to the South, he took me with him. Unfortunately, at Bibiani my father didn't have time to teach me. One year when my father came back to Dagbon for the Damba Festival [an annual celebration of the birth of The Holy Prophet Muhammed], he told my grandfather, Lun-Naa Neindoo, "If I keep Abubakari at Bibiani, it will be bad. I want to leave him at home. I don't want him to be a southern boy."

I began learning our drumming talks and the singing. Lun-Naa Neindoo started me with **Dakoli Nye Bii Ba,** the beginning of drumming [that is, the first repertory learned by young *lunsi*]: "God is the Creator. He can create a tree, He can create grass, He can create a person." You drum all before you say, "A

FIGURE 3.7

Studio portrait of Abuba-kari as a young man.

There are significant differences of ecology, history, and culture between what Abubakari calls "the North" and "the South."

Whereas his father comes from a long line of drummers, Abubakari's mother comes from a royal family.

FIGURE 3.8

Studio portrait of Lun-Naa
Wombie, Abubakari's
father.

Just as the royals of Dagbon
have an elaborate hierarchy of
chieftaincies, so the *lunsi*
have a pyramidlike system of
titled positions of authority.

Mba means "father"; for a *lunga*
drummer, your teacher becomes
your teaching-father.

According to Dagbamba etiquette, children never question
the orders of their father.

Creator, God, created our grandfather, Bizung
[the first *lunga*]." The elders have given *Dakoli Nye
Bii Ba* to the young ones so that they can practice
in the markets. When they know that you are
improving, they start you with drumming stories
and singing stories. On every market day we, the
young drummers, came together and drummed
by ourselves.

When the Woriboggo chief made my father
Sampahi-Naa, the drum chief second to the *Lun-
Naa* [the highest rank of drum chief], he could not
go back to Bibiani. My father said, "Now, I am
going to work with you on our drumming history
talks." He began with the story of Yendi [seat of the
paramount chieftaincy of Dagbon]: how Dagbon
started, how we traveled from Nigeria and came to
Dagbon, how we became drummers, how it
happened that our grandfather Bizung made himself a drummer. If he gave me a story today,
tomorrow I did it correctly.

I was with my father for a long time, more
than five years. My father was hard. I faced
difficulty with my father because of his way of
teaching. My father would not beat the drum for
you. He would sing and you had to do the same
thing on *lunga.* If you couldn't do it, he would
continue until you got it before adding another.

[Later] . . . my father sent me to my teaching-
father, Ngolba. He had a good voice, a good
hand—every part of drumming, he had it. He had
the knowledge, too, and people liked him. When
he was drumming, he would make people laugh.
People would hire him: "We are having a funeral
on this day. Come and help us." I traveled with
him, carrying his *lunga.* Because of his drumming,
Ngolba never sat at home; every day we went for drumming. That was how people
got to know me. Any time I was walking, people started calling, "Ngolba, small
Ngolba." And with my sweet hand and my quick memory, everyone liked me.

Already I knew something in drumming, so for him to continue with me was
not hard. I only had to listen to his story and follow him. When we went to a
place and he told stories, I tried to keep it in my mind. When we were resting that
night, I asked him, "Oh, my uncle, I heard your talk today. Can you tell me
more about it?" There, he would start telling me something. That is how I
continued by education with Mba Ngolba. I was very young to be drumming the
deep history rhythms with a sweet hand.

My father called Ngolba and advised him, "I am not feeling happy about
all the traveling you and Abubakari are doing. Drummers are bad. Somebody
might try to spoil your lives. Find something to protect yourself. And protect
Abubakari too." Father Ngolba—I can never forget him. Sometimes, when I was
sitting at home, he would call me to get something to drink. I couldn't ask
him, "Father, what is this?" In Dagbon, you can't ask him—you have to drink it.
My Mba Ngolba did it for me several times.

Another reason why I liked my teacher, my Father Ngolba, is that despite his
quick temper, he didn't get angry with me. He loved me. He didn't take even one
of his ideas and hide it from me. Even if I asked him about something common
that many drummers know, the thing left—he didn't hide it. He would tell me, "I

have reserved something. If you bring all your knowledge out in public, some people with quick learning can just collect it."

I respected Ngolba like my father. During farming time I got up early in the morning and went straight to the farm. When he came, he met me there already. If it was not farming time, I would go to his door, kneel down, and say good morning to him. I would stay there, not saying anything until at last he would ask me, "Do you want to go some place?" Only then could I go. Teachers can give you laws like your own father. That is our Dagbamba respect to teachers.

Father Ngolba died in the South. When an old drummer dies, we put a *lunga* and a drumstick in the grave. The man who was with Ngolba when he died told me, "Your father said, 'Only bury me with this drumstick—don't add my *lunga* to bury me. Give my *lunga* to Abubakari.'" I said thank you for that. We finished the funeral back in Dagbon. The second brother to Ngolba spoke to all their family, "Ngolba told me that if it happens he dies, Abubakari should carry on with his duties. He should take his whole inheritance. And Ngolba had nothing other than his *lunga*." I have his *lunga*; it is in my room now. [See Figure 3.9 for a recent photo of Abubakari and members of his family.]

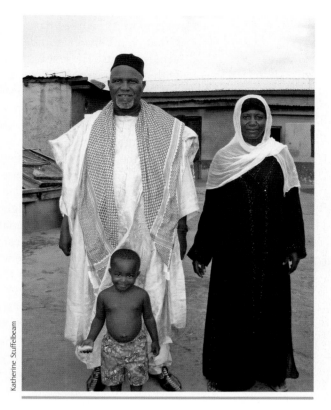

Katherine Stuffelbeam

FIGURE 3.9

Abubakari Lunna with his wife Fusena and son Wahidu, 2005.

Shona Mbira Music

The recording of "Nhemamusasa" (CD 1, Track 19) features another uniquely African type of musical instrument. It is known outside Africa as "thumb piano"; speakers of the Shona language call it *mbira* (mmm-*bee*-rah). The "kaleidophonic" sound of its music (Tracey 1970:12) provides us with another insight into the musical potential of 3:2 rhythmic structures. Further, the *mbira* tradition shows another way African music can transform a group of separate individuals into a participatory polyphonic community. Information for this section draws primarily on the research of the ethnomusicologist Paul Berliner (1993).

CULTURAL CONTEXT

History

The Shona, who live in high plateau country between the Zambezi and Limpopo Rivers, are among the sixty million Bantu-speaking people who predominate in central and southern Africa. Since about 800 C.E., kingdoms of the Shona and neighboring peoples have ruled large territories; stone fortresses such as the Great Zimbabwe number among Africa's most impressive architectural achievements. These kingdoms participated in a lively Indian Ocean commerce with seafaring powers such as the Arabs, Persians, and Indians (Mallows 1967:97–115). The Portuguese arrived about 1500. Eventually, the large-scale Shona states faded under pressure from other African groups, notably the more militaristic Ndebele in the 1800s. The Shona became a more decentralized, agricultural people.

At the turn of the twentieth century, English-speaking settlers took over the land and imposed their culture and economy on the local Africans. The colonial period in what was then called Rhodesia was brief, but it radically affected most local institutions. As in neighboring South Africa, a systematic policy of land grabbing left Africans materially impoverished. Racist settlers scorned African culture; many local people came to doubt the ways of their ancestors. For two decades after the independence of other contemporary African nation-states in the 1950s and 1960s, white Rhodesians maintained their dominance. Finally, a war of liberation (1966–1979) culminated in majority rule and the birth of the nation-state Zimbabwe in 1980.

Music played a part in the struggle. Popular and traditional songs with hidden meanings helped galvanize mass opinion; **spirit mediums** were leaders in the war against white privilege (Frye 1976; Lan 1985). After decades of denigration by some Africans who had lost faith in traditional culture, the *mbira* became a positive symbol of cultural identity.

Shona Spirits

From the perspective inherited from the Shona ancestors, four classes of spirits (literally *mweya,* or breath) affect the world: spirits of chiefs (*mhondoro*), family members (**mudzimu**), nonrelatives or animals (**mashave**), and witches (*muroyi*) (Lan 1985:31–43). Although invisible, the ancestral spirits nonetheless have sensory experience, feel emotions, and take action to help and advise their beloved descendants. *Mbira* music helps connect the living with their ancestors.

Humans and spirits communicate by means of possession trances. In possession, a spirit enters the body of a living person, temporarily supplanting his or her spirit. Once embodied in its medium, an ancestral spirit can advise his or her living relatives, telling them things they have done wrong and how to protect themselves and ensure good fortune. Similarly, a *mhondoro* spirit may advise a gathering of several family groups regarding matters that affect the entire community, such as the coming of rain. Possessions occur at **mapira** (singular *bira*), all-night, family-based, communal rituals. *Mbira* music and dancing are significant elements in these events (Berliner 1993:186–206; Zantzinger n.d.).

THE *MBIRA*

Construction

Mbiras of many different styles of construction occur throughout Africa and its diaspora. Most *mbiras* have four features of construction: (1) a set of long, thin keys made of metal or plant material, (2) a soundboard with a bridge that holds the keys, (3) a resonator to shape and amplify the sound of the plucked keys, and (4) jingles that buzz rhythmically when the keys are plucked. Like the *kora,* the instrument matches the bilateral symmetry of the human body; that is, left-side keys are for the left thumb, right-side keys are for the right thumb and index finger. The longer, bass keys lie toward the center of the soundboard; the shorter, treble keys toward its edges (Berliner 1993:8–18).

On our recording of "Nhemamusasa," we will hear an instrument that is frequently used at spirit possession ceremonies: the **mbira dzavadzimu,** literally "**mbira** of the ancestors" (mmm-*bee*-rah dzah-vah-*dzee*-moo). Figure 3.10 shows a characteristic layout of its keys and one tuning arrangement.

In performance, musicians place the *mbira* within a large gourd resonator (*deze*) that brings out the instrument's full tone; when playing for personal pleasure or during learning-teaching sessions, the resonator may not be needed (see Figure 3.11).

Bottle cap rattles or snail shells attached to the soundboard and resonator provide the important buzzing ingredient to the music. Performances usually include hand clapping, singing, and a driving rhythm played on a pair of gourd rattles called a *hosho.*

FIGURE 3.10

A tuning plan for the *mbira dzavadzimu.*

FIGURE 3.11

Younger *mbira* players
Luken Kwari (left) and
Cosmas Magaya (right)
emulate the demonstration
of their elder, John Kunaka
(center).

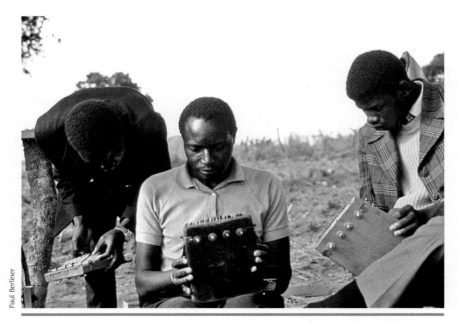

Paul Berliner

Tuning (Chuning)

Shona musicians refer to the tonal qualities of an *mbira*'s sound with the
English word *tuning* or the modified term *chuning*. Artists use **chuning** to refer
not only to interval configurations but also to qualities of tone, sound
projection, pitch level, and overtones (Berliner 1993:54–72). The *mbira
dzavadzimu* is tuned to a seven-pitch scale over a range of three octaves;
interval size varies among different *chunings*. Musicians debate the affective
quality of different *chunings* and symbolically link the *mbira* keys with features
of culture such as family relationships, emotional or physical responses to
music, and animal imagery.

The Player and the Instrument

In performance, the instrument faces toward the player. Repeatedly plucking the
keys in prescribed patterns, musicians establish cycles of harmony, melody,
rhythm, and counterpoint. Each key on the *mbira* emits a fundamental pitch and a
cluster of overtones; the resonator shapes, reinforces, prolongs, and amplifies this
complex tone. The buzzing bottle caps not only provide rhythm to the music's
texture but also add to the instrument's array of tuned and untuned sounds. Tones
overlap. The *mbira*'s sound surrounds the player. In this music, the whole is far
more than the sum of the parts (Berliner 1993:127–35).

Creative, participatory listening is an essential aspect of this music-culture.
Performer and audience must hear coherent melodies in the *mbira*'s numerous
tones. Many pieces exploit the creative potential of 3:2 relationships; often one
hand is "in three or six," while the other is "in two or four." Hand-clapping
phrases provide a good way to join in the performance and experience this
polymetric feeling (see Transcription 3.17).

TRANSCRIPTION 3.17
Hand-clapping phrases
for *mbira* music.

For players immersed in the process, the *mbira* takes on a life of its own. Here is how Dumisani Maraire, one of the first teachers of Shona music to non-Africans, explains it:

> When a mbira player plays his instrument . . . he is . . . conversing with a friend. He teaches his friend what to do, and his friend teaches him what to do. To begin with, the mbira player gives the basic pattern to the mbira; he plays it, and the mbira helps him produce the sound. He goes over and over playing the same pattern, happy now that his fingers and the mbira keys are together. So he stops thinking about what to play, and starts to listen to the mbira very carefully. (Maraire 1971:5–6)

"NHEMAMUSASA"

According to the Shona, ancestral spirits love to hear their favorite *mbira* pieces. Musical performance is an offering that calls them near, thus making possession more likely. Because of its important social use, this repertory remains stable over many generations. Pieces for *mbira dzavadzimu,* most of which have been played for centuries, are substantial musical works with many fundamental patterns, variations, styles of improvisation, and so forth. These pieces have two interlocking parts: *kushaura,* the main part, and *kutsinhira,* the interwoven second part. Since each part is polyphonic in its own right, the interaction of parts creates a wonderfully multilayered sound. The vocal music, which has three distinct styles—*mahonyera* (vocables), *kudeketera* (poetry), and *huro* (yodeling)—adds depth to the musical texture and richness to the meanings expressed in performance. In our discussion here, we only scratch the surface of the *kushaura* part of one piece.

On CD 1, Track 19, we hear "Nhemamusasa" (*neh*-mah-moo-*sah*-sah), revered by the Shona as one of their oldest and most important pieces (see the Close Listening guide). It was played for **Chaminuka,** a powerful spirit who protects the entire Shona nation. The song title literally means "Cutting Branches for Shelter." One of Berliner's teachers reports that "'Nhemamusasa' is a song for war. When we [the Shona] were marching to war to stop soldiers coming to kill us, we would cut branches and make a place [tent shelter] called a *musasa*" (John Kunaka, quoted in Berliner 1993:42). In 1991 Erica Kundizora Azim, an

CD 1:19

"Nhemamusasa" (lit. "Cutting Branches for Shelter"), *kushaura* section (2:39). Traditional Shona. Field recording by Paul Berliner. Zimbabwe, 1971.

experienced American student of *mbira,* heard a contemporary interpretation of the song's meaning from a female Shona friend:

Text, "NHEMAMUSASA"   Homeless people sit in their shantytowns with nothing to do.
No work.
Trouble is coming.

Evidently the piece evokes profound feelings. For the Shona, sentiments evoked by pieces such as "Nhemamusasa" make them effective for use in rituals of spirit possession. Even for those of us without inside knowledge of Shona cultural history, the musical surface of "Nhemamusasa" sparks powerful feelings.

Rhythm

Tapping out a four-stroke plucking pattern—right index, left thumb, right thumb, left thumb—provides insight into a Shona *mbira* player's experience of the *kushaura* part of "Nhemamusasa." When the pattern repeats over and over, any of the four actions may be taken as the first one. Within this circular structure that has no beginning or end, melodies arise from the *mbira* as players apply the plucking pattern to the appropriate keys.

Each melodic phrase requires three repetitions of the 4-pulse pattern; four of these 12-pulse phrases make one pass through "Nhemamusasa's" principal musical unit (see Transcription 3.18). From the perspective of playing technique, the pulse structure can be expressed in the equation $(3 \times 4) \times 4 = 48$; in other

TRANSCRIPTION 3.18
Plucking pattern for the *kushaura* part of "Nhemamusasa."

Close Listening

"NHEMAMUSASA"
("CUTTING BRANCHES FOR SHELTER")

CD 1:19

COUNTER NUMBER	COMMENTARY
0:00–0:46	*Kushaura mbira* **part by itself.**
0:00	Fade in during fourth 12-pulse phrase.
0:04–0:13	First full occurrence of 48-pulse cycle.
0:04	First 12-pulse phrase.
0:06	Second 12-pulse phrase.
0:08	Third 12-pulse phrase.
0:10	Fourth 12-pulse phrase.
0:13–0:20	Second occurrence of 48-pulse cycle.
0:13	First 12-pulse phrase.
0:15	Second 12-pulse phrase.
0:17	Third 12-pulse phrase.
0:19	Fourth 12-pulse phrase.
0:20	Third occurrence of 48-pulse cycle; 12-pulse phrases approximately every two seconds.
0:28	Fourth occurrence of 48-pulse cycle.
0:36	Fifth 48-pulse cycle.
0:43	Sixth occurrence of 48-pulse cycle.
0:47	*Kutsinhira* **part enters.**
0:51	Seventh occurrence of 48-pulse cycle.
0:59-	Eighth occurrence of 48-pulse cycle.
1:07	Ninth occurrence of 48-pulse cycle.
1:14	Tenth occurrence of 48-pulse cycle.
1:22	Eleventh occurrence of 48-pulse cycle.
1:30	Twelfth occurrence of 48-pulse cycle.
1:38	Thirteenth occurrence of 48-pulse cycle.
1:45	Fourteenth occurrence of 48-pulse cycle.
1:46	*Hosho* **(rattle) enters.**
1:54	Fifteenth occurrence of 48-pulse cycle.
2:01	Sixteenth occurrence of 48-pulse cycle.
2:09	Seventeenth occurrence of 48-pulse cycle.
2:17	Eighteenth occurrence of 48-pulse cycle.
2:24	Nineteenth occurrence of 48-pulse cycle.
2:32	Break in temporal flow to announce end of performance.

words, four phrases, each with 12 pulses that are grouped into 3 quaternary beats (equivalent to $\frac{3}{2}$ meter). Given the right-left alternation in the plucking pattern, we can also interpret the pulse structure as $(6 \times 2) \times 4 = 48$; in other words, the 12 pulses within each phrase are grouped into 6 binary beats (equivalent to $\frac{6}{4}$ meter). In Transcription 3.18 these ways of hearing the music's meter are notated with half notes and quarter notes above and below the four-line staff. The music's most fundamental **time-feel** does not derive from playing technique, however. Instead, players feel a steady flow of ternary beats, that is, 3 pulses per beat. Within each 12-pulse melodic phrase, the three explicit 4-pulse plucking units are felt in terms of four implicit 3-pulse beats. From the perspective of the player's inner feeling, the pulse structure is $(4 \times 3) \times 4 = 48$. Transcription 3.18 shows the several ways one 12-pulse phrase can be felt: x-shaped note heads are beamed together in groups of three to show the player's basic four-feel; different placements of crossing time-feels "in three" and "in six" are suggested by brackets above and beneath the staff. Please note that the plucking sequence begins with a right index finger on the 11th pulse within the phrase.

The flow of ternary beats is emphasized audibly by the *hosho* and the *kutsinhira mbira* parts. In our recording (CD 1, Track 19), the coexistence of the two different pulse structures generates a powerful musical effect. The musical example highlights the interaction of *kushaura* and *kutsinhira:* It begins with the *kushaura* part by itself, then the *kutsinhira* joins and the whole ensemble swings into action. I hear the music "in three" at the start and then find myself reoriented to the four-feel when the other parts enter.

Melody

Table 3.1 illustrates how a polyphonic texture is generated within this rhythmic and tonal environment. First, consider melodies closely connected to the movements of a player's fingers. Over the course of a 48-pulse cycle, the plucking pattern generates five pitch rows, one each from keys plucked by (1) right index, (2) first left-thumb stroke, (3) right thumb, (4) second left-thumb stroke, and (5) right index and right thumb as a pair. Read Table 3.1 from left to right to get the pitch sequence of each row; read rows 1–4 from top to bottom, left to right to get the pitches in the sequence of four-unit plucking patterns. For example, in the first sequence, (1) the right index plays c′, (2) the first left-thumb stroke plays c, (3) the right thumb plays g, and (4) the second left-thumb stroke plays C. Row 5, which reads left to right, indicates the melody created by as the player rocks between index finger and thumb of the right hand.

TABLE 3.1 Pitch sequence in "Nhemamusasa."

	1 2 3 4	1 2 3 4	1 2 3 4	1 2 3 4	1 2 3 4	1 2 3 4	1 2 3 4	1 2 3 4	1 2 3 4	1 2 3 4	1 2 3 4	1 2 3 4
1)	c′	c′	b	c′	c′	b	c′	c′	c′	d′	d′	c′
2)	c	e	d	c	e	e	c	f	e	d	f	e
3)	g	g	g	g	g	a	g	a	a	a	a	a
4)	C	e	d	C	e	e	C	f	e	d	f	e
5)	c′ g c′ g b g	c′ g c′ g b a	c′ g c′ a c′ a	d′ a d′ a c′ a

Without rhythm these pitch rows are musically incomplete. When set in a polymetric context, melodies emerge. The plucking pattern suggests melodies "in three" and "in six," but the inner feeling guides the ear to melodies "in four." By creatively combining these time-feels in their musical imaginations, experienced Shona listeners hear many interweaving melodies. For example, the tied eighth-notes in Transcription 3.19 visually emphasize the four-feel; three-feel and six-feel conceptions emerge by isolating the notes played by each finger.

TRANSCRIPTION 3.19
The *kushaura* melody in "Nhemamusasa."

Many melodies emerge from the crossover between hands. Transcription 3.20 shows one such "inherent" melody (see Kubik 1962).

x = left thumb y = left thumb z = right thumb

TRANSCRIPTION 3.20
An inherent melody in "Nhemamusasa."

The right-thumb "voice" functions like a drone (first on g, then on a) in relation to the steady movement of the two left-thumb "voices." Because of their proximity in pitch, the ear hears the tones sounded by the first left thumb and the right thumb as cohesive rhythmic figures that articulate the upbeats of a three-feel unit ($^3_2$ time) marked off by the second left-thumb stroke—3-4-ONE, 3-4-TWO, 3-4-THREE. The multiple possibilities of beginnings and endings are evident in the pattern of octave leaps in the left thumb: Does the lower pitch anticipate the higher? Does the higher note echo the bass?

THOMAS MAPFUMO AND *CHIMURENGA* MUSIC

This section on Shona music-culture closes with an example of what might be termed modern traditional music: "Nyarai" by Thomas Mapfumo and Blacks Unlimited on CD 1, Track 20. Mapfumo has dubbed this style *chimurenga* music. With its pop band instrumentation and studio production, the music sounds new, but Mapfumo and his audience hear its links to *mbira* music (Bender 1991:163; Eyre 1991:51). Mapfumo and his guitarist, Jonah Sithole, intentionally model their arrangements on traditional music (Eyre 1988:87–88). Like some types of *mbira* music, "Nyarai" is recreational music for dance parties that also comments on topical issues.

Chimurenga music helps us realize that centuries-old traditions need not be obsolete or nostalgic (Waterman 1990). The word **chimurenga** ("struggle") refers both to the war against the white regime in Rhodesia and to a style of music that rallied popular support for the cause (Bender 1991:160–65; Eyre 1991; Manuel 1988:104–6). In the 1970s the music became popular among Africans despite white censorship of song lyrics and an outright ban on artists and recordings. Just as African slaves in the Americas encoded their own meanings in the texts of African American spirituals, African freedom-fighting songwriters used allusion to make their points. The baffled censors knew a song was subversive only when it was on everyone's lips, but by then the word was out.

Thomas Mapfumo remembers the development of the *chimurenga* music in the following interview with the music journalist Banning Eyre (square brackets mark Eyre's comments, curly braces mark mine):

> I grew up in the communal lands, which used to be called reserves, for the African people. . . . I grew up with my grandparents who were very much into traditional music. Each time there was an *mbira* gathering, there were elder people singing, some drumming, some clapping. I used to join them. In the country, there were no radios, no TVs. . . .
>
> {Later Mapfumo lived with his parents in the city and joined bands doing rock and roll covers.}
>
> I was into a lot of things . . . even heavy metal. There were rock band contests held in Salisbury {now Harare}. . . . Some South African bands would cross the Limpopo [River] into Rhodesia to compete. There were a lot of black bands playing rock 'n' roll music, and we were one of them. But not even one black band ever won a contest. And I asked myself: "What are we supposed to be if this isn't our music? If they [the whites] claim it to be their music, then we have to look for our own music." As a people who had actually lost our culture, it was very difficult to get it back. . . .
>
> {After several years of singing with different bands that toured the beer halls of Rhodesia in the early 1970s, Mapfumo began writing more-serious lyrics.}
>
> One afternoon, we came up with a nice tune opposing Mr. Ian Smith [the final prime minister of white-minority-ruled Rhodesia]. . . . This tune was called "Pa Muromo Chete," which means "It Is Just Mere Talk." Mr. Smith had said he would not want to see a black government in his lifetime, even in a thousand years. So we said it was just talk. We were going to fight for our freedom. This record sold like hot cakes because the people had got the message. Straight away, I composed another instant hit called "Pfumvu Pa Ruzheva," which means "Trouble in the Communal Lands." People were being killed by soldiers. They were running away from their homes, going to Mozambique and coming to live in town like squatters. Some people used to cry when they listened to the lyrics of this record. The message was very strong. . . .
>
> The papers were writing about us. . . . Everyone wanted to talk to us about our music, and the government was very surprised, because they had never heard of a black band being so popular among their own people. They started asking questions. . . .
>
> {In 1979 Mapfumo was detained by the police. After liberation, the popularity of the *chimurenga* style declined, but in the late 1980s he regained local popularity with songs that criticized corruption.}

We were not for any particular party.... We were for the people. And we still do that in our music. If you are a president and you mistreat your people, we will still sing bad about you. Never mind if you are black or white or yellow....
    {His lyrics still make social comment.}
    Today, Zimbabwe is free.... So we are focusing our music worldwide.... We have been in a lot of world cities. We have seen people sleeping in the streets and governments don't look after these people. That is what our music is there for today. We will never stop singing about the struggle. (Eyre 1991:78)

"Nyarai" ("Be Ashamed") was recorded after the government headed by Robert Mugabe came to power in Zimbabwe. Our recording (CD 1, Track 20) is an excerpt from the longer recorded version. Its traditional stylistic features include musical form based on an 8-beat melodic/harmonic cycle (I–IV–I–V), polyphonic interplay of melodies on two guitars and bass, collective improvisation, occasional climaxes using higher register, and insistent articulation by percussionists of the onbeats and selected offbeats (see the Close Listening guide). The lyrics celebrate victory and chide people ("Be ashamed") who are unreconciled to change. The song is a praise poem for the warriors, their leaders, their families, and their supporters. Although on this recording Mapfumo praises Mugabe for his role in the war of black liberation, subsequent events in Zimbabwe have brought mixed reviews for Mugabe's leadership of that troubled country.

CD 1:20

"Nyarai" ("Be Ashamed"), excerpt (2:29). Thomas Mapfumo. Performed by Thomas Mapfumo and Blacks Unlimited. *Thomas Mapfumo: The Chimurenga Singles, 1976– 1980.* Gramma Records Zimbabwe. Shanachie CD 43066.

Close Listening

"NYARAI" ("BE ASHAMED")

CD 1:20

COUNTER NUMBER	COMMENTARY
0:00	Fade-in
0:08	8-beat cycles begin
1:16	Vamp on word *Nyarai*
1:33	"Shout out" to war heroes
1:48	Guitar solo break
2:01	Brass enters; fade-out

We are celebrating the birth of Zimbabwe	Text,
Mothers are proud of Zimbabwe	"NYARAI"
Fathers are proud of Zimbabwe	
We boys are proud of Zimbabwe	
Girls are proud of Zimbabwe	

Congratulations comrades
And congratulations to all the others
Who fought the *Chimurenga* war
To liberate Zimbabwe
All our ancestral spirits give thanks
The whole nation gives thanks
Congratulations to Mr. Mugabe
And many others
Who fought the liberation war
They liberated Zimbabwe
All ancestral spirits adore the liberators
Congratulations Mr. Machel
And many others who fought the *Chimurenga* war
They liberated Zimbabwe
But there are some reactionaries
Who don't like to be ruled by others
What sort of people are you?
Why are you not ashamed, when you have been defeated
Be ashamed
Be ashamed
Be ashamed
When you have been defeated
Get out
When you have been defeated

Who do you want fight with?
Isn't the war over?
What is left to be done in Zimbabwe?
Mr. Mugabe has won
He has brought peace
Congratulations to the *povo* [black liberation soldiers]
You fought in the *Chimurenga* war
You liberated Zimbabwe

Text translation, "Nyarai" by Thomas Mapfumo courtesy of the Information Office, Zimbabwe High
Commission, London.

The BaAka People Singing "Makala"

Our final example of African music-culture differs dramatically from the traditions of the Ewe, Mande, Dagbamba, and Shona. It brings us full circle to the communal, inclusive spirit of African music so clearly present in the music of the Ghanaian postal workers. Information for this section relies on the field research of Michelle Kisliuk (Kisliuk 1998).

On CD 1, Track 21, we hear the singing, hand clapping, and drumming of the BaAka (*bah*-ka) people. The immense, ancient, thickly canopied tropical forest exerts a powerful influence on life in central Africa. The BaAka are one of several distinct ethnic groups who share certain physical, historical, cultural, and social features as well as adaptations to the natural world (Turnbull 1983). Here I will refer to these groups collectively as **Forest People.** Because of their physical size, non-Africans have called the Forest People "Pygmies." It is an ethnocentric label; their size is a benefit in the forest and plays a minor role in the way they are viewed by their larger African neighbors.

For millennia the Forest People existed in ecological balance with their environment. Sheltered in dome-shaped huts of saplings and leaves, they lived with kin and friends in small, loose-knit groups. Because these hunting bands needed only portable material possessions, they could easily shift their encampments every few months according to the availability of food. They obtained a healthy diet through cooperative hunting and gathering, allowing them ample time for expressive, emotionally satisfying activities such as all-night sings. The social system was informal and flexible: men and women had roughly equal power and obligations, consensus decisions were negotiated by argument, children were treated gently. Individuals were not coerced by formal laws, distant leaders, or threatening deities. The forest was God, and people were children of the forest (Turnbull 1961:74).

At this point you may be wondering why the preceding paragraph was written in the past tense. During the colonial and postcolonial eras, external forces have confronted the Forest People to a degree unprecedented in their history. They now live within nation-states forged in violent anticolonial wars; multinational timber and mining companies are at work in the forest; scholars and adventurers visit some of them regularly. In short, the Forest People now face great changes.

Earlier I mentioned the Western ethnocentric view of the Forest People. Throughout history, other peoples have drawn on this culture in various ways. Let us now look at three images that reflect the conflicting roles that the Forest People play in the world's imagination.

THREE IMAGES OF THE FOREST PEOPLE
Primal Eden

For thousands of years, members of the world's imperial civilizations have found renewal in the music of the Forest People. In 2300 B.C.E. an Egyptian pharaoh wrote to a nobleman of Aswan who had journeyed south to the Upper Nile:

> Come northward to the court immediately; thou shalt bring this dwarf with thee, which thou bringest living, prosperous and healthy from the land of the spirits, for the dances of the god, to rejoice and (gladden) the heart of the king of Upper and Lower Egypt, Neferkere, who lives forever. (Breasted 1906, in Davidson 1991:55)

Today, aided by books and recordings, the Forest People continue to exert a pull on the world's imagination. In particular, the beautiful life of the BaMbuti recounted in Colin Turnbull's *The Forest People* has entranced many. Recordings by Simha Arom have introduced listeners to the intricacy of BaAka vocal polyphony (Arom 1987). For many people, this music-culture evokes cherished values—peace, naturalness, humor, community. In the music of the Forest People we want to hear an innocence lost to our complex, polluted, violent world.

Primitive Savage

Paired with this image of primal utopia is the notion of primitive savagery. According to this view, Pygmies represent an early stage of cultural evolution, a primitive way of life associated with the Stone Age. By definition primitives do not know the achievements of "high" civilization—science, mathematics, engineering, philosophy; they have no electricity, no industry, no nations, no armies, no books. If this is the stuff of civilization, then like other native peoples in remote locations on earth, the Forest People must be "primitive."

But calling a human group "primitive" establishes a dangerous inequality. It can justify genocide; enslavement; servitude; colonialism; underdevelopment; land grabbing for lumbering, mining, agriculture, and tourism; and reculturization through evangelism, schooling, wage labor, and military service. From this imperialist perspective, cultures that differ from the "modern" way must change or be eradicated.

Unique Culture in a Global Village

Instead, we can characterize the Forest People with concepts that are less emotionally charged. They are nonliterate and nonindustrial, with a relatively unspecialized division of labor and a cashless barter/subsistence economy; theirs is a homogeneous society with small-scale, decentralized social institutions, egalitarian interpersonal social relations, and relative gender equality. Their God is everywhere in this world, and they exist within the web of nature.

Forest life is not an idyllic paradise, however. Hunters sometimes share meat from the day's hunt only after other members of their group complain about its unfair distribution. People suffer from disease, hunger, violence, and anxiety. For the past four hundred years they have shared the forest with Bantu and Sudanic agriculturalist villagers; more recently, they have adjusted to international forces. Compared to one's own culture, the Forest People may seem better in some ways, worse in others. Undoubtedly, their culture is unique.

The next section presents a detailed description of a BaAka song. This will set the stage for seeing how the music-culture of the Forest People functions as a resource in their adaptation to change.

"MAKALA," A *MABO* SONG

Setting

CD 1:21

"Makala" (name of unknown person) (2:20). Traditional BaAka song. Field recording by Michelle Kisliuk. Central African Republic, 1988.

The performance-studies scholar and ethnomusicologist Michelle Kisliuk recorded "Makala" (*mah*-kah-lah) in December 1988 in the Central African Republic (see the Close Listening guide). The setting was a performance event, or *eboka,* of *Mabo* (*mah*-boh), a type of music and dance associated with net hunting (see Figure 3.12). Hunting not only provides food but is a key cultural institution as well. At this performance, novices (*babemou*) and their entourage from one group had walked to a neighboring camp to receive hunting medicine and related dance instruction from experts (*ginda*). Over the course of two days, performers presented *Mabo* for this ritual purpose as well as for the pleasure of learning new songs and dance flourishes. At times a small-scale affair involving only the *Mabo* specialists and their students, the *eboka* sometimes swelled into a much larger social dance attended by a crowd of BaAka and villagers. Kisliuk recorded this song on the evening of the first day (1998:98ff.).

Close Listening

"MAKALA"

CD 1:21

COUNTER NUMBER	COMMENTARY
0:00	Music takes shape as male singers, drummers, and women gradually join in.
0:16	Melodic and text theme is sung once.
0:20	Theme is elaborated in rich multipart chorus.
0:55	Prominent high-pitched yodeling.
1:16–1:33	Different drumming and prominent countermelody.
1:46	Theme stands out.
1:52	Hand clapping joins in until recording fades out.

Form and Texture

An *eboka* of *Mabo* consists of sections of singing, drumming, and dancing. Each song has a theme, that is, a text and tune. By simultaneously improvising melodic variations, singers create a rich polyphony. After five to fifteen minutes of play with one song, they begin another. From time to time, the *eboka* is "spiced up"

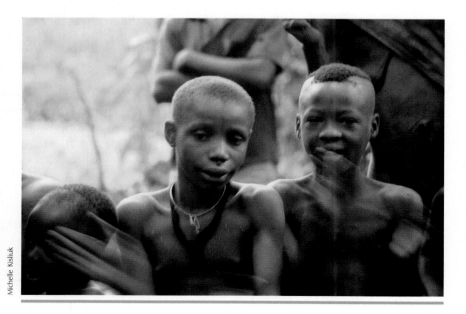

Michelle Kisliuk

FIGURE 3.12

BaAka in performance.

with an *esime,* a section of rhythmically intensified drumming, dancing, and percussive shouts (Kisliuk 1998:40–41).

Timbre

Men and women of all ages sing "Makala." Using both chest and head voices, they obtain a great variety of tone colors that range from tense/raspy to relaxed/breathy. One striking feature, yodeling, involves quick shifts between head and chest voices. Musical instruments include drums and hand claps. Two different drum parts are played on the drum skins that cover the ends of carved, cone-shaped logs. Often, Forest People enrich the percussion by rapping with wooden sticks on the drum's body and striking together metal cutlass blades; Transcription 3.21 visualizes some of their favorite polyrhythmic combinations. Forest People also make music with instruments such as flutes, trumpets, and harps, but not in *Mabo.*

TRANSCRIPTION 3.21 Charted BaAka poly- rhythms. (Arom 1991:305. Used with permission.)

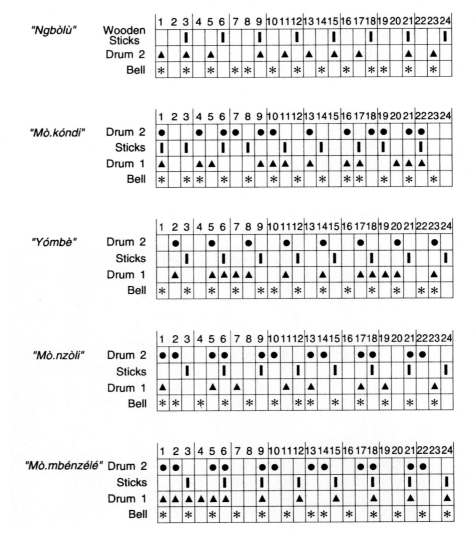

Theme

Transcription 3.22a shows the main melody of "Makala" (adapted from Kisliuk 1991:219; see Kisliuk 1998:98). Transcription 3.22b shows an excerpt from a version of the theme and a variation of it. Because many different parts occur simultaneously, just listening to the recording does not easily reveal the song's melodic theme. Kisliuk learned the theme when hearing it sung in isolation from other parts by a young woman walking along a path. Singers often do not raise the theme until they have established a richly interwoven polyphony; even then, they are free to improvise on its melodic features.

ee ya ee ya Ma _ ka - la eh   ee ya na le le oh _ ho ho

TRANSCRIPTION 3.22a
Isolated melodic theme of "Makala."

Ma _ ka - la o ah ee ya na le le oh _ ho

ah _ ah _ ah oh ee ya _ oh _ ho

TRANSCRIPTION 3.22b
Excerpt of a version of the theme (first staff) and variation (second staff) of "Makala."

Makala's theme establishes several important musical features of "Makala." The song's musical form relies on the continuous reiteration of the 8-beat phrase. The melody's intervals may be written with four pitches, given here as D, C, B♭, G. Shaped into two 4-beat motives, the tune oscillates between movement and repose: The B♭ on beat 4 moves toward a cadence at beat 8 on C. The tune's rhythm moves toward the cadences on beats 4 and 8.

As in Native American songs, singers mostly use vocables (see Chapter 2). The sparse text of "Makala" is typically cryptic (Kisliuk 1998:99).

moto monyongo	beautiful person	**Text,**
Makala	name of an unknown deceased person from the Congo, where *Mabo* originated	**"MAKALA"**
na lele, oh	I cry [implying a funeral setting in this song]	

Turnbull reports that songs of the BaMbuti often mean "We are children of the Forest" or "The Forest is good." In troubled times they sing a longer text: "There is darkness all around us; but if darkness is, and the darkness is of the forest, then the darkness must be good" (Turnbull 1961:93).

Polyphony

The polyphonic texture of this choral music is complex (see Transcription 3.23). Like a well-made multitrack rock and roll recording, the layered parts in "Makala"

TRANSCRIPTION 3.23
Polyphony in "Makala."

TRANSCRIPTION 3.23
(*continued*)

sound fresh with each listening. Forest People use many different qualities of multipart song. I hear musical processes that can be labeled as heterophony, drone/ostinato, layering, counterpoint, and accompaniment. Happily, reality confounds neat analysis; there are no absolute distinctions among these polyphonic devices.

MUSIC-CULTURE AS AN ADAPTIVE RESOURCE

Restoring Balance

The active force of music-making contributes to the Forest People's enduring yet ever-changing way of life. The BaMbuti encode the practical, moral effect of song in their words for conflict and peace: *akami,* noise or disordered sound, and *ekimi,* silence or ordered sound (Turnbull 1983:50–51). Troubles arise when synergy among people and symbiosis with the forest is disrupted. Communal singing "wakes the forest," whose benevolent presence silences the *akami* forces (Turnbull 1961:92). With yodels echoing off the trees, the forest physically becomes one of the musicians.

Enacting Values and Creating Self

Improvised, open-ended polyphony embodies egalitarian cultural values such as cooperation, negotiation, argument, and personal autonomy. By making social relations tangible, performance helps individuals develop identity within a group. Kisliuk gives a firsthand report of her participation:

> My senses tingled; I was finally inside the singing and dancing circle. The song was "Makala," and singing it came more easily to me while I danced. As I moved around the circle, the voices of different people stood out at moments, affecting my own singing and my choices of variations. I could feel fully the intermeshing of sound and motion, and move with it as it transformed, folding in upon itself. This was different from listening or singing on the sidelines because, while moving with the circle, I became an active part of the aural kaleidoscope. I was part of the changing design inside the scope, instead of looking at it and projecting in. (1998:101)

Autonomy Within Community

Most members of a BaAka community acquire music-making skills as they grow up (enculturation). During times of crisis, the group needs the musical participation of every member. For example, in a memorable scene from *The Forest People,* even when others in the hunting group insult and ostracize a man for setting his hunting net in front of the others', he joins the all-night singing and is forgiven (Turnbull 1961:94–108).

Although collective participation in performance is highly valued, individuals may stand out. Kisliuk writes that the community knows the composers of individual songs and originators of whole repertoires such as *Mabo.* Explicit teacher–student transmission does take place between the old and young of one group and among members of groups from different regions. Turnbull wrote of an acclaimed singer/dancer who seems particularly emotional and prone to time/space transformation during performances: "He was no longer Amabosu; he had some other personality totally different, and distant" (Turnbull 1961:89). BaAka repertory has a varied history and a dynamic future. Music connects the people to their past, while helping them negotiate their present.

Conclusion

Contrary to the images of chaos and despair conveyed by international mass media, we have encountered African music-cultures of stability, resourcefulness, and self-respect. Abubakari Lunna's life story reveals the rigor of an African musician's education. The erudition, commitment, suffering, and love are profound. Although he says good drumming is "sweet," clearly it is not frivolous or just fun. We could call it "deep," like the music of Frank Mitchell (see Chapter 2). We have seen that many Africans value the achievements of their ancestors. The Ewe rigorously study *Agbekor* and recreate it with passionate respect in performance. Innovative *chimurenga* music draws its inspiration from classics of Shona repertory. Mande songs link the wisdom of the elders to the problems of today.

African music-cultures are strongly humanistic. The human body inspires the construction and playing technique of musical instruments such as the *mbira* and *kora*. The spontaneous performances of postal workers and the ritual ceremonies of Forest People point out an important feature of many African music-cultures: Music serves society. As we have experienced, many kinds of African music foster group participation.

Although I encourage African-style musicking, musicians who cross cultural borders need sensitivity to limits and contradictions. To me, nothing approaches the power of time-honored repertory performed in context by the people born into the tradition, the bearers of culture. The history of an African musical heritage like Mande *jaliya* casts a humbling light onto recent idioms. When non-Africans play African music, especially those of us with white skin, the legacy of slavery and colonialism affects how an audience receives the performance. Thomas Mapfumo, who as a young rock and roller faced discrimination, now competes in the commercial marketplace with international bands that cover African pop songs. How many enthusiasts for African music love its aesthetic surface but regard spirit possession as superstition?

Music is a joyful yet rigorous discipline. The hard work of musical analysis yields important benefits. By making clear the sophistication of African musical traditions, analysis promotes an attitude of respect. Analysis helps us understand the inner structure of music; it provides an ear map for appreciative listening and informed performance. This chapter has emphasized notation examples with rhythms based on 3:2. As we have seen, this profound and elemental timing ratio animates many African traditions.

Analysis of musical structure raises big questions that resist simple answers: Can thought be nonverbal? What approach to music yields relevant data and significant explanation? By treating music as an object, does analysis wrongly alienate music from its authentic cultural setting? How can people know each other? Each chapter in this book benefits from this type of questioning. We seek to know how people understand themselves, but we must acknowledge the impact of our own perspective. Not only does an active involvement in expressive culture provide a wonderful way to learn about other people, but it can change a person's own life as well. From this perspective, ethnomusicology helps create new and original music-cultures.

Inquiry into music-cultures need not be a passive act of cultural tourism. On the contrary, a cross-cultural encounter can be an active process of self-development. When we seek knowledge of African music-cultures, we can also reevaluate our own. As we try our hands at African music, we encounter fresh sonic styles and experience alternative models of social action. Just as African cultures are not static, each student's personal world of music is a work in progress.

Book Companion Website

You will find tutorial quizzes, Internet links, and much more at the Book Companion Website for *Worlds of Music,* Fifth Edition, at **academic.cengage.com/music/titon/worlds_5**

North America/Black America

JEFF TODD TITON

CHAPTER 4

Music of work, music of worship, music of play: The traditional music of African American people in the United States has a rich and glorious heritage. Neither African nor European, it is fully a black American music, forged in America by Africans and their descendants, changing through the centuries to give voice to changes in their ideas of themselves. Through all the changes, the music has retained its black American identity, with a core of ecstasy and improvisation that transforms the regularity of everyday life into the freedom of expressive artistry. Spirituals, the blues, jazz—to Europeans, these unusual sounds are considered America's greatest (some would say her only) contribution to the international musical world.

Of course, modern black music does not sound unusual to North Americans. This is because the black style has been so pervasive for many years. Locate a CD reissue of some popular music from the first decade or two of the twentieth century. This music will sound stilted, square, extravagantly dramatic, unnatural, and jerky—not because of the recording process, but because of the influence of grand opera singing and marching band instrumental styles of the period. But in the 1920s, aptly called the Jazz Age, Bessie Smith and other African American jazz and blues singers revolutionized the craft of singing popular music. Not only that, but their performances from the stage and on recordings "helped to carve out new space in which black working people could gather and experience themselves as a community" (Davis 1999:137). Their approach lay close to the rhythm and tone of ordinary talk, and this natural way of singing caught on. Blues, gospel, jazz, swing, bop, rhythm and blues, rock and roll, funk, soul music, Motown, Muscle Shoals, disco, rap, hip-hop: The currents of African American music in the twentieth century transformed popular music first in North America, then in Europe, and eventually throughout the world.

Music of Worship

The easiest way to get acquainted with a music-culture in the United States is to survey its popular music on the radio. Most North American cities have one or two radio stations programming African American music. Listen for a couple of

145

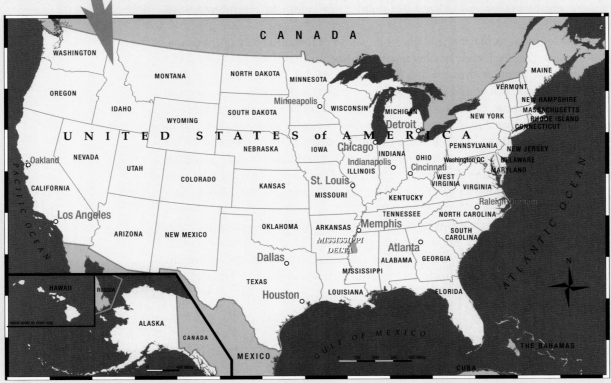

weeks; you will hear mostly contemporary black music, with occasional side trips into older forms and styles. But on Sundays the standard fare is recorded religious music, along with remote broadcasts of worship services from black churches in the city and surrounding suburbs. These live church broadcasts showcase a broad spectrum of black religious music: modern gospel quartets, powerful massed choirs, and soloists whose vocal acrobatics far exceed those of their counterparts in nonreligious music. Some of these broadcasts include congregational singing: camp-meeting choruses, particularly among Pentecostals, and **hymns** (songs of praise to God), particularly among Baptists.

Listen now to a hymn sung by a black Baptist congregation in Detroit (CD 1, Track 22). It is the first verse of the familiar Christian hymn "Amazing Grace," but the rhythm, melody, and performance style are unfamiliar to most people outside the black church. A deacon leads the hymn. Because the microphone was placed next to him during the recording, his voice is heard above the rest. He opens the hymn by singing the first line by himself: "Amazing grace how sweet it sound." The congregation then joins him, and very slowly they repeat the words, sliding the melody around each syllable of the text. Next, the deacon sings the second line by himself: "That saved a wretch like me"; then the congregation joins him to repeat it, slowly and melismatically (see Chapter 3). The same procedure finishes the verse (see the Close Listening guide).

That one verse is all there is to the performance. The singers do not use hymnbooks; they have memorized the basic tune and the words. Notice that the congregation, singing with the deacon, do not all come in at the same time; some lag

CD 1:22

Amazing Grace (2:36). Traditional. Performed by deacon and congregation of the New Bethel Baptist Church. Field recording by Jeff Todd Titon. Detroit, Michigan, 1977.

Close Listening

"AMAZING GRACE"

CD 1:22

COUNTER NUMBER	COMMENTARY	LYRICS
0:00	Leader gives out the first line.	Amazing grace how sweet it sound
0:09	Congregation joins leader to repeat first line, to a very slow and elaborate melody, with many melismata.	Amazing grace how sweet, ah
0:45	Leader gives out the second line.	That saved a wretch like me!
0:49	Congregation joins leader to sing second line.	That saved a wretch like me!
1:14	Leader gives out the third line.	I once was lost but now am found,
1:20	Congregation joins leader to sing third line.	I once was lost but now am found,
1:56	Leader gives out the fourth line.	Was blind but now I see.
2:01	Congregation joins leader to sing fourth line.	Was blind but now I see.

Marion Post Wolcott. Courtesy of the Library of Congress, FSA-OWI Collection.

FIGURE 4.1

Abandoned rural black church in Manning, South Carolina, June 1939.

behind the others a fraction, singing as they feel it. Not everyone sings exactly the same tune, either. Some ornament the basic tones with more in-between or melismatic tones than others do. The singers improvise their ornamentation as they go along. It is a beautiful and quite intricate performance; try singing along. Probably you will find it difficult. Transcription 4.1 shows one way of singing the first two lines. This may be helpful, but after listening many times you may be able to sing it even without reading the transcription; after all, the people in the congregation learned it by ear. This way of organizing the singing in church, in which a leader sings a line and then repeats it with the congregation, is called **lining out**. Lining out psalms and, later, hymns was a standard practice in colonial America. Black slaves and freedmen worshipped with whites and picked up the practice from their example. The influence then became mutual. Today you can still hear lining out in a great many black Baptist churches throughout the United States, particularly in the rural South (Figure 4.1). (Among white churches it survives chiefly among Old Regular Baptists in the coal-mining country of the southern Appalachian mountains.)

TRANSCRIPTION 4.1
"Amazing Grace" as sung at the New Bethel Baptist Church.

Notation in this chapter employs an arrow above a note head to indicate a pitch slightly higher (or lower) than notated but insufficiently high or low to be notated by the neighboring chromatic step. A solid line between successive note heads indicates a vocal glide. Time value of grace notes should be subtracted from the previous note. An *x* on a staff space or line indicates the approximate pitch of an unstable, half-spoken syllable. A fermata above a note head indicates a pitch held slightly longer than notated; an inverted fermata indicates a pitch held slightly shorter than notated. This additional notation is an attempt to make the Western staff-scale notation system more responsive to world music styles.

Recorded and transcribed by Jeff Todd Titon, Detroit, Michigan, June, 1978.

This version of "Amazing Grace" has many characteristics typical of African American music in the United States. The words are sung in English, and they fall into **stanzas** (verses or strophes), as most English folk songs do. But the style of the performance is black African:

> *Movement:* The singers sway freely to the music, dancing it with their bodies.
> *Social organization of the singing group:* As we saw in Chapter 3, the leader-chorus call-and-response is the predominant African group vocal organization.
> *Timbre:* The singing tone quality alternates between buttery smooth and raspy coarse.
> *Pitch:* The pitch is variable around the third, fifth, and seventh degrees of the scale. The tune is playful—ebbing and eddying like the ocean tide.

We can understand these attributes of traditional African American music more clearly if we contrast this version of "Amazing Grace" with a British American version of the same hymn, from a church in northwestern Virginia (CD 1, Track 23). The white song leader stands erect like the soldier of the cross he is, chest out, eyes front, unmoving save for his hand, which marks the regular and clearly audible beat. Leader and congregation sing together instead of in call-and-response alternation. The choral texture is polyphonic instead of heterophonic. Transcription 4.2 of the first two lines compares his singing with the tune as it is printed in the church hymnbook (Transcription 4.3).

The song leader's tone quality is unvaryingly coarse, giving an impression of energetic seriousness rather than playful ecstasy. His tune is stately, measured, and decorated. His slight variations are deliberate, and they differ slightly from one another in each of the four verses that make up the performance. But they are restrained compared with the melodic decoration sung by the black deacon. Here the two music-cultures have a very different idea of how to worship in song. Worshippers whose idea of religious music is that it should be solemn and serious may suspect that African American musical styling in music for worship, particularly in gospel music, is more like entertainment than proper worship. They do not understand that the black aesthetic requires styling and soul to bring music to life. On the other hand,

CD 1:23

Amazing Grace (2:52). Traditional. Performed by the congregation of the Fellowship Independent Baptist Church, led by Rev. John Sherfey. Field recording by Jeff Todd Titon. Stanley, Virginia, 1977.

AS SUNG:

A - maz - ing ___ grace how ___ sweet the ___

AS WRITTEN:

sound   That ___ saved   a ___ wretch   like ___ me!

TRANSCRIPTION 4.2
"Amazing Grace" as sung at the Fellowship Independent Baptist Church. The transcription follows the melody as sung by the song leader. For comparison, the lower staff shows the melody as written in their church hymnal. (See also Transcription 4.3.)

Recorded and transcribed by Jeff Todd Titon. Stanley, Virginia, August 1977.

TRANSCRIPTION 4.3
"Amazing Grace" from
Church Hymnal.

John Newton   Wm. Walker

Tennessee Music and Printing Co., Cleveland, Tennessee, 1951.

worshippers whose idea of religious music is that it should praise God with as much style, feeling, and even ecstasy as the singers can express may find this British American example of "Amazing Grace" dull and lifeless by comparison. Yet, a few more hearings of this British American example reveal subtleties such as the upward catch on the release of certain tones, as, for instance, at the end of the word *grace* in the first line. Certainly the singers are no less full of feeling in their experience of this music, even though their expressive styles are so different. Try imitating each version of this well-known song; both are much admired examples of their kind. Your efforts to sing will increase your understanding of the musical styles as well as your pleasure in the musical experience.

As suggested earlier, a radio survey of black music reveals a vital church music-culture. Suppose we enter the black church where I recorded the first song and observit firsthand (Figure 4.2). It is a Baptist church with a large sanctuary, seating perhaps fifteen hundred on this warm Sunday morning. The men are dressed in blue or black vested suits, with black socks and shoes. A few of the younger men are conspicuous in tan, baby-blue, or burgundy suits with matching shoes. The women wear dark suits or dresses, and many have on fashionable hats; all of them wear stockings and dress shoes. Choir members wear green robes over

Jeff Todd Titon

FIGURE 4.2

A young deacon chants an improvised prayer. The microphone connects with the church's public address system. Detroit, Michigan, 1978.

their formal attire. To keep a breeze, they swing cardboard fans supplied by the funeral homes that have printed their advertisements on them.

When we hear "Amazing Grace," we have come to the **deacons' devotional,** an early part of the worship service consisting of old-time congregational hymn singing, scripture reading, and a chanted prayer offered by a deacon while the rest hum and moan a wordless hymn in the background. The praying deacon improvises his chanted prayer—the words and tune—which begins as speech and then gradually turns to a chant with a definite tonal center, moving at the close in a regular meter; the congregation punctuates the deacon's phrases with shouts of "Yes," "Now," and so forth, which are intoned on the tonal center (C in the transcription). This, of course, is another example of call-and-response. Transcription 4.4 shows the closing section of chanted prayer. The congregation's response (Yes!) is in brackets; the transcription follows the melody (lines 3–10 in the text) as chanted by the deacon, who improvises the words and tune as the spirit moves him.

TRANSCRIPTION 4.4
Lines 3–10 from chanted prayer by deacon and congregation at the Little Rock Baptist Church.

Recorded and transcribed by Jeff Todd Titon. Detroit, Michigan, October 1977.

Text,
CLOSING SECTION
OF CHANTED PRAYER

O Lord. (Congregation: *Yes!*)
Have mercy today, Father. *(Yes!)*
You know where we at. *(Yes!)*
You know our hearts. *(Yes!)*
5   You know our hearts' desire. *(Yes!)*
Please Jesus! *(Yes!)*
Please Jesus! *(Yes!)*
Go with us today. *(Yes!)*
I know you know me. *(Yes!)*
10 You know all about me. *(Yes!)*
Now Lord. *(Now Lord!)*
Now Jesus. *(Now!)*
When we can't pray no more *(Yes!)*
over here. *(Yes!)*
[spoken] Give us a home somewhere in thy kingdom.

The deacons lead the devotional from the altar area, and after the devotional is through, the activity shifts to the pulpit, where announcements are made, offerings are taken up, and responsive reading is led. Interspersed are modern, lively **gospel songs,** sung by soloists and the high-spirited youth choir, accompanied by piano and organ. The preacher begins his spontaneous sermon in a speaking voice, but after about fifteen minutes he shifts into a musical chant (Transcription 4.5), all the while improvising and carrying on his message.

Text,
SERMON

Nicodemus was a ruler.
He was a
rich man.
You know everybody loves money.
5   Everybody loves to look, be looked upon.
Everybody loves to be called somebody.
Ah I imagine Nicodemus was ah in that category.
And ah he heard about God.
I don't know where he heard about him back but he heard of
10 something about God
What he was doing.
And ah
he
made it up in his
15 mind
that he was going to see God.
And ahh he made
an appointment with him.
And ahh the Scripture says that it was at night.

```
20  It's all right
    in the midnight
    to make appointment with him.
    It's all right
    to make appointment with him
25  if it is at noon day.
    You should make appointment with him.
    I made appointment with him one day
    and ahh
    I told him my situation.
30  Oh Lord.
    And everything went all right.
    Mmm
    hallelujah.
    And Nicodemus said,
35  he said, "I know
    that no man can do these things
    except God be with him."
    You know God says
    in the
40  Scripture here,
    he say you can do all things.
    "You can do all things in my name
    if you'll vow in me
    and I'll abide in you."
45  You should get in Christ.
    You should get in touch with God.
    Learn a little more about him.
    And when you've found Christ
    just wrap around him and
50  and everything will be all right.
```

Transcription by Jeff Todd Titon. Minneapolis, Minnesota, August 1968.

TRANSCRIPTION 4.5
Lines 20–25 from chanted portion of sermon delivered by Rev. George Trawick. In reading the words, pause about one-half second at the end of each measured line.

Recorded and transcribed by Jeff Todd Titon. St. Mark's Baptist Church, Minneapolis, Minnesota, August 1968.

Our excerpt comes from the chanted portion of a sermon by Rev. George Trawick, Pastor of St. Mark's Baptist Church, Minneapolis, Minnesota, which I recorded in August 1968. Transcription 4.5 (lines 20–25) follows the melody as chanted by the preacher, who improvises the words and tune, as the Spirit moves him, rather than reading from a printed text. This style of sermon delivery was at least 150 years old at the time of my recording, and forty years later it can still be heard among black, Baptist ministers. The change from speech to chant (the chant is sometimes called **whooping**) is accompanied by a change from a playful timbre that alternates between clear and buzzy, light and coarse, to a rather continuously hoarse timbre. As they did for the praying deacon, the congregation responds to the preacher's phrases with shouts of "Well," "Yes," and so forth, on the tonal center. Sometimes the preacher fits his chant into a regular meter for brief periods, lasting from perhaps ten seconds to a minute. But more often the chanted phrases are irregular. Still, compared with phrases in ordinary conversation, they are relatively uniform and, when punctuated by the congregation, they give the impression of regularity.

The Reverend C. L. Franklin of Detroit (Figure 4.3) spoke to me of the rhythm of his whooped preaching: "It's not something I can beat my foot to. But I can feel it. It's in me." It is also in the members of the congregation who sway back and forth with each phrase. Rev. Franklin's sermons were extraordinarily popular—he toured the nation to preach in the 1950s and 1960s, often with his daughter, Aretha. Recordings of his sermons can often be found in the gospel bins in record stores in black communities.

Eventually the sermon closes and an invitational song follows, led by a soloist from the choir. Three or four people heed the invitation and come

FIGURE 4.3

Reverend C. L. Franklin, pastor, chanting ("whooping") as he delivers the sermon's climax. New Bethel Baptist Church, Detroit, Michigan, 1978.

Jeff Todd Titon

FIGURE 4.4

Religious music quickens the Holy Spirit and sends a woman into trance. Detroit, Michigan, 1977.

forward to join the church. A final offering is taken up, the preacher gives the benediction, and the choir comes down from the choir stand, locks arms in the altar area facing the pulpit, and joins the congregation in singing "Amen."

Altogether, song and chant have taken up at least half the running time of the worship service: the old-style singing of the deacons' devotional, the traditional chant of the prayer and sermon, and the modern gospel songs. The music is literally moving; it activates the Holy Spirit, which sends some people into shouts of ecstasy, swoons, shakes, holy dance, and trance (Figure 4.4). If they get so carried away that they are in danger of fainting or injuring themselves, they are restrained by their neighbors until members of the nurses' guild can reach them and administer aid. In this setting, music is an extremely powerful activity—and the church is prepared for its effects.

Much of the music of black Christian worship in the United States is traditional. We have seen that the lining-out tradition dates from colonial America, and many of the hymns sung have the same vintage. The Negro spiritual developed later, born of the camp-meeting revivals in the late eighteenth and early nineteenth centuries. The delivery style of these chanted prayers and sermons is at least as old as the early nineteenth century, and probably older, though of course the deacons and preachers improvise the content. Today they can be heard in their most traditional form as the "choruses"—one verse repeated several times—in Pentecostal services, while in black Baptist and Methodist services they are featured in carefully arranged, multiversed versions sung by trained choirs in a tradition that hearkens back to the Fisk Jubilee Singers of the late nineteenth century (see Transcription 4.6).

TRANSCRIPTION 4.6
"Swing Low, Sweet
Chariot."

Swing low, sweet char - i - ot, __ Com-ing for to car-ry me home,

Swing low, sweet char - i - ot, __ Com-ing for to car-ry me home.

1. I   looked   o   - ver Jor - dan, and   what did   I   see, __
2. If   you   get   there be - fore __ I   do, __
3. The   bright - est   day   that   ev - er __ I   saw, __
4. I'm   some - times   up   and __ some - times   down, __

Com - ing for   to   car - ry   me   home? A   band __ of   an - gels
Com - ing for   to   car - ry   me   home, Tell   all __ my friends I'm
Com - ing for   to   car - ry   me   home, When Je - sus wash'd my
Com - ing for   to   car - ry   me   home, But   still __ my soul feels

com - ing af - ter me, __ Com - ing for to car - ry me home.
com - ing   too, __ Com - ing for to car - ry me home.
sins __ a - way, __ Com - ing for to car - ry me home.
heaven - ly   bound, Com - ing for to car - ry me home.

G. D. Pike, *The [Fisk] Jubilee Singers* (Boston: Lee and Shephard, 1873), 166.

Music of Work

A **work song,** as the name suggests, is a song workers sing to help them carry on. It takes their minds off the tiring and monotonous bending, swinging, hauling, driving, carrying, chopping, poling, loading, digging, pulling, cutting, breaking, and lifting (Figure 4.5). A work song also paces the work. If the job requires teamwork, work song rhythms coordinate the movements of the workers (Figure 4.6).

Jack Delano. Courtesy of the Library of Congress, FSA-OSI Collection.

FIGURE 4.5

Chopping cotton on rented land, near White Plains, Greene County, Georgia, June 1941.

Work songs were widely reported among black slaves in the West Indies in the eighteenth century and in the United States in the nineteenth. Most scholars believe black work songs must have been present in the American colonies, even though the documentary evidence is thin. While African American work songs may have been influenced by British work songs (sea chanteys and the like), the widespread, ancient, and continuing African work song tradition is the most probable source.

Work music is hard to find in the United States today. Where people once sang, machines now whine. But in an earlier period, African Americans sang work songs as they farmed and as they built the canals, railroads, and highways that became the transportation networks of the growing nation. This daily music helped make the

Frederic Ramsey, Jr.

FIGURE 4.6

Workers lining track. Alabama, 1956.

African American sound what it was then and what it is now. In his autobiography *My Bondage and My Freedom* (1855), ex-slave Frederick Douglass wrote,

> Slaves are generally expected to sing as well as to work. A silent slave is not liked by masters or overseers. "Make a noise," "make a noise" and "bear a hand," are the words constantly addressed to the slaves when there is silence amongst them. This may account for the almost constant singing heard in the southern states.

After Emancipation, the singing continued whenever black people were engaged in heavy work: clearing and grading the land, laying railroad track, loading barges and poling them along the rivers, building levees against river flooding, felling trees hauling nets. This included the inevitable farm work: digging ditches, cutting timber, building fences, plowing, planting, chopping out weeds, and reaping and loading the harvest. The words and tunes of these work songs, or **field hollers,** fit the nature of the work. People working by themselves or at their own pace in a group sang slow songs without a pronounced beat; the singer hummed tunes or fit words in as desired, passing the time.

Close Listening

FIELD HOLLER (WORK SONG)

CD 1:24

COUNTER NUMBER	COMMENTARY	LYRICS
0:00	Caston sings first line, drawing out the length of tones as he wishes.	Hey, one of these mornings, mornings, and it won't be long;
0:10	Second line; like the first and all others in a flexible rhythm without a steady beat. Here, "captain" means boss.	You're gonna look for me, captain, and up the road I'll be gone.
0:17	Caston speaks.	"And this other guy named Curtis used to sing a song, says,"
0:21	Caston sings first line of second verse. Notice the melismata in "-try" of "country."	I'm goin' up the country, baby, and I can't take you.
0:33	Caston sings second line of second verse.	There's nothing up the country that a monkey woman can do.

Additional verses

Hey—captain don't you know my name?
I'm the same old fellow who stole your watch and chain.

I'm going away, baby, to wear you off my mind.
You keep me worried and bothered all the time.

As a farm boy Leonard "Baby Doo" Caston learned to sing these field hollers by copying the practice of older farmhands (CD 1, Track 24). In the background you can hear the sound of a stereo playing in the room where the recording was made. A "monkey woman" is a woman without common sense; a "captain" is a boss. Try singing along with Baby Doo Caston. The free rhythm makes it difficult to do, even when you read along with Transcription 4.7. See the Close Listening box, then make up a verse and try singing it by yourself.

Not surprisingly, the words of these songs show that the singers wanted to be elsewhere, away from work. In group labor that required teamwork and a steady pace, people sang songs with a pronounced beat, which coordinated their movements. About forty years ago a rowing work song, "Michael, Row the Boat Ashore," was recorded by a group of white singers who had probably never come any closer to the work than crewing on the Connecticut River, but their version became a best-selling record on the popular music charts. The song was first reported in the 1867 collection *Slave Songs of the United States* (Transcription 4.8). The words to work songs are open-ended; that is, the song leader can improvise new lines ("Michael, row the boat ashore" or "O you mind your boastin' talk") and repeat old ones until his stock is exhausted and his voice gives out, while the rest of the workers merely sing the responsorial burden ("Hallelujah!") after each line, in a call-and-response pattern. Today, an African American group of former menhaden fishermen, the Northern Neck Chantey singers, preserve and perform worksongs at folk music festivals.

CD 1:24

Field Holler (0:43). Traditional solo work song. Performed by Leonard "Baby Doo" Caston. Field recording by Jeff Todd Titon. Minneapolis, Minnesota, 1971. (Background noise from the apartment is audible.)

TRANSCRIPTION 4.7
Field holler as sung by Leonard "Baby Doo" Caston.

Hey one of these_ morn-ings_____ morn - ings and it won't be long._____ You're gon-na look for me cap - tain _____ and up the road I'll be gone. _____

Recorded and transcribed by Jeff Todd Titon. Minneapolis, Minnesota, May 1971. (Titon 1974a)

TRANSCRIPTION 4.8
Lines 1–2 from "Michael, Row the Boat Ashore."

1. Mi - chael row de boat a - shore. Hal - le - lu - [Cho.] jah! 2. Mi-chael boat a gos-pel boat. Hal - le - lu - jah! [Cho.]

Slave Songs of the United States, compiled by William Francis Allen, Charles Pickard Ware, and Lucy McKim Garrison (New York: A. Simpson & Co., 1867), 23–24.

**Text,
"MICHAEL, ROW THE
BOAT ASHORE"**

3. I wonder where my mudder deh (there). (*Hallelujah!*)
4. See my mudder on de rock gwine home.
5. On de rock gwine home in Jesus' name.
6. Michael boat a music boat
7. Gabriel blow de trumpet horn.
8. O you mind your boastin' talk.
9. Boastin' talk will sink your soul.
10. Brudder, lend a helpin' hand.
11. Sister, help for trim dat boat.
12. Jordan stream is wide and deep.
13. Jesus stand on t' oder side.
14. I wonder if my maussa deh.
15. My fader gone to unknown land.
16. O de Lord he plant his garden deh.
17. He raise de fruit for you to eat.
18. He dat eat shall neber die.
19. When de riber overflow
20. O poor sinner, how you land?
21. Riber run and darkness comin'.
22. Sinner row to save your soul.

What makes a good song leader? What is the purpose of work songs? Collecting work songs in 1947 inside the Mississippi State Penitentiary at Parchman, Alan Lomax asked these questions of the African American inmates whose singing he recorded:

LOMAX: Do you think it makes work easier when you sing?

INMATE: Yessir.

LOMAX: Do you think you can do more or do you think you can slack off when you sing?

INMATE: Nosir, what makes it go so better—when you're singing, you forget, you see, and the time just pass on 'way; but if you get your mind devoted on one something, it look like it will be hard for you to make it, see—make a day—the day be longer, look like. . . . So to keep his mind from being devoted on just one thing, why, he'll just practically take up singing, see. . . .

LOMAX: What's the most important thing about a good leader . . . does he have a real good voice or a strong voice or what?

INMATE: Well . . . now it wouldn't just exactly make any difference about the dependability of his voice or nothing like that, boss; but it would, it take the man with the most experience to my understanding to make the best leader in anything. You see, if you'd bring a brand new man here, if he had a voice where he would sing just like Peter could preach, and he didn't know what to sing about, well, he wouldn't do no good, see, but here's a fellow, he, maybe he ain't got no voice for singing, but he's been cooperating with the peoples so long and been on the job so long till he know just exactly how it should go, and if he can just mostly talk it, why, and you understand how to work, well it would go good with you—it don't make any difference about the voice....

LOMAX: You mean he has to know the timing?

INMATE: Yessir... that's what it takes, the time, that's all it is. You can just whistle and, if you know the time and can stay in time with the axes, you can whistle and do, cut just as good as you can if you were singing... but you have to be done experienced.

(Lomax 1976. © Alan Lomax. Used by permission.)

The aesthetic standards of the African American work song call for a good sense of the beat and the ability to time it to the work at hand. A sweet-sounding voice that is always in tune may be desirable in other situations, but it is not important in the group work song tradition.

In some southern prisons black inmates sang work songs. For example, the song "Rosie" (CD 1, Track 25) was used to regulate the axe blows when the workers were felling large trees. Sometimes as many as ten men circled the tree and chopped, five pulling their axes out just before the other five all struck at once. Axes were swinging through the air at all times, back and forth; the work was dangerous and the timing was crucial. Without work songs, the white and Latino inmates chopped two to a tree. With work songs, the black inmates chopped four, six, eight, or ten to a tree. The work went faster and better, and the singing group felt pride and solidarity in its accomplishment. See the Close Listening guides and Transcription 4.9.

In the words of Bruce Jackson, a collector of prison work songs,

CD 1:25

"Rosie" (2:50). Traditional work song. Performed by prisoners at Mississippi State Penitentiary. Field recording by Alan Lomax. Parchman, Mississippi. 1947.

The songs [may] change the nature of the work by putting the work into the worker's framework rather than the guards'. By incorporating the work with their song, by, in effect, co-opting something they are forced to do anyway, they make it theirs in a way it otherwise is not. (1972:30)

Close Listening

"ROSIE"—EXCERPT FROM FIRST VERSE WITH CALL-AND-RESPONSE

CD 1:25

COUNTER NUMBER	COMMENTARY	LYRICS
0:01	Axes sound, call (leader).	Be my woman, gal I'll
0:04	Axes sound, response (leader and group).	Be your man.
0:07	Axes sound, call (again).	Be my woman, gal, I'll
0:11	Axes sound, response (again).	Be your man.

Close Listening

"ROSIE"

CD 1:25

COUNTER NUMBER	COMMENTARY	LYRICS
0:00	Verse 1	Be my woman, gal, I'll be your man. Be my woman, gal, I'll be your man. Be my woman, gal, I'll be your man. Every Sunday's dollar in your hand. In your hand, lordy, in your hand. Every Sunday's dollar in your hand.
0:39	Verse 2	Stick to the promise, gal, that you made me. Stick to the promise, gal, that you made me. Stick to the promise, gal, that you made me. Wasn't going to marry till I go free. I go free, lordy, I go free. Wasn't going to marry till I go free.
1:17	Verse 3	Well, Rosie, oh lord, gal. Ah, Rosie, oh lord, gal.
1:29	Verse 4	When she walks she reels and rocks behind. When she walks she reels and rocks behind. Ain't that enough to worry a convict's mind? Ain't that enough to worry a convict's mind?
1:53	Repeat verse 3	Well, Rosie, oh lord, gal. Ah, Rosie, oh lord, gal.
2:05	Verse 5	Be my woman, gal, I'll be your man. Be my woman, gal, I'll be your man. Be my woman, gal, I'll be your man. Every Sunday's dollar in your hand.
2:29	Repeat verse 3	Well, Rosie, oh lord, gal. Ah, Rosie, oh lord, gal.

Collected by Alan Lomax; transcribed by Mieczyslaw Kolinksi. From Courlander 1963. Reprinted courtesy of Columbia University Press.

In African American music, whether of work or worship, calls answered by responses emblematize the social nature of this music. This is not a predictable and predetermined music. **Improvisations** in lyrics and melodies, created at the moment of performance, as well as changes in timbre, show the high value African Americans place on innovation, creativity, and play.

M. K.

TRANSCRIPTION 4.9
"Rosie." Worksong sung by inmates of Mississippi State Penitentiary, Parchman, Mississippi, 1947.

TRANSCRIPTION 4.9
(*continued*)

I go free, Lor - dy, _____ I go free,

weren't gon - na mar - ry till ___ a ___ I go free.

Well _____ Ro - sie O Lord, gal.

ah _____ Ro - sie _____ O Lord, gal.

Collected by Alan Lomax; transcribed by Mieczyslaw Kolinski. From Courlander 1963.
Reprinted courtesy of Columbia University Press.

Music of Play

As we have seen, the performance of religious songs and work songs in the black tradition includes elements of play. For example, churchgoers admire the beautiful performance of a verbally adept preacher as he plays with the resources of language and gesture, and they clap their approval as a solo singer sustains a climactic pitch or goes through intricately improvised melodic variations with great feeling. Work songs introduce a playful, distancing attitude toward the labor at hand. Like call-and-response, this sort of play with pitch, timbre, and rhythm characterizes both African and African American music.

Although African American religious songs and work songs contain elements of play, their main purpose is to aid in worship and work. In contrast, music of play serves primarily as entertainment, performed mainly for pleasure even when its effect is also educational, cathartic, or ecstatic.

Imagine that we are walking through the black neighborhood outside the church after the service we "attended" earlier in the chapter. We find ourselves surrounded by the music of play. Children skip rope on the side streets, chanting jump rope rhymes and taunts at one another. Teens walk down the street listening to CD players. Deep bass tones boom out through powerful car stereos that throb with the latest hip-hop hits. Jukeboxes can be heard in the bars and barbecue joints that line both sides of the main street. When night falls, some of the bars have live entertainment—a local band that plays the blues, or a nationally known jazz combo in a fancy nightspot. Downtown in the city auditorium a nationally known artist is scheduled, while in the public gardens a concert of classical music offers the premiere performance of an electronic composition by a black composer who teaches at the city university.

Blues

Clearly, the music of play in black America offers a dizzying array of genres. The rest of this chapter focuses on just one African American music of play: blues. The blues is a music familiar to many, but its very familiarity presents problems. Chief among them is the current emphasis on blues as a roots music. If blues is the root, then rock is the fruit—or so the story goes in the films and radio programs produced in 2003 (see "Further Listening" and "Further Viewing" at the end of the chapter), which the U.S. Congress declared the "year of the blues." (We will see more about blues and roots music near the end of this chapter.) But blues is a music in and of itself. It is wrapped tightly around the history and experiences of African Americans in the United States and deserves to be understood in this light. Blues is tied intimately to African American experience and cannot be understood without reference to its historical development within African American culture.

A second area of confusion about blues arises over the relationship between blues and jazz. Is blues a part of jazz? Did the stream of blues flow into the river of jazz? That common metaphor is not accurate. Historically, blues and jazz are more like parallel highways with crossroads between them. Blues can be understood as a feeling—"the blues"—as well as a specific musical form. Jazz, which engenders complex and varied feelings, is best thought of as a technique, as a way of forming. Jazz musicians applied their technique to the blues form, as to other musical forms.

Muddy Waters (Figure 4.7), Howlin' Wolf (Figure 4.17), B. B. King, Albert Collins, John Lee Hooker (Figure 4.22), and Buddy Guy (Figure 4.21), who rose to national prominence as blues singers, came from a vital tradition. For decades, the blues music-culture—with its singers, country juke joints, barrelhouses, city rent parties, street singing, bar scenes, nightclubs, lounges, recordings, and record industry—was a significant part of the black music-culture in the United States. In the 1960s, when desegregation and the Civil Rights Movement changed African American social and economic conditions, blues faded in popularity among African Americans while it gained a large and appreciative white audience. Nowadays the blues music-culture incorporates white as well as black musicians and includes a worldwide audience.

BLUES AND THE TRUTH

The best entry into the blues is through the words of the songs. It is hard to talk at length about words in songs, and harder still to talk about music. As Charles Seeger, one of the founders of the Society of Ethnomusicology, reminds us, it would be more logical to "music" about music than to talk about it (Seeger 1977:16). And in the blues music-culture, when the setting is informal, that is just what happens when one singer responds to another by singing verses of his or her own. Another common response to blues is dancing. Dancers and listeners as a rule have no interest in an articulate body of blues criticism.

FIGURE 4.7

Muddy Waters (McKinley Morganfield) relaxes between songs at the Ann Arbor Blues Festival, 1969.

Jeff Todd Titon

Speaking of **oral literature** (literature spoken or sung and passed along without writing or musical notation) as a whole, Dennis Tedlock points up the paradox with gentle irony:

> Members of primary oral cultures generally limit themselves to brief remarks about performances when they say anything at all, and such remarks are quickly forgotten. There is no such thing as an oral performance of the great critical discourse of the past. (Tedlock 1977:516)

The most common response to blues music is a feeling in the gut, dancing to the beat, nodding assent, a vocalized "that's right, you got it, that's the truth"—not unlike the black Christian's response to a sermon or a gospel song. A good, "deep" blues song leaves you feeling that you have heard the truth in a way that leaves little more to be said.

Yet much *can* be said about the words to blues songs. Because the words pass from one singer to another as a coin goes from hand to hand, they become finely honed and proverbial in their expression: economical, truthful. Response to the words of the songs can be talked about in words. Moreover, blues lyrics have a legitimate claim to be considered as serious literature. As the literary critics Cleanth Brooks, R. W. B. Lewis, and Robert Penn Warren have written,

FIGURE 4.8

Lazy Bill Lucas. Minneapolis, Minnesota, 1968.

Jeff Todd Titon

In the world of music the recognition of blues as art is well established. But waiving their value as musical art, we may assert that they represent a body of poetic art unique and powerful.... No body of folk poetry in America—except, perhaps, the black spirituals—can touch it, and much of the poetry recognized as "literature," white or black, seems tepid beside it. (Brooks, Lewis, and Warren 1973:II, 2759)

We begin by taking an extended look at a single blues performance, "Poor Boy Blues," by the Lazy Bill Lucas Blues Band (Figure 4.8). Bill Lucas is the vocalist; he accompanies himself on electric guitar. He is joined by two other musicians, one on acoustic guitar and the other on drums. Listen to the recording now (CD 1, Track 26), and look at the Close Listening guide, paying particular attention to the lyrics.

CD 1:26

"Poor Boy Blues" (3:16). Performed by Lazy Bill Lucas Trio. Field recording by Jeff Todd Titon. Minneapolis, Minnesota, 1970.

RESPONSE TO THE LYRICS OF "POOR BOY BLUES"

I did not choose "Poor Boy Blues" because the words were outstanding; they are typical. For me, some of it is good, some not; some of it works, some does not. "I'm

Close Listening

"POOR BOY BLUES"

CD 1:26

COUNTER NUMBER	COMMENTARY	LYRICS
0:00	Instrumental introduction led by guitar.	
0:13	Lucas sings verse 1. Drums play mostly long-short figures; guitar plays mostly Da-da-da, Da-da-da figures when Lucas is silent between lines.	I'm just a poor boy; people, I can't even write my name. I'm just a poor boy; people, I can't even write my name. Every letter in the alphabet to me they look the same.
0:50	Lucas sings verse 2. Accompaniment as for verse 1.	Mother died when I was a baby; father I never seen. Mother died when I was a baby; father I never seen. When I think how dumb I am, you know it makes me want to scream.
1:26	Lucas sings verse 3. Interplay of the two guitars when Lucas is silent between lines.	Ever since I was the age around eleven or twelve, Ever since I was the age around eleven or twelve, I just been a poor boy; ain't caught nothing but hell.
1:59	Lucas speaks, signaling an instrumental break. "Lay your racket" means "play your instrument."	"Lay your racket, boy, lay your racket."
2:03	Instrumental break the length of one verse. Da-da-da figures mostly throughout on guitar.	"Have mercy."
2:36	Lucas sings verse 4.	When I was a child Santa Claus never left one toy. When I was a child Santa Claus never left one toy. If you have any mercy, please have mercy on poor boy.

Used with permission of William Lucas.

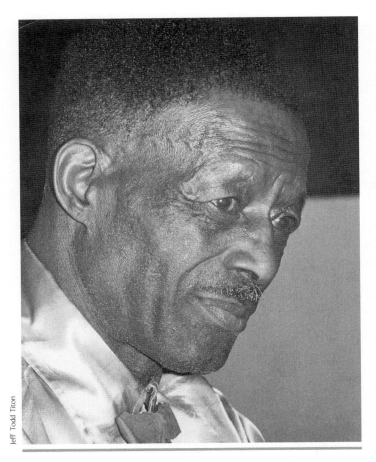

Jeff Todd Titon

FIGURE 4.9

Eddie "Son" House. Minneapolis, Minnesota, 1971.

just a poor boy; people, I can't even write my name" produces an automatic response of sympathy for the poor boy, but it is not a deep response. I am sorry for the poor boy's illiteracy, but, heck, everyone has problems. When the line repeats I am anxious to hear how the stanza will close. "Every letter in the alphabet to me they look the same" brings to my mind's eye a picture of a strange alphabet in which all letters look alike or, rather, in which the differences in their shape have no meaning. The image is clear, it works, and it involves me. This poor boy may be illiterate, but he is perceptive. And not only does the image itself succeed, but the delay of the most important word in the line, *same,* until the end, and the impact of its rhyme with *name,* convinces me I am hearing the truth. Blues singer Eddie "Son" House (Figure 4.9) told me about how he put his blues stanzas together: "I had enough sense to try to make 'em, rhyme 'em so they'd have hits to 'em with a meaning, some sense to 'em, you know" (Titon 1994:47). The inevitable rightness of the rhyme—you expect it and it rewards you—hits harder than an unrhymed close, particularly because the end rhyme always falls, in blues, on an accented syllable.

I do not respond to "Mother died when I was a baby"; I resist a statement that sounds sentimental. This is not because I think of myself as some kind of tough guy, but because I want the sentiment to be earned. I much prefer the statement at the close of the line: "father I never seen." The effect is in the contrast between the mother who died and the father who might as well be dead. In the image of the father who has never been seen is the mystery of not knowing one's parents. It is not just missing love; for all we know the poor boy was raised by loving relatives. But a child takes after parents, inherits the biology, so to speak; without knowing your parents you do not fully know yourself. That is the real terror of the poor boy's life. "When I think how dumb I am, you know it makes me want to scream" is a cliché; the rhyme is forced. Okay, scream. Nor do I respond to the third stanza when I hear it; but when I think about it, it seems curious that the poor boy says he began to catch hell from age eleven or twelve. I guess that he was catching it all along but did not fully realize it until then. That is a nice point, but a little too subtle to register during a performance. I would have to sing it several times myself to appreciate that aspect of it.

The final stanza takes great risk with sentimentality, calling up Christmas memories, but it succeeds by a matter-of-fact tone: "When I was a child Santa Claus never left one toy" dispels the scene's stickiness. Santa Claus never left a toy for anyone, but a child who believes in Santa can enjoy an innocent world where presents reward good little boys and girls. If he could not believe in Santa, I wonder if he ever had any part of the innocent happiness people seem to need early, and in large doses, if they are going to live creative lives. Or it could have been the other way around: He believed in Santa, but Santa, never bringing him a toy, simply did not believe in him.

The song now leads up to its final line, a plea for mercy. "You" are addressed directly: If you have any mercy, show it to the poor boy. Will you? If you heard this from a blind street singer, would you put some coins in his cup? Would you be more likely to show mercy to the poor boy than to someone down on his luck who just walks up and asks for spare change? The song will strike some people as sentimental, calling up an easy emotion that is just as quickly forgotten as it is evoked. T. S. Eliot, in a widely influential argument, said that in a work of literature any powerful emotion must have an "objective correlative"; that is, the work itself must demonstrate that there is good reason for the emotion (Eliot [1920] 1964). Has "Poor Boy Blues" given you good reason for mercy? Have you been told the truth, or were you played for a sucker?

AUTOBIOGRAPHY AND THE BLUES

We have been considering the words in a broad, English-speaking context. Considering the effect of "Poor Boy Blues" on a generalized listener can take us only so far. What do the words mean to someone in the blues music-culture? What do they mean to Lazy Bill Lucas? Does the "I" in the "Poor Boy Blues" represent Lucas? What, in short, is the relationship between the song and the singer?

More than any other subject, the correspondence between the words to blues songs and the lives of the singers has fascinated people who write about the blues. The blues singer's image as wandering minstrel, blind bard, and untutored genius is idealized, but, according to Samuel Charters, "There is no more romantic figure in popular music than the bluesman, with everything the term involves. And it isn't a false romanticism" (1977:112). The result is that most books on blues are organized biographically. Some writers have gone so far as to derive the facts of an otherwise obscure blues singer's life and personality from the lyrics of his or her recorded songs. On the other hand, published life stories of blues singers in their own words are rare (see, for example, Brunoghe 1964; Titon 1974b). If we read these first-person life stories properly, we can understand them as far more reliable expressions of the blues singer's own personality than song lyrics are, because the lyrics are often borrowed from tradition. Nonetheless, most people assume that the lyrics of a blues song do speak for the singer. Paul Oliver wrote, for example, "One of the characteristics of the blues is that it is highly personalized—blues singers nearly always sing about themselves" (Oliver 1998:33). If that is true, then "Poor Boy Blues" should reflect the life and thoughts of Lazy Bill Lucas.

I was a close friend of Bill Lucas's for six years, playing guitar in his blues band for two of them. During the course of our friendship I tape-recorded his recollections of his life, edited and excerpted for publication first in *Blues Unlimited* (Titon 1969), a British blues research journal, and later in the accompanying notes to his first American LP (Titon 1974a). Let us look, then, at parts of Lucas's life history and see if "Poor Boy Blues" speaks for him.

The Life History of Bill Lucas, Blues Singer

I was born in Wynne, Arkansas, on May 29, 1918. I never heard my mother say the exact *time* I was born: she was so upset at the time I guess she wouldn't remember. I have two sisters and three brothers; I was third from my baby sister, the third youngest.

Ever since I can remember, I had trouble with my eyesight. Doctors tell me it's the nerves. I can see shapes, I can tell colors, and I know light and dark, but it's hard to focus, and no glasses can help me. An operation might cure it, but there's a chance it could leave me completely blind, and I don't want to take that gamble.

My father was a farmer out in the country from Wynne. He was a sharecropper, farming on the halvers. In 1922 we moved to Short Bend, Arkansas, but my father wanted to get where there were better living conditions. A lot of his neighbors and friends had come up to Missouri and told him how good it was up there.

About every two or three years we moved from one farm to another. Some places you had good crops, according to the kind of land you had. Some places we had real sandy land, and that wasn't good; but in the places that were swampy, that black land, that was good. You know when you're sharecropping cotton and corn you look for the best location and the best living conditions. And you could move; you didn't have a lease on the place.

So my family moved to Advance, Missouri, in 1924. We moved by night but that doesn't mean we had to slip away. They loaded all our stuff in a wagon and we caught the ten o'clock train. That was my first train ride; I loved the train then. Advance was about twenty-five miles west of the river; it wasn't on the highway, just on the railroad. It was a little town of five hundred; it consisted of two grocery stores and a post office which doubled over into a saloon. We never did go to town much except on Saturdays. In the summertime we'd go in about every week to carry our vegetables to sell in a wagon: watermelons and cabbage and stuff.

My father wanted to own his own farm, but that was impossible. That was a dream. He didn't have enough money to buy it and there weren't any loans like there are nowadays. We owned cattle, we owned pigs. We had about thirteen milk cows, and we had leghorn chickens that gave us bushels of eggs. We were better off than our neighbors because we would sometimes swap our eggs for something we didn't have. We were blessed with eggs and chickens and milk. We were blessed. I tried to, but I never did learn how to milk. I wasn't too much use on the farm. I did a lot of babysitting but not too much else.

There weren't many guitars around, but in 1930 my daddy got me a guitar. I remember so well, just like it was yesterday, he traded a pig for it. Money was scarce down there; we didn't have any money. The boy wanted $7 for it. We didn't have money but we had plenty of pigs. Our neighbors had some boys that played guitar, but they never did take pains and show me how to do it. I would just watch 'em and listen. I learned from sounds. And after they were gone, then I would try to make the guitar sound like I heard them make it sound. It was easier to play single notes than chords. Right now till today I don't use but two fingers to play guitar; I don't play guitar like other people. I wanted the guitar because I liked the noise and it sounded pretty.

After I got it and come progressing on it, a tune or two here or there, my dad and mama both decided that would be a good way for me to make my living. I knew all the time I wanted to make a career out of it, but after I came progressing on it, well they wanted me to make a career out of it too. But they said I had to be old enough and big enough to take care of it, not to be breaking strings and busting it all up.

My father got me a piano in 1932 for a Christmas present. That was the happiest Christmas I ever had. He didn't trade pigs for that; he paid money for it. Got it at our neighborhood drugstore. It was an upright. It had been a player piano but all the guts had been taken out of it. Well, at the time I knew how to play organ, one of those pump organs; I had played a pump organ we had at home that came about the same time as the guitar. A woman, she was moving, she was breaking up housekeeping, and she gave us the organ. It had two pedals

Halvers: A sharecropping arrangement in which the landlord supplied the tenant with a shack, tools, seed, work animals, feed, fuel wood, and half the fertilizer in exchange for half the tenant's crop and labor.

on it and you'd do like riding a bicycle. So it didn't take me long to learn how to bang out a few tunes on the piano.

I didn't know what chords I was making. We got a little scale book that would go behind the keyboard of the piano and tell you all the chords. It was a beginner's book, in big letters. I could see that. You know, a beginner's book is in big letters. And I wanted to learn music, but after I got that far, well, the rest of the music books were so small that I couldn't see the print. And that's why I didn't learn to read music.

I did learn to read the alphabet at home. My parents taught me, and so did the other kids. I used to go to school, but it was just to be with the other kids, and sometimes the kids would teach me. I was just apt; I could pick things up. I had a lot of mother-wit.

So I bumped around on the piano until 1936, when we left the country and came to Cape Girardeau, Missouri. I had to leave my piano; we didn't have room for it. I almost cried. That was when I started playing the guitar on street corners. My dad had day work; that was the idea of him moving to the city, trying to better his living conditions. I forget what he went to work as: I think he worked in a coal yard. We stayed at my sister's house; one of my oldest sisters was married. But we had to go back to Commerce, Missouri. My dad couldn't make it in Cape Girardeau so we went to Commerce. I don't know what he thought he was going to do there because that was a little hick town, wasn't but about three hundred in population there. He didn't farm there; I vaguely can remember what we did now.

At that time I didn't know too much about blues. We had a radio station down there but they all played big band stuff and country and western music. But we didn't call it country and western music back then; we called it hillbilly music. Well, hillbilly music was popular there and so I played hillbilly music on the guitar and sang songs like "She'll Be Coming 'round the Mountain" and "It Ain't Gonna Rain No More" and "Wabash Cannonball." The only time I heard any blues was when we'd go to restaurants where a jukebox was and they'd have blues records. And my daddy had a windup phonograph, and we had a few blues records at home by Peetie Wheatstraw and Scrapper Blackwell and Curtis Jones—the old pieces, you know. So I learned a little bit about blues pieces off the records I'd hear around home. I heard Bessie Smith and Daddy Stovepipe and Blind Lemon Jefferson.

At that time I didn't have any knowledge of music. I liked any of it. I even liked those hillbilly songs. And when I heard the blues I liked the blues, but I just liked the music, period. And when I played out on street corners, I'd be playing for white folks mostly, and that was the music they seemed to like better, the hillbilly music. So I played it because I'd been listening to it all the time on the radio and so it wasn't very hard for me to play. The blues didn't *strike* me until I heard Big Bill Broonzy; that's when I wanted to play blues guitar like him.

We lost our mother in 1939. We buried her in Commerce, and we left Commerce after she died. My dad, he went to St. Louis in 1940, still trying to find better living conditions. Later that year he brought me to St. Louis, and that's where I met Big Joe Williams. At that time he wasn't playing in bars or taverns; he was just playing on the street. So he let me join him, and I counted it an honor to be playing with Big Joe Williams because I had heard his blues records while I was still down South. And so we played blues in the street.

But I didn't stay in St. Louis long. My dad and I came to Chicago the day after New Year's in 1941. Sonny Boy Williamson was the first musician I met with up there. I met him over on Maxwell Street, where they had all their merchandise out on the street, and you could buy anything you wanted on a Sunday, just like you could on a Monday. They had groceries, clothes, hardware, appliances, right out on the street, where people could come to look for bargains. That was a good place to play until the cops made us cut it out. I played a lot with Sonny Boy. Little suburban places around Chicago like Battle Creek, and South Bend. We were playing one-nighters in taverns and parties. Sonny Boy would book himself, and I went around with him. There wasn't much money in it; Sonny

Sonny Boy Williamson: Harmonica player John Lee Williamson (d. 1948).

"I didn't have a name": He means that the name Bill Lucas was unknown to the blues audiences.

Little Walter: Walter Jacobs, the most imitated blues harmonica player after World War II.

Boy paid my expenses and a place to stay with his friends. He was known all up around there. He played with me when he couldn't get nobody else. I didn't have a name at the time. But I had sense enough to play in time and change chords when he changed; it wasn't but three changes anyhow. We didn't play nothing but the funky blues. He just needed somebody to keep time, back him up on guitar.

Big Bill Broonzy was my idol for guitar, and I'd go sit in on his shows. He'd let me play on the stand between times; I'd play his same songs. Bill knew I couldn't do it as well as he did, so he wasn't mad. In fact he appreciated me for liking his style. I also liked T-Bone Walker (Figure 4.25), but he made so many chord changes! I was unfortunate to learn changes; I never did know but three changes on the guitar.

I used to play with Little Walter on the street, too, in the black section, where they wanted the blues. I quit playing that hillbilly music when I left St. Louis. In St. Louis I was getting on the blues right smart after I met up with Big Joe Williams. But white folks in Chicago or here in Minneapolis don't like hillbilly music. They tell you right away. "What you think I am? A hillbilly?"

I started in my professional career in 1946 when I joined the union. We all joined the union together, me and Willie Mabon and Earl Dranes, two guitars and a piano. We took our first job in 1946 on December 20, in the Tuxedo Lounge, 3119 Indiana, in Chicago. They paid union scale, but scale wasn't much then. The leader didn't get but twelve dollars a night, the sidemen ten dollars. We worked from 9 P.M. until 4 A.M. It was a real nice club. These after-hours clubs always had good crowds because after two o'clock everybody would come in. We had a two-week engagement there, and I thought it was real good money. But then we were kicked back out on the street.

Little Walter and I used to play along with Johnny Young at a place called the Purple Cat—1947. That's where he gave me the name "lazy" at. We'd been there so long Little Walter thought I should go up and turn on the amps, but I never did go up and do that thing, so that's why he started calling me "lazy" Bill, and the name stuck.

In 1948 I started in playing with Homesick James, and sometimes also with Little Hudson. I started out Little Hudson on playing. When I first met him in Chicago around 1945 or 1946 he wasn't playing. Of course he had a guitar, but he wasn't doing nothing. I started him and encouraged him and so he'd come and sit in with me and Sonny Boy or me and Willie Mabon or whoever I'd be playing with. He just started like that. And when he got good he was respected. He had a right smart amount of prestige about him, Hudson did. I switched to playing piano in 1950 because they had more guitar players than piano players. But of course I'd been playing piano all along—just not professionally, that's all. Little Hudson needed a piano player for his Red Devils trio. Our first job was at a place called the Plantation, on Thirty-first Street, on the south side of Chicago.

I don't know where he got the idea of the name from, but the drummer had a red devil with pitchforks on the head of his bass drum. And he played in church, too! Would you believe they had to cover up the head of the drum with newspapers? He'd cover the devil up when he'd go to church.

I had a trio, Lazy Bill and the Blue Rhythm, for about three or four months in 1954 [Figure 4.10]. We were supposed to do four records a year for Chance, but Art Sheridan went out of business and we never heard about it again. We did one record [see CD 1, Track 27].

Well, I didn't keep my group together long. You know it's kind of hard on a small musician to keep a group together in Chicago very long because they run out of work, and when they don't get work to do, they get with other guys. And there were so many musicians in Chicago that some of 'em were underbidding one another. They'd take a job what I was getting twelve dollars for, they'd take it for eight dollars.

Courtesy of Jo Jo Williams.

FIGURE 4.10

Lazy Bill and His Blue Rhythm, studio photo. Chicago, Illinois, 1954. From left to right: Lazy Bill Lucas, James Bannister, "Miss Hi-Fi," and Jo Jo Williams.

I was doing anything, working with anybody, just so I could make a dime. On a record session, any engagement at all. For a while I was working with a disc jockey on a radio station. He was broadcasting from a dry cleaners and he wanted live music on his broadcast. I did it for the publicity; I didn't get any money for that. Work got so far apart. Every time I'd run out of an engagement, it would be a long time before another one came through. And so Mojo and Jo Jo, they had come up here to Minneapolis. They had been working at the Key Club, and they decided they needed a piano player. I wasn't doing anything in Chicago; I was glad to come up here. I had no idea I was going to stay up here, but I ended up here with a houseful of furniture.

Mojo and Jo Jo: George "Mojo" Buford, harmonica player, and Joseph "Jo Jo" Williams, bass player.

©1974 by William Lucas and Jeff Todd Titon. A fuller version accompanies Titon 1974a.

Lazy Bill Lucas and "Poor Boy Blues"

Bill Lucas's account of his life ends in Minneapolis in 1964. The following year I began my graduate studies at the University of Minnesota and met him at a university concert. By that time he had two audiences: the black people on the North Side of the city who still liked the blues, and the white people in the university community. The 1960s was the period of the first so-called **blues revival** (Groom 1971), during which thousands of blues records from the past four decades were reissued on LPs, dozens of older singers believed dead were "rediscovered" and recorded, and hundreds of younger singers, Bill Lucas among them, found new audiences at university concerts and coffeehouses and festivals. The revival, which attracted a predominantly young, white audience, peaked in the great 1969 and 1970 **Ann Arbor (Michigan) Blues Festivals,** where the best of three generations of blues singers and blues bands performed for the more than ten thousand fans who had traveled thousands of miles to pitch their tents and attend these three-day events. Bill Lucas was a featured performer at the 1970 festival. For his appearance he received $400 plus expenses, the most money he ever made for a single job in his musical career.

FIGURE 4.11

Lazy Bill Lucas in his apartment. Minneapolis,
Minnesota, 1971.

In the 1960s and 1970s Bill Lucas could not support himself from his musical earnings. A monthly check (roughly a hundred times the minimum hourly wage) from government welfare for the blind supplemented his income in Minneapolis (Figure 4.11). Most of Minneapolis's black community preferred soul and disco music to blues, while others liked jazz or classical music. Nor was there sufficient work in front of the university folk music audience for Bill. He sang in clubs, in bars, and at concerts, but the work was unsteady. When I was in his band (1969–1971), our most dependable job was a six-month engagement for two nights each week in the "Grotto Room" of a pizza restaurant close to the university. Classified by the musicians' union as a low-level operation, it paid the minimum union scale for an evening's work from 9:00 P.M. to 1:00 A.M.: $23 for Bill, $18 for sidemen. On December 11, 1982, Bill Lucas died. A benefit concert to pay his funeral expenses raised nearly $2,000. Subsequently, he was memorialized by a weekly blues radio show in the Minneapolis bearing his name, while in 2003 the Greater Twin Cities Blues Music Society presented a concert and conference entitled "Remembering Lazy Bill Lucas."

His life history not only gives facts about his life but also expresses an attitude toward it. We can compare both with the words of "Poor Boy Blues" to see whether the song speaks personally for Bill Lucas. Some of the facts of the poor boy's life correspond, but others do not. I asked him whether the line about all the letters in the alphabet looking the same held any special meaning for him, and he said it did. Unless letters or numbers were printed very large and thick, he could not make them out. On the other hand, unlike the poor boy in the song who never saw his father, Lucas and his father were very close. Moreover, his Christmases were happy, and one year he received a piano then. What about the attitudes expressed in the song and in the life history? Neither show self-pity. Bill did not have an illustrious career as a blues singer; he scuffled during hard times and took almost any job that was available. Yet he was proud of his accomplishments. "I just sing the funky blues," he said, "and people either like it or they don't."

"Poor Boy Blues" cannot therefore be understood to speak directly for Bill Lucas's personal experience, but it does speak generally for it, as it speaks for tens of thousands of people who have been forced by circumstances into hard times. Thus, in their broad cultural reach, the words of blues songs tell the truth.

LEARNING THE BLUES

One question that bears on the relation between Lazy Bill Lucas and "Poor Boy Blues" is the authorship of the song. In fact, Lucas did not compose it; St. Louis

Jimmy Oden first put it together and later recorded it in 1942. Lucas learned the song from the record. Learning someone else's song does not, of course, rule out the possibility that the song speaks for the new singer, for he or she may be attracted to it precisely because the lyrics suit his or her experiences and feelings.

In the African American music-culture, almost all blues singers learn songs by imitation, whether in person or from records. There are no formal lessons. In his life history, Lucas tells how he listened to neighbors play guitar and how he tried to make it sound like they did. After he developed a rudimentary playing technique, he could fit accompaniments behind new songs that he learned from others or made up himself.

Unquestionably the best way to come to know a song is to make it your own by performing it. Listen once again to "Poor Boy Blues" (CD 1, Track 26) and concentrate now on the instrumental accompaniment. The guitarists and drummer keep a triple rhythm behind Lucas's singing. When Lucas pauses, the guitar responds with a sequence of single-note triplets (Transcription 4.10).

Transcribed by Jeff Todd Titon.

TRANSCRIPTION 4.10
Rhythmic outline, "Poor Boy Blues."

This triplet rhythm is a common way of dividing the beat in slow blues songs. When accented monotonously, as in many rock and roll tunes from the 1950s, it becomes a cliché. Music students familiar with dotted rhythms (from marches and the like) should resist the temptation to hear this as a dotted rhythm. Recordings of white musicians before World War II attempting to play blues and jazz very often do not flow or "swing," because the musicians are locked into dotted rhythms.

Next listen to the rhythm of Lucas's vocal, and try to feel both rhythms, vocal and accompaniment, at the same time. You might find this attempt difficult. The reason is that Lucas seldom sings squarely on the beat. Transcription 4.11 of his melody is an oversimplification for the sake of readability, but even here we see a great deal of syncopation, in delayed entrances or anticipations of the beat. Lucas is not having a hard time *finding* the beat; on the contrary, he deliberately avoids it.

The musical brilliance of "Poor Boy Blues" rests on the difference between vocal and instrumental rhythms. Accents contrast; at times each part has its own meter. While the accompanying instruments stay in triple meter, Lucas sings in alternating duple and triple. In other words, passages of two-against-three polymeter (especially apparent at the outset of measures 1, 5, and 9 in Transcription 4.11) alternate with passages of three-against-three single meter. I have written 4.11 in $\frac{4}{4}$ to bring out the contrast. One feels that Lucas initiates each vocal phrase in triple meter, then quickly shifts to duple, hurrying his phrasing in imitation of speech rhythm.

In Chapter 3, we saw that two-against-three polymeter characterizes black African music. Here we see a deep connection between African and African American music: rhythmic complexity and polymeter. But our example from the

TRANSCRIPTION 4.11
"Poor Boy Blues," stanza
3, as sung by Lazy Bill
Lucas.

Poor Boy Blues

Lazy Bill Lucas

Recorded and transcribed by Jeff Todd Titon. Minneapolis, Minnesota, May 1970.

blues does not reflect continuous polymeter, as in Africa. Rather, blues music (and jazz, and reggae) *shifts* into and out of polymeter, playfully teasing the boundary. When these shifts occur rapidly, the boundary between single meter and polymeter breaks down. The result is a new sense of time: the graceful forward propulsion we hear as "swing" that makes us feel like moving our whole body in response.

To sing "Poor Boy Blues" as Lucas does, begin by simply *saying* the words (page 167) to get a feel for the speech rhythms. If you read music, use Transcription 4.11 as a guide, but always follow the recording. Listen to the way he slides up to the high G in measures 2, 6, and 10, indicated on the transcription by a solid line just before the note heads. Then hear how he releases "poor" (measure 9) and slides directly afterward into "boy." This sliding and gliding is another type of musical "play," this time with the pitch, not the beat. Finally, listen to him attack the word "twelve" (measures 3 and 7) just ahead of the bar rather than as written.

THE BLUES SCALE

Lucas sings "Poor Boy Blues" in a musical scale I have called the **blues scale** (Titon 1971).

TRANSCRIPTION 4.12
The blues scale (key
signature of G for
convenience).

This scale typifies blues, jazz, spirituals, gospel tunes, and other black American music. An original African American invention, the blues scale also is the most important scale in rock music. It differs significantly from the usual Western diatonic major and minor scales, and it does not correspond to any of the medieval European church modes. The blues scale's special features are the flatted seventh and the presence of both the major and minor third. (Another special feature, seemingly a later development, is the flatted fifth.) A typical use of this double third, sometimes called "blue note" by jazz writers, is shown in measure 8 of Transcription 4.11: Lucas enters on the minor third and proceeds directly to the major third. This is yet another example of "playing" with the pitch in black American music.

If you are a guitarist, you can easily play along with the record by following Transcription 4.11 and reading the chord diagrams in Figure 4.12. Lucas plays "Poor Boy Blues" in the key of G. With the exception of his G and G^7 chords, he employs standard first-position fingering. He prefers the dominant to the dominant seventh (here D instead of D^7) on guitar, but the opposite when he plays piano. He makes most of his single-note runs in the first position, but sometimes he moves up the guitar neck on the first two strings to play the highest notes. If you pick out the accompaniment from the record by ear, you will be learning blues guitar in one of the traditional, time-honored ways.

Lucas accompanies himself on piano in another rendition of "Poor Boy Blues," on *Lazy Bill Lucas*, Philo LP 1007.

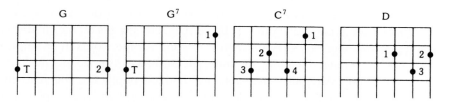

FIGURE 4.12

Guitar chord positions for "Poor Boy Blues."

COMPOSING THE BLUES

Besides learning blues songs from other singers and from records, blues singers make up their own songs. Sometimes they think a song out in advance; sometimes they improvise it during performance. Often a performance embodies both planning and improvisation. The blues song's first composition unit is the line. If you sing the blues most of your life, blues lines will run through your mind like proverbs, which many indeed are: for instance, "You never miss your water till your well runs dry." A male singer might rhyme it with a line like, "Never miss your woman till she say good-bye." (A female singer's rhyme: "Never miss your good man till he say good-bye.") The singer has just composed his stanza:

> You never miss your water till your well runs dry,
> No, you never miss your water till your well runs dry,
> I never missed my baby till she said good-bye.

A blues singer rarely "composes" self-consciously. Instead, lines and stanzas seem to "just come," sometimes in a rush but more often one at a time and widely spaced. The blues singer Booker White called the songs he made up "sky songs": "I have an imaginary mind to do things like that. Didn't have nary a word written down. I just reached up and got 'em" (Evans 1971:253). Another blues singer, Robert Pete Williams, described how his songs came to him:

> The atmosphere, the wind blowing carries music along. I don't know if it affects you or not, but it's a sounding that's in the air, you see? And I don't know where it comes from—it could come from the airplanes, or the moaning of automobiles, but anyhow it leaves an air current in the air, you see? That gets in the wind, makes a sounding, you know? And that sounding works up to be a blues. (Wilson 1966:21)

Statements such as these show the universal aspect of the blues and present the singer as an interpreter of the natural world. The sounding airplane and the moaning automobile trace a human pattern in the surrounding atmosphere that only the gifted interpreter, the translator, the blues singer can hear. When the singer turns it into a song for all to hear, the universal truth is apparent.

If the blues singer plans the stanzas in advance, he or she memorizes them, sometimes writing them down. As we have seen, the stanzas may or may not speak directly for the personal experience of the singer. St. Louis Jimmy, the author of "Poor Boy Blues," said this about another of his songs, "Goin' Down Slow":

> My blues came mostly from women.... "Goin' Down Slow" started from a girl, in St. Louis—it wasn't me—I've never been sick a day in my life, but I seen her in the condition she was in—pregnant, tryin' to lose a kid, see. And she looked like she was goin' down slow. And I made that remark to my sister and it came in my mind and I started to writin' it.... I looked at other people's troubles and I writes from that, and I writes from my own troubles. (Oliver 1965:101–2)

Songs that blues singers memorize usually stick to one idea or event. A memorized song, Lucas's "Poor Boy Blues" has four stanzas on the circumstances leading to the poor boy's cry for mercy. In contrast, the words in an improvised song seldom show the unity of time, circumstances, or feeling evident in a memorized song. After all, unless you have had lots of practice, it is hard enough to improvise rhymed stanzas, let alone keep to a single subject (compare McLeod and Herndon 1981:59 on improvised Maltese song duels). So an improvising singer usually throws in some memorized, traditional stanzas along with stanzas he or she puts together on the spot.

A BLUES SONG IN THE MAKING

Today a few blues songs are improvised in performance, but most are memorized beforehand. This memorization reflects a later trend in the history of the blues and results from the impact of commercial blues records, which began in the 1920s, on singers born after about 1910. Singers who wanted to make records studied them and got the idea that a song ought to last about three minutes (the length of a 78-rpm record) and stick to one theme—as most recorded blues songs did. So they composed and memorized their songs, and they memorized other singers' songs. Of course, they could not avoid learning traditional stanzas and building a mental storehouse of them, but more and more they sang from memory instead of improvising. Today the influence of recordings is overpowering, so singers seldom change lyrics when learning other people's songs. Further, like rock bands trying to "cover" hit records, they copy the instruments, too. In short, most blues singers today think a blues song should have a fixed, not variable, text.

In 1954 Art Sheridan, the owner of Chicago-based Chance Records, asked Lazy Bill Lucas to make a record. During the early 1950s Lucas had played piano as a sideman on several of Homesick James Williamson's recordings, and he was a member of the Blues Rockers, a group with the minor recording hits "Calling All Cows" and "Johnny Mae." For his own session as leader, Lucas was billed as "Lazy Bill and His Blue Rhythm." He chose an original song, "She Got Me Walkin'." Lucas composed the lyrics in advance and memorized them for the recording session.

The first thing you may notice in "She Got Me Walkin'" (CD 1, Track 27) is that the stanza form differs from that of "Poor Boy Blues." In that song Bill Lucas sang a

CD 1:27

"She Got Me Walkin'" (3:01). William "Lazy Bill" Lucas. Performed by Lazy Bill and His Blue Rhythm: Lazy Bill Lucas, piano and vocal; Louis Myers, guitar; Elga Edmonds, drums. Chance 10" 78-rpm record. Chicago, Illinois, 1954.

line, then more or less repeated it, and closed the stanza with a rhyming punch line. Most blues stanzas fall into this three-line pattern, particularly traditional stanzas. But some, like stanzas 2 and 3 of "She Got Me Walkin'," fall into a different line pattern consisting of a *quatrain* (four lines rhymed abcb) and a rhymed two-line *refrain* that follows to close out each stanza (see the Close Listening guide). You can easily hear the contrast between the **three-line stanza** and the **quatrain-refrain stanza.** The quatrain fits four short bursts into the first four measures (bars) of the twelve-bar blues, while the refrain fits into the last eight bars. The quatrain-refrain pattern became popular after World War II. It usually offers vignettes in the quatrain to prove the truth of the repeated refrain. Because any stanza form is by nature preset, it acts as a mold into which the improvising singer pours his or her words. Of course just any words will not do, because the refrain has to repeat, lines must rhyme, and the whole thing has to make sense.

Lucas told me that he thought getting the names of some of his musician friends into "She Got Me Walkin'" would make the song more popular. The uninitiated listener would find the nicknames a little mysterious and might be intrigued. "Snook" was the harmonica player Snooky Pryor. James Williamson had recorded under the name "Homesick James" and was well-known to the people who frequented the Chicago bars and clubs to hear blues. When I asked Lucas whether the lyrics were based on a true story, he replied, "More or less." The "she" of the song turns out to be none other than Johnny Mae, whom Bill had sung about for The Blues Rockers a few months earlier. Johnny Mae was Homesick James's girlfriend.

As Lucas's lyrics show, during the years following World War II blues musicians in Chicago formed a social as well as a musical community. They kept each other company, played on each other's recordings, substituted for one another at various club dates, and both competed with and supported one another in the music business and social world. These relationships persisted for years. For example, Muddy Waters and Howlin' Wolf were rivals. Even as late as 1970, at the Ann Arbor Blues Festival, this rivalry was evident. Waters was scheduled to come onstage after Wolf's set, but Wolf prolonged the set well beyond the agreed-on ending time in a bid to steal time from Waters (Gordon 2002:215–16; Segrest and Hoffman 2004:261–62).

Close Listening

"SHE GOT ME WALKIN'"

CD 1:27

COUNTER NUMBER	COMMENTARY	LYRICS
0:00	Instrumental introduction.	
0:14	Lucas sings verse 1. Interplay among all accompanying instruments.	My baby got me walkin' all up and down the street. My baby got me walkin' all up and down the street.

	Instrumental response to the vocal "calls" (instruments respond when Lucas pauses between phrases and lines).	She left me for another man 'cause she wanted to be free.
0:56	Lucas sings quatrain starting verse 2.	My baby told me one day, And I laughed and thought it was a joke; She said I'm going to leave you, You don't move me no more.
1:09	Refrain, verse 2.	She got me walkin' all up and down the street; She left me for another man 'cause she wanted to be free.
1:35	Lucas speaks, signaling an instrumental break.	"Play it for me, boy."
1:37	Instrumental break.	
2:17	Quatrain starting verse 3. "Snook" is James "Snooky" Prior.	I don't want to see Snook, Not even Homesick James; The way my baby left me, I really believe he's to blame.
2:30	Refrain, verse 3.	She got me walkin' all up and down the street; She left me for another man 'cause she wanted to be free.

Words and music by William Lucas. Used by permission.

The life histories and social ties of blues singers have clearly influenced their music. Our discussion to this point has focused on the lives and songs of blues musicians. The next sections provide a close look at an instrument associated with the early blues. Following the blues tradition of learning by doing, we will begin by learning how to build a one-stringed diddly-bow (see Figure 1.13).

HOW TO MAKE AND PLAY A ONE-STRINGED DIDDLY-BOW

The musical bow, a single string stretched on a frame of some kind, like a hunting bow, is a widespread tribal musical instrument. Related to it is the one-stringed **diddly-bow,** a traditional African American instrument usually strung with thick wire held on supports out from and parallel to a barn wall (see Figure 1.13). Many blues singers who grew up on Southern farms recall it as their first musical instrument (CD 2, Track 1), and rock and roll singer Bo Diddley took his stage name from it.

Despite its simple construction and playing technique, the diddly-bow produces a very satisfactory blues sound. It is easy to build and learn to play it even if you have never built an instrument before. Figure 4.13 provides a list of building materials and a construction diagram for a portable diddly-bow, smaller and handier than the traditional instrument that was affixed to the wall of a barn. You can get free wood from the scrap pile of a sawmill or lumberyard. For a few dollars, any musical instrument store should be able to supply you with a single guitar machine head, some hard plastic material for the bridge and nut, and a steel string. Try to get a banjo string with a "loop end" that will fit easily over the wooden screw at the bridge end of the instrument.

FIGURE 4.13

How to make a portable, one-stringed diddly-bow.

Saw a notch for the nut near one end of the piece of wood, then cut the wood back to the end. Glue a piece of scrap wood to the bottom of the cutaway. Drill a hole for the string anchor pole and attach the machine head to the scrap-wood bottom. Make sure that the top of the string anchor pole is lower than the top of the nut (Figure 4.14).

FIGURE 4.14

Close-up of nut end of diddly-bow.

Glue the nut flush against the notch so that the top of the nut is about $\frac{1}{8}$ inch higher than the string board. Saw a notch for the bridge near the other end of the string board, and glue in the bridge so that it is about $\frac{1}{4}$ inch higher than the string board. Insert a small wooden screw between the bridge and the short end of the string board, leaving about $\frac{1}{16}$ inch clearance between the board and the head of the screw to fit the string loop on. Glue two pieces of scrap wood underneath the string board to serve as a table rest. Attach the loop end of the banjo string over the wooden screw, then push the other end through the machine head anchor pole, taking up most of the slack. Knot the string around the anchor pole and turn the machine head knob, tightening the string until, when you pluck it, it produces the same pitch as the tonic (here, the lowest and most frequently played tone) on One-String Sam's accompaniment for "I Need $100" (CD 2, Track 1). Check the pitch against the recording.

CD 2:1

"I Need $100" (2:59). Performed by One-String Sam, c. 1956. Detroit, Michigan. Reissued on *Detroit Blues: The Early 1950s.* Blues Classics LP, BC-12.

Play your diddly-bow by plucking the string near the bridge with the thumb of one hand. The other hand will slide a smooth device such as a bottleneck, lipstick case, piece of copper tubing, pipe tool, or closed pocket knife atop the string; for now, concentrate on the hand that does the plucking, and leave the sliding hand out of it entirely. Hold the diddly-bow with the heel of your plucking hand falling just between the wooden screw and the bridge; slight pressure will prevent the instrument from moving on the table. Turn your hand counterclockwise and make a half-fist with your fingers loosely tucked so that your thumb is parallel to the string and can pluck the string comfortably in a motion away from your body. Once you have played on your own a bit, listen to the CD track. Use the transcriptions to work out the rhythms, and then learn more about the slide technique.

One-String Sam accompanied himself on a small, portable diddly-bow as he sang "I Need $100" in Detroit in the 1950s (CD 2, Track 1). I could not make out the lyrics of stanza 2 with much confidence (see the Close Listening guide).

Close Listening

"I NEED $100"

CD 2:1

COUNTER NUMBER	COMMENTARY	LYRICS
0:00	Introductory accompaniment on the diddly-bow	
0:05	Sam sings quatrain of verse 1.	You know I talked with mother this morning, mother talked with the judge. I could hear her, eavesdropping, you know I understood their words.
0:17	Sam sings refrain of verse 1. Diddly-bow finishes the line after "You know I . . ." "Go my baby's bond" means pay the bail bond to set my friend free from prison	She said, "I need $100. You know I . . . You know I need $100 just to go my baby's bond."
0:41	Sam sings quatrain of verse 2.	You know me and my little girl got up this morning. She said she wanted to freeze to death. Told her in the icebox to look in, baby I freeze my ice myself.
0:53	Sam sings refrain of verse 2. Again, the diddly-bow ends the first line instrumentally.	I just need $100. I say I need . . . You know I need $100 just to go my baby's bond.
1:13	Sam plays a few extra riffs on the diddly-bow.	

1:23	San sings quatrain of verse 3.	You know I left your mother standing, baby, In her doorway crying. Come begging and pleading don't mistreat your little girl of mine.
1:35	Sam sings refrain of verse 3.	I said, "Mother-in-law I need $100. All I need's . . . All I need $100 just to go my baby's bond."
1:59	Sam takes longer instrumental break; he speaks in the middle of it.	[spoken] Yeah, you know I need your $100.
2:22	Sam sings quatrain of verse 4.	You know my houselady come telling about want to talk for an hour, want to go to the Red Cross people you know want a sack of Red Cross flour.
2:34	Sam sings refrain of verse 4.	I told her all I need's $100. All I need's . . . Baby if I had $100, I could go and go my baby's bond.
2:56	Engineer fades to end.	

The rhythm that One-String Sam uses in "I Need $100" is the same triplet rhythm that Bill Lucas used in "Poor Boy Blues": CHUNG, k'CHUNG, k'CHUNG, k'CHUNG, and so on:

The simplicity of the instrument allows us to invent a diddly-bow notation that shows how to play "I Need $100" or any other song. In the diddly-bow notation each triplet beat will be marked with a box (see Transcription 4.13).

TRANSCRIPTION 4.13
Diddly-bow notation.

The basic rhythm for "I Need $100" comes out like Transcription 4.14.

TRANSCRIPTION 4.14
Basic rhythm, "I Need $100."

CHUNG   k' CHUNG   k' CHUNG

With your thumb plucking away from your body, play the diddly-bow in that rhythm for a while until it is comfortable. If your hand gets cramped, stop and shake it out. Keep it loose; move the whole thumb as a unit, not just the upper part above the knuckle. Come back to playing it every so often, and by the end of a day it will have become second nature.

That is about all there is to the right-hand part (or left-hand part, if you are left-handed) of "I Need $100." The other hand's part is even simpler; in fact, most of the time it does nothing at all while you pluck the tonic as you have just been practicing. At other times it slides a bottleneck or other smooth device along the top of the string to make the whining, zinging sounds you hear on the record.

Traditionally, the diddly-bow is played with a **bottleneck** slide. Any hard object that can be held easily in your hand will serve, but glass makes the best sound. Find a bottle with a cylindrical neck (Figure 4.15). You can find a glass cutter at a hardware store or a specialty shop. Glass cutters give a sure, neat cut, but be careful not to cut yourself. If this traditional method does not appeal to you, you can buy a machine-made one in a store that sell guitars.

Cut about two inches

Cut here

Cylindrical neck

But *not* this kind

FIGURE 4.15

Choosing the right bottle.

Hold the bottleneck comfortably in your hand so you can rest it and slide it gently but firmly up and down the string of the diddly-bow from the nut to the area where your other hand plucks the string. If you press too hard, the string will touch the fingerboard and the sound of the plucked string will be muffled. Gentle pressure gives a clear, ringing tone.

Practice sliding the glass on the diddly-bow. Make certain you have a good grip on the bottleneck so you can take it off the string when playing the tonic and can put it on the string at various locations. Pluck the string as you slide.

Now, find the various simple pitch intervals with the slide on the string (Figure 4.16). The octave will sound when the slide is about halfway between the nut and the bridge. With a pen or pencil, mark this point on the string board with the number 2 (for one-half the distance to the bridge). The perfect fifth will be sounded when the slide is one-third of the distance between the nut and bridge. Mark this point on the string board with a 3. The perfect fourth will be sounded when the slide is one-fourth the distance between the nut and bridge. Mark this point on the string board with a 4. The major third will be sounded when the slide is one-fifth the distance between the nut and bridge. Mark this point with a 5. These will be your reference points for the intervals used in "I Need $100," and of course they will come in handy when you want to play other songs.

FIGURE 4.16

Marking intervals on the diddly-bow.

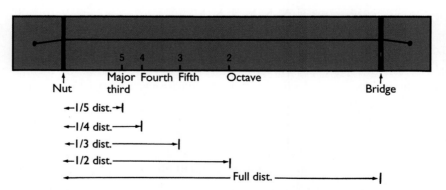

The marks you have just made on your string board will easily be incorporated in our diddly-bow notation to indicate where to place the slide. A dot inside the notation box indicates that the slide is off the string; this is the tonic. A number inside a notation box tells you where to place the slide as you pluck the string with the other hand. Try this:

TRANSCRIPTION 4.15
Four-tone sequence on the diddly-bow.

This four-tone sequence is one of Sam's typical moves in "I Need $100." He plucks the tonic for a count of one triplet, then puts on the slide at 4, plucks the string, and holds the tone for a count of two triplets. Next he moves the slide on the string back to 5—actually, slightly to the nut side of 5, because he uses a neutral rather than a major interval of a third—and plucks the string for a count of one triplet. Finally, he takes the slide off and plucks the tonic for a count of two triplets. Listen to the recording again and pick out the spots where he plays this sequence.

When you have mastered this four-tone sequence, you will be well on your way to Sam's accompaniment for "I Need $100." Transcription 4.16 offers box notation for the accompaniment Sam uses in the first stanza. The wavy lines after 3 and 2 indicate a vibrato, which Sam makes by quickly wiggling the slide back and forth on the string in the general area of the string board mark. Now turn on the recording once again and play along with One-String Sam.

SOCIAL CONTEXT AND THE MEANING OF THE BLUES

Blues is best understood as both a musical form and a feeling. The blues songs we have taken a close look at, "Poor Boy Blues," "She Got Me Walkin'," and "I Need $100," are typical and can bring us toward a structural definition of blues as a song form. Textually, blues songs consist of a series of rhymed three-line or quatrain-refrain stanzas, each sung to more or less the same tune. Blues tunes usually consist of twelve-measure (bar) strophes, and they employ a special scale, the blues scale (Transcription 4.12). They are rhythmically complex, employing syncopation and, at times, differing rhythms between singing and instruments. Many other attributes of blues songs—melodic shape, for instance, or the typical raspy timbre—lie beyond the scope of an introduction but may be followed up elsewhere (see Titon 1994).

Although the emotional aspects of blues are embodied in such musical aspects as the singer's delivery and in the way the musicians "play around" with the blues scale and rhythmic syncopation, the most direct expression of blues feeling comes from the lyrics. Most blues lyrics are about lovers, and they fall into a pattern arising from black American life. The blues grew and developed when most African Americans lived as sharecroppers on Southern cotton farms, subject to segregation, Jim Crow laws, and violence, from late in the nineteenth century until just before World War II, when farm mechanization began to displace the black workers, and factory work at high wages in the Northern cities attracted them (Gussow 2002:5–6). Down home, young men and women did not marry early; they were needed on the farm. If a young woman became pregnant, she had her baby and brought the child into the household with her parents. She did not lose status in the community, and later she often married the father of her child. When a woman did marry young, her partner usually was middle-aged and

TRANSCRIPTION 4.16
Diddly-bow accompaniment for "I Need $100," as played by One-String Sam on CD 2, Track 1.

Transcribed by Jeff Todd Titon.

needed a woman to work and care for his children from a prior marriage. It was good to have plenty of children; when they came of age to work, more hands could go into the cotton and corn fields. Adoption was common; when families broke up, children were farmed out among relatives.

Sociologists and anthropologists, some of them black (such as Charles Johnson), studied this sharecropping culture in the 1920s and 1930s. Interested in patterns of love, marriage, and divorce, the fieldworkers found that partners separated because one could not live with the other's laziness, violence, or adultery. These reasons added up to **mistreatment,** the very word they used. A woman was reported as saying her current lover was "nice all right, but I ain't thinking about marrying. Soon as you marry a man he starts mistreating you, and I ain't going to be mistreated no more" (Johnson [1934] 1966:83). Blues songs reflected these attitudes; mistreatment was the most common subject. Once the subject was established, people began to expect mistreatment as the appropriate subject for blues songs, and although many blues were composed about other subjects, the majority had (and still have) to do with lovers and mistreatment. After World War II the sharecropping culture was less important; the action now took place in the cities where most black people had gone: Atlanta, New York, Washington, Detroit, Memphis, St. Louis, Chicago, Dallas, Houston, Los Angeles, Oakland. But black family patterns per-sisted among the lower classes in the urban ghettos, and so did the blues.

FIGURE 4.17

Howlin' Wolf (Chester Burnett). Ann Arbor Blues Festival, 1969.

Blues lyrics about mistreatment fall into a pattern. The singer casts himself or herself in the role of mistreated victim, introduces an antagonist (usually a mistreating lover), provides incidents that detail the circumstances of the mistreatment, and draws up a bill of indictment. Then, with the listener's tacit approval, the victim becomes the judge, and the drama turns on the verdict: Will he or she accept the mistreatment, try to reform the mistreater, or leave? Resigned acceptance and attempted reform resolve a minority of blues songs. Most often the victim, declaring independence, steps out of the victim's role with an ironic parting shot and leaves. "Dog Me Around," as sung by Howlin' Wolf (Figure 4.17), is typical in this regard.

---

1. How many more years have I got to let you dog me around?
   How many more years have I got to let you dog me around?
   I'd just as soon rather be dead, sleeping way down in the ground.
2. If I treat you right you wouldn't believe what I've said.
   If I treat you right you wouldn't believe what I've said.
   You think I'm halfway crazy; you think I ought to let you have your way.
3. I'm going upstairs, I'm going to bring back down my clothes.
   I'm going upstairs, I'm going to bring back down my clothes.
   If anybody asks about me, just tell 'em I walked outdoors.

Text,
"DOG ME AROUND"

"Dog Me Around," by Howlin' Wolf (Chester Burnett). Copyright © 1974, Modern Music Publishing Co., Inc. Used by permission.

In stanza 1 the singer complains of mistreatment, saying his lover treats him like a dog. We learn in stanza 2 that the singer may also be guilty; "If I treat you right" implies mistreatment on both sides of the relationship. (Stanza 2 could be interpreted

FIGURE 4.18

Dancing at a juke joint.
Alabama, 1957.

Frederic Ramsey, Jr.

as dialogue spoken by the singer's mistreating lover, but without an obvious clue like "she said," point of view seldom shifts in blues lyrics.) The singer resolves the drama in stanza 3 when he declares that he will leave his lover. "Just tell 'em I walked outdoors" is an understatement that shows how little the affair means to him.

Blues music helps lovers understand each other. Because the themes are traditional and shared by the community, blues songs also give listeners community approval for separation in response to mistreatment. The listener who recognizes his or her situation in the lyrics of a blues song receives a good definition of that situation and a possible response to it. At a Saturday night party, or at home alone, a mistreated lover finds consolation in the blues (Figure 4.18).

Of course, mistreatment is not the only theme in blues lyrics. They portray virtually all kinds of relationships among partners. For example, in "Kokomo Blues" (CD 2, Track 2), Fred McDowell (Figure 4.19) sings about a joyful place called "Kokomo" in a way that also describes their relationship.

 CD 2:2

"Kokomo Blues" (2:40). Fred McDowell. Performed by Fred McDowell, vocal and guitar; Jeff Todd Titon, guitar; Mitchell Genova, drums. Field recording by Michael Justen. Minneapolis, Minnesota, July 1970.

McDowell was notable for his rural Mississippi juke-joint guitar style. In contrast to the solo flights of the lead guitar in a typical urban blues or rock band, McDowell's guitar playing is based on short, repeated melodic phrases (**riffs**) whose infectious rhythms are well suited to dancing. His riff-based style of accompaniment with its descending bass line is free of the constraints of bar lines and chord changes, which makes it difficult for the accompanying musicians to anticipate phrase entrances and timings until they get used to playing along with the leader. This is an example of **downhome blues,** or early blues, chiefly sung by men accompanying themselves on acoustic guitar. It is sometimes called "country blues" even though the music was sung and played in cities and by people who grew up there. "Kokomo Blues" dates to the early twentieth century and was revived by R. L. Burnside, Junior Kimbrough, and the Mississippi All-Stars in the 1990s, getting a good deal of attention from alternative-rock fans. While listening to "Kokomo Blues" you may find it hard to keep still. These short repeated riffs put the musicians and dancers into a rhythmic groove. This rhythmic technique can be found in all genres of African American music, including jazz, gospel, soul, disco, and hip-hop. Magic Sam uses a similar riff-based accompaniment in "You Don't Love Me" (CD 2, Track 4).

THE BLUES YESTERDAY

In this chapter we have approached blues as an African American music. And that is historically true: African Americans invented blues music. But many non-African American readers of this book already know something about blues, because blues today extends well beyond the boundaries of the African American music-culture. Today more people recognize the name of the British blues singer-guitarist Eric Clapton than the names of Muddy Waters and Buddy Guy. About thirty-five years ago blues entered mainstream U.S. culture, and in our mass-mediated global village today blues is an attractive commodity. You can hear blues played in Prague, Dar es Salaam, and Tokyo by citizens of Czechoslovakia, Tanzania, and Japan. Nowadays blues is regarded as a universal phenomenon, accessible to all.

It is true that African Americans invented blues, and it is also true that early on people outside the black communities were attracted to it. The white folklorist Howard Odum, for example, collected blues songs in the South prior to 1910. The African American composer W. C. Handy popularized blues in the 1910s with songs such as "St. Louis Blues," but white singers such as

Jeff Todd Titon

FIGURE 4.19

Fred McDowell. Minneapolis, Minnesota, 1970.

Close Listening

"KOKOMO BLUES"

CD 2:2

COUNTER NUMBER	COMMENTARY	LYRICS
0:00	Fred McDowell speaks to introduce the song and cues the band.	[spoken] Now this is "Kokomo." What I'm going to play. The song about the lights. Let's go, guys.
0:07	McDowell begins an introduction with his electric guitar, establishing the descending melodic riff that will accompany the song. Drum and second guitar enter a few seconds later.	
0:15	McDowell stops the riff to tune his low D string for a couple of seconds. His guitar is in G tuning (DGdgbd[1]). He resumes the riff at 0:18.	

0:22	McDowell sings quatrain of verse 1 while the second guitar and drum improvise an accompaniment to fit McDowell's riff.	Well kokomo me baby, kokomo me right, kokomo your daddy, he'll be back tomorrow night.
0:32	McDowell sings refrain of verse 1, alternating the riff with other melodic figures.	Crying, I, Baby don't you want to go. Down to that eleven light city, sweet old Kokomo.
0:57	McDowell sings quatrain of verse 2, with an accompaniment that mimics the vocal melody.	Well, kokomo me baby, kokomo me twice, kokomo your daddy, I'll be back tomorrow night,
1:08	McDowell sings refrain of verse 2, after a few seconds' delay while he plays a different rhythmic riff, then goes back to the descending riff. The other musicians try to follow.	Crying, I, Honey don't you want to go. Down to that eleven light city, sweet old Kokomo.
1:34	McDowell sings quatrain of verse 3.	Well I ain't never loved a ——— Hope I never will; Thisaway you got of loving, crying, [will] get somebody killed.
1:43	McDowell sings refrain of third verse. Again he delays his entrance after "I . . ."	Crying, I, Baby don't you want to go. Down to that eleven light city, sweet old Kokomo.
2:04	McDowell sings quatrain of verse 4.	Well, one and one is two; three and more makes six; Keep messin' around, baby, you're gon' get somebody's trick.
2:13	McDowell sings refrain of verse 4.	Crying, I, Baby don't you want to go. Down to that eleven light city, sweet old Kokomo.
2:37	Engineer fades song out.	

"Kokomo Blues" by Fred McDowell. © 1996 Tradition Music (BMI), administered by BUG. All rights reserved. Used by permission.

Sophie Tucker recorded blues songs before African American singers were permitted to do so. African American blues queens such as Bessie Smith made blues the most popular African American music in the 1920s, attracting a small white audience as well as a large black one. The 1920s also brought the first recordings of downhome blues: Blind Blake, the greatest ragtime guitarist; Charley Patton, a songster regarded as the father of Mississippi **Delta blues** (downhome blues from the Mississippi Delta); and a host of others brought the music out of the local juke joints and house parties and onto recordings that were circulated back into the black communities (Titon 2002:15). Jimmie Rodgers, the first star of country music, whose brief career lasted from 1927 through 1933, sang many blues songs, particularly his "blue yodels."

Rodgers, a white Mississippian, learned many of his songs and much of his relaxed singing style from black railroad men. Blues has remained an important component within country music ever since. African American rhythms, jazz instrumental breaks, and the blues scale were critical in the formation of bluegrass, which ironically is usually regarded as an Anglo-American musical tradition (see Cantwell 1984). Further, the banjo—the quintessential bluegrass instrument—was derived from an African instrument.

Blues has always been a popular form within jazz and remains so today. In the 1930s and 1940s, blues "shouters" such as Jimmy Rushing with Count Basie's orchestra bridged the line between blues and jazz. African American rhythm and blues of the 1940s followed in the tradition of these blues shouters, such as Wynonie Harris, Tiny Bradshaw, and Joe Turner, along with crooners such as Charles Brown. In the meantime an **urban blues** sound arose featuring singers with small bands led by electric guitar. Aaron "T-Bone" Walker (Figure 4.25) invented it in the 1940s, Riley "B. B." (Blues Boy) King made it immensely popular in the 1950s, and it gained strength on the West Coast through singer-guitarists such as Pee Wee Crayton (Figure 4.20). Rock and roll in the 1950s began as a white cover of black rhythm and blues, but by the early 1960s black Americans competed well in that arena, and singers such as Ray Charles and Motown groups like Diana Ross and the Supremes became immensely popular. Ray Charles's biggest hit, "What'd I Say," was a blues song; blues such as "Maybellene" were among Chuck Berry's best-selling recordings; it even became possible for downhome blues singers such as Jimmy Reed, whose "Big Boss Man" climbed high on the pop charts, to cross over into the white music charts.

Blues played a crucial role in British rock during the 1960s. Groups such as the Rolling Stones (whose name came from one of Muddy Waters's songs and whose early albums featured covers of **Chicago blues***) participated in the British blues revival. Dozens of British blues bands could be found in such cities as London and Liverpool, and talented instrumentalists such as John Mayall and Eric Clapton arose from this ferment in the 1960s. An American blues revival in the same decade gave the white musicians Paul Butterfield and Charlie Musselwhite a start, and a new phenomenon appeared: bands whose personnel included a mixture of black and white musicians. Muddy Waters, for example, featured the white harmonica player Paul Oscher and in the 1970s had a white guitarist, Bob Margolin, in his band. Lazy Bill Lucas, the leader of the band I played in during the 1960s, led an integrated band. At the 1970 Ann Arbor Blues Festival, Luther Allison and Johnny Winter sang and played a set together (Figure 1.3).

Jeff Todd Titon

FIGURE 4.20

Pee Wee Crayton in performance at the Ann Arbor Blues Festival, 1969.

---

*While Chicago has been an important blues city ever since the 1920s, "Chicago blues" refers to a sound that arose among musicians who had migrated from Mississippi and were living in Chicago just after World War II. Pioneers of this sound included Muddy Waters, Little Walter, and Howlin' Wolf.

Jeff Todd Titon

FIGURE 4.21

Buddy Guy performs at the
Ann Arbor Blues Festival, 1970.

Since the late 1960s many white American rock bands have covered black blues hits from the 1950s and 1960s. The screaming guitar lines of heavy-metal music are an interpretation (some would say a misinterpretation) of the blues lead-guitar styles of B. B. King, Albert King, Freddy King, Elmore James, and others. Most rock fans do not realize the debt that rock owes to blues and the African American community. But in the 1960s most of black America saw blues as old-fashioned. Outside of strongholds in the Mississippi Delta and Chicago, blues accounted for a small proportion of jukebox records and received little radio airplay. Black intellectuals dismissed blues as a music of resignation, unfit for the contemporary climate of civil rights and black power. **Soul music**—the most popular African American music in the 1960s, recorded for companies like Stax-Volt and Atlantic by artists such as James Brown, Aretha Franklin, and Otis Redding—proved much more attractive. Yet during this same decade many blues singers revived their careers, finding a new audience. The blues revival of the 1960s brought commercially recorded blues music and black musicians before a largely white public in North America and Europe. Buddy Guy, popular today, was active but overshadowed in the 1960s revival (see Figure 4.21).

The revival of the 1960s was in fact a renewal, a reinvigoration of blues, as the older musicians like Howlin' Wolf and Muddy Waters found a new audience. In the film *The Road to Memphis* (2003), B. B. King speaks of his awe at the standing ovation he received at the Fillmore Theatre in San Francisco in 1968 when he sang for this white audience. But in the 1960s it was still possible to speak of blues as a community-based music among the older African Americans who had grown up with it. I had participated in this blues music culture when I got to know and to play music with Lazy Bill Lucas and his friends in Minneapolis in the 1960s. In the 1970s and 1980s that generation passed away while blues fell out of popularity except among a small group of aficionados, largely white, some of whom, like Bonnie Raitt and Stevie Ray Vaughn, became professional blues and rhythm and blues musicians themselves. By the end of the 1980s the movie *The Blues Brothers* had restored blues to the common culture, but in a way that foregrounded white musicians as well as black, with a predominantly white audience, while emphasizing the urban, soul music side of blues. Meanwhile on the downhome end of the blues spectrum, the reissue of the complete recordings of the Delta blues singer-guitarist Robert Johnson fed, and spread, his legend while in the 1990s downhome musicians such as Junior Kimbrough and R. L. Burnside were promoted and achieved success with the alternative-rock audience. The continuing careers of some **source musicians,*** such as John Lee Hooker (Figure 4.22) and B. B. King, coupled with the arrival of new, young black musicians such as Alvin Youngblood Hart, Corey Harris, and Keb' Mo', continued to invigorate this small corner of American vernacular music. By now it was no longer possible to speak of

---

*Elder musicians thought to be authentic by virtue of birthright and participation in the music-culture during its golden age, rather than its present-day revival.

blues as a community-based music among African Americans, as it had been earlier in the twentieth century. Rather, these young black musicians came at the music as revivalists, seeking out recordings and source musicians just as their young white counterparts like myself had done a generation earlier.

Magic Sam, B. B. King, Muddy Waters, and Howlin' Wolf represented variety in the modern electric blues sound, while singers who had made recordings before World War II performed acoustically on the folk music circuit, sounding much as they had decades ago: Roosevelt Sykes, Mississippi John Hurt, Son House, Skip James, John Lee Hooker, Lightnin' Hopkins (Figure 4.23), Big Joe Williams, and Booker White, to name a few. Few blues singer-guitarists were more highly sought after during the 1960s blues revival than Johnny Shines (Figure 4.24), a man with roots in the Mississippi Delta and a direct connection to the legendary bluesman Robert Johnson.

Jeff Todd Titon

FIGURE 4.22

John Lee Hooker and admirer. Ann Arbor Blues Festival, 1970.

FIGURE 4.23

Sam "Lightnin'" Hopkins performs at the Ann Arbor Blues Festival, 1969.

Johnny Shines

Johnny Shines (1915–1992) was born in Frazier, near Memphis, Tennessee. As a teenager he liked to listen to blues records by Charley Patton and Blind Lemon Jefferson; in 1932 he heard Howlin' Wolf in person and bought his first guitar.

> I was sitting and watching Wolf every night—that is every night I could get where he was—all night long, too. Finally one night everything just fell in place and I started playing. I had no lessons or nothing, nobody taught me anything. Even the whole time later when I ran around with Robert [Johnson], he never took the time to show me nothing. I just picked up things as I went along. (Personal communication, 1991)

Shines traveled and played blues with Johnson from about 1935 to 1937. Years later, after Johnson's tragic death, Shines moved to Chicago where he made a few outstanding recordings of his own. Never able to support himself full-time as a musician, he did construction work and quit the music business altogether in the 1950s, but like so many other blues singers he was "rediscovered" and found a new audience among young, white blues aficionados during the 1960s blues revival.

Like Robert Johnson, Shines had a light, tense voice and often pitched his songs at the top of his vocal range, going into falsetto at times. Shines ornamented his vocal melodies more than most blues singers did. His guitar playing, whether acoustic or electric, owed a debt to Johnson and to the early Chicago blues guitarists, but he never developed the solo lead guitar technique of a T-Bone Walker (Figure 4.25) or a B. B. King.

Jeff Todd Titon

Jeff Todd Titon

FIGURE 4.24

Johnny Shines at the Smithsonian Institution's Festival of American Folklife, 1991.

CD 2:3

"From Dark Till Dawn" (3:27). John Ned "Johnny" Shines. Performed by Johnny Shines, vocal and guitar. Field recording by Jeff Todd Titon. Beloit, Wisconsin, March 1970. (Background noise from the audience is audible.)

The subjects of Shines's lyrics were more varied than those of most singers. Listen now to his version of a blues that he told me he learned from a relative: "From Dark Till Dawn" (CD 2, Track 3). Shines's lyrics offer an example of "signifying" a way of speaking or writing indirectly about something, using figurative language in a code whose key is hidden from some listeners. It can be as simple as a euphemism for sex ("How do you want your rollin' done?") or a boast ("I'm gonna build me a mansion out on some old lonesome hill"). In blues, signifying can involve coded language for sex but it also takes the form of ironic understatement or overstatement directed at lovers, bosses, or both. In Baby Doo Caston's field holler (CD 1, Track 24), the lyrics refer to the boss as "captain," a word that sounds respectful to the boss whereas among the black community it is understood to be sarcastic.

Language codes are not limited to Africans or African Americans; coded speech characterizes any group that feels oppressed or that wants to hide something from others nearby. Adolescents, criminals, working-class people—these, for example, have their own particular vocabulary and ways of communicating meaning that are hidden from adults, police, or bosses. Down east Maine natives who serve tourists and summer people vacationing from New York and Boston sometimes call a wealthy man from away "cappy" (short for "captain") with a similar kind of irony that Baby Doo Caston sings in the field holler, but the man from away doesn't understand the double meaning. Within African American communities, signifying developed into a fine art. Woven into the thread of black music, whether in the spirituals, blues, jazz, or hip-hop, it has been an effective survival mechanism.

Although mistreatment is the subject of most blues lyrics, others boast of the singer's talents as a lover. Songs like Muddy Waters's "Hoochie-Coochie Man" are filled with bravado, and at first glance "From Dark Till Dawn" seems to fall into the same category. But if you think about the lyrics more carefully (see the Close Listening guide), you realize that the point of the first stanza is not so much that the singer is a capable lover, but that he is sensitive enough to want to please his lover, even if it takes all night. Further, the second stanza admits the possibility that he might not be pleasing to all women. The third, on the other hand, is a boast; yet it is the boast of someone standing in a line of tradition, crediting his father, who showed him what it meant to love a woman. In this context "love" becomes more than simply "rolling from dusk till dawn."

Of all the blues musicians I met, Shines was the most artistically self-conscious. He was thoughtful and articulate about his musical compositions, his career, and his place in blues history. Performing was difficult for him; it required great effort. At the Wisconsin Delta Blues Festival, where I recorded him singing "From Dark Till Dawn"

Close Listening

"FROM DARK TILL DAWN"

CD 2:3

COUNTER NUMBER	COMMENTARY	LYRICS
0:00	Shines speaks introduction to song.	[spoken] This is a very old song. This is a song that my mother's cousin used to sing when I was a little bitty—well, it don't have to be that old though, do it!—I was just a little fellow, you know. I used to stand in the field and listen to her sing this song, you know. And I thought it sounded so pretty, and I didn't forget it.
0:25	Shines plays the song's melody on the guitar as an instrumental introduction.	
1:03	Shines sings verse 1. Verses are in the AAB form, not the quatrain-refrain form.	Won't you tell me, mama, how you want your rollin' done? Won't you tell me, mama, how you want your rollin' done? I'm gonna please you, mama, if I have to roll from dusk to dawn.
1:41	Shines sings verse 2.	I'm gonna build me a mansion out on some old lonesome hill, I'm gonna build me a mansion out on some old lonesome hill, Where if one woman don't like it, there'll be a hundred and five that will.
2:12	Shines plays the song's melody as an instrumental break between verses.	
2:46	Shines sings verse 3.	Well, I was born in Tennessee, down on a cotton farm. I'm my daddy's own child; I am his only son. Well, he taught me how to love; and I swear that is a job well done.

"From Dark Till Dawn," words and music by John Shines. © Uncle Doris Music, ASCAP. Used by permission.

in 1970, he told me he was resentful that more blues fans were interested in what he could tell them about the legendary Robert Johnson than in Shines's own compositions and performance. Irony was his way of dealing with that situation. He would not always tell interviewers the right answers to their questions.

FIGURE 4.25

Action at the Ann Arbor
Blues Festival, 1969, which
took place on the same
weekend as the legendary
rock festival in Woodstock,
New York. Big Mama
Thornton sings while
T-Bone Walker plays guitar.

Jeff Todd Titon

He invited me to visit him at his home in Alabama, and when I did so a few
months later, he was much more relaxed than when he had been on the road. He
showed me portions of the autobiography he was writing; he spoke with conviction
about racism in the record industry. He listened patiently while I played some pieces
on my guitar for him, and he gave me a few suggestions about how to make them
better. A year before his death in 1992, I spent a week with him at the Smithsonian
Folklife Festival, where he was a featured artist. In the last years of his life he used his
music to help educate people (black people in particular) about black history. He
found it unsettling that white America had adopted blues music as its own. The
festival was a good vehicle for him because in this museum setting he could present
his ideas on how African Americans must look to black music as a primary resource
in order to understand black history in a racist society.

Magic Sam

Blues has its share of heroes and heroines who died too young. John Lee (Sonny Boy)
Williamson, stabbed to death in Chicago in 1947, was an outstanding singer and
blues harmonica player. Robert Johnson, poisoned in his twenties by his girlfriend's
jealous husband, would have changed the course of blues history had he lived. As it
was, although he had only two recording sessions, his impact on post–World War II
Chicago blues was immense. We turn now to the music of another Mississippi-born
blues singer-guitarist who died before his time: Magic Sam (Sam Maghett, 1937–
1969). His first instrument was the diddly-bow. As a young teenager he moved to
Chicago with his family. His club and record career began in the 1950s when he was
still a teenager. After a stint in the armed services, he returned to the clubs on the
West Side of Chicago, where his generation of musicians was moving Chicago blues
toward soul—the music of James Brown, Otis Redding, Aretha Franklin—the most
popular African American music of the 1960s. Magic Sam recorded three albums for
Delmark in Chicago, where he had made a reputation for his soaring vocals and
flashy guitar playing. But those who had heard him in the clubs said these studio
albums failed to capture the brilliance of his live performances.

Magic Sam's luck changed abruptly at the 1969 Ann Arbor Blues Festival in Michigan (Figure 4.25). B. B. King, Howlin' Wolf, Muddy Waters, Albert King, John Lee Hooker, Freddy King, James Cotton, Big Mama Thornton, Otis Rush, T-Bone Walker, Lightnin' Hopkins—virtually all the major contemporary blues artists performed at this three-day affair. Roosevelt Sykes, Big Joe Williams, Sleepy John Estes, and Son House represented an older generation whose careers had begun before World War II. Luther Allison, Jimmy Dawkins, and Magic Sam were among those representing the future. It was a huge "cutting" contest, as each artist tried to outdo the others. Writing about this event, the blues critic John Fishel concluded, "If one set [stood] out as surpassing all others in excitement and virtuosity, it [was] Magic Sam's" (Fishel 1981).

It was Sunday afternoon, August 3, the last day of the festival, about three o'clock—not prime time. Casual in the extreme, Sam arrived a half-hour late. He had to borrow a drummer from another band. Yet somehow in the performance they came together at the highest heat. It was all the more remarkable because of the sparse instrumentation: guitar, bass, and drums. Yet Magic Sam was no ordinary guitarist. On "You Don't Love Me" (CD 2, Track 4) recorded at the festival from the audience, Sam played his guitar as both a lead and rhythm instrument, catching a riff that both hearkened back to the deepest blues of the Mississippi Delta and pointed forward to the grooves of the future. Over it all Sam's voice carried effortlessly to the audience of ten thousand, who picked up the groove and, as if lifted to their feet by some unseen force, danced for the remaining twenty minutes of his set.

This is truly a masterful performance (see the Close Listening guide). It's unfortunate that the only two recordings made of it (or of Sam's entire set, heard on Delmark CD DE-645, *Magic Sam Live*) were from the audience. Yet despite the poor technical quality of the recording, we can hear just what caused the audience to respond as if in a single body. First there is Sam's unerring groove and rhythmic sense, matched perfectly by his band. Second, by alternately playing both lead and rhythm styles of guitar, Sam controls the groove better than if he had a second guitarist. Third, Sam's riff (compare it with Fred McDowell's) is based in the Delta boogie riffs and owes something to the songwriter-guitarist who first recorded it (Willie Cobbs), but Sam has sped it up and, by playing it for hundreds of hours in bars and clubs, he has perfected its rhythms until they are second nature. Fourth, Sam's melodic playing behind (and interplay with) his singing is inventive and extremely effective, both foregrounding the melody and responding to it. His string-bendings to change the pitch are perfectly timed to the rhythms in the melody, while his timbral changes during the riffs (achieved by damping the strings with his left hand) add to the interest of the piece and make Sam sound like the one-man band that, in the West Side bars of Chicago where he played, he frequently was. Finally, his voice just floats over the instruments, in a time zone of its own. The crowd responded instinctively and joyfully. While anyone can appreciate this performance, knowledgeable blues guitarists listening to Sam here will shake their heads in amazement and smile broadly in recognizing Sam's great achievement, one that carried throughout the entire festival set. The blues journalist and producer Dick Shurman later wrote about Magic Sam as a postmodern master:

> His music had roots in the boogie he loved and in the tension and challenge created by the distraction of a noisy, bustling bar. He was able, par excellence, to turn the response of the audience into a foil and a force in the music. Partly because of his reliance on whatever equipment was available (like amps without

CD 2:4

"You Don't Love Me" (3:35). Lyrics by Willie Cobbs. Performed by Magic Sam (Sam Maghett), vocal and guitar; Sam Lay, drums; unknown bass player. Field Recording by Jeff Todd Titon. Ann Arbor, Michigan, August 1969.

Close Listening

"YOU DON'T LOVE ME"

CD 2:4

COUNTER NUMBER	COMMENTARY	LYRICS
0:00	Fade into Magic Sam playing the riff, twice.	
0:06	Magic Sam sings last two lines of verse 1, playing melody while he sings each line and playing the riff twice after each line, varying the timbre and volume both electronically and by damping the strings with his left hand.	Ah, ah, ah, you don't love me yes I know. But since you have left me, baby, now I have no place to go.
0:30	Magic Sam sings verse 2, playing melody while he sings each line and playing the riff after each line. Drummer Sam Lay responds to the guitar licks and varies the timbre of his drum sounds.	Yes I love you and I'll do anything you say. Yes I love you and I'll do anything you say. And if you will love me, baby, I'll get on my knees and pray.
1:07	Magic Sam repeats verse 1. His voice floats high on the word "love."	Ah, ah, ah, you don't love me yes I know. Ah, ah, ah, you don't love me yes I know. But since you have left me, baby, now I have no place to go.
1:40	Magic Sam shouts "Oh yeah," signaling that an instrumental break is coming.	
1:43	Magic Sam plays the verse on his electric guitar, varying the timbre and volume greatly to distinguish the melody from the riff.	
2:19	Magic Sam repeats verse 1.	
2:53	Ending: Magic Sam repeats the last line of the verse with variations. The meaning of the last line changes in a new context. He accompanies these lines with the riff.	I don't have no place to go Lord, I don't have no place to go. Don't you know that I love you, but I don't have no place to go. Won't you find me a place to go, Won't you find me a place to go.
3:25	Coda: Magic Sam signals the end of the song with a formulaic melody and a change of timbre.	

reverb units and borrowed guitars) and partly because of the loose circumstances and the long nights (usually playing until 4 A.M.), Magic Sam was a world apart from the studio's time limits, structures, and formulas. (1981)

Sam's career took off immediately after Ann Arbor. In the next month he toured the European blues clubs, a sure sign that he had arrived. But on December 1, 1969, he died of a heart attack. He was thirty-two years old.

THE BLUES TODAY

For an example of contemporary blues, we turn to a masterpiece by an older singer, Otis Rush (Figure 4.26). "Ain't Enough Comin' In" was voted the outstanding blues recording of the year 1994 by the readers of *Living Blues* magazine. This piece, which Rush wrote and arranged, is as outstanding a performance of contemporary urban blues as can be heard today, more than ten years after it was recorded.

FIGURE 4.26

Otis Rush performing at the Ann Arbor Blues Festival, 1969. Note that he plays left-handed.

    Listen now to CD 2, Track 5. The song starts with an authoritative drumbeat, and immediately the electric bass sets a heavy rhythmic riff that repeats until the end of the song, changing pitch when the chords change. In its rhythmic constancy the bass provides something akin to the bell pattern in *Agbekor* (see Chapter 3) that anchors the entire performance. The drummer plays simply but forcefully and unerringly, marking the beat 1–2–3–4, with the accent on 3. A rock drummer would be busier than this— and a lot less relentless. The electric bass is louder than the drums, which is characteristic of black popular music since the 1970s.

    Listeners who can recognize the difference between major and minor chords will realize that this is a minor blues, built on the minor i-iv-v chords instead of the major ones. The first chorus is instrumental (see the Close Listening guide). Rush plays the electric guitar lead above a riffing rhythm section that includes a trumpet and saxophone as well as an organ. The direct, spare playing here sets a somber mood for his powerful vocals that follow. The song features a bridge section ("Now when it's all over...") that departs from the usual twelve-bar blues pattern, but you will recognize that otherwise (except for the minor key) the song has a typical blues structure. After the vocals Rush takes the tune twice through with a guitar solo, and this is followed by two choruses in which a saxophone leads, taking some of Rush's ideas and developing them. The bridge returns, followed by two more verses, and Rush takes it out with one more instrumental chorus. Hear how the sound of the guitar vibrates at the beginning of the last chorus. This is a *tremolo,* and Rush is known for getting this effect by pushing his fingers from side to side on the strings (a hand tremolo) rather than using the tremolo bar attached to the electric guitar.

    Rush's vocal style is striking. Like many blues singers he hoarsens his voice at times to show great emotion, but he also makes his voice tremble at times, an effect that mirrors his guitar tremolo (and vice versa). Blues writers have called Rush's voice "tortured" with a "frightening intensity" and a "harrowing poetic terror" (Rowe 1979:176) and "tense and oppressive" (Herzhaft 1992:300). There is

CD 2:5

"Ain't Enough Comin' In" (5:53). Otis Rush. Performed by Otis Rush on *Otis Rush: Ain't Enough Comin' In.* Mercury CD 314518769-2. 1994.

Close Listening

"AIN'T ENOUGH COMIN' IN"

CD 2:5

COUNTER NUMBER	COMMENTARY	LYRICS
0:01	Instrumental introduction.	
0:09	Rush's guitar takes the lead and is accompanied by the band for one verse.	
0:35	Rush sings first verse, with band accompanying.	Oh, I ain't got enough comin' in to take care of what's got to go out. It ain't enough love or money comin' in, baby, to take care of what's got to go out. Like a bird I got my wing clipped, my friends; I've got to start all over again.
1:02	Rush sings second verse.	If the sun ever shine on me again, Oh lord if the sun ever shine on me again. Like a bird I got my wing clipped, my friends; I've got to start all over again.
1:28	Bridge section (third verse)-different melodic and harmonic structure.	Now when it's all over and said and done, money talks and the fool gets none. The tough get tough and the tough get goin'; come on baby let me hold you in my arms.
1:46	Rush sings fourth verse while band continues to back him up as in the second verse.	It ain't got enough comin' in to take care of what's got to go out. Ain't enough love or money comin' in, baby, to take care of what's got to go out. My friends, I got my wings clipped; I've got to start all over again.
2:12	Rush takes the lead on the electric guitar for an entire verse, accompanied by the band.	
2:38	Rush continues to play an instrumental lead for another verse. Listen to how he "bends" the pitch of some notes by pushing the string to the side.	
3:05	Tenor saxophone lead for a verse; notice the deliberately raspy, buzzy tone.	
3:31	Tenor sax lead for another verse.	

3:57	Rush repeats bridge (third verse).	When it's all over and said and done, money talks and the fool gets none. The tough get tough and the tough get goin'; come on baby let me hold you in my arms.
4:16	Rush sings sixth verse.	Ain't got enough comin' in to take care of what's got to go out. It ain't enough love or money comin' in, baby, to take care of what's got to go out. Like a bird I got my wings clipped, my friends; I've got to start all over again.
4:40	Rush sings seventh verse.	If you don't put nothing' in you can't get nothin' out; You don't put nothin' in, baby, you can't get nothin' out; Like a bird I got my wings clipped, my friends; I've got to start all over again.
5:07	Rush plays instrumental lead guitar to ending fade out. Notice the vibrating guitar (hand tremolo).	

"Ain't Enough Comin' In" written by Otis Rush. © 1994 Otis Rush Publishing (BMI)/Administered by BUG. All Rights Reserved. Used by permission.

no denying that Rush has a full, powerful voice. Its vehemence and falling melodic curve may remind you of the Navajo Yeibichai singers (Chapter 2).

Rush's lyrics are clever and subtle. In the beginning of his career he relied on the professional songwriter Willie Dixon, but after his first hit songs he decided that he could "write one better than that" (Forte 1991:159). When I hear the first line, I think "ain't enough comin' in" refers to money; but in the second line Rush lets me know that I should think of the parallel between love and money: The singer feels that he's giving too much and not getting enough of either in return.

Who is Otis Rush? Is he the latest singer-guitarist to capitalize on the blues revival of the 1990s? Not at all: Otis Rush has been a blues legend since the 1950s, well-known to musicians and serious blues aficionados if not to the general listening public. Stevie Ray Vaughn named his band Double Trouble in honor of Rush's finest song from that decade. Led Zeppelin covered Rush's "I Can't Quit You Baby," with the guitarist Jimmy Page lifting Rush's instrumental break note-for-note (Forte 1991:156). Rush's guitar playing turned Eric Clapton into a disciple. When Rush met Clapton in England in 1986 he called Clapton a "great guitar player" and modestly went on, "Everybody plays like somebody. It's good to know that somebody's listening. To me, I'm just a guitar player. I'm not trying to influence nobody, I'm just trying to play, and play well. And hopefully I can sell some records" (Forte 1991:161).

Otis Rush was born in Philadelphia, Mississippi, in 1934 and began playing at age ten. Left-handed, he plays the guitar upside-down, with the bass strings closer to the ground; this accounts for some of his special sound (see Figure 4.26). For example, to "bend" a note on the treble strings, Rush pulls the string down, whereas a right-handed guitarist must push the string up (harder to do). Like Bill Lucas, he first sang country music, not blues. It was not until the late 1940s, when he came to Chicago and began visiting the blues clubs, that he decided to sing and play the blues.

Although B. B. King, T-Bone Walker, and Magic Sam were among the musicians who influenced him most strongly, Rush developed his own version of modern blues guitar. His style is subtle, spare, cool—the instrumental equivalent of caressing a lover. There is nothing egotistical about it, no showing off. His use of silence is brilliant. "Well, I can play fast stuff, but I try to take my time and make you feel what I'm doin'," he told Jas Obrecht. "You can play a bunch of notes so fast, but then you turn around, and somebody out there listening says, 'What did he play?' Sound good, but can't remember nothin'. Take your time and play. Measure it out enough where they got time to hear what you're doing" (2000:243). Like a fine aged wine at its peak, at its best his music has great presence, neither understated nor flashy: substantial, direct, powerful, and commanding respect.

Rush takes risks onstage and in recordings. Often he would rather try something new than stick with the same old thing. "I can make that guitar say what you sayin' right now," Rush told Obrecht. "I can say The Lord's Prayer on my guitar and you'll say, 'That's every word of it.' Just like you talkin' there? I can make my guitar say just what you said. . . . I can sing with my guitar, just like I sing with my voice" (2000:243). Rush's guitar isn't merely imitating his vocals. It replies to them and extends them, in another example of the African call-and-response aesthetic. The album from which "Ain't Enough Comin' In" is taken represented a long-overdue turning point in Rush's career. He is, today, one of the very best of the older generation of blues singer-guitarists, a generation whose music was formed prior to the blues revival of the 1960s.

A Few Final Words

At the turn of the millennium, blues became swept up in the **roots music** phenomenon, as the term *folk music* no longer seemed useful as a descriptive or marketing category to describe twenty-first-century American vernacular and ethnic musics that had long outgrown the classic "folk" characteristics (see Chapter 5). "Blues, hillbilly, country, zydeco, Cajun, Tejano, Native American, and rockabilly" were the major early forms of roots music according to Robert Santelli and Holly George-Warren (2002:12). To that list we can add gospel, jazz, rhythm and blues, and bluegrass, as well as polka, klezmer, Irish, and various musical expressions of different American ethnic groups. Whereas folk music was associated with rural farm villages, roots music matured in cities; whereas folk musicians learned their craft primarily from family and neighbors, roots musicians embraced the commercial recording culture that began recording American vernacular music in the 1920s and gradually spread local and regional styles across the nation. Whereas folk musicians were largely illiterate and without much formal education, roots musicians, particularly in the late twentieth century, were literate and educated, even if they did not have formal musical training. In addition, the folk musician traditionally regarded the music she or he played as the music of the community; it did not require labeling according to genre—it was simply "music" or "our music." The roots musician, on the contrary, is well aware of genre and style, usually makes a living from music (or hopes to do so), and "is conscious of being part of the American music tradition. Often he or she feels a personal responsibility to carry on that tradition" (Santelli and George-Warren 2002:13). This self-conscious identification with a tradition and a desire to perpetuate it is not a characteristic of the musician in a folk society, whose music is an expression of its time and place. Finally, according to Santelli and George-Warren, "The roots artist writes and sings songs that reflect such themes as gender and class relationships, regional and historical issues, and racial and ethnic tensions" (Ibid.). The researchers' language reflects this shift from folk to roots. Whereas the early blues artist Son House (b. 1902) told me he sang about "men and women and the troubles they have getting along with each other," the contemporary roots music-culture thinks that blues are about "gender and class relationships." This self-reflexivity reflects the postmodern quality of the roots music movement. Yet marketing blues as a roots music has its drawbacks. Claiming that blues is important chiefly because it shaped and influenced what came after it relegates blues to the past.

Consider what happens once any musical genre has been popularized by the mass media, written about, studied, and defined. Some of that interpretive activity is carried back to performers, and people come to expect the music to conform to those definitions. Record producers, promoters, writers, and lately scholars are partly responsible for codifying the rules of the blues genre. Few of them were raised in African American communities. How, once standardized, can blues music change and grow, yet still remain blues? Must singers stay with the old forms, changing only their contents—new wine in old bottles; new lyrics, new instrumentation, in old settings? Must festival promoters choose blues singers on the basis of how well they conform to the genre? Should a folklore police enforce the rules?

Today's most active blues music-culture is in Chicago, a city with a history of great hospitality to the blues (see Grazian 2003), where blues is presented to tourists in highly mediated forms. Dozens of blues clubs may also be found in such cities as Houston; St. Louis; Memphis; Clarksdale, Mississippi; Oakland–San Francisco; and Detroit. Well-known blues singers such as B. B. King and Buddy Guy tour nationally and, sponsored by the U.S. Department of State, as goodwill ambassadors abroad.

Not long ago I was at a club in Chicago and heard a woman blues singer with a powerful voice, backed by a four-piece band. It turned out she had studied voice in preparation for the opera, then decided she would have a better career singing blues. Do these historical, economic, and audience changes mean we should abandon our music-culture models (Chapter 1) in the face of real-world complications? No, but we need to keep in mind that it is a *model*, an ideal. Music-cultures are not isolated entities—they respond to economic, artistic, and interpretive pressures from without as well as within. Their histories reveal that response to these pressures; "catching" or defining a music at any given time comes at the expense of the long view.

www Book Companion Website

You will find tutorial quizzes, Internet links, and much more at the Book Companion Website for *Worlds of Music,* Fifth Edition, at
academic.cengage.com/music/titon/worlds_5

Europe/Central and Southeastern Regions

TIMOTHY J. COOLEY

On a chilly February afternoon in **Podhale,** a region in the alpine Tatra Mountains of southern Poland, a young couple climbs into a horse-drawn carriage and joins a procession from the village church to the village firehouse, where two large rooms have been rented for a banquet and dance (Figure 5.1). It is their wedding, a full day and night with a sequence of rituals beginning at the groom's house, then processing to the bride's house (which in this case is replaced by a larger rented hall at the village firehouse), to the local Roman Catholic church, and then back to the bride's house or rented hall for a banquet, dancing, and several additional ritual ceremonies. The wedding celebration continues throughout the night. In many cases, the wedding party and guests will return to the bride's house or rented hall for several more nights of celebrating, including nearly constant live music and dancing.

Listen to CD 2, Track 6, recorded during the procession of the wedding couple from church to banquet hall. The first part of the recording features the singing of two ceremonially dressed men (Figure 5.2) who lead the procession on horseback, singing at the top of their lungs. These two men are called *pytace* (askers, announcers, criers), and they are hired for their ability to sing and ride well. First we hear the horses' hooves on the road, then the *pytace* singing as they pass by the microphone. In the middle of their song we hear clanking sounds made by two local boys dressed up as Romani (Gypsy) beggars, beating metal pails with sticks as they demand tips from the wedding party. The boys have stretched a rope across the road—a gate that they will not open unless they are paid. The *pytace* respond with a sung threat (all in jest) before bribes are paid and the gate is removed. You may have noticed a low rumble at the beginning of the track; this was caused by wind in the microphone. The audio for this track comes from a video of the procession recorded outdoors on a breezy day with a handheld camcorder. Ethnomusicologists often conduct fieldwork alone, carrying and operating their own equipment (video and still cameras, audio recorders, notebooks, micophones, and so forth). The results are rarely "studio quality," but they can capture some of the spirit (and noise) of the moment (see Chapter 11 for more on doing this sort of research).

The *pytace* are followed by the carriage with bride and groom, which is immediately followed by a horse-drawn wagon bearing a regional-style string band

CD 2:6

Wedding procession (1:33). Singers (*pytace*) Stanisław Krupa and Jan Krzeptowski-Sabała; string band consisting of Stanisław Styrczula-Masniak, lead violin; Sebastian Karpiel-Bułecka, lead violin; Jurek Niton, second violin; Andrzej Frączysty, second violin; Henryk Krzyptowski-Bochač, second violin; and Tadeusz Styrczula-Maśniak, *basy*. Field recording by Timothy J. Cooley. Olcza, Poland, 1995.

205

FIGURE 5.1

Carriage carrying bride
Wioleta Karpiel-Replon,
groom Andrzej Skupien,
and family members
between the church
ceremony and the wedding
banquet, village of Olcza,
Poland, 1995.

Timothy J. Cooley

FIGURE 5.2

Pytace Stanisław Krupa and
Jan Krzeptowski-Sabała
leading the wedding pro-
cession, village of Olcza,
Poland, 1995.

Timothy J. Cooley

playing music as they ride (Figure 5.3). On the second half of the CD track, you will hear this band as they pass by my microphone (see the Close Listening guide). Several other carriages convey members of the wedding party and relatives of the bride and groom while guests follow on foot or in cars. The sonic image of the recording captures this festive occasion with the sounds of horses, ersatz "Gypsies," people talking excitedly while walking, and the occasional automobile. Although important, the music serves as only one part of the complex soundscape represented on this field recording.

Timothy J. Cooley

FIGURE 5.3

Musicians playing while riding in a horse-drawn wagon in the wedding procession, village of Olcza, Poland, 1995.

Close Listening

WEDDING PROCESSION

CD 2:6

COUNTER NUMBER	COMMENTARY/TEXT	TRANSLATION*
0:00	Sounds of horses' hooves and wind in the microphone	
0:02	*Pytace* singing	
	Łotwórz ze siy łotwórz	Open, open
	Ej, ty cygańsko bramo	Gypsy gate
	Jak siy nie łotwórzys	If you do not open
	Ej, bedziys porombano	You will be chopped up
	(Clanking of sticks on pails, the string band and other procession noises audible.)	
0:42	String band, riding in a horse-drawn wagon, draws closer to the audible foreground.	
0:52	Beginning of a melodic phrase (*nuta*, or note) and ostinato pattern by the string band.	
1:08	Beginning of a variation on the melodic phrase and ostinato pattern by the string band in audible foreground.	

*All Polish song texts were transcribed and translated with the help of Anna Gąsienica-Byrcyn, Marcin Gąsienica-Byrcyn, Anna Styrczula-Maśniak, and/or Dorota Dutsch.

Most of you reading this book have been to a wedding, maybe even to a Roman Catholic wedding like the one described here. However, the musical practices were probably quite different. Looking at the photos and hearing the music, would you be able to identify the event as a wedding procession if you had not read this description? If so, your conclusions may have been based on what you saw instead of what you heard. For example, you might have picked up on the use of the color white, which is symbolic of a bride in many parts of Europe, though not in all European traditions. Look again at Figure 5.1. The two horses pulling the bride and groom are white; all other horses in the procession are brown or black. Though partially covered by a dark fleece coat, the bride is wearing a white dress, the white ribbon from her wreath drapes over her right shoulder, and she is carrying a bouquet of white flowers. Now look at the groom. Note that the capelike jacket over his shoulders is tied with a white ribbon (traditionally cut from the same stock as the bride's wreath). All the other men who wear similar capes, such as the musicians seen in Figure 5.3, tie them with red ribbons. Even if you had not been told that this was a wedding, the attention focused on a young couple and the emphasis on the color white may have given you that idea.

In most societies weddings serve as excellent places to experience music. They tend toward the traditional, are often religious, bring together several generations of two families, and can be quite nostalgic. As such, the music at weddings must accommodate the needs of solemn ritual and a celebratory party, the young and the old, as well as ideas about tradition and new beginnings. Taken as a whole, wedding music says much about a people's history, belief systems, and ideas about community, family, and place.

Yet, is the music one experiences at a wedding necessarily "wedding music"? In many societies, the answer would be both yes and no. For example, the music most associated with weddings in America is a composition by Richard Wagner known as the "Bridal Chorus" from his opera *Lohengrin,* first produced in 1850. Think of the lyrics "Here comes the bride, all dressed in white..." and you may be able to recall the tune. Even without the lyrics, when you hear the tune, you probably think of weddings. On the other hand, much of the rest of the music you are likely to encounter at a wedding in America consists of popular or religious songs and tunes that are usually not specific to weddings. The same music may be used in other contexts and does not symbolically reference a wedding.

Though a few stages of weddings in the Tatras feature music considered specific to wedding rituals, nothing about the music on CD 2, Track 6—other than the text sung by the men on horseback—makes it unique to weddings. The musical sounds on this track can be divided into two general categories. First we hear the unaccompanied, unmetered singing of the *pytace.* Such singing by a pair of men on horses suggests a wedding, but the same stylized, drawn-out, loud singing is used in other ceremonial occasions, not just weddings. The *pytace* are doing their job well by bringing attention in a particularly striking way to an important event, but without understanding the text we cannot know for certain that the event is a wedding. The second musical sounds on the same CD track are of the string band as they pass by in their special wagon during the wedding procession. Their instrumental music is metered, in contrast to the criers' singing, and there is no musical hint in what they play that this is music for a wedding. For both the songs and the instrumental music, the context determines the function of the music. (See Chapter 1 for more on meter.)

This brief sketch from a wedding in Poland illustrates several themes important to this chapter as well as the book. First is the great *diversity of cultural practices* found within Europe. Many wedding rituals throughout the continent are similar in structure, yet the musical practices essential to the wedding ritual vary greatly. Even among people who share the same religion, the music they associate with weddings may be completely different. The Poles married in our example are Roman Catholic, but their wedding shared no music with a comparable wedding among Roman Catholics in either Italy or Ireland, for example. Further, with the exception of some of the music used in the church itself, the music at this wedding in the Polish Tatras is even unlike wedding music in other regions of Poland.

The second theme is *cultural context.* Context is essential for understanding the function and meaning of musical sounds. The musical sounds on CD 2, Track 6, do not tell us that this is a wedding procession (exclusive of the sung text); the same tunes and styles are used in other contexts. However, when combined with a few images and even a minimum of cultural background, we understand the music as integral to a wedding celebration. Concerning the particular tradition featured in this introductory vignette, we can go further and correctly surmise that music is pervasive and needed at all stages of the wedding, even during what otherwise would be a transitional moment between ceremonial spaces (the church and the banquet hall in this case).

The third theme is *music and identity.* A fundamental principle of ethno-musicology is that people realize and express identities, both personal and collective, through music. Therefore we can know something of an individual's identity through the music they create, employ, and enjoy. We have already seen that without prior cultural knowledge, the musical sounds alone on our first recording would not inform us that this is a scene from a wedding; yet many of us probably could identify the society behind the musical sounds as European. What about the sounds suggests that they are European? The first sounds we hear are two human voices, but unless you recognize the language as a Slavic dialect, voices alone do not mark the music as European—all peoples of the world use their voice in special ways that we might call song. The way the two men sing together in polyphony (see Chapter 1) does suggest Europe, in that polyphonic singing appears in many European traditions. However, this sort of singing appears in other parts of the world as well. We might also experience the string band as European. Certainly, violins are used throughout Europe, but they are also featured elsewhere such as in India, Latin America, and North America. Yet again, the way the string band from the Tatras played together in a meter easily divided by 2, and with a distinct melody accompanied harmonically by the other violins and a basslike instrument, can be identified as European (though the harmonic and melodic structures do not fit well into what musicians trained in the European classical music tradition might call "common practice"). You can see that the issue of identity raises as many questions as answers. After considering Europe as a geopolitical and cultural region, we will return to this point and try to better understand what makes the musics of Europe "European."

Europe: An Overview

When someone mentions Europe to you, what comes to mind? A particular country such as France or Germany? Maybe a large city such as Vienna, London, Moscow, or Paris? What sounds play in your mind's ear when you think about "European music"? Some of you might think of a symphony by Mozart or Beethoven, a Chopin etude you played in piano lessons once, or the popular singer Björk, the band U2, or even the Beatles. But these last two bands are from Ireland and England, islands off the coast of the continent of Europe. Should they be included in our definition of "Europe"? If Europe is defined as a landmass, the European continent extends from Portugal in the west to Asia in the east. This certainly extends beyond the concept of Europe most of us have. Perhaps a cultural definition of Europe will clarify our position and help us get on with the study of "European music." But what about North America? Isn't there much that is "European" about the institutions and cultural practices of the United States, Canada, and Mexico? Defining Europe as a culture area has its own pitfalls.

The way we conceive of regions of the world rarely depends solely on physical geography; the human capacity for categorization, naming, and dividing inevitably comes into play. Like music, Europe exists as a concept as well as a concrete object—what Benedict Anderson famously calls "imagined communities" (1991). For our purposes, the concept of Europe includes several island nations (Iceland, the United Kingdom and Ireland), and the nation-states on the western end of the European continent from Portugal in the west to at least the western parts of Russia in the east. In the north are the countries of Norway, Sweden, and Finland; in the south are Spain, Italy, and Greece. At the moment of this writing, Turkey is being considered for membership in the European Union; should it be included in our definition of Europe? Of course North America is technically not part of Europe, but in Chapter 1 of this book we read about Euro-American music-culture, sometimes called Western music. Just as we can identify many different music-culture practices in the United States alone, there are literally hundreds of distinct musics in the nations of Europe. Nonetheless, certain ideas about music and certain ways of creating and organizing sounds can be identified as European. The European settlement of the Americas, not surprisingly, results in many shared musical practices there as well, and for this reason in this chapter we will occasionally reference and compare music in North America and Europe.

Social and Political Organization

We have many ways of understanding the social and political organization of Europe. For instance, we can view Europe as a collection of independent democratic nation-states, but to the extent that this is true, it is a fairly recent phenomenon. For much of its history, most of Europe's population and land was organized into fiefdoms that were often governed by loosely defined kingdoms and later empires. As a way of thinking about Europe as a whole, though, we might more fruitfully begin by focusing on religion—for its sweeping, long-term influence on the social, political, and musical practices of Europe. Then we will consider the more recent manifestations of nationalism for their influential effect on contemporary ideas about music from various regions of Europe.

RELIGION AND SOCIETY

The three predominant religions in Europe, though by no means the only religions practiced, are Judaism, Christianity, and Islam—all monotheistic religions with roots in the Middle East and with significant shared texts (the Torah or Old Testament). Despite what these religions have in common—or perhaps because of this—the differences between them tend to receive emphasis and shape individuals' and society's interactions. Tensions between Christian Europe and Muslim Europe in particular did much to define the politics, societies, and cultural practices of the region in the distant and recent past (Davies 1996:253–58). Divisions between different sects of Christianity are similarly influential in Europe, as illustrated recently in Ireland. Here we will consider how these tensions and ideas of difference have played out in Europe and how they have affected music-culture practices.

Of these three religions, Christianity is the largest and longest established in Europe. Spread throughout Western Europe most effectively by the Roman Empire, Christianity became the dominant religion in all of Europe by the fourth century. For most of its history in Europe, Christianity has been divided into several politically and socially significant categories: Roman Catholicism, Orthodoxy (primarily in the east and southeast), and various sects of Protestantism (strongest in northern Europe and the United Kingdom).

Judaism is practiced almost exclusively by ethnic Jews, who over time have formed a loosely linked European community. Jews never obtained a political state within Europe, a quality that they share with European Roma. Both Islam and Christianity, on the other hand, enjoyed the benefits of becoming state religions. Judaism was introduced to Europe as early as 70 C.E. when Jews, forced into diaspora by the Romans after the destruction of the Second Temple, settled in Mediterranean Europe, and in subsequent centuries moved into Central and Western Europe with the Roman Empire. Though several waves of persecution and expulsion diminished Jewish communities over the centuries, significant communities were established by the eighteenth-century Enlightenment era. In most of Europe, the Holocaust nearly annihilated Jewish communities during World War II (Bohlman 2000b:248–49). Some communities are slowly rebuilding, and the influence of Jewish music remains strong in many parts of Europe (Rice 2000:11).

Muslim* communities have flourished in Europe since the Moorish Andalusian Empire (eighth to thirteenth centuries) on the Iberian Peninsula, and the Turkish Ottoman Empire (fourteenth to twentieth centuries) in southeastern Europe. Muslim individuals and communities form important components of most European nation-states today, and Islam is a dominant religion in some countries and regions (Albania and Bosnia, for example). Like Jews, however, Muslims have

---

*Muslim is the term used for one who follows Islam.

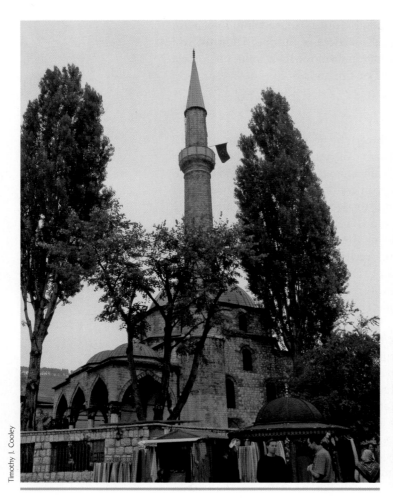

Timothy J. Cooley

FIGURE 5.4

Mosque in Sarajevo. Bosnia,
2004.

been periodically persecuted and driven from Europe. For example, both Jews and the Muslim Moors were expelled from Andalusian Spain in 1492. Muslim communities are historically strong in many Southeastern European nations, such as Bosnia (see Figure 5.4), and communities of more recent immigrants are found throughout Europe.

What effect does religion have on musical practices? Answering this question is difficult, even though the influences are believed to be many, great, and varied. As we can see in Chapter 10, the relationship between Islam and ideas about music is important but contentious for many Muslims. In fact, what may be the most influential sonic production of Islam—the recitation of the Qu'ran (Koran)—is not considered music. Nonetheless, the rules for properly reciting the Qu'ran are reflected in the modal practices of Muslim classical musicians, and these rules also influence vocal ornamentation in some forms of folk music. The Call to Prayer, given five times each day, is part of the soundscape of Muslim communities still thriving in parts of Southeastern Europe, as well as in Muslim neighborhoods in many other European metropolitan centers.

Muslims have also influenced European musical instruments. Both the guitar and the violin descended from Middle Eastern instruments. The guitar in particular is believed to be a descendant of the 'ud, which was probably introduced to Spain by the Moors.

Jewish music and musicians are integrated into the musical practices of many parts of Europe (see Armistead 1979; Bohlman 2000a, 2000b). Jewish music in Europe includes two major traditions, the Sephardic and the Ashkenazic traditions. The Sephardic Jews are originally from the Iberian Peninsula, but were expelled in the fifteenth century. Many moved to the Balkans in Southeastern Europe, some settled in the British Isles or the Netherlands, while others left Europe. The Ashkenazic Jews were most prominent in Germany, Australia, and Eastern Europe. Identity for European Jewry centered on religion, language, and other cultural practices rather than on association with a particular location, country, or kingdom. Yet music expressive of a distinctive Jewish cultural identity developed in response to the inventions of national traditions in the 1800s (Bohlman 2000b:249). Examples include the instrumental ensembles called **klezmer,** which provided music for ritual and secular events both inside and outside Jewish communities. In many parts of

Eastern Europe, Jewish musicians were essential for non-Jewish weddings, and in may cities and regions across Europe, Jewish musicians were among the most highly sought-out musicians until the Holocaust. Wheras a high degree of integration with other European musics characterized the aesthetic of many Jewish instrumentalists, vocal music served to define a specific Jewish identity through the use of language (Yiddish for many Ashkenazic Jews, Ladino for Sephardic Jews, as well as Hebrew from religious and secular texts). "Oifn Pripetshik," discussed later, is an example of a Yiddish language song from an Ashkenazic tradition.

Aligned with the ruling powers that experienced the greatest successes, Christianity has maintained the political advantage in much of Europe. Like mosques and synagogues, Christian churches have served as institutions for spreading sociocultural ideas and practices over wide regions, between kingdoms and across national borders. For example, the official language of the Roman Catholic Church is Latin. Even though Vatican II reforms, instituted in the 1960s, allowed the mass to be conducted in the local vernacular, music with Latin texts is still common in churches around the world. Another example is a particular approach toward ideas about scale and modality (the organization of pitches typically used in a melody; see Chapter 1) that spread across Europe with the church.

Churches also fostered traditions of literacy, including musical literacy. The system of notating music still used in many parts of the world today (the five-line system used in this book) developed in Europe as early as the eleventh century and settled into the form used today in the early seventeenth century. The ability to notate accurately many aspects of music (notably pitch, rhythm, and duration) subtly changes one's conception of music itself and forms one of the ideological divisions between "classical," "popular," and "folk" music in Europe. Notation also facilitates the conception and composition of large-form abstract music (music without texts, for example, such as a concerto or symphony), and to some extent, the phenomenon of harmony discussed later.

In more regionally specific contexts, church traditions encouraged certain types of musical practices. For example, Roman Catholic brotherhoods in Spain have a tradition of snare and bass drum performances reserved for two days of the year during Holy Week, an annual Church holiday including Easter (see Plastino 2001, 2003 for a colorful ethnography and recordings of some of the dynamics of this drumming tradition). The Roman Catholic Church in particular has many holidays and processions that serve as occasions for special music. The Protestant Reformation, beginning in the sixteenth century, divided much of Western Europe into Protestant denominations (mostly in Northern Europe) and Roman Catholic churches (primarily in the south). The Protestant churches created new musical forms, notably chorales that the entire congregation sang. Some of these chorales were based on vernacular texts or common melodic formulas (Schulenberg 2000:74). For an example of a Lutheran chorale, see "A Mighty Fortress," discussed later (Transcription 5.3).

All three of the religions considered here have clearly influenced the music-culture of Europe. However, the greatest and most pervasive influences on musical practices are the social qualities of organized religions. One is the social structure a religion provides for the society as a whole, or in some cases for a religious community within a society. The second is the influence of the weekly worship services, or in the case of Islam, daily sound-art events such as the Call to Prayer and recitation of the Qu'ran. These musical practices—approaches toward melody, rhythm, formal structure; the instruments used or prohibited; gendered practice imposed on communities; and so forth—feed the societies' soundscape in inescapable ways. Though religions' influences on musical practices are wide-spread, it would be a mistake to assume that most music in Europe can be labeled exclusively Christian, Jewish, or Muslim. Musical practices tend to be ecumenical and worldly in the sense that they spread freely from mouth to ear around the world, respecting no religious or political borders.

NATIONALISM AND NATION-STATES

Kingdoms and empires as the predominant social and political organizational units in Europe gradually gave way to the modern nation-states that characterize Europe today beginning only in the late eighteenth and the nineteenth centuries. Key and early events effecting this change include the 1776 American Declaration of Independence (not in Europe, but a declaration of independence from a European monarchy), and the 1789 French Revolution. The idea of a nation-state differs fundamentally from the idea of a kingdom or empire (and other forms of dynasties) in that the authority resides in the people of the state, rather than in the dynastic rulers of a kingdom. Another difference is that dynasties, like religions, usually claimed to have divine right to rule and govern (White 2000:45–49). Nation-states usually do not claim divine right, though even modern societies today may claim divine authority to support their agendas.

Nationalism as an idea grew out of Enlightenment and Romantic philosophy in Western Europe, including ideas about rational scientific authority, the rights of individuals, and the good of the entire society.* This new way of conceiving of social organization from the people up, rather than from the king, emperor, or God down, required new ways of defining social units. The polity was no longer peoples on the lands controlled by a king, but ideally a group of people meaningfully linked together through cultural practices such as language, music, costume, and religion. Today such social groupings into nations may seem both obvious and problematic. After all, we expect Germans to speak German, the French to speak French, Poles to speak Polish, and so forth. But national languages did not grow out of the soil; they are the products of national education as well as forced resettlements and ethnic cleansings. Still, not all nation-states insist on a unique language. For example, the Swiss speak French, German, and Italian (there is no language called "Swissish"); German is the official language in Austria; and so forth.

The challenges to the idea of "nation" (a significantly united people) and "nation-state" (a political unity with a state) become evident upon even a cursory look at any modern nation-state. One common theme in current theories of nationalism is that nations are not natural, inherent, or immutable but must be

*For theories of nations and nationalism, see Anderson 1991; Gellner 1997; Hobsbawm 1990; Hutchinson and Smith 1994; Smith 1998. For statements specifically on music and nationalism, see Austerlitz 2000; Bohlman 2004; Frolova-Walker 1998.

"invented" (Hobsbawm and Ranger 1983) and "imagined" (Anderson 1991). As Philip Bohlman explains (2004:35–80), music has played an important role in creating national myths ever since the rise of nationalism. As a result, many of our ideas about music in Europe are strongly influenced by a belief that music informs us about the essence of a people (a nation), and that as one moves from nation-state to nation-state, one can expect the change to be reflected in the "national" music. To the extent that this is true, it is the result of nationalism—of proactive national imaginations and inventions. In other words, the notion of national musics is itself a human invention, just like all other cultural practices.

Though cultural practices are invented and not necessarily natural, they are nonetheless real. We will consider examples of music that are Polish, Bosnian, German, Jewish, Turkish-Romani, and Bulgarian. Our approach will be to consider the music in its local context, the individuals who created the music, and what we can learn about those people and the place they live from their musical practices.

The Sounds of European Music

In this book, written for the English-speaking world and marketed largely in North America and Europe, identifying common elements in European music, much of which is familiar to our readers, may seem unnecessary. Yet because ethnomusicologists study all musical cultures, including Euro-American ones, it is interesting to see what happens when we ask the same questions of a familiar music that we ask of an unfamiliar one. Sometimes the results are quite surprising. Taking the four aspects of musical sound introduced in Chapter 1 (rhythm and meter, melody, harmony, and form), we will consider what unique contributions Europeans may have made to the world of music.

RHYTHM AND METER

Listen again to CD 2, Track 6, paying special attention to the rhythm. The first part featuring men on horseback singing can be interpreted as being in free rhythm, or unmetered. Though repeated listening may reveal a slow pulse, this pulse is uneven and flexible. The second part of this selection, featuring the string band, is clearly metered; that is, there is an obvious pulse beat organized in a repeating pattern. The music is not always easy to hear over the clomping of the horses, cars, wind, and excited wedding guests, but careful and repeated listening will reveal an ostinato (a bass line that is played again and again) by a three-stringed cello-sized instrument called *basy*, and a repeating melodic idea played by two lead violinists. If we assign the value of a quarter note to the steady sawing of the *basy*'s bow, and decide that each measure or bar of music receives 2 quarter-note beats ($\frac{2}{4}$ time), we might be able to hear that the pattern repeats after 5-bar phrases. As you try to hear the music in this way, be warned: The violinists and the *basy* player are some of the best from Podhale, and as is the practice there, they never play the same thing twice in exactly the same way. Variation is considered the sign of a true musician in Podhale.

This method of analyzing rhythm is useful when considering European music. First, determine if the music has a pulse or beat; second, if it does, determine if and how the beat is organized into measures or bars; third, determine how the bars are grouped to form phrases. This type of focused listening takes some practice, but if you spend the time to gain this skill you will be able to make sophisticated observations about the form and structure of much European music.

The string-band portion of CD 2, Track 6, illustrates some of the most common rhythmic features found in European music—folk, popular, and classical. These features, explained in Chapter 1, are shared by most music heard in America. The second part of CD 2, Track 6's music has a steady pulse or beat (first level of rhythmic analysis) that is easily organized into bars of two beats each (second level of rhythmic analysis). This is an example of *duple meter,* meaning that the number of pulses in each bar is divisible by 2 (usually just 2 or 4 beats per bar). The most common metrical structure in European music is duple meter. When we apply the third level of rhythmic analysis—the number of bars grouped to form a musical phrase—to the string-band portion of our selection, however, we find a phrase structure that is not common in Europe. Melodic units beginning at 0:52 and 1:08 are indicated in the Close Listening guide. Each phrase in this example is five-bars long, a relatively unusual phrase-length in European music, and the entire melodic idea takes three phrases (15 bars total). Music with 5-bar phrases forms an important genre in the music along the Polish and Slovakian border, but in Europe as a whole, 4-bar phrases are much more common, sometimes rendered as 2- or 8-bar phrases.

The next most common metrical structure in European music consists of bars with a number of beats divisible by three, called *triple meter.* Music for a waltz is a good example of triple meter: (ONE-two-three, ONE-two-three, etc.). The Yiddish song "Oifn Pripetshik" (CD 2, Track 7) is an example of triple-meter

CD 2:7

"Oifn Pripetshik" (3:49). Mark Warshawsky. Katherine Meizel, voice; Lillie Gordon, violin; and Ralph Lowi, guitar. Arranged by Meizel, Gordon, and Lowi. Studio recording by Kevin Kelly. University of California, Santa Barbara, 2006.

Close Listening

"OIFN PRIPETSHIK"

CD 2:7

COUNTER NUMBER	COMMENTARY/TEXT	TRANSLATION*
0:00	Instrumental introduction, guitar and violin	
0:09	Verse 1 *Oifn pripetshik brent a fayerl* *Un in shtub iz hés,* *Un der rebe lerent kléne kinderlach* *Dem aleph béz.* (repeat last 2 lines)	In the stove a little fire burns And in the house it is warm, And the rebbe is teaching the little children The alphabet.

0:33	Refrain	
	Zét zhe kinderlach gedenkt zhe tayere	See now children, remember dear ones,
	Vos ir lerent do	What you are learning here
	Zogt zhe noch a mol un take noch a mol	Repeat it again and again
	Komets aleph o. (repeat last 2 lines)	*Komets aleph o.* [alphabet chant]
1:05	Verse 2	
	Lernt kinder mit grois chéshek	Study, children, with great desire
	Azoi zog ich aich on	That is what I tell you
	Ver s'vet gicher fun aich kenen ivre	He who'll know his Hebrew first
	Der bakumt a fon. (repeat last 2 lines)	Will win a banner for a prize.
1:29	Refrain	
2:01	Verse 3	
	Az ir vet kinder elter vern	Children, only when you get older
	Vet ir alén farshtén	Will you understand
	Vi fil in di oisyes lign trern	How many tears lie in the letters of the alphabet
	Un vi fil gevén. (Repeat last 2 lines.)	And how much weeping.
2:26	Refrain	
2:58	Verse 4	
	Az ir vet kinder dem goles shlepn	Children, when you grow tormented
	Oisgemutshet zain	With the struggle of exile
	Zolt ir fun di oisyes koach shepn	Looking to the letters of the alphabet
	Kukt in zé arain. (Repeat last 2 lines.)	You will draw strength.
3:22	Refrain	

*English translation by Katherine Meizel and Arthur Schwartz.

rhythmic organization, though it does not sound like a waltz. As the phrase markings in Transcription 5.1 indicate, each phrase is 4 bars long, illustrating the most common European phrase structure.

The carol "Joy to the World" used in Chapter 1 to illustrate the most common Western scale structure also illustrates common European rhythmic tendencies. The melody for this carol was composed by an American, Lowell Mason (1792–1872), but Mason was a deliberately "European" American composer who used his influence as a music educator to replace the uniquely American fuguing-tunes and anthems from the eighteenth century with what he considered to be "correct" European styles (McKim 1993:47). In addition, "Joy to the World" quotes two melodic ideas from the oratorio *Messiah* by George

TRANSCRIPTION 5.1
"Oifn Pripetshik" by Mark
Warshawsky. Text and
melody adapted from
Pasternak (1994:72–73).

Frederick Handel (1685–1759). Even if penned in America, "Joy to the World" is a very European-style composition and illustrates typical European melody and rhythm.

With your attention on rhythm, sing through the carol using Transcription 5.2 as a reference. The carol is in duple meter $\left(\frac{2}{4}\right)$, and all but one of the phrases occupies 4 bars. (Note that with the exception of the first phrase, each phrase begins one eighth note ahead of the bar line. This is called a "pickup.") The second phrase, on the words "let earth receive her king" stands alone as a 3-bar phrase. A much more typical phrase structure is found in "A Mighty Fortress," a hymn composed by the German Martin Luther (1483–1546), one of the leaders of the Protestant Reformation and the founder of the Lutheran church. This is a duple-meter tune with 4-bar phrases, each divided into two 2 bar subphrases (Transcription 5.3). However, the very last phrase is only 2 bars, and is a melodic quote of the second half of the first phrase. These three examples taken from Yiddish, European/American, and German traditions illustrate the general tendency in European music for duple or triple meter organization of pulse, grouped most often into 4-bar phrases.

TRANSCRIPTION 5.2
"Joy to the World"
by Lowell Mason, text by
Isaac Watts.

TRANSCRIPTION 5.3
"A Mighty Fortress"
by Martin Luther.

CD 2:8

Ruchenitsa (2:14). Performed by
Yanko Atanasov Kumitov,
gaida; Georgi Mitov Uchkov,
kaval; Vladi Dimitrov, *gudulka;*
and Panyo Georgiev Gurgov,
tupan. Field recording by
Timothy Rice. Tenevo, Yambol
region, Bulgaria, 1969.

As a counterexample, listen to CD 2, Track 8, a wedding dance from Bulgaria called a *ruchenitsa.* The ethnomusicologist Timothy Rice recorded this example in 1969 at a wedding in the village of Tenevo near the town of Yambol in the Thracian region of Bulgaria (for more, see Rice 1994:16–18). The dance is played by a traditional band consisting of a *gaida* (bagpipe), *kaval* (end-blown, bevel-edged flute), *gudulka* (bowed, pear-shaped fiddle), and *tupan* (cylindrical, double-headed bass drum, played with a large stick in one hand and a thin wand in the other). We instinctively hear this example as having a pulse beat and as being danceable, but we might have trouble identifying or describing the meter. Is it in duple or triple meter? Or is that even the right question? A *ruchenitsa* is a genre of dance music played at village weddings in Bulgaria and is also a common staple among international dance clubs in America that include what are often called Balkan dances in their repertory. Dancers typically describe these meters as composite groups of short (S) and long (L) beats or pulses (Rice 1994:73). Using this system, a *ruchenitsa* consists of three beats, two short and one long: S-S-L, S-S-L, S-S-L, and so on. Sometimes these meters are called "additive meters" and each beat is conceived of as two or three equal beats (Rice 2004). In the additive meter system, a *ruchenitsa* would be counted **1212123, 1212123,** and so forth (2 + 2 + 3), with the total number of beats per cycle adding up to seven. In this system, one might say that a *ruchenitsa* is "in seven." However, the tempo on CD 2, Track 8, is so fast that it is nearly impossible to count the individual beats. You will find it much easier to find the S-S-L, S-S-L pulse pattern. Listen to the selection again, and try to tap out the S-S-L beat pattern or, even better, dance across the room in a repeating series of two short steps and one long step. Note that the example begins with the sounds of the bagpiper filling his instrument with air and starting the drone and chanter pipes. The melody and meter begin a split second before 0:04 seconds into the track (see the Close Listening guide).

Close Listening

RUCHENITSA

CD 2:8

COUNTER NUMBER	COMMENTARY
0:00	Filling bagpipe with air and starting the drone and chanter pipes
0:04	**Theme 1,** 8-bar phrase
0:11	Theme 1 repeated
0:17	**Theme 2,** 8-bar phrase
0:24	Theme 2 repeated
0:30	**Theme 3,** 8-bar phrase

0:37	Theme 3 repeated
0:43	**Theme 4,** 8-bar phrase
0:49	Theme 4 repeated
0:55	**Theme 5,** 4-bar phrase
0:59	Theme 5 repeated
1:02	Theme 5 repeated
1:05	Theme 5 repeated
1:08	**Theme 6,** 4-bar phrase
1:11	Theme 6 repeated
1:14	Theme 6 repeated
1:17	Theme 6 repeated
1:20	**Theme 7,** 4-bar phrase
1:23	Theme 7 repeated
1:26	Theme 7 repeated
1:29	Theme 7 repeated
1:32	**Theme 8,** 8-bar phrase
1:38	Return to **theme 3,** variation
1:44	Theme 3 repeated
1:50	**Theme 4** repeated
1:56	Theme 4 repeated
2:02	**Theme 5** repeated
2:05	Theme 5 repeated
2:08	Theme 5 repeated
2:11	Theme 5 repeated

This type of additive meter, often called "asymmetrical," is common the Balkan region of Europe, as well as throughout much of the Middle East. As we have seen, a *ruchenitsa* when transcribed is usually rendered in $\frac{7}{8}$, each short beat receiving two eighth notes, and the long beat receiving three for a total of seven eighth notes per measure (see Transcription 5.4). And though presented as a counterexample to the European tendency toward duple or triple meter, it corresponds perfectly with the European propensity for organizing metrical units into phrases of 4 or 8 bars (recall that the third level of rhythmic analysis is phrase structure). Take a close look at Transcription 5.4 as you listen to the *ruchenitsa*. Notice that each repeating theme consists of 8-bar units. The 8-bar phrases can be interpreted as two 4-bar phrases, the second phrase beginning like the first but ending differently. Thus, one can hear the entire performance in phrases of 4 bars each—very typical of European phrase structures. To aid your listening, the melodic themes are numbered (1–8) and lapsed minutes and seconds when each theme begins are indicated in the transcription.

TRANSCRIPTION 5.4

Ruchenitsa. Transcribed by Timothy Rice.

TRANSCRIPTION 5.4
(*continued*)

PITCHES, SCALES, AND MELODY

In Chapter 1, you read that Euro-Americans prefer a particular way of organizing pitches into scales, the most common scale in the Euro-American system being what we call a major scale. This is also true for most European music. "Joy to the World" serves as an example, beginning with a melody that simply steps down the major scale. The next most common scale featured in European music systems is the minor scale; "Oifn Pripetshik" provides a melody in this scale. Though there are numerous additional scales or pitch sets employed, the vast majority of European music uses either major or minor scales. Readers of this book will know that, in the world of music, there are many varied ways of deriving pitch sets for music, and Europe's contribution to pitch and scale varieties is quite limited. Europe's unique contributions to the world of music lie elsewhere.

Scales alone do not make for very interesting melodies. Beautiful, memorable, striking melodies are created in the navigation of scales. In European music, this includes different ways of emphasizing particular pitches in the scale. Again, the decidedly European-style American composition "Joy to the World" illustrates melodic tendencies for European music. Composers achieve melodic emphasis in several ways. Being first or the last in a phrase gives a pitch a type of emphasis. Holding a pitch longer than others also gives it emphasis, as does placing it in a strong metrical position. Emphasis, then, is often related to rhythm, since metrical position and the time a pitch is held are both aspects of rhythm.

Which pitches are emphasized in the first phrase of "Joy to the World"? The pitches to the first and last words, *joy* and *come,* receive emphasis, and both are on the pitch "do" or the 1st and 8th scale degrees; that is, they are the first and eighth notes of the scale. They receive the same pitch name because they are an octave apart. In Europe, as in most world-music systems, pitches an octave apart are closely related and often receive the same scale name. See for example Transcription 6.1 in the chapter on India. The pitch "sa," which corresponds in function to the pitch "do" in the European system of solfège, receives the same name even though it is an octave higher or lower. Which pitches of "Joy to the World" receive emphasis by being held the longest? Looking at Transcription 5.2, we see that the words *world* and *come* are held the longest. *Come* is on the pitch "do," the 1st scale degree, and "world" is on "so," the 5th scale degree. At this point, we can see that "do" and "so" are important pitches in this short phrase of a well-known song. The 5th scale degree, called the "dominant," is the second most important pitch in much European music.

While singing the phrase again, tap your foot on the words *joy, world, Lord* and *come.* You will note that you are tapping evenly, setting up the sort of symmetrical rhythmic pattern or meter we discussed earlier. This metrical stress, then, produces another means of emphasizing certain pitches. Again, "do" and "so" are emphasized, as well as the pitch "mi" for the word *Lord.* Considering all these different ways to emphasize certain pitches of a scale, we can conclude that the pitch "do" receives the greatest emphasis, "so" the second greatest, and "mi" a third level of emphasis. These pitches played together create a chord—two or more pitches sounded together to create a deliberate harmonic sound. In fact, they emphasize the chord built on the "do" pitch, or the first scale degree, which functions as the tonic or home pitch of this particular major scale (see Chapter 2). We can summarize that melodic pitches emphasize the most important pitches of a scale, and these in turn function in the harmonic structure of the music. We will turn to the concept of harmony after we consider a few additional European melodies.

Return again to "A Mighty Fortress" by Martin Luther. Though writing songs for the Protestant church, Luther often derived his melodies from existing secular songs, even folk songs sung in drinking halls or bars. "A Mighty Fortress" ("Ein feste Burg" in the original German) is probably an original melody, though based on a common melodic formula that moved deliberately down the major scale (Marshall and Leaver 2001). In this way it is similar to Mason's "Joy to the World," yet the melodies differ greatly. Looking at Transcription 5.3, you can see that the first phrase shares at least one thing in common with the first phrase of "Joy to the World": both begin on "do" and end on "do" an octave lower. "A Mighty Fortress" also fills in all the pitches of a major scale, but the melody meanders. By contrast, the first phrase of "Joy to the World" steps directly down the scale, one note per scale degree.

Another similarity between the first phrases of the two melodies is that they both emphasize the 1st and 5th scale degrees. We can divide the first phrase of "A Mighty Fortress" into two subphrases, marked in the transcription and text with a comma. The first half of the phrase begins on "do" and ends on "so"; the second half also begins on "do" but then moves down the scale in a stepwise manner to end an octave lower, almost like "Joy to the World" except for the step up on the word "ne-ver." Sing the second half of this phrase ("a bulwark never failing") and the first phrase to "Joy to the World," one right after the other. You will see that these melodic fragments are very similar, yet easily distinguished by slight differences in rhythm ("A Mighty Fortress" is marchlike, while "Joy to the World" with its skipping rhythm is, appropriately, more joyful) and the brief interruption in the otherwise stepwise descent from "do" to "do" in "A Mighty Fortress."

"Oifn Pripetshik" illustrates what is known as a "minor" mode, identified by a lowered 3rd scale degree. The minor mode is the second most common melodic mode found in European music. Originally titled "Der alef-beyz" or "The ABC," "Oifn Pripetshik" is a Yiddish-language song by popular Eastern European Jewish songwriter Mark Warshawsky (1840–1907) (Rubin 1979:270, 272–74). His most popular song, "Oifn Pripetshik" is comparable to "A Mighty Fortress" in that both are in vernacular or folk styles, and within broad communities the melodies are very well known even if most individuals do not know the identities of the composers. The minor "Oifn Pripetshik" melody has been used in a film drawn from the life story of George Gershwin, as well as more recently in Steven Spielberg's 1993 film *Schindler's List.* The version on your CD was recorded for this chapter by three graduate students in ethnomusicology at the University of California–Santa Barbara. Though each of the performers has considerable scholarly interest and performance experience in Jewish, European, and tangentially related Middle Eastern musics, the performance on your CD does not represent a particular Yiddish tradition.

HARMONY

The examples used to illustrate melody in Europe also illustrate one of this region's most unique contributions: harmony. Recall from Chapter 1 that harmony is created by two or more different pitches sounded intentionally at the same time for the purpose of the sound they make together. This can also be called a *chord,* a term familiar to guitar players that is derived from *accord,* implying that the pitches sound pleasant together—in accord with one another. However, exactly which intervals sound "in accord" depends on interpretation, and we will see that not all music practices in Europe share the same aesthetics of harmony. Europe is not the only part of the world that independently devised ways to combine different pitches simultaneously, but it does seem to have most fully developed the concept of simultaneous pitches that create meaningful sounds independent of melody.

In its most fully realized state, harmonic music is said to have "harmonic rhythm": the movement of harmonic sounds or chords in time. The chord patterns played by a guitar for a particular song provide an example of harmonic rhythm. In Chapter 4 we learned about common harmonic patterns in African American blues, patterns that are directly related to European harmonic practices. In fact, much popular music in Europe and America of the nineteenth and twentieth centuries relies heavily on the concept of harmony. This is not the case in all Euro-American music, and harmony is of decreasing concern in certain forms of popular music (drum and bass dance music, and some rap, for example, reconceive of or dispense with harmony). Classical or "art" music in Europe also moved away from harmony. Nonetheless, harmony remains a key feature of much European music—folk, classical and popular.

Consider "Joy to the World" again. The letters C, F, and G represent a simplified version of the chords, or triadic harmonies, that accompany this melody. "Joy to the World" is given here in the key of C, and these three chords are built on the 1st (C), 4th (F), and 5th (G) scale degrees of that key. This is the same basic chordal relationship employed in the blues, for example, and the basis of the harmonic system favored in much of Europe since the eighteenth century. Using a guitar or piano, play these chords while you sing the melody. The sounding of the different chords in time is the harmonic rhythm of "Joy to the World," also represented in Transcription 5.5.

TRANSCRIPTION 5.5
Harmonic rhythm of "Joy to the World." Each box represents one quarter-note beat in $\frac{2}{4}$ time.

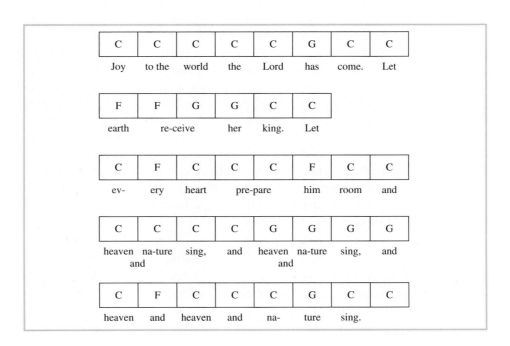

Some musics of Europe take radically different approaches toward harmony, such as the music heard on CD 2, Track 9, "Sister, Hold Your Chastity." This is European music, to be sure, but it employs a different aesthetic from most other European musics with regard to vocal timbre, melody, rhythm, and harmony. This is an example of a song genre called *ganga* from the Central European nation-state Bosnia and Herzegovina. It was performed by three girls from the village of Umoljani (Figure 5.5). As is the practice for female *ganga* singers, these girls are close friends who have been singing together from a young age. Like the music from the Polish Tatras, this is considered mountain music, the language is a related Slavic language, and the texture of the singing is polyphonic—more than one melodic line performed simultaneously. They are also similar in that the singers take great pleasure in the physical and aesthetic sensation of singing together with loud, powerful voices. But what is considered beautiful and consonant harmonically is quite different in Bosnia and Herzegovina than in Poland. In the Polish example, the singers sing unison or at an interval of a third, harmonies generally interpreted as consonant in European music. In the *ganga* example, there are three voices, a leading voice and two accompanying singers who enter on the second melodic phrase. They begin in unison with the lead singer, move together up a step (from G to A), but then the two accompanying voices remain on the A while the lead singer moves back down to the G, the interval of a major second (Transcription 5.6; Close Listening guide). An American listener might consider this harmony harsh or dissonant, but it is considered pleasing or consonant to the singers, and therefore is consonant in that regional European music tradition. What is consonant and dissonant in music is an aesthetic evaluation, not a law of nature.

CD 2:9

"Sister, Hold Your Chastity" (0:38). Traditional women's *ganga* song. Performed by Azra Bandić, Mevla Luckin, and Emsija Tetarvoić. Field recording by Mirjana Laušević. Umoljani village, Bosnia, 1990.

Mirjana Laušević

FIGURE 5.5

The singers of CD 2, Track 9, the highlander women's *ganga* song. From left to right, Azra Bandić, Mevla Luckin, and Emsija Tatarović, near the village of Umoljani, 1989.

TRANSCRIPTION 5.6

Ganga, "Sister, Hold Your Chastity," as sung by Azra Bandić, Mevla Luckin, and Emsija Tatarović.

Čuvaj se-ko poš-ten-je   ko su-ze, ko te lju-bi   (hh)

(oj) taj _____ te ne-će u-ze' čuvaj se-ko poš-te-

eh _____

(oj)-nje — — ko su-ze ko te lju-bi.

Close Listening

"SISTER, HOLD YOUR CHASTITY"

CD 2:9

COUNTER NUMBER	COMMENTARY/TEXT	TRANSLATION
0:00	Lead singer sings first line. *Čuvaj seko poštenje ko suze, ko te ljubi,*	Sister, hold your chastity like tears, the one who kisses you,
0:12	Lead singer begins second line and is joined by the other two singers. *(oj) taj te neće uze', čuvaj seko pošte-*	he will not take you, sister, hold your
0:26	Third line *(oj) -nje ko suze, ko te ljubi.*	chastity like tears, the one who kisses you.

SUMMARY

We can now draw some general conclusions about European musics, though, as we have seen, each conclusion has its exceptions. When compared with music throughout the rest of the world, most music in Europe has relatively simple symmetrical structures in rhythm and in overall form. European music tends toward rhythmic organization of even pulses in repeating groups of two or three beats. Similarly, melodic structures tend toward pairs of melodic ideas (A and B phrases) and repeating structures (such as the strophic song form). The same can be said about the pitch content of most European music. The major, diatonic scale is the most prominent scale; the minor scale is the second most common. Other scales and modes are used, but they tend to emerge from specific regions and groups of people, or from distant historical practices. Much of the beauty of European music comes in the subtle variation and ornamentation of these simple structures.

If European musicians have made any unique contribution to world music, it is the concept of harmony and harmonic rhythm. Polyphony is another hallmark of European music, though it is not unique to Europe. Most colleges and universities offer classes on European polyphony and harmony, and we have only touched on the complexity of these systems here.

Though we have focused on general tendencies in European musics, Europe is host to an amazingly rich variety of regional music styles, genres, and associated cultural practices. While religious and political institutions have contributed to the unification of some musical practices across broad swaths of Europe, much of the music maintained and created anew in any given location provides exceptions to the tendencies described here.

In this chapter, I downplay the usual division of European musics into classical, popular, and folk; examples that span the gamut are used instead. However, these categories do have some meaning and utility. Classical music can be described as those musical practices that receive significant institutional support and that frequently rely on written sources including music notation and written treatises about the music. Institutional support includes the financial support of governments and other social organizations such as religious institutions, schools, and universities. This sort of support, combined with a long tradition of musical literacy, facilitates large ensembles (symphonic orchestras and opera companies are examples) and complex musical forms prescribed in writing (musical scores). Popular music receives similar support, but the institutions involved are generally commercial: They exist to make money. Popular music is thus mediated by some form of commercial interest. Folk music, or "music of the people," as it is expressed in many European languages, tends to be more regional and may or may not have commercial or institutional support. For example, a community will have its own musicians, and members of that community are likely to know those musicians personally and experience their music firsthand.

In this book, the authors emphasize music as human behavior. Of course categorizing musical practices and repertories as classical, folk, and so forth is itself meaningful human behavior and it does affect how we conceive of music, but music practice itself tends to thwart geographic and conceptual borders. Your school probably offers classes on specific European-style music repertories and genres, but in this chapter we will try to take a broad view of music in Europe, illustrated with a few very specific case studies.

Case Study: Podhale, Polish Tatra Region

This chapter started with a musical excerpt from a wedding in the Tatra Mountains of Poland. We now return to the Tatras and ask what makes the musical practices of that region in Europe what they are today. How do they resemble yet differ from the European musical practices just described? What can we learn about the people from this part of Europe by the way they make music? We start with the mountains themselves, as environment impacts a people's cultural practices.

The Tatra Mountains are the tallest mountains in Central Europe (Figure 5.6), forming a natural border between the southern tip of Poland and Slovakia (Map 5.1). They are part of the Carpathian mountain range that begins in Romania, crosses through the southwest corner of Ukraine, then follows the border between Poland and Slovakia before it turns southwestward between the Czech Republic and Slovakia, ending just north of Vienna. The highest peaks reaching over 8,700 feet (2,655 meters) are on the southern, Slovak, side of the Tatras. The tallest peak on the Polish side is almost 8,200 feet (2,499 meters) above sea level. Though not as tall as the Rocky Mountains or the Alps, the Tatras are steep rocky, alpine-type mountains that dramatically affect how people live. Here we consider some of the ways that this mountain environment has influenced culture to this today.

The social and emotional interpretation of mountains has changed over time. Many of us today think of mountains as beautiful, dramatic landscapes—locations of desire where we travel to ski in the winter and hike in the summer. This, however, is a relatively modern view of mountains created only since the late eighteenth century, when traveling to mountainous regions for scientific reasons,

FIGURE 5.6

View of Giewont, one of the peaks of the Tatra Mountains viewed from the village of Kościelisko, 1995.

Timothy J. Cooley

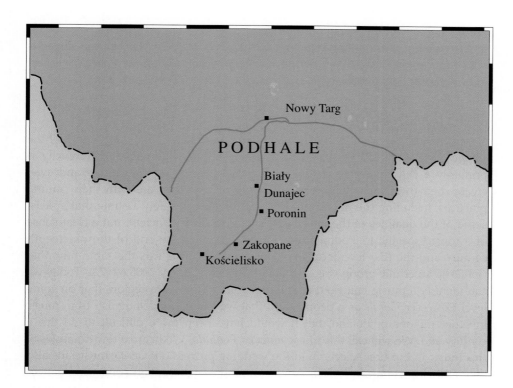

MAP 5.1

Podhale region of Poland.

for leisure, or for adventure was a new thing in Europe (Hall 1991:41). Before that time, mountains were feared and avoided—natural borders only to be crossed at great peril (Cooley 2005:74). Improved roads and the introduction of train service into mountain areas encouraged tourism in the late nineteenth century, further changing the popular image of mountains into a destination of desire. Of course, mountains still do hold real dangers—a fall during a hike in the mountains rings alarms in our minds that are not sounded when we contemplate a fall during a hike across a valley—but in the era of "extreme sports" these dangers, too, form part of mountains' attraction. In the modern world, mountains still symbolize danger, but this danger creates excitement instead of dread. Though mountains often serve as natural borders, they often evoke a sense of freedom and escape rather than containment.

The changing meaning of mountains in the modern world influences cultural practices among mountain residents in interesting ways. The geographic span of the Carpathians is especially interesting culturally, because over the centuries migrants carried lifeways along the Carpathian chain, resulting in similar cultural practices throughout the mountains and across several national borders. For example, traditional music, dance, and clothing in the Polish and Slovak Tatras are closely related. The relative height and rugged conditions of the jagged Tatras also discouraged people from settling there, so that they were some of the last places in Central Europe to receive permanent settlements (from about the thirteenth century; see Cooley 2005:66–67). People who did settle in the Tatras used shepherding methods appropriate for high mountains as practiced all along the Carpathians from as far away as Romania. The clothing, food, dance, and music indigenous to the region has more in common with Slovakia, Hungary, and

Romania than with other regions of Poland. The Tatra region is usually considered unique owing to mountain isolation (Czekanowska 1990:84), but the music is linked in significant ways to other European musical traditions and, as we will see, most recently to "worldbeat" music.

PEOPLE AND MUSIC IN PODHALE

Górale means "mountaineer(s)" (*góra* means "mountain"), and many consider the *Górale** of Podhale to be a particular ethnic group within Poland. Ethnicity is primarily a cultural rather than a biological category. *Górale* express and even create their own and others' understanding of who they are with their cultural practices, including the music that they make. We can safely assume that at least some of the qualities of the music that *Górale* make are ancient, but a clear sense of a music specific to Podhale did not emerge until the end of the nineteenth century and the first few decades of the twentieth. This was the same time that *Górale* as an ethnic group was also being defined (Cooley 2005:67–72). Today we can identify a music-culture that is indigenous to the Tatra region, that on some level expresses *Górale* as a people, and that we can easily distinguish from music in other regions of Poland, but it would have been more difficult to do this a century ago. We will call this music **muzyka Podhala.** We heard a few examples of this music in our first selection, in the wedding procession. *Górale* musicians also play and sing common Polish, American, and pan-European songs and dances (waltzes, polkas, *csárdáses,* for example), as well as popular and classical music from Europe and America, but a core repertory of *muzyka Podhala* is still actively performed by and identified with *Górale.*

Remembering that any individual or collective group's musical practices are complex and often open-ended, not bounded by categories and genres, we can identify a set of core practices that make up *muzyka Podhala.* To help organize our thoughts about what may be some very new musical ideas and sounds, we will divide *muzyka Podhala* into two categories: music for listening and music for dancing. Both categories have vocal and instrumental music, and much of the repertory can fall into either category, depending on use. One general principle that informs all performances of *muzyka Podhala* is the *nuta* concept. **Nuta** (plural *nuty*) literally means "note," but *Górale* musicians use it to refer to a melodic idea or tune family. The point is that any given *nuta* is not a fixed melody, but an idea that is realized only in performance, and is varied with each repetition. Any audio recording or transcription of a *Górale nuta* presents one realization of the melodic idea, not a final, fixed melody.

GENRES OF *MUZYKA PODHALA*

The array of music within even a narrow definition of *muzyka Podhala* includes an impressive number of named genres. Here we will learn a few of these genres, though the border between genres is not always clear and many tunes can be classified in several ways. The fluid nature of *Górale* ideas about music is

---

*Following Louise Wrazen (1991:175), I use the plural Polish word *Górale* as both noun and adjective, singular and plural. For an explanation of *Górale* as an ethnic category, see Cooley 2005:67–72.

illustrated here with three versions of the same *nuta,* but each version falls within a different genre depending on how it is performed and how it functions.

Listen to CD 2, Track 10, recorded at a festival in Podhale in 1992. It is performed by the men of a song-and-dance troupe from Kraków, one of Poland's largest cities. Though Kraków is not in Podhale, most of the members of the troupe are from Podhale and going to college in Kraków. The piece starts with one singer, then a second joins, and then others join, singing in harmony (Transcription 5.7). This style of staggering the beginning to songs and instrumental music is typical. Lead singers or violinists rarely announce what they will perform; they simply start and others follow when they recognize the *nuta* and text. Our CD selection illustrates the typical way in which singers improvise harmony parts to the lead singer's melody, but all end together in unison. The rhythm of this piece is free; it has a pulse, but is not clearly metered. Try to tap your foot to the music. You can do it, but your taps will not be even. This style of performance is called **pasterska** (pastoral) and is considered outdoor music to be sung in a full, open voice. The poetic texts typically have two parts, the second set of lines repeated (ABB form). The *nuta* is repeated three times with some variation (AAA musical structure; see the Close Listening guide).

CD 2:10

Pasterska (pastoral) (0:29). Performed by the troupe Skalni at a festival in Zakopane, Poland. Field recording by Timothy J. Cooley, 1992.

TRANSCRIPTION 5.7
Pasterska, performed by the troupe Skalni.

Close Listening

PASTERSKA

CD 2:10

COUNTER NUMBER	COMMENTARY/TEXT	TRANSLATION
0:00	Lead singer begins the first couplet, followed by other singers a few seconds later, singing in harmony.	
	Hej, juhasicek biedny,	Hey, poor shepherd boy,
	Nie obłapi nigdy.	He never hugs (cuddles).
0:08	Second couplet	
	Hej, owiecki paść musi	Hey, sheep he must pasture
	Choc go dziewce kusi	While a girl seduces him.
0:17	Repeat of the second couplet	

Wierchowa (0:52). Performed by Góralska Kapala, from Chicago: Boguslawa Łowisz, voice; Jan Rózalowski, lead violin; Stanislaw Zatłoka, second violin; Andrzej Tokarz, *basy*. Field recording by Diana Lantz. University of California, Santa Barbara, 2003.

CD 2, Track 11, features the same *nuta* but performed in a style typical of the *wierchowa* genre. A *wierch* in *Górale* dialect is a mountain peak or ridge, and *wierchowe* (plural) are mountain peak songs or *nuty*. Though clearly based on the same *nuta*, or melodic idea, the *wierchowa* clearly differs from the *pasterska* (CD 2, Track 10). In the *wierchowa*, we can hear an ensemble of instruments. This is a typical *Górale* **kapela** or string band: a lead violin, one or more accompanying violins, and a *basy* (see Figure 5.7, though this is not a photograph of the band heard on Track 11). The accompanying instruments play an ostinato (see the Close Listening guide). Listen to the *basy*, which plays the pitches DD EE DE AC# DD over and over again. Like Track 10, one person begins the piece, and others join in after a few beats. But with Track 11, it is a violin that begins, not a singer, and you will notice that the pulse is much more even—not perfectly even (that would be boring), but you can easily tap your foot to this example. After the band plays through the *nuta* three times (AAA form, the same as Track 10), a female singer enters, accompanied by the band (Figure 5.8).* The pulse slows down, but

Close Listening

WIERCHOWA

CD 2:11

COUNTER NUMBER	COMMENTARY/TEXT	TRANSLATION
0:00	The lead violin begins the *nuta* (melodic idea); the rhythm is metered.	
0:03	The other violin and the *basy* join in, providing a harmonic accompaniment.	
0:09	Repetition of the same *nuta*, slight variation; 5-bar ostinato pattern established.	
0:17	Second repetition of the *nuta* with some variation.	
0:25	Singer begins, using the same 5-bar *nuta*. She is accompanied by the string-band. The tempo slows, but the pulse remains steady. Much of the text is unintelligible. *Ej, śpiewam jo se śpiewam* *Ciese (?_____)*	Hey, I sing, I sing (unintelligible text)
0:35	Singer continues with the second couplet, same *nuta*. *Ej, ło dam nie Janicku* *(?_____)*	Hey, _____ Jack . . . (unintelligible text)
0:44	Singer repeats the second couplet using the same *nuta*.	

---

*During a conversation with *Górale* musician Krzysztof Trebunia-Tutka, I played this recorded example and asked about my *pasterska, wierchowa, ozwodna continuum* theory (discussed shortly; see Table 5.1). Krzysztof believes that the particular *wierchowa* example I use here represents a relatively recent style created for a folk opera, *Jadwisia spod regli* by Julian Reimschüssel (1908–1984).

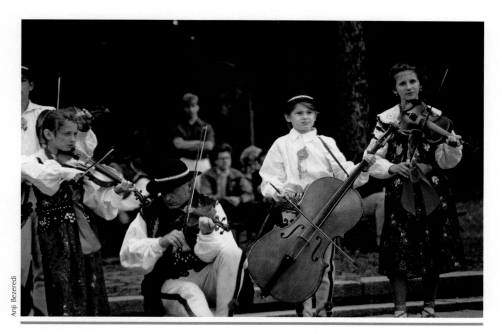

FIGURE 5.7

Górale kapela, led by Józef Staszel (sitting), at a festival for children's troupes in Poronin, Poland, 1992.

Anji Bezeredi

remains relatively steady. Whereas the *pasterska* is free meter, the *wierchowa* is metered in $\frac{2}{4}$ time (Transcription 5.8). Each musical phrase has 10 beats, divided into 5 bars. The poetic text containts two lines, the second line repeated to create an ABB poetic form, the same as in the *pasterska* example.

The next example (CD 2, Track 12) again uses the same *nuta,* but this time it illustrates the characteristics of the **ozwodna** genre. The meaning of the dialect term *ozwodna* or *rozwodna* is unclear, but *Górale* have suggested "slowly" and "in a circle, turning." In the context of *muzyka Podhala,* however, the term refers to a genre of dance music. An *ozwodna* is usually instrumental, though the lead dancer will often call for the tune by singing it, as we hear in our selection. The rhythm is metered and the tempo is relatively fast; each phrase has 10 beats divided into 5 bars, though many *ozwodne* have different phrase lengths. Notice that this time

CD 2:12

Ozwodna (1.05). Performed by the troupe Skalni at a festival in Zakopane, Poland. Field recording by Timothy J. Cooley, 1992.

TRANSCRIPTION 5.8

Wierchowa, sung by Bogusława Łowisz.

FIGURE 5.8

Bogusława Łowisz and Zdzisław Miernicki in a recording studio at the University of California, Santa Barbara, 2003.

Timothy J. Cooley

the singer-dancer sings two poetic lines (AB poetic structure) to the same music (AA melodic structure) and does not repeat the second line (see the Close Listening guide). However, the lead violinist renders the *nuta* differently: The first time through he plays essentially the same melodic shape that the singer used, but he ornaments it in a way idiomatic of this style of violin playing. The second and third time through the 5-bar phrase, he varies the *nuta*, emphasizing a lower register, for example, for much of the first three bars of the phrase, creating an ABB melodic phrase structure (Transcription 5.9). The ostinato pattern is the same as it is on the *wierchowa*, with the *basy* playing DD EE DE AA DD repeatedly (the second A replaces the C♯ played by the *basy* on CD 2, Track 11).

Close Listening

OZWODNA

CD 2:12

COUNTER NUMBER	COMMENTARY/TEXT	TRANSLATION
0:00	Lead singer-dancer calls the *nuta* by singing a song. The *nuta* is the same as in CD 2, Tracks 10 and 11. It is clearly metered. *Hej, ani jo nie juhas, Ani jo nie baca.*	Hey, I am not a shepherd apprentice, I am not a chief shepherd.
0:02	Violins and *basy* join, playing an accompanying part to the singer.	

0:06	Singer, still accompanied by the string band, sings the second couplet, repeating the same *nuta*.

Hej, sama mi ciupaska   Hey, my hatchet by itself
Owiecki nawraco.   Takes care of the sheep.

0:11	Phrase A. Lead violin picks up the same *nuta* while the singer begins to dance. The violinist varies the *nuta*, emphasizing a slightly higher register. Someone whistles rhythmically.
0:15	Phrase B. Lead violinist plays the 5-bar pattern again, emphasizing a lower register.
0:19	Phrase B. Lead violinist plays a third 5-bar phrase, again emphasizing a lower register.
0:22	Phrase A. Lead violinist plays 5-bar phrase, very similar to what he played at 0:11, emphasizing the higher register.
0:26	Phrase B. Lead violinist a plays 5-bar phrase, lower register.
0:30	Phrase B. Lead violinist plays 5-bar phrase, lower register, confirming the ABB melodic phrase structure
0:34	Phrase A variation.
0:37	Phrase B variation.
0:40	Phrase B variation.
0:44	Phrase A variation.
0:47	Phrase B variation.
0:51	Phrase B variation; someone whistles.
0:54	Phrase A variation; whistle continues.
0:57	Phrase B variation.
1:01	Phrase B variation.

The distinctions between the *pasterska, wierchowa,* and *ozwodna* genres can be considered as points along a continuum (see Table 5.1). A *pasterska* is typically unmetered, vocal, and performed for the pleasure of singing and listening. A *wierchowa* may be metered or unmetered and is typically for listening, but the term also refers to dance pieces; further, it may be sung, played on instruments, or both, as in our example. An *ozwodna* is always metered, generally refers to music intended for dancing, and is instrumental, though a singer may introduce the *nuta,* as we heard. Tracks 10 and 11 illustrate the ambiguity of the categories. Track 10 has a fairly pronounced pulse and could be classified as a sung *wierchowa.* Track 11 has some of the *rubato* typically associated with the *pasterska* genre. Track 12, on the other hand, was played for a dance (at the same performance by the college-aged troupe featured in Track 10) and that places it

TRANSCRIPTION 5.9
Ozwodna, performed by
the troupe Skalni.

clearly in the *ozwodna* category, though some *Górale* refer to this family of *nuta* as
"*wierchowa* for dancing."

TABLE 5.1 *Pasterska—Wierchowa—Ozwodna* Continuum

Pasterska	*Wierchowa*	*Ozwodna*
Typically unmetered	Unmetered or metered	Metered
For listening	For listening or dancing	For dancing
Vocal	Vocal and/or instrumental	Instrumental

MUSIC FOR DANCING

Górale in Podhale dance many different styles, from disco to polka, but we will
focus on several genres considered indigenous to the region. Most characteristic is
a couples' dance called *góralski* or *po góralsku* (in the *Górale* manner or style). The
góralski differs from most social dancing that you might be familiar with in that
the focus is on a single couple—one man and one woman—though the woman is
always introduced to the dance area by a second man or by a group of women. In
contrast, waltzes, polkas, and other dances at gatherings of *Górale* have many
couples on the dance floor at once. The *góralski* dance and the accompanying
music are highly improvised yet fall within elaborate structures. Improvisation is

always governed by rules—it is never completely free of preexisting forms, gestures, and melodic ideas. We will consider three integrated layers of this elaborate *góralski* structure here: the social, the musical, and the physical (the dance itself).

Danced primarily by a single couple, the *góralski* may first appear to be social interaction between one man and one woman, but on closer observation one sees that it requires the active participation of additional dancers, musicians, and the circle of onlookers. The dance suite begins when a male dancer approaches the band (the traditional string band or *kapela*) and requests a dance, usually by slipping some money into one of the f-holes of the *basy* and singing a song to the tune to which he intends to dance. This first *nuta* is invariably an *ozwodna*. Meanwhile, a second male dancer is seeking out and inviting to dance the woman with whom the primary male dancer desires to dance. (The first male dancer arranged this with the second beforehand.) The second man brings the chosen woman to the dance floor and "turns her out." Then he exits the dance floor, leaving the woman to dance with the primary male dancer. After each *nuta* in the suite, the primary female dancer leaves the immediate dance area, perhaps having a seat or chatting with her friends. In other words, she moves back into the community, which literally surrounds the dance. For each subsequent dance within the suite, she is reintroduced to the dance floor either by the secondary male dancer, or more typically by a group of female dancers. In either case, the same basic dance steps are used as the dancers turn together first clockwise, then counterclockwise before the primary female dancer is spun and left to dance with the primary male dancer. When the primary male dancer decides he has danced enough, he calls for one of the two closing tunes called **"zielona"** (literally "green") while continuing to dance with his partner. When the band hears the call for "green," they shift to the new *nuta* without pausing, and touching for the first time, the couple turns together using the same steps employed when others introduced the female dancer to the dance floor.

Music for the *góralski* consists of a series of distinct *nuty* as called by the primary male dancer and played by the *kapela*. With the exception of the last tune, which is performed as a type of coda attached to the penultimate tune, each dance tune is usually clearly separated from the previous dance (listen to CD 2, Tracks 13–17). Dances may have many seconds or even several minutes between each *nuta*, yet the separate *nuty* and dances are considered to be within the same suite or dance-sequence. They are distinct events within the larger suite that go together and have a clear beginning and end.

A *Góralski* dance suite always begins with an *ozwodna*. The most common metrical structure of an *ozwodna* is built around 5-bar structures with two pulses in each bar (CD 2, Tracks 13 and 14). Though unusual for dances in Western Europe, this metrical structure is common in the Tatras and some of the other Carpathian Mountain regions. The opening *ozwodna* is followed by a sequence of tunes/dances that may include additional *ozwodne*, and **drobne** ("small") and/or **krzesane** ("striking"). *Drobne* and *krzesane* are closely related tune types combining virtuosic violin playing with elaborate and athletic dancing by the man. They often have 4-bar phrases, but many have unusual phrase structures. As we have seen, each dance cycle ends with one of two tunes, or a medley of both, called "zielona" while the dance couple touches for the first time and dance a specific turning step. See Table 5.2 for a summary of the structure of the *góralski* dance suite.

TABLE 5.2 Structure of the *góralski* dance suite.

Genre	Description	Key Structural Points
Ozwodna	Opening *nuta*/dance	Second male dancer "turns" the female dancer onto dance area.
Krzesana, drobna, or *ozwodna*	Any number in any order	Usually a group of women reintroduce the primary female dancer to the dance area for each subsequent dance.
"Zielona"	Closing song/*nuta* and dance gesture	No break in the music or dance. Lead male dancer "turns" the female dancer and the dance suite ends.

Taken together, CD 2, Tracks 13–17, represent a complete *góralski* dance suite as performed in the village of Kościelisko, Poland, by three members of the Trebunia-Tutka family: Krzysztof on lead violin, his brother Jan on accompanying violin, and their cousin Paweł on *basy.* They were recorded in the home of Ewa and Wojtek Styrczula-Maśniak, where I was staying for a few days in August 2005. I asked Ewa and Wojtek's daughter, Anna, and one of her brothers, Marcin, to dance to inspire the *kapela* while it played and to allow us to hear the sounds of the dancers' shoes on the wooden floor and their occasional claps. Their cousin, Aniela Styrczula-Maśniak, also helped out by turning Anna out onto the dance floor after the first *ozwodna.* Anna, Marcin, and Aniela wore what they had on when I asked them to dance, except they changed into their **kierpce,** tooled-leather shoes with hard leather soles and straps that wrap up the ankles (Figure 5.9). We recorded a suite of dance *nuty* without the dancers, and then one with them. The musicians exclaimed that they played much better with the dancers because the dancing gave them drive and energy. Interaction between musicians and dancers is part of the aesthetic of the music that helps generate pleasure as well as beauty.

FIGURE 5.9

Aniela Styrczula-Maśniaka (left) turning out her cousin Anna Styrczula-Maśniaka (center), who will then dance with her brother Marcin (right). This photograph was taken during the session when CD 2, Tracks 13–17, were recorded in the Styrczula-Maśniaka home in Kościelisko, Poland, 2005.

Timothy J. Cooley

Listen carefully to the accompanying ostinato pattern for the first *ozwodna* (CD 2, Track 13) and compare it to CD 1, Track 12. The ostinatos are essentially identical though the *nuty* differ. The shared ostinato pattern is a typical 5-bar *ozwodna* type (note the identical *basy* pattern: DD EE DE AA DD). See the Close Listening guide.

CD 2:13

Góralski suite part 1: *Ozwodna* (0:57). Performed by Krzysztof Trebunia-Tutka, lead violin; Jan Trebunia-Tutka, second violin and voice; Paweł Trebunia-Tutka, *basy*; with Anna, Marcin, and Aniela Styrczula-Maśniak dancing. Field recording by Timothy J. Cooley. Kościelisko, Poland, 2005.

Close Listening

GÓRALSKI SUITE PART 1: *OZWODNA*

CD 2:13

COUNTER NUMBER	COMMENTARY/TEXT	TRANSLATION
0:00	Singer Jan Trebunia-Tutka calls for the dance by singing a couplet. The lead violin and *basy* join in on the fifth metrical pulse (third bar) playing the accompanying 5-bar ostinato pattern. *Ej, dziwcyno kochanie* *Nie lygoj na sianie*	 Girl my love Don't lie in the hay
0:06	Jan sings the second couplet, using the same *nuta*. *Ej, bo ciy sianko zdradzi* *Bedom chłopcy radzi*	 The hay will betray you The boys will be happy.
0:11	Krzysztof Trebunia-Tutka, lead violinist, takes over the melodic lead and plays a variation of the same *nuta*, phrase A. Marcin Styrczula-Maśniak begins to dance with his sister. We can hear his shoes stomping on the wooden floor.	
0:16	Lead violin plays a variation of same *nuta* over the same 5-bar ostinato, but his variation differs enough that we will call it phrase B.	
0:20	Variation of phrase B, establishing ABB melodic phrase pattern.	
0:24	Phrase A variation.	
0:27	Phrase B variation.	
0:31	Phrase B variation.	
0:35	Phrase A variation.	
0:38	Phrase B variation.	
0:42	Phrase B variation. Dancer Marcin heard clapping while he dances.	
0:45	Phrase A variation.	
0:49	Phrase B variation; dancers heard stomping.	
0:52	Phrase B variation.	

CD 2:14

Góralski suite part 2: *Ozwodna* (1:07). Performed by Krzysztof Trebunia-Tutka, lead violin; Jan Trebunia-Tutka, second violin and voice; Paweł Trebunia-Tutka, *basy*; with Anna, Marcin, and Aniela Styrczula-Maśniak dancing. Field recording by Timothy J. Cooley. Kościelisko, Poland, 2005.

The second dance in the suite (CD 2, Track 14) is an additional *ozwodna*, also in 5-bar phrases, but the ostinato differs significantly. The *basy* plays a variation of this pitch pattern—three phrases, each 5 bars long: DD DE DD ED EE, DE EE AA BC# EE, DD EE DE AA DD. This dance is not introduced by a song (see the Close Listening guide).

Close Listening

GÓRALSKI SUITE PART 2: OZWODNA

CD 2:14

COUNTER NUMBER	COMMENTARY
0:00	Lead violinist Krzysztof introduces the *nuta*. The accompanying violin and *basy* join on beat 5 (third bar). Nuta is three 5-bar phrases long, ABB variation pattern. The ostinato differs slightly in each 5-bar phrase, repeating every 15 bars.
0:05	Phrase B, 5 bars
0:09	Phrase B, 5 bars
0:13	Phrase A; *basy* pattern DD EE DD ED EE
0:17	Phrase B; *basy* pattern DE EE AA BC# EE
0:21	Phrase B; *basy* pattern DD EE DE AA DD
0:25	Phrase A (ABB repeats)
0:29	Phrase B
0:33	Phrase B
0:37	Phrase A (ABB repeats)
0:41	Phrase B
0:45	Phrase B
0:49	Phrase A (ABB repeats)
0:52	Phrase B
0:56	Phrase B
0:59	Phrase A
1:03	Phrase B and end

The third dance tune is a *krzesana* called "trzy a ros" ("three and one"). As with many of the *krzesana* genre tunes, the name refers to the structure of the *nuta* and ostinato. Listen to CD 2, Track 15, and pay careful attention to the accompanying *basy* that changes pitch on the third and fourth beat as follows: DD AD, DD AD, DD AD, and so on. In every 4-beat section, there are three D pitches and one A pitch, hence the name "three and one." The accompanying violin in this example plays a more elaborate "harmonic" ostinato (see the Close Listening guide). (Harmony is a concept that fits only awkwardly with *muzyka Podhala*. The *basy* and accompanying violin pitch and chord changes function to mark time and musical structure rather than to create the harmonic pull of most European classical music and some Euro-American popular music.)

CD 2:15

Góralski suite part 3: *Krzesana* "trzy a ros" (1:26). Performed by Krzysztof Trebunia-Tutka, lead violin; Jan Trebunia-Tutka, second violin and voice; Paweł Trebunia-Tutka, *basy*; with Anna, Marcin, and Aniela Styrczula-Maśniak dancing. Field recording by Timothy J. Cooley. Kościelisko, Poland, 2005.

Close Listening

GÓRALSKI SUITE PART 3: *KRZESANA* "TRZY A ROS"

CD 2:15

COUNTER NUMBER	COMMENTARY/TEXT	TRANSLATION
0:00	Jan Trebunia-Tutka introduces the dance by singing. The string-band joins in the third bar.	
	Aśtajrom, aśtajrom,	(nonsense vocables)
	Sto śtyrdziyśi kacek mom.	I have one-hundred and forty ducks.
0:05	Second sung couplet.	
	A te kacki mojyj Kaśki,	Those ducks belong to my Kate,
	Jo siy z Kaśkom dobrze znom.	I know my Kate very well.
0:09	Krzysztof plays a variation of the same *nuta* on the violin. Note the unvarying basy/ostinato pattern: DD AD, DD AD, etc.	
0:33	Note how the string band adjusts tempo to the audible steps of the male dancer.	
0:58	Following the lead violinist, the string band modulates down to the key of G. The *basy* ostinato pattern becomes GG DG, GG DG, etc.	
1:12	The piece modulates back up to the key of D before ending.	

Close Listening

GÓRALSKI SUITE PART 4: KRZESANA "PO DWA"

CD 2:16

COUNTER NUMBER	COMMENTARY
0:00	Dance called, not by singing, but by calling out *"po dwa!"* The lead violinist begins the tune; the accompanying *basy* and violin join in third bar. *Basy* ostinato pattern: DD AA DD AA, etc.
0:15	Beginning of second variation cycle. Each phrase is 4 bars long. Variation cycles usually begin with a phrase emphasizing a higher register.
0:28	Beginning the third variation cycle. Note that the number of 4-bar phrases varies in each variation cycle.
0:44	Beginning of fourth and final variation cycle.

CD 2:16

Góralski suite part 4: *Krzesana* "po dwa" (0:54). Performed by Krzysztof Trebunia-Tutka, lead violin; Jan Trebunia-Tutka, second violin and voice; Paweł Trebunia-Tutka, *basy*; with Anna, Marcin, and Aniela Styrczula-Maśniak dancing. Field recording by Timothy J. Cooley. Kościelisko, Poland, 2005.

CD 2:17

Góralski suite part 5: *Krzesana* "ze stary" and "zielona" (2:07). Krzysztof Trebunia-Tutka, lead violin; Performed by Jan Trebunia-Tutka, second violin and voice; Paweł Trebunia-Tutka, *basy*; with Anna, Marcin, and Aniela Styrczula-Maśniak dancing. Field recording by Timothy J. Cooley. Kościelisko, Poland, 2005.

The fourth dance in the suite (CD 2, Track 16) is another *krzesana* called "po dwa" ("in two"). The accompanying violin and *basy* change chords every two beats (chords DD AA DD AA, etc.), hence "in two." See the Close Listening guide.

The next dance is also a *krzesana,* this to a modulating sequence of *nuty* with a changing ostinato pattern called "ze stary" ("the old one") (CD 2, Track 17). Then without stopping, at exactly 1:43 seconds into the track, the lead dancer gestures for the end of the dance, and the band immediately shifts into "zielona," the closing coda. Recall that the "zielona" *nuta* marks the end of the dance sequence and the moment when the lead male dancer turns the lead female dancer, ostensibly making physical contact with her for the first time during the dance. See the Close Listening guide.

We can make several preliminary interpretations about the social meaning of *góralski* dancing based on the structure alone. Before we do this, however, we should remember that *Górale* of Podhale are modern Europeans who share much culturally with other Europeans and many Americans. Yet traditional cultural practices, such as the *góralski* dance, contain information concerning core values and ideas about what it means to be *Górale* in the twenty-first century, even if such practices do not describe how any one individual lives his or her life. With this in mind, we can note that within the overall structure of the dance, the primary male dancer exercises considerable freedom and control (Wrazen 1988:197). He determines what dance tunes will be used, with whom he will dance, and for how long they will dance together. The primary female dancer must express herself by the way she dances within the context controlled by the man. Her options are limited, but her intentions can be read by the community as

Close Listening

GÓRALSKI SUITE PART 5: KRZESANA "ZE STARY" AND "ZIELONA"

CD 2:17

COUNTER NUMBER	COMMENTARY/TEXT	TRANSLATION
0:00	Jan introduces the fifth dance with two sung couplets. The string band, as usual, joins in the third bar.	
	Ej se ino cina cina	Hey, only "cina cina" (nonsense vocables)
	Lepso Kaśka niż Maryna	Kathy is better than Mary
	Kaśka uprać, Kaśka usyć	Kathy does laundry, Kathy sews
	Maryniy siy nie kce rusyć.	Mary does not want to move.
0:10	Krzysztof on lead violin picks up the *nuta* with its 4-bar phrases and plays for the dance. Note the *basy* ostinato pattern: AA AE, AA AE, etc.	
0:22	Following a melodic cue played by Krzysztof, the ostinato pattern changes to EE AA, EE AA, etc.	
0:38	Following the lead violinist again, the ostinato pattern changes back to AA AE, etc.	
1:06	The *nuta* modulates up to D with a *basy* ostinato pattern: DD DA, DD DA, etc.	
1:28	The *nuta* modulates to G, with a *basy* ostinato pattern: DD GG, DD GG, etc.	
1:43	Following a visual cue given by the lead dancer, the *nuta* abruptly changes "zielona" for the ending turn of the dancers.	

they observe how she responds to the male dancer with her body language, facial expressions, and general interactions with her partner. Remember that only one couple dances at a time while all others are free to watch—and they usually do so with great interest. As might be expected, dancing *po góralsku* entails a certain amount of showing off within one's own close circle of friends, family, and community. Especially for the man, it is a vigorous and athletic dance that requires skill and stamina in addition to thorough knowledge of the music.

LIFE STORY: KRZYSZTOF TREBUNIA-TUTKA

A violinist and singer featured on several of the CD tracks for this chapter, including the dance suite we just analyzed, Krzysztof Trebunia-Tutka embodies many of the themes of this chapter. He is a traditional musician in the sense that he comes from a long line of family village musicians, he is respected in Podhale as one of the finest musicians and dancers in the *muzyka Podhala* style, and he is an excellent teacher. "Traditional" in this sense means doing things as they were done in the past, the way one's parents, grandparents, and as in Krzysztof's case, even great-grandparents did things. Yet Krzysztof is a modern, cosmopolitan, twenty-first-century global citizen. He has shared with me in interviews and informal conversations that he believes traditions must change and adapt in order to stay alive in the present day. Therefore, Krzysztof is comfortable and capable playing the violin, shepherd's flute, or dancing *po góralsku* in a local-style costume as his great-grandfather would have done, and on the same day playing on a festival stage before thousands of fans with a reggae band from Jamaica or a rock-fusion band from Warsaw (Figure 5.10).

I met Krzysztof in Podhale in 1992. He was performing with his father Władysław and sister Anna at an informal celebration after a small folk festival in the village of Poronin, right next to his home village of Biały Dunajec (Figure 5.11). At the time he was twenty-two years old, a university student in Kraków, and recognized at least locally as an accomplished violinist, dancer, and tradition bearer. That summer I interviewed Krzysztof, and we enjoyed many informal meetings and conversations as

FIGURE 5.10

The Trebunia-Tutka family band performing in a fusion concert in Zakopane, Poland, 2005. Władysław Trebunia-Tutka is on the left, Krzysztof is dancing in the middle, and his sister Anna is playing *basy*. Note the electric bass and the drum set barely visible behind Krzysztof, along with a Hungarian cymbolum to the right of Anna.

Timothy J. Cooley

well. I have continued to correspond with and visit him in the intervening years. During this time, Krzysztof became a household name in all of Poland and a popular worldbeat music performer and recording artist with several CDs that made the charts in Western Europe. Yet he remains grounded in the Podhale region where he actively teaches local children how to play *muzyka Podhala,* sing, and dance.

This brief biography is based on my interviews and conversations with Krzysztof. In our interviews and conversations over the years, two themes have consistently emerged: first, deep knowledge of the cultural practices of Krzysztof's ancestors is very important for his self-conception and his understanding of his own musical activities; second, while grounded in this sense of musical heritage, he believes it is his right and perhaps responsibility to experiment with his music.

Krzysztof was born in 1970 and raised in the small Tatra village of Biały Dunajec, Poland. Whether in conversations with me, in the introductions he makes when

Timothy J. Cooley

FIGURE 5.11

From right to left: Andrzej Polak, Władysław Treubnia-Tutka, Krzysztof, and Anna partially blocked by Krzysztof's violin and arm. Poronin, Poland, 1992.

performing on stage, or in the liner notes of a published recording, Krzysztof is quick to reference a long line of ancestors who played *muzyka Podhala*. His great grandfather Stansław Mróz was a shepherd and a respected bagpipe player.* Mróz is mentioned in the writings of the Polish musicologist Adolf Chybiński, who worked in Podhale before World War I (Chybiński [1923] 1961:362), and he was acquainted with the famous Polish composer Karol Szymanowki, who frequently visited Podhale. Krzysztof's grandfather Jan Trebunia-Tutka (b. 1898) was also a musician, as was his brother Stanisław (b. 1907). Jan and his wife had nine children, four boys and five girls. All of the boys were musicians, including the youngest, Władysław (b. 1944), Krzysztof's father. By the 1950s Władysław was already recognized as a skilled violinist, and the Trebnia-Tutka family band was making a name for itself at the local and national folk music festivals and contests that mushroomed in postwar Poland. When Krzysztof told me about this long line of musicians, he noted with a sense of pride and amusement that in the 1950s there were so many family musicians that the Trebunia-Tutka family could produce three bands to simultaneously play three different weddings or parties.

Here Krzysztof explains how his father reluctantly began teaching him how to play violin:

> When I was about six years old, Mama asked Dad to teach me to play. He gave me a little *złóbcoki* to play [boat-shaped folk violin; see Figure 5.12]; he did not want me to break a real violin. I did not like it that much, and he did not want to teach me. But little by little I learned, and he would every now and then suggest that we play a tune together. He would tell me how to do something, what I was doing wrong. (Interview with author, August 23, 2005)

Even though his father was and excellent music teacher with other people's children, Krzysztof found it challenging to learn from him at first. However, he did teach Krzysztof how to dance the difficult *ozwodna* steps by the time he was seven.

---

*Bagpipes are often associated with shepherding cultures. The bags themselves are made from the hides of sheep or, as in the case of *Górale* pipes, from goats.

FIGURE 5.12

Władysław Trebunia-Tutka playing a *złóbcoki*. Poronin, 1992.

That same year Krzysztof joined a local school song-and-dance troupe that he enjoyed very much, in part because of the camaraderie with friends. Thanks to his father's teaching, Krzysztof became one of the best dancers in the school.

At that time in the 1970s it was quite common for schools, villages, and even businesses to sponsor regional song-and-dance troupes. Poland was then governed by the Communist Party, which encouraged folk music troupes as ideologically appropriate expressions of "the people." Whether or not any individual in a troupe accepted that ideology was beside the point since all businesses, schools, and organizations were associated with the government on some level. Krzysztof as a young boy was probably not that politically aware, and he recalls appreciating the song-and-dance troupes for the social and traveling opportunities they provided. He recalls traveling with his school troupe at age eight or nine to Germany and how inspired he was to meet musicians and dancers from around the world. In the 1980s, Poland was under martial law as the Communist Party attempted to resist the SOLIDARITY* movement that led to the end of communist hegemony in 1989. During martial law, travel outside of the country was severely restricted, but Krzysztof was able to travel around Europe with his troupe.

Krzysztof's father took a greater interest in his son's abilities when he saw him perform with the school group, as Krzysztof relates:

> He showed me how to play on the *fujarka* [wooden flute associated with shepherds]. I liked that very much. I could very quickly learn how to play the tunes. I won first place at a contest on that *fujarka*. That was great motivation, and I would play whenever I had a moment: waiting for my Mama, who worked at the hospital, waiting at a bus stop, whenever I had a moment. And all the time I was getting better at the *złóbcoki*. (Interview with the author, August 23, 2005)

In 1982, when Krzysztof was about twelve, his father brought him with the family band to a national folk festival up in central Poland. Krzysztof recalls the inspiration he received when the family won first prize at the contest. At that time he also started attending a local music school where he learned how to read music, the basics of European common practice music theory, and the rudiments of playing the piano. Though he did not stick with the music school, he continues to

---

*The *Solidarność* movement (SOLIDARITY in English, and typically written in capital letters) achieved free elections and won those elections in 1989. This set off a wave of anticommunist movements throughout Central Europe.

apply these basic skills to his music. For example, he can read the musical notations in books about *góralska muzyka* and uses these books to supplement his understanding of the repertory he learned from his family and community teachers.

When he was thirteen, Krzysztof received an accordion from his father; with his piano keyboard skills, he quickly learned how to play tunes on this new instrument. Though not considered traditional in *Górale* music, and though the equal-tempered tuning of the accordion conflicts with *Górale* tuning practices, the instrument is very useful for pan-European social dance music such as waltzes and polkas. These pan-European dance tunes play an important role at local weddings, and Władysław began taking his son and his accordion with him when he played wedding parties. Wedding celebrations in Podhale typically go on for several days, lasting until the early morning hours each day. Though Krzysztof was young for this type of work, he was tall enough to seem a bit older and, besides, he was with his father.

During these years, Krzysztof gained musical knowledge and skill. He played with his family's band in several school troupes, and occasionally in other families' bands (many regional bands draw most of their players from extended families). As he matured, he shifted his energies back to violin playing and dancing—perhaps the most respected skills for a young man in this region. By the time he was twenty, he was considered one of the best young regional musicians in Podhale. While attending college in Kraków, Krzysztof became the musical director of Skalni, an influential *Górale*-style song-and-dance group that drew its members from university students of the various institutions in Kraków. In 1990 he started a band under his own name (Kapela Krzysztofa Trebuni-Tutki) that recorded a cassette released in 1992, *Żywot Janicka Zbójnika.*

At about the same time, Krzysztof was involved in another recording project with his immediate family—father Władysław and sister Anna—that opened the doors to many new musical opportunities. In 1991 the Trebunia-Tutka family band made a worldbeat fusion recording with a Jamaican reggae band based in London called the Twinkle Brothers. The cassette that resulted made the popular music chants in Europe and launched Krzysztof's second career as a professional musician, which included several additional recordings with the Twinkle Brothers (Figure 5.13). The first recording features *muyzka Podhala* including traditional texts in what we might call a

FIGURE 5.13

CD cover to *Trebunie-Tutki w Sherwood.* Kamahuk 1996. From left to right: Della Grant, Krzysztof, Norman "Twinkle" Grant (in *Górale* costume), Anna, and Władysław Trebunia-Tutka.

Photograph by Piotra Gronau; graphic design by Kinga Mazurek-Sforza. CD conception and compilation by Włodzimierz Klescz and Krzysztof Trebunia-Tutka. Used with permission.

reggae dub sonic context with Jamaican patois glosses on the *Górale* poetry. We will learn more about this worldbeat fusion recording later in this chapter. In my interviews with Krzysztof, he consistently notes that while some may criticize the popularizing of versions of *muzyka Podhala,* he believes that he always treats the music with respect, never performing a parody of his own heritage. Additionally, the experience has prompted him to be creative, writing new texts about contemporary life in Podhale, as well as writing new tunes in the *Górale* style. Krzysztof's first new composition was "Kochaj a buduj," a song about building a traditional wooden house; Krzysztof is an architect by profession, specializing in designing modern houses using the traditional log construction technique.

Now the Trebunia-Tutka family tours the world playing a deliberate mix of very traditional-style music using *złóbcokis,* wooden flutes and bagpipes; modern adaptations of older music; and entirely new compositions that add an electric bass and drum set to the more-traditional ensemble of violins and *basy* (Figure 5.10).

Krzysztof is a legitimate pop star in Poland, a household name with records in most every CD store. Yet he still takes time to teach groups of children the basics of *muzyka Podhala.* When I asked him about this, he responded that the pay for this teaching is very low and he does not have much time, but that teaching children is a mission. Besides, he says, he has an ability to teach, and many of his students go on to make him quite proud.

Krzysztof teaches his students how to read and write music using cipher notation. His introduction of a level of literacy to a musical practice that emphasizes oral transmission is consistent with Krzysztof's interpretation of his own worldbeat fusion projects, as well as new compositions that reference traditional style. Deep knowledge of one's own heritage is essential for responsible musical self-representation. This knowledge is also liberating. Grounded in *muzyka Podhala,* Krzysztof is free to go beyond the repertory and style of his ancestors—to play music from Slovakia, lowland Poland, and Hungary and to collaborate with musicians from Jamaica and elsewhere. As a performer whose popularity extends well beyond his home mountain region and nation, Krzysztof takes seriously the responsibility to educate people about *muzyka Podhala*—what it is as well as what it is not—and he demands the freedom to do this respectfully on his own terms.

EUROPEAN VILLAGE MUSIC ON STAGE AND IN YOUR NEIGHBORHOOD

If you travel to Podhale as a tourist, you will very likely experience regional music in restaurants and at festivals. This is true in many parts of Europe, not just the Tatras. A quick perusal of almost any travel guide will reveal regional festivals where you can find local foods, arts, and music. Though festivals in the Tatras have taken place only since the mid-twentieth century, they are an important part of the way music is remembered and understood today. Elsewhere I have explained why I believe these modern-day festivals are deeply meaningful for *Górale* today (Cooley 1999; 2001; 2005:217–38). They are modern rituals, where ideas about what it means to be *Górale* of Podhale are presented, preserved, and remembered in the context of a globalizing world. Some of the music from Podhale featured in this chapter was recorded at festivals (CD 2, Tracks 10 and 12).

As a nation of immigrants from around the world, the United States hosts many festivals where European music is heard. Many immigrants also choose to have weddings in America that incorporate traditions from their heritage home. Immigrants have continued to cultivate European folk music traditions on this side of the Atlantic (Titon and Carlin 2002). My first experiences with *muzyka Podhala* were in Chicago, at festivals and at weddings. Boasting the largest concentration of Polish *Górale* outside of Poland, Chicago has dozens of Tatra-style string bands and song-and-dance troupes. In fact, song-and-dance troupes from America fairly often participate at folk music festivals in Podhale. When Louise Wrazen conducted a study of Polish *Górale* musicians and dancers in Toronto and Chicago, she found that children who learned the musical practice in North America tended to experience the music as a static icon of the past and of their self-conscious ethnicity (Wrazen 1991, 2007). Musicians and dancers who learned in Poland before moving to the United States or Canada, on the other hand, were much more likely to retain the fluid semi-improvised performance still common in Podhale. However, since 1989, travel between America and Central and Eastern European nations has increased. It may be that the musical connections have increased as well. Take a look at your local newspapers, phone books, and even television programs for information about how European immigrant groups in your neighborhood represent themselves musically. Festivals are an excellent place to begin.

European Regional Musics on the Global Stage: Three Case Studies

You may have noticed that this chapter has not emphasized the "purity" of music. Since the 1970s, ethnomusicologists have generally not believed in musical *purity*—music that is created by an isolated group of people reflecting no outside influences. Certainly in Europe it has been a long time since any group of people have lived isolated from others. The Tatra Mountains are often described as isolated, but even there people (with their musical ideas) have come from distant locations to settle, and since the late nineteenth century the region has been a popular tourist destination. There are qualities of *muzyka Podhala* that are unique and distinct, but not isolated, and certainly not pure.

Technology makes the exchange of musical sounds easier today than ever before. Even if people have little contact with others from distant places, they have probably heard radio broadcasts or recordings of music from different parts of the world. Here we examine music that deliberately brings together local and distant musical ideas and sounds.

This book's chapters offer many examples of the impact of globalization on musical practices. The chapters on South India and Indonesia in particular describe some of the ways that musics from those parts of the world have been combined with Western popular music. This type of synthesis has many names—from fusion, hybrid, and syncretism to creole. I use the term *fusion* because it suggests the combination of different elements through heat, or in the case of cultural practices, through intense contact and interaction. Another useful term is **worldbeat,** a wide category that combines popular genres of music that have a level of international recognition with a local or indigenous music usually considered "exotic." Other terms used to refer to the same phenomena are *world music, global music,* and *global pop* (for discussions of these terms, see Taylor 1997:1–3; Erlmann 1996:467; and Feld 2001:191). Perhaps most interesting in the context of this book are the perspectives of the indigenous musicians as they embrace globalization. On closer looks and listenings, one usually discovers that imitation of Western popular music is not their objective, but rather they intend to stake out a local identity in the context of global media.

MUZYKA PODHALA AND REGGAE

Both the discovery of the music of Podhale in Chicago and Krzysztof's life story raise interesting and important questions concerning the relevancy of so-called traditional musical practices in the twenty-first century. One of the premises of this book—indeed, of ethnomusicology itself—is that music is conceived of and constructed differently in different regions of the world. Music may change in meaning while maintaining its form when carried with immigrants from the Tatra Mountains to the urban landscapes of Chicago or Toronto. But what happens when a family band of "traditional" *Górale* musicians decides to join forces with another family band, this time of reggae musicians with roots in Jamaica? How does a local musical practice adapt to a globalizing world?

"Krzesany Po Dwa" (CD 2, Track 18) features the Trebunia-Tutka family band together with the Twinkle Brothers band, introduced above. It exemplifies both the process and some of the issues raised by worldbeat fusions (see Figure 5.13). Considering the music-sound itself, we have a piece that is easily recognized as fitting within the popular genre of reggae. But what makes it *sound* like reggae? Is it possible to *hear* it as *muzyka Podhala* instead of reggae, or even simultaneously as reggae?

To answer these questions, we might begin by determining what makes it sound like reggae in the first place. Listen carefully to the first few seconds of "Krzesany Po Dwa" ("Going to the Village"; CD 2, Track 18) and follow the Close Listening guide. First we hear a 2-second drum introduction, which alone tells us that this is not traditional *muzyka Podhala*—there are no drums traditionally in Podhale. The drum introduction is followed by what a reggae musician might call the *dub,* a rhythmic/harmonic ostinato played on drum set, electric bass, electric guitar, and piano. The first four bars of this ostinato are represented in Transcription 5.10; subsequent repeats are variations on this ostinato, with a few modulations into different tonal areas. What most identifies this dub as reggae is the piano emphasis on the second beat of each measure, supported by the snare drum, which also accents this beat. The second beat of a duple-meter measure (or the second and fourth beats in $\frac{4}{4}$ meter) is usually felt as a weaker beat, and when it is accented, often with a relatively high-pitched instrument, a lilting feeling is created that induces movement in listeners' bodies. This regular marking by a medium- to high-pitched sound of a typically unaccented metrical position is also what makes a polka a polka. There are differences (a polka is

CD 2:18

"Krzesany Po Dwa" ("Going to the Village") (5:04). Music and words adapted by Władysław Trebunia and Norman Grant from traditional songs. Performed by the Twinkle Brothers band and the Trebunia-Tutka family band. Produced by Norman Grant and Włodzimierz Kleszcz. Released by Kamahuk (www.kamahuk.net), Tutki (www.trebunie.pl), and Twinkle Music (www.twinklemusic.com) in 1992 on *Twinkle Inna Polish Stylee: Higher Heights* and rereleased on *Twinkle Brothers. Trebunia-Tutki Greatest Hits* on CD in 1997.

"KRZESANY PO DWA" ("GOING TO THE VILLAGE")

CD 2:18

COUNTER NUMBER	COMMENTARY/TEXT
0:00	Drum introduction.
0:02	Reggae "dub" established by drum, bass, electric guitar and piano. Spoken d in English: "Hey Johnny, where you goin', man?" "To the village." And so forth.
0:15	*Krzesany* "po dwa" *nuta* played on violins introduced.
0:25	The Twinkle Brothers begin singing in harmony: "Comin' from the mountains . . ."
0:41	The Trebunia-Tutka family sings the *Górale* dialect original text (paraphrased in the English texts sung by the Twinkle Brothers).
0:48	The Trebunia-Tutka family band plays a second *nuta* using the same "po dwa" ostinato: DD AA, DD AA, etc.
0:52	More spoken dialogue in English by the Twinkle Brothers.
1:01	Twinkle Brothers sing a second verse: "The boys are down there drinkin' . . ."
1:14	Modulation to the key of G, same "po dwa" ostinato: GG DD, GG DD, etc. Spoken dialogue by the Twinkle Brothers.
1:27	Reggae dub, whistle, and vocal call of a sort used by *Górale* in the Tatras.
1:36	Violin playing a "po dwa" *nuta* over the reggae dub. More vocal calls in *Górale* dialect.
1:56	Reggae band drops out, leaving the *Górale kapela* playing "po dwa" alone.
2:03	Reggae band returns as one of the Trebunia-Tutka family members sings a couplet.
2:37	*Górale kapela* drops out, modulation from key of D to G. Reggae band bass and drum play dub.
2:50	Sung *Górale* text accompanied by reggae drum and bass alone.
3:03	Modulation to C, ostinato: GG CC, GG CC, etc. Full reggae band and *Górale kapela* return.
3:24	*Górale* dialect texts sung. Accompanied by both the Reggae band and *Górale kapela*.
3:32	Modulation back to D, ostinato: DD AA, DD AA, etc. Both family bands playing.
4:18	Bass and drum dub only.
4:36	*Górale* dialect couplet sung over bass and drum dub.
4:54	*Górale* violin returns for a few phrases before the end.

TRANSCRIPTION 5.10
"Krzesany Po Dwa"
("Going to the Village"),
"dub" ostinato played
by the Twinkle Brothers'
rhythm section.

typically much quicker, and the marked position is on an "upbeat" rather than on the beat as is the case with reggae, for example), but the principle is the same.

Almost immediately, as the reggae dub is being established, a voice is heard asking, "Hey Johnny, where you goin', man?" to which a second, lower voice responds, "To the village." There is nothing particularly "reggae" about this spoken dialogue, yet the use of the English language again reminds us that this is not *muzyka Podhala.* In fact, there is nothing Polish at all about the music to this point, except for the whistle and vocal call heard in the background starting at 5 seconds. But most of us would not be able to identify the whistle and call as specifically Polish, and the music remains sonically reggae. Not until 15 seconds into the piece do our ears receive any real hint that this is not traditional reggae. At this moment we hear a *Górale* string ensemble playing *Krzesana* "po dwa," one of the *góralski* dance tunes introduced earlier. Listen to CD 2, Track 16, and you will hear the same ostinato and *nuta* heard on Track 18, beginning at 0:15. "Po dwa" means "in two," and careful listening will confirm that the *basy* and accompanying violins, as well as the bass guitar, piano, and electric guitar, change harmony every two beats: two beats on D, two beats on A.

At 0:25 seconds, two singers in harmony sing "Comin' from the mountains, Johnny the outlaw . . . " over the reggae dub and *Górale* string ensemble mix. The English dialect verse is a loose translation of the original *Górale* dialect text, *Idzie z góry zbójnici. . . ,* that we hear at 0:41. By now it is clear that this is fusion: music we hear as reggae combined with music from the Polish Tatra Mountains. The music is multivalent, that is, we can hear and interpret it in many ways. The dub establishes the sound as reggae; the violins, the tune that they play, and *Górale* dialect text signal worldbeat fusion; a Polish listener and others familiar with *muzyka Podhala* will experience the piece as *Górale* at least on some level. Keep listening, and at 1:56–2:02 the reggae dub drops out completely leaving only the *Górale* ensemble. If someone began auditioning this piece here, it would sound like traditional *muzyka Podhala,* at least for six seconds.

As with all music, the sound of this reggae/*muzyka Podhala* fusion is just part of the story. A critical listener wants to know what brought the Trebunia-Tutka family and the Twinkle Brothers together in the first place. The impetus behind this particular worldbeat fusion was Włodzimierz Kleszcz, a politically active radio producer from Warsaw. From 1948 to 1989 Poland was a communist country under the influence of the former Soviet Union. As a way of protesting against the Communist Party, Kleszcz actively promoted certain forms of popular and folk music, especially what he called black and pan-African influenced music associated with struggles for human independence. His interest in reggae derived from these concerns, but until the end of communist political hegemony in 1989, he avoided Polish folk music because he associated it with communist propaganda (interview with the author, March 22, 1995). Dramatic social change requires dramatic change in the use and conception of musical practices as well. After the fall of communism in 1989, Kleszcz reassessed his relationship with Polish folk music and became concerned that the Western popular music that he promoted might threaten the music he formerly shunned. His idea was to combine a Polish folk genre with a popular genre to create something that Poland's youth would listen to, with the hope that this would increase their interest in Polish folk music. In 1991 Kleszcz came up with the idea of trying to combine a traditional *Górale* band made up of a father, Władysław Trebunia, and two of his children, Anna and Krzysztof, with a traditional reggae band, the Twinkle Brothers. He had been bringing the Twinkle Brothers to Poland since the mid-1980s, and during one of their trips to Poland, he arranged for the leader of the band, Norman Grant, and bassist, pianist, guitarist Dub Judah to visit the Trebunia family in their Podhale home. There they jammed for a few days before they all traveled to Warsaw and then separately recorded raw tracks at Polish Radio; the *Górale* band recorded tracks, and the reggae band recorded separate tracks. The two bands did very little if any playing together at that recording session. The raw tracks were later "fused" in a London mixing studio and then released on a cassette called *Twinkle Inna Polish Stylee: Higher Heights* in 1992. The cassette, which centers on the legend of Juraj Jánošík (translated as "Johnny" in the English portions of our example), an early-eighteenth-century *zbójnik* (high-way robber) today employed as a Robin Hood-like symbol of freedom and justice, rose to number nine on the World Music Charts Europe in October 1993. (See Cooley 2005:162–202 for a full account and interpretation of this fusion project.)

This fusion of *Górale* music with reggae tells us many things about Podhale in the late twentieth and early twenty-first centuries. First, if Podhale ever was a truly isolated corner of Europe, it can hardly make that claim now. People from all around the world travel to the Tatra Mountains, and even family musicians regionally recognized as local culture bearers are now free to create music with internationally known reggae musicians. Second, ancient stories such as the *zbójnik* legends from Slovakia and Poland can be reinterpreted and given modern meaning. The desire for economic and individual independence, as well as the perils of betrayal, at the center of the *zbójnik* legend are still relevant in Poland, and they resonate with Jamaican Rastifarians as well as an international worldbeat audience. Both *Górale* and Jamaican Rastifarians have traditions of music about independence. Third, though the human desire for independence is probably universal, no single music system is universal. The fusion of reggae and *muzyka Podhala* required outside mediation from Kleszcz, the Warsaw radio producer, and a group of studio mixers in Warsaw and London. In other words, the *Górale* and reggae musicians were not able to play together at first—only later, when they recreated their hits for concert performances, did they learn to play together live.

The Trebunia-Tutka family musicians went on to create numerous additional fusion recordings, ranging from jazz to modern choral arrangements, with the Twinkle Brothers and with other Polish musicians. A partial listing of their recordings, as well as additional fusion projects, is provided in the Further Listening section at the end of this book.

BALKANSKI DZHAZ (BALKAN JAZZ), YURI YUNAKOV, AND IVO PAPASOV

On CD 2, Track 8, we were introduced to the Bulgarian wedding dance called *ruchenitsa* and the concept of "asymmetrical" or "additive" meters. The *ruchenitsa* with its seven-beat (2 + 2 + 3) or short-short-long metrical pattern is seemingly at odds with the European tendency toward simpler duple- or triple-meter structures. For those of us not familiar with this type of dance music, it may be difficult to count at first, but once we get the hang of it, the short-short-long meter makes us want to dance. If you have ever danced a Balkan open-ended circle dance, you know the pleasures of repeating patterns of short and long steps. Try stepping to the *ruchenitsa* on CD 2, Track 19, starting with your left foot, l-r-L, r-l-R, l-r-L, etc. (the capital L's and R's correspond to the long pulses of the pattern). You will find it easier to start at 7 seconds into the track, where the *ruchenitsa* pattern is established. Do not get discouraged if you lose the pattern at 21 seconds into the track, when the introductory material returns. This example has the same short-short-long metrical pattern heard on Track 8 and is just as fast, almost too fast for dancing.

"Kurdzhaliiska Ruchenica" (CD 2, Track 19) features two Bulgarian superstars, Yuri Yunakov and Ivo Papasov, each of whom has his own wedding band, but they occasionally perform together (Figure 5.14). Here they are joined by Neshko Neshev and Salif Ali, stars in their own right who have been playing with Yunakov and Papasov for years creating the sort of folk-jazz-rock fusion heard here. As exciting as the music is to listen to, the history and social meanings of this Bulgarian wedding music make it all the more fascinating.

Yunakov and Papasov are of Turkish Romani ancestry, and both come from musical families with long histories of playing music for Romani and Turkish weddings and other ceremonies where dance music is required. Therefore, in their persons, the communities they serve, and the music they play they are

CD 2:19

"Kurdzhaliiska Ruchenica" (7:10). Music and arrangement by Ivo Papasov. *Yuri Yunakov & Ivo Papasov: Together Again.* Ivo Papasov, clarinet; Yuri Yunakov, saxophone; Neshko Neshev, accordion; Salif Ali, drum set; Kalin Kirilov, guitar, bass; and Seido Salifoski, *tarabuka.* Traditional Crossroads (BMI), CD 4330. 2005.

multicultural, bridging Europe with the Turkish Middle East and aspects of Romani culture that are woven throughout Northern India, the Middle East, Europe, and beyond.

"Kurdzhaliiska Ruchenica" illustrates this. The dance form *ruchenitsa* is considered Bulgarian (the musicians playing a village version of this dance heard on CD 2, Track 8, are ethnically Bulgarian). Romani musicians playing music marked as ethnically Bulgarian is not new or strange. In fact, this practice became mandatory in the 1980s when the Bulgarian government sought to erase traces of ethnic minorities. Romani and Turkish Muslim minorities were forced to change their names to approved Bulgarian names, such as those considered Christian, and cultural displays of "Oriental" identity were banned by law, including musical forms and the Turkish language (Rice 2004:72). Ivo Papasov began his life as Ibryam Hapazov, but changed his name in response to Bulgaria's draconian antimulticultural laws.

Courtesy of Traditional Crossroads. Used with permission.

FIGURE 5.14

Ivo Papasov (clarinet) and Yuri Yunakov (saxophone), 2005.

"Kurdzhaliiska Ruchenica" also shows the influence of jazz, another music banned by the communist government in Bulgaria during most of their 1944–1989 reign, probably because of the improvisational qualities of jazz and its association with the United States. Papazov likes to call his music *balkanski dzhaz* (Balkan jazz) (Slobin 2002:237; Buchanan 1996). Like many of the Turkish forms played by Yunakov and Papasov, jazz performance typically highlights improvisation, a musical practice interpreted as expressive of ideological and political freedom.

Listen again to "Kurdzhaliiska Ruchenica," paying close attention to the texture (see Chapter 1). What instruments are playing together, and how do they relate to one another? When musicians play in close unison or polyphony, they are probably not improvising but have worked out the music beforehand —they have arranged the music in some way or another. This does not mean that they perform the prearranged music with a musical score—they generally perform from memory. The Close Listening guide shows where the melody instruments are playing precomposed or arranged material, and where they improvise over what rock and jazz musicians might call a "vamp" provided by the percussion, bass, and electric guitar.

Certainly the energetic, powerful, improvisatory performances of Papasov, Neshev, Yunakov, and the other band members stand in stark contrast to the highly arranged and polished versions of folk music that the communist-led government heralded as representing the ideal vision of Bulgaria. Therefore, even if the form *ruchenitsa* was politically acceptable, the jazz and Turkish styles fused by Yunakov and Papasov were politically suspect. When the government

Close Listening

"KURDZHALIISKA RUCHENICA"

CD 2:19

COUNTER NUMBER	COMMENTARY
0:00	Introduction, clarinet, saxophone, and accordion in unison.
0:07	*Ruchenitsa* dance 7-beat pattern established (S-S-L or 2 + 2 + 3 beats).
0:21	Repeat of introduction; *ruchenitsa* pattern suspended.
0:28	Repeat of main theme; return of *ruchenitsa* pattern.
0:42	Melody instruments beak into homophonic polyphony (same rhythm but different pitches, usually at an interval of a third).
0:56	Melody instruments again in unison.
1:57	*Ruchenitsa* again suspended for a bridge section.
2:10	Percussion, bass, and electric guitar set up rhythmic "vamp" in *ruchenitsa* pattern. Yuri Yunakov improvises on themes with his saxophone.
3:32	Saxophone and accordion join clarinet for a precomposed section.
3:50	Clarinet performs a call-and-response with the saxophone and accordion.
4:03	Return of rhythmic vamp. Neshko Neshev improvises on accordion.
4:54	Clarinet and saxophone return for another precomposed bridge section.
5:07	Beginning with Papasov on his clarinet, the three lead instruments trade short improvised phrases.
5:18	Ivo Papasov improvises extended section on clarinet.
5:39–5:54	Melodic suggestion of Turkish music.
6:39	Return of saxophone and accordion, precomposed closing coda.

banned listening to jazz, Yunakov and Papasov had to learn it by clandestinely tuning in to Turkish radio broadcasts of jazz and by obtaining contraband records. The risks to musicians were real—both Yunakov and Papasov spent time in jail for their politically inappropriate performances of the wedding music. Despite this oppression, the wedding music pioneered by Yunakov and Papasov swelled in popularity during the 1980s and remains popular today, in part because of its historical referencing of political resistance and ideas about freedom and independence.

RIFFING ON MUSIC FROM THE "SOUTHERN SLAVS"

Return for a moment to CD 2, Track 9. This example of *ganga* singing was sung by Azra Bandić, Mevla Luckin, and Emsija Tatarović in 1990 on Mount Bjelašnica, south of the capital city Sarajevo, in the independent state of Bosnia and Herzegovina. Formerly one of the six republics of Yugoslavia (literally "land of the south Slavs") from 1945 to 1991, Bosnia and Herzegovina is a relatively pluralistic society with three predominant ethnic groups: Bosniaks, Serbs, and Croats. All three groups in Bosnia and Herzegovina speak closely related Slavic dialects, the official language being Serbo-Croatian. These distinct ethnic identities are tied to histories of religious and other cultural practices rather than to biological differences or origins in different parts of the world. Bosniaks are traditionally Muslims whose ancestors converted to Islam during the 425-year occupation of the area by the Ottoman Empire. Serbs are related historically and culturally to Eastern Orthodox Christianity, and Croats are associated with Roman Catholicism (see also Petrović 2000:962–65). However, it would be a mistake to assume, for example, that all Serbs are practicing Orthodox Christians or that all Bosniaks are Muslim—just as one would not assume that Roman Catholicism defines the identity of all Italians. Yet, because religious institutions have a profound influence on cultural practices and societies in general, they can play key roles in the development of ethnic concepts as well as interethnic tensions.

Following the 1991 dissolution of Yugoslavia, ethnic tensions were exploited by those in power, and a regional war erupted between 1992 and 1995 that devastated most Bosnian villages, killing or scattering many of their inhabitants. Thus, the physical and social context in which children would have learned *ganga* was fundamentally altered. For example, Umoljani, the village where "Sister, Hold Your Chastity" was recorded in 1990, was burned down in 1992. Fortunately the three girls who sang the *ganga* on CD 2, Track 9, survived and were again singing together as young women in 2000 (see Slobin 2002:233–35 in the fourth edition of this book for a recording of these same individuals in 2000). This story provides hope for the survival of individuals and musical practices. Nonetheless, wars, death, and displacement do create musical change (see Pettan 1998 for more on the impact of war on music in Croatia).

Here we will consider two examples of change, both resulting from people and music moving from villages to urban centers and around the world. The first has to do with a long practice in Europe of celebrating "folk" music and adapting it for use in institutions of higher learning, the bastions of "classical" or "art" music. In 2005 I visited Sarajevo where the devastation of the recent war literally touched every building. Even the Academy of Music has a large hole created by a missile in a wall of their performance hall. At this academy, college-aged students are taught to sing *ganga* and other regional music genres, as well as the same European classical repertory found in elite music schools. Emblematic of a cosmopolitan commitment to religious/ethnic tolerance that defines the spirit of Sarejevo, young Bosniak, Serb, and Croat women sang *ganga* together, socialized together, laughed together. While cognizant of the real tensions and animosities that drive politics in many parts of the world, musical sounds and practices that travel with people from village to city and from country to country may offer counternarratives and cause for renewed hope.

Is *ganga* sung by a few friends in a village the same music as *ganga* sung by a cosmopolitan collection of individuals in a choir at an urban academy? The structure of the music is sonically identical: A lead singer introduces a song and is joined by two or more additional singers who perform "cutting" or "sobbing" accompanying patterns, producing the characteristic close harmonic intervals. However, as cultural practice, the rural and academic *ganga* are quite distinct, reflecting dramatically different ideas about music and activities involving music, especially when we understand *ganga* as gendered practice. Men and women do not sing *ganga* together, and their styles and approaches toward the genre differ. For girls and women in a traditional rural Bosnian context, *ganga* is typically performed by a close group of friends who sing together almost exclusively from the time they are small children until they are married. Men and boys, on the other hand, are socially free to sing *ganga* with different groups and with singers from other villages. In Sarajevo, this freedom to exchange singing partners is extended to young women, and sometimes contentious ethnic identities are redefined at least momentarily as diverse groups join their voices together.

The second example also comes from an elite institution of education, this time in Middletown, Connecticut. It also illustrates a dramatic change in musical structure from traditional Bosnian singing to what we are calling worldbeat fusion and to the aesthetic joining of individuals with diverse backgrounds. "Žuta Baba" (CD 2, Track 20) was recorded in 1997 by a group of students associated with Wesleyan University who formed a band called Žabe i Babe ("frogs and grandmothers" in Serbo-Croatian, roughly equivalent to the American phrase "oranges and apples"). Not unlike the students who learned to sing *ganga* at the Academy of Music in Sarajevo, the individuals in Žabe i Babe learned to sing *ganga* at Wesleyan's Music Department from a Bosnian student, Mirjana Laušević, the same woman who made the field recording reproduced as CD 2, Track 9.*

"Žuta Baba" (CD 2, Track 20) is a version of a genre of traditional Bosnian village singing called *šaljive pjesme* (joking songs). This genre is considered appropriate for elderly women or men, and employing double entendre, the texts are often lascivious. The singing shares some of the musical qualities of *ganga* (CD 2, Track 9): loud, open-throated, powerful, and direct singing; an emphasis on close harmonic intervals considered dissonant in other European music systems; and phrases ending with a slow downward glissando or a high yelp (see the Close Listening guide). The musicians in Žabe i Babe also enjoyed playing and singing American rock music and felt these traditional Bosnian music genres shared many of the same sonic qualities, especially the powerful, direct singing and pleasure in harmonic intervals considered

CD 2:20

"Žuta Baba" (2:59). Traditional words and music, arranged by Mirjana Laušević, Tim Eriksen, and Peter Irvine. Performed by Bosnian/American fusion band *Žabe i Babe*. Tim Eriksen (electric guitar), Peter Irvine (drums), Donna Kwon (voice), Mirjana Laušević (voice, keyboards), and Tristra Newyear (voice). Bison Publishing, BP 110857, 1997.

---

*Mirjana Laušević was the source of almost all of the material and information for this interpretation of *ganga* and Bosnia and Herzegovina. I am deeply indebted to her for permission to use her recordings and for her suggestions for improving this chapter. This chapter is dedicated to the memory of Mirjana, who died much too young. Transcriptions and translations of the texts are by Laušević with additional assistance from Marcel Dražila.

dissonant in other contexts. With members from several continents, these musicians did what people have been doing for centuries, combining sounds from distant sources to create something new—a musical fusion.

Close Listening

"ŽUTA BABA"

CD 2:20

COUNTER NUMBER	COMMENTARY/TEXT	TRANSLATION
0:00	Instrumental introduction (guitar and drums)	
0:25	Vocal introduction *Oja, oja, oja* (x4)	Nonsense vocables
0:38	Refrain *Oja, nina, oja, ne, oja nina, oja* *Oja, nina, oja, ne, oja nina, oja*	Nonsense vocables
0:51	Verse 1 *Žuta baba snutak snuje, kre, kre, kre* *Žuta baba snutak snuje, hm, hm, hm* *U barici na kladici, kre, kre, kre* *U barici na kladici, hm, hm, hm*	Yellow grandma dreams a little dream, ribbit, ribbit, ribbit (frog sounds) In a puddle on a little log, ribbit ...
1:03	Refrain	
1:17	Verse 2 *Otud ide rak na konju, kre, kre, kre* *Otud ide rak na konju, hm, hm, hm* *Sta to viče tupa-lupa, kre, kre, kre* *Sta to viče tupa-lupa, hm, hm, hm*	A crawdad on a horse is coming, ribbit ... What is it that yells bum-bop, ribbit ...
1:30	Instrumental (guitar riff, followed by clackers)	
1:55	Refrain	
2:08	Verse 3 *Sta to viče tamo-vamo, kre, kre, kre* *Sta to viče tamo-vamo, hm, hm, hm* *Sta to liječe gori-doli, kre, kre, kre* *Sta to liječe gori-doli, hm, hm, hm*	What is it that yells here-there, ribbit ... What is it that flies up-down, ribbit ...
2:20	Refrain	
2:33	Verse 1 repeated	
2:46	Coda *Oja, oja, oja* (x3)	

Reinterpreting Europe

What can we learn from the musics of Europe about the place called Europe and its peoples? One thing we learn is that there is no single way of being European. We find some general tendencies within European musical practices, but every generalization can be countered with examples from a European musical tradition that does things differently. *Ganga* singing in Bosnia, for example, is every bit as European as Mozart's compositions, even though what constitutes "consonant" singing differs greatly from Mozart's Salzburg to villages in Bosnia. Whereas some musical characteristics extend to a majority of musical practices in Europe, we can usually associate them with sweeping social and political forces such as the relatively recent institutions of nation-states and the much older influence of religions, especially Judaism, Christianity, and Islam.

Ethnomusicologists find it most satisfying to look at music among particular groups of people in specific locations. Even then they find great diversity of cultural practices, sometimes within individuals. Krzysztof Trebunia-Tutka represents the younger generation of a long line of family musicians in the well-defined region of the Polish Tatras, yet he performs with his own identity across national and ethnic borders. Balkan wedding music as played by Yuri Yunakov and Ivo Papasov draws on American jazz, Turkish musical styles, and Bulgarian folk dance forms. And though we tend to assume these types of fusions are new, they are not. The *muzyka Podhala* now considered traditional in the Polish Tatras derives from diverse sources across Central and Southern Europe. The nineteenth-century carol "Joy to the World" was composed in America with a text from Britain by Isaac Watts and melodic ideas from the German/English composer George Frederick Handel. We can conclude that the diversity of cultural practices presented as one of the themes of this chapter extends to even the most local of musical traditions.

Yet even when a performance practice draws on sources from around the world for inspiration, knowledge of the local context (the second theme of this chapter) is essential for understanding musical practice. *Ganga* singing for girls and women in Bosnia is more than an expression of musical aesthetics—it is a way of interacting with one's closest friends. To dance a *góralski* in the Polish Tatras requires knowledge of a series of dance steps and the tune types to which they are danced. Jazz is now a truly international musical form, but in Bulgaria it references ideas about freedom and independence that two decades ago would have landed a musician in jail. Though two young couples, one in Ireland and the other in Poland, may both practice Roman Catholicism, their weddings will require musical practices that differ greatly.

The third theme of this chapter is music and identity. What can we know about the identity of Europeans through the music they produce and enjoy? Merely determining from our listening that music and musicians come from a European music-culture can be challenging, though in some cases we can make a tentative identification. The violin ensembles of the Tatras "sound" European, for example. On closer examination of that music, we learn how *Górale* situate themselves in Poland, culturally and geographically on the edge looking south and east toward the Balkans. In the Balkans, musical practices can also inform us about the Romani and Turkish heritage of some musicians. Yet no musician simply inherits a musically articulated identity. All musicians make choices and perform their identity musically to reference place, religion, and ideologies as they see fit.

Book Companion Website

You will find tutorial quizzes, Internet links, and much more at the Book Companion Website for *Worlds of Music,* Fifth Edition, at **academic.cengage.com/music/titon/worlds_5**

India/South India

DAVID B. RECK

Imagine in your mind's eye approaching, from the air, the vibrant city of Chennai in southern India. You first notice in the east the rich blue of the ocean—the Bay of Bengal—spreading out to the horizon. Along the coastline is a white ribbon of sand. Facing the sea and on broad avenues stretching inland are huge whitewashed government buildings designed by the British, and the orientalist spires and domes of the High Court and University of Madras. Finally you would see modern glass-and-concrete office buildings, stores, hotels, and apartment complexes jutting up from a green sea of tropical foliage.

The colonial British had named their provincial capital "Madras," but it had always been called simply Chennai—"the city"—in Tamil, the language of the region and the state of Tamil Nadu. The climate, similar to that of coastal Central America, is described jokingly by local citizens as having three seasons: "the hot, the hotter, and the hottest!" In truth, November through January—the season of festivals of music and dance—can be quite pleasant and Caribbean-like, with a sea breeze in the evenings and the temperatures dipping into the low seventies at night.

In the old days Madras was a leisurely and genteel city. Most houses and buildings were one and two stories, with only the temple *gopurams*—ornately sculpted towers of Hindu temples—projecting up overhead (see Figure 6.1). Coconut palm, banyan, neem, jacaranda, and other trees shaded houses and streets, while an array of tropical plants filled every yard and garden (and still do in many neighborhoods). Classical Indian music, religious songs, and vintage pop songs echoed from radios, temples, and outdoor concert halls. Each morning the day might begin in the cool hours as early as 4:30 A.M. And each evening the town would shut down by 9:30 or 10:00. At night one slept under the perfume of flowering jasmine and to the songs of nightingales.

In Chennai today, with its estimated population of up to 7 million, modern buildings—apartment high-rises, hotels, shopping centers, offices, and corporate headquarters—increasingly give the city a generic urban look. The chaotic traffic of cars, buses, trucks, vans, auto rickshaws, motorcycles, mopeds, bicycles, and

The author wishes to thank Lalitha Muthukumar, M. Muthukumar, Nalini Easwar, and Easwar Iyer for help in Tamil translations and with the Glossary. Thanks also to David P. Nelson and Dan Reck for clarification of rhythmic concepts.

FIGURE 6.1

A *gopuram* at the entrance to Sri Kapaleeshwara temple in the Mylapore section of Chennai is typical of those soaring over every city and town in South India.

Photo © Carol Reck 2005. All rights reserved.

pedestrians clog the streets as they move in a cacophony of horns beneath a carbon monoxide haze. There is even an appropriately named Hotel Traffic Jam!

Overhead each day dozens of domestic and international flights approach the busy airport. A host of local television stations vie with international channels such as the BBC, ESPN, Nickelodeon, MTV, or Hong Kong's Star Channel. Sari-clad models posing as homemakers plug instant soup, shampoo, gadgets, face powder, or dishwashing detergent. Shop windows display refrigerators, air conditioners, TV sets, VCRs, automobiles, kitchen appliances, furniture, shoes, silks, and ready-made clothing. Pizza Hut and Kentucky Fried Chicken sit amidst Indian restaurants with their pungent array of curries and vegetarian fast foods. Modern hospitals equipped with the latest medical technology and world-class doctors are spaced throughout the city. Massive factories and mills produce fabric, steel, automobiles and trucks, polymers, motorcycles, electronic goods, and railway locomotives. Computers and software are everywhere as, here and throughout the planet, India establishes itself as the place where excellent technical schools train a generation whose expertise and innovation feed the global high-tech industry.

Billboards and palatial movie theaters, popular magazines, radio, and TV proclaim the cultural dominance of the film industry. Songs from the latest hit movies in Tamil, Hindi, or other South Asian languages blare from tea stalls, from makeshift loudspeakers at gatherings, and from homes.

Down the block from the air-conditioned supermarket, the video store, or the modern pharmacy, one can still find the crowded shops of the bazaar—spices and grains piled high in pyramids, exotic perfumes in dozens of colors and fragrances, finely woven rugs, and exquisite hand-loomed silks and cotton fabrics spread out like a rainbow. On every street corner, a woman sits with a basket of fragrant flowers woven into strands for women's hair or garlands for the gods. In towns and villages, the skilled craftsmen for which India is famous follow the trades of their forefathers: carving in stone or sandalwood, weaving, making intricate jewelry, hammering out fine metalwork in brass or copper, painting, carving, engraving, or making musical instruments. In homes and restaurants, a seemingly infinite variety of traditional deliciously spiced dishes in regional styles continue to make South Asia a paradise of fine cooking. Somehow, magically, these ancient traditions persist in a radically changing world, the new and old, the traditional and the innovative, thriving in a unique coexistence.

Everywhere, jarring juxtapositions confront the visitor. A farmer in a turban and loincloth plows behind bullocks in a field next to an airport runway as a Boeing 787 roars by. Mud and thatch huts sit in the shadow of luxury high-rise apartments. A nuclear power station, its machinery garlanded with flowers, is dedicated at an hour set by astrologers to 3,000-year-old Hindu chants. A traditional classical music performance takes place around the corner from a trendy coffee shop blasting out the latest American rap.

Jawaharlal Nehru, independent India's first prime minister, liked to describe his culture as a palimpsest, a manuscript parchment written on again and again in which everything written before is never fully erased. Everything written earlier is somehow still there, visible and readable, blurred perhaps, but never fully replaced or forgotten. The new is constantly added on, but the old, the traditional, continues. The multifaceted and complex nature of Indian civilization is one characteristic that makes it so rich in comparison with the increasingly monolithic nature of much of rest of the modern world.

In the flash and color and familiarity of the modern it is easy to forget that South Asia—India, Pakistan, Bangladesh, Nepal, Sri Lanka, and several smaller countries—is home to one of the world's most ancient civilizations.

History, Culture, and Music

The facts about India are staggering. Its population of more than a billion people live in an area a third the size of the United States. The country has fifteen major languages, almost as many alphabets, and many regional dialects. It is the world's largest democracy. Its history running back thousands of years makes newer countries such as Canada or the United States seem like mere blips on the cosmic screen.

One of the oldest land masses on the planet, South Asia stretches at latitudes that, if superimposed on the western hemisphere, would stretch from Oklahoma (where the Himalayas would be) south through Texas, Mexico, and Central America (see the map at the beginning of this chapter). Perhaps owing to its geography—a huge diamond cut off from neighboring lands by the ocean, deserts, impenetrable jungle, and the highest mountains in the world—greater India, despite outside influences, has developed cultures and lifeways that are distinctly its own.

THE INDUS VALLEY CIVILIZATION (c. 2500–c. 1700 B.C.E.)

The region's continuous history goes back five thousand years and beyond, disappearing into time. Stone Age encampments uncovered by archaeologists point to early human habitation, but the retrievable story begins in collective myth and legend preserved in oral traditions for centuries before being written down. High culture begins with the Indus Valley Civilization, which flourished for 800 years from 2500 B.C.E. and was roughly contemporary with that of

Drawing by Navarana. © Navarana Reck 2001. All rights reserved.

FIGURE 6.2

Dancing Girl. Mohenjo Daro, bronze, third millennium B.C.E.

Babylon and other cities in the fertile crescent between the Tigris and Euphrates rivers in current Iraq. The walled cities of Mohenjo-Daro and Harappa in current Pakistan boasted well-planned grids of streets, an advanced drainage system, palaces, warehouses, public baths, and a written language (as yet indecipherable). Sophisticated art in clay and metal portrays elephants, tigers, deer, the familiar Indian cows with their shoulder hump, realistic human portraits, and dancing girls. As to music, aside from some clay whistles (toys perhaps), no instruments or performances are portrayed in art. But the four-inch bronze dancing girl of Figure 6.2 is intriguing. What music did she dance to?

THE ARYANS (c. 1700–c. 500 B.C.E.)

Toward the end of the Indus Valley period, a migration (or invasion) of people from Central Asia who called themselves Aryans moved into the northern plains of the subcontinent (like later invaders) through the mountain passes between Afghanistan and Pakistan. Linguistic analysis has proven that groups of the same people also migrated south into Persia and west into Europe. Thus Sanskrit, Hindi, Farsi, Greek, Latin, German, French, Spanish, Italian, and English are all part of the same Indo-European language family.

The warlike and pastoral Aryans, with their chariots and herds of cattle, brought to India its first extant literature, the four **Vedas** (*vay*-dahs), sacred books of prayers, incantations, and rituals still chanted today. Prototypes of the Hindu gods appear in these texts, along with seeds of later philosophical thought. Musicians today tell their pupils that India's classical music originated in the chanting of the Vedas by priests, the four notes of chant gradually expanding to the myriad scales in the rich tapestry of the *raga* (*rah*-gah) system, discussed later in this chapter. This belief—along with another origin myth describing performing arts as a gift of the gods—illustrates an important concept: *in India, musical expression has a strong underpinning of the sacred, the ancient, the timeless.*

KINGDOMS THROUGH THE CLASSIC AND MEDIEVAL PERIODS (500 B.C.E.–c. 1400 C.E.)

A great many kingdoms, such as that of the great Buddhist emperor Ashoka (268–231 B.C.E.) or of Chandragupta II (c. 340–c. 415 C.E.), appeared in the succeeding centuries. Like Latin in medieval Europe, Sanskrit became the common language of the educated. Remarkable works on religion and philosophy such as the *Upanishads* (the "forest books") explored the nature of reality and, through introspection, the self. Sages invented the physical and mental discipline of yoga, now practiced around the world. Siddhartha Gautama Buddha (fifth century B.C.E.) expounded the new compassionate faith we know as Buddhism, eventually to spread throughout Asia. The various *Puranas* fleshed out the myths of the gods and goddesses of the Hindu pantheon, forming the basis of popular Hinduism today.

The greatest of the kingdoms provided royal patronage to the arts. The massive technical book of theater, music, and dance, the *Natya Sastra* (perhaps as early as 200 B.C.E.), describes performance, theory, and professional training in great detail. (The current-day classification of instruments into strings, winds, drums, and solid-body percussion follows the guidelines established in that work.) Many more music-theory books—such as Sarangadeva's twelfth-century *Sangeeta Ratnakara* ("Crest-Jewel of Music")—follow the development of Indian music over the centuries.

Along with the sciences, literature also flourished. Much Sanskrit poetry was actually lyrics to songs, but without notation the music has long been forgotten. The two great epics, the Ramayana and the Mahabharata were written, remaining important even today as source material for theater, dance, and lyrics in music. The great poet and playwright Kalidasa (mid-fourth to early fifth centuries) wrote works that, like Shakespeare's, have been translated into dozens of languages.

Painting, sculpture, and architecture also reached pinnacles of achievement. The murals in the Caves of Ajanta and Ellora, the remarkable stupa (hemisphere) at Sanchi, or the breathtakingly beautiful sculptures at temples such as Konarak, Khajaraho, and Mahabalipuram are treasures of world art. Although many musicians are portrayed in paint and stone, their instruments and music are silent, lost in time (Figure 6.3). While Europe suffered through its Dark and Middle Ages, successive Indian civilizations were among the most advanced on earth.

THE MOGHULS (1527–c. 1867)

Beginning in the twelfth century, Muslim traders and warlords from Central Asia and Afghanistan appeared on the scene. The warlords periodically swept into the plains as far as Delhi, sacking cities and leaving devastation in their wake before

Photo © Carol S. Reck 2005. All rights reserved.

FIGURE 6.3

Two flutists, two drummers, and a *veena* player (right, the *veena* is played over the shoulder) provide music for a dancer (center). Detail of frieze from temple, Rajasthan. Late tenth century.

returning to their homelands. However, in 1527 a remarkable general, Babur—a descendent of the Mongol Genghis Khan and a lover of poetry, books (though he could not read), music, and formal gardens—decided to stay. The result was the powerful Moghul dynasty, centered in Delhi and Agra, which dominated much of North India until a period of decline beginning in the 1700s. The Moghuls were Muslim and, though brutal in war, were lavish patrons of the arts, making their courts centers of learning and culture. Emperors such as Akbar the Great (reigned 1556–1605) and Shah Jahan (reigned 1628–1658) imported scholars, painters, musicians, writers, and architects from as far west as Arabia. To this day stories are told of legendary singers such as Tansen of Akbar's court who in performance could miraculously light lamps or cause cooling breezes simply through the power of his sound and command of music.

The great monuments of Moghul architecture such as the palace at Fatehpur Sikri or Shah Jahan's tomb for his wife—the Taj Mahal—illustrate the Moghuls' most impressive artistic accomplishment: the remarkable integration of characteristics indigenous to India with elements derived from the Islamic world of Persia and beyond. This synthesis can be seen in the tradition of miniature paintings, which were originally book illustrations but now serve as masterpieces of art dispersed in museums and collections around the globe. This synthesis can also be heard in music. The melodic concepts of the *raga* system, soaring improvisations, and the singing of beautiful poetry, particularly in North Indian classical music, connect with elements found in Persian, Turkish, and Arabic musical traditions. The connection can also be seen in hybrid musical instruments such as the ***sitar*** (sih-*tahr;* a plucked twenty-two–string classical instrument) and ***tabla*** (*tahb*-blah; a set of two small drums, one of metal and pot shaped, the other of wood and cylindrical, played with fingers and palms), which have country cousins in the *setar* of Central Asia or the *tabala* of North Africa.

There is an important principal at work here, as true today as at the time of the Moghuls. Again and again over the centuries, foreign cultural ideas have migrated into India. Once there they have been absorbed, assimilated, digested, played with, and combined with indigenous cultural elements, merging eventually in a new and undeniably Indian synthesis.

Finally, the Moghul Era established a division in India's two related but different classical music systems. In the north in areas under Moghul rule, musical influences from the Islamic world interacted more strongly with native traditions to form the Hindusthani (hindu-*stah*-nee) music tradition. By contrast, in South India, staunchly Hindu, conservative, and only marginally affected by Moghul invasions, the Carnatic (car-*nah*-tik) music tradition predominates.

THE PERIOD OF BRITISH COLONIZATION (1600S–1947)

In 1498, only six years after Columbus's epic voyage, Vasco da Gama touched down in Kerala on India's southwestern coast. He had found what Columbus was looking for. The Age of Sail had begun. Unlike previous invaders the British came by sea, at first as traders along with the Dutch, French, and Portuguese. The East India Company and later the British government, through wars and enforced alliances with native maharajas, finally emerged as paramount colonial rulers.

In spite of economic exploitation and the inherent racism of any colonial regime, the British did make some significant contributions to the subcontinent. They built railways, communications, and administrative and civic infrastructures, and they set up universities introducing English as the medium of study. (The widespread working knowledge of English has served Indians well in the globalization processes of recent years.) Education also helped to create a political movement that led eventually to independence with leaders such as Mahatma Gandhi (1869–1948) using nonviolent resistance to confront political and social injustice. Gandhi's influence, which inspired Martin Luther King Jr. in the American civil rights movement, continues to this day.

Musically the contributions of the British regime are less obvious. In the heyday of the colonial era, the British cut themselves off from meaningful contact with "native" culture. Rather, they imported pianos and other instruments from home for their dance orchestras and military bands. The establishment of a Pax Britannica, however, provided a peaceful environment in which Indian arts flourished. The so-called golden age of South Indian classical music (c. 1700–c. 1900) occurred under British rule, unnoticed by the foreign missionaries and bureaucrats. In the 1920s a recording industry led by H.M.V. in Calcutta made it possible to listen to performances of Indian music again and again, a substantial change in an oral tradition in which music, never written down, was learned by rote from a **guru** (teacher who passes on knowledge to disciples), or tangentially at concerts. When "talkies" replaced silent films around 1930 the movie industry, drawing on traditional theater, was quick to incorporate songs into every film. Movie songs remain the source of most pop music today.

In 1936 a national radio, All-India Radio (AIR), based on the BBC model, was established. Under enlightened directorship, AIR produced hundreds of broadcasts of Indian classical music each year, including a prestigious weekly national concert.

Perhaps the most important development, however, was the discovery by Indian musicians that they could adapt some European instruments to playing music in Indian style. The piano was summarily rejected, but the violin, **harmonium** (portable small reed organ), clarinet, and even the banjo became, in essence, Indian instruments. Again as in the Moghul era we can see the process of synthesis by which India adopts foreign elements and "Indianizes" them.

INDEPENDENCE AND THE MODERN PERIOD (1947–PRESENT)

In 1947 British India—now India, Pakistan, and Bangladesh—achieved independence; Sri Lanka (formerly Ceylon) became independent in 1948. The transition from colonies to nation states has had many ups and downs. Wars and social unrest have interrupted efforts at industrialization. Strong traditions have resisted change. Yet modernization has occurred, slowly at first, but at lightning speed since the 1980s.

We have seen that religion and the arts in India, especially music and dance, are inseparable. Today the polytheistic gods of Hinduism are alive and well, venerated in homes, temples, cycles of religious festivals, and music. Yet, about a tenth of the population is Muslim, giving India a larger Islamic population (120 million) than all but one of the Muslim countries of the world, Indonesia.

Caste and Community

The social system of hereditary caste, though changing, still plays a role in politics, in marriage, in household customs, and in music. In South India—in contrast to North India where many prominent musicians are Muslim—the majority of classical musicians have been high-caste Brahmins. However, the Devadasi, a caste of women dedicated to service in temples, along with their families, have also been among the most celebrated in music and dance traditions. The internationally esteemed diva, M. S. Subbulakshmi (1916–2004), South India's greatest dancer, T. Balasaraswati (1918–1984), and the eminent flutist/educator T. Viswanathan (1927–2002) were all born into this community.

Members of the barber's caste are known for playing the double-reed *nagasvaram* (*nah*-gah-svah-rum) and *tavil* (*tah*-vil) drum associated with temples, weddings, and other sacred events. A few musicians from minority communities, such as *nagasvaram* virtuoso Sheik Chinnamoulana, a Muslim, and the singer Jesudas, a Christian, are lionized. In popular music today A. R. Rahman, a Muslim, and Illaiyarajan, from the lowest (untouchable) Harijan community, are acknowledged masters. Genius, it seems, can transcend caste or background.

In the late twentieth and early twenty-first centuries, the tradition of highly valuing the arts has continued in India. As one traveler comments: "When I came into U.S. customs and told them I was a musician I was strip-searched. By contrast, when I arrived in India and said I was a musician, the customs official expressed his delight, wrote down a list of the best musicians and festivals, and waved me through."

Culture has been one of modern India's most prestigious exports. Contemporary authors such as Salman Rushdie (*Midnight's Children*) or Arundhati Roy (*The God of Small Things*) are among the most famous writers in English today. Since the 1960s, many extraordinary filmmakers have also appeared. Perhaps the best known is Satyajit Ray (1921–1992), whose works from *The Apu Trilogy* to *Charulata* have gained him recognition as one of a handful of masters of contemporary art cinema. Dancers such as Balasaraswati or Mrinalini Sarabhai have performed all over the world. Musicians such as Ravi Shankar, Ali Akbar Khan, and Zakir Hussain are megastars East and West.

In India, government support of music remains strong (dwarfing the miniscule government support of music in the United States). The Sangeet Natak Academy in Delhi oversees prestigious and substantial awards to prominent writers, actors, poets, and musicians. State governments do the same.

Today, tens of thousands of cassettes, CDs, DVDs, and videotapes are available covering every imaginable style. Musicians now have unlimited access, not only to their own traditions but also to music around the globe. Indian violinists may work a little of Vivaldi's *Four Seasons* into an improvisation, drummers might try out a few rock and roll riffs. Or they may jam with visiting jazz musicians from New York, Paris, or Helsinki.

Instruments such as the saxophone, electric guitar, mandolin, and electronic keyboard have joined the earlier Western instruments adopted into Indian music. With globalization, Indian music is absorbing the new, as it always has. Yet the old, the traditional, remains. In the palimpsest that is South Asia, the interplay between the ancient and the modern continues through all the changes of time and history. This coexistence of the old and the new is part of the world of amazement that is India.

Many Musics

If you were to stroll through one of the residential neighborhoods of Chennai, you might come into contact with many types of musical sound. In the mornings come the vendors, each pushing a cart—the vegetable man, the pots and pans salesman, the fruit lady, the waste newspaper collector, the coconut man (who will climb your tree for a fee)—and each has a distinctive (and musical) call recognized by the local housewives.

As the day wears on, a mendicant may appear, chanting a sacred song and playing a small gong or the sacred conch shell trumpet. Once in a great while a snake charmer may walk the street with his bag of cobras. Unforgettable is the distinctive nasal whine of his snake-charming music on the *punji* (*pun*-jee)—a double-reed instrument with two pipes (for melody and drone). Other wandering minstrels come and go. Clearly, in this place we are in the rich realm of Indian folk music (Figure 6.4).

POP MUSIC

On TV, over the radio, or blasting from the neighborhood snack shops, one can hear Indian popular music, also called "cine songs" because almost all popular music originates in movies. The Indian film industry, incidentally, is the largest in the world. Each film features despicable villains, fearless and clever heroes, gorgeous heroines, romance (always rocky), family problems, utterly surprising plot twists, broad comedy, heart-stopping fight scenes, and sexy dances. In virtually all movies, songs periodically interrupt the plot with MTV-like visuals in exotic settings or elaborate song-and-dance production numbers. The actors and actresses always lip-sync the words, which are actually sung by "playback singers," who along with the "music director" (composer/arranger) and lyricist are the true stars of India's pop music scene.

Cine music is to some ears a curious and sometimes bizarre blend of East and West. Choppy and hyperactive melodies often in "oriental" scales are belted out by nasal-sounding singers over Latin rhythms and an eclectic accompaniment that may include Western instruments mixed with an array of folk and classical Indian instruments. It is an anything goes, "if it sounds good, use it," approach to music. The "anything" today might include harmony and counterpoint, rap, rock, symphony music, and jazz, as well as Indian styles and sounds.

The lyrics, like those of pop music everywhere in the world, tend to focus on the eternal emotions and complications of love and romance. A duet/dialogue between female and male singer is thus the norm. But lyrics can also be comic, religious, ethical, family centered, highly poetic, or deeply philosophical.

A good place to start is to watch videos (extracted from movies) of several contemporary songs by the great A. R. Rahman. In "Kannalane" ("O Eyes, Look Truly," Song 2 from the film *Bombay*), an eloquent and lilting love song is backed

Photo © Carol S. Reck 2005. All rights reserved.

FIGURE 6.4

P. Ahmed, an itinerant street minstrel, pipes on the *nagasvaram* minus the usual accompaniment of *tavil* drum.

by traditional Indian instruments as dancers swirl in brightly colored skirts in a palatial setting, that of a Moslem wedding. "Sutram Boomi" ("Precept Earth," Song 2 from *Dum Dum Dum*) and "Azhegama Raatchasiye" ("O Beautiful Demoness," Song 3 from *Mudalvan*) emphasize folk music and instruments in their sound and are set appropriately in agricultural and rural village festival locales.

"Desinghu Raja" ("King Desinghu," Song 3 from *Dum Dum Dum*) transforms modern hero and heroine into king and queen of ancient Tanjore. The elaborate production number is filmed in the spectacular temples and palaces of that city. American rock/Indian style along with English phrases appear in "Shakalaka Baby" (Song 1 from *Mudalvan*) and "Urvasi Urvasi! Take It Easy" (Song 1 from *Kadalan*) as hip college students dance their heads off. Tamil rap interspersed with a folk tune hilariously interrupts a classical dance scene in "Petta Rap" ("Neighborhood Rap," Song 3 from *Kadalan*).

Listen to "Engal Kalyanam" ("Our Wedding") on CD 3, Track 8. This vintage song takes a lighthearted look at the commotion and excitement of an Indian wedding, with the ever-present relatives and the joyful feelings of the happy couple.

CD 3:8

"Engal Kalyanam" ("Our Wedding"), cine song (3:25). Music by M. S. Viswanathan, lyrics by Vali. Performed by P. Susheela, T. M. Soundararajan, P. B. Sreenivos, and L. R. Eswari. From *Hits from Tamil Films*, Vol. 6. EMI Odeon (India) EAECS 5519. LP. Calcutta, India, 1969.

Text, "ENGAL KALYANAM"

(Chorus) Our wedding is a "confusion wedding"!

1. Sons-in-law put up the money,
   And the father-in-law puts up the canopy to receive the gifts.[1]
   Morning is the wedding, and evening is the wedding night!
   Enliven! A love marriage![2]
   Tomorrow at the altar we'll exchange garlands, won't we?
   And won't the drums play with the pipes?[3]
2. The lovers' tale is performed in the eyes.
   It's a great struggle—to perform in the eyes!
   A colorful chariot is running beside me;[4]
   Heaven is coming to us!
3. Mother-in-law puts on eye makeup,
   While the sons-in-law stare at her mirror;
   The [wedding] procession winds along the street with firecrackers,
   While everyone gives their blessings.
   Shall we have ten to sixteen children?
   Shall the trimness of our [youthful] bodies be lost?
4. You claimed you hated men,
   Yet you gave me desire!
   If I am like Kama, the god of love,
   You are the reason!
   Your [blushing] cheeks invite me;
   Your thoughts ask for me, I can tell!
   Your eyes—are like bright lightning . . .
   What are the pleasures we haven't experienced?
5. The bride's father had prayed to the god of Tirupati
   That the marriage might be performed there,
   So the bride and groom might have auspicious lives.[5]

The sons-in-law better come home now
And give a send-off to the bride's father,
So that he can take up *sanyasin!*[6]

Free translation from the Tamil by S. B. Rajeswari (1989).

_____

1. The ceremony takes place under a canopy of banana stalks, bamboo, and cloth.
2. Spouses traditionally are chosen by parents. A "love marriage" as in Europe and the Americas is unusual, except in the movies.
3. "Drums . . . pipes" these are *tavil* and *nagasvaram* with their sacred and auspicious sound.
4. The groom is like an ancient god-hero riding a chariot.
5. Tirupati is the hilltop site of the most popular temple in South India.
6. Now that the bride's father has managed the tension and complications of his daughter's wedding, it is humorously suggested that he can become a recluse (*sanyasin*) meditating in a hermitage. In sacred texts, this is the last stage of human life.

Close Listening

"ENGAL KALYANAM" ("OUR WEDDING")

CD 3:8

COUNTER NUMBER	COMMENTARY	SECTION
0:00	Chorus: *Engal kalyanam . . .* ("Our wedding . . .")	A
0:18	Instrumental break	
0:32	Verse 1: Male-female duet in musical dialogue over "walking" bass line	B
0:49	Instrumental break	
0:53	Chorus (repeat): *Engal kalyanam . . .*	A
1:02	Instrumental break	
1:10	"Woody Woodpecker" call from U.S. cartoon.	
1:14	Verse 2: Duet over drum accompaniment, new sound	C
1:42	Verse 3: Duet over "walking" bass line	B
2:12	Verse 4: Duet over drums accompaniment	C
2:35	Verse 5: Duet over "walking" bass line	B
3:14	Chorus: *Engal kalyanam . . .* and quick fade-out	A

Although the style of "Our Wedding" is a "golden oldie," one might notice certain strong characteristics that mark this song as unmistakably Indian: the frenetic pace of the clap-hammer rhythms, the alternating male and female voices with backup chorus, an eclectic orchestra, and the culturally specific references in the lyrics.

There are three musical sections to the song:

A: The chorus (*Engal kalyanam* . . .).
B: Marked by a jazzlike "walking" bass, before moving on.
C: Marked by a accompaniment exclusively of drums, a very different sound. Sections B and C both carry the verses of the song. Instrumental interludes (one with a quote from an American cartoon) occur between the first four vocal sections.

Older Indian pop music as heard in films from the 1940s, 1950s, and 1960s may approach the semiclassical or even classical in style and instrumentation, as in the classic film *Thillana Mohanambal* (1968) about the romance between a famous dancer and a *nagasvaram* virtuoso.

The timbres, forms, and instrumentation of Indian pop music continue to evolve in extremely varied and creative ways, especially when compared with the rigid industry-controlled formulas for most American pop songs. The more one listens to Indian pop music, the more one can appreciate its unique qualities, enjoy the beauty of its lyrics and themes, and gain a better understanding of why this is the favorite music of a billion people, old and young, rich and poor, educated and uneducated. Perhaps some day the great contemporary Indian songwriters such as A. R. Rahman and Ilaiyaraja will gain the recognition that they deserve on the world scene.

RELIGIOUS MUSIC

Religious music is another important category of music in India. Among the dozens of other devotional traditions of South Asia—folk, pop, or classical, primarily Hindu but also Moslem or Christian—is that of **bhajan** (*bhah*-juhn). A *bhajan* is a song, devotional in nature and relatively simple technically, that is sung primarily as an offering to God. *Bhajans* might be sung by a soloist with a backup of violins, flutes, harmonium, and drums (or a small cine orchestra), with additional rhythmic support coming from small ringing bell-cymbals, clackers, or hand claps. A *bhajan* can be sung straight through as a song, or sung in a congregational call-and-response manner with a leader singing out verses, while the group responds with either a repetition or a refrain. A member of the responding group thus need not be trained in music, but can participate simply by mimicking the words and tune of the leader.

As noted earlier, the ensemble of two or more *nagasvaram* double-reed pipes with *tavil* drums is associated with temple worship, religious processions, weddings, and auspicious occasions of all kinds. (Similarly, the sound of a pipe organ has religious connotations in the West.) But the music that the *nagasvaram* plays is largely that of South Indian classical music (Figure 6.4 and DVD movie *Thillana Mohanambal,* Scene 1).

Classical Music

The classical music of South India is called ***karnataka sangeeta*** (car-*nah*-tuh-kah sahn-*gee*-tah, with a hard "g") or in English simply **Carnatic music.** The roots of this music lie in the distant past, in the courts and palaces of rajas and maharajas, in the great southern kingdoms and in the stately southern temple complexes built between the eighth and nineteenth centuries.

Sculpture in the ancient temples and palaces as well as murals and miniature paintings give us vivid visual images of the instruments, orchestras, dance styles, and the where and how of musical performance through several thousand years. Although the stone and painted images are silent, they bear a striking resemblance to what is seen in performance today (compare the dancers in Figures 6.3 and 6.6). Books also give us descriptions of music and performance. But the actual sound and style of pre–twentieth-century music exists only in conjecture.

Any oral tradition, such as that of Indian classical music, lives primarily in the hands, voices, memory, and creative imagination of individual human beings. In this tradition, the music can never be frozen in time, either by being written down (in words or notation) or by being preserved as a visual entity (as in a painting or photograph). The music, in a sense, lives uniquely in each performance, in the unique rendition of a song on a particular day, at a particular hour, and in the ephemeral spontaneity and creativity of improvisation. Today, videos and CDs can preserve a particular performance, but whether this fixity, this documentation, will change the essentially oral nature of Indian music and the liquid way musicians approach their tradition remains to be seen (Figures 6.5 and 6.6).

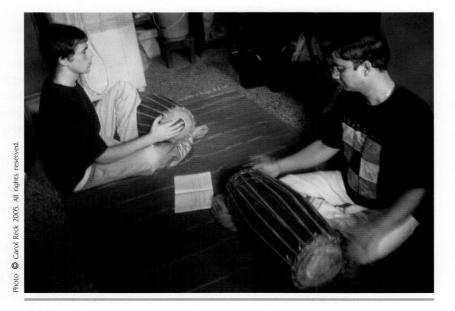

Photo © Carol Reck 2005. All rights reserved.

FIGURE 6.5

Umayalpuram Mali gives a lesson on *mridangam,* South Indian drum, to a student. Music is transmitted orally and by example, with notation as in the book on the floor used only as a memory aid.

FIGURE 6.6

The renowned Guru Sudharani Raghupathy (seated in chair) gives a *bharata natyam* dance lesson to Priya Murle. Seated on the floor are vocalist Krishnaveni Sundarajan (left), dancer Aruna Subbiah (third from left), who is chanting dance rhythms, and composer and drummer K. S. R. Aniruddha (fourth from left).

Photo © Carol Reck 2005. All rights reserved.

Music for South India's dance traditions—particularly in *bharata natyam* (bha-ruh-tah *nah*-tyam)—is similar in style to that of classical concert music. The forms of the songs, however, are unique to dance and may include sections where a specialist sitting among the musicians chants out rhythmic syllables—*nattu-vangam* (naht-tu-*vahn*-gum)—to match the intricate footwork of the dancer (Figure 6.6). Musical phrases may be repeated again and again as the dancer interprets and reinterprets the meaning of lyrics in a visual language of hand gestures, facial expressions, and body movement. In several genres of dance music the lyrics are beautiful love poetry, as often as not exploring the erotic myth of the sensuous god Krishna and his earthly lover, the beautiful Radha. Songs borrowed from the dance tradition are commonly included toward the end of classical music concerts.

As noted earlier, the Carnatic style of the south contrasts with the Hindusthani tradition of the north. In **Hindusthani music,** expansive improvisations move gradually from near immobility to sections of great speed and virtuosity. In contrast, the Carnatic music is built around an immense repertoire of precomposed Hindu devotional songs. The musical texture is more busy, and improvisations fall into blocklike sections.

Carnatic music began to take its present shape in the "golden age" of the late eighteenth and early nineteenth centuries. Three great saint-poet-composers dominate this period: Syama Sastry (1762–1827), Tyagaraja (1767–1847), and Muttuswamy Dikshitar (1776–1836). Like singer-songwriters today, these composers wrote both the melodies and the lyrics to their songs.

A clever proverb describes the trademark of each. Dikshitar's songs are like a coconut: The "hard shell" of his intellectual music structures and scholarly song texts must be broken to get to the sweetness inside. Sastry's music is like a banana: The flavorful fruit is not so difficult to get to, but one must still peel off the bitter "skin" of tricky rhythm. But Tyagaraja's songs are like a mango: The "sweet fruit" of both poetry and music are immediately accessible. It is no wonder then that Tyagaraja's songs dominate the repertoire today, cherished by musicians and audiences alike.

THE SOUND WORLD

Listen to "Devi Niye Tunai," a classical song in **kriti** (*krih*-tee) form composed by the twentieth-century composer Papanasan Sivan (CD 3, Track 9). *Kriti* is the principle song form of South Indian classical music. The singer is Shobha Vasudevan, a graduate of the University of Madras. She has sung recitals at Brihaddhvani and at other venues. The *mridangam* accompanist David Nelson is Artist in Residence at Wesleyan University, where he received his Ph.D., and a senior disciple of the great drummer T. Ranganathan. Nelson has accompanied T. Visnathan and others in India, the United States, and tours of Europe and China. The song text is in the Tamil language and praises the goddess Meenakshi with fish eyes (always open), who is worshipped in the magnificent temple in the southern city of Madurai.

CD 3:9

"Devi Niye Tunai" ("O Devi! With Fish-Shaped Eyes") (4:37). Papanasan Sivan. Performed by Shobha Vasudevan, vocal, and David P. Nelson, *mridangam*. Recorded for author by recording engineer Owen Muir. Amherst, Massachusetts, January 2001.

---

1. *devi neeye tunai ten madurai vaazh meena lochani*
2. *devaati devan sundaresan cittam kavar bhuvana sundari—amba*
    (Repeat 1)
3. *malayadhvajan maadavame kaancana maalai pudalvi mahaaraagjni alaimahal kalaimahal pani keervaani amudanaya iniya muttamizh valartta*
    (Repeat 1)

1. O Devi, with fish eyes! One who dwells in the south, in Madurai, protect me.[1]
2. You are the one great beauty in the world who has captured the heart of the Lord of Lords, Sundaresa.[2]
3. O, the One born out of the penance of the Lord of the [Himalaya] Mountains, Daughter of the mountains, great in wisdom, O Devi, [even] the daughter of waves and the daughter of the arts bow in respect to you.[3]

Free translation from the Tamil by Shobha Vasudevan.

---

1. *Devi* (related to the English *diva*) means "goddess." Meenakshi is one of many manifestations of the goddess Parvati, wife of Siva.
2. Similarly, Sundaresa is a manifestation of the great god Siva.
3. The "daughter of waves" is Lakshmi, goddess of wealth; the "daughter of the arts" is Saraswati (Figure 6.15).

Text, "DEVI NIYE TUNAI"

You may notice that each line is repeated (with successive variations) several times and that the *kriti* is in three sections. The opening phrase (beginning *devi niye tunai. . .*) is repeated after sections 2 and 3 as a refrain. The *raga* is **Keeravani** (keer-uh-*vaw*-nee) with a scale (if one disregards the intensive ornamentation) similar to the European harmonic minor scale:

sa   ri   ga   ma   pa   da   ni   sa

TRANSCRIPTION 6.1
Scale of *Keeravani raga*.

Close Listening

"DEVI NIYE TUNAI" ("O DEVI! WITH FISH-SHAPED EYES")

CD 3:9

COUNTER NUMBER	COMMENTARY
0:00	Electronic *tambura* drone background.
0:07	Brief *alapana* improvisation introduces *raga*.
0:28	1. *Pallavi* ("sprouting") section. Song and *tala* cycle begin. Drum enters. Each phrase and variation of the phrase is sung twice.
1:36	2. *Anupallavi* ("after sprouting"), second section of the *kriti.* Each phrase and variation sung twice.
2:11	**Reprise** of final variation of (1). *Pallavi.*
2:31	3. *Charanam* ("foot"), third section of *kriti.*
3:00	Singer puts brief improvised phrase into song.
3:24	Song continues with melody of (2). But the melody is set to new words here in the *Charanam*.
4:04	**Reprise** of final variation of (1). Pallavi and improvised final vocal phrase.
4:22	Listen for the drum's three-times-repeated rhythm, which signals closure.

The *tala* (time cycle) is **Adi tala** (*Ah*-dee *tah*-luh), the most common of the South Indian time cycles. It has 8 beats subdivided 4 + 2 + 2 . (See Figure 6.12 for instructions in counting *tala.*)

If you think about the song "Devi Niye Tunai," you will notice that it is marked by an environment of sound—like the spices of curries or the brilliantly colored silk saris worn by South Asian women—that signals at once where on the planet it is from. First, there is, the incessant, unchanging sound of a *drone* with a nasal buzz. Against this unchanging background a *single melody unfolds.* This melody differs greatly from tunes of Western classical or popular music: Its lines are sinuous and complex, marked by subtle bends and slides, with *intense ornamentation* in sharp contrast to the "plain" notes of most Western music (Figure 6.7).

The notes of its scale may also zigzag through intervals unfamiliar to Western ears, in tones flatter or sharper than those of the piano keyboard. A

A "note" in Indian music

A note on the piano

Melodic movement
in Indian music

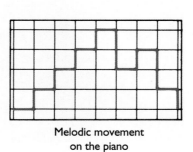

Melodic movement
on the piano

FIGURE 6.7

Notes and melodic movement in Indian music compared with those of the piano.

"note"—called a *svara* (*svah*-rah)—in Carnatic music is quite different from the fixed, stable note in Western music. A "note" can be a tiny constellation of ornamented pitches. Further, movement from one *svara* to the next may be sliding or gliding rather than the stepwise movement between Western notes (Figure 6.7).

Improvisation plays a key role in performance in Indian music. All musicians must be able to invent music on the spot. In "Devi Niye Tunai" the singer improvises briefly only twice, but the drummer is improvising throughout.

An interesting timbre, or tone color, strikes us. This sound world distinctly prefers *nasal timbre,* whether in the human voice or in musical instruments. Even adopted European instruments such as the clarinet or violin are played in a manner to increase their "nasalness."

In performance, music paper or notation is nowhere to be seen: The performers are clearly *working by ear in an oral tradition.* There is no conductor, but each performer has a comfortable and well-defined role to play.

When the drum comes in, we are immediately struck by the energy and *complexity of the drummer's rhythms,* played with the fingers and hands. We can sense a strong beat, but the metrical unit—*tala*—seems to be longer and more complicated than those we are used to (3/4, 4/4, etc.).

Finally, *lyrics in classical music are touchstones to Hindu mythology.* Lyrics reference details in the stories of the gods and goddesses, their attributes, and their relationship to human devotees. For South Indians these references can be read easily since they are part of the culture they have gown up with. (Similarly, we "read" the Woody Woodpecker reference in the pop song.)

CONCERTS

Concerts usually begin between 5:30 to 6:30 in the evening except at music festivals, when they occur from morning until late night. Programs are sponsored

FIGURE 6.8

An ensemble in concert. The principal artist, the great flutist N. Ramani, sits in the middle of the stage at Sri Ranjana Sabha. Behind him a student plays the drone *tambura*. Violin accompanist S. D. Sridhar sits at the right. The remarkable T. K. Murthy, assisted by a student (behind), plays *mridangam* on the left. Over their heads are prints of great composers with Tyagaraja, Dikshitar, and Syama Sastry in the middle.

Photo © Carol Reck 2005. All rights reserved.

by *sabhas* (*sah*-bhahs), cultural clubs that bring to their members and the general public music, dance, plays, lectures, and even an occasional movie. The large and prestigious *sabhas* have their own buildings, often large shedlike structures with overhead fans and open sides to catch the evening breeze. Other *sabhas* may use an auditorium, a lecture hall, or a temple. The audience may sit in rattan chairs or, as in the past, on large striped rugs or mats spread on the floor. The musicians sit on a raised platform or stage, and they are sure to have cronies or fellow musicians sitting in close proximity in front to offer reactions and encouragement through stylized motions like head wobbling, enthusiastic verbal comments, or tongue clicking (which, in contrast to Western culture, means "Awesome!").

Musicians sit on a rug on a stage or platform with the principle musician always in the middle, the drummer on stage left, and the violinist or other accompanist on stage right. Other musicians, if any, sit in the rear (Figure 6.8).

Compared with classical music concerts in the West, these concerts are relaxed and informal. Members of the audience may count time with their hands, periodically exchange comments with friends, or occasionally get up to buy snacks at the refreshment stand. Usually there are no printed programs. A knowledge-able audience is familiar with the repertoire of songs, *ragas* (melodic modes), and *talas* (time cycles). A concert lasts from one-and-a-half to three hours without an intermission.

THE ENSEMBLE: MUSICAL TEXTURE

In a concert each musician and instrument has a role to play. These roles, creating the musical texture, might be described as functional layers: (1) the melody layer, (2) the background drone, and (3) the rhythm/percussion. Within each layer there may be one or more musicians (Figure 6.9).

The Melodic Layer

The *principal melodic soloist* dominates the ensemble. A disciple may support the principal melodic soloist in the background. A singer is principle melodic soloist in maybe 80 percent of all concerts, but instruments such as violin, bamboo flute, saxophone, *veena,* or mandolin may be featured.

The next important role within this layer is the *melodic accompanist.* In South India this is usually a violinist, partly because the violin is always used to accompany a vocalist, and most concerts feature voice. The melodic accompanist plays three important roles: He or she must (1) play along on all the songs (following the notes of the soloist instantaneously); (2) echo and support the soloist's improvised phrases in the *alapana* (*ah-lah*-puh-nuh) (which frequently precedes the song), adding a short *alapana* of his or her own; and (3) alternate with the soloist in later improvisations, which bring the performance to a climax. In instrumental concerts, an instrument duplicating that of the soloist might provide the melodic accompaniment, for example, violin + violin, veena + veena, etc.

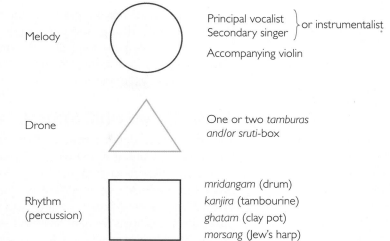

FIGURE 6.9

The functioning layers in Carnatic music.

The *Sruti* Layer

The drone, or **sruti** (*sroo*-tee), layer includes one or more specialized instruments. The *tambura* (tahm-*buh*-ruh) is a four-stringed plucked instrument tuned to the tonal center and fifth. Its buzzing timbre is created by inserting a small length of thread under each playing string on the slightly rounded top of the bridge, creating a rich blend of overtones. This sound is perhaps the most recognizable "Indian" sound of all. The tuned reed **sruti-box** can also be used. Played with a bellows, it gives a continuous reed organ sound. Today most musicians use small synthesizers that can duplicate electronically the sound of either instrument.

The Rhythm/Percussion Layer

Finally, there is the bedrock of the ensemble, the percussion. The double-headed, barrel-shaped **mridangam** (mrih-*dun*-gum) drum is the *principal accompanying percussion* instrument (and often the only percussion) in Carnatic music (Figure 6.5). When other *subordinate percussion instruments* are added, their players must follow the signals of the *mridangam* player, who tells them when to play together or singly, or when to drop out. The other percussion instruments used in classical music performance are the **ghatam** (*gah*-tum), a large clay pot with a ringing, metallic sound (Figure 6.13); the **kanjira** (kahn-*jih*-rah), a tambourine with a snakeskin head and jangles; and the **morsang** (*mor*-sang), a Jew's (or jaw's) harp that is played in the same rhythms as the other percussion instruments.

In the CD examples (CD 3, Tracks 9 and 10), note that there are only two performers: singer/*mridangam* and *veena/mridangam,* respectively. In both cases, an electronic *sruti*-box supplies a drone background. Thus, all three functioning layers—melodic, drone, and percussion—are represented.

Now that we have looked at the makeup of a South Indian ensemble, we need to explore two concepts that are central to an understanding of India's classical music: *raga* and *tala*.

RAGA: THE MELODIC SYSTEM

The ancient texts define a ***raga*** as "that which colors the mind." In fact, in Sanskrit the primary meaning of the word is "coloring, dying, tingeing." This connection with generating feelings and emotions in human beings—with "coloring" the mind and the heart—is important because a *raga* really has no equivalent in the West. A *raga* is an expressive entity with a "musical personality" all its own. This musical personality is, in part, technical—a collection of notes, a scale, intonation, ornaments, resting or pillar tones, and so on. Most of all, it includes a portfolio of characteristic musical gestures and phrases—bits and pieces of melody—that give it a distinct and recognizable identity. Each *raga* has its rules about the way a musician may move from one note to another and particular ways of ornamenting certain notes with slides and oscillations. But, aside from its scale, a *raga* cannot be written down; it is part of the oral tradition. One gets to know a *raga* gradually—by hearing one's guru or other master musicians perform it over many years. It is said that getting to know a *raga* is like getting to know a close friend: beginning with the face and voice, one eventually perceives the inner personality with all its quirks, puzzles, and delights.

Traditional texts associate particular *ragas* with human emotions: the nine traditional ***rasas*** (*rah*-sahs; "flavors")—love, anger, sadness, fear, disgust, wonder, heroism, laughter, religious devotion—plus a possible tenth, utter peacefulness. *Ragas* may also be associated with colors, animals, deities, a season of the year, a time of day (like late at night or early morning), or certain magical properties (causing rain, calming the mind, auspiciousness, and so forth). Because of these many extramusical associations, there is a genre of miniature paintings of *ragas* called ***raga-mala*** (*rah*-gah *mah*-lah). In the painting of *raga* Goda (Figure 6.10), the mood of the *raga* is created through two colorfully dressed figures in the foreground—a woman playing a frame drum and a dancing nobleman, both frozen in movement—against a dark background. Delicate green leaves connect to a vine wrapping around a tree, a symbol of lovers.

Musicians know these associations and the many folkloric tales about them: *ragas* charming cobras, causing rain, bringing peace of mind, raising the dead, healing sickness, causing a rift with one's guru. One amusing tale even illustrates that if a particular *raga* is sung in the morning, the singer will go hungry the rest of the day. What is clear in all this is that in India *ragas* are seen as powerful and full of expressive force; they touch deep emotions within the human heart as well as deeper realities at the very core of existence.

THE *MELAKARTA* SYSTEM

In Carnatic music, all *ragas* relate to a ***melakarta*** (*may*-luh-*car*-tah), a basic "parent" or "mother" scale. There are seven notes in each *melakarta* scale—(1) *sa* —(2) *ri* —(3) *ga*—(4) *ma*—(5) *pa*—(6) *da*—(7) *ni*. In the system (Figure 6.11) the

285

Photo © Carol Reck 2005. All rights reserved.

FIGURE 6.10

A *raga-mala*, a painting of the *raga* Goda. A courtier dances delicately while a lady plays drum. The images and colors establish the expressive mood of the *raga*. Basohli School, late seventeenth century.

tonal center—(1) *sa*—and the perfect fifth above—(5) *pa*—never change since they coincide with the drone. The other five notes mutate in a complex system to create different scales.

Your teacher will guide you through the simplified chart given as follows (Figure 6.11). Following the lines from left to right, one can discover that there are seventy-two possible tracks, and therefore seventy-two basic seven-note "parent" scales in the system. These scales of seven notes up and the same seven down—with the other elements that form a *raga* added to them—are known as the *seventy-two melakarta ragas*.

But the system does not end here. Dozens of other *ragas* may derive from each of the seventy-two *melakarta* "mothers" by creating other characteristics: (1) omitting notes in ascent and/or descent, (2) zigzagging the scale in ascent and/or descent, (3) adding "visiting" notes from other scales, and (4) adding other distinguishing elements such as unusual ornaments, intonation, or special melodic phrases.

FIGURE 6.11

The *melakarta* system
(tracks read from left to
right)

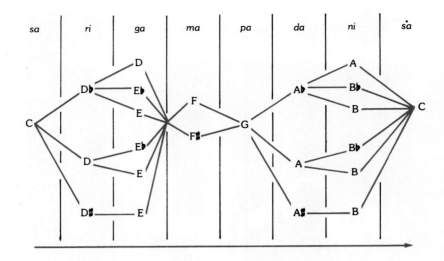

There are thus hundreds of *ragas* in common use—and potentially many more. Some *ragas* are popular, while others are rare; some are "major," others are "minor"; some are deep and complicated, others are "light." Some have been in the Carnatic music tradition for centuries, while others are recent. Some have traveled down from North India or even from as far away as Cambodia.

As one begins to listen seriously and in depth to Carnatic music, one discovers that the seemingly infinite variety of *ragas* and the expressive use musicians make of them, shaping them into beautiful melodic compositions or spinning them out in improvisation, form the heart and soul of India's classical music.

FIGURE 6.12

Counting *talas.*

Adi tala (fast or slow tempo): 4 + 2 + 2 = 8 beats

```
  1  .  2  .  3  .  4  . /5 . 6 . /7 . 8 . //
 (&)   (&)   (&)   (&)    (&)  (&)   (&)  (&)

Clap ─────────────────Clap        Clap
        Finger count        Wave       Wave
```

rupaka tala: 1 + 2 = 3 beats

```
  1   /2   3   //
Clap Clap
         Wave
```

(khanda) chapu tala: 2 + 3 = 5 beats

```
  1   2  /3   4   5   //
Clap  *  Clap Clap  *

*space (i.e., nothing)
```

misra chapu tala: 3 + 2 + 2 = 7 beats

```
  1   2   3  /4   5  /6   7   //
Clap Clap  *  Clap  *  Clap  *
```

TALA: THE TIME CYCLE

Tala, the organization of time in music, is part of a conceptual spectrum in Indian thought that moves from a fraction of a second—as the ancient texts picturesquely put it, the time it takes a pin to puncture a lotus petal—to the great **yugas** (*you-*gahs), or "ages," which like geological time periods span millions of years. The musician regards time initially as a beat, or regular pulse. On the larger level, beats are grouped into regularly recurring metric cycles. These cycles are called **talas.** In theoretical texts there are hundreds, but in Carnatic music today only four *talas* predominate in common practice (Figure 6.12).

Except for the **khanda chapu tala** (*kahn*-dah *chah*-pu *tah*-lah) and **misra chapu tala** (*mis*-rah *chah*-pu *tah*-lah), which are generally performed at a brisk tempo, all *talas* may be performed at fast, medium, or slow tempo. In slow tempo there are two pulses per beat, as in "1 & 2 & 3 & 4 . . ." and so forth.

The *tala* cycles differ from the common Western time signatures in that *tala* accents occur in uneven groupings (4 + 2 + 2, or 3 + 2 + 2, or 1 + 2, and so on). These groupings are marked by the accent of hand claps.

THE DRUMMER'S ART

In performance the *mridangam* player and other percussionists play in an improvisatory style based on hundreds of rhythmic patterns and drum strokes that they have learned, invented, absorbed, and stored in their brains and hands (Figures 6.5 and 6.13). In performance the percussionist may use precomposed patterns, arranging them in predictable or unpredictable groupings. Or he may create entirely new patterns, spontaneously, but within the limits and grammar of his rhythmic language.

The drummer's art centers on drum strokes— distinctive individual tones produced on different parts of the drumhead by different finger combinations or parts of the hands. These strokes, individually and as part of rhythmic patterns, can be expressed *sollukattu* (sol-lu-*kaht*-tu), spoken syllables that duplicate drum strokes and rhythmic patterns. Some patterns with *sollukattu* drawn from elementary lessons are given in Transcription 6.2.

The drummer's art is complex. At first he must accompany songs, the *kritis,* and other compositions of the Carnatic music tradition. He must know each song, picking up the flow and feeling, shaping his accompaniment to the internal rhythm of the song.

The drummer emerges from the background during long-held notes in the melody, or at cadences, marking endings with a formulaic threefold repetition called a **mora** (*mo*-ruh) or *korvai* (*kor*-vai). When the melodic soloist is improvising within the *tala* cycles, the alert drummer is quick to recognize and respond to patterns, to echo them, or to ornament them rhythmically. The South Indian percussionist, however, does not merely "play off the top of his head." Through years of training, study, and listening, his brain in a sense has been programmed with hundreds of rhythmic building blocks, formulas, and possibilities for larger combinations. He is also calculating constantly, like a master mathematician, how his formulas and patterns of asymmetrical lengths will fit into the *tala* cycles to come out right at the end.

Although we have only touched the surface of the drummer's art, we can begin to appreciate a rhythmic system as complicated as any on earth, a counterbalance to the melodic beauties of the *raga* system. As an old Sanskrit verse says, "Melody is the mother, rhythm is the father."

Photo © Carol S. Reck. 2005. All rights reserved.

FIGURE 6.13

N. Govindarajan practices the clay pot *ghatam* at home.

TRANSCRIPTION 6.2
Drum rhythms in
sollukattu.

LEVEL I:

Basic drumstrokes and sound on the *mridangam*——2 or 3 for the left hand, about 14 for the right hand and fingers.

ta - di - tom - nam - etc.

LEVEL 2:

Tiny cell-like rhythmic patterns, such as:

connected with various stroke arrangements:

ta - ki-ta	*ta - ka - di-mi*	*ta-lan - gu*
di - ki-ta	*ki - ta - ta-ka*	
tom - ki-ta	*na-ka-tan-gu*	
nam - ki-ta		

etc.

LEVEL 3:

Brief rhythmic patterns of several (or more) beats built from combinations of rhythmic cells, like:

na-ka-tan-gu ki - ta - ta - ka

or:

din - ta-din - ta - ta-din - ta - ta-din - ta - ki - ta

LEVEL 4:

Longer strings of rhythmic pattern combinations, and *moras* (3-times-repeated ending formula) like:

Do 3 times:

di - tan - ki-ta   na-ka-tan-gu   ki-ta-ta-ka   tom- -

tan-gu   ki - ta - ta-ka   tom- -

tan-gu   ki - ta - ta-ka   tom-   Resolution

The above small *korvai* pattern (LEVEL 4) is ten beats long and is played three times (10 + 10 + 10 = 30 beats). It resolves on a final "tom" *after* the third repetition. In *rupaka tala* (3-beat cycle) begin the pattern on the first beat. (Note that the first repetition begins on the second beat of a *tala* cycle, and the final repetition begins on the third beat of a *tala* cycle. The final "tom" will resolve on the first beat of an additional *tala* cycle.) One can also try doing the pattern in double-time (twice as fast). The final "tom" will still resolve on the first beat of the *tala* cycle.

A Carnatic Music Performance

A concert in South India is marked by a string of songs, each in a specific *raga* and *tala.* While the song may be performed alone for its own intrinsic beauty, the principle musician may choose to perform one or more forms of improvisation before, within, or after the rendition of the song. In a concert, several song forms

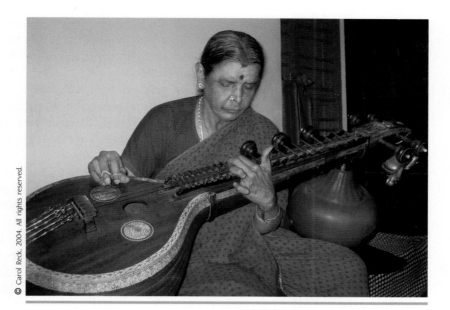

© Carol Reck. 2004. All rights reserved.

FIGURE 6.14

Ranganayaki Rajagopalan with the *veena* she has played since she was a small girl.

are used. A *varnam* (etude) usually begins a concert. Then a string of contrasting *kritis* build up to the "main item," the climax of the concert with the most extensive improvisations and a drum solo. (The "main item" may have a stately *kriti* in a "major" *raga* at its core, or it may be in a mostly improvised genre known as **ragam-tanam-pallavi** [*rah*–gam, *tah*-num, *pawl*-luh-vee]). Then the last half hour or so of a concert has a more relaxed atmosphere with "lighter" *bhajans* and other devotional music, **slokam** (*shlo*-kahm), religious verses chanted recitative-style in *ragas* of the singer's choice, or songs from the classical dance tradition.

Listen to a performance of a *kriti* with improvisations and drum solo (CD 3, Track 10) played on the plucked *veena* by Ms. Ranganayaki Rajagopalan accompanied by Mr. Srimushnam V. Raja Rao playing the *mridangam* drum. Before examining the performance itself, however, we must meet the musicians.

Ms. Ranganayaki (Figure 6.14), now more than seventy years old, in 1936 was a very unruly child. Her parents had sent her to live with a childless uncle and his wife in the prosperous southern town of Karaikudi. The uncle was the friend of a great *veena* virtuoso, Karaikudi Sambasiva Iyer. (You will notice that South Indian musicians often take their hometown as a "first name.") The wealthy merchants and financiers of the town, many of whom had traveled to Singapore, Hong Kong, or other outposts of the British Empire to make their fortunes, were great supporters of music.

As the story goes, one day Ranganayaki's uncle appeared with his four-year-old niece at the great musician's house. As the elders were talking about music, Sambasiva Iyer sang a tone. To his surprise, the young girl, playing nearby, sang the same tone. Sambasiva sang another note. The girl duplicated that note. Recognizing a rare talent, the musician took the little girl into his household, into an apprenticeship known as the **gurukula** (gu-ru-*koo*-lah) **system.**

The discipline was extremely rigorous, with lessons beginning at 4:30 in the early morning and continuing throughout the day, as the stern guru taught her and other youngsters living in the household. Mistakes or laziness were met with painful slaps from a bamboo rod. Effort and accomplishment were rewarded not

CD 3:10

"Sarasiruha" ("To the Goddess Saraswati") (22:32), *Kriti* in Natai *raga, Adi tala.* Pulaiyur Doraismy Ayyar. Performed by Ranganayaki Rajagopalan, *veena;* Raja Rao, *mridangam.* Recorded for author by recording engineer Rahul K. Raveendran, Chennai, India, 2001.

with praise, but with subtle gestures such as the guru himself serving food on a student's banana-leaf plate. Ranganayaki describes her life during that period as "not a normal childhood. I had no playmates or anything. It was *asura sadhakam* ('devil's practice')" (Personal communication 2000).

Ranganayaki's musical genius gradually developed. By age twelve she was accompanying her guru in concerts, and soon thereafter she was giving solo recitals. The close relationship continued after her marriage at age fifteen, through a move to the big city of Chennai, and up until Sambasiva Iyer's death in 1958. The apprenticeship had lasted twenty-two years.

Over the years Ms. Ranganayaki has enjoyed a distinguished career. She has been recognized as dedicated to her tradition and as one of the great *veena* virtuosi of her time. With her phenomenal memory she is a rare repository of the songs played by the Karaikudi tradition, while her skills and creativity at improvisation —always avoiding the preplanned and formulaic—are remarkable. She has toured Europe and the United States, and has been regularly featured in the prestigious AIR national radio broadcasts. After a string of previous honors, in 2000 she received one of India's highest artistic awards—the National Award for Music— from the Sangeet Natak Akademi in Delhi.

Speaking of the *veena* tradition of which she is one of the greatest living exponents, she has said, "Words cannot describe it. One can only feel it while listening to it. It is just like this: you can *say* that sugar is sweet. But you can only really understand the sweetness by tasting it" (Personal communication 2000).

Ms. Ranganayaki's instrument, the **veena,** has three drone strings and four playing strings. Its carving and ivory trim make it a work of art, and testimony to the skill of the hereditary craftsmen who made it. The chromatically placed brass frets are set in black wax, which is scalloped to allow room for the fingers to bend the strings in ornamentation. A set of complex fingerings, slides, and pulled multipitched ornaments enable the musician to interpret the character of each *raga* and its subtle intonation.

Women in Music

A note on women in South India's classical music is in order. As we can see by our two listening examples (devotional songs to the goddesses Meenakshi and Saraswati), worshipping God in a feminine form is common in Hindu India. Given this highest form of respect, it is perhaps no surprise that women are accepted into most professions and have been prime ministers in India, Pakistan, and Sri Lanka. In music, two of the greatest poet-composers—the Rajasthani princess Mirabai (1504–1550) and the Tamilian saint Andal (early eighth century)—were women. In the contemporary scene many of the leading musicians are women, especially as singers (M. S. Subbulakshmi, D. K. Pattammal are examples), but also on instruments such as violin (T. Rukmani), flute (the Sikkul Sisters), and *veena* (Rajeeswari Padmanabhan, Kalpakam Swaminathan). On the other hand, women do not tend to play reed instruments such as the clarinet, *nagasvaram*, or saxophone. Nor do they tend to play percussion instruments. But there are exceptions to this mold, such as Kaleeshabi Mahaboob Subhani (*nagasvaram*) and Sukanya Ramgopal (*ghatam*), and certainly in the future women will break through these barriers.

The drummer is Srimushnam (his ancestral village) V. Raja Rao on the *mridangam.* He is one of the great contemporary performers on his instrument. Known as "a musician's musician," he has accompanied most of the leading singers and instrumentalists of Carnatic music in India and abroad in Europe, the Americas, and Asia. He takes particular pride in his ability to accompany the soft tones of the *veena* with a light yet precise touch of fingers and hands on the drumheads. In the CD example (CD 3, Track 10), he illustrates both the art of accompaniment and a brief drum solo.

Raja Rao's instrument, the *mridangam,* has a barrel-shaped body carved from jackwood. Both of its heads are made from multiple layers of leather, the outer layers cut with a circular hole in the middle. The lower (untuned) left-hand head has a blob of damp wheat paste applied to its center to give it a booming sound. The center of the right-hand head (which is tuned) has a hard metallic black spot made of many polished layers of rice paste and other ingredients. The use of the fingers as miniature drumsticks allows the drummer to play passages of incredible speed and virtuosity.

The performance begins with two improvised sections—*alapana* and *tanam*—for *veena* alone. *Alapana* (in free time, with "breath" rhythms and no regular pulse) and *tanam* (marked with strong, energetic, and irregular rhythms) must precede a song and introduce the listener to the *raga* in which the song is set. The beginning of the song in *kriti* form, "Sarasiruha" in Natai *raga, Adi tala,* is marked by the entrance of the drum. A lively improvised section for *veena* with drum accompaniment called *kalpana svaras* follows, with a brief drum solo, the **tani avartanam,** at the end.

We will now look at the five sections of "Sarasiruha" and its improvisations in performance (see the Close Listening guide).

Close Listening

"SARASIRUHA" ("TO THE GODDESS SARASWATI")

CD 3:10

COUNTER NUMBER	COMMENTARY
Alapana (improvised)	
0:00	*Veena* alone (with drone), Free rhythm (no regularly recurring beat). Introduces the melodic characteristics of Natai *raga.* Begins slowly in the lower range of the instrument, then moves higher and faster to explore the middle and high ranges.
2:05–3:15	Peak of *alapana.* Reaches highest note. Then descends to conclusion.
Tanam (improvised)	
3:18	*Veena* alone (with drone). Irregular beat. Rhythmic exposition of Natai *raga.* Listen for the phrases to begin low in the range, then work their way to middle and high range.
7:48–8:18	*Veena* switches back to *alapana* style for descent and close.

***Kriti* (composed song) "Sarasiruha"**

8:25   Song begins in *Adi tala* (4 + 2 + 2). Drum enters.

13:31   Repeated variants of musical phrase—invocation of Saraswati, then song continues to the end.

***Kalpana svaras* 1 (improvised, short—one cycle or less)**

14:45   Lively improvised section. Begins with four short *svara* improvisations of less than a half *tala* cycle, each returning to the *idam* "place."

***Kalpana svaras* 2 (improvised, extended)**

15:10–17:48   Three extended *svara* improvisations of six and one-half-, seven and one-half-, and ten and one-half-*tala* cycles respectively, each returning to *idam* "place."

***Tani avartanam* (drum solo)**

18:00   Improvised and precomposed rhythmic solo by the *mridangam. Adi tala* continues.

21:30   Listen for the *mora* or *korvai,* a formulaic rhythmic pattern repeated three times that signals the end of the drum solo.

***Kriti* return and close**

22:22   *Veena* joins back in with *kriti*'s first bit of melody and an improvised close.

ALAPANA

The first section of the performance (CD 3, Track 10) is an ***alapana*** (*ah-lah-pah-nah*), a free-flowing exposition and exploration of the *raga* its facets and phrases, its ornamentation, its pushes and pulls of intonation, as well as its mood and character. An *alapana* is nonmetrical, that is, it has no regular beat or recurring *tala* cycles. Instead, its phrases evolve in flowing proselike "breath rhythms," phrases that eventually come to rest on important pillar tones, or resting notes.

An *alapana* has a general plan set both by the tradition as a whole and by the improvisational habits of the musician. In general, the phrases of an *alapana* begin slowly and gradually increase in speed and complexity as they move higher and higher in the range of the voice or instrument. After a peak there is a descent back to the lower register with an ending on the tonal center (*sa*). The voice or (as in this case) melodic instrument always performs against the drone background.

The *raga* of the *alapana* is derived from that of the *kriti,* the song composition, which it precedes. In our performance the *raga* is **Natai** (*nah*-tai), an ancient and powerful *raga* associated with the great god Siva in the form of Nataraja (nah-tuh-*rah*-jah)—"the Lord of Dance." The Dance of Siva is said to shake the universe with its power and fury. The basic scale of Natai is as follows:

TRANSCRIPTION 6.3
Scale, Natai *raga.*

The most noteworthy characteristic of this *raga* is the shake or oscillation on the second note of the scale, *ri* (D♯ in our notation) as it descends downward to the tonal center *sa* (C). It is a sound startlingly similar to the major/minor "blues" third found in the African American tradition (Chapter 4). If you listen carefully or hum along with the performance, eventually you will begin to recognize the series of musical phrases and gestures that give Natai *raga* its character or "musical personality."

TANAM

Tanam (*tah*-nam) is a highly rhythmic exposition of the *raga*. It is usually played or sung only once in a concert and is placed after the *alapana* and before the *kriti*. On the *veena* the musician plucks the playing and drone strings in asymmetrical improvised patterns while simultaneously working through the various phrases of the *raga*. Although there are no *tala* cycles in *tanam*, there is a strong sense of beat. Just as in *alapana* the overall shape of a *tanam* follows the range of the instrument from low to high in graduated steps and back down again. The Karaikudi tradition is famous for its *tanam*.

KRITI "SARASIRUHA"

All compositions in Carnatic music are songs, melodies with words. Because they are not precisely notated but, rather, taught and learned orally, songs do not have definitive versions. But within a specific guru's style, students will be expected to follow the guru's version. As a song is passed down from strings of gurus to disciples on its journey over hundreds of years to the present, many variant versions appear. Yet the composition remains recognizably itself—the main turns of phrase and the lyrics remain despite the variations in detail.

The *kriti* (composition) is the major song form of Carnatic music performance. (The word *kriti* is linguistically related to the same Indo-European root *kr* as the English word *creation*.) A brief *kriti* might be as short as four minutes; a long *kriti* in slow tempo could last for fifteen minutes or more. The structure is amazingly flexible—it may be contracted or expanded in an almost infinite number of ways.

The melody and lyrics of "Sarasiruha" (*sah*-rah-see-*roo*-ha) are by the nineteenth-century composer Pulaiyur Doraisamy Ayyar. The song is addressed to the goddess of music and learning, Saraswati (Figure 6.15). A free translation of its text follows:

FIGURE 6.15

Saraswati, goddess of music and learning.

Drawing © Navarana Reck 2001. All rights reserved.

NAVARANA

1. O Mother who loves the lotus seat,
   Ever delighting in the music of *veena*,
   Ever joyful, and ever merciful to me.
2. Save me who have taken refuge in you!
   O You with feet as tender as sprouts,
   You charm the hearts of poets.
   You dwell in the lotus.
   You of the jeweled bracelets.
   (reprise) 1. O Mother who loves the lotus seat . . .

Text, "SARASIRUHA"

3. Lotus-eyed Mother who is gracious to the lowly who seek your mercy,
   Mother with a face as lovely as the autumn moon,
   Pure Lady! O Saraswati, chaste, ever fond of learning,
   Lady with breasts like ceremonial vessels,
   Complete Being, who holds a book in her hand which bestows all dominion.
   (reprise) 1. O Mother who loves the lotus seat . . .

Free translation by Indira Viswanathan Peterson.

Although the words of the song are not audible in an instrumental performance, the musicians and knowledgeable members of the audience know the song text well. The importance of this knowledge can be seen in the performance of "Sarasiruha": At the place in the lyrics where the name of the goddess "O Saraswati . . ." appears (CD 3, Track 10, 14:33–15:10), Ms. Ranganayaki repeats the musical phrase over and over again—a multiple invocation of the goddess' name—before she moves forward to the completion of the *kriti*.

KALPANA SVARAS

Kalpana (kahl-pah-nuh) means literally "imagined," and *svaras* (*svah*-ruhs) are the "notes" of the scale of the *raga* being performed. This section of improvised "imagined notes" occurs either in the latter part of the *kriti* rendition or after the *kriti* has been completed. Identifying this section in a vocal performance is easy, because the performer sings the names of the notes of the *raga* scale—*sa, ri, ga, ma, pa, da,* or *ni*—instead of lyrics. In an instrumental performance, the musicians articulate or pluck each note.

The *kalpana svaras* always return to a phrase from the *kriti,* a familiar island in a sea of improvisation. This phrase, its beginning note, and the place where it begins in the *tala* cycle are important, because ultimately each turn of the *kalpana svaras* will lead back to it. Indeed, it is called the **idam** (ih-*dum*), the "place." In Ms. Ranganayaki's performance the "place" is the opening phrase of the *kriti*:

TRANSCRIPTION 6.4
The opening phrase of "Sarasiruha" is the *idam* ("place") for the resolution of *kalpana svaras.* It begins on the second pulse of the downbeat after the first beat of the *tala,* its first pitch is *pa,* both "places" in time and space to which the conclusion of each improvisation must lead. After the first few of its notes the *idam* may be slightly varied in performance.

At first, the improvised *svaras* will be short, perhaps only filling the last four of one *tala* cycle before returning to the phrase of the *idam*. As time goes on, the improvisations will grow in length and complexity, extending through more and more cycles of the *tala* as the performer's imagination runs free. A final extended improvisation will bring the *kalpana svara* section to a climax before its final return to the *idam* and the song.

THE DRUM SOLO: *TANI AVARTANAM*

As a conclusion of the "main item" in a concert, the *mridangam* player (and other percussionists, if any) come to the foreground with an extended solo. In a full concert, this solo will extend for ten to fifteen minutes or more. In our performance, Raja Rao's solo is concise. As noted earlier, the drum solo gives the percussionist the chance to display the full range of his skills and rhythmic imagination. In each section of the solo the drummer will explore a certain range of patterns and architectural ideas. Finally, the solo will end on an extended *korvai* (*kor*-vai), a big pattern repeated three times. This pattern leads back to an entrance of the *kriti* by the melodic soloist and the conclusion of the performance.

One form of improvisation not used in our performance, *niraval* (*nih*-rah-vahl), is a set of improvisations based on a phrase from the *kriti* and its song text which can precede the *kalpana svara* section.

On another occasion, at another performance, the musician might decide—using the same *kriti* as a centerpiece—to shape the performance in a different way. The song might be performed alone, for example, after a perfunctory *alapana* of a few phrases. Or the *tanam* and drum solo might be omitted. While the shape of the *kriti* will remain basically the same, the nature of the improvisations might vary as the musician draws on the procedures, ideas, and performance habits stored in his or her memory and on the interpretation of a particular *raga* on a particular day. This fluidity of performance sparked by the creative instincts of the South Indian musician is one of the delights of the Carnatic music tradition.

Indian Music and the West

As noted earlier, India's culture has long assimilated outside influences and made them its own. The presence of the violin, saxophone, guitar, and mandolin in Carnatic music, and the all-inclusive nature of South India's cinema/pop music industry are obvious examples. As the globalization of music through television, movies, CDs, cassettes, and travel continues, mutual influences between India and the West are bound to increase.

Since the 1970s, South Indian musicians have seen the connections between jazz improvisation and India's classical music traditions. From that awareness the genre known as "fusion" was born, an interface between East and West that continues to excite a younger generation of musicians and listeners. The Carnatic violinists L. Shankar and L. Subramanian have worked extensively with American and European jazz and rock musicians over the past thirty years, as has the *tabla* wizard Zakir Hussain. In the 2000s, the Australian singer Susheela Raman fused Carnatic *kritis* with an electric, hard-driving Chicago blues style (as in her album

Salt Rain). She also has composed original songs reflecting her multicultural background. The talented American jazz pianist Vijay Iyer, whose parents are from South India, has worked with saxophonist Rudresh Mahanthappa and others to bring into jazz a subtle integration of Carnatic music rhythm and improvisational procedures, creating a unique style that defies definition (see the album *Reimagining,* 2005).

In the late twentieth and early twenty-first centuries, an increasing number of South Asians have been working, studying, and living abroad. Cohesive communities of transplanted Indians, many trained in music, now appear in almost every major city or university town on earth. The children of first-generation immigrants often find themselves in a bicultural world where the "Indianness" of their home and family must be balanced against the pervasive dominance of the mainstream culture of their adopted country. Cultural clubs, temples, and mosques support the study and presentation of concerts of classical Indian music and dance. Various Indo-pop styles, such as "bhangra" in Great Britain (note Panjabi MC's self-named album *Panjabi MC Beware*) or "tassa-beat soca" in Trinidad, have also evolved. Here the drones, scales, and sometimes the instruments and languages of Indian music fuse with the beat and electric sound of mainstream rock and pop styles.

Indian music has infiltrated the West since the late 1950s. The *sitar* virtuoso Ravi Shankar is a seminal figure. Having spent years in Paris as a boy with the dance troupe of Uday Shankar, he has been able to move with ease in the elite worlds of Western classical and pop music. By the late 1960s his concerts with the *tabla* virtuoso Alla Rakha at venues as varied as the Edinburgh Music Festival and the Monterey Pop Festival eventually gave him superstar status in Europe and the United States, as well as in India.

Over the years Ravi Shankar has released many collaborative recordings. These include the *West Meets East* dialogues with famous Western musicians— among them the classical violinist Yehudi Menuhin, the flute virtuoso Jean-Pierre Rampal, and the jazz musician Paul Horn. In the album *East Greets East* (1978) he performed with traditional Japanese musicians. His *Shankar Family and Friends,* an early 1970s recording made in San Francisco with several dozen Indian and Western musicians (including one listed enigmatically as "Harris Georgeson") includes some fascinating music.

In the mid-1960s, Ravi Shankar acquired the most illustrious of his students, George Harrison of the Beatles. Harrison's interest in Indian classical music and religious philosophy resulted in a series of finely crafted Indian-based songs ranging from "Love You To"* and "Within You, Without You" to "The Inner Light" (recorded in Bombay) and the post-Beatles "My Sweet Lord."

In "Love You To," from the Beatles 1966 album *Revolver*, the *sitar* begins with a brief introduction of the notes of a *raga*-like scale in unmeasured time—a hint of an *alapana.* A background drone of *tambura* and bass guitar continues throughout. The *tabla* drumbeat enters, establishing a driving metrical pulse of *tala*-like cycles. Harrison's vocal line is sung in flat tones and ends with a descending melisma of distinct Indian vocal sound. In the second section of the song, the repetitive riffs

---

*The song was incorrectly listed in its 1966 Decca American release as "Love You Too."

alternating between *sitar* and voice reflect the "question and answer" interplay of Indian musicians in performance. Then there is an instrumental break with the *sitar* and *tabla* improvising first in cycles of seven beats, then in five, and finally in three, all of which leads to a final rendition of chorus and verse. A fast instrumental post-lude corresponds to the ending climactic sections of a North Indian performance. All of this in a three-minute song!

Many of John Lennon's songs of the mid-sixties also had Indian influences, such as "Across the Universe" with its Sanskrit phrases or the beautiful song "Rain." Lennon often used Indianlike sound and textures to indicate the trippiness of drug-induced states (as in "Lucy in the Sky with Diamonds"). In the musical texture of "Tomorrow Never Knows," built over a hair-raising drone and Ringo's hypnotic beat, Lennon (with producer George Martin) uses exotic riffs and Indian instruments floating in a hallucinogenic collage of backward tapes and sound effects (described by one critic as "a herd of elephants gone mad!"). All of this backs the otherworldly dream state of the lyrics inspired by the *Tibetan Book of the Dead* as interpreted by the LSD guru Timothy Leary.

Indo-pop music has continued to flourish in Great Britain, where large immigrant communities from the former colonies continue to generate new genres and sounds. The filmmaker Vivek Bald, in his groundbreaking documentary *Mutiny: Asians Storm British Music,* has brilliantly surveyed the Indo-Brit scene in the late twentieth century.

The singer and composer Sheila Chandra, born in 1965, has treated diverse influences from East and West with intelligence and sensitivity. Trained in both Western and Indian music, in the 1980s she joined with Steve Coe and Martin Smith to form an innovative East/West fusion band, Monsoon (see *Silk,* 1991). In the exquisite song "Ever So Lonely/Eyes/Ocean" from the 1993 album *Weaving My Ancestor's Voices,* she sets her English lyrics to *raga*-based melody, drone, and synthesizer. In "Speaking in Tongues" I and II from the same album, Chandra adapts the lightning-fast language of spoken Indian drum patterns with great ingenuity, moving from traditional *sollukattu* to whispers, clicks, and playful gibberish. In her more recent work, Chandra has focused on the unique qualities of her voice set against electronic and acoustic drones and explored the synthesis of world vocal traditions from the British Isles, Spain, North Africa, and India.

In South India, the film composer and songwriter Ilaiyaraja is a superstar (Figure 6.16). Born in a village in 1943 to a poor family in the lowest stratum of society, Ilaiyaraja left high school to join a band formed by his stepbrother to provide entertainment at political rallies and festivals. Seeking his musical fortune in Chennai, he apprenticed himself to "Master" Dhanaraj, a composer for one of the big film studios. The eccentric "Master" taught him not only the skills of writing songs and film scores but also Carnatic music, Western music notation, harmony, and the classical European music of Bach, Mozart, and Beethoven. Meanwhile, Ilaiyaraja supported himself by playing guitar in studio orchestras. In his spare time he arranged pop songs by the Beatles, Paul Simon, and others.

Ilaiyaraja's break came in 1976 when he was hired to write songs and background music for the hit movie *Annakili* ("The parrot Annam"). In contrast to the "classical-lite" pop songs of his day, Ilaiyaraja echoed the earthy South Indian rural theme of the film with folklike melodies backed by driving village rhythms and an orchestra filled with folk instruments. His music with its folk roots and

FIGURE 6.16

Composer Ilaiyaraja's head dominates a billboard for the movie *Kadagattam-kari* ("Kadagattam-girl"). *Kadagattam* is a South Indian folk genre in which the female dancer must balance a clay pot on her head as she dances.

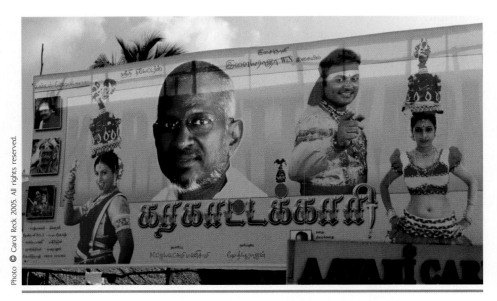

Photo © Carol Reck 2005. All rights reserved.

vibrant sound took the country by storm, blaring from radios and bazaar loudspeakers, admired by men, women, and children of all classes, rich and poor—taxi drivers, coolies, villagers, and urban intellectuals alike.

In the ensuing years, Ilaiyaraja has written songs and background music for more than seven hundred films. He is so famous that his name precedes those of movie stars.

In his composition "I Met Bach at My House," Ilaiyaraja illustrates the facility by which he can flit from East to West. After a brief violin *alapana* in Carnatic music style, a string orchestra enters playing an arrangement of a Bach prelude (from the Third Partita for violin). The solo violin enters again, flitting through the contrapuntal texture like a soloist in a Baroque concerto grosso, but the violin's sound, style, intonation, and ornamentation are pure South Indian.

As Indian classical and popular musicians continue to absorb the varied musics of the world around them, and as world musical traditions continue to be instantaneously accessible, perhaps the ancient traditions of classical Indian music North and South, Hindusthani and Carnatic, will continue to find echoes, reflections, interpretations, and responses in the music of the West.

Book Companion Website

You will find tutorial quizzes, Internet links, and much more at the Book Companion Website for *Worlds of Music*, Fifth Edition, at **academic.cengage.com/music/titon/worlds_5**

Asia/Music of Indonesia

R. ANDERSON SUTTON

Indonesia is a country of astounding cultural diversity, nowhere more evident than in the stunning variety of musical and related performing arts found throughout its several thousand populated islands. Known formerly as the Dutch East Indies, Indonesia is one of many modern nations whose boundaries were formed during the centuries of European colonial domination, placing peoples with contrasting languages, arts, systems of belief, and conceptions of the world under a single rule. The adoption of a national language in the early twentieth century was a crucial step in building the unity necessary to win a revolution against the Dutch (1945–1949). Today, a pan-Indonesian popular culture has been contributing to an increased sense of national unity, particularly among the younger generation. Nevertheless, recent strife between ethnic groups, which dominated international headlines about Indonesia at the turn of the millennium, has challenged this sense of unity. Indeed, though we can identify some general cultural traits, including musical ones, shared by many peoples of Indonesia, to speak of an "Indonesian" culture or style of music is problematic. Regional diversity is still very much in evidence.

Most Indonesians' first language is not the national language (Indonesian) but one of the more than two hundred separate languages found throughout this vast archipelago. Further, although many are familiar with the sounds of Indonesian pop music and such Western stars as Beyoncé and Justin Timberlake, they also know their own regional musical traditions. In Indonesia many kinds of music exist side by side in a complex pluralism that reflects both the diversity of the native population and the receptiveness of that population to centuries of outside influences. Indonesia is, then, a country truly home to worlds of music.

What first impression might this country give you? You would probably arrive in the nation's capital, **Jakarta** (jah-*kar*-tah), a teaming metropolis of more than ten million people—some very wealthy, most rather poor. Jakarta is near the western end of the north coast of **Java,** Indonesia's most heavily populated (but not largest) island. (See the map on the following page.) The mix of Indonesia's many cultures among themselves and with Western culture is nowhere more fully realized than in this special city. Many kinds of music are heard here. Western-style nightclubs, karaoke bars, and discos do a lively business until the early hours of the morning. Javanese *gamelan* (*gah*-muh-lahn; percussion ensemble) music accompanies nightly performances of *wayang orang* (*wah*-yang *oh*-rang) theater,

an elaborate type of dance-drama from central Java. You might also run across Jakarta's own *gambang-kromong* (*gahm*-bang *kroh*-mong; small percussion ensemble) and perhaps a troupe from Bali, Sumatra, or any of the many other islands performing at the national arts center Taman Ismael Marzuki or the Indonesian cultural park Taman Mini. As you begin to find your way around the city by taxi, bus, or three-wheeled *bajaj*, you may develop a taste for highly seasoned food. You will certainly get a sense of Indonesia's many cultures by roaming this complex city. Much of what you encounter, however, has a strong presence in the various regions in which it is rooted.

Central Java

Java is an island about the size of New York State (just less than 50,000 square miles). With over 100 million people, Java is one of the most densely populated regions in the world. (Indonesia's total population is about 220 million.) Most of the central and eastern two-thirds of the island is inhabited by Indonesia's largest ethnic group, the Javanese, roughly 75 million people who share a language and other cultural traits, including music, though some local differences persist. In **Sunda,** the western third of the island, live the Sundanese, who have a language and arts distinct from those of the Javanese. Despite its dense population, Java remains mostly a farming society, with wet-rice agriculture as the predominant source of livelihood. Although most Javanese profess to be Muslim, only a minority follow orthodox practice. Many adhere to a blend of Islam with Hinduism and Buddhism (introduced into Java over one thousand years ago) and with what most scholars believe to be an even earlier layer of belief in benevolent and mischievous spirits and in ancestor veneration. The worldview that embraces these many layers of belief is often referred to as *kejawèn*—literally, "Javanese," or "Javaneseness," a term that indicates its importance in Javanese self-conception. Since the mid-1980s, however, Javanese have increasingly embraced a less syncretic and more orthodox Islam.

From Jakarta a twelve-hour ride on bus or train through shimmering wet-rice fields, set in the plains between gracefully sloping volcanic mountains, leads to **Yogyakarta** (often abbreviated **Yogya** and pronounced *jog*-jah). Yogya is one of two court cities in the cultural heartland of Central Java. The other, about forty miles to the northeast, is **Surakarta** (soo-rah-*kar*-tah or soo-raw-*kar*-taw; usually called "Solo"). Most Javanese point to these two cities as the cultural centers where traditional *gamelan* music and related performing arts have flourished in their most elaborate and refined forms. These courtly developments contrast with the rougher styles associated with the villages and outlying districts.

Yogya is a sprawling city with a population of about 500,000. It has several multistory malls and hotels but few other buildings taller than two stories. Away from the several major streets lined with stores flashing neon signs and blaring popular music, Yogya in many ways resembles a dense collection of villages. Yet at its center stands one of Java's two main royal courts, the official home of the tenth sultan (His Highness Hamengku Buwana X; hah-*muhng*-koo bu-*waw*-naw). Unlike any Western palace or court, this is a complex of small buildings and open pavilions appropriate for the tropical climate. It was not designed merely for comfort, however. Endowed with mystical significance as an earthly symbol of the macrocosmos (the ordered universe), the court is oriented to the cardinal directions. The ruler, whose residence is located at the very center of the court, is imbued with divine powers, as were the Hindu-Javanese kings many centuries ago.

In many of these pavilions are kept the court *gamelan* ensembles. Some date back many centuries and perform only for rare ritual occasions, while others have been built or augmented more recently and are used more frequently. Like other treasured heirlooms belonging to the court, most of these sets of instruments are believed to contain special powers and are shown respect and given offerings. Also kept in the palace are numerous sets of finely carved and painted **wayang kulit** (*wah*-yang *koo*-lit; puppets made of water buffalo hide) used in all-night performances of highly sophisticated and entertaining shadow plays. Classical Javanese dance, with *gamelan* accompaniment, is rehearsed regularly and performed for special palace functions.

Though the court is still regarded as a cultural center, it is far less active now than it was prior to World War II (during which the Japanese occupied Indonesia). Much activity in the traditional Javanese arts takes place outside the court and is sponsored by private individuals and by such modern institutions as the national radio station and public schools and colleges. In the rural villages, which long served as a source and inspiration for the more refined courtly arts, a variety of musical and related performing arts continue to play a vital role in Javanese life.

GAMELAN

The word *gamelan* refers to a set of instruments unified by their tuning and often by their decorative carving and painting. Most *gamelans* consist of several kinds of metal slab instruments (similar in some ways to the Western vibraphone) and tuned knobbed **gongs.** The word "gong" is one of the few English words derived from Indonesian languages. (Two others are "ketchup" and "amok.") In English, "gong" may refer to any variety of percussion instrument whose sound-producing vibrations are concentrated in the center of the instrument, rather than the edge, like a bell. In Javanese, it refers specifically to the larger hanging knobbed gongs (see Figure 7.1) in *gamelan* ensembles and is part of a family of words relating to largeness, greatness, and grandeur—*agung* ("great," "kingly"), *ageng* ("large"), and *gunung* ("mountain"). In addition to gongs and other metal instruments, a *gamelan* ensemble normally has at least one drum and may have other kinds of instruments: winds, strings, and wooden percussion instruments (xylophones).

Some ancient ceremonial *gamelans* have only a few knobbed gongs and one or two drums. The kind of *gamelan* most often used in central Java today is a large set, comprising instruments ranging from deep booming gongs three feet in diameter to high-pitched gong-chimes and slab instruments, with three drums, several bamboo flutes, zithers, xylophones, and a two-stringed fiddle.

Instruments in the present-day *gamelan* are tuned to one of two scale systems: **sléndro** (*slayn*-dro), a five-tone system made up of nearly equidistant intervals, normally notated with the numerals 1, 2, 3, 5, and 6 (no 4); and **pélog** (*pay*-log), a

Arthur Durkee, EarthVisions Photographics

FIGURE 7.1

The *gamelan* Kyai Kanyut Mèsem ("Tempted to Smile") in the Mangkunegaran palace, Surakarta, Central Java. In foreground: *gong ageng* and *gong siyem*.

seven-tone system made up of large and small intervals, normally notated 1, 2, 3, 4, 5, 6, and 7. Some *gamelans* are entirely *sléndro,* others entirely *pélog,* but many are actually double ensembles, combining a full set of instruments for each system. A Western piano can replicate neither of these scale systems. Transcription 7.1 shows the Western major scale, consisting of "whole tone" and "half tone" intervals (that is, eight adjacent white keys on the piano, starting with C as "do"), in comparison with sample intervals for one instance of *sléndro* and one of *pélog* (these are not entirely standardized, as I explain further on).

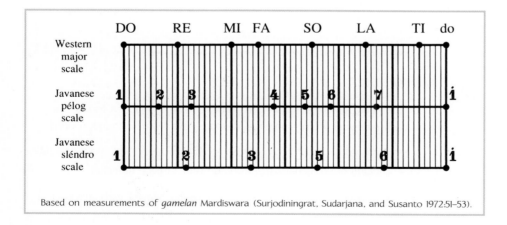

Based on measurements of *gamelan* Mardiswara (Surjodiningrat, Sudarjana, and Susanto 1972:51–53).

TRANSCRIPTION 7.1

Western scale and representative *pélog* and *sléndro* scales.

GAMELAN INSTRUMENTATION

The instrumentation of a full *sléndro-pélog gamelan* varies slightly, but it usually includes all or most of the instruments given in the list (see instruments boxes on pages 304–306). Most of these are illustrated in Figure 7.2.

Drawing by Peggy Choy

FIGURE 7.2

Central Javanese *gamelan* instruments.

Knobbed-Gong Instruments

gong ageng	Largest of the hanging gongs, suspended vertically from a wooden frame; one or two in each *gamelan*; often simply called gong; played with a round, padded beater.
siyem (*see*-yuhm)	Middle-sized hanging gong; usually from one to four in each *gamelan*.
kempul (kuhm-*pool*)	Smallest hanging gong; from two to ten per *gamelan*; played with a round, padded beater.
kenong (kuh-*nong*)	Largest of the kettle gongs, resting horizontally in a wooden frame; from two to twelve per *gamelan*; played with a padded stick beater.
kethuk (kuh-*took*)	Small kettle gong; one for each scale system; played with a padded stick beater.
kempyang (kuhm-*pyahng*)	Set of two small kettle gongs, for *pélog*; played with padded stick beater.

bonang barung (*bo*-nahng *ba*-roong)	Set of ten, twelve, or fourteen kettle gongs resting horizontally in two parallel rows in a wooden frame; one set for each scale system; often simply called *bonang*; played with two padded stick beaters. *Barung* indicates middle or lower register.
bonang **panerus** (*pa*-nuh-roos)	Smaller member of the *bonang* family; same as *bonang barung* but tuned an octave higher; one for each scale system. *Panerus* indicates highest register.

Metal-Keyed Instruments

saron demung	Largest member of the **saron** (*sah*-ron) family; six or seven thick metal keys resting over a trough resonator; usually one or two for each scale system; often simply called *demung*; played with a wooden mallet.
saron barung	Like *saron demung* but an octave higher; usually from two to four for each scale system; often simply called *saron*.
saron peking	Like *saron barung* but an octave higher; often simply called *peking*.
gendèr slenthem (guhn-*dehr sluhn*-tuhm)	Six or seven thin metal keys suspended by strings over cylindrical resonators made of bamboo or metal; one for each scale system; often simply called *slenthem*; played with a padded disc beater.
gendèr barung	Thirteen or fourteen thin metal keys, suspended over cylindrical resonators; one for *sléndro*, two for *pélog*: **bem** (buhm; with tones 1, 2, 3, 5, and 6 in each octave) and *barang* (with tones 2, 3, 5, 6, and 7 in each octave); often simply called *gendèr*; played with two padded disc beaters.
gendèr panerus	Like *gendèr barung* but an octave higher.

Other Melodic Instruments

gambang (*gahm*-bahng)	Seventeen to twenty-three wooden keys resting over a trough resonator; one for *sléndro*; one or two for *pélog*; if two, like *gendèr barung* and *gendèr panerus*; if only one, exchange keys enable player to arrange instrument for *bem* (with scale 1, 2, 3, 5, and 6 in each octave) or for *barang* (with 2, 3, 5, 6, and 7); played with two padded disc beaters.
celempung (chuh-*luhm*-poong)	Zither, usually supported at about a thirty-degree angle by four legs, with twenty to twenty-six strings arranged in ten to thirteen "double

	courses" (as on a twelve-string guitar); one for *sléndro*, one or two for *pélog* (compare *gambang*); plucked with thumbnails.
siter (*si-tuhr*)	Smaller zither, resting on floor or in horizontal frame, with from ten to twenty-six strings in single or double courses, one for *sléndro*, one or two for *pélog* (compare *gambang* and *celempung*); plucked with thumbnails.
suling (*soo*-leeng)	End-blown bamboo flute; one for *sléndro*, one or two for *pélog*.
rebab (ruh-*bab*)	Two-stringed fiddle; one or two per *gamelan*.

Drums

kendhang gendhing (kuhn-*dahng* guhn-deeng)	Largest of the hand drums; two leather heads, laced onto a barrel-shaped shell; one per *gamelan*.
kendhang ciblon	Middle-sized hand drum; like *kendhang gendhing*; often simply called *ciblon*; one per *gamelan*.
kendhang ketipung	Smallest hand drum; often simply called *ketipung*; one per *gamelan*.
bedhug	Large stick-beaten drum; two leather heads tacked onto a cylindrical shell; one per *gamelan*.

There is no standard arrangement of these instruments in the performance space except that they are almost always placed at right angles to one another, reflecting the Javanese concern with the cardinal directions (see Figure 7.3). Generally the larger gong instruments are in the back, with the *saron* family immediately in front of them, *bonang* family and *bedhug* drum to the sides, other melodic instruments in front, and *kendhang* drums in the center. The placement of the instruments reflects their relative loudness and their function in the performance of pieces, to be discussed shortly.

The *gamelan* instruments are normally complemented by singers: a small male chorus (*gérong*) and female soloists (*pesindhèn*). Java also supports a highly developed tradition of unaccompanied vocal music, which serves as a major vehicle for Javanese poetry. Although Javanese have recorded their sung poetry in several writing systems for over a thousand years, these are normally sung rather than read silently or aloud. Even important letters between members of the nobility were, until the twentieth century, composed as poetry and delivered as song. Although the postal system has eliminated this practice, vocal music, whether with *gamelan* or unaccompanied, enjoys great popularity in Java today.

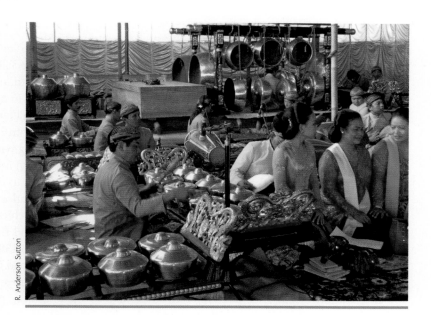

R. Anderson Sutton

FIGURE 7.3

Members of the Pujangga Laras *karawitan* group performing at a wedding in Eromoko, Wonogiri, Central Java, August 3, 2006.

The relation between vocal and instrumental orientations in *gamelan* music is reflected in the two major groupings of instruments in the present-day Javanese *gamelan:* "loud-playing" and "soft-playing." Historical evidence suggests that these two groupings were once separate ensembles and were combined as recently as the sixteenth or early seventeenth century. Associated with festivals, processions, and other noisy outdoor events, loud-playing ensembles were strictly instrumental. Soft-playing ensembles were intended for more-intimate gatherings, often indoor, and involved singing. Even today, performance style distinguishes these two groupings. In loud-playing style, only the drums and louder metal instruments are used (see the left-hand column of Table 7.1). In soft-playing style, these instruments, or most of them, are played softly, and the voices and instruments listed in the column on the right are featured.

TABLE 7.1 The Two *Gamelan* Instrument Groups.

Loud-Playing Instruments	Soft-Playing Instruments
gong ageng	gendèr barung
siyem	gendèr panerus
kempul	gambang
kenong	celempung
kethuk	siter
kempyang	suling
bonang family	rebab
saron family	
slenthem	
kendhang family	
bedhug	

GAMELAN CONSTRUCTION

Bronze is the preferred metal for *gamelan* manufacture, owing both to its durability and to its rich, sweet sound quality. Brass and iron are also used, especially in rural areas. They are considerably cheaper than bronze and easier to tune but less sonorous. Bronze *gamelan* instruments are not cast but instead forged in a long and difficult process. Though the metal worker in many societies occupies a low status, in Java he has traditionally been held in high regard. Forging bronze instruments not only requires great skill but also retains a mystical significance. Working with metals, transforming molten copper and tin (the metals that make bronze alloy) into sound-producing instruments, is believed to make one especially vulnerable to dangerous forces in the spirit world. For this reason the smiths make ritual preparation and may actually assume mythical identities during the forging process. The chief smith is ritually transformed into Panji, a powerful Javanese mythical hero, and the smith's assistants to Panji's family and servants (see Becker 1988; Kunst 1973:138).

The largest gongs may require a full month of labor and a truckload of coal for the forge that heats the metal. Only after appropriate meditation, prayer, fasting, and preparation of offerings does a smith undertake to make a large gong. The molten bronze is pounded, reheated, pounded, reheated, and gradually shaped into a large knobbed gong that may measure three feet or more in diameter. A false hit at any stage can crack the gong, and the process must begin all over.

GAMELAN IDENTITY

A *gamelan*, particularly a bronze set with one or two fine large gongs, is often held in great respect, given a proper name, and given offerings on Thursday evenings (the beginning of the Muslim holy day). Though *gamelan* makers have recently begun to duplicate precise tuning and decorative designs, each *gamelan* is usually a unique set, whose instruments would both look and sound out of place in another ensemble. Formerly it was forbidden even to attempt to copy the tuning and design of palace *gamelan* instruments, as these were reserved for the ruler and were directly associated with his power.

The variability in tuning from one *gamelan* to another certainly does not stem from a casual sense of pitch among Javanese musicians and *gamelan* makers. On the contrary, they take great care in the making and in the occasional retuning of *gamelan* sets to arrive at a pleasing tuning—one that is seen to fit the particular physical condition of the instruments and the tastes of the individual owner. For example, I spent one month with a tuner, his two assistants, and an expert musician as they gradually reached consensus on an agreeable tuning, and then altered the tuning of the many bronze gong and metal slab instruments through a long process of hammering and filing—all by hand. Bronze has the curious property of changing tuning—rather markedly during the first few years after forging and more subtly over the next twenty to thirty years, until it has finally "settled." It might seem that the lack of a standard tuning would produce musical chaos, but the actual latitude is rather small.

GAMELAN PERFORMANCE CONTEXTS

Despite the changes wrought by modern institutions in the contexts of music making and the ways music is understood, Javanese music is more closely interrelated with other performing arts and more intimately bound to other

Arthur Durkee, EarthVisions Photographics

FIGURE 7.4

Musicians playing the *gamelan* Kyai Kanyut Mèsem. Mangkunegaran palace, Surakarta, Central Java. In foreground: *Sarons, kempul,* and gongs on left; *saron peking* and *bonangs* on right.

aspects of life than are the arts in the West. Concerts of *gamelan* music, with an audience sitting quietly and paying close attention to the music, have only recently appeared and serve mostly to present new, experimental works. In contrast, presentations of the more traditional *gamelan* music are best understood as social events that involve *gamelan* music. They usually commemorate a day of ritual importance, such as a birth, circumcision, or wedding. Normally a family sponsors such an event and invites neighbors and relatives, with others welcome to look on and listen. The invited guests are served food and are expected to socialize freely throughout the duration of the event. No one expects the guests to be quiet during the performance of pieces or to pay rapt attention to them the way an audience does at a Western concert. Rather, the music, carefully played though it may be, is seen to contribute to the festiveness of the larger social event, helping to make it *ramé* (lively, busy in a positive way). Connoisseurs among the guests will ask for a favorite piece and may pay close attention to the way the ensemble or a particular singer or instrumentalist performs, but not to the exclusion of friendly interaction with the hosts and other guests. Although the music is intended to entertain those present (without dance or drama), it also serves a ritual function, helping to maintain balance at important transitional points in the life of a person or community.

More often, *gamelan* music is performed as accompaniment for dance or theater—a refined female ensemble dance (*srimpi* [*sreem*-pee] or *bedhaya* [buh-*daw*-yaw]; see Figures 7.5 and 7.6); a flirtatious female solo dance; a vigorous, martial lance dance; or an evening of drama based on Javanese legendary history, for example. A list of traditional genres currently performed in Central Java with *gamelan* accompaniment would be long. Some are presented primarily in commercial settings, with an audience buying tickets. Others most often involve a ceremony.

The genre held in the highest esteem by most Javanese, and nearly always reserved for ceremony, is the shadow puppet theatre or *wayang kulit* (see Figures 7.7 and 7.8),

FIGURE 7.5

Dancers at Pujokusuman in Yogyakarta perform a *srimpi*, female court dance.

Peggy Choy

which dates back no fewer than one thousand years. Beginning with an overture played on the *gamelan* during the early evening, shadow puppet performances normally last until dawn. With a screen stretched before him (almost all Javanese puppeteers are male), a lamp overhead, and puppets to both sides, one master puppeteer (*dhalang*) operates all the puppets, performs all the narration and dialogue, sings mood songs, and directs the musicians for about eight hours with no intermission.

Although the musicians do not play constantly throughout the evening, they must always remain ready to respond to a signal from the puppeteer. He leads the musicians and accents the action of the drama through a variety of percussion patterns he plays by hitting the wooden puppet chest to his left and the clanging metal plates suspended from the rim of the chest. If he is holding puppets in both hands, he uses his foot to sound these signals. He must be highly skilled as a manipulator, director, singer, and storyteller.

The puppeteer delivers not a fixed play written by a known playwright but rather his own rendition of a basic story—usually closely related to versions performed by

FIGURE 7.6

Dancers at the Pakualaman palace in Yogyakarta perform a *bedhaya*, female court dance, here with innovative costumes.

other puppeteers, but never exactly the same. It might be a well-known episode from the **Ramayana** (rah-mah-*yah*-nah) or **Mahabharata** (ma-hah-bah-*rah*-tah), epics of Indian origin that have been adapted and transformed in many parts of Southeast Asia and have been known in Java for one thousand years.

During a shadow puppet performance, the *gamelan* plays music drawn from a large repertory of pieces, none specific to a single play and many of which are played in other contexts as well. A good musician knows many hundreds of pieces, but like the shadow plays, the pieces are generally not totally fixed. Many regional and individual variants exist for some pieces. More importantly, the very conception of what constitutes a *gendhing* (guhn-*deeng*)—a "*gamelan* piece" or "*gamelan* composition"—differs from the Western notion of musical pieces, particularly within the Western "classical" tradition.

FIGURE 7.7

Puppeteer Ki Gondo Darman performing *wayang kulit* at the ASKI Performing Arts Academy in Surakarta.

GAMELAN MUSIC: A JAVANESE *GENDHING* IN PERFORMANCE

We can best begin to understand what a Javanese *gendhing* is by considering one in some detail—how it is conceived and how it is realized in performance. Listen to *Bubaran* "Kembang Pacar" (CD 2, Track 21). This is from a tape I made in a recording session in Yogya with some of the most highly regarded senior musicians associated with the court. It was played on a bronze *gamelan* at the house of one of Yogya's best known dancers and choreographers, R. M. Soedarsono, who founded the National Dance Academy (ASTI) in Yogya and recently retired from serving as Rector of the Indonesian Institute for the Arts (ISI).

Note that it is an example of loud-playing style throughout, in the *pélog* scale system, with small and large intervals. It uses the tones 1, 2, 3, 5, and 6, with an occasional 4, but no 7. Javanese normally refer to *gendhing* by their formal structure, in this case **bubaran** (boo-*bah*-ran; meaning 16 beats per *gongan*, 4 *kenong* beats per *gongan*); the name of a particular melody, here, **"Kembang Pacar"** (kuhm-*bahng pah*-char; a kind of red flower); the scale system (*pélog*); and the modal category (**pathet nem** [*pah*-tuht nuhm]).

What about its structure? How does this piece—or, more precisely, this performance of this piece—organize the sounds it employs? Unless they are connected directly to a previous piece in a medley sequence, Javanese *gendhing* begin with a solo introduction, played on one instrument or sung by a solo singer. Here a short introduction (*buka*) is played on the *bonang* by the well-known teacher and musician Pak Sastrapustaka (1913–1991). Refer to the Close Listening guide for the timings of the various sections.

During the latter portion, this *bonang* is joined by the two drums *kendhang gendhing* and *ketipung,* played (as is customary) by one drummer—in this case, the court musician Pak Kawindro. The drummer in a Javanese *gamelan* acts as a conductor, controlling the tempo and the dynamics (the relative levels of loudness and softness). He (or she) need not be visible to other musicians, since the "conducting" is accomplished purely through aural signals. The drummer does not stand in front of the ensemble but sits unobtrusively in the middle of it.

Although we discussed the choice of *Bubaran* "Kembang Pacar" at this recording session, experienced musicians recognize the identity of the *gendhing* from the introduction and do not need to be told what piece is about to be performed. The *bonang* player (or other musician providing an introduction) may simply play the introduction to an appropriate piece and expect the other musicians to follow. At the end of the introduction, most of the rest of the ensemble joins in, the large gong sounds, and the main body of the *gendhing* begins.

The structure of this main body is based on principles of balanced, binary (duple) subdivision and of cyclic repetition. The basic time and melodic unit in *gendhing* is the *gongan,* a phrase marked off by the sound of either the largest gong (*gong ageng*) or the slightly smaller *gong siyem.* For most *gendhing* these phrases are of regular length as measured in beats of the *balungan,* the melodic part usually played on the *slenthem* and the *saron* family—almost always some factor of two: 8 beats, 16 beats, 32 beats, 64 beats, 128 beats, 256 beats. (In the genre of pieces that serve as the staple for accompanying dramatic action, as we will see later, *gongan* are of irregular length, and the regular unit is marked instead by the smaller gong *kempul.*)

CD 2:21

Bubaran "Kembang Pacar" ("Red Flower"). *pélog pathet nem* (3:04). Central Javanese *gamelan* music in loud-playing style, performed by musicians affiliated with the royal palace in Yogyakarta. Field recording by R. Anderson Sutton. Yogyakarta, Java, Indonesia, 1980.

Close Listening

BUBARAN "KEMBANG PACAR"

CD 2:21

COUNTER NUMBER	COMMENTARY

Buka (introduction)

0:02	Initiated by *bonang barung.*
0:05	*Kendhang* joins in and slows the tempo.
0:10	Other instruments join in, gong marks end of *buka.*

Statement 1 of main body of the piece

0:11	1st *gongan* (major phrase) begins.
0:24	2nd *gongan* begins.
0:37	3rd *gongan* begins.
0:51	4th *gongan* begins.

Statement 2 of main body of the piece

1:04	1st *gongan* begins.
1:17	2nd *gongan* begins.
1:30	3rd *gongan* begins.
1:44	4th *gongan* begins.

Statement 3 of main body of the piece

1:56	1st *gongan* begins.
2:07	2nd *gongan* begins.
2:18	3rd *gongan* begins.
2:29	4th *gongan* begins.
2:30	Tempo begins to slows in response to *kendhang.*
2:49	Final gong beat marks the end of this performance.

The *kenong* subdivides a *gongan* into two or four shorter phrases, and these are further subdivided by *kempul, kethuk,* and in some lengthier pieces *kempyang.*

These structural principles result in a pattern of interlocking percussion that repeats until an aural signal from the drummer or one of the lead melodic instruments (*bonang* in loud-playing style, *rebab* in soft-playing) directs the performers to end or to proceed to a different piece. Whereas in Western music composers must provide explicit directions for performers to repeat a section (usually by means of notated repeat signs), in Javanese *gamelan* performance, repetition is assumed.

As we speak of "phrases" in describing music, borrowing the term from the realm of language, Javanese also liken the *gongan* to a sentence and conceive of the subdividing parts as "punctuation." For *Bubaran* "Kembang Pacar," after the gong stroke at the end of the introduction, the pattern of gong punctuation shown in Transcription 7.2 is repeated throughout. (See the Close Listening guide for timing of the progression in this performance from introduction through the three statements of the four *gongan*.)

TRANSCRIPTION 7.2
Interlocking punctuation pattern.

```
                                      .   .   .   .   .   .   .   .
   t = kethuk                       t w t N t P t N t P t N t P t N
   N = kenong                                                     G
   P = kempul
   G = gong or siyem
   w = rest
   . = one beat in balungan melody
```

The time distribution of these punctuating beats is even, but the degree of stress or weight is not (even though no beat is played louder than any other on any single instrument). Javanese listeners feel the following progression of stress levels (Transcription 7.3), based on the levels of subdivision.

TRANSCRIPTION 7.3
Stress levels in punctuation pattern.

```
   SUBDIVISIONS
   full gongan:                                                    G
   1st level:              N           N           N              N
   2nd level:      w           P           P           P
   3rd level: t        t       t       t       t       t       t

             ----------------------------------------------------------
             wk  md  wk  str wk  md  wk  str wk  md  wk  str wk  md  wk  xstr

   beat no.   1   2   3   4   5   6   7   8   9  10  11  12  13  14  15  16


             (wk = weak; md = medium; str = strong; xstr = very strong)
```

The strongest beat is the one coinciding with the largest and deepest-sounding phrase marker, the gong (G), and with the *kenong* (N), at the end of the phrase. Javanese would count this as one, *two,* three, *four,* and so on, with the strongest beat being the sixteenth. This is the only beat where two punctuating gong instruments coincide. This "coincidence" releases the rhythmic tension that has built up through the course of the *gongan,* giving a sense of repose.

Although in the West we may dismiss events as "mere coincidence," in Java the simultaneous occurrence of several events, the alignment of days of the week and dates (like our Friday the 13th), can be profoundly meaningful. It is not uncommon to determine a suitable day for a wedding, or for moving house, based on the coincidence of a certain day in the seven-day week with a certain day in the Javanese five-day market week, and this in turn within a certain Javanese month (in the lunar calendar, rather than the solar calendar used in the West). The simultaneous occurrence of what to Westerners would seem to be unrelated (and therefore meaningless) events—such as the sounding of a certain bird while a person is carrying out a particular activity—can be interpreted in Java as an important omen.

This deep-seated view of the workings of the natural world is reflected in the structure of *gamelan* music, where coincidence is central to the coherence of the music. The sounding of the gong with the *kenong* marks the musical instant of greatest weight and is the only point at which a *gendhing* may end. Other, lesser points of coincidence also carry weight. If we consider the piece in terms of the *balungan* melody, the next strongest stress comes at the coincidence of the *balungan* with the *kenong* strokes. And in pieces with longer *gongan* (for example, 32, 64, or 128 beats), many of the *saron* beats do not coincide with any punctuating gong, making each *kenong* stroke and even each *kethuk* stroke an instance of stress and temporary repose.

The ethnomusicologist Judith Becker and her former student Stanley Hoffman represent the cyclic structure of *gendhing* by mapping patterns onto a circle, relating the flow of musical time to the recurring course traced by the hands of a clock. The pattern used in *Bubaran* "Kembang Pacar," then, can be notated as shown in Transcription 7.4.

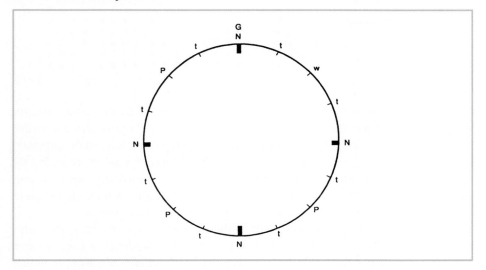

TRANSCRIPTION 7.4
Punctuation pattern of *Bubaran* "Kembang Pacar" represented as a circle.

Becker argues convincingly that the cyclic structure of Javanese *gendhing* reflects the persistence of Hindu-Buddhist conceptions of time introduced to Java during the first millennium C.E. and not wholly eliminated by the subsequent adoption of Islam. (For an elaboration of this theory, see Hoffman 1978, Becker 1979, and especially Becker 1981.)

In the performance of many pieces today, the players of most of the punctuating instruments have a choice of pitch. Their choice is normally determined by the *balungan* melody tone played simultaneously or the one about to be emphasized in the following phrase. However, when performing in loud-playing style, musicians sometimes use a single pitch throughout; this reflects the practice of earlier times, when only one *kempul* and one or two *kenong* were made for each *gamelan.* Here the musicians opt for this older practice; they use *kempul* tone 6 throughout and a special *kenong* tuned to tone 5 in the octave below the other kenong. The *kethuk,* as is customary in Yogya, is tuned to tone 2. The gong player chooses to sound the *gong ageng* for only the first and last gong strokes; otherwise he plays the smaller *gong siyem,* tuned to tone 2.

Let us now consider the *balungan* melody of this piece (CD 2, Track 21) performed on the *saron* and *slenthem* and notated as in Transcription 7.5. The system used here and elsewhere in this chapter is the cipher notation system now widely used throughout central and eastern Java. Dots in place of numerals indicate the sustaining of the previous tone. A dot below a numeral indicates the lower octave and a dot above indicates the higher octave. An extra space or two is often given after groups of four beats as a means of marking a "measure"—though in Java the stress is on the last beat, not the first. Today many Javanese musicians refer to notation to learn or to recall particular pieces, but they do not generally read from notation in performance. Further, the notation usually includes only the *balungan* melody and introduction; the parts played on other instruments are recreated in relation to the *balungan* melody and are open to some degree of personal interpretation.

TRANSCRIPTION 7.5
Introduction and *balungan* melody in the Javanese cipher notation system.

```
                                                                              G
                                                                              N
    Introduction           (on bonang):   5 3 5 .   2 3 5 6   2 4 5 4   2 15555


    Main Body                                                                 G
    punctuation (same each gongan):       t w t N   t P t N   t P t N   t P t N
                         1st gongan:       3 6 3 5   3 6 3 5   3 6 3 5   6 5 3 2
                         2nd gongan:       6 5 3 2   6 5 3 2   6 5 3 2   5 3 5 6
                         3rd gongan:       2 1 2 6   2 1 2 6   2 1 2 6   3 5 3 2
                         4th gongan:       5 3 5 .   2 3 5 6   2 4 5 4   2 1 6 5
```

The piece consists of four *gongan* (each, of course, with the same *bubaran* structure), played one after the other. Each of the first three begins with a measure that is played three times in succession and ends on the same tone as the previous gong tone. This kind of regularity enhances the balanced symmetry provided by the punctuation structure. The fourth *gongan,* which stands out with its one sustained note (fourth beat) and lack of internal repetition, is melodically quite similar to the introduction and leads right back into the first *gongan.*

To help you distinguish the sounds of the different layers of punctuation and melody in this piece, listen to a rendition performed by students in the Javanese *gamelan* performance ensemble at the University of Wisconsin–Madison, in which you will first hear just the *balungan* melody, then the other parts added one by one (CD 2, Track 22). Note that, because *gamelan* tuning is not standardized, the exact pitches of the *pélog* tones in the *gamelan* you hear in Track 22 of CD 2 differ noticeably from those of the *gamelan* in Track 21 of CD 2. Neither is considered "out of tune"; they merely differ.

The four-*gongan* melody of *Bubaran* "Kembang Pacar" is first played alone, with no punctuation, drum, or elaboration. As the four-*gongan* melody (or "statement") repeats, one layer of punctuation, drum pattern, or elaboration is added with each *gongan.* There are four full statements in this selection (see the Close Listening guide).

CD 2:22

Demonstration: *Bubaran* "Kembang Pacar," *pélog pathet nem* (3:55). *Balungan* melody alone, followed by addition of other instruments one by one. Performed by University of Wisconsin–Madison Javanese *gamelan* ensemble, directed by R. Anderson Sutton. Recorded at the University of Wisconsin, Madison, December 2000.

Close Listening

BUBARAN "KEMBANG PACAR"

CD 2:22

COUNTER
NUMBER   COMMENTARY

Main melody—*Gongan* A through D

0:02   *Saron* and *slenthem* play major phrase A, 1st statement, 16 beats.
              (metal slab instruments)

0:17   *Gongan* B, 1st statement, 16 beats.

0:32   *Gongan* C, 1st statement, 16 beats.

0:46   *Gongan* D, 1st statement, 16 beats.

1:00   *Gong* enters, marking end of *gongan* D.
              (Large hanging gong; marks the ends of all major phrases)

Gongan A, 2nd statement

1:04   *Kenong* enters, playing on every 4th beat.
              (Large kettle, horizontally mounted; subdivides the major phrase)

Gongan B, 2nd statement

1:20   *Kempul* enters, playing on the 6th, 10th, and 14th beats.
              (Medium hanging gongs; subdivides the major phrase)

Gongan C, 2nd statement

1:30   *Kethuk* enters, playing on the 1st and 3rd beat of every group of 4 (every other beat
              throughout).
              (Small kettle; subdivides the *kenong* phrase)

Gongan D, 2nd statement

1:43   *Kendhang* (kuhn-*dahng*) enters, playing rhythmic patterns that fill the length of each
              major phrase (16 beats).
              (Set of large and small barrel drums; directs tempo and dynamics)

Gongan A, 3rd statement

1:56   *Saron peking* enters, echoing each tone of the main melody.
              (Smallest, highest pitched *saron*, metal slab instrument; doubles main melody except at
              slower tempos, when it usually varies the melody)

Gongan B, 3rd statement

2:09   *Bonang barung* enters, playing variations and embellishments.
                (Larger, lower-pitched gong-chime; elaborates the main melody and subdivides its
                beats)

Gongan C, 3rd statement

2:21   *Bonang panerus* enters, playing variations and embellishments twice as fast as the
                bonang barung earlier.
                (Smaller, higher-pitched gong-chime; elaborates the main melody)

Gongan D, 3rd statement

2:34   Full instrumentation.

2:38   Drummer speeds up tempo nearing the end of major phrase D.

Gongan A, 4th statement

2:45   Full instrumentation.

Gongan B, 4th statement

2:56   Full instrumentation.

Gongan C, 4th statement

3:06   Full instrumentation.

Gongan D, 4th statement

3:17   Full instrumentation.
                Drummer signals slowing of tempo to end the piece.

The main body can be repeated as many times as the drummer desires or as is appropriate to the context in which it is performed. Pieces in *bubaran* form are normally played at the end of performances (*bubar* means "to disperse"). The guests or audience are expected to leave during the playing of the piece; thus the number of repetitions may depend on the length of time it takes those in attendance to get up to leave.

Having explored the structure of this piece as performed, let us focus our attention on the part played by the drummer, using the smallest and largest drums in combination. Throughout the piece he plays a pattern generic to the *bubaran* form. That is, the drumming for any of the forty or so other pieces in this form would be the same: a particular introductory pattern, several variant patterns for the main body, and a special contrasting pattern that is reserved only for the final *gongan* and that, together with the slowing of tempo, signals the ending. The patterns comprise a series of drum strokes. Each stroke has a name that imitates the actual drum sound: *tak, dung,* and *dang*—T, d, and D (see Transcription 7.6).

```
Introduction:                                          _____  N/G
     5   3   5   .     2   3   5   6     2   4   5   4     2   1 5 5 5 5
                                         T   T   d   D     T   d   d   .

Main Body:
         t   w   t   N   t   P   t   N   t   P   t   N   t   P   t  N/G
 (e.g.)  3   6   3   5   3   6   3   5   3   6   3   5   6   5   3   2
 A:      d   d   d D .   d   d   d D .   d   d   d D .   d D d D   d D .
                                         (played in 1st, 2nd, & 4th gongan)

         2   1   2   6   2   1   2   6   2   1   2   6   3   5   3   2
 B:    T d D . T d D .   T d D . T d D .   T d D . T d D .   d D d D   d D .
                                         (played in 3rd gongan)

         5   3   5   .   2   3   5   6   2   4   5   4   2   1   6   5
 Ending: T d d   d   D   T d d D T d D   d D T d T d T  D d   D   d d .
                                         (played in 4th gongan, last time)
```

TRANSCRIPTION 7.6
Bubaran drum patterns— a generic vocabulary of drum strokes, each with an onomatopoetic name that imitates the actual drum sound (*tak, dung,* and *dang*—T, d, and D). T—*Tak* is a short, crisp sound produced by slapping the smaller head of the *ketipung* with the palm. d—*Dung* is a high, resonant sound produced by one or two fingers striking the larger head of the *ketipung.* D—*Dang* is a deep sound produced by hitting the larger head of the *kendhang gendhing,* often in combination with *tak* on the *ketipung.*

It is the drummer who first begins to play faster, thereby signaling the ensemble to speed up at the end of the second time through the large cycle of four *gongan.* As a warning that he or she intends to end, the drummer alters the last few strokes in the penultimate *gongan* (in this case from dDdD dD. to dDdD TdD [not shown in the transcription]). This way the other musicians all know to slacken the tempo, though the precise rate is determined by the drummer. The playing of the ending pattern through the last *gongan* confirms his or her intentions.

We have seen how the punctuating gong parts and the drumming fit with the *balungan* in *Bubaran* "Kembang Pacar." We can now turn to the elaborating melodic instruments—here the middle-range *bonang* (*barung*) and higher-range *bonang* (*panerus*)—which normally play at a faster rate, subdividing the *balungan* part and providing variations based on the *balungan* melody. In pieces with *balungan* played at slower tempos, the highest-range *saron* (*peking*) also provides a limited degree of melodic elaboration, but in Yogyanese court style it is sometimes omitted (as it is here).

I mentioned earlier that the only part normally notated is the *balungan.* Other melodic parts are derived through processes generally understood by practicing musicians. Ideally, all musicians can play all the parts. In reality, this is true only in the best professional groups; however, most musicians have at least a passive knowledge of the workings of all the instruments and know how to respond to various signals and nuances.

The two *bonang* here perform in a style called "walking," usually alternating left and right hands in sounding combinations of tones derived from the *balungan.* Transcription 7.7 shows the *bonang barung* part as it is played the first time through the four *gongan.* The arrangement of kettle gongs on the instrument is given in the upper portion of the transcription; the lower portion shows the actual *bonang* playing in relation to the *balungan.*

TRANSCRIPTION 7.7
Cipher notation for the *bonang barung* part as played the first time through the four *gongan*—"walking" style.

```
                              4̇    6̇    5̇    3̇    2̇    i    7̇
Kettles on bonang:
                         1    7    2    3    5    6    4


Bonang Playing in Bubaran Kembang Pacar:

balungan:    3    6    3    5    3    6    3    5    3    6    3    5    6    5    3    2

bonang:    3 6 3 6 3 5 3 5   3 6 3 6 3 5 3 5   3 6 3 6 3 5 3 5   6 5 3 5 6 . 6 .
                                                                          2   2

balungan:    6    5    3    2    6    5    3    2    6    5    3    2    5    3    5    6

bonang:    6 5 3 5 6 . 6 .   6 5 3 5 6 . 6 .   6 5 3 5 6 . 6 .   5 3 5 3 6 6 6̇ .
                    2   2             2   2             2   2                   6

balungan:    2    1    2    6    2    1    2    6    2    1    2    6    3    5    3    2

bonang:    2̇ i 2̇ i 5 6 i 6   2̇ i 2̇ i 5 6 i 6   2̇ i 2̇ i 6 6 6̇ .   3 3 3̇ . 2 2 2̇ .
                                                              6         3         2

balungan:    5    3    5    .    2    3    5    6    2    4    5    4    2    1    6    5

bonang:    5̇ 3 5̇ 3 5 5 5̇ .   2̇ 3 2̇ 3 5 6 5̇ 6̇   2̇ 4 2̇ 4 5 4 5̇ 4̇   2̇ i 2̇ i 6 5 3 5
                          5
```

In subsequent repetitions, the *bonang barung* part is similar but not identical. The variations reflect the sensibilities of the player, who both adjusts to tempo changes and alters his or her patterns purely for the aesthetic enjoyment of variation. The *bonang* player has not learned a particular *bonang* part or set of variations, note for note, for this one piece. Rather, the player has thoroughly internalized a vocabulary of patterns known by tradition to fit with certain phrases of *balungan.* What the player usually will have learned about the particular piece, other than its *balungan,* is the octave register in which to play variations (for example, 3 6 3 6 rather than 3̇ 6̇ 3̇ 6̇).

The *bonang panerus* plays similar sorts of variations of the *balungan* melody but at twice the rate of the *bonang barung.* Transcription 7.8 gives *balungan, bonang barung,* and *bonang panerus* parts for the first *gongan.* The arrangement of kettles on the *bonang panerus* is identical to that of *bonang barung,* with each tuned an octave higher than the corresponding *bonang barung* kettle.

TRANSCRIPTION 7.8
Bonang barung and *panerus* parts for *Bubaran* "Kembang Pacar," first *gongan.*

```
balungan:    3    6    3    5    3    6    3    5    3    6    3    5    6    5    3    2

bon. bar.:  3 6 3 6 3 5 3 5   3 6 3 6 3 5 3 5   3 6 3 6 3 5 3 5   6 5 3 5 6 . 6 .
                                                                          2   2

bon. pnr.:  363.3636353.3535  363.3636353.3535  363.3636353.3535  656.6535626.626.
```

You can see in Transcription 7.8 how the two *bonang* vary by repetition: 3 6 in the *balungan* becomes 3 6 3 6 in the *bonang barung* part and 363.3636 in the *bonang panerus* part—all heard simultaneously. The players do not mechanically repeat this pattern throughout, however; they can substitute alternate tones (such as 6 5 3 5 instead of 6 5 6 5) and make other choices. In any case, we can see why the Javanese refer to the *saron* and *slenthem* melody as *balungan.* The term literally means "outline" or "skeleton," and the *balungan* provides just that for the elaborating instruments (and for voices, in soft-playing style). The degree to which the *saron* and *slenthem* part actually sounds like an outline depends on its tempo and the resulting levels at which the elaborating instruments subdivide it.

IRAMA LEVEL

In the performances of *Bubaran* "Kembang Pacar" (CD 2, Tracks 21 and 22), the *bonang barung* plays at twice the density of the *balungan*, subdividing it by two. This ratio defines one of five possible levels of *balungan* subdivision known as **irama** (ee-*raw*-maw) levels. If the tempo had slowed sufficiently (as we will see in the next piece), the *bonang barung* would have doubled its ratio with the *balungan*, subdividing each beat by four. Ward Keeler aptly likens the process to a car shifting gears, in this case downshifting as it goes up a steep grade (Keeler 1987:225). To maintain its relationship with the *bonang barung,* the *bonang panerus* would double as well, resulting in an eight-to-one ratio with the *balungan.* At the slowest *balungan* tempo, the *bonang barung* would have a ratio of 16 beats to 1 *balungan* beat; and the *bonang panerus,* along with several of the soft instruments, would play a full 32 beats for each *balungan* beat!

PERFORMING YOUR OWN *GAMELAN* MUSIC

To get the feeling of *gamelan* ensemble performance, all you need is a group of seven or eight people. You can either use available percussion instruments, such as Orff, or simply use your voices. Start by assigning each punctuating instrument to one person. The gong player can simply say "gong" (in a low, booming voice), the *kempul* player "pul" (middle voice), the *kenong* player "nong" (long and high), and the *kethuk* player "tuk" (short and low). Another can be assigned to play the drum pattern (saying the syllables given in the Transcription 7.6 patterns). Then the remaining performers can divide among themselves the *balungan* melody and, if they are inclined, some *bonang* elaboration. With a larger group, people can double up on all instruments except the drum.

First try the piece we have listened to, because the tune is familiar. The "drummer" should control the tempo and play the ending pattern, slowing down, to end. Try different versions, with different numbers of repetitions. You can end at any gong tone, not just at the end of the fourth *gongan.* Then try the piece given in Transcription 7.9, called *Bubaran* "Udan Mas" (literally, "Golden Rain"). You can hear it on the CD recording *Javanese Court Gamelan* from the Pura Paku Alaman (Nonesuch 72044). The gong punctuation is the same as in *Bubaran* "Kembang Pacar," but the melody differs. The sequence is as follows: introduction, first *gongan* twice, second *gongan* twice, first *gongan* twice, second *gongan* twice, and so on, until your drummer signals an ending. Try to learn it well enough not to need the notation so that, like a Javanese musician, you will be using your ears rather than your eyes.

TRANSCRIPTION 7.9
Bubaran "Udan Mas,"
pélog pathet barang.

```
Introduction:                                                          N/G
              7   7   7   5   6   7   2̇   2̇   7   6   5   6   7   6   5
                                        T   T   d   D   T   d   d

Main Body:
            t   w   t   N   t   P   t   N   t   P   t   N   t   P   t   N/G
(balungan:) 6   5   3   2   6   5   3   2   3   3   2   3   6   5   3   2

(bonang:) 6 5 6 5 2 . 2 .  6 5 6 5 2 . 2 .  3 3 3 . 3 3 . .  6 5 6 5 2 . 2 .

(balungan:) 7   5   6   7   5   6   7   2   2   7   6   5   6   7   6   5

(bonang:) 7 5 7 5 6 7 6 7  5 6 5 6 7 2̇ 7 2̇  2̇ 7 2̇ 7 6 5 6 5  6̲ 7 6 7 5 5 5 .


Approximate equivalents in Western pitches for pélog scale:

(1 = D), 2 = E, 3 = F, (4 = A♭), 5 = A, 6 = B♭, 7 = C  (1 and 4 not used here)
```

A JAVANESE *GENDHING* IN SOFT-PLAYING STYLE

CD 2:23

Ladrang "Wilujeng" ("safe, secure"), *pélog pathet barang* (8:47). Central Javanese *gamelan* music in "soft-playing" style. Performed by musicians of Ngudya Wirama *gamelan* group under the direction of Ki Suhardi. Field recording by René Lysloff. Yogyakarta, Java, Indonesia, 1980.

Listen to the next recording, *Ladrang* "Wilujeng," *pélog pathet barang* (CD 2, Track 23). *Wilujeng* literally means "safe" or "secure." The piece is often performed at the beginning of ceremonies or rituals to ensure the safety of not only the community involved but also the ceremony or the performance itself. The recording was made at the house of my teacher Suhardi, who lived just outside of Yogya and directed the professional *gamelan* musicians at the Yogya branch of the national radio station, Radio Republik Indonesia (R.R.I.). Some of the performers were professional musicians (at R.R.I. and elsewhere); others were Suhardi's neighbors who gathered at his house for regular weekly rehearsals on his *gamelan*.

The instruments, which filled much of his modest house when they were spread out for playing, are mostly iron and brass. Perhaps you noticed the contrast in sound quality as the metal percussion instruments first entered. For soft-playing style, however, the quality of singing and the various soft-sounding instruments matters the most, rendering the contrast between bronze and other metals far less significant than it is in loud-playing style. For this reason, some Javanese say that the soft-playing music is more a music of the common people (who cannot afford large bronze ensembles) and the loud-playing music more a music of the court and nobility.

PATHET

Like *Bubaran* "Kembang Pacar," *Ladrang* "Wilujeng," *pélog pathet barang* uses the *pélog* scale system, but it is classified as *pathet barang*. Javanese generally identify three *pathet* in each of the two scale systems, ordered in relation to the progression in which they are featured in the all-night shadow puppet performances (see Table 7.2).

TABLE 7.2 *Pathet* in Shadow Puppet Performance.

Sléndro pathet	Pélog pathet	
About 9:00 P.M.–midnight	nem	lima
About midnight–3:00 A.M.	sanga	nem
About 3:00 A.M.–6:00 A.M.	manyura	barang

In actual shadow puppetry today, the first phase may start before 9:00 P.M. and last until well after midnight. The second often begins as late as 2:00 A.M. and the third as late as 4:30. Several schemes are given for music performed outside of the shadow puppet context, but current practice indicates little relation between time of day and *pathet*. Instead, pieces in *sléndro pathet nem* or *pélog pathet lima*, which are usually calm and subdued, tend to be played relatively early in a performance, regardless of the time of day.

Much effort has been spent in defining *pathet* with reference to the melodies of *gamelan* pieces, particularly the *balungan*. The famous Dutch ethnomusicologist Jaap Kunst noted that certain phrase finals were more common in one *pathet* than another, especially for pieces played primarily in *sléndro* (Kunst 1973). Mantle Hood, one of Kunst's students and a major force in establishing ethnomusicology in the United States, devoted an entire book to the subject, concluding that *pathet* can be distinguished by different cadential patterns in the *balungan* part and the avoidance of certain tones (Hood 1954).

With a larger body of data than was available to Hood, Judith Becker found *pathet* to be "based upon three interlocking factors: (1) melodic pattern, formula, or contour, (2) the pitch level of that pattern and (3) the position of the pattern within the formal structure of a piece" (Becker 1980:81). In *sléndro*, for instance, a measure with the contour of three conjunct steps downward can occur in any *pathet*. Measures beginning on tone 5 and descending to 1 (5 3 2 1) are relatively common in both *sléndro pathet manyura* and *sléndro pathet sanga*, but in *manyura* they normally do not end in a strong position (for example, with a gong stroke), whereas in *sanga* they often do. Measures with the same descending contour, but beginning on tone 6 and descending to 2 (6 5 3 2) are common in both *pathet manyura* and *pathet nem*, but those ending in gong position are more likely to be *pathet nem*.

Javanese often speak of register or pitch level in relation to *pathet*, likening it in some ways to Western concepts of key. Indeed many *gendhing* are played in several *pathet*, just as Western popular tunes are often transposed from one key to another. The relationship to key is most apparent not in the single-octave *balungan* melody but in the parts played on instruments with wider ranges and in the singing. Instrumentalists and singers learn a vocabulary of melodic patterns, which they can readily transpose up or down—and even between scale systems. For example, the pattern one uses to arrive at tone 6 in *sléndro pathet manyura* can be realized one tone lower, with the same physical processes, to end on 5 in *sléndro pathet sanga*. In fact, most Javanese say that *pathet sanga* is simply *pathet manyura* down one tone. But musicians often describe *sléndro pathet nem*, the lowest of the three *sléndro pathet*, as consisting of an ambiguous mix of phrases from the other two *sléndro pathet*, as is the case in our third example (discussed later).

Pélog pathet are understood slightly differently. *Pathet barang* is easily distinguished by the presence of tone 7 and the avoidance of tone 1. Differentiating *pathet lima* from *pathet nem* presents greater problems, since both avoid tone 7, employ the other six *pélog* tones, and do not seem to be simply one or more tones above or below the other. Javanese musicians often disagree over which of these two is the correct *pathet* category for a given piece. Perception of a piece's mood, which is determined by other factors besides melodic contour and register, may also contribute. The calmer pieces would be classified as *lima* and livelier ones as *nem*.

The point here is not to try to present a thorough survey of the many ideas about the concept of *pathet*. Rather, I hope you have learned that *pathet* is somewhat more complicated than its Western counterpart, "mode." The word *pathet* literally means "limit" and is related to other Javanese words for stopping or delimiting. In many ways it indicates something about the limitations of the piece in question— the tones that will be played or emphasized in the *balungan* melody, the pitch level of the other parts, the mood, and (especially for shadow puppetry accompaniment) the time of day or night at which it is appropriately played. Although the association with mood and time of day suggests comparison with Indian *raga* (see Chapter 6), *pathet* is actually a very different concept. *Ragas* are differentiated from one another by details of interval structure and ornament, as well as contour, but not by register. Hundreds of *ragas* are known, thousands theoretically possible. Indian musicians do not, however, transpose pieces from one *raga* to another, because the *raga* is essential to the aesthetic impact of the piece. *Pathet* is a far more general concept. Only a few *pathet* are identified for each of the two scale systems, and transposition from one *pathet* to another occurs with some frequency.

A CLOSE EXAMINATION OF *LADRANG* "WILUJENG"

Ladrang "Wilujeng" (CD 2, Track 23) differs from *Bubaran* "Kembang Pacar" in many ways. It is in soft-playing style, featuring voices and the various soft-sounding instruments. The introduction is played on the *rebab* (fiddle), with the subtle slides and nuances one could not produce on a fixed-pitch instrument such as the *bonang*. The pattern of punctuation (*ladrang*) is nearly the same as in the previous piece, but it is expanded to fit with *gongan* phrases of 32 beats rather than 16. The players of the *kempul* and *kenong* do not limit themselves to one tone, but instead use a variety of tones, matching or anticipating important tones in the melody.

Instrumental Playing in *Ladrang* "Wilujeng"

Ladrang "Wilujeng" is often performed in *sléndro pathet manyura* as well as *pélog pathet barang* simply by transferring the melodic patterns from one system to the other. Transcription 7.10 presents the introduction, the *balungan,* and the gong punctuation (with pitch choices for *kempul* and *kenong*).

TRANSCRIPTION 7.10 *Ladrang* "Wilujeng," *pélog pathet barang.* For each section (A and B) the gong punctuation is shown on the first line (letters and numerals) and the *balungan* on the second.

```
                                              ___N/G
Introduction:        7 3 2  6 72. 3  7 7 3 2  7 67276

A: (umpak section)

    t    w    t  N3   t  P6   t  N5   t  P3   t  N6   t  P3*  t  N6/G
   2 7 2 3  2 7 5 6  3 3 . .  6 5 3 2  5 6 5 3  2 7 5 6  2 7 2 3  2 7 5 6
                                            *(if going to ngelik, P6)

B: (ngelik section)
    t    w    t  N6   t  P7   t  N6   t  P6   t  N7   t  P6   t  N6/G
   . . 6 .  7 5 7 6  3 5 6 7  6 5 3 2  6 6 . .  7 5 7 6  . 7 3 2  . 7 5 6
```

This piece is considerably more challenging to follow than *Bubaran* "Kembang Pacar." It slows and changes *irama* level in the third measure (3 3 . .), settling by the end of the first *gongan* to a tempo of about 36 *balungan* beats per minute. *Irama* is a level of subdivision of the main melody beat by elaborating instruments. The first section (A) is played twice, then the second (B) once, then first twice again, the second again, and so on, ending in the first: A A B A A B A A B A. For the final two *gongan,* the tempo first speeds up (but with no change in *irama* level) to about 42 beats per minute and then slows gradually to the final gong. A solo female singer (*pesindhèn;* puh-*seen*-den) sings for most of the first two *gongan.* At the beginning of the first B and from then on, all the singers join in unison. Further, the *balungan* part is no longer played explicitly. Instead the *balungan* instruments play simple variations based on the *balungan.* (See the Close Listening guide.)

Close Listening

LADRANG "WILUJENG"

CD 2:23

COUNTER NUMBER	COMMENTARY
0:00	Beginning of introduction, played on *rebab* (fiddle).
0:07	Gong at end of introduction, the rest of the ensemble enters.
0:18	Change of *irama* level from level 1 to level 2.
0:49	Gong at end of first statement of *gongan* A.
1:41	Singers enter in unison, just prior to the end of *gongan* A.
1:42	Gong at end of second statement of *gongan* A.
2:36	Gong at end of first statement of *gongan* B.
3:30	Gong at end of third statement of *gongan* A.
3:58	End of first verse of unison singing.
4:23	Singers enter in unison, singing second verse.
4:24	Gong at end of fourth statement of *gongan* A.
5:17	Gong at end of second statement of *gongan* B.
6:11	Gong at end of fifth statement of *gongan* A.
6:39	End of the second verse of unison singing.
6:44	Drummer signals acceleration in tempo.
7:01	Gong at end of sixth statement of *gongan* A.
7:46	Gong at end of third statement of *gongan* B.
8:11	Drummer signals gradual slackening in tempo.
8:41	Final gong at end of seventh statement of *gongan* A.

The drummer, with the same two drums used in the previous example (*kendhang gendhing* and *ketipung*), plays standardized patterns specific to *ladrang* formal structure: a *ladrang* introduction, a *ladrang* slowing-down pattern (in the first *gongan*), standard patterns for most of the rest of the performance (with a standard variation each time the B section is played), and finally an ending pattern during the final *gongan.* In accord with the soft-playing style, the drumming is softer and sparser than in loud-playing style. Transcription 7.11 presents the standard pattern used, with minimal variation, throughout all the A sections but the final one.

TRANSCRIPTION 7.11
Drum pattern, *Ladrang*
"Wilujeng," *irama dadi.*

```
    2   7   2   3     2   7   5   6     3   3   .   .     6   5   3   2
    .   .   .   .   .   d   d   .   d   D   .   .   .   .   .   d   .   d   .dDd.Dd   .  .  .  d  D  .  d  D

    5   6   5   3     2   7   5   6     2   7   2   3     2   7   5   6G
    d   D   .   d   .dD  .  T   d   d   d   D   d  .dD  d  .dD  dD.dD.dD.dD   .  .  .  d  .dD  d  D
```

Other instrumentalists play variations of the *balungan* melody, producing such a complex heterophony that some scholars identify *gamelan* music as polyphonic, noting the stratification of layers: parts moving at a wide variety of tempi—some at a much faster rate or higher density than others. Generally the smaller, higher-pitched instruments play at the faster rates and the larger, deeper ones at the slower rates. One can get a sense of this stratification by considering the frequency with which the gong is struck, comparing it with *kenong* (here four times per gong), then *balungan* (here eight times per *kenong*), and then the subdividing parts (*bonang barung* and *saron peking* four times per *balungan* beat; *bonang panerus* and many of the soft-playing instruments eight times per *balungan* beat). Thus the instruments playing at the fastest rate, mostly those of higher pitch, actually play 256 beats for every one beat of the gong!

I mentioned earlier that in this example the *balungan* is varied even on the instruments that usually sound it explicitly. After the first two *gongan*, where the *balungan* is played normally, the *saron* play simple variations, adding neighboring tones, while the *slenthem* lags by a quarter beat, all of which contributes to a dreamy blurring that allows the vocal melody to assume prominence.

The combination resulting from the interlocking of *slenthem* and *saron* here is identical to what the much higher-pitched *saron peking* plays, duplicating and anticipating the *balungan* tones in a manner that also resembles closely the "walking" style of *bonang* playing. This means of varying the *balungan* characterizes *peking* playing generally; it is not limited to the few cases where the *balungan* is only implied. (See Transcription 7.12.)

TRANSCRIPTION 7.12
Saron peking passage,
Ladrang "Wilujeng."

```
(balungan:    3   5   6   7P   6   5   3   2N)

saron peking:   3355335566776677 6655665533223322
```

Throughout *Ladrang* "Wilujeng," the *bonang*s play in walking style, mixed with occasional reiteration of single tones or octave combinations, as found in the first example, *Bubaran* "Kembang Pacar." The lengthier time interval between *balungan* beats here, however, provides an opportunity for greater melodic and rhythmic independence from the *balungan* melody. For example, the following phrase is played (with occasional variation) on the *bonang barung* with the *balungan* 2 7 5 6. (See Transcription 7.13.)

```
balungan:          2      7      5      6N
bonang barung:   2̇ 7 7̄5̄5 5 7 . . 5 7 7̄5̄. 6 7 . 6
```

TRANSCRIPTION 7.13
Bonang barung passage,
Ladrang "Wilujeng."

The various soft-playing instruments provide more-elaborate variations that are more independent of the *balungan* part and often inspired by phrases in the vocal parts. Because they blend together in the thick texture of soft-playing style, distinguishing all the soft instruments is difficult. As an example, consider the *gambang* (xylophone), which plays mostly "in octaves"—the right hand usually sounding the same tone as the left, but one octave higher. The excerpt is from the middle of the A section, fourth statement (4:05 to 4:20 on CD 2, Track 23). (See Transcription 7.14.)

```
balungan:          5              6              5              3P
r.h.   2̇ 3 2̇ 3 5 5 5̇ 3 5 5 3 5 3 5 3 5 6 2̇ 7 6 5 3 5 2̇ 7 6 6 6 2̇ 2̇ 7 2̇ 3
l.h.   2 3 2 3 5 2 3 5 2 3 5 3 2 3 5 6 2̇ 7 6 5 3 5 2 7̣ 6̣ 7̣ 6̣ 2 6̣ 7̣ 2 3

balungan:          2              7              5              6
r.h.   3̇ 5̇ 6̇ 7̇ 6̇ 2̇ 7 6 5 6 3 2̇ 7 3 2̇ 7 7 2̇ 7 2̇ 7 6 5 3 3 5 3 5 6 6 5 6
l.h.   3 5 6 7 6 2̇ 7 6 5 6 3 2 7̣ 3 2 7̣ 3 2 7̣ 2 7̣ 6̣ 5̣ 3 3 5 3 5̣ 6̣ 3 5̣ 6̣
```

TRANSCRIPTION 7.14
Gambang passage,
Ladrang "Wilujeng."

In other statements of this passage, the *gambang* part is similar, but not identical. Good players draw from a rather large vocabulary of patterns and vary the repeated passages in performance with a degree of individual flexibility, though not with the range of spontaneity associated with improvisation in jazz or Indian music. The *gambang* player, like the other *gamelan* musicians whose part is not completely fixed, operates with a system of constraints (not quite "rules" or "laws"). At the end of a measure, the *gambang* and *balungan* tones almost always coincide; at the midpoint (second beat), they usually do; on other beats they often do not, even though the *gambang* sounds eight (or in some cases as many as thirty-two) times as many tones as the *balungan*.

Singing in *Ladrang* "Wilujeng"

Solo singing with *gamelan* is also based on notions of flexibility and constraint. During the first two *gongan* one of the female vocalists sings florid vocal phrases that weave in and out of the *balungan* part. Although her part employs a much freer rhythm than the steady pulsation of most of the instruments (for example, the *gambang* discussed earlier), her melody is also constructed from phrases that usually end on the same tone as the *balungan* phrase, even though in current practice she often reaches that tone a beat or two later than most of the other instruments. Although her phrases resemble those of other singers, in some small ways they are her individual patterns. The vocal text used by the solo singer (difficult to determine in this recording) is not specific to the piece; it is one of many in a well-known verse form fitted to the structure of this *ladrang* and to many pieces in this and other forms.

In contrast to the soloist, the chorus sings a precomposed melody. The text, although agreed on before performance, is again a generic one, used in many *gamelan* pieces and having no connection with the meaning of the title of this piece. To a great degree, Javanese melodies and texts lead independent lives. For example, one may sing a single melody with a variety of texts or sing a single text in a variety of *gamelan* pieces; such choices depend on the wishes of the performers or sometimes (but rarely) the requirements of a particular dramatic scene.

The choral text presents many riddles in which the meaning of seemingly unrelated phrases in the first part suggests the meaning or sound of words or phrases in the second part. The Javanese greatly enjoy this kind of literary indirection, which we can see as an aesthetic expression of the high value placed on subtlety and indirection in daily life. To understand the connections, one must know traditional Javanese culture rather well: history, legends, nature, foods, place-names (in both the real and the mythological worlds), and the Javanese shadow puppet tradition with its many hundred characters. Javanese poetry is difficult to render in English. In the following, the Javanese is given first, with word-by-word translation second (with some double meanings), followed by a freer translation.

Text,
LADRANG "WILUJENG,"
PÉLOG PATHET BARANG

1. *Manis rengga, satriya ing Lésanpura*
    sweet decoration (colorful sweet snack), knight of/in Lésanpura
    Beautifully adorned, the knight from Lésanpura. [a kingdom in the Mahabharata]
    Setyanana yèn laliya marang sira
    Be loyal if forget to you
    You should be loyal, even if you forget yourself.

2. *Tirta maya, supaya anyar kinarya*
    Water pure, so that quickly be made
    Beautiful clear water, let it be done quickly.
    Ning ing driya, tan na ngalih amung sira
    purity/emptiness of/in heart, not exist move only you
    With the purifying of my heart, there is nothing that moves, only you.

3. *Kala reta, satriya ngungkuli jaya*
    Time red (centipede), knight surpass glory/victory
    At dawn, the knight proves exceptional in his glory.
    Sun mbang-embang hamisésa jroning pura
    I hope/yearn for have power within domain/palace
    I yearn to exercise power here in this domain.

Some of the riddles here are obscure even to most Javanese. An explanation of two of them should give you an idea of how they work. In the first line of stanza 1, the words *satriya ing Lésanpura* (a knight in the kingdom of Lésanpura) suggest the sound of the first word of the second line *setyanana,* as the shadow puppet character named Setyaki is a well-known knight who came from Lésanpura. *Kala reta*, in the first line of the third stanza, suggests not the sound but one meaning of the root particle in the compound *mbang-embang* in the second line. Though the two-word expression *kala reta* can mean "centipede," the two words translate individually as "time" (*kala*) and "red" (*reta*). *Bang*, the root of *mbang-embang*, is another word for red, and *bang-bang wétan* (literally "red-red east") is a Javanese expression for dawn. In this example, as is common in pieces where male and female singers join to sing, the text is interspersed with extra words and syllables whose meaning may be obscure (underlined in Transcription 7.15), and portions of the text may be repeated. These characteristics strongly suggest the relatively greater importance of what we would call the "musical" elements (pitch and rhythm) over the words, with the words' meaning often obscured and the words serving primarily as vehicles for beautiful melody. Transcription 7.15 shows the scheme for the first stanza (with *balungan* and gong punctuation given above the vocal line).

TRANSCRIPTION 7.15
First stanza, choral vocal part, *Ladrang* "Wilujeng."

The second stanza operates the same way, with repetition of the last four syllables at the end of one A section and repetition of the first four syllables of the second line in the next A. Only the final stanza (here the third, but this could have gone on for many more stanzas) ends after one B and one A and thus does not reach the "*Adèn, adèn*" interjections and the repetition of the first four syllables we would expect in the next A if the performance did not end where it does.

BIOGRAPHY OF KI NARTOSABDHO—A *GAMELAN* MUSICIAN, COMPOSER, AND PUPPETEER

So far we have focused mostly on musical sound and its structure. But what of the people who are most drawn to this music—the musicians themselves? Javanese and foreign scholars alike have often mentioned the close interrelationship among the arts in Java. In fact, the status of "musician" does not preclude one from dancing or performing puppetry. Many of the better performers in one art are quite competent in several others. In the following pages a consummate artist, one famous as a *gamelan* musician, composer of new pieces, and shadow puppeteer, speaks for himself.

The biography provided here is based on an interview my wife and I conducted with the late Ki Nartosabdho in 1979. (His music is discussed at length in Becker 1980.) We began by asking him how he became a shadow puppeteer. He proceeded to tell us the story of his life from early childhood memories, with just a few questions from us, which I have omitted here.

> Since I sat at my school desk in second grade, I had a knack for the arts. Which ones? Painting. Children's paintings, but even so, with cubist style, realism, expressionism, and my own creations: for instance, a lamb being chased by a tiger, things like that. Now, they really did not give lessons in those kinds of painting for children my age, but I made every effort to see duplications of pictures made by other painters at that time. After beginning to learn to paint, I began to learn classical style dance. I'd dance the role of a monkey, an ogre, and so forth. We actually learned a lot about classical dance—not everything, but a good deal. At that time I lived in my small village, in the Klatèn area [between Yogya and Solo]—called Wedhi. I was born in Wedhi on August 25, 1925. There, when I was twelve years old and in third grade, we had a teacher who gave dance lessons. He was from Solo. We studied so hard that we were able to put on quite an impressive show. It was really rare for village children to have the opportunity to study with a "classical" dance teacher from Solo.
>
> After dance, I began to learn Western music—violin, guitar, cello, and *keroncong*. [The *keroncong* is a small chordophone, like an ukulele, played in the Western-influenced Indonesian genre of the same name. The violin, guitar, and cello he studied were for this same genre, and not for "classical" Western music.] By village standards I did just fine, but not by city standards. After that, I studied *gamelan* music. All these interests took their toll—requiring one to spend time, emotions, and especially money. Especially for musical instruments, what was I to use to purchase one? A guitar in 1937 cost six gulden—Dutch money—or we would say six *rupiah* [Indonesian currency]. I was the eighth of my brothers and sisters; I was the youngest. And I was born into a family that was poor—lacking in possessions, in work, and especially in education. So it is clear that, no matter how much I wanted something, I could not continue my education without any income. My father died just after I began second grade, and my mother, a widow, was already old. So I earned money by making masks—yes, masks in order to

be able to continue school. And I managed to finish fifth grade. And I used to have Dutch language classes after school, but they cost 1.25 gulden each month, so I only took Dutch for two months. They threw me out—because I couldn't pay!

Now, rather than hang aimlessly about the house, when I was a teenager, I took off, without even asking my mother's permission. Where in the world would I go, I didn't know. Like a bird in flight, not knowing where I might perch. It was as if I needed some time to suffer. —Excuse me, I don't usually come out with all this about myself, but today I am.— Anyway, like a bird in flight, no idea where I should perch. I might even be called a *gelandangan* [homeless street person]. If not a *gelandangan,* then an outcast, or a forgotten soul.

I felt that the perch I should take was only to join and follow performing groups: both *kethoprak* [musical drama, with stories from Javanese legendary history] and *wayang orang* [musical dance-drama, based on the same Indian epics as shadow puppetry]. First I joined a *kethoprak* group, working as an actor and as a *gamelan* musician. But what I got for it was very minimal—both artistically and financially. And what was more, the coming of the Japanese reinforced my feeling that I had to keep drifting. A life of wandering about, and in tattered clothing. There were lots of clothes then that no human being should have to wear [burlap bags, etc., as the Japanese took much of the cloth during their occupation], but like it or not, circumstances required it. In Javanese there is a the saying: *nuting jaman kalakoné* ["following the times is the way to act"—or, "go with the flow"]. There are lots of sayings and stories that still have mystical content in Indonesia, still plenty. And you should know, even though in your country there is so much great technology, in Indonesia traditional and mystical matters still persist, and are even gaining in strength.

So, I played with about ten *kethoprak* groups: only one month, then move, three months and move, at the longest, only four or five months, then move. It is called *lècèkan*—not taking care of oneself. Then one day I was playing drum for a *kethoprak* group named Sri Wandowo, playing in Klatèn. This was in 1945, just before the Proclamation of Independence [August 17]. There was a manager, the manager of the Ngesthi Pandhawa *wayang orang* troupe, who happened to be eating at a little eating stall behind the *kethoprak* stage where I was playing. As he ate, he heard my drumming and it made an impression. After going home—from eating frogs' legs—he called three of his troupe members and asked them to find out who it was playing *kendhang* for the *kethoprak.* After that, in brief, I left Sri Wandowo and joined Ngesthi Pandhawa. And what startled the other members was that I was the only member who was nervy enough to play drum at his first appearance. I had lots of experience drumming, but what I knew needed "upgrading."

Now, this guy named Narto [Nartosabdho] was a man without upgrading. Three quarters of the Ngesthi Pandhawa members scorned me, ridiculed me, and seemed disgusted by my behavior. A new member already nervy enough to direct and play drum? Now, in the old days, Ngesthi Pandhawa was just an ordinary *wayang orang* troupe, with lots of free time in its schedule. Well, I took steps for "evolution"—not "revolution," but "evolution." Where was our "evolution"? On the stage of Ngesthi Pandhawa, both in the *gamelan* music and in the dance, and in the new pieces I composed—I should say "we" composed. These were very popular with the public, with the audience. From village tunes to new tunes unknown in Java, such as waltz-time. [Several other composers have also experimented with *gamelan* music in triple meter, including the Yogyanese Hardjosoebroto. It is not clear who can rightfully claim to have done it first.] The piece was *Sang Lelana* ["The Wanderer"]. Also there was *Aku Ngimpi* ["I Dream"] and *Sampur Ijo* ["The Green Scarf"], even for dance!

And [the vocal parts] for these waltz pieces could be duet or trio: one, two, or three voices [singing different melodies]. When we tried these out at Ngesthi

Pandhawa, there were people who predicted that I would go crazy. My response was that we are all human. God gives us cattle, not beefsteak. Once we are given cattle by God, we have the right to transform it into something that is appropriate and useful, in accordance with our taste. All the better if we can bring in rhythms (meters) from outside Indonesia, as long as we don't change or destroy the original and authentic Indonesian rhythms. For example [Nartosabdho taps—on the "x"s in Transcription 7.16—and hums],

TRANSCRIPTION 7.16
Ki Nartosabdho's demonstration of *gamelan* with triple meter.

```
        x    x    x    x    x    x    x    x    x

 Gong . .  3 5 7 6 6  . 5 3 6 5 5  . 3 2 7̣ 2  . .  5 6 5 3N

     . .  7̣ 2 6̣ 7̣ 7̣  . 3 2 7̣ 2P
```

Yes, three-four. Now in the old days this didn't exist. And even now, when it does, it causes hassles for all the instruments played with two hands—drum, *gendèr, gambang*—hassles, but it turns out it is possible. At first [they played] only the simplest of patterns; now it is enjoyed by many listeners: experts [players] and those who only wish to listen. Now obviously I faced some defiance, lots of criticism that I was destroying [tradition]. I was called "destroyer." But I didn't take it just as criticism, but rather as a whip—to push me to find a way. Indeed the criticism was justified. So maybe not only in my country, but in yours too, if there is something startling and seemingly irrational suddenly applied [in the arts], it gives rise to much protest and criticism, right? So maybe the life of mankind everywhere is the same. What differs is just their appearance, their language, their traditions, but life is the same, right?

As it turned out I did okay. My manager gave me something: not money, but a name. Before, I had been Sunarto, now Nartosabdho [from *sabda*—see later]. I gratefully accepted this honor, though not without careful consideration of its justification. In Indonesia often a name is taken from one's profession. For example, Pak Harja Swara [*swara* = "voice," "sound"] works as a vocalist, *gérong*. Then Harjana Pawaka. *Harjana* means "safe" [cf. *wilujeng*], and *pawaka* means "fire"; he was on the fire brigade, someone who puts out fires. Wignya Pangrawit: *wignya* means "skilled," and *pangrawit* "a *gamelan* player"; so he was someone skilled at playing *gamelan*. Then Nyata Carita: *nyata* is "clear," "evident," and *carita* is "story"; he was a puppeteer who was accomplished, skilled in storytelling. And I was given the addition *sabda*. *Sabda* is "the speech of a holy man." But here I was a composer and drummer at Ngesthi Pandhawa, specializing in *gamelan* music. It did not seem possible that I would utter such speech. I taught singing and *gamelan*. So I wondered how my profession might fit with this name *sabda*.

[In *wayang orang*, one person sits with the musicians and acts as a *dhalang*—not operating puppets, but providing narration and singing the mood songs known as *sulukan*. We learned from interviewing other members of the Ngesthi Pandhawa troupe that, one night when the usual *dhalang* was unable to perform, Nartosabdho took over and, to the amazement of the audience, showed himself to have a fine voice, facility with the somewhat archaic *dhalang*'s language, and a thorough knowledge of the story. This preceded his debut as a *wayang kulit dhalang*/puppeteer.]

Well, on April 28, 1958, I earned the title *dhalang* [here, puppeteer for *wayang kulit*, not *wayang orang*] in Jakarta, at R.R.I. People heard that I was learning to do shadow puppetry, and in January 1958 I was called by the broadcast director, Pak Atmaka—he's still alive. Would I do a broadcast? [Javanese shadow puppetry, though it uses beautifully carved and painted puppets, is often broadcast over the radio. The audience follows the story by recognizing the particular vocal quality given to each character by the puppeteer, and they also enjoy the music.] I replied that I would not be willing right away. The broadcast would be heard all over Indonesia, maybe even outside the country. This was before all the private radio stations, so broadcasts from the central studio could be heard clearly [at great distances]. I agreed to perform in a few months, in April. What shape should my puppetry performance take, how classical, how innovative? Could I match the quality of my accomplishments in *gamelan* music? How to proceed, it is always a puzzle. There was a woman, a singer (*pesindhèn*) who made a promise: if I could perform shadow puppetry all night, she would give me a kiss. A kiss of respect, right, not an erotic kiss, not a "porno" kiss!

Sometime after coming home to Semarang from performing in Jakarta, I had a guest. His name was Sri Handaya Kusuma, and he came on behalf of the Medical Faculty in Yogya. He wanted a performance around Christmas time. [Though few Javanese are Christian, Christmas is a holiday, and schools are normally on a short break beginning shortly before Christmas and lasting until after the New Year.] I was asked to perform a "classic" story. Now requests began to come in one after the other: Jakarta, Yogya, Surbaya, Solo. Yes, I was earning money, but more importantly I was also earning my name. Nowadays I perform once or twice a week, but have more requests than that. I have even played at the presidential palace in Jakarta for Pak Harto [former President Suharto] four times.

How did I learn? I am what you would call an "autodidact." I read and so forth, but it also took looking at a lot of shadow puppetry performances. I would watch all the puppeteers I could, not only the older ones, but also the younger. And each performance, by whatever puppeteer, offered something new that I could and should incorporate in my own performance.

What about musicians? When I first played in Jakarta, it was the R.R.I. musicians who accompanied me. Elsewhere, I would take a few of those closest to me, my *gendèr* player, Pak Slamet, who came from Yogya and still plays at R.R.I. Semarang. And my drummer was the late Pak Wirya. Since 1969 I have had my own group, Condhong Raos, mostly younger musicians, under thirty-five years of age.

In the early 1970s I began to make cassettes, first of my new *gamelan* pieces, then of full-length shadow puppet performances. There were some discs produced by Lokananta [the National Recording Company] in the 1960s, too. My first set of *wayang* cassettes was the story "Gatutkaca Sungging," recorded in 1974, if I remember correctly. Not so long ago. I don't really have a favorite story—how can you say one is better than another? If someone wants to hire a puppeteer and asks for "Parta Krama," ["Parta, i.e. Arjuna, gets married"] for example, no puppeteer should say he doesn't like that story. That wouldn't be very good!

What changes do I foresee in the next five or ten years? It may be possible to predict changes in technology, but not in culture, not in the arts. Some people think *wayang kulit* should be given in Indonesian language. To me, if a change adds to the beauty of the art, then it can be accepted. If not, then it cannot be. In Javanese there are many ways to say "eat," or "sleep." [He goes on to give examples. Different honorific levels of vocabulary permeate Javanese but are almost entirely absent from Indonesian. Nartosabdho implies, without stating explicitly, that he finds *wayang* more beautiful in Javanese and would like to keep it that way.] I have taken *gamelan* music from various areas of Java, even Sunda and Bali, and used them in the *gara-gara* [a comic interlude occurring at the beginning of the *pathet sanga* section, around 1:00 A.M.]. Not only have I studied these different songs, but I have even taken liberties with them. But other aspects of my puppetry have not been influenced by other regional styles. My style is basically Solonese. Who can predict if it will change, or how it will change?

The preceding few pages have presented my English translation of much of what Ki Nartosabdho told my wife and me when we visited him in his modest home in Semarang. Though he was still giving one or two strenuous all-night *wayang* performances per week, he was already suffering from a kidney disease. In late 1985 Ki Nartosabdho died and left a legacy of hundreds of new *gamelan* vocal pieces, hundreds of musical recordings, and close to one hundred recordings of all-night *wayang* performances. His group Condhong Raos still performs music, but at present no one stands out as such a clear "superstar" within the world of traditional Javanese performing arts—a world that, until the era of mass media, really knew no "star system" at all.

GAMELAN MUSIC AND SHADOW PUPPETRY

Now that we have had a glimpse of a man deeply involved in both *gamelan* music and shadow puppetry, it is fitting to consider some of the music most closely associated with shadow puppet performance (Figure 7.8). Both the pieces we have studied so far are seldom played for dance or dramatic accompaniment. The musical staples of the shadow puppet repertory are pieces with dense *kenong* and *kempul* playing and *gongan* of varying length—pieces that generate a level of excitement, partly because of the dense gong punctuation. Each *pathet* includes at least three of these staple pieces: relatively calm, somewhat excited, and very excited. The gong punctuation is densest in the very excited pieces and least present in the calmest pieces. The puppeteer determines which piece is to be played; he must be just as thoroughly at home with the *gamelan* music as he is with the many hundreds of characters and stories that comprise this tradition.

We are going to listen to two versions of one of these pieces, the Yogyanese **Playon "Lasem"** (*plah*-yon *lah*-suhm), *sléndro pathet nem* (CD 3, Tracks 1 and 2),

CD 3:1

Playon "Lasem," sléndro pathet nem, Rendition 1 (1:20). Central Javanese *gamelan* music for shadow puppetry. Performed by *gamelan* group under the direction of Ki Suparman. Field recording by R. Anderson Sutton. Yogyakarta, Java, Indonesia, 1974.

FIGURE 7.8

Dhalang (shadow puppeteer) Ki Bawor, performing an all-night *wayang kulit* near the town of Purwokerto, western Central Java, July 18, 2006.

R. Anderson Sutton

which exemplifies the "somewhat excited" category. Depending on the mood the puppeteer wishes to establish, the piece can be played in loud-playing or in soft-playing style, or switched at any point. (The calmest of the three is usually in soft-playing style; and the most excited is always performed in loud-playing style.) Also, the length of the piece can be radically tailored to suit the needs of the dramatic moment. Sometimes it may go on, through repetition of a central section, for five or ten minutes. During the course of the all-night performance at which I recorded these examples, the puppeteer (Ki Suparman) signaled this piece to be played eighteen times—all, of course, within the *pathet nem* section of the night, which lasted from about 9:00 P.M. to about 1:30 A.M.

Transcription 7.17 gives *balungan* notation for the entire piece, as well as the *gong ageng* or *siyem* sound at the end of each line, as written. The *kenong* plays on every *balungan* beat, the *kempul* every second beat (except where the gong sounds), and the *kethuk* between the beats.

```
   Introductory portion:        (signal....)  5          Length of Gongan
                      6 5   6 5 6 5   2 3 5 6              10 beats
              1 6 5 6   2 3 5 3   2 1 2 1                  12 beats
              2 1 2 1   6 5 3 5   2 3 5 6                  12 beats
              1 6 5 6   5 3 2 3   1 2 3 2**                12 beats

   Repeated portion:
      [: 5 6 5 3   5 6 5 3   6 5 2 6   5 2 3 5*           16 beats
                      3 2 3 2   6 5 2 3                     8 beats
      5 3 5 3   5 2 3 5   1 6 5 3   2 1 3 2               16 beats
                      6 6 1 2   3 5 6 5                     8 beats
              2 1 2 1   2 1 3 2   5 6 1 6                  12 beats
                      3 2 5 3   6 5 3 2 :]                  8 beats
   Endings:
      *  from gong tone 5 (first rendition):    2 1  3 2 1 6
      ** from gong tone 2 (second rendition):   5 3  2 1 2 6

- - - - - - - - - - - - - - - - - - - - - - - - - - - - - - - - - - - - -

   Punctuation Pattern for playon/srepegan form:

      kempul & gong:         P  (repeat x ?)    G      e.g.:   P  P  P  P  G
      kenong & kethuk:    tNtN  (repeat x ?)  tNtN            tNtNtNtNtNtNtNtN
      balungan:            . .  (etc.)          . .            6 5 6 5 6 5 2 3 5 6
```

TRANSCRIPTION 7.17
Balungan notation for
Playon "Lasem," *sléndro*
pathet nem.

Notice that here the frequency of "coincidence" between gong punctuators is very high: every second beat! To Javanese, this makes for exciting music, appropriate for scenes charged with emotion, even for fights. Quick rapping on the puppet chest signals the musicians to play. The drummer, playing the middle-sized drum (*ciblon*), and sometimes the *kenong* player as well, enter just before the rest of the ensemble.

The first rendition we will hear takes a little over a minute, only beginning to repeat when the puppeteer signals the playing of a special ending phrase. All the musicians must know one or two of these ending phrases for each gong tone and be ready to tag the appropriate one onto any *gongan* if the signal comes. This first rendition begins in soft-playing style but speeds and gets loud by the end of the first *gongan*, then proceeds through the entire melody, begins to repeat the main section, and ends, on signal, after the first *gongan*. (See the Close Listening guide.)

Close Listening

PLAYON "LASEM," RENDITION 1

CD 3:1

TIME	COMMENTARY	PHRASE IN MAIN MELODY
Introduction		
0:00	Puppeteer knocks on puppet chest to signal musicians to play.	
0:03	Full *gamelan* ensemble begins to play in soft-playing style, including female singer (*pesindhèn*).	Phrase A, 10 beats of the main melody.
0:11	Puppeteer clangs loudly on metal plaques. *Gamelan* speeds up and switches to loud-playing style. Female singer and soft instruments drop out.	Phrase B, 12 beats.
0:18	Brief shouts by the puppeteer as rival characters engage in fight.	Phrase C, 12 beats.
0:24	Continued clanging on metal plaques accompanies the fight.	Phrase D, 12 beats.
Central section (repeatable)		
0:31	Drumming and clanging on metal plaques accentuate fight action.	Phrase E, 16 beats of the main melody.
0:38	Lively accompaniment continues.	Phrase F, 8 beats.
0:41	More loud shouts by puppeteer.	Phrase G, 16 beats.
0:50	Lively action and accompaniment continue. Drumming is especially active here.	Phrase H, 8 beats.
0:53	Lively action and accompaniment continue	Phrase I, 12 beats.
1:00	Lively action and accompaniment continue.	Phrase J, 8 beats.

Repeat

1:04	Section repeat begins; lively action.	Phrase E, 16 beats of the main melody.
1:10	Puppeteer performs pattern of knocks that signal *gamelan* musicians to move to ending phrase (K).	Two beats before the end of Phrase E.

Coda

1:12	Puppeteer's signal knocks continue, confirming his intention to end the piece.	Phrase K, 6 beats of the main melody.
1:15	Performance of *Playon* "Lasem" ends; puppeteer continues knocking on puppet chest to set mood, and he begins to speak.	

CD 3:2

Playon "Lasem," *sléndro pathet nem,* Rendition 2 (0:33). Central Javanese *gamelan* music for shadow puppetry. Performed by *gamelan* group under the direction of Ki Suparman. Field recording by R. Anderson Sutton. Yogyakarta, Java, Indonesia, 1974.

In the second rendition (CD 3, Track 2; see the Close Listening guide), entirely in loud-playing style, the musicians never even reach the "main" section. To add variety to this rendition, played quite late during the *pathet nem* section (around 12:30 A.M.), the *saron* players play variant phrases for some of the passages notated earlier, although the *slenthem* player holds to the previous version.

Close Listening

PLAYON "LASEM," RENDITION 2

CD 3:2

COUNTER NUMBER	COMMENTARY	PHRASE OF MAIN MELODY
Introduction		
0:01	Puppeteer knocks on wooden puppet chest and metal plaques to signal musicians to play.	
0:03	Full *gamelan* ensemble begins to play in loud-playing style.	Phrase A, 10 beats of main melody
0:08	*Gamelan* continues in loud-playing style, puppeteer continues rapid knocking on metal plaques.	Phrase B, 12 beats

0:14	(same)	Phrase C, 12 beats
0:20	(same)	Phrase D, 12 beats
0:25	Approaching the gong beat, the puppeteer performs short pattern of knocks that signal *gamelan* musicians to move to coda.	One beat before end of Phrase D

Coda

| 0:26 | Puppeteer's signal knocks continue, confirming intention to end the piece | Phrase K' (coda), 6 beats |
| 0:29 | Without any gradual slowing down, *gamelan* ends on final beat of coda. | |

Even without such change, we can see that this one piece has the potential for a great variety of renditions, through changes in tempo, instrumentation, and ending points. This is the essence of shadow puppet music—a very well known piece, played over and over, but uniquely tailored each time to fit precisely with the dramatic intentions of the puppeteer and kept fresh by the inventiveness of the instrumentalists and singers who constantly add subtle variations.

Bali

Just east of Java, separated from it by a narrow strait, lies the island of **Bali** (*bah-lee*). The unique culture and spectacular natural beauty of this island have fascinated scholars, artists, and tourists from around the world. In Bali almost everyone takes part in some artistic activity: music, dance, carving, painting. Although the Balinese demonstrate abilities that often strike the Westerner as spectacular, they maintain that such activities are a normal part of life. The exquisite masked dancer by night may well be a rice farmer by day, and the player of lightning-fast interlocking musical passages who accompanies him may manage a small eating stall.

Most of the several million people inhabiting this small island adhere not to Islam, Indonesia's majority religion, but to a blend of Hinduism and Buddhism resembling that which flourished in Java prior to the spread of Islam (fifteenth to sixteenth century C.E.). In this the Balinese and Javanese share elements of a common cultural heritage. As in Java, we find percussion ensembles known as *gamelan* (or *gambelan*), with metal slab instruments and knobbed gong instruments that look and sound quite similar to those of the Javanese *gamelan.* Some of the names are the same (*gendèr*, gong, *gambang, saron, suling, rebab*) or similar (*kempur, kemong*). Most ensembles employ some version of the *pélog* scale system (some with all seven tones, others with five or six). The accompaniment for Balinese shadow puppetry (as in Java, called *wayang kulit*) employs the *sléndro* scale system, although the instruments used consist only of a quartet of *gendèrs* (augmented by a few other instruments for Ramayana stories). Many Balinese pieces employ gong punctuating patterns similar in principle to those of Java. The Balinese play *gamelan* for ritual observances, as in Java, though usually at temple festivals, or in procession to or from them, rather than at someone's residence.

Nevertheless, certain characteristics clearly distinguish the musics of these two neighboring cultures. For example, the Balinese maintain a variety of ensembles, each with its distinct instrumentation and associated with certain occasions and functions. There is no single large ensemble that one can simply call "the Balinese *gamelan.*" However, the style of music one hears performed in most ensembles in Bali shares several characteristics: (1) strictly instrumental, (2) characterized by changes in tempo and loudness (often abrupt), and (3) requiring a dazzling technical mastery by many of the musicians, who play fast interlocking rhythms, often comprising asymmetrical groupings of two or three very fast beats. People often comment that Balinese music is exciting and dynamic in comparison with other Indonesian musics, exploiting contrasts in the manner of Western art music.

They may also comment on the "shimmery" quality of the many varieties of bronze ensembles. This quality is obtained by tuning instruments in pairs, with one instrument intentionally tuned slightly higher in pitch than its partner. When sounded together, they produce very fast vibrations. In the West, piano tuners rely on these same vibrations, called "beats," to "temper" the tuning, although on a piano it is intervals that are made intentionally "out of tune" rather than identical strings sounding the same tone. Of course, the intentionally "out-of-tune" pairs of metallophones are perceived to be "in tune" (that is, "culturally correct") in Bali, just as the piano is in Western culture.

The most popular ensemble in Bali today is the *gamelan gong kebyar* (kuh-*byar*), which developed during the early twentieth century along with the virtuosic dance it often accompanies (also called *kebyar*—literally, "flash," "dazzle"). *Kebyar* music is indeed "flashy," requiring not only great virtuosity of the players, but also a consummate sense of ensemble—the ability of many to play as one.

Listen to "Kosalia Arini" (ko-*sal*-yah a-*ree*-nee; CD 3, Track 3), a piece composed by the prolific Balinese composer and skilled drummer Wayan Beratha in 1969 for a *gamelan* festival. This piece demonstrates features typical of *gamelan gong kebyar* (Figure 7.9), many of which contrast markedly with Javanese *gamelan* music and with older styles of Balinese music. These include episodic structure—the piece is clearly divided into sections with contrasting instrumentation, rhythm, and texture. Portions of the piece involve cyclic repetition, but the overall design is neither cyclic nor rigidly binary as in Javanese *gamelan* pieces.

Michael Tenzer, a U.S. scholar, composer, and performer of Balinese *gamelan gong kebyar,* has provided a detailed analysis of this piece (Tenzer 2000:367, 381–83), from which the following much briefer commentary derives. Most basic are the contrasts between what Tenzer calls "stable" (cyclic) and "active" (noncyclic) sections.

The overall piece proceeds through four main sections (see the Close Listening guide). As you listen, notice the changes (often abrupt) in tempo,

CD 3:3

"Kosalia Arini" (10:48). *Gamelan gong kebyar.* Composed by Wayan Beratha. Performed by STSI (Sekolah Tinggi Seni Indonesia) *gamelan* musicians, directed by Nyoman Windha and Pande Gde Mustika. Recorded by Michael Tenzer and Ketut Gde Asnawa, with Yong Sagita. STSI campus, Denpasar, Bali, August 1998.

FIGURE 7.9

The *gamelan gong kebyar* of Bali.

Wayne Vitale

instrumentation, dynamics, and register (high pitch or low pitch). Each section is identified not only by characteristic rhythm and texture but also by tonal center. Though repetitive in some sections, the whole piece is much more like a fantasia or an exuberant study in contrasts (especially in dynamics and in rhythm) than even the most dramatic renditions of Javanese pieces.

Close Listening

"KOSALIA ARINI"

CD 3:3

COUNTER NUMBER	COMMENTARY	TONAL CENTER
Noncyclic section		
0:00	*Gendèrs* (metal slab instruments) at different pitch registers play fragments of asymmetrical phrases. Mostly soft dynamic level. Occasional louder and flashy full-ensemble fragments (*kebyar* interruptions).	C#
0:46	Partial *kebyar* interruption.	
1:43	Full *kebyar* interruption.	
2:16	Flute solo, with low-register *gendèr*. Very soft.	D

Transition

| 2:41 | Higher-pitched *gendèrs* enter, marking transition to next section. Mostly soft. | D |

Cyclic section

| 2:49 | *Gendèrs* play 4-beat phrases; highly repetitive; alternates between soft and medium dynamic level. | D |

***Kebyar* interruption**

| 4:39 | Full ensemble. Sudden, loud flash. | D |
| 4:41 | Short passage featuring the *reyong* (*ray*-yong) (kettle gong-chime played by four musicians). | D |

Cyclic section

| 4:53 | Drum variations (by two drummers) open second cyclic section. Loud and fast, then softer. | D |
| 5:13 | *Gendèr* and *reyong* alternate. Mostly soft, fast tempo. Section stops abruptly, with no *gong*. | E |

Transition

| 7:22 | *Gendèrs* play transition to third cyclic section. | E |

Cyclic section

| 7:34 | *Gendèrs* now play in 8-beat phrases. Mostly loud, full instrumentation, alternating with some soft passages. | C# |

Coda

| 10:30 | 12-beat coda, full ensemble. | C# |

North Sumatra

Going from Bali or Java to North **Sumatra** (soo-*mah*-trah) involves a considerable distance, both culturally and geographically. Although influenced to some degree by Indian culture during the first millennium C.E., the Batak people, the main inhabitants of the province of North Sumatra, have largely converted to Protestant Christianity or to Islam. The Christian Bataks sing hymns at their Sunday church services with an exuberance and an accuracy of pitch that would put most Western congregations—and even many choirs—to shame. In addition, many indigenous musical genres still thrive among the Batak, and many of these are central to rituals only marginally related to Christianity or Islam, if at all. Just as the majority

FIGURE 7.10

Tukang Ginting plays the Karo Batak *kulcapi.* Kabanjahe, North Sumatra.

of Javanese Muslims partake in rituals involving *gamelan* music and Hindu-based shadow puppetry, so the Batak Christians adhere in varying degrees to beliefs and ritual practices that were prevalent prior to the coming of Christianity.

The most celebrated Batak ensembles are the varieties of percussion and wind ensembles known as *gondang* or *gordang,* which usually include a set of tuned drums that are counterparts to the kettle gong-chimes (*bonang* or *trompong*). These can be heard on several fine recordings available commercially (see end of book). Our brief encounter with music in North Sumatra is from a ritual observance I attended among the Karo Batak, who live in the highlands west of Medan and north of the large and beautiful Lake Toba (see Figure 7.10).

A woman in the town of Kabanjahe was planning to open a beauty parlor in part of her house and wished to have the space ritually purified and to secure blessing for her new business by seeking harmony with the spirit world. This she hoped to accomplish by sponsoring and participating in a ceremony involving music and dance and during which she would contact her immediate ancestors through the help of a spirit medium. Members of her family gathered, along with sympathetic neighbors (but not some of the more orthodox Christians, who were not so sympathetic) and even a few foreign visitors, including myself. To my surprise I was urged to take photographs and record the event.

The ceremony lasted for nearly five hours, with several long sections of continuous music. Family members and some neighbors joined the woman in a traditional line dance. The spirit medium sang incantations, sometimes while dancing. He spoke gently to the woman and sometimes loudly to the spirits. With some difficulty the woman eventually went into trance, and the evening was deemed a success.

The musical group engaged for the evening (Figure 7.11) was a small ensemble performing *gendang keteng-keteng,* a form of traditional Batak music employing a small two-stringed, boat-shaped lute (*kulcapi*); two bamboo tube

FIGURE 7.11

Members of Tukang Ginting's *gendang keteng-keteng* group, playing the bamboo tube zither (*keteng-keteng*). Kabanjahe, North Sumatra.

zithers (*keteng-keteng*); and a porcelain bowl (*mangkuk*). On each of the tube zithers, thin strips had been cut and stretched, forming taut filaments. A small bamboo disk was attached to one filament on each. These remarkable instruments create a kind of interlocking percussive filagree. In addition, when the filaments with the disks are struck, they vibrate over a hole cut in the bamboo to produce a deep, vibrato sound remarkably like a small gong. The ensemble played continually for many hours, with the spirit medium singing part of the time. Melody, filling in, gong punctuation—here were the essential elements, it seemed, for music making not only throughout much of Indonesia but much of Southeast Asia as well.

The few excerpts I provide on the recording (CD 3, Track 4; see the Close Listening guide) cannot give a real sense of the long ritual, but they offer an introduction to musical sounds that contrast with the *gamelan* ensembles we have heard and yet bear a distant likeness to them. The first excerpt is from the early part of the ceremony. The *kulcapi* player, Tukang Ginting, provides what is basically a repeating, cyclic melody that he varies. The "clickety" sounds are the two percussionists playing the two *keteng-keteng*, filling in the texture to give constant "busy" sound, which seems to characterize much music throughout Indonesia. What is especially remarkable, in light of the other music we have heard, is how the porcelain bowl and the gong sounds relate. The gong sound occurs at regular intervals, as one so often finds in Java and Bali. It is subdivided by the porcelain bowl sound, which coincides with the gong sound and at the midpoint between them like a *kenong* subdividing and coinciding with a gong in Java.

CD 3:4

Gendang keteng-keteng, two excerpts (1:58). Traditional Batak music. Performed by ensemble led by Tukang Ginting on *kulcapi*. Field recording by R. Anderson Sutton. Karo Batak highlands of North Sumatra, 1979.

Close Listening

GENDANG KETENG-KETENG, TWO EXCERPTS

CD 3:4

COUNTER NUMBER	COMMENTARY
0:00	Fade in to performance with *kulcapi*, two *keteng-keteng*, and porcelain bowl.
0:03	1st gong sound (from *keteng-keteng*), together with porcelain bowl, which also sounds midway between gong sounds throughout the performance; *kulcapi* plays melody.
0:08	2nd gong sound; *kulcapi* continues to play melody.
0:13	3rd gong sound; *kulcapi* plays variations of previous melody.
0:18	4th gong sound; *kulcapi* continues variations of melody.
0:23	5th gong sound; *kulcapi* plays very similar variation of previous melody.
0:28	6th gong sound (same).
0:33	7th gong sound (same).
0:38	8th gong sound (same).

0:43	9th gong sound (same).
0:45	Fade out.
0:48	Fade in to later stage of the performance: same instrumentation, faster tempo.
0:49	1st gong sound; *kulcapi* plays variation of previous melody, but faster.
0:51	2nd gong sound (same).
0:54	3rd gong sound (same).
0:56	4th gong sound (same).
0:58	5th gong sound (same).
1:00	6th gong sound (same).
1:03	7th gong sound (same).
1:05	8th gong sound (same).
1:06	Tempo suddenly doubles; gong sound and porcelain bowl double density (gong sound approximately once every second); *kulcapi* switches to rapid playing, repeating same tone many times.
1:54	Fade out.

The second excerpt is from a climactic moment in the evening when the woman first thought she was going into trance. (She did not succeed at this point but did an hour or so later.) The players increase the musical intensity by compressing the time interval between gong beats; the tempo speeds up and then doubles during this excerpt. The porcelain bowl consistently subdivides the time between gong beats, even in the very fast portion, resembling structurally the *wayang kulit* music of Java (like the *playon* we studied earlier).

With its gong punctuation, coincidence, cyclic melody, binary rhythms, and fast-moving and dense percussion playing, this music seems clearly a relative of the *gamelan* music we heard earlier. Although this discussion has stressed the similarities, realize that these are only structural similarities, easy to identify from a theoretical perspective. The differences are so profound that the Batak and Javanese care little for each other's music. To the Javanese, clacking bamboo is no substitute for the varied drum strokes of the *kendhang*, the interlocking melodies of the *bonang*, or the heterophonic wanderings of the various soft-playing ensemble instruments in the Javanese *gamelan*. To the Batak, the thick-textured and often mighty sound of a full Javanese *gamelan* cannot attain the personal intimacy of the small *gendang keteng-keteng* ensemble nor the spontaneity of the *kulcapi* player.

Perhaps these few examples of traditional music from several regions of Indonesia will help you begin to understand the national motto *Bhinneka Tunggal Ika*—an Old Javanese phrase meaning "Unity in Diversity." In the arts we indeed find great variety, but the underlying elements that these arts share attest to the appropriateness of the motto. As we turn to examples of recent popular music, we find another layer of Indonesia's musical diversity—one that many Indonesians experience and that is especially meaningful to younger Indonesians from many regions.

Indonesian Popular Music

Most of the music Indonesians would identify as "popular" is, like most popular music anywhere in the world, characterized by the use of at least some Western instruments and Western harmony (see Hatch 1989). Essentially a commercial genre, it is disseminated through the mass media and performed by recognized stars. Unfortunately, space does not allow us to explore the interesting history of Western-influenced music in Indonesia, which has primarily been in the popular vein. We will, however, consider three superstar individuals or groups that represent each of three contrasting styles within the "pop" music world in Indonesia.

RHOMA IRAMA, *DANGDUT*

The first contemporary style is called *dangdut,* in imitation of the sound formerly made on hand drums and more recently on trap set and electric guitar. The musician known during the 1970s and 1980s as the "king of *dangdut*" was Rhoma Irama. Born in 1947 in West Java, he learned to play electric guitar and showed greater interest in music than in the formal schooling his mother struggled to afford. In his late teens he dropped out of school and joined the underground music movement, heavily influenced by Western rock (and banned by then-president Sukarno).

Irama soon became disenchanted with rock. By his own account, he then consciously set out to create a sound that would satisfy the craving of Indonesian youth for a "modern" musical style but that would also sound clearly Indonesian (or at least "Eastern") in contrast to Western rock (Frederick 1982:109). He turned to a Western-influenced genre, *orkès melayu* music, which originated in the urban areas of North and West Sumatra. This genre incorporated influences from the soundtracks of the many Indian films that have long enjoyed wide popularity in Indonesia (see Chapter 6). Even with its quasi-Western harmonic basis, this music was clearly Eastern, characterized by highly ornamented singing and flute playing.

Rhoma Irama set out to make a commercial mark, and he succeeded spectacularly. Like most pop stars, he has sung about love, but he has also presented forthrightly his own ideas about his country and, perhaps most persistently, about his religion. He was one of the first Indonesian popular artists to make the pilgrimage to Mecca, and he has used both his music and his films to spread his Islamic message. One of his first hits (1977) was a piece about greed, entitled "Rupiah" (the national currency). It was banned by government officials who thought it "debased the national currency" (Frederick 1982:117). Another early song, also banned, was "Hak Azasi" ("Basic Rights"), which described human rights—including freedom of religion and freedom of speech.

Listen to "Begadang II" (CD 3, Track 5), which was the most popular song of 1978 and established Irama as a star. The song bears the same title as the hit film for which it served as the theme song. Begadang is a Jakarta term for staying up all or most of the night, usually to socialize with friends. This song provides a typical example of the *dangdut* musical sound as Irama developed it. The text shows Irama's clear orientation toward lower-class youth (see the Close Listening guide). Like most of his music, it appeals to the youthful urge to dance and often accompanies popular social dancing akin to rock or disco dancing in the West.

CD 3:5

"Begadang II" ("Staying up All Night") (3:33). Popular *dangdut* music. Performed by Rhoma Irama and his Soneta Group. *Begadang II.* Yukawi Indomusic. 1978.

Close Listening

"BEGADANG II"

CD 3:5

COUNTER NUMBER	SECTION/TEXT	TRANSLATION
0:00	Instrumental introduction, featuring Rhoma Irama on electric guitar	
0:22	Verse 1	
	Apa artinya malam minggu	What good is Saturday night
	Bagi orang yang tidak mampu?	For those who are not well-to-do?
	Mau ke pesta tak beruang;	Want to go to a party, but have no money;
	Akhirnya nongkrong di pinggir jalan.	Wind up squatting by the side of the road.
0:48	Refrain	
	Begadang, marilah kita begadang,	Stay up, let's stay up,
	Begadang sambil berdendang;	Stay up and sing;
	Walaupun kita tidak punya uang	Even though we don't have money
	Kita juga bias senang.	We can still have fun.
1:02	Verse 1 (same text and music as earlier)	
1:26	Instrumental break, featuring Rhoma Irama on electric guitar	
1:50	Bridge 1	
	Bagi mereka yang punya uang	Those who have money
	Berdansa-dansi di nite club;	Dance at night clubs;
	Bagi kita yang tak punya uang	Those of us who have no money
	Cukup berjoget disini.	Just dance here [by the road].
2:03	Short instrumental break	
2:10	Bridge 2	
	Bagi mereka yang punya uang	Those who have money
	Makan-makan di restoran;	Always eat in nice restaurants;
	Bagi kita yang tak punya uang	Those of us who have no money
	Makannya di warung kopi.	Just eat at makeshift roadside stalls.
2:27	Verse 1	
2:57	Refrain	
3:04	Verse 1	
3:29	Sudden stop at the end of Verse 1	

"Begadang II" by Rhoma Irama. Used by permission.

Twenty-five years after this hit, Irama was still producing cassettes, although he no longer dominated the market. He has also starred in several films in which—to the chagrin of more conservative Indonesian Moslems—he proselytizes for Islam through his loud, electric *dangdut* music. Unlikely as it may seem, then, Rhoma Irama gained his fame as an Islamic rock star and enjoyed enormous commercial success. His passion for communicating his vision of a more perfect society, holding closely to the teachings of Islam, led him into the realm of politics. In 1982 he endorsed the Islamic opposition party and played at a rally in Jakarta that erupted in violence shortly before the elections took place. Yet by the early 1990s he had, most likely with some reluctance, joined the incumbent political party and even played at functions of the very body that represented the clearest threat to Islamic political power in Indonesia: the army. More recently, Irama has become one of the most outspoken critics of younger *dangdut* singers who emphasize sexually provocative movements on stage, and he was a leader in the failed effort to have the Indonesian government adopt what was labeled as an "antipornography" law but, in fact, would have banned hundreds of Indonesian performing art forms—traditional as well as modern—in which the costumes of female performers do not cover the shoulders or legs.

RESPONSES TO GLOBALIZATION

From Irama's *dangdut*, we now turn to two more recent examples of popular music (one released in 2000, the other in 1998). The forces of globalization have intensified since the 1980s, inundating the Indonesian marketplace with the commercial cultural products of the West, including various forms of American pop, rock, and jazz. Our final two musical examples represent different responses to this process. The first, by a group called **Krakatau** (named after the famous volcanic island lying just west of Java), involves a careful synthesis of Sundanese (West Javanese) *gamelan* and fusion jazz. The second, by a rock group known as Ahmad Band, represents a full embrace of Western alternative and heavy-metal styles, with a strong element of political and social protest in the lyrics.

Krakatau, Sundanese *Gamelan*, and Fusion Jazz

Krakatau (Figure 7.12) was founded in the late 1980s by **Dwiki Dharmawan** (*dwee*-kee dar-*ma*-wan), a jazz keyboardist whose skill in imitating the styles of Joe Zawinul (Weather Report) and Chick Corea won him an award from the Yamaha Music Company of Japan in 1985. The early recordings of Krakatau present original fusion jazz tunes with complex harmonies and rhythms. They include jazz songs, some in English, sung by a female Javanese-Sundanese singer, **Trie Utami,** who offers polished and sophisticated imitations of African American jazz vocal styles. Yet beginning around 1993 and 1994, members of the group, particularly Dharmawan and Utami, grew tired of merely imitating the music they admired from the West. Because the core members had all spent much of their youth in West Java (Sunda), they decided to incorporate Sundanese musical elements into their music, adding local experts on *saron, bonang, rebab,* and *kendang.* In short, they set out to create a hybrid variety of music, mixing Western and indigenous Indonesian musical instruments and elements.

Experiments in such combinations have been taking place in Indonesia for centuries. Special challenges are posed by the fact that many Indonesian instruments

FIGURE 7.12

Krakatau in performance.

Courtesy of Krakatau (Dwiki Dharmawan).

and songs use tunings and scales, such as *sléndro* and *pélog,* that are not compatible with Western ones (take a look back at Figure 7.2). In the nineteenth century, brass band instruments were played with *pélog gamelan* instruments in the courts of Central Java, representing a symbolic fusion of Javanese and Dutch power. In the early twentieth century, Javanese composers began to write pieces combining Javanese singing with Western instruments.

In the 1990s, Indonesia saw a sudden growth in experimental combinations of pop/rock instruments and indigenous Indonesian ones. The musician often acknowledged as the inspiration for this trend is **Guruh Sukarno Putra** (*goo*-rooh soo-*kar*-no *poo*-tra), who produced *Guruh Gipsy,* a landmark album in 1976 involving piano, synthesizers, and rock instruments playing along with Balinese *gendèrs* and drums and incorporating Central Javanese vocal styles and West Javanese scales and melodies. Guruh is the youngest living son of the founding father of the Republic of Indonesia, President Sukarno. His music has sometimes been referred to as *pop berat* (literally "heavy pop"; see Hatch 1989), a music more varied and challenging to listen to than the easy rhythms of *dangdut.* But where Guruh drew on various regional Indonesian styles, the members of Krakatau have attempted to focus on their own region, Sunda.

In 1994 they released *Mystical Mist,* in which some pieces sounded more like jazz fusion and others more Sundanese. In their most recent release, *Magical Match,* the blend is more even throughout. One of the ingenious ideas they have employed is the tuning of their Western instruments to the scales of Sundanese traditional music. Dwiki programmed in a complex alteration of pitches for his keyboard and worked out special fingerings so that when he strikes certain combinations of black and white keys on his keyboard, he can produce the tones of *sléndro, pélog,* or other scales typical of Sundanese traditional music. The bass player uses an electric bass with no frets (the horizontal metal strips found on guitars that facilitate production of the Western scale). With skillful placement of his fingers, he can play bass patterns in *sléndro* and other non-Western scales. On this album Trie Utami sings not like a jazz singer but with the distinctive timbre of a Sundanese female singer (*pesindhèn*). The example on our recording, however, is purely instrumental, illustrating most clearly the skill of the musicians in creating a piece that tries to be not just Sundanese and not just Western but a "magical match" of the two.

Listen to "Shufflendang-Shufflending" (CD 3, Track 6) and follow it with the Close Listening guide. The title mixes the English word *shuffle* (a type of African American ecstatic song/dance combination performed in worship, also known as "ring-shout") and the Sundanese words for drum (*kendang*) and *gamelan* musical piece (*gendhing*). Krakatau is joined by Zainal Arifin, Adhe Rudiana (who teaches traditional music at the Indonesian College of Performing Arts in Bandung, West Java), and recent graduates Yoyon Darsono, Elfik Zulfiqar, and Tudi Rahayu.

While it is possible to enjoy the sounds and the rhythm without knowing their origins, the meaning this music has for Krakatau members and for their fans in Indonesia is its ability to "Sundanize" jazz or pop music and to "jazz" or "modernize" Sundanese music at the same time. Its ambiguity provides a bridge between the seemingly incompatible worlds of local Indonesian/traditional culture and Western/modern culture. Dharmawan and other members of the group, whom I got to know in August 2000, did not have a clear sense of what to call their music. We talked about "new age," "world music," and "ethno-pop." They clearly hope that this music will reach beyond Indonesia to attract listeners from around the world, not only to their own music but also to the rich treasury of Indonesia's traditional music.

CD 3:6

"Shufflendang-Shufflending" (4:11). Ethno-jazz fusion, Sundanese. Performed by Krakatau: Dwiki Dharmawan, keyboard; Pra Budidharma, fretless bass; Budhy Haryono, Western drum set ("traps"); joined by Yoyon Darsono, *rebab* and flute; Adhe Rudiana, *kendang*; Elfik Zulfiqar and Tudi Rahayu, *saron*; Zainal Arifin, *bonang. Magical Match.* Kita Music. 2000.

Close Listening

"SHUFFLENDANG-SHUFFLENDING"

CD 3:6

COUNTER NUMBER	COMMENTARY
0:00	Western instruments open piece with a repeating short musical phrase.
0:15	Hints of a *pèlog* scale (small and large intervals between tones).
0:42	Abruptly, *sarons* (metal slab instruments) play in *slèndro* scale (near equidistant tones).
0:50	*Sarons* play in *pèlog* scale.
0:59	*Sarons* return to play in *slèndro* scale.
1:09	Switch to *rebab* (two-string fiddle) playing in *pèlog* scale.
1:35	Back to fusion jazz style, as in beginning, although not exact repetition. Similar rotation of scales continues through excerpt.

Courtesy of Ahmad Band (Ahmad Dhani).

The Ahmad Band: Indonesian Rock Music

Let us turn now to an example of alternative rock, performed by the Ahmad Band on *Ideologi Sikap Otak*, released in 1998 just as Indonesia was undergoing extraordinary political upheaval, with student demonstrations and confrontations that led to the resignation of Indonesia's authoritarian president, Suharto, in May of that year. The Ahmad Band is named for its founding songwriter, Dhani Ahmad Manaf (Figure 7.13), one of the core members of Dewa 19, an enormously popular (and more mainstream) group, whose many singles and albums have topped the Indonesian charts since the mid-1990s. Several other musicians joined Dhani (as he is known) to form the Ahmad Band: Andra Ramadhan (guitarist for Dewa 19), Bimo (drum), Bongky (bass), and Pay (guitar). Dhani invited me to his studio several times, and we talked at great length about music. It was clear from the start that he had almost no interest in indigenous Indonesian "traditional" music of any kind. He said it was hard enough to write and produce good rock songs, let alone try to mix in traditional instruments or other stylistic elements. Some of his music, especially the music he composes and performs with the popular Dewa 19, presents the usual pop themes of love and youth. Dhani also has strong political convictions, however, which he has expressed musically with his alternative group, Ahmad Band.

FIGURE 7.13

"Dhani" (Dhani Ahmad Manaf) in performance with the Ahmad Band.

CD 3:7

"Distorsi" ("Distortion") (5:19). Indonesian rock music. Performed by Ahmad Band: Dhani Ahmad Manaf, vocal; Andra Ramadhan, guitar; Bimo, drum; Bongky, bass; Pay, guitar. *Ideologi Sikap Otak.* Aquarius P 9173. 1998.

Listen to "Distorsi" (CD 3, Track 7), an alternative-rock protest song about hypocrisy and corruption. The song does not mention specific names (Suharto, for example, or his cabinet ministers, or his rich business cronies). To do so would have risked immediate and severe measures—not only censorship but imprisonment. Instead, like other protest music in Indonesia, this song makes bitter complaints without pointing a finger. However, Indonesian listeners understand and are moved to action by this and other protest songs, just as much as they are by impassioned speeches at political rallies. (See the Close Listening guide.)

Close Listening

"DISTORSI" ("DISTORTION")

CD 3:7

COUNTER NUMBER	SECTION/TEXT	TRANSLATION
0:00	Instrumental introduction, featuring Dhani Ahmad Manaf on electric guitar	
0:10	*Maunya selalu ...* (x5)	They always want ...

0:36	Verse 1	
	Maunya selalu memberantas kemiskinan,	They always want to combat poverty, but
	Tapi ada yang selalu kuras uang rakyat.	there's always someone who siphons off the
		people's money.
0:51	*Maunya selalu ... (x3)*	They always want ...
0:59	Verse 2	
	Ada yang sok aksi buka mulut protas protes,	There are show-offs who open their mouths in protests,
	tapi sayang mulutnya selalu beraroma alcohol.	but it's a shame their mouths always smell of alcohol.
1:18	Refrain	
	Yang muda mabuk, yang tua korup, (x2)	The youth are drunk, the elders corrupt,
	Mabuk terus, korup terus.	continually drunk, continually corrupt.
	Jayalah negeri ini,	Great is this country,
	jayalah negeri ini.	great is this country.
1:37	Verse 3	
	Maunya selalu menegakkan keadilan,	They always want to strengthen justice,
	Tapi masih saja ada sisa hukum rimba.	But there is still the residue of the law of the jungle.
1:53	Verse 4	
	Ada yang coba-coba sadarkan penguasa	There are those who try to make [our] ruler[s] aware
	Tapi sayang yang coba sadarkan sadar 'aja ndak pernah.	But it's a shame that those who try have never been aware [themselves].
2:10	Bridge 1	
	Setiap hari mabuk,	Every day drunk,
	ngoceh soal politik;	babbling about politics;
	setiap hari korup,	every day corrupt,
	Ngoceh soal krisis ekonomi.	babbling about the economic crisis.
2:29	Refrain	
2:47	Instrumental interlude	
3:00	*Maunya selalu ... (x5)*	They always want ...
3:15	Verse 5	
	Perut kekenyangan bahas soal kelaparan.	Those with full stomachs discuss hunger.
	Kapitalis sejati malah ngomongin soal keadilan social.	True capitalists even talk about the matter of social justice.
3:34	Bridge 2	
	Selalu monopoli!	Always monopoly!
	Ngoceh soal pemerataan,	Babble about even distribution,
	setiap hari tucau,	every day shooting up [narcotics],
	ngomel soal kebobrokan.	grumbling about collapse.

4:01	Refrain	
4:16	Refrain	
4:32	*Maunya selalu . . .* (x11)	They always want . . .

"Distorsi" by Dhani Ahmad Manaf. Used by permission.

These three examples of popular music from Indonesia offer some important contrasts in style and message. The contrasts among them can begin to give you an idea of the complexity of Indonesia's popular music—still mostly unexplored by research scholars. Despite his political shift in the early 1990s, Rhoma Irama remains a strong Muslim. His roots are humble and he speaks to the disenfranchised masses. Krakatau's public image is secular and at once regional (Sundanese *gamelan*) and international (jazz fusion). Both Irama and Krakatau perform music that has developed from a blend of disparate musical elements. Ahmad Band, in contrast, strives consciously to create within the stylistic norms of Western alternative rock, producing confrontational music. Where Irama's *dangdut* music has consistently and consciously been molded by mass taste and has found popularity throughout the entire nation, the others appeal to a narrower market: sophisticated urbanites (especially Sundanese and Javanese) for Krakatau and disaffected urban youth for Ahmad Band.

All three have aspired to use their music to do more than entertain. Through different approaches, Irama and Ahmad Band offer a social message to their listeners and followers. Krakatau provides a bridge between local tradition and international modernity. Each carves out a social place for its music and maintains a separate artistic style as a result. Despite the upheaval and frequent unrest in parts of Indonesia today, this country still prides itself on its people's ability to tolerate diversity and coexist. These three popular examples offer a glimpse of that diversity and show us that it applies not only to traditional regional culture but also to popular music disseminated nationally.

 Book Companion Website

You will find tutorial quizzes, Internet links, and much more at the Book Companion Website for *Worlds of Music,* Fifth Edition, at
academic.cengage.com/music/titon/worlds_5

East Asia/China, Taiwan, Singapore, Overseas Chinese

JONATHAN P. J. STOCK

The Chinese cultural world includes a distinctive cross-section of peoples in mainland China, as well as Taiwan, Singapore, and other diasporic groups around the globe. In the People's Republic of China, at the heart of this international constituency, we can hear the echoes of long-standing traditions from one of the great historical centers of civilization. We can also see how these echoes underpin the fast-paced musical multiplicities of a large, contemporary nation and major world market for new expressive forms. Concentrating on mainland China, but touching on other places along the way, this chapter explores the Chinese musical present by looking at how today's musical styles emerge from and resonate with their particular historical pathways.

The relationship between the past and the present is a fascinating topic for music research anywhere—especially so in China because of the rich historical documentation there. The musical present exists in a permanent state of counterpoint with the musical past, an image we can explore with a concept from the school of Chinese philosophy known as **Daoism** (sometimes written as **Taoism**). This is the idea of **yin and yang,** literally the female and male principles, sometimes symbolized ☯. The idea is that any entity comprises not only a principal object but, at the same time, its complementary opposite. The new is not just new, but a reaction to the old, which was itself once new. The category "male" seems distinct enough from "female," yet both emerge from the interaction of female and male, so much so that imagining a moment when the categories were truly separate is difficult. The following paragraphs apply this outlook to Chinese society, geography and history, language, formative philosophies and religion, and political organization.

China has the largest population of any country in the world (more than 1.3 billion in late 2004, with one newborn every two seconds). We can find enormous cultural variety within this huge population. China has long been ethnically diverse; the Chinese state officially recognizes fifty-five "nationalities" as well as the majority Han people, who form around 92 percent of the total. Also, the population is unevenly distributed. Most of the Han Chinese inhabit the

The author wishes to acknowledge the assistance of the following: Carlton Benson, Chou Chiener, Pete Fletcher, Gu Chenyuan, Hsu Shuo-Wen, Frank Kouwenhoven, Lee Yachen, Dave Moore, Antoinet Schimmelpenninck, Hera Tang, Wang Tingting, Samuel Wong, and Zhao Yue.

rich agricultural lands in the eastern one-third of the country—to get a sense of the resulting population density, imagine a billion people living in the United States between the Mississippi River and the Atlantic coast. Meanwhile, Han and many of the other nationalities (including Zhuang, Uighur, Hui, Yi, Tibetans, Miao, Manchu, and Mongols) are spread across the extensive deserts and oases of the west, the mountain ranges and grasslands of the north, and the tropical jungle and mountains of the southwest. Differing ways of life occur in each of these environments. Furthermore, although around 60 percent of the population is rural, inhabiting a social milieu formed primarily around family work and other concerns at the village level, only a generation ago 75 percent of people worked on the land. This trend reflects the rapid and significant urbanization and industrialization of the nation. One more generation will see rural Chinese as a minority. Of course, there were huge cities, elaborate courts, temples, and factories in historical China, and so urban, professional, and elite musics are every bit as well established as the music of the agricultural classes is. There have been significant overseas Chinese communities for several centuries, and any account of Chinese music in the present day needs to consider this large and varied diaspora. Most prominent are populations in Taiwan and Singapore. Overseas Chinese are significant markets for Chinese musical trends: Some sustain traditions now little found in the mainland, and many have originated new musical expressions, some of which have become popular in the mainland in turn.

The diaspora speaks of the changing geographic bounds of the Chinese world through time. The historical record (Table 8.1) shows that the territory we now know as China has several times been unified by military force into a single nation and at other moments fractured into separate self-governing states. Around 221 B.C.E., for example, the ruler of a state named Qin defeated his rivals across much of present-day China, taking for himself the title of First Emperor (*Qin* is pronounced "chin"—the origin of the term *China*; see the box "Mandarin Chinese Pronunciation"). His important legacy ranged from attempts to standardize the language across the nation to rebuilding and extending the northern defenses, thus forming the Great Wall. Conquest of a different kind occurred in the early thirteenth century, when Genghis Khan led a Mongolian invasion that temporarily unified an enormous portion of Eurasia. A further northern invasion occurred in the mid-seventeenth century, when the Manchus swept southward to found the Qing Dynasty, which endured until 1911. Fragmentation remains part of the contemporary situation. In 1912 the Nationalist Party established a Republic of China and, following Japanese invasion and a bitter civil war, a People's Republic led by the Chinese Communist Party was established in 1949. At this time, the Nationalists retreated to the island of Taiwan, which the Qing had ceded to Japan in 1895 and was reclaimed by the Republic of China in 1945 after Japan's defeat in World War II. Recent years have seen a thawing of the economic and cultural relationship between Taiwan and China, but political reunification remains distant and contested. Meanwhile, a century and a half of British colonial activity in this area encouraged many Chinese to migrate to Southeast Asia; one consequence is that the city-state of Singapore has a majority population of ethnic Chinese.

The field of language reflects a similar duality of divergence and accord. Younger Han people in China today mostly speak the national language, Mandarin

TABLE 8.1 Chinese Dynasties.

Zhou	11th century B.C.E.–221 B.C.E.
Qin	221–207 B.C.E.
Han	206 B.C.E.–220 C.E.
Tang	618–907 C.E.
Song	960–1279
Yuan (Mongols)	1271–1368
Ming	1368–1644
Qing (Manchu)	1644–1911
Republic of China	1912–present (continuing in Taiwan)
People's Republic of China	1949–present

Chinese, and also a regional variety of Chinese particular to the locality where they were brought up. These regional dialects are often mutually unintelligible, although they all share some words and grammatical structures. Importantly, these are **tone languages,** which means that the pitch (high, low, rising, falling, etc.) at which a syllable is pronounced is as important in determining its meaning as its combination of other components (duration, stress, and the sounds equivalent to consonants and vowels). This characteristic has significant implications for vocal music, as we will see. In contrast to spoken Chinese, writing across the Chinese world has long been unified in a single system of characters (apart from small-scale exceptions such as the *nüshu* script known to certain women only). These characters consist of pictorial, phonetic, and other elements; their primary distinction from alphabetic languages is that each written character equals a whole word (with a few exceptions). For centuries, these characters were used across East Asia as the principal form of written language. There are also the native languages of the many minority groups, such as Uighur or Mongol, learned by those of that ethnicity and often by their neighbors as well.

Many within the Chinese world can disseminate ideas widely in Mandarin Chinese and can read the writings of fellow citizens past and present, but this hardly means that the Chinese have a single outlook on the world. On the contrary, there have always been conflicting schools of thought. **Confucianism,** which emerged from the writings of Kong Fuzi (literally Lord Kong, c. 550–479 B.C.E.), argued that good governance required a fixed social hierarchy in which loyalty flowed upward from wife to husband, son to father, common man to ruler, and ruler to heaven. Social responsibility then passed downward, with each individual obliged to care for those on the next stratum below. Confucius saw human nature as basically good but easily corrupted by poor leadership. Meanwhile, Daoists argued for self-cultivation and the importance of severing one's personal ties to an imperfect world. Both systems aimed to explain humanity's place in the universe. However, neither depended on religious belief in the Indo-European sense, although Daoism later cross-fertilized with local folk religions, including spirit and **ancestor worship.** These forms of worship involve rites to pay respect to natural and supernatural forces and to one's forefathers. **Buddhism,** a third major outlook, came from India to China early in the first millennium C.E. This doctrine held that human beings were inherently imperfect but, through religious practice, could embark on a journey of gradual self-improvement through multiple incarnations toward a purified future.

Each of these doctrines was overlaid by an imperial context that itself varied widely. At times, a landed aristocracy held the most power; during other periods, the imperial court ruled through a professional elite of scholar-officials selected by public examination and dispatched to oversee districts far from their own homes. Today the political organization of the Chinese world is no more straightforward. The administrative elite in mainland China is formed principally by members of the Chinese Communist Party. This political system emphasizes social equality, the shared ownership of property, strong central planning, and state control. However, recent decades have seen the encouragement of private enterprise and the rise of business interests, and corruption and the abuse of privilege by those in power has remained a problem. Since 1997 the former British colony of Hong Kong has returned to Chinese rule, with a governor appointed in Beijing but otherwise having a political system somewhat separate from that of the rest of the mainland. The Taiwanese have a recently established multiparty democracy. Chinese in most other countries are typically minority groups with little political say, except in the city-state of Singapore, where the Chinese form the majority population. Singapore is run as a democracy, but the government is notably authoritarian, and the same party (indeed, often the same few families) has held power since independence from Britain half a century ago.

In sum, the Chinese world comprises many highly varied locations even while people within this zone sometimes choose to perceive themselves as a single cultural entity. Chinese language and thought rely on shared principles and structures but equally have always sustained diverse perspectives. This same duality applies to Chinese musical culture: On the one hand, there are few musical features that are both uniquely and universally Chinese—characteristics shared in all this music but uncommon in East Asia or more globally; on the other hand, the *idea* of Chinese music is more universal, forming a significant category in Chinese discussions about music, identity, and international cultural contact. Like many around the world, the Chinese believe that their music makes them special and distinct from everyone else. We return to this issue at the end of the chapter.

Mandarin Chinese Pronunciation

Today, Mandarin Chinese is commonly transliterated into an alphabetical system called Pinyin to help those who cannot read Chinese characters. Many Pinyin letters sound similar to their English equivalents. Common sounds requiring special attention are listed here, with approximate English pronunciations.

Pinyin	English Sound	Example	Approximate Pronunciation
a	ah	*Zhang*	"jahng"
ai	eye	*kuai*	"kwhy"
ao	ow	*jiao*	"jee-ow" (rhymes with "cow")

e	uh	*ge*	"guh"
ei	a (long)	*Bei*	"bay"
i	ee/ir	*ni, shi, dizi*	"nee," "shir," "dee-zuh"—*i* has an "ee" sound except after c, ch, r, s, sh, z, & zh, when it is "ir" or "uh" if unstressed
ü	like *ü* in German	*Lü*	"lue"—shape your lips as if to say "oo" but compress the vocal cavity as in "ee"
c	ts	*can*	"tsahn"
q	ch	*qin*	"chin"
r	s (as in "pleasure")	*ren*	"rjun"
x	sh	*xi*	"she"
y	ee	*yan*	"yen"
zh	j	*zhi*	"jir"

Speech tones are normally omitted in Pinyin (but are very important in pronouncing a word correctly). Most syllables are equally stressed (for example, Abing is ah-bing, not AH-bing or ah-BING). A full guide is at http://en.wikipedia.org/wiki/Pinyin. Note that Chinese names are written with family name first, then personal name.

A Musician Between Traditional and Modern Worlds

FIGURE 8.1

Abing on the first page of a Chinese music dictionary (*Zhongguo yinyue cidian*, Beijing, 1985).

To illustrate in musical terms the interweaving of the historic and the modern, the traditional and the newly composed, the national and the regional, the Chinese and the foreign, let us consider a musician named Abing (Figure 8.1). Abing's music is frequently performed, recorded, and broadcast in China, and his pieces are studied by amateurs and professionals alike within China and overseas.

Born in the 1890s and named Hua Yanjun, Abing was brought up in a Daoist temple in Wuxi, Jiangsu Province, not too far from Shanghai. The Daoists accompanied their rites with a large-scale musical ensemble, and some of them were highly accomplished musicians. Abing soon became one himself. In early adulthood his sight declined and he took to performing songs and instrumental pieces in the streets, using the name Blind Abing. In 1950, the year of his death, Chinese musicologists visiting Wuxi on another research project recorded him. Abing played three solos on the pear-shaped lute *pipa* (Figure 8.2) and three on the two-stringed fiddle *erhu,* apparently from his street-music repertory. These performances were quickly published in music notation as solos for study by high school and conservatory musicians— until recently, most undergraduate music students in China studied with teachers at specialist music conservatories and arts institutes, so writers on Chinese music often refer to them as conservatory musicians.

FIGURE 8.2

Singaporean *pipa* musician Samuel Wong in a recording session.

Courtesy of Samuel Wong.

CD 3, Track 11, presents an excerpt from Abing's own recording of his *pipa* solo "Great Waves Washing the Sands." The instrument's name is onomatopoeic, combining terms that imitate the sounds of strokes across the strings (*pi*) and back (*pa*). The *pipa* has an extensive history, having been introduced to Chinese court music from Central Asia during or before the seventh century C.E. In the following centuries, it was often performed by specialist entertainers, and so its solo music became display oriented. Early illustrations of the *pipa* show it sounded by a large, handheld plectrum or pick, but as the *pipa* became more of an entertainment instrument, performers came to use false fingernails of bone, horn, or tortoise-shell, tied or taped on prior to performance. Because each finger could now pluck independently, more varied and virtuosic playing became possible. Standard strokes today include the following:

CD 3:11

"Da lang tao sha" ("Great Waves Washing the Sands"), excerpt (1:06). Abing [Hua Yanjun]. Performed by Abing, *pipa*. Field recording by members of the Music Research Institute. Wuxi, China, 1950.

- *Tan,* a rightward pluck with the index finger
- *Tiao,* a stroke in the opposite direction with the thumb
- *Gun,* a "roll" formed by quick repetition of *tan* and *tiao*
- *Lun,* or "wheel," which involved plucking the string alternately and continuously with all the fingers in rapid and smooth succession

The *pipa* can also sound multiple pitches at once: For instance, accompanying a melody on the highest-pitched string by strums across the lower three. Additional performance techniques include the use of harmonics (by lightly stopping a string at certain points) and pressing a stopped string sideways to increase its tension, resulting in a rise in pitch or a *bend.* The player may also slap the body of the instrument to simulate battlefield noises. If you have a guitar or another stringed instrument, try out these techniques; some, particularly *lun,* are difficult to master without training and long practice.

The *pipa*'s wide technical range is immediately apparent in "Great Waves Washing the Sands." Historically, solos for *pipa* included both short, free-standing pieces and compilations of several of these into suites. (Many were written in scores somewhat similar to the notation shown in Transcription 8.8.) Often, a short piece or a section of a suite was exactly sixty-eight *ban* in length (*ban* are metrical strong beats, equivalent to a Western measure), as in the first section of "Great Waves Washing the Sands" (see the Close Listening guide and Transcription 8.1). Pieces depicting romantic or natural scenes like this are categorized as "civil" (*wen*), while "military" (*wu*) pieces recount battles. In fact, many of the same performance techniques are found in both civil and military pieces, although they may be combined differently in each.

Close Listening

"DA LANG TAO SHA" ("GREAT WAVES WASHING THE SANDS")

CD 3:11

COUNTER NUMBER	SECTION	COMMENTARY
0:00	End of section 1, slow	*Lun* occurs on the very first note and many offbeat notes after that. We can also hear some double stopping (sounding two notes at once, generally those an octave apart in this passage). The music is based on a pentatonic scale of D, E, F#, A, and B.
0:40	Section 2, faster	Brief, repeated melodic motifs emphasizing a few notes in turn over an offbeat repeated A-string. Note the temporary modulation here: the C½# C½# C½# B A motif has a bluesy sound. (Instruments of Abing's day had just one fret pitched midway between high C and C#, both of which were rarely played notes then—today's instruments have two frets, one for C and one for C#.) There is a slight increase in tempo as the section progresses.
1:01	Start of section 3	A brief, stylistically unified fast-tempo section.

Despite its title, the music does not specifically suggest waves or a beach. Analysts have found melodic resemblances between this piece and an older one entitled "Autumn Moon over the Han Palace," which portrays the emotions of a neglected court concubine. In fact, there is controversy over exactly what happened in the recording session when these pieces were collected; it may be that the present title was created on the spot by the visiting musicologists, not given by Abing.

Listening to the old recording gives a sense of the traditional music sphere that was even then being transformed in much of China by strong currents of musical modernization. Published for conservatory-based performers all over China shortly after it was recorded, Abing's music too was thrust into these

TRANSCRIPTION 8.1
Passage from "Great
Waves Washing the
Sands."

transformations. Established from the 1920s on, Chinese music conservatories relied on Western models for the training of performers and composers. Music like Abing's appealed for nationalistic reasons rather than purely for its traditional flavor, and in the conservatories it was played on instruments redesigned for virtuosic performance skills, equal-tempered tuning, and concert-hall performance. Further, the music was edited: Accompaniments were freely added, tempo was held back to allow a more dramatic range of expression, improvisatory street performance was reshaped into notated music with a fully fixed structure, and picturesque titles or even revolutionary stories were provided in program notes to suggest interpretations of the music. Nevertheless, keep in mind that many conservatory musicians in the 1950s and since have seen themselves as the inheritors of older, regional folk styles, explaining their adjustments as modernizations and improvements of the original raw material.

Abing's image changed along with his music, a process that produced a wide variety of images because strikingly few details of his life were recorded. He would come to represent the archetypal Chinese folk musician to some, an oppressed revolutionary to others, to yet others a romantic visionary, and to still others a dubious figure connected with urban subcultures of drug abuse and prostitution. In fact, the Communist system regularly puts forward individual life stories as examples to help educate the citizens at large, somewhat like the use of stories of saints in Catholic communities, and so an element of poetic license is understandable in some of the revisions of his life that occurred. Chinese biographies of Abing are numerous and include movies and journalistic writings as well as academic studies. Here are compressions of four of them to show the range of lives put forward for this enigmatic musician.

1. *The Daoist:* Adopted at an early age, Hua Yanjun became a leading member of the Daoist temple ensemble. Then, lacking the money to treat an eye infection, he slowly lost his sight. Unable to play in the temple ensemble any longer, he scraped out an existence by performing on street corners. Retaining his Daoist faith to the end, he was buried in the local temple cemetery. He learned a huge repertory of traditional pieces and was deft at refashioning traditional melodic ingredients into instrumental solos, a few of which were recorded shortly before his death.

2. *The Revolutionary:* Abing began life as a Daoist. However, his interest in the entertainment music of the masses led to his expulsion from the temple. Beaten senseless by the lackeys of a reactionary landlord who lusted after the poor musician's attractive wife, he was left for dead. He survived but was blinded, and he was forced to become a street musician. Naturally, his sense of social justice was strong after this, and he was eager to repeat stories that discredited the reactionary bourgeois classes. When the Japanese invaded, he broadcast in song the news of Communist guerrilla victories not reported in the newspapers. When the People's Republic was established, he was offered a post as tutor in a local music conservatory, though he died before he could take it up. Fortunately, six of his pieces, which express the innermost aspirations of multitudes of laboring peoples, have been preserved for posterity.

3. *The Romantic:* Abing lost his mother almost at birth. Deprived of her love, his one solace was his father's lute playing, which helped put the lonely child to

sleep each night. After discovering his illegitimacy from his classmates' taunts, he gradually developed a stubborn, uncommunicative character. Musical instruments were his only true friends, and it was through them that he poured out his emotions. When his father died, he carelessly frittered away his inheritance and contracted a disease that led to the loss of his sight. Many times, remorse and pain made him want to kill himself, but music was the only thing that stopped him—he just could not bear to be parted from his instruments. From then on, he remained part of the lowest echelon of society, living in darkness among the miserable, oppressed laboring classes. Yet, without this experience, he would never have created the compositions he did, his music representing the beautiful scenery of his home town, scenes that now he saw only in his mind's eye.

4. *The Drug Addict:* Brought up by Daoist priests, the young Abing showed much talent and quickly mastered all the local instruments and the semi-improvisatory styles with which they were performed. As a young man he inherited both money and property, but frequent visits to brothels and opium dens gradually exhausted his funds, and syphilis left him blind. He was forced to rely on his musical talents to survive. Ever resourceful, he began to sing salacious gossip in the market place. Anything juicy or gory would do, especially if it concerned the sex lives of local personalities, or the foiling of the hated Japanese invaders. He even managed to maintain his opium habit by playing background music in smoking dens, for which he received free drugs. His most famous piece is actually based on a well-known prostitute's song. This was recorded by a team of Communist musicologists, though the musician was wise enough not to tell them the source of his inspiration, and they did not mention it when they published his solos. He died some months later, allegedly of an opium overdose.

These examples show how authors select evidence from what is known, interpret that evidence depending on how they feel about it, draw in frameworks from the wider cultural beliefs around them, and shape the account with a view to how a target audience will respond. Look at how second and third biographies portray Abing's fall to the lowest social level. In the second, his fall justifies the continued performance of his music—Abing becomes a man of the people, and his music comes to reflect and represent their spirit. This is a tenet of Marxist theory, which sees every cultural artifact as imbued with the class outlook of its creator. According to this theory, the best music to play in a Marxist state emerges from the working classes. By way of contrast, the third biography presents Abing's creativity as an escape from his difficult life—he is put forward as a tortured genius, rather like the German composer Beethoven who similarly struggled against deafness from midlife on. Behind this image is the nineteenth-century romantic idea that outstanding inspiration results from confrontation with the toughest situations: if art reflects life, the greatest art emerges only from the most heroic life. (For more on Abing's life, see Stock 1996, which also has recordings of his music.)

It was through processes of reinvention like these that a traditional folk musician and his music have become, and still remain, part of the modern Chinese musical world. We will see similar processes of transformation at play throughout this chapter.

A Cross-Section of Chinese Music

We just saw a specific example of Chinese music—how street-begging music (itself perhaps derived from a classical piece) can change quickly into a modern concert-hall art work. But is there a way to approach Chinese music overall? How can we begin to grasp this immense subject area? Table 8.2 gives an overview by listing types of music found across the Chinese world today, with a range of imported and newly created genres shown alongside selected age-old, historical styles. Many are reproduced on the CDs with this book, and the discussion that follows introduces each in turn (except for "Great Waves Washing the Sands," which we have already encountered.)

TABLE 8.2 Some Examples of Chinese Music.

Number	Song Type	Song Title
1	Folk song 1	"Weeding Song" (CD 3, Track 12)
2	Folk song 2	"Releasing the Horse into Pasture" (CD 3, Track 13)
3	*Sizhu* ensemble music	"Song of Happiness" (CD 3, Track 15)
4	*Beiguan* processional music	"Seven-Inch Lotus" (CD 3, Track 17)
5	Beijing opera	*Third Wife Teaches Her Son* (CD 4, Track 1)
6	Ballad singing	"Scholar Qian" (CD 4, Track 2)
7	*Qin* solo	"Three Variations on Yang Pass" (CD 4, Track 3)
8	*Pipa* solo	"Great Waves Washing the Sands" (CD 3, Track 11)
9	*Erhu* solo	"Festival Night Canzonetta"
10	Piano solo	"The Joyous Festival of Lunar New Year's Day" (CD 4, Track 4)
11	Buddhist chant	From the Greater Water and Land Dharma Assembly
12	Ritual song	*Pasibutbut* (CD 4, Track 5)
13	Christian hymn	"Praise from Heaven and Earth" (CD 4, Track 6)
14	Film song	"Full Moon and Blooming Flowers"
15	Pop song	"Scent" (CD 4, Track 7)
16	New folk music	"Miracle"

Listing the items in this way, however, overly separates each. In practice, in China as elsewhere, different kinds of music share many features. Figure 8.3 maps these same examples onto a grid, showing various ways that we might group them according to certain shared characteristics. For example, we might place them by instrumentation into vocal, vocal-instrumental, or instrumental categories. The two folk songs (1 and 2) are performed without instrumental backing and fall into the category of vocal music, as does the ritual song (12). The former were rural forms originally performed during agricultural labor, so it is little surprise that they omit instrumentalists—people needed their hands free to take part in the work—and the latter came from a society of hunter-gatherers who join their hands while singing, as we will see later on. Meanwhile, much music

FIGURE 8.3

Grid of selected genres of Chinese music.

combines vocal and instrumental forces, including all the entertainment genres, from Beijing opera (5) to film song (14). Some music, though, is designed for instruments alone, such as the solos for the stringed instruments *qin* and *pipa* (7 and 8) or the *beiguan* ensemble music (4), although this is a porous boundary in many cases—some *qin* and *beiguan* pieces include singing.

On the same figure, we might instead choose to divide Chinese music into forms intended for the people at large and those aimed at more elite types of listeners. If so, the folk song examples and ritual chant are now joined by several other mass entertainment forms such as Beijing opera (5) and the pop song (15) as well as religious forms such as Buddhist chant (11) and the Christian hymn (13). Meanwhile, the contemporary piano solo (10) is an example of a music mastered only by a specialist minority in China, which places it alongside the *qin* solo, among other examples. None of these categories is static, though. Folk song and

Beijing opera are becoming musics of specialist choice in China today, as we will see, and piano learning seems so fashionable in many parts of China that it nearly equals a mass music—there may well be more piano students in China than anywhere else in the world today.

Yet another way to approach these examples is to look at whether each is predominantly rooted in indigenous traditions or was significantly inspired or impacted by Western models. In this case, the two folk songs can now be placed in the indigenous category along with the socially elite solos for the stringed instruments *qin* and *pipa,* among others. The pop song and Christian hymn, though, arise from imported musical models. We could go beyond these categorizations, dividing up the great mass of Chinese music again and again by musical material, performance context, social function, and the performers' social class or perhaps relating one division to another to see what patterns emerge. As Figure 8.3 shows, categorization is not only a tool for organizing knowledge but also an analytic device, which we can deploy to focus in on selected deep musical continuities.

Folk Song

Today the widespread distribution of playback technology has allowed listening to recorded or broadcast music to replace much day-to-day personal music making. Before such technology, singing played an integral role in many events or situations, including courting, funerals, and child care. A Chinese example is the marriage lament tradition.

THE MARRIAGE LAMENT TRADITION

In the past, and still sometimes today, a bride in many parts of China had to abandon her original home when she was transferred through arranged marriage to another family; she was permitted to return just once a year. The bride burst into song as she finally left her parents, putting her full emotions into the performance. Bridal laments allowed women to express thoughts that normally remained unspoken, and both the lyrics and the emotional performance stimulated all who were present to reflect on the difficult situation of the socially marginalized woman. In the following verse, a bride describes her new family as bandits as she laments painfully to her father's sister:

> Oh Aunt,
> Please feel sorry for your poor niece.
> I am so heartbroken that I cannot comb my hair.
> Because these bandits are making trouble,
> I am crying day and night.
> From now on I will fade and fall into pieces (cited in Watson 1996:116).

LADY MENGJIANG

Although songs like these had an important social function, their musical design was often just as important if not more so. This is true of the next song, which is also the song of an unhappy woman, the chief character in the lyrics. "Lady Mengjiang" describes a lonely newlywed whose husband was sent to construct the Great Wall. Each verse treats one month in turn as Mengjiang imagines what she and her husband would do if only he were home. Transcription 8.2 presents the first verse of the song in staff notation, with a few additional analytic markings.

> The first month brings new year. Every home is decorated with a red lantern. Other couples are together. Lady Mengjiang's husband has gone to build the Great Wall.

Text
"LADY MENGJANG"

TRANSCRIPTION 8.2
One verse of "Lady Mengjiang."

The first detail to notice is that there are four phrases of two measures each. We can see that by reading the lyrics. Some analysts assume therefore that the song has four musical components and use a model from Chinese literature—start, development, transformation, synthesis—to describe its structure. We will proceed instead by noticing how the pitch ending each phrase is repeated to start the next phrase. Arrows have been added to the notation to emphasize this, and you can see the repeated pitch even if you cannot read staff notation. This technique smoothes the phrases together and, with the evenly balanced duration of each phrase, gives the song a lyrical rather than a dramatic character. Looking more closely at these phrase-ending pitches, we can detect a two-part musical structure superimposed onto the four-line text. See how the ends of lines 2 and 4 reach the same note (D), whereas lines 1 and 3 contrast (A in line 1, E in line 3). Building on that observation, notice that the melody in the second half of line 2 is almost identical to that in the second half of line 4. Again, you can see the close match even if you cannot read staff notation. You can also recognize that measures 1 and 5 (the start of lines 1 and 3, respectively) are related. The only major difference is the first beat of those measures: measure 5 continues from the end pitch of measure 4, while measure 1 (when repeated) marks a clean break from the end of measure 8. This makes musical sense, marking the start of each verse clearly each time the singer goes onto a new month in the lyrics.

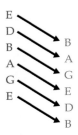

FIGURE 8.4

The relationship between measures 2–3 and 6–7 in "Lady Mengjiang."

That just leaves measures 2–3 and 6–7 (marked with a box labeled "X"). There is a relationship here too, although you may need to be confident with staff notation (or like deciphering codes) to spot it. Measures 6–7 are actually a lower-pitched version of measures 2–3. Correspondence is not 100 percent exact—the singer decorates the melody differently each time—but if we write the pitches used in measures 2–3 from highest to lowest (E, D, B, A, G, and E, the left-hand column in Figure 8.4) and then move down that series by two steps (as in the right-hand column), we see how measures 6–7 emerge from measures 2–3.

One detail not explained yet is why we also find the note F# in measures 6 and 7. According to Chinese music theory, a pentatonic tune (a melody using a five-note scale) can "borrow" one or two extra notes. They are used in certain places to increase the musical affect (see Transcription 8.3). That is what happens here: F# appears just twice as a means of approaching low E. Each time it substitutes for G, as used throughout the rest of the verse. Play or sing the tune with G in place of F#: The melody sounds good, but the overall expressive impact is reduced.

TRANSCRIPTION 8.3
The pentatonic scale with two optional tones.

Overall, measures 5–8 are a transformation of measures 1–4, being more similar at each end and more contrasting in the middle. Again, the song has a two-part melodic structure even though there are four lines of lyrics in each verse.

This song shows the following characteristics common to many other examples of Chinese music:

- The end tone of one line may be reused to start the next.
- A pattern of contrasting cadence tones lends variety to the music.
- A pentatonic scale is used much of the time, but optional extra notes add expressive interest.
- The melody has both consistency (through reuse of material) and variety (through transformation).
- Melodic structure is not necessarily identical to textual structure.

"Lady Mengjiang" is a **strophic** song sung by a single person throughout. This format is used for many kinds of counting and listing songs, each verse introducing the next item in a series—the singer's dreams for each successive month, in this case. It can be used in riddle songs as well, in which each verse answers the preceding one and poses a new question. Certain strophic songs have instrumental accompaniment, which has led some scholars to call them urban folk songs, the idea being that there are more instruments available in the towns. However, people in the countryside own instruments too, even if they do not take them to the fields when laboring. The most crucial difference may be the contexts in which songs with and without instrumental accompaniment are sung, the former being well suited for use during work and the latter being effective for leisure or entertainment.

SHAN'GE (SONGS OF AGRICULTURAL WORK, FLIRTING, AND COURTING)

Of course, one can find numerous regional folk song traditions across China, all with distinct characteristics of their own. Work songs form one significant subcategory of these. Some work songs contain alternating solo and group phrases allowing for the synchronization of manual work (see also Chapter 4). The two folk song examples we will listen to here come from what is probably the most widespread subcategory, **shan'ge:** outdoor songs for agricultural work, flirting, and courting. This is a logical grouping: In the past, young people spent much of their time working in the fields, a process they enlivened by singing to the others around them. Sometimes, shan'ge verses are sung alternately by a boy and a girl, and they tease each other, improvising new verses in an ongoing battle of wits.

First, we have a song from Jiangsu Province, East China (CD 3, Track 12). It is performed by Jin Wenyin (b. 1927; Figure 8.5), a singer from Qiandai Village, to the east of the city of Suzhou. He worked as a village school teacher and local cultural officer until he became an agricultural laborer during the Cultural Revolution (1966–1976), when many of those associated with cultural activities found themselves fiercely criticized in public meetings, physically maltreated, and thrown out of their former posts. In 1979 he regained cultural employment and actively gathered songs and texts of all kinds from his friends and neighbors.

CD 3:12

"Yundao ge" ("Weeding Song") (1:33). Traditional Jiangsu folk-song. Performed by Jin Wenyin. Field recording by Antoinet Schimmelpenninck and Frank Kouwenhoven, Qiandai, China, 1987. *Chinese Folk Songs and Folk Singers: Shan'ge Traditions in Southern Jiangsu.* Leiden, 1997.

Courtesy of Antoinet Schimmelpenninck.

FIGURE 8.5

Folk singer Jin Wenyin.

The excerpt that Jin sings is from a rice-weeding song (Transcription 8.4). It combines moments where Jin cries out, using syllables like "e-he-hei," and those where he sings simple lyrics describing the task of weeding a rice paddy.

TRANSCRIPTION 8.4 "Weeding Song" by Jin Wenyin. The original pitch is one octave lower. Extended lines show each line of lyrics; all other syllables are sung calls.

Transcription after Schimmelpenninck 1997:258.

The musical phrases are initially difficult to distinguish in Transcription 8.4, but comparison with many other examples (a standard ethnomusicological technique) reveals how Jin has elaborated a simpler model of two phrases, each with two segments (see the Close Listening guide). The Dutch ethnomusicologist Antoinet Schimmelpenninck, who researched folk singing in East China, discovered that singers there do not so much memorize different songs but instead flexibly rework one primary tune to suit multiple texts, using such techniques as partial repetitions and inserted calls. You can find in this example the musical principles listed after "Lady Mengjiang" (smooth melodic links, contrasting cadences, and so forth).

Weeding was arduous but essential work during the hot summer months, and all present joined in the calls as they uprooted weeds. The leader improvised lyrics to help the workers forget the heat of the day and their weariness. Jin Wenyin sang alone when he recorded this song in 1987, but had he been singing while weeding, he would likely have developed a short story over several verses or started to challenge other singers within earshot to improvise riddle songs. Jin told Schimmelpenninck, "Sometimes we sang songs in the fields until we knew

Close Listening

"YUNDAO GE" ("WEEDING SONG")

CD 3:12

COUNTER NUMBER	COMMENTARY	LYRICS AND TRANSLATION	
0:00	Opening calls	*e hehe hehei*	
0:09	Line 1 of the lyrics, musical phrase 1a	*yingdao ei . . .*	If you're weeding, sing a weeding song,
0:19	Extension of the phrase by repeating a few words from line 1	*yingdao ei . . .*	weeding . . .
0:27	Further repetition	*aya yingdao ei . . .*	weeding . . .
0:34	Line 2, phrase 1b	*liang pang mei . . .*	With knees bent, squelching in the mud,
0:51	Line 3, phrase 2a	*ngei gwa ei . . .*	I see a six-foot plot, full of weeds,
1:01	Line 4, phrase 2b	(1st time) *se zi . . .*	my ten fingers hold six seedlings.
1:12	Like the opening calls but leads to a repeat of line 4 and phrase 2b	*ei hei hei . . .*	

no more texts. What to do about it? Well, we could sing 'Shi zhi taizi' ['Ten Tables,' a song counting famous historical and legendary figures one by one]. That gave us ten more songs." Or, before marriage, he might have begun to sing about the beauty of one of the girls nearby in the hope of sparking her romantic interest or at least of initiating some amusing teasing. Jin noted that girls were shy and sang less than men, but if the girl wished, she might sing a verse in reply, and the duet would continue until one singer lost inspiration (and so lost the contest) or a third person chipped in with a verse.

In the same interview, Jin Wenyin noted that the rise of chemical weed killer meant that few people now sang weeding songs. Mechanization also played a part, as did the drift of people to industrial work and the reorganization of land ownership after the 1980s. Before then, much of the land was worked collectively, first by teams of laborers for landlords and later by groups of commune members. From the 1980s on, however, many families were allocated individual plots, with the result that they organized separate work schedules. A better standard of living has resulted, but so has a decline in collective singing. *Shan'ge* are no longer a normal part of work activities, being sustained in some rural areas only by folklore enthusiasts like Jin Wenyin.

But decline is not the full picture, since *shan'ge* have a long history of spreading to new contexts. In ancient China, the emperor sent out officials to gather song texts to help him judge whether the people were happy or not. The seventeenth century saw a literary movement in which certain Chinese authors collected and published songs that they felt had an attractive local character, particularly those with erotic content. The most famous of these writers was Feng Menglong (1574–1646), who published the words of over three hundred *shan'ge*. Feng argued that the songs showed sincere feelings, unlike the contrived, self-conscious love affairs of the social elite. During the 1910s and 1920s, following the example of Christian missionaries and school reformers, social activists of various political outlooks took up mass singing to instill group solidarity or to help their followers disseminate a message. Folk song tunes were often chosen—the activists saw that use of a familiar tune helped people take in the new words. The movie *Yellow Earth* (directed by Chen Kaige, 1984) tells the story of a Communist soldier sent in 1939 to collect village folk songs for just such a purpose. In the 1950s many of these tunes, with their new lyrics, were published for educational use across the nation. The new social order meant that the lyrics of love songs were largely omitted or rewritten as hymns of admiration for Chairman Mao Zedong (Mao Tse-tung, 1893–1976) and his Chinese Communist Party. Nevertheless, *shan'ge* tunes survived, and songs related to work patterns were sometimes left intact in these collections.

The second recorded example, "Releasing the Horse into Pasture," illustrates this recent situation (CD 3, Track 13). Zhao Yue (b. 1977; Figure 8.6) learned this song, which is from Yunnan Province, Southwest China, as a student at the Shenyang Conservatory of Music, in distant Northeast China (Transcription 8.5).

Courtesy of Jiang Shu.

FIGURE 8.6

Singer Zhao Yue.

TRANSCRIPTION 8.5
"Releasing the Horse into Pasture" as sung by Zhao Yue.

Zheng-yue fang ma wu-lu-lu de zheng yue zheng yao, Gan-qi ma lai deng-lu cheng, yao e, deng-lu cheng.
phrase 1   phrase 2

Verse 1 only

CD 3:13

"Fang ma shan'ge" ("Releasing the Horse into Pasture") (0:58). Traditional Yunnan folksong. Performed by Zhao Yue. Field recording by Zhao Yue. Sheffield, UK, 2007.

"Releasing the Horse into Pasture" shares with the weeding song a two-phrase design and use of vocal cries alongside singing. Yet the two differ significantly. First, this song has a more straightforward structure than the weeding song does. Second, the greatest contrast is in meter: Jin's *shan'ge* is in free meter, as opposed to Zhao's clear duple meter. Third, Zhao's repertory includes songs from all across China (and overseas), unlike that of Jin, who learned a local set of tunes and songs. Fourth, Jin learned informally in the fields to reshape one main melody to fit a wide range of different song texts, whereas Zhao

Close Listening

"FANG MA SHAN'GE" ("RELEASING THE HORSE INTO PASTURE")

CD 3:13

COUNTER NUMBER	COMMENTARY	LYRICS AND TRANSLATION	
0:00	Verse 1 (7 measures long, divided into a 3-measure phrase and a 4-measure phrase): Phrase 1: a, a', b a is a falling pattern and appears in form a and the more-elaborate a'; b is a sequence pitched a step below	*Zhengyue . . .*	In the first month I release the horse to pasture,
0:06	Phrase 2: a, b', c, b' b' has one extra note than b to set an extra syllable; c is two rhythmic cries, one to each beat	*Ganqi ma . . .*	I encourage the horse to go into the field.
0:14	Verse 2: Music as verse 1	*Dama ganzai shantou shang,* *Xiaoma ganlai sui hou gen.*	The big horse climbs the mountain, The little horse follows on behind.
0:26	Verse 3: Music as verse 1	*Eryue fang ma baicao fa,* *Xiao ma chi cao shenshanli pao.*	In the second month I feed the horse every kind of grass, The little horse eats grass and gallops in the mountain valleys.
0:43	Verse 4; a, a', b a, b', b', c (the final two elements are reversed to create a distinctive ending)	*Ma wu yecao bu hui pang,* *Cao wu lushui bu hui fa.*	Without grass the horse won't get fat, Grass without dew won't grow well.

memorized in the classroom a contrasting series of fixed-format songs. Fifth, while Jin sings in his local Wu dialect, Zhao performs her songs in Mandarin Chinese.

Still, we would be mistaken to describe Zhao's rendition as "inauthentic" compared with Jin's. After all, neither performance occurred in an agricultural setting, and in the past *shan'ge* were mostly sung by young, single people, much closer in age to Zhao than to Jin. Instead, each performance sustains the tradition in a new setting, Jin's as folkloric hobby and Zhao's in the sphere of music education.

Instrumental Ensemble Traditions

China is rich in instrumental ensemble traditions. These have deep roots in many areas, although their history has been far from static. Ancient paintings and court records reveal fascinating details of early ensembles. Other traditions have come down to us through archaeological findings, one of the most remarkable of which is a set of musical relics from the tomb of Marquis Yi, the ruler of a small Chinese state called Zeng.

In winter 1977, a unit of the Chinese People's Liberation Army was called in to level a small, unremarkable hill north of the city of Wuhan in Hubei Province so that a factory could be built. After breaking into a previously unknown burial pit, the soldiers quickly called in the archaeologists. The discovery that followed remains unparalleled among any of the other ancient cultures in Asia, Africa, Europe, or the Americas.

Laid out as a classical Chinese palace, the stone-lined tomb contained everything the Bronze Age despot would need for an upwardly mobile afterlife: an ornately lacquered wooden double coffin to shield both his bones and his dignity; weapons, armor, and bronze chariot fittings; the skeletons of twenty-one women and a dog; and a full set of ritual musical instruments, including a sixty-five-piece ensemble of studded bronze *zhong* bells and thirty-two tuned *qing* chime stones. Each woman lay next to an instrument, on which had been inscribed its tuning. Beside the bodies were illustrations of the musicians in performance, though sadly no musical notation. Inscriptions recorded that the bell set was presented to Marquis Yi in 433 B.C.E. by his powerful neighbor the King of Chu.

Superbly preserved in the central "ceremonial courtyard" of the subterranean palace (Figure 8.7), each bell could produce two pitches, depending on where it was struck. The set had a range of over five octaves, much of it fully chromatic in semitones. The bells were inscribed with the names of the tones they produced in both **absolute** and **relative pitch.** This means we can today relate the ancient names of notes to their actual pitch levels (absolute pitch) and understand how they fit together into a tonal system (relative pitch). The inclusion of five sets of beaters suggests how many musicians might have performed the bells at once. Some of the instruments or other ritual materials found in the tomb bore scenes depicting the making of music, providing further clues about performance practice. Drums, strings, and wind instruments, along with the chime stones, completed the ensemble.

FIGURE 8.7

Excavation of the tomb of Marquis Yi (So 2000:15).

A smaller musical ensemble was laid at the foot of the Marquis's coffin in his personal chamber. This comprised a transverse flute, panpipes, two mouth organs, *sheng* (an instrument that would inspire the invention of the accordion), a small drum, three zithers of twenty-five strings with movable bridges, a ten-stringed type of *qin* zither (later in this chapter we discuss its better-known seven-stringed form), and a five-stringed zither, which appears to have been struck with a handheld stick. All these instruments were very well preserved. The *qin*, for instance, survived with several of its tuning pegs intact, allowing historians to date that technology to at least this period. Coffins of eight young women were close at hand, suggesting that eight of these instruments were played at once to the fortunate Marquis. As if these treasures were not enough, the archaeologists uncovered a second tomb just a few years later. This was thought to be that of the Marquis's consort or close descendant. Here were yet further instruments and more clues to Chinese court music-culture of more than two millennia past.

The large, carefully crafted bronze bell set was a hugely expensive gift, and we might wonder what Marquis Yi was doing with such a set—according to Confucian orthodoxy, the largest sets were reserved for kings and emperors. It was also an incredible item to take to the afterlife, not to mention the sacrifice of all those young women (and the dog). This was conspicuous consumption long before Thorstein Veblen coined the term in the last years of the nineteenth century. Veblen linked conspicuous consumption with conspicuous leisure and conspicuous waste. In this view, artistic production is deliberately expensive, time-consuming, splendid, and useless. Useless, that is, in the narrow sense of propelling immediate human survival, but useful indeed in projecting one's elevated wealth, fitness, or status, since only the most superior human being had the surplus time to invest in such cultural display, or, indeed, the authority to take it with him to the grave. If this is so, perhaps the bell ensemble's musical performances were similarly display oriented, being musically virtuosic and intended primarily to project the Marquis's regal ambitions.

This interpretation of the music played by these ensembles differs from the one put forward in historical writings, which predominantly describe ritual music. Yet we know the ancient Chinese had entertainment-oriented music. The philosopher Mozi (c. 470–c. 390 B.C.E.) made a point of rejecting that music as a wasteful drain on the state and called for the execution of professional musicians. The ancient record of court music, the *Yueji*, described another Marquis with a love for contemporary entertainment music. His sentiments may be familiar to many music students worldwide:

> Marquis Wen of Wei asked Zixia, "When I don my ritual regalia and listen to the ancient music, the only thing I fear is that I will keel over [from boredom]. But when I listen to the tones of Zheng and Wei, I never feel the least bit sated with it. May I be so bold as to ask why the ancient music is that way when the new is not? (DeWoskin 1982:94)

The regal bell set may have allowed Marquis Yi to signal royal status when he reached the afterlife, but its power perhaps extended beyond the symbolic. Music is in many senses the least concrete of all the arts. Its sounds—particularly those of the large bells (Figure 8.8)—are readily felt in and around the body while remaining invisible to the eye. Music's special appeal to us as listeners and

FIGURE 8.8

Replica bell modeled on those
discovered in the tomb of
Marquis Yi.

"feelingful invisibility" seems to parallel the agency of the supernatural, which many ancient peoples believed to be present, powerful, and unseen. It is no wonder that music plays a regular role in religious services and funeral ceremonies worldwide, and that people see it as a bridge to the otherworldly.

Because we have no surviving music from 433 B.C.E., but only instruments, tunings, and illustrations, the remainder of this section studies two much more contemporary traditions, Jiangnan *sizhu* from the Shanghai region of East China and *beiguan* from the city of Jilong in Northern Taiwan. These allow us to focus on contrasting aspects of Chinese ensemble music as found today.

JIANGNAN *SIZHU*

Several instrumental traditions are found in and around Shanghai, among them **Jiangnan** *sizhu* (Figure 8.9). Its name means the silk and bamboo music of the Jiangnan region, in East China around the lower reaches of the Changjiang (Yangtze River). The phrase *silk and bamboo* refers to the two major categories of instruments used in this music, silk-stringed instruments and bamboo-tubed wind instruments. The ancient Chinese recognized eight categories of sound-producing materials: silk, bamboo, metal (as in the bells described above), stone (as in tuned chimes), gourds (hollowed out to make the body of a mouth organ), earth (baked into clay ocarinas), leather (stretched to make drumheads), and wood (as in clappers). *Sizhu* ensembles are widely distributed across China, their exact instrumentation varying from place to place. In Jiangnan, the ensemble is flexible, but it often includes one or two of each of the following instruments: *erhu;* **sanxian** (three-stringed, long-necked lute), *pipa, ruan* (four-stringed, round-bodied lute), *yangqin* (hammered dulcimer), and *dizi* (transverse bamboo flute); it also includes the *sheng* (mouth organ), and a percussionist plays woodblock and clappers. Sometimes, the

FIGURE 8.9

Sizhu performance in a
Shanghai tea shop. The
back row has an *erhu*
player on the left (partially
covered), next to him a
pipa player, and then a
yangqin. The front musicians are a percussionist
(left) and a player of the
sanxian (we can see the
top of its neck only).

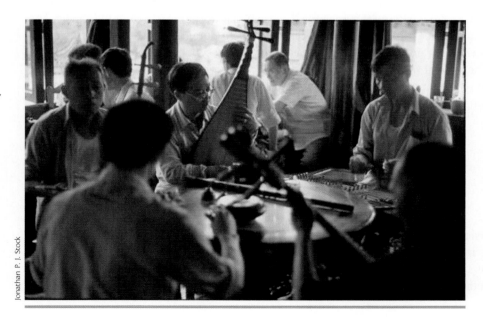

ensemble adds a *zheng* (also called *guzheng*; a bridged zither with usually twenty-five strings), and in soft pieces a *xiao* (bamboo end-blown vertical flute) replaces the more effervescent *dizi*.

Jiangnan *sizhu* music used to be played by hired instrumentalists at weddings and in local opera but it is better known as an amateur music today, most typically being performed in tea shops by groups of friends who have formed a music club, rather like Irish music sessions in pubs but with tea as the main drink, not beer. This change reflects a process of gentrification quite widely found in the history of Chinese music. In China, the skills of professional performers have always appreciated, but music professionals themselves were typically held in low esteem before the twentieth century, which meant that amateur musicians wanted to learn the music but not be taken for professionals. One means of marking their social distance was to transfer the performance to a new context distant from the commercial situations of hired wedding bands or the theater.

In tea shop performances of Jiangnan *sizhu*, musicians seat themselves around a table and play primarily to one another, taking turns as the event proceeds. Other people sit around, possibly listening to the ensemble but more often chatting, smoking, and drinking tea. The brief excerpt recorded on CD 3, Track 14, illustrates how the music actually sounds at a tea shop; see the Close Listening guide, then compare this track with the next one, from a studio recording.

The music on CD 3, Track 15, gathers three excerpts from a performance of "Song of Happiness" ("Huanle ge") by *dizi, erhu, sanxian, yangqin, pipa,* and percussion. "Song of Happiness" is one of the primary eight pieces that together comprise Jiangnan *sizhu*'s core repertory. It used to be played to accompany a bride on the wedding procession to her new home, although, and as we saw

CD 3:14

Jiangnan *sizhu* (0:28). Performed by musicians at the Huxin Tea Shop. Field recording by Jonathan Stock. Shanghai, China, 1990.

CD 3:15

"Huanle ge" ("Song of Happiness")(1:24). Jiangnan *sizhu*. *Musique de la region du fleuve Yangtze.* Playasound PS65048.

Close Listening

JIANGNAN *SIZHU*

CD 3:14

COUNTER NUMBER	COMMENTARY
0:00–0:28	Listen first to the duple meter of the percussion part. There are two kinds of sounds, a "tick" from the woodblock and a "tock" from clapper (played, one to each hand, by the same musician).
	Listen to the melody, which is heterophonic; that is, each musician plays the same tune at once in a version specific to his or her instrument. The *dizi* can be heard clearly, as can some plucked and bowed strings.
	Then consider the background sound—this is not music for a passive audience. Or is it the music that is the background sound?

earlier in the chapter, not every bride was entirely happy to make the journey. A complete performance of "Song of Happiness" is a suite of three renditions of essentially the same melodic material played slowly, moderately, and quickly in turn (see the Close Listening guide). But because there are more decorations at the slower speed, the overall flow of the music actually sounds somewhat similar from one rendition to the next, even though the players perceive the three as having quite different tempos. Transcription 8.6 transcribes the start of the melody as presented by the *dizi* player in each rendition. The moderate and fast versions of the tune have been stretched horizontally to better show the close relationship among all three renditions.

Close Listening

"HUANLE GE" ("SONG OF HAPPINESS")

CD 3:15

COUNTER NUMBER	COMMENTARY	
0:00	Start of first rendition	Note how the instruments share the same overall tune; note also a gradual pickup in speed.
0:48	Start of second rendition	Same tune, about twice as fast the first rendition; somewhat less ornamented.
1:16	Start of third rendition	Same tune, about twice as fast again, with much less surface decoration.

TRANSCRIPTION 8.6
Dizi performance at the start of each rendition in "Song of Happiness" (notated one octave below actual pitch).

Jiangnan *sizhu* illustrates several characteristics of Chinese ensemble music in general:

- Heterophonic performance style—multiple instruments share the same melodic line.
- Variation during performance—the surface details of the music are not entirely fixed, with room for spontaneous ornamentation and interplay with other musicians.
- Notation is used when players learn the music, but they perform from memory rather than by reading scores; this increases flexibility but constrains the size of the repertory.
- Much music is in suite form: a gradual progression from slow, expanded tunes to fast, compressed versions of the same tune.
- Performance is very much part of a wider social event, not a rendition to a paying audience; in the *beiguan* ensemble in the next section, performance is part of religious ritual, perhaps the most widespread traditional context for ensemble music in China and Taiwan.

BEIGUAN

The *beiguan* ensemble on CD 3, Tracks 16 and 17, is a band of wind and percussion players who perform outdoor ritual music, predominantly at funerals and temple festivities. Though *beiguan* sounds quite unlike Jiangnan *sizhu,* this contrast is not due to geography or local cultural preference—both Taiwan and Jiangnan have well-blended, introspective indoor ensembles and strident outdoor wind-and-percussion groups. Instead, the two examples allow us to experience the breadth of musics that make up the category of instrumental ensemble traditions.

Beiguan music emanates a muscular self-confidence that perfectly matches its outdoor setting. Here is an extract from my field notes when I began to study *beiguan*. My aim was to capture in words the impression of being surrounded by this remarkably stirring music. Incidentally, field notes like this normally are not intended for direct publication, and you can see that I was experimenting with a personal, even novelistic style here, one which perhaps even jars with the careful writing more normally put forward in textbooks. Still, the idea of using lively prose to directly communicate the sensation of music making is one that has attracted many ethnomusicologists in recent years.

> Standing near the ensemble, or better taking part as a musician, my ears ring. During and afterward. It could be a rock concert, but it is actually someone's funeral. At the epicenter of the band the air seems to thicken and boil, as streams of molten sound tumble into one another, jostling for supremacy. Each beat of the huge frame gong is felt in the body as much as heard by the ears; the heart thrills to the brilliant clash of the paired cymbals, shot through from moment to moment by the sweet rising tones of the hand gong. Meanwhile, two slim sticks dance balletically on the bald pate of the single-skinned drum. Dance is the word. The movements are visual as well as sonic, signaling the other musicians in a supple staccato punctuated by silent gesticulations and underpinned by the direct rhythmic tattoo of the low-pitched barrel drum or its flat-toned, circular neighbor. But atop all this is the thick, vibrant keening of the massed double-reeds. Blown in near unison, they achieve a visceral resonance I can almost taste. Melodic phrases cascade out of the double-reed instruments, powered by robust circular breathing and a microcosm of swirling grace notes. This is indeed music to stir the soul, music to die to. (Field notes, September 10, 1999)

However imperfectly I could capture it in words, my moment-to-moment enjoyment of musical sound fueled my recognition of the dedication and skills of the *beiguan* musicians whom I had met at the Juleshe ensemble in Baifushequ, Jilong, North Taiwan. They appeared to have memorized vast tracts of technically demanding musical repertory, including numerous suites of up to an hour in length, an achievement about which they were quite nonchalant. Admiring the artistry of these humble experts, I wished both to join such a group to learn performance myself and to better understand *beiguan* through discussion, reflection, and contextual study. In fact, musical participation, human fellow-feeling, and analytic reflections effect a kind of circular process, each reinforced by its predecessor and inspiring more of the next in turn.

The rich personal and intellectual development spurred by such musical experiences is just one reason why ethnomusicologists, and educators more generally, argue that we should learn by doing whenever we possibly can. We can try this approach by learning to sing the first tune taught to newcomers at Baifushequ. This melody is called "Seven-Inch Lotus" ("Qi cun lian"; CD 3, Track 16) and it is often used in celebratory performances (Transcription 8.7). The lotus is a flower, but the piece is not a depiction of nature. Instead, its name is just a label that helps musicians remember which tune is which, each tune referred to by its own name. This practice is in line with a widespread tradition in Chinese music to reuse tunes in different musical situations.

CD 3:16

"Qi cun lian" ("Seven-Inch Lotus") (0:25). Performed by Wu Wanyi. Field recording by Jonathan Stock. Jilong, Taiwan, 1999.

TRANSCRIPTION 8.7 The *beiguan* tune "Seven-Inch Lotus" in staff notation.

cei gong liu u liu,　　xiang u liu gong liu　　cei, gong liu u liu gong　　cei, liu gong cei gong liu

xiang, gong cei xiang u liu　　xiang, gong cei xiang u xiang　　liu,　u liu u liu gong

"Seven-Inch Lotus" is fairly easy to sing, particularly in a group, although there are one or two wide leaps and memorizing the names of each pitch takes a little while. These names are actually notes in a Chinese notational system called *gongche. Gongche* is similar in principle to the Western do-re-mi system: Each symbol records a tone's position in the scale (that is, its relative pitch, not its absolute pitch), and the main overall function of the notation is to help people learn and recall tunes. Traditionally, *gongche* notation is written in columns, starting on the right-hand side (see Transcription 8.8).

The main characters in each column each represent one note. Markings in smaller print record metrical details and a few other details. Musicians learn by singing again and again from the score. In learning it in the classroom, the best way is for students to keep repeating the tune together, without paying attention to anyone else's mistakes. If necessary, someone can play the tune once or twice on an instrument so that the class can become familiar with its shape. Remember that vocal quality is not important—formal performances are instrumental, not vocal. Nor is exact pitch: I have heard one very good musician sing softly a fifth higher

TRANSCRIPTION 8.8
"Seven-Inch Lotus" in *gongche* notation.

than her ensemble colleagues because that pitch level suited her voice better. None of the other musicians gave any sign of complaint, although it would be distracting if everyone sang at different pitch levels at once. To help keep time, the musicians also beat the tabletop on the main beat of each metrical unit, waving on the off beat (see the Close Listening guide). Try singing it now with CD 3, Track 16.

Close Listening

"QI CUN LIAN" ("SEVEN-INCH LOTUS"), VOCAL VERSION

CD: 3:16

COUNTER NUMBER	COMMENTARY	
0:00	First rendition	Wu Wanyi sings through the notation, beating the start of each measure on the table top; another player warms up his reed in the background.
0:20	Start of a second rendition	Recording fades out after a few seconds.

Beiguan musicians try hard to be considerate to one another and to be inclusive in their performance activities. They see themselves as members of a community organization, and male members refer to one another as brothers. But they are also serious about their art, and every ensemble recognizes one or two senior players as teachers. It is their responsibility to maintain standards, as shown in this further extract from my field notes.

> Mr You, the teacher, stops the ensemble and scolds the young drummer for slipping up. The drummer looks contrite, hanging his head. Two of his friends leap to their feet. "It doesn't matter," one of them cries, "He's trying!" You shakes his head: "He's not memorized it properly. How can other people keep together with him like this?" Discussion ensued, although I suspect You had intended the question to be rhetorical. Everyone agreed they wanted to include the drummer in the forthcoming processional performance. The drummer admitted that he couldn't play the *suona* [double-reed] part either, so he couldn't transfer to that instead. It was decided that a more experienced player should take over, while the beginner sat nearby, imitating his movements closely and drumming onto the back of a nearby wind-player's chair. This would be his final chance to memorize the drum part if he wanted to perform publicly this time. (Field notes, August 3, 1999)

Once a tune is fully internalized—that is, it can be sung without reference to the notation—the musicians transfer it onto the ensemble's double-reed instrument, or *suona* (Figure 8.10). To do so, they need to convert the vocal melody into a full-scale instrumental piece. They add notes to fill any gaps in the melody (there is one after the fifth note of "Seven-Inch Lotus") and decorate the surface of the melody with grace notes. The percussionists add their parts too, which are taught through use of a second kind of notation, drum syllables that compress the essential features of the music's percussion patterns into a few **onomatopoeic syllables:** syllables that sound like the sounds they represent ("kuang" represents a strike of the large gong, for example, and "tak" a dry-sounding stoke on the single-skinned drum).

On CD 3, Track 17, we hear a performance of "Seven-Inch Lotus" by the Baifushequ musicians (Figure 8.10). See the Close Listening guide for more.

CD 3:17

"Qi cun lian" ("Seven-Inch Lotus") (1:47). Performed by Baifushequ Juleshe Beiguan Troupe. Field recording by Jonathan Stock. Jilong, Taiwan, 2001.

FIGURE 8.10

Members of Baifushequ Juleshe *beiguan* ensemble playing *suona*.

Jonathan P. J. Stock

Close Listening

"QI CUN LIAN" ("SEVEN-INCH LOTUS"), ENSEMBLE VERSION

CD 3:17

COUNTER NUMBER	SECTION	COMMENTARY
0:00	Percussion passage linking this tune to the preceding one	Begins with a slowly accelerating pattern on the barrel drum. The single-skinned drum joins in, with its distinctive high-pitched click. The cymbals and gongs pick up its cue. The cymbals play regular pulses in time with the single-skinned drum. The higher gong plays a partially syncopated pattern; the large gong reinforces every other beat of the cymbals. The leader slows the speed down to cue the wind instruments.
0:15	"Seven-Inch Lotus"	Gradual entrance of all the *suona*. The percussion continue, and a simple duple meter is established.
0:39	Second rendition	There is a slight increase in speed; small details differ in each rendition—note, for example, the second drummer switch briefly from barrel drum to bass drum at 0:56.
0:57	Third rendition	
1:16	Fourth rendition	
1:34	End pattern	The *suona* end by drawing out the first note of the tune followed by a note a step below. The percussion then provide a linking passage to the next tune.

Often, a *beiguan* group is affiliated with a local temple, which provides rehearsal space in return for the ensemble's participation in rites and processions. This was once common in mainland China and may now be returning in many areas, though the political suppression of religious activities there in much of the second half of the twentieth century hit ritual musics particularly hard. In Taiwan, *beiguan* musicians will approach successful businessmen and ask them to act as heads of troupes, providing funding to support the ensemble's activities and regularly inviting all members to dine or socialize together, thereby cementing human relations within the group as a whole.

Earlier, I mentioned the gentrification of the Jiangnan *sizhu* tradition as it turned from the entertainment music of low-class professionals into the repertory of respectable amateur enthusiasts. *Beiguan* offers similarities and contrasts in this regard. Members of the Baifushequ group are proud of their amateur status, and the music has roots in opera performance. But the opera from which *beiguan* emerged was performed primarily by the sons of the social elite for ritual display. In the last generation or two, opera performances have become rare, leaving the instrumental accompaniments as the main musical repertory. Many *beiguan* musicians today have manual trades: construction workers, market stall owners, taxi or truck drivers, and shop workers. The social elite in Taiwan are more likely to send their children for lessons in piano or violin than to apprentice them to a *beiguan* troupe these days, which they perceive as old-fashioned, working class, and associated primarily with rural funerals.

Opera and Ballad Traditions

In this section we compare two narrative forms, *jingju* (Beijing opera) and **Suzhou** *tanci* (Suzhou ballad-singing). Narrative forms in China range from storytelling with little or no musical setting to fully staged opera with large amounts of singing and acrobatics. There are now several hundred distinct traditions across the whole of China. The two genres to be discussed illustrate the great range within this broad category.

JINGJU (BEIJING OPERA)

In our look at *jingju,* we will focus on the speech and singing typical of the *qingyi* role. A *qingyi* is a serious heroine, and good actresses are reputed not only for their vocal powers but also for their evocative use of stance and gesture, which an audio recording obviously cannot capture. I have selected an excerpt with relatively little stage movement so that less is lost overall. However, you will gain a deeper appreciation of *jingju* if you see it performed live or on film. (Several internationally distributed Chinese films contain excerpts of *jingju.* For example, *Farewell My Concubine* follows the lives of two singers caught up in the great social changes of the mid-twentieth century.)

The recorded excerpt from the drama *Third Wife Teaches Her Son* occurs when the heroine Wang Chun'e introduces herself and her difficulties since her husband's death. Men in Confucian society were permitted multiple wives, who were expected not to remarry after their husband's death. In this opera, however, wives one and two have quickly remarried, leaving the dutiful Chun'e to bring up her husband's son by one of the other wives. Wang Chun'e is played by the actress Li Shiji. Li is a singer of the Cheng school of performance, which means that she favors a lyrical, graceful style modeled on that of Cheng Yanqiu (1904–1958), a male actor famous for his female impersonations. (In other words, Li is a woman who imitates a man who imitates a woman.) CD 4, Track 1, provides a few phrases of a kind of musical speech and then the start of a song (see also Transcription 8.9).

CD 4:1

Sanniang jiao zi (Third Wife Teaches Her Son), excerpt (4:33). Performed by Li Shiji and the Beijing Jingju Troupe. *Sanniang jiao zi.* 1962. China Record Company HD-128.

TRANSCRIPTION 8.9
Two lines of *erhuang manban* from *Third Wife Teaches Her Son* as performed by Li Shiji.

TRANSCRIPTION 8.9
(*continued*)

Text	
THIRD WIFE TEACHES HER SON	[1] Wang Chun'e, leave the sewing room, thinking and sighing to myself. Recalling my deceased husband, I am deeply grieved.

The remarks in the Close Listening guide present what Chinese musicians would call the "pitch skeleton" of the *erhuang manban* tune as performed by a *qingyi* singer. Although E♭ is the first note of the scale employed, the most important tone is actually B♭, the fifth degree of that scale. Many phrases begin and end with B♭, and they all involve its alternation with other significant notes (E♭ and C). We can make a distinction between scale and mode here, the *scale* being the set of notes and the *mode* being the particular weighting of them employed in this case that treats B♭ as the overall target pitch for this music.

In the past, tunes like *erhuang* were reused from one drama to another—the idea of hiring a composer to write each new opera gained influence in China only

Close Listening

SANNIANG JIAO ZI ("THIRD WIFE TEACHES HER SON"), EXCERPT

CD 4:1

COUNTER NUMBER	SECTION	LYRICS	COMMENTARY
0:00	Declamatory speech		The usual speech tones of Chinese are heightened to produce a theatrical effect.
0:28	Instrumental introduction		Start of Transcription 8.9. The tune is *erhuang manban* (slow-beat *erhuang*), one recognized by accustomed listeners for its expressive qualities. The lead accompaniment instrument is the *jinghu,* a small two-stringed fiddle with a forceful tone. Other instruments can be heard. Underneath its highly decorated surface, the instrumental introduction continually returns to emphasize B♭.

Line 1 of the song text

COUNTER NUMBER	SECTION	LYRICS	COMMENTARY
1:04	Measures 10–11, first vocal phrase		
		Wang Chun'e	Vocalist and fiddle player track each other closely, although they sometimes differ in details and the fiddle player continues when the vocalist breaks off to rest. The phrase starts and ends on B♭.
1:19	Measures 12–14, second vocal phrase	*zuo caotang*	Leads from B♭ up to E♭.
1:41	Instrumental interlude		Percussionist plays more elaborate rhythms when the singer rests. B♭-dominated.
2:01	Measures 18–24, third vocal phrase	*zi si zi tan*	Reiterates the overall B♭ to E♭ shape of phrase 2, but then, to reinforce the sad mood of the lyrics, there is a fall from E♭ to a new emphasis on C.

2:50	Instrumental interlude		Returns emphasis to B♭.
Line 2 of the song text			
3:20	Measures 29–38	*Xiang qi le wo di fu hao bu canran*	Alternates emphasis of B♭ and C. E♭ is occasionally substituted by D, a tone that nearly always falls back to C rather than rising up to E♭ as it might in Western music.

from the mid-twentieth century. Reusing music allowed performers to avoid unpaid rehearsal time, and it also encouraged them to develop multiple versions of each tune to better express the needs of the scene in question. Thus, there are fast versions of *erhuang*, free-meter versions, and so on, each of which shares the outline just introduced (or varies it in a patterned way) and adds a distinct set of surface features.

In *jingju*, onstage characters are classified according to role type: *sheng* male, *dan* female, *jing* painted-face, and *chou* clown. There are subcategories within each type: for example, the *dan* designation includes the *qingyi* (as in our example), *wudan* (military woman), *huadan* (flirtatious maid), *laodan* (elderly woman), and *caidan* (comic woman), among others. Conventions for costumes and makeup vary according to the role type and are often elaborate and expensive, requiring considerable skill in their correct application prior to performance (see Figure 8.11). These identify the role type to accustomed viewers.

Though *Jingju*'s costuming and makeup are rich, scenery and stage props are often simple, the former consisting perhaps of only a table and two chairs. With the aid of various drapes, these simple objects represent settings from a mountain pass to a courtroom, a palace, a bedchamber, or an inn. Up to the mid-twentieth century, troupes were often migratory, traveling from place to place to perform. As such, it made sense that they took with them only the most basic scenic props.

FIGURE 8.11

Cao Man fixes her head-dress prior to performing the *wudan* role of Green Snake.

M. Azadehfar

But explanations for this are not purely logistical. *Jingju* combines four basic expressive means: singing, speech, acting, and fighting (*chang, nian, zuo,* and *da*). Singing and speech embrace a range of modes of voice production, from melismatic arias to the declamation of poems and everyday conversational speech. Acting and fighting cover a gamut extending from facial expressions to postures, gestures, mime, and choreographed fighting and acrobatics. Each role type draws distinctly on these four expressive means—as a serious heroine, the *qingyi* is normally a specialist in singing and speech, with important acting skills but little scope to fight. Elaborate stage props would limit the chance for performers to display their skills in mime or acrobatics.

The professionals who took part in opera performance in imperial China were much admired for their skill but held low status. Some, male and female alike, engaged in prostitution, and officials regularly condemned opera performances as rowdy occasions that encouraged gambling and debauchery. At times, legal restrictions on mixed troupes led performers to form male-only or female-only troupes. In these cases, some actors or actresses specialized in the impersonation of characters of the other gender. In modern times, some of the most famous singers were men who took female roles, for example, Mei Lanfang (1894–1961) and Cheng Yanqiu.

Touring troupes vied for employment at urban theaters and teahouses, aristocratic residences, village fairs, and temples. A wide range of occasions called for opera—from birthday celebrations and funerals to agricultural rites, religious festivals, and clan anniversaries. As a result, operas frequently projected a moral message, presenting tales that promoted Confucian virtues such as filial duty and female chastity, as in the example here. The performance of a single story could stretch over several days.

Several significant developments occurred in the twentieth century. The rise of the recording and broadcasting industries, starting in the 1920s, allowed actors to discover something of the musical and dramatic styles of their distant counterparts, and audiences began to select entertainment from a much broader spectrum than before. Some opera ensembles adopted Western musical instruments, and the opening of Western-style theaters led to the greater use of purpose-built scenery and props. Specialist directors, scriptwriters, and, by the 1940s, composers were employed to provide new dramatic materials. Developing a tendency already present in certain regional styles, some of the new operas explored contemporary social themes, although historical settings predominated.

After the founding of the People's Republic in 1949, the Chinese Communist Party called for an increase in the number of operas with contemporary themes and working-class characters, as opposed to those peopled with historical heroes and villains, and for some years during the Cultural Revolution only a small number of "model operas" could be performed. The music of these dramas largely resembled that of preceding decades, but the stories described Chinese revolutionary struggles and the war against Japan (1937–1945). In fact, Mao Zedong remained a considerable fan of traditional opera. One official who had worked then at the Ministry of Culture told me how he had produced traditional opera tapes for Mao's private listening, sometimes calling performers in to make new recordings. The actors were very frightened, since Mao's government had forbidden performance of those dramas at this time. After the end of the Cultural Revolution in 1976, the presentation of mythical and historical tales (or newly written stories with a historical setting) resumed, with contemporary settings largely left to other genres.

SUZHOU *TANCI* (SUZHOU BALLAD SINGING)

A similarly complex historical background underlies Suzhou *tanci*. After emerging from a series of older ballad-singing genres, the tradition in Suzhou underwent a three-way split during the mid-nineteenth century:

- Male storytellers dominated the public teahouses, enlivening their renditions with jokes and spicy love stories. Even a subject as simple as climbing the stairs could lead to ribald remarks: the male character might ask the female character whether she would like the man to go up on top or prefer him to come up from behind.

- A new class of women performers arose. These were highly cultivated courtesans, prized for their artistic and musical aptitude as well as their beauty; their performances occurred in private for their patrons.

- Publishing *tanci* scripts became popular and profitable. Authors wrote scripts not for live performance but to be savored as literature by the nonperforming connoisseur.

By the 1930s, *tanci* was a primary form of entertainment across East China; judging from its share of radio airtime, it appealed to more people than any other musical genre did. But over the next fifty years, *tanci* gradually slipped from prominence. Today it is a specialist interest sustained largely by dedicated enthusiasts, among them the American historian Carlton Benson (see Figure 8.12). Exactly why this decline occurred seems not to have been fully analyzed yet. Educational change promoted the use of Mandarin Chinese rather than regional dialects, and many Chinese began to look to new forms of entertainment, such as film, television, and popular music. Also, the political climate became at times highly unsympathetic to traditions that focused on the past and to the bawdy, improvised humor of the teahouse. There is an analogy to be drawn with the rapid rebuilding of Suzhou in recent years. The city was once famous for its elegant gardens and canals, which are still there but now hard to find amid the large-scale concrete and glass of Suzhou's contemporary cityscape.

Suzhou *tanci* is most often performed by a single musician who speaks, sings, and plays a musical instrument, usually a three-stringed, long-necked *sanxian* or possibly the four-stringed lute *pipa*. Sometimes, multiple musicians perform together, in which case the additional players accompany while the first sings. The storyteller may also make hand gestures, rap the tabletop with a woodblock, or wave a fan, but he or she normally remains seated beside a table while performing rather than getting up to act out the story.

The accompanying recording (CD 4, Track 2) features Zhang Jianting (1909–1984; Figure 8.13), who sings an excerpt from "Scholar Qian: Yanda Looks in the

FIGURE 8.12

Carlton Benson (with *sanxian*) gives a *tanci* performance at an amateur club in Shanghai in 1993.

CD 4:2

"Qian xiucai: Yanda zhao jing" ("Scholar Qian: Yanda Looks in the Mirror"), excerpt (1:25). Performed by Zhang Jianting. *Pingtan: Zhang Jianting chang-duan jing pin.* 1962. Shanghai Audio Book Company X-4012.

Close Listening

"QIAN XIUCAI: YANDA ZHAO JING"
("SCHOLAR QIAN: YANDA LOOKS IN THE MIRROR")

CD 4:2

COUNTER NUMBER	SECTION	COMMENTARY
0:00	Speech	Zhang speaks in the local dialect and rough tones of a comic character, and the audience responds warmly to his witty description; he warms up his fingers on the *sanxian*.
0:29	Start of the *sanxian* music	Listen to the 5-beat pattern in the instrumental accompaniment at 0:33. Like many originally improvisatory musics worldwide, *tanci* music relies greatly on the use and reuse of short phrases. It is constructed mainly from the tones D, F#, and A (or do-mi-sol in the mode of the excerpt). It recurs in various transformations: Some last just three beats whereas others last five—using units of five and three gives rhythmic syncopation to the flow of the music, which is in quadruple meter.
0:42	Entrance of the voice	There are two phrases, A and B, which alternate in varied form as the singing progresses, with short instrumental interludes. There are relatively fixed positions for the lyrics in each phrase so that different texts can be performed to the same tune.

Mirror," a short, humorous story concerning a man who notices his own reflection for the first time in twenty years and is shocked not to find the handsome, trendy young man of his youth.

The accompaniment figure here is constructed mainly from the tones D, F#, and A. This is a major triad, and is quite standard in Western music but uncommon in Chinese melodies. Four versions are marked with brackets in Transcription 8.10.

Zhang was one of Suzhou *tanci*'s preeminent musicians, and his career typifies those of many professional musicians in mid-twentieth century China. Zhang began by gaining experience in several of the popular entertainment forms of his youth. His professional career began at age nine, when he traveled from one village to another with his uncle, disseminating ballads on religious themes. Over the next several years he performed in operatic and ballad genres across East China, including *jingju*, mastering several dialects and

FIGURE 8.13

Zhang Jianting from a cassette cover.

TRANSCRIPTION 8.10
Sample pattern of accompaniment. Recorded pitch is slightly lower than notated.

learning much new melodic material. That he chose to develop an adult career in *tanci* was due to that genre's public prominence, which drew skillful musicians from other genres. The best performers in this style competed for attention and reputation at venues in Shanghai and other large cities in the region. Competition drove stylistic innovation, with performers introducing new features to stand out from their rivals. Radio also facilitated change, allowing *tanci* musicians to be broadcast directly into the homes of thousands of listeners. Domestic daytime listeners included many women who would have felt uncomfortable in the male-dominated atmosphere of the teahouses, and competition for this audience influenced the content and format of the performances in turn.

By the formation of the People's Republic in 1949, Zhang had become a major star. He was a founder member of a leading state-run troupe in 1951 and developed several new *tanci* on revolutionary themes at this time. He also revised the classical repertory he had inherited, developing new versions of many of these stories. In this process he drew on his wide study of other traditions. He is particularly noted for having formed a musical style that is highly melodic, emotionally direct, clear in enunciation, and imbued with the vigorous timbre of the painted-face vocal role from *jingju*. In his later years, experts began to speak of the Zhang school of performance, referring to his particular combination of vocal, instrumental, and interpretative style, which many performers of following generations imitated.

Opera and ballad traditions saw some of their greatest development and sharpest decline in the twentieth century. Many genres that dominated mainstream performance venues and the airwaves two generations ago survive presently only as niche entertainments for enthusiasts. In fact, some of the expressive skills built up in these genres have been transferred to new media, most obviously, the acrobatic style of fighting as applied in such Chinese films as *Crouching Dragon, Hidden Tiger*, directed by Ang Lee (2000). But the traditional opera and ballad performances themselves still repay attentive listening and viewing. Even without understanding the lyrics, we can appreciate the smooth blending of skills—vocal, instrumental, visual, gestural, and so forth—that make a top-level performance successful.

Solo Instrumental Traditions

One of the most famous *tanci* tales is *The Tale of the Western Chamber,* which concerns a young woman who plays the seven-stringed zither *qin* while thinking about the man with whom she has just fallen in love. In the Chinese imagination, however, the *qin* is usually a vehicle for more spiritual reflections. Here is a poem from Wang Wei (699–759; cited by DeWoskin 1982:145) that captures the classical image of the role of the instrument (see also Figure 8.14):

> Sitting alone in the dense bamboo groves,
> I strum my *qin* and accompany with long whistles;
> No one to see this deep in the trees,
> Only the bright moon appears to shine.

FIGURE 8.14

Detail from Zhao Ji's painting *Listening to the* qin.

ZITHER (QIN) SOLOS

The *qin* (also called *guqin*) has an ancient design (a modern *qin* appears in Figures 8.16 and 8.17). Seven-stringed zithers date from over two thousand years ago, and those with different numbers of strings existed even earlier, as we have seen. The *qin* consists of a convex length of wood, narrower at one end than the other. A baseboard, into which two sound holes have been cut, is fixed underneath, leaving a small hollow cavity between the two boards as resonating chamber. Makers use old, well-seasoned wood, which produces the best resonance. While selling me a *qin,* the Shanghai-based player Dai Xiaolian told me that the particular instrument she was offering used wood from an old coffin. Catching my surprised look she added, "Don't worry, they clean it first."

Whatever their prior use, the boards are fitted together and coated with a dark lacquer. The seven strings, which differ in thickness, are looped around two feet near the narrower end of the *qin* and drawn across the length of the front board before passing over a low bridge toward the other end. Each string then passes through a hole drilled in the board and is secured by a tuning peg on the underside. Decorative tassels are often attached to the pegs. Traditionally, the strings were made of silk, but recent decades have seen metal strings substituted in China's music conservatories. These are more durable and give a louder tone, but some musicians prefer the timbre of silk strings, and some enthusiasts still employ them today. Alongside the strings lies a row of thirteen inlaid studs. These function as a guide to the performer, showing where to stop the strings. Nearly every part of the *qin* is given a symbolic name. For instance, the two sound holes on the underside of the instrument are know as "dragon pool" and "phoenix pond," respectively, a selection that implies a male-female dualism. The square-shaped and rounded pillars that attach the baseboard to the top board represent earth and heaven, respectively—earth has its bounds, whereas heaven stretches on without end.

Although its design is simple, the *qin* is rich in timbres. The strings can be plucked singly, plucked in combination, strummed one after another, and played both open and stopped. Harmonics are sounded by lightly stopping a string while plucking it. The instrument is also rubbed, tapped, and struck by the fingers, and experts claim to be able to produce as many as sixty different kinds of vibrato by moving the finger that stops a string. Different plucking techniques (described later) and slides add further sonic variety.

We can see much sonic variety in the recorded example, which is the third variation and coda of "Three Variations on Yang Pass" (CD 4, Track 3; see also Transcription 8.11; another player's performance occurs in Yung 2002:162–4). Like many *qin* pieces, it is generally performed solo, although there are also songs with *qin* and duos with the vertical bamboo flute *xiao*. The piece's whole musical structure— a very short introduction, three main sections (which successively develop and extend the same musical material), and then a coda with a free-meter feel and use of harmonics—also makes it representative of *qin* music more widely (see the Close Listening guide). Larger pieces typically have more sections and vary musical material from one section to the next but are otherwise similar in many respects.

CD 4:3

"Yangguan san die" ("Three Variations on Yang Pass"), third variation and coda (1:55). Performed by Wang Tingting, *qin*. Field recording by Jonathan Stock. Sheffield, UK, 2005.

TRANSCRIPTION 8.11
Final section of "Three Variations on Yang Pass" for *qin*.

For much of its extensive history the *qin* was associated with the elite scholar-officials who governed the Chinese empire. These administrators, often referred to as the literati, included many highly cultivated amateur musicians.

Close Listening

"YANGGUAN SAN DIE" ("THREE VARIATIONS ON YANG PASS")

CD 4:3

COUNTER NUMBER	SECTION	COMMENTARY
0:00	Mini introduction	Uses harmonics—note that the music is very soft. (This is disguised on some recordings by putting the microphone close to the instrument—play this track as softly as you dare.)
0:07	Start of third variation	Switches to normal tones—note also the legato sound (multiple tones coming from one pluck) and the alternation of high and low tones. The music is in free time—it has a regular pace, but there may not be an equal number of beats in each phrase.
0:32		Speed increases. The music is lower pitched overall and gains an insistent quality—this is the most impassioned part of the piece.
0:47		Notes are played here in pairs (B♭, B♭; D, D; C, C) with a different playing technique the second time— it might be played on an open string first and then on a stopped string, or plucked softly and then plucked strongly with a fingernail, or played cleanly once and then approached with a slide.
1:09		Passage where each tone is plucked simultaneously on two strings at once. Then, speed decreases.
1:33	Coda	Harmonics

As an amateur pastime, the *qin* was played either alone for self-cultivation or among a small group of like-minded friends. Even today, some *qin* players call their meetings *yaji,* "elegant gatherings." For this reason, the *qin* was never subject to pressure, until recently, to produce a louder volume in order to entertain a massed audience. Instead, and even when the instrument is placed on a specially designed table that acts as an amplifier, the player remains the one who hears the music the best.

The literati brought to the *qin* several ideals from their broader societal setting. Poetry and music were combined as *qin* songs, the music of which was designed to bring out the inner spirit of the poetic text. Calligraphy interfaced with *qin* performance. *Qin* techniques were directly stimulated by the hand postures and brush strokes of Chinese calligraphy, and aesthetic dualisms such as movement-stillness or solidity-emptiness were transferred to the musical domain. Since so many performers of the instrument were expert writers who were used to commenting explicitly on the aesthetic qualities of their artworks, it is not surprising that they developed both a sophisticated notational system for the *qin* and a substantial body of accompanying knowledge in the form of paintings, essays, poems, and instructional books.

Like paintings, many *qin* pieces centered on historical or programmatic scenes. Famous examples include "Flowing Waters" and "Geese Landing on a Sandy Beach." Other pieces attempted to capture occurrences from the emotional world of the literati. "Three Variations on Yang Pass" drew on a poem by Wang Wei to portray the feelings of parting friends. One has been assigned to a post in a distant region, and they recognize that they may never meet again. Their emotions become successively less restrained with each of the three final cups of wine they take together.

Music like this is written in a score called *jianzipu* (literally, "abbreviated-character notation"). *Jianzipu* scores are conventionally laid out in columns starting on the right-hand side of the page, like classical Chinese writing. Each column consists of a series of symbols, many of them derived from Chinese characters, that tell the performer which string to pluck, how to pluck it, where to stop the string, which stopping technique to employ, and what ornamentation to add, if any. Figure 8.15 shows an example. In the central lower part of the symbol is the Chinese number 2: 二 (*er*). This tells us to play string 2. Curving around this indication is an abbreviated version of the Chinese word for hook: 勹 (from 钩 *gou*). This informs us to employ the right-hand middle finger to pluck string 2 inward toward the body. The upper left element is the character 大 (*da*, big), which means the left-hand thumb must stop string 2. Finally, the Chinese number 7 (七, *qi*) appears at top right: string 2 should be stopped at the 7th stud (which is exactly halfway along its length). Distinct string tunings are used in different pieces, but often the strings are tuned to C (two octaves below middle C), D, F, G, A, c, and d. If so, the note produced here is actually D below middle C.

Generally speaking, the right hand is used to pluck or strum the strings near the bridge of a *qin*. Any of the right-hand digits can be called on to pluck a string. The resulting timbre reflects the amount of nail or flesh that strikes the string as well as the force and direction of the finger or thumb. Meanwhile, the left hand moves up, down, and across the surface of the instrument as necessary to produce stops, slides, and vibrato. Occasionally, a left-hand pluck occurs as a special effect. The hands of Wang Tingting, the performer on CD 4, Track 3, are shown in Figure 8.16; she appears more completely in Figure 8.17.

Some books claim that *qin* notation "lacks" indications of rhythmic duration. This is partially true, but *jianzipu* is better thought of as a complete system in its own right. In fact, rhythmic durations are important in *qin* music, but that does not mean that they have to be fixed in writing. When *qin* players learn, they generally approach a senior musician for lessons. They also gather books of music in tablature and study the accompanying essays that describe the artistic image and technical details of each composition. Relying on their experience, some *qin* performers use a process known as *da pu* (literally, "beating the score") to generate their own realizations of compositions; others gradually depart from

FIGURE 8.15

A sample *jianzipu* symbol.

Jonathan P. J. Stock

FIGURE 8.16

The hands of a *qin* player.

Jonathan P. J. Stock

FIGURE 8.17

Wang Tingting playing the *qin*.

their teacher's version to a more personal rendition over time. Bell Yung (2002:161) counted thirty-three different versions of "Three Variations on Yang Pass" in scores dating from 1491 to 1922. The musician, then, brought both literary and oral knowledge to the act of reading *qin* music, as well as the expectation that he or she had some scope to invent a personal interpretation. The omission of rhythmic detail in *jianzipu* scores left room for this creative flexibility.

Today, few people play the *qin*. The scholar-administrators whose emblem it was are long gone, swept away in revolutions and political reorganizations a century ago, and this restrained, sensitive, and flexible solo music seems out of place in today's fast-paced, energetic China. As the *qin* expert Liang Mingyue says,

> The small volume of the *qin* stimulates the development of one's subjective auditory sensibility by means of concentration. In fact, there may be a real problem in that today's industrial surroundings, which are full of people and noises, have made us insensitive to a lower sound volume, and that our ancestors of a thousand or more years ago had a more acute sense of hearing than present-day listeners. Therefore, listening with increased concentration and cultivating the "way of the *qin*," that is, listening with the ear, the heart and the mind, has as much relevance today as it did two thousand years ago. (Liang 1985:211)

What Liang is saying is that learning to listen to the *qin* is potentially very rewarding indeed, drawing us into a special space of heightened sensitivity. Of course, this is not the only music worldwide that can do this. Other examples of musics that invite close listening include many string quartets, Scots fiddle tunes designed "for listening," contemporary electroacoustic compositions, and the "songs of contemplation" performed by Gbaya men in the Central African Republic. (The wide geographic distribution of these examples reminds us to remain wary of such stereotypes as the passive, mystical East; active, rational West; or energetic, body-driven Africa.) Certainly, learning to listen very carefully is a precondition for many kinds of heightened musical experiences. The soft refinement of the *qin* emphasizes this quality in a particularly outstanding way.

A further pair of instrumental solos illustrates a trend in new music in the twentieth century that accompanied the major social changes mentioned earlier. The first is for a Chinese stringed instrument, the two-stringed fiddle *erhu*, and was composed by Liu Tianhua (1895–1932). The second is a piano piece by Liao Shengjing (b. 1930). These two solos exemplify what is sometimes called "national music" (*guoyue*), a style like so many in the twentieth-century world that drew on aspects of Western means while attempting to preserve and develop national musical content as an alternative to Western music (see Stock 2004). *Guoyue* includes ensemble pieces and those for a full orchestra of Chinese instruments, but here we will only look at solo pieces within this category. Strictly speaking, many Chinese would put music for Western instruments outside the bounds of national music, but I include a piano solo here because the national music played on Chinese instruments and the Chinese compositions written for Western instruments overlap significantly. The example also reminds us that China has served as a significant center for the composition and consumption of Western music for the last eighty or more years.

Early national music solos were often very similar to traditional creations such as "Great Waves Washing the Sand" which we met at the start of this chapter. Yet, as these pieces became fixed in detailed notation (earlier *gongche* scores recorded the main outline of the piece only), they became more and more identified with the authoritative figure of a composer or arranger, as in Western classical music. Instruments were redesigned to produce greater volume and cover a wider range, and musicians used them to perform in the contemporary contexts of the recital, recording studios, broadcasts, and Western-style classes at schools and music conservatories. Some of the students in these institutions even came to look down on their forebears outside the conservatories, dismissing their performances as crude and out of tune. Our discussion of the *qin* emphasized the importance of learning to listen closely, but this point was missed by the 1930s musician Ying Shangneng: "The 7-chord *ch'in* [*qin*] has hardly any sound at all. No wonder, therefore, in the annals of Chinese music, there is no Beethoven or Schubert" (Jones 2001:39). As this patronizing comment suggests, musicians like Ying were unaware of the characteristics of the traditions they were turning away from.

Critics of hybridized musics like national music point out that in music "means" and "content" are not easily separated. Redesigning an instrument to play in equal temperament strips away some of its distinctive character and charm, and training players intensively to read notation and follow a conductor may mean they do not develop oral learning, memorization, or improvisatory skills. Successful national styles can obscure and even threaten well-formed local traditions, leading to fears of musical impoverishment, cultural "grey-out," as Alan Lomax once put it (1968:4). Yet these critics can overstate the case, too: Is it really fair for us to describe Chinese musicians who adopt staff notation and Western harmonies, African musicians who use the synthesizer, or folk musicians with electric guitars, as culturally "inauthentic"? Is it not possible that skilled and thoughtful musicians will be original and creative with the new means they have adopted? For their part, the musicians concerned may see the adoption of technology such as the electric guitar or staff notation as no more than an essential process of keeping up with the times. In exploring music-cultures, we have to pay careful attention to what people say and do in the new social contexts thrown up by intercultural contact, just as in other musical situations, since only when we understand people's intentions can we see why they produce, value, and consume music in the ways that they do.

ERHU SOLOS

The *erhu* is a present-day version of a two-stringed fiddle believed to have been imported along the Silk Road. Exactly when this instrument reached China remains unclear, but accounts of what may be early bowed instruments appear from the eleventh century onward. Perhaps the world's earliest music encyclopedia, Chen Yang's *Book of Music* (the *Yue shu,* completed in 1101), described such an instrument as played by members of the Xi tribe, nomads from the Northwest who had later settled in central China. The two-stringed fiddle proliferated in numerous varieties over the next millennium in China, many instruments using local materials. The dominant consideration was tone quality: For instance, the strident *jinghu* was tailored to provide a counterpart to the voice in the noisy theaters where Beijing opera was performed. Versions of the instrument were also found in many traditional music ensembles and taken up by beggars as well.

In the early years of the twentieth century, a large-scale movement of cultural reform began; those involved believed that China's "unscientific" culture was holding it back, and yet they were strongly nationalistic and did not wish to simply discard Chinese culture. In the sphere of music, reformist musicians applied what they had learned about Western instruments to Chinese music, creating new fusions in the process. For example, in the 1920s Lü Wencheng (1898–1981), one of the originators of an urban entertainment genre called Cantonese music, replaced the higher-pitched of the two silk strings on his own small-sized *erhu* with a violin's E-string. Cantonese music was fashionable, and *erhu* players in other Chinese cities followed Lü's innovation, finding the steel string more durable and smoother in sound across the whole register. Variable tuning was largely superseded by the selection of d' and a' as standard pitches for the open strings, and larger-sized instruments were invented to act as viola, cello, and bass in the bowed string section of the modern Chinese orchestra. This shows how the idea of the violin as one of a family of instruments of different sizes was as influential as its specific performance techniques.

Liu Tianhua was one of the most prominent of the early twentieth-century national music reformists. He composed ten solos for *erhu* as well as one of the first sets of technical etudes for the instrument. He performed the solos in concerts and in radio broadcasts, and his pupils studied them at the small number of higher education courses in music that were then appearing at selected Chinese colleges and universities. Generally speaking, Liu's solos are like their traditional predecessors for *pipa* or *qin,* being short, sectional compositions with pictorial titles. Fingering patterns are mostly conventional, allowing the players to add traditional-style decorations, such as slides. Their novelty lay in the following: (1) the way in which notation showed every detail, (2) the use of new techniques (stopping the strings with the tips of the fingers, for example, and violin-style vibrato), (3) the use of Western musical ingredients (such as minor key and compound time), and, most of all, (4) Liu's playing of the pieces in new, elite settings.

In Transcription 8.12, we can see how Liu attempted to create elegant music that would distance this instrument from its association with beggars. The example shows the opening of *Festival Night Canzonetta,* a piece that refers to the Lunar New Year's Eve, when the whole family should draw together as one. Such occasions are joyful but potentially tinged with nostalgia for relatives no longer present or unavoidably absent. (This piece is not on the accompanying CD, but Liu's music is widely available on commercial recordings.)

TRANSCRIPTION 8.12
Liu Tianhua's *Festival Night Canzonetta,* measures 1–32.

PIANO SOLOS

Liao Shengjing's piano piece takes the same theme as Liu's composition, now transposed to the village sphere and entitled "The Joyous Festival of Lunar New Year's Day" (CD 4, Track 4). This is the first of *Twenty-four Preludes for Piano* subtitled *Chinese Rural Scenes in 24 Solar Terms* (see the Close Listening guide and Transcription 8.13).

From one point of view, Liao's piece exemplifies the socialist realist style that predominated in China from the 1940s until the early 1990s. The socialist realist movement, which Mao Zedong adopted from the Soviet Union, gave artists an important role in society. Their task was to inspire social change by providing positive images of the new society toward which reform aimed, perhaps contrasting these with negative images of the past. Art was not to be created for art's sake—this slogan was criticized as a smokescreen offered by middle-classes artists who wished to foist their own class-based values onto the ordinary

CD 4:4

"Li chun: Xinnian jiajie" ("The Joyous Festival of Lunar New Year's Day") (1:24). Liao Shengjing. Performed by Hsu Shuo-Wen, piano. Field recording by Jonathan Stock. Sheffield, UK, 2005.

Close Listening

"LI CHUN: XINNIAN JIAJIE" ("THE JOYOUS FESTIVAL OF LUNAR NEW YEAR'S DAY")

CD 4:4

COUNTER NUMBER	SECTION	PART (MEASURES)	COMMENTARY
0:00	A	First part (mm. 1–10 on Transcription 8.13)	Opening figure switches from simple to compound duple time in measure 5. Despite some chromatic notes, the music is in C major. According to a program note on the score, the music represents a village band merrily playing and people enjoying the festive atmosphere.
0:11		Second part (mm. 11–18)	Repeats and develops the earlier material.
0:21		Third part (mm. 19–24)	Repeats and develops the earlier material, this time without switching to compound duple meter.
0:28	B		Softer music with a shift to G minor.
0:53	A		Repeats section A. The first two parts are repeated exactly as before; the third part is modified to lead to a loud ending.

TRANSCRIPTION 8.13
Liao Shengjing's "The Joyous Festival of Lunar New Year's Day," measures 1–24.

people at large, thereby obstructing real social change. Instead, novels, movies, plays, poems, and music were to be open to the understanding of everyday people. For several decades, students and professionals in the arts were regularly sent to work on the land or in factories and barracks, seeking the comments and suggestions of ordinary people on draft versions of new compositions. The socialist realist style overlapped with national music in several ways; for example, the music had to express a Chinese theme and use the full range of modern methods and techniques while remaining accessible to ordinary listeners.

The happy village scene described in Liao's piece fits the requirement of providing a positive image of life under socialism. The short duration and simple ABA plan helps create music an untrained listener can immediately comprehend and follow. The same can be said of its predominantly tonal orientation.

From another perspective, though, the idea of writing solo piano music like this shows the composer's close ties to European classical music. There are sets of twenty-four piano preludes by Hummel, Chopin, and Debussy, the number twenty-four allowing the composer to explore each major and minor key in turn. (The equal-tempered piano, of course, is an ideal tool for this kind of exploration.) Liao's set is exploratory, too, but he employs not the twenty-four major and minor keys of Western music but a set of twenty-four pentatonic-based modes that he developed after investigating Chinese pentatonic modal systems in 1985. Liao's preludes reflect his search for a new system of composing music that is both inherently Chinese and also intrinsically modern. And while the title of our example prelude calls to mind the positive imagery important in social realism, the set as a whole points back to presocialist Chinese tradition: Each prelude takes the name of one of the twenty-four phases of the lunar calendar. Much music created in present-day China draws similarly on multiple sources of inspiration.

Religious Traditions

We have already met one specifically religious tradition, the music of the *beiguan* ensemble, and several of the other musics already described have connections with China's religious culture. This short section marks the continued existence—in some cases, the resurgence or transformation—of religious musics in China today.

Communist-led reforms in the middle years of the twentieth century considerably affected the large sphere of Buddhist music. Some reforms were positive, such as the new state supporting researchers who investigated and recorded Buddhist musicians. But many were negative. For example, a large-scale movement against superstition had monks persecuted and forcibly dismissed from their posts. Many temples today struggle to maintain their activities, which traditionally included large amounts of chanting and, in some cases, instrumental ensemble performance. Some ceremonies were large-scale, elaborate affairs that required numerous participants; an example is the Greater Water and Land Dharma Assembly, which could last over a week. Faced with Communist suppression, some monks moved to Taiwan, a migration that fired a renewal of Buddhist traditions there. A few Buddhists already in pre-Communist Shanghai had begun to disseminate a new kind of Buddhist art music outside the temples. In Taiwan a Buddhist music industry has arisen, and its commercial products now range from recordings of chants and rituals to New Age–inflected music and DVDs of large-scale dance extravaganzas.

Instead of delving further into Buddhist religious music, however, we look here at two smaller-scale examples that hint at the variety of religious music in the

Chinese world. The first is an excerpt from *Pasibutbut* singing from the Bunun people who inhabit central Eastern Taiwan. All the examples given so far have featured the music of the Han Chinese majority, so this excerpt contributes the sounds of one of the many ethnic minority groups across this region. Like many peoples worldwide who depend on agriculture and hunting (rather than trade) for their food, the Bunun have traditionally prayed for good harvests and good fortune in the hunt. Certain of these prayers have been enhanced by being set to music, and since both agriculture and hunting are group acts, the prayers are sung collectively.

CD 4, Track 5, is a short excerpt from the *Pasibutbut,* or *Prayer for a Rich Millet Harvest.* Sung in ritual agricultural or hunting contexts at the start of the New Year, the *Pasibutbut* involves some six or more men who don traditional robes and face inward, placing their arms around one another's backs (Figure 8.18). They may also revolve slowly as a group while singing. The overall pitch rises very slowly, and the music forms an offering designed to satisfy the Sky God, Dehanin. One Bunun singer told me in March 2006 that song should be "stable, like a mountain going up to the sky." The Bunun recognize four different vocal parts in the group, each of which can be taken by multiple singers and plays a distinct role in the musical prayer (see the Close Listening guide).

CD 4:5

Pasibutbut (Prayer for a Rich Millet Harvest), excerpt (1:15). Traditional Bunun chant. Performed by villagers from Mingde, Taiwan. Field recording by Wu Rung-Shun. *Bunong zhi ge.* 1993. Wind Records Co. Ltd. TCD1501.

Close Listening

PASIBUTBUT (PRAYER FOR A RICH MILLET HARVEST), EXCERPT

CD 4:5

COUNTER NUMBER	COMMENTARY
0:00	First voice enters with an "oh" sound, quickly followed by a second voice a fifth lower singing "eh."
0:06	Third voice enters to "oh," close in pitch to the first; a fourth voice enters singing "eh" a fifth above.
0:13	One voice sings an octave above the starting pitch, quickly falling back to a fifth above—this is a way of marking the climax of a phrase.
0:17	New series of entries; the overall pitch has now slipped up a semitone, one of the special characteristics of this singing style.
0:33	Notice the overlapping entries of voices—the music never falls completely silent.
0:58	A voice farther from the microphone marks the climax of a phrase; again the music slips up a semitone.

FIGURE 8.18

Bunun men from Haiduan district performing the *Pasibutbut*. Taidong, 2005.

C. Chou

Like many other Taiwanese aboriginal societies, the Bunun are now heavily influenced by Christian missionization, primarily evangelical, and according to some sources an estimated 25 percent of Taiwan's aborigines attend church. The Bunun village where I lived for two months has two churches, both well attended. However, it was clear that the church has not served merely as a force for change. The industrialization of Taiwan during the latter half of the twentieth century saw considerable numbers of younger aboriginals migrate to the towns and cities. There was little demand for speakers of aboriginal languages in those locations, and urban schools did not provide mother-language teachers until recently. Language loss among the younger generations has become a serious issue, and some village communities now lack the younger and middle generations so vital for social cohesion and cultural continuity. In this environment, churches have often become community-based cultural centers, using their premises for language education, the promotion of traditional music, and the sustenance of community spirit, as well as for direct Christianization through worship (see Mayuan 2005).

Christian churches are well established in many other parts of the Chinese world, too. If the Bunun example shows the church as an environment supporting wider cultural stability, the following example, from a Hong Kong–based Baptist church, demonstrates the indigenization of Christian music in East Asia. Western missionaries turned their attention to Hong Kong only after the island was ceded to Britain following the Opium War in 1841. Church music was introduced as a means of encouraging converts (and any other listeners) to memorize religious texts that explained tenets of the Christian faith. At first, Chinese musicians did not participate in the creation of new hymns. Instead, new texts were set to well-known local tunes, or Chinese words were fit to Western melodies provided by the missionaries.

This was a challenging task in that the speech tones of the lyrics had to match the rise and fall of the melody if the words were to be clearly discerned. The Hong Kong church musician Hera Tang (2005:66) provides an example of the confusion that might arise in these situations. In one song she found the words "Lord's

CD 4:6

"Tindei jaan mei" ("Praise from Heaven and Earth") (1:16). Music by Joseph Chi. Lyrics by Chor-ping Chang. Performed by Cherith Baptist Church. Field recording by Hera Tang. Hong Kong, China. 2005.

heart" set to a low, level melodic phrase. The meaning is clear when it is sung in Mandarin Chinese, but if sung in Cantonese, the dialect spoken in Hong Kong, the words sound like "pig's heart."

To avoid this problem, Hong Kong Christians have increasingly written their own hymns and praise songs, a process assisted by the appearance over the past several decades of institutions offering music training in the city. Joseph Chi's "Praise from Heaven and Earth" (CD 4, Track 6) forms a specific example (see the Close Listening guide and Transcription 8.14).

Close Listening

"TINDEI JAAN MEI" ("PRAISE FROM HEAVEN AND EARTH")

CD 4:6

COUNTER NUMBER	SECTION	LYRICS AND MEASURES	COMMENTARY
0:00	A	Verse 1; mm. 1–6: *Dei yu hoi . . .* (romanized according to Cantonese pronunciation)	Three kinds of snappy rhythms with offbeat syncopations give the hymn a strong Christian praise song flavor (m. 1 beats 1–2, m. 3 beats 3–4, and m. 5). The hymn sets a whole phrase of text to each measure until the final phrase of each verse, which is extended—this gives the song's pace variety and fits closely with the song text.
0:20	A'	Verse 2; repeat of 1–6, going on to 8: *Jung jaan sing . . .*	Note that the song is largely syllabic in nature—one note per syllable; compare it with the folk song in Transcription 8.4 or the *jingju* in Transcription 8.9. This puts an emphasis on the words as a text that listeners are supposed to hear clearly, as well as helping the congregation to sing together.
0:43	BA"	Verse 3; end of 8–17 *Yeung jaanmei . . .*	The text demonstrates some elements of rhyme (*mei-fei-mei-hei* in mm. 9–12, for instance). Reuse of the A material from measure 13 on means the song can be learned quickly. The song's range covers just an octave and a third, avoiding notes too high or too low for the majority of the congregation. These characteristics suit it for church use, where there is little rehearsal time and a need to vary songs by season and theme.

TRANSCRIPTION 8.14
Hymn "Praise from Heaven and Earth" by Joseph Chi.

Let the earth and sea proclaim a song of praise,
Let the sky and the rocks sing their praises,
Wind, rain and lightning also sing out,
The clouds and mist send forth a eulogy,
Let all the earth make a powerful sound beyond compare.

The sounds of praise will never wane,
The whole earth bows in reverence,
Sing to God in the highest,
Glory without limit,
Everything of my Lord reveres Jesus.

Let the praises fly forth like the wind on the sea,
Let the praises rise up like the ripples around a boat on the sea,
Sing to God in the highest,
Glory without limit,
Everything of my Lord reveres Jesus!

Text
"PRAISE FROM HEAVEN AND EARTH"

At first hearing, this is much like a Western song of praise, with only the Cantonese lyrics pointing to its place of origin. Yet such a song's "non-Chinese" musical language can be interpreted locally exactly as proof of its aptness for use in Hong Kong. As the pastor and choir advisor Alep Gung comments,

I do not like the church music in Chinese style and I do not think that this style represents our cultural identity. I think pop music can show such identity because it has taken a main part in Hong Kong's musical mainstream in the past decades. Chinese music is only a small part, and not a popular style in Hong Kong. (Tang 2005:96)

Nevertheless, even a song like this one employs Chinese cultural features, as its lyrics particularly show. The hymn starts with lines of seven syllables, the most usual line structure in classical Chinese poetry, and its opening image in the words *Dei yu hoi* (literally, "earth and sea") is a typically Chinese construct suggesting the combination of opposites. We can compare it with the yin and yang dualism or with the title of the Buddhist Water and Land rite mentioned briefly at the start of this section. Later imagery (ripples around a boat on the sea) can be compared with those in a traditional Chinese painting, which illustrates its theme by picking out details rather than giving a full rendition of its scene. These details distinguish this hymn from a Western-language one translated into Cantonese and demonstrate the indigenization of Christian music in this location. That being said, there is an international Christian music industry that links churches in Taiwan, Hong Kong, and Singapore; those among the overseas Chinese in North America and Europe; and, increasingly, those in mainland China itself. CDs and sheet music are widely disseminated, and professional groups tour actively.

Popular Music

FIGURE 8.19

Zhou Xuan in a 1930s' publicity photo.

As we saw in the preceding example, some consider popular music to be the most representative kind of local music in Hong Kong. Popular music is strongly established across much of the rest of the Chinese world as well, although the exact histories of this differ markedly by location. You can locate much of this music, and a large amount of material relating to it, by searching the Internet. Among Chinese commentators, the relationship between national and international ingredients in the music has generated great interest. Meanwhile, many Westerners have looked into the relationship between rock music and politics.

Historians date the rise of Chinese popular music to the 1930s. This decade saw the rise of a film industry in China, centered in Shanghai, and popular music was strongly associated with Chinese film almost from its beginning. The roots of film song lay largely in the ballroom and cabaret music of Shanghai's entertainment industry in the 1920s. Many film songs were performed by a small band using idioms influenced by jazz and Tin Pan Alley to accompany a mostly pentatonic vocal melody sung in Mandarin by a female film star. Lyrics dealt with charming, romantic images appropriate both to the flirtatious world of ballroom dance and to the storylines of many films. A minority of film songs drew on Chinese folk tunes accompanied by Chinese instruments or by a mixed Chinese-Western ensemble. Some of these were romantic in tone, but others were produced by left-wing artists who hoped to stir up a progressive social awareness among their listeners by pointing out social inequalities. Many musicians recorded, and the music industry promoted, both kinds of songs.

Among the numerous film music singers of this age, Zhou Xuan (1918 or 1920–1957; Figure 8.19) has received the most attention. She led a precarious childhood, narrowly avoiding being sold to a brothel at age ten. Instead she was apprenticed to the Mingyue Song and Dance Troupe based at Shanghai's somewhat notorious Great World Entertainment Center. Zhou graduated from the children's troupe into the ensemble of film actors and musicians managed by the prominent composer Li Jinhui (1891–1967). Her move in 1932 coincided with Japanese military action in Shanghai, which stimulated a new genre of patriotic film. Zhou Xuan also acted in romantic films, and in all appeared in forty-two films, recording over a hundred songs and earning the accolade "golden voice."

"Full Moon and Blooming Flowers" (a title derived from a Chinese idiom for conjugal bliss) is representative of her style. (See Shanghai 2005 for an online recording labeled "Flowers under a Full Moon.") Zhou's husband, Yan Hua, composed the piece for her to sing in a movie version of the classic romance *The Tale of the Western Chamber* and uses the lyrical jazz style found in so many Shanghai film songs. Zhou's pentatonic tune is supported by a large-scale band, including bowed strings, flute, clarinet, muted trumpets, trombone, piano, percussion, and mandolin (Transcription 8.15).

Music like this was all but swept away after 1949 in mainland China, to be replaced by the more martial strains of massed song and by further developments of the nationalistic songs already mentioned. The latter were infused with yet more patriotic intensity and increasingly came to be sung by members of state-run entertainment ensembles. Like the earlier film music, these songs were widely broadcast; they still occupied much of the public entertainment sphere in the early 1990s. Unlike the film songs, though, they did not compete in a commercial market for audiences. Instead, they played a prominent role in the soundworld the state produced to teach its citizens roles and feelings appropriate to their lives in socialist China.

The popular music industry shifted to Taiwan and Hong Kong. There, Shanghai-derived film music gradually changed through contact with new trends in Western and Japanese popular music, by the rise of new production techniques, and by the region's changing commercial opportunities. In Hong Kong, for instance, singers initially dropped Mandarin in favor of Cantonese, since this was the native language for most in Hong Kong. Later, with the rise of television, soap operas played a major role in popularizing certain types of songs and their singers. Recently, Korean soaps have become much admired across Chinese-language television networks, leading to a growing Chinese interest in Korean singers and their songs. Film remains a significant part of the equation as well, and many of the most prominent singers of Cantopop (Cantonese-language pop song) are, were, or aim to become prominent movie stars. Examples from the 1980s and 1990s include Jacky Cheung, Andy Lau, Anita Mui, and Faye Wong. Meanwhile, the gradual reintegration of the mainland as a market from about 1980 saw many singers produce Mandarin versions of their songs for sale there as well as Cantonese versions for sale in Hong Kong, and sales of the former now exceed those of the latter.

The return of popular music to the mainland cities coincided with a gradual decline of the state-sponsored music and a regrowth of a commercial music industry within China itself. These changes were spurred by the economic liberalization that Premier Deng Xiaoping introduced in the 1980s. Among the new local styles were such as the *xibei feng* ("Northwest wind" or "Northwest style"), which featured a deliberately rough solo vocal timbre suggestive of

TRANSCRIPTION 8.15
Excerpt from "Full Moon
and Blooming Flowers"
by Yan Hua, as sung
by Zhou Xuan.

northwestern Chinese folk singing, along with lyrics that commented not so much on romance (as in the Hong Kong and Taiwan songs) or on a positive political message (as in the state-supported light music) but on the hardships of contemporary life. Though some political leaders denied the existence of any such hardships under Communism, the new economic climate allowed the music to spread among China's urban youth.

Although rock has yet to become part of the musical mainstream in China, many commentators outside of China have written about the rock singer Cui Jian. His brand of Chinese rock, including his rough vocal style, became deeply associated with prodemocracy protests, which sparked military suppression in 1989. Cui denied that his songs criticized government policies, but his co-option of many of the most potent symbols of the Chinese revolution (red flags, the long march, etc.) clearly raises interpretations that extend beyond the meanings government authorities habitually accorded to those symbols. Moreover, his use of pronouns rather than actual names in certain songs means that a line like "But you always laugh at me," from the song "I Have Nothing," might be taken by different listeners as either a reference to a troubled personal relationship or a complaint about the attitude of the ruling authorities.

The speed with which young people across the country adopted such styles, and the depth of affection they generated, worried government officials. The ideological positions of some songs seemed to them potentially damaging to younger listeners' moral outlook, and thus to the socialist state. On the other hand, these same officials wanted China's music industry to become economically self-supporting, and they recognized that this meant record companies had to be allowed to sell music that people wanted to buy. An outright ban would simply alienate the youth, who would then duplicate and share cassette copies anyway; only the state's music industry would lose out. Their solution has been to allow nearly all music, whether home-produced or imported, to be distributed and sold but to restrict access to the state-run broadcast media for genres that they viewed with suspicion (such as rock). Periodic campaigns have been initiated against "spiritual pollution" and "bourgeois liberalization." Some politicians have claimed that love songs make young people selfish: Love of the Communist Party and of the state should come before romantic love for another individual. A selection of Zhou Xuan's more patriotic songs, long forbidden in Shanghai, reappeared in the 1980s as part of one such campaign. They were offered as good examples of a kind of nationalistic popular music, but their appeal for many lay more in their nostalgia value, not as alternatives to pop imported from Taiwan and Hong Kong.

Over the longer term, government campaigns against spiritual pollution have faltered. In 1994, for example, the highly sentimental song "Scent" (CD 4, Track 7) won a major mainland song prize. Performed by the Taiwanese singer Winnie Hsin (Xin Xiaoqi; Figure 8.20), this song well represents the sentimental mainstream of popular music at that time.

CD 4:7

"Weidao" ("Scent") (1:42). Music by Huang Guolun, lyrics by Yao Qian. Performed by Winnie Hsin, voice; Ni Fanglai, guitar; and Tu Ying, keyboards. *Xin Xiaoqi: Weidao.* 1994. Rock Records (Taiwan) Co. Ltd. RD1296.

FIGURE 8.20

Cover of Winnie Hsin's CD featuring the song "Scent."

Close Listening

"WEIDAO" ("SCENT")

CD 4:7

COUNTER NUMBER	SECTION	LYRICS	TRANSLATION
0:00	Instrumental introduction		
0:33	Verse	*Jintian wanshang de xingxing hen shao, Bu zhidao tamen pao na qu liao.* *Chiluoluo de tiankong, xingxing duo jiliao.* *Wo yiwei shang xin keyi hen shao, Wo yiwei wo neng guode hen hao.* *Shei zhidao yixiang ni sinian ku wu yao, Wu chu ke tao.*	This evening the stars are very few, I don't know where they have run off to. An empty sky, where the stars are so lonesome. I thought my sorrow would get less, I thought I could get through this. Who could know my every thought is of you, I long for you so bitterly, I can't escape from it.
1:17	Chorus	*Xiangnian ni de xiao, Xiangnian ni de waitao, Xiangnian ni baise wazi, He ni shenshang de weidao.* *Wo xiangnian ni de wen, He shouzhi dandan yancao weidao.* *Jiyizhong ceng bei'aide weidao.*	I miss your smile, I miss your coat. I miss your white socks, and your body's aroma. I miss your kiss, and the light tobacco smell on your fingers. The once-beloved scent is in my memory.

Quite a few websites describe this song, using adjectives like *touching* to refer to its emotional world. When the song was released, Hsin emphasized an autobiographical aspect, putting forward an account of her relationship with a man who treated her badly but whom she could not get out of her system. While there is no reason to doubt her words, the story allows her to claim an emotional authenticity that establishes this as her own song, not simply one written for her to perform (see the Close Listening guide). This staking of a personal claim will be familiar to many listeners to Western popular music. Singers there also put themselves forward as "emotional experts" whose primary task is not to recount dramatic action but to explore deeply an emotional state. Contrast this with many kinds of African popular music in which the singer is a "moral expert," a wise man or woman who advises the listener on how best to act in the difficult situations life generates.

The song's music reinforces the compulsive, self-destructive love revealed in the lyrics and described by Hsin in interviews. Instrumentation, blend, and vocal-instrumental balance are carefully deployed to mold a soft, dreamlike shell around the singer's perfectly formed voice, embracing it and protecting it by sealing off the outside world. This kind of obsessive reverie, where a singer lovingly catalogs the traces of her lost love rather than taking action to set matters right, is exactly the kind of emotional state that the Communist Party officials had described as unhealthy. It also, of course, makes the song a suitable vehicle for karaoke performance, one of the main ways in which songs like this are popularized across the Chinese-speaking world. By stepping into Hsin's place in karaoke performance, other women put themselves forward as maltreated but unfaltering lovers, claiming an emotional position parallel to (but updated from) the one expressed in the wedding lament text cited earlier in this chapter.

This last similarity might suggest that little has changed in the world of Chinese gender relations, with women remaining the objects of widespread mistreatment by men. Whether or not this is true, the twentieth century saw the rise of many new opportunities for female musicians and performers. Prominent today is an ensemble called the Twelve Girls Band (Figure 8.21). Formed in June 2001 from graduates of several of the capital's top conservatories and colleges, the band is one of several groups to have established a niche within the popular music market through playing electronically mediated arrangements on Chinese instruments, such as *erhu, zheng, pipa,* and *dizi.* Many of their works are available on CD and DVD. Even here the long shadow of China's historical past is clear. The Twelve Girls Band use a classical term (*yuefang*) for the word *band,* which reminds the Chinese speaker of the imperial court entertainers of the ancient past. Despite the rhythm section, electric bass, lights show, updated costuming, and elements of virtuosic display, the instrumental arrangements lie close indeed to the style of the national music compositions described earlier. However, the continued strength of national sentiment in contemporary musical settings in China todayhas not limited the success of groups like this overseas. The case of

FIGURE 8.21

Stage photo of some of the Twelve Girls Band from the *Beautiful Energy* DVD (JSCP 2003).

the Twelve Girls Band illustrates the ongoing internationalization of contemporary musics from China. Clearly, music is actively flowing from China to the outside world.

Chinese Music/World Music?

Toward the start of this chapter, I commented that few musical features are both uniquely and universally Chinese. The examples given bear this out: We cannot set all or most Chinese music apart from other music around the world simply by analyzing sonic ingredients. Although pentatonic melodies are widespread, not every example here has them, nor are they confined to China. The same is true for heterophonic textures, for sectional pieces with pictorial titles, and for Chinese instruments (many of which occur in various forms across East and Southeast Asia). Neither can we define Chinese music tidily on simple geographic terms. As the last examples of popular music emphasize, much of China's contemporary entertainment arises outside the borders of the People's Republic of China, while performers like the Twelve Girls Band tour worldwide. The same was true in centuries past, which saw widespread musical exchanges, albeit at a slower pace.

We nevertheless encounter in the social world a *concept* of Chinese music, as occurs when Chinese people try to explain what makes their musical lives distinct from those of other peoples. In doing this, they refer not only to sonic and geographic characteristics but also to contexts and usages of performance and to the emotional and social content generated through acts of music making. Their comments often involve comparison, as in "Chinese music is like this, foreign music is like that," and they put forward a statement that is as much about the qualities and experiences of life as about music. We return to the model of yin and yang here, but this time on two levels. On the first, "music" and "life" are opposed but inherently interlinked, and any account of the specific sound materials of Chinese music necessarily reflects Chinese life more generally. On the second, "China" is opposed to but conceived in direct acknowledgement of "the foreign." From this perspective, studying Chinese music offers a position from which to gain insight not only into Chinese life but also to comment on trends in global musical culture.

www Book Companion Website

You will find tutorial quizzes, Internet links, and much more at the Book Companion Website for *Worlds of Music,* Fifth Edition, at **academic.cengage.com/music/titon/worlds_5**

Latin America/Chile, Bolivia, Ecuador, Peru

JOHN M. SCHECHTER

Latin America is a kaleidoscope of cultural and ecological patterns, producing a myriad of distinctive regional lifeways. It comprises a continent and a half with more than twenty different countries in which Spanish, Portuguese, French, and dozens of Native American languages in hundreds of dialects are spoken. It is at once the majestic, beautiful Andes mountains, the endless emptiness of the Peruvian-Chilean desert, and the lush rain forests of the huge Amazonian basin. Native American cultures that were not eradicated by European diseases have in many cases retained distinctive languages, belief systems, dress, musical forms, and music rituals. Most Latin American cultures, though, share a common heritage of Spanish or Portuguese colonialism and American and European cultural influences. For instance, several ports in Colombia and Brazil served as major colonial centers for the importation of black slaves; Latin America thus remains a rich repository of African and African American music-culture traditions, including rituals, musical forms and practices, and types of musical instruments.

In Latin American culture, mixture is the norm, not the exception. When you walk through the countryside of Ecuador, for example, you hear a Spanish dialect borrowing many words from Quichua, the regional Native American language. The local Quichua dialect, conversely, uses many Spanish words. South of Ecuador, in the high mountain regions of Peru, the harp is considered an Indigenous instrument, although European missionaries and others in fact brought it to Peru. In rural areas of Atlantic coastal Colombia, musicians sing songs in Spanish, using Spanish literary forms, but these are accompanied by African-style drums and rhythms and by Amerindian flutes and rattles. In northern highland Ecuador, African Ecuadorians perform the *bomba,* a type of song that features African American rhythms, Quichua Indian melodic and harmonic features, and Spanish language—with sometimes one or two Quichua words. Overall, it is hard to maintain strict cultural divisions because the intermingling of Iberian (Spanish and Portuguese), African, and Native American strains is so profound in the Latin American experience.

When you first think of Latin American music, you might hear in your mind's ear the vibrancy of the rhythms in salsa. There is an enormous variety of beaten and shaken rhythm instruments, such as claves, bongos, congas, and maracas, both in salsa and throughout Latin America. In distinctive sizes and shapes, the

guitar figures prominently in Latin American folk music. In Peru and Bolivia, for example, a type of guitar called the *charango* (cha-*ran*-go) may have as its body the shell of an armadillo. There are other types of Latin American music with which you might also be familiar, including bossa nova, calypso, and tango.

In this chapter, we will take a close look at musics of four Latin American countries: Chile, Bolivia, Ecuador, and Peru. We will study songs in both the Spanish language and the **Quichua** (*kee*-chooa), or Quechua, language—an Indigenous tongue of the Andes, spoken by some six to eight million people in Bolivia, Peru, Ecuador, and Argentina. (In Peru and Bolivia, the language is called Quechua; in Ecuador, the dialects are called Quichua.) We will listen to pieces by a solo harpist, a bereaved mother, two duos and several ensembles—musics that are either notably traditional or markedly contemporary. The nine pieces we will address speak eloquently to their own cultures' means for expressing profound grief, to their political concerns, to their "social" forms of music making (Andean panpipe playing), to their histories and ecologies, or, in one case, to the composer's autobiography. A central theme in several instances is that of praise and esteem for one's beloved.

Chilean Nueva Canción

VÍCTOR JARA AND INTI ILLIMANI

We begin with a contemporary, politically aware music: a powerful folk song composed in 1967 by a great figure in Chilean modern music, Víctor Jara (1938–1973). Trained in acting and directing, Jara ultimately became a great figure in the modern song movement, *Nueva Canción* (noo-*ay*-va kan-*syon*), or "New Song," of Chile and, sometimes under a different genre name, of all Latin America. (See Jara 1984 for a full discussion of his life and career, including an accounting of his evolving political consciousness, in a biography written by his wife, Joan.)

Nueva Canción is a song movement through which people stand up for their own culture—for themselves as a people—in the face of oppression by a totalitarian regime or in the face of cultural imperialism from abroad, notably the United States and Europe. It developed first in the southern cone of South America—Argentina, Chile, and Uruguay—during the 1950s and 1960s, and it has since spread throughout Latin America. As we know from U.S. history, the 1960s in particular witnessed violent upheavals. Latin America echoed the assassinations and urban violence in the United States: Nearly every country in South America, as well as Cuba and the Dominican Republic in the Caribbean, saw revolution, massacre, underground warfare, or other forms of violent social and political confrontation at that time. For a fuller discussion of the philosophy, political contexts, songs, composers, and ensembles of Chilean *Nueva Canción*, Argentine *nuevo cancionero argentino*, and Cuban *nueva trova*, see Schechter 1999b:425–37; this discussion incorporates study of several Víctor Jara songs, including "Preguntas por Puerto Montt," "Plegaria a un labrador," and "Despedimiento del angelito." You can find a discussion of Jara's song "El lazo" at Schechter 2002:388–91.

For now, let us look closely at one of Víctor Jara's best-known compositions, "El aparecido" (ell a-pa-reh-*see*-doh), as interpreted here by the noted Chilean *Nueva Canción* ensemble Inti Illimani (*Inti* = Quechua for "sun"; *Illimani is* the name of a mountain in Bolivia). The Close Listening guide provides the full text of "El aparecido" and illustrates the formal structure of this modern-day, composed Chilean *cueca* (*kweh*-ka).

Close Listening

"EL APARECIDO" ("THE APPARITION")

CD 4:8

COUNTER NUMBER	COMMENTARY	LYRICS	TRANSLATION
Introduction			
0:00	Ensemble enters in the song's minor home key, 6/8 meter. *Kena* (flute) plays melody and suggests the shape of the vocal stanzas to come.		
1st stanza			
0:10	*Sesquialtera* meter. Kena "tail" repeats opening segment of the introduction.	*Abre sendas por los cerros Deja su huella en el viento, El águila le da el vuelo Y lo cobija el silencio.*	He opens pathways through the mountains, Leaves his mark on the wind, The eagle gives him flight And silence envelops him.
2nd stanza			
0:36		*Nunca se quejó del frío Nunca se quejó del sueño. El pobre siente su paso Y lo sigue como ciego.*	Never has he complained of the cold, Never has he complained of lack of sleep. The poor man senses his step And follows him like a blind man.
Refrain			
0:58	Melody changes to a major key; concludes in minor.	*¡Córrele, córrele, correlá, Por aquí, por aquí, por allá. ¡Córrele, córrele, correlá, Córrele, que te van a matar, Córrele, córrele, correlá, Córrele, que te van a matar, Córrele, córrele, correlá!*	Run, run, run, Here, here, over there. Run, run, run, Run or they'll kill you, Run, run, run, Run or they'll kill you, Run, run, run!

Instrumental interlude

1:18	*Kena* repeats melody of introduction with first three pitches an octave higher.

3rd stanza

1:29	Minor key. *Kena* "tail".	*Su cabeza es rematada* *Por cuervos con garra de oro:* *Como lo ha crucificado* *La furia del poderoso.*	His head is finished off By ravens with talons of gold: Like the fury of the powerful has crucified him.

4th stanza

1:57	Minor key.	*Hijo de la rebeldía* *Lo siguen veinte más veinte.* *Porque regala su vida* *Ellos le quieren dar muerte.*	Son of rebellion Twenty, and twenty more pursue him. Because he offers his life They want his death.

Refrain

2:17	Melody changes to major key; concludes in minor home key.

Instrumental interlude

2:37	Minor key. *Kena* repeats melody of Introduction with first three pitches an octave higher.

4th stanza repeats

2:48	Background voices sing stanza in counterpoint with soloist.

Refrain

3:09	Major key. Concludes in the minor home key.

This Inti Illimani version—music and text—can be found at Acevedo et al. [1996?]:118–23.

When you listen to Inti Illimani's version (formulated by that ensemble in 1971) of "El aparecido" (CD 4, Track 8), you may wonder about the metrical rhythm of the piece (recall the discussion of rhythm and meter in Chapter 1). You may think that you hear the music at one moment in moderate $\frac{3}{4}$ meter, 1-2-3, 1-2-3—but at the next moment, in lively $\frac{6}{8}$ meter, **1**-2-3-**4**-5-6, **1**-2-3-**4**-5-6. This version of a traditional Chilean rhythm known as the *cueca* in fact juxtaposes both of those types of metrical rhythm at the same time. When this occurs—and it happens in many types of Latin American folksong, musics heard from Mexico all the way down to Chile and in many countries in between—it is referred to as *sesquialtera* metrical rhythm: roughly, the simultaneous feeling of $\frac{3}{4}$ and $\frac{6}{8}$ meter. This metrical-rhythmical ambiguity is the heart and soul of much, though not all, Hispanic-derived Latin American regional folk music. You will hear it in Mexican *son huasteco*, in Colombian *bambuco*, in Ecuadorian *albazo*, in Peruvian *marinera*, in

CD 4:8

"El aparecido" ("The Apparition") (3:33). Chilean *cueca*. Víctor Jara. Inti Illimani ensemble: Max Berrú, Horacio Durán, Jorge Coulon, José Miguel Camus, José Seves, Horacio Salinas. Monitor Presents *Inti-Illimani 2: La Nueva Cancion Chilena*, 1991.

Argentinian *chacarera*, in Chilean/Bolivian *cueca*, and in many other genres as well.

When you look at the Close Listening guide, you may also wonder about the terms *major* and *minor key* (or *scale*). Chapter 1 explained the concept of the major scale, with the example of the C Major scale built on the consecutive white keys of the piano. Specifically, it noted that the interval between each pitch is not the same. It spoke of this Euro-American major scale, but also of the Javanese *sléndro* and *pélog* scales (see Chapter 7 as well). Different scale types reflect different organizing principles behind the relationships and sequence of their constituent pitches.

"El aparecido" uses variants of the minor scale as well as the major scale. The vocal stanzas and instrumental sections use two forms of the minor scale, while the refrain moves into different major keys, only to conclude on the minor home key. One will often encounter this mix of scales in traditional musics of the Andes region, including Chilean folk music; when Chilean *Nueva Canción* musicians compose contemporary interpretations of traditional musics, they reflect that cultural sensitivity to major and minor keys.

Note that in the listening chart the word **counterpoint** refers to combining two or more melodic parts. On the repeat of stanza 4 ("Hijo de la rebeldía"), the voices divide, so that one group seems to "follow" the other, with the same text fragments, yet different melodic fragments; thus, we have an example of counterpoint— contrapuntal, or polyphonic, texture.

As you can see, the lyrics of "El aparecido" reflect the turbulence of the times. Written by Víctor Jara in 1967, "El aparecido" was dedicated "to E.(Ch.)G."— Ernesto Che Guevara. Now famous in this interpretation by Inti Illimani, the piece speaks of this revolutionary figure's eluding his pursuers; the music reaches a climactic point in its chorus: "¡*Córrele, córrele, correlá; córrele, que te van a matar; córrele, córrele, correlá!*" ("Run, run, run; run, for they are going to kill you; run, run, run!") (Schechter 1999b:428–29).

As noted earlier, the 1950s to 1970s in Latin America was a period of violent upheaval, witnessing the Plaza de Mayo massacre in Buenos Aires and the subsequent fall of Perón in Argentina (1955); the fall of Cuba's Batista government and the victorious Cuban Revolution (1959); the fall of the João Goulart government in Brazil (1964), beginning a fifteen-year hard-line era; the U.S. intervention in Santo Domingo (1965); an increase in guerrilla activity in Peru, Colombia, and Bolivia; the death of Ernesto Che Guevara in Bolivia (1967); the subsequent spread of guerrilla fighting in Central America and Venezuela, and the Tlatelolco massacre in Mexico (1968); and the victory of the Unidad Popular in Chile (1970), initiating three years of government under Salvador Allende, followed by the 1973 military coup (Schechter 1999b:428, citing Carrasco Pirard 1982:604).

I described in the fourth edition of *Worlds of Music* (Schechter 2002:390–94) how metaphor plays a major role in songs by Víctor Jara, Violeta Parra, and Atahualpa Yupanqui. A **metaphor** is an assertion that one thing is also something else, a comparison that typically enhances meaning. So, here, in "El aparecido," Guevara is depicted as a mythological figure ("*Abre sendas . . . en el viento*"), one of great power and respect ("*El águila le da el vuelo*"); one of mystery ("*lo cobija el silencio*"); and one pursued by many ("*Lo siguen veinte más veinte*") of the powerful, of the wealthy ("*Su cabeza es rematada/Por cuervos con garra de oro*"). "El aparecido" falls within an established Latin American tradition of praising in song individuals—often being pursued—whom some might consider to be outlaws;

others, to be heroes. Among the protagonists of the Mexico-Texas border *corrido* (ko-*rree*-do; ballad) tradition, one could point to "Gregorio Cortez" (Paredes 1958; 1976:31) and to two songs about Robin Hood figures, "Joaquín Murieta" and "Heráclio Bernal" (Schechter 1999a:8–10, citing McDowell 1972:208–14 and Sonnichsen 1975:5); a Robin Hood figure of twentieth-century Argentina is Juan Bautista Bairoleto (Moreno Chá 1999:267–70).

As to Inti Illimani, they were victims of the 1973 Chilean coup (see later for a fuller discussion). One of the original members, Horacio Salinas, recalls, "We were in Italy, on a three-month tour that lasted 15 years. Against our will, we were very far from our country and alone with our music" (Manz 2005:27). They returned from Italy on Chile's Independence Day, September 18, 1988 (greeted by a crowd of some five thousand, at the airport), after fifteen years in exile, during which they toured more than sixty countries (Ibid. 27, 28).

In February 1994, I heard them perform at the University of California at Berkeley. This concert showed how much the ensemble had evolved since a group of Santiago Technical University engineering students had created it in 1967. In addition to the familiar *Nueva Canción* panpipes, *charango*, and **kena** (*ke*-na; Andean vertical notched flute), the seven-member aggregate now incorporated instruments native neither to Chile nor the Andes: hammered dulcimer and soprano saxophone. The ensemble's multi-instrumentalists now performed sophisticated, tailored arrangements, featuring contemporary, highly coloristic harmonizations of traditional Andean and Caribbean genres. To these points, Inti Illimani musicians have remarked that the ensemble's extended years in exile—nearly half their total years of existence—have led them to more universal creative roots (González 1989:272–73). In addition to their renowned version of "El aparecido," the group's repertoire in this highly polished performance was remarkably variegated, showcasing the breadth of Latin American (if elaborately disguised) forms: hocketing panpipes (see the discussion on *k'antu*, next), Peruvian *wayno* (discussed later), Venezuelan *joropo*, Chilean *cueca*, Ecuadorian *sanjuán* (discussed later), Cuban *son*, and Mexican *ranchera*. The ensemble toured the United States in fall 1995, performing in Nebraska, Michigan, Wisconsin, Missouri, Illinois, and Washington, D.C. In 2001–2002 the group toured Italy, Spain, South America, Mexico, and North America (University of Iowa 2003). On October 17, 2004, with many newer members, Inti Illimani performed a concert in Santa Cruz, California. Early in 2005 Inti Illimani member and originating director Horacio Salinas taught a seminar entitled "La *Nueva Canción* and Popular Movements in Latin America" at the Center for Latin American Studies, University of California, Berkeley.

VIOLETA PARRA

Horacio Salinas recently summarized the contribution of our next major figure of the *Nueva Canción* movement, Violeta Parra, in these words:

> What she did was to democratize music. Before her, songs were not about the people's problems. For the first time, songs spoke of social problems in very poetic terms. They were not only about love, which has always been present in song lyrics, but also about the human condition, the social condition, the exploitation of the people. The protest song was born [in Chile]. Songs became a vehicle of humanization, and music contributed in a notable way to a moment of liberation of the spirit." (Manz 2005:27)

In Chile, Violeta Parra was a fundamental moving force in the development of *la Nueva Canción Chilena*. A multifaceted artist—musician, poet, painter, tapestry embroiderer, sculptor, potter—Violeta Parra immersed herself in the folklore of Chile, initially in her home region of Chillán in southern Chile, then in Santiago Province, and ultimately throughout the length of the country. Her enormous collecting efforts significantly helped make Chilean folk songs legitimate and known on the national level. In 1964 she set up a cultural center in La Reina, on the outskirts of Santiago, where she coached musicians. Both here and at the Peña de los Parra—a coffeehouse focusing on folklore, run by Isabel and Ángel, her two oldest children—the *Nueva Canción* movement took shape in the 1960s. Many of its pioneering artists had done their own fieldwork, traveling widely through the Chilean countryside to hear and document principally rural traditions in music and music-related customs. Thus, the *Nueva Canción* musicians sought to reproduce authentic, traditional styles (such as Jara's *cueca* "El aparecido") and to use traditional instruments (such as Violeta Parra's preference for the *charango*) to express their views on contemporary events and issues. The 1969 Primer Festival de la Nueva Canción Chilena, sponsored by the Universidad Católica in Santiago, gave the now recognizable movement a name (Morris 1986:119–20).

Like Jara's "El lazo," a musical tale of an aged lasso-maker on a poor ranch in Jara's childhood village of Lonquén, Violeta Parra's songs may sometimes draw on natural contexts. For example, "Rin [a Chilean rhythm] del angelito" (1964–1965) depicts the joyous atmosphere of a Chilean wake for a dead child. This subject also drew Víctor Jara to compose a song ("Despedimiento del angelito" ["Farewell of the Little Angel"]); we look more closely at a child's wake later in this chapter. On the other hand, Parra's music may be highly satirical, as in her composition "¿Qué dirá el Santo Padre?" ("What Will the Pope Say?"), written around 1957.

Partial text from "¿QUÉ DIRÁ EL SANTO PADRE?"

Miren cómo nos hablan de libertad
Cuando de ella nos privan en realidad.
Miren cómo pregonan tranquilidad
Cuando nos atormenta la autoridad.

Look how they speak to us of liberty
When really they deprive us of it.
Look how they proclaim peace
When the authorities torment us.

Chorus

¿Qué dirá el Santo Padre que vive en Roma
Que le están degollando sus palomas?

What will the pope, who lives in Rome, say
To the fact that they are beheading his doves?

Miren cómo nos hablan del paraíso

Cuando nos llueven penas como granizo.

Look how they speak to us of paradise
When afflictions rain down on us like hail.

The Chilean writer Fernando Alegría comments that Parra first cries out here against injustice, then appeals to the pope to make a statement on these conditions—yet he remains silent throughout the song. Like the majority of Latin Americans, most Chileans are Roman Catholics; the Catholic Church has frequently stood in the forefront of the struggle for human rights in Latin America. Violeta

Parra's plea ultimately brought a response from the Vatican: In April 1987 Pope John Paul II visited Chile, spoke out against conditions of oppression, and met with Indigenous peoples, encouraging them to sustain their cultural values (Levy 1988).

Finally, though by no means have we exhausted the full range of song types produced by this great artist, Violeta Parra also has composed love poetry. In the highly moving "Gracias a la vida," written, ironically, just before her 1967 suicide, the artist thanks life for having given her the eyes, ears, words, feet, heart, laughter, and weeping through which she might perceive and approach the man she loves.

THE FRONT LINES OF SOCIAL CHANGE

In songs such as Jara's "El lazo" (composed c. 1964, about the Lonquén lasso-maker) and "Angelita Huenumán" (composed in 1969, about a Mapuche blanket-maker), *Nueva Canción* artists sought to reinvoke and revalidate traditional lifeways of forgotten but valued individuals and peoples. Yet, as with Jara's "El aparecido" and Parra's "¿Qué dirá el Santo Padre?" *Nueva Canción* musicians also expressed their social consciousness, speaking out in a clear voice against conditions of oppression and advocating social change. Martha Nandorfy, in comparing the philosophical stances of these two artists, notes that, where Parra "rail[ed] against functionaries, bureaucrats, and politicians, in short, against government, and Jara . . . oppos[ed] the ruling class through organized party politics—both fought to defend cultural survival, recognizing that social justice and human rights must be defined and defended within popular culture" (2003:203). In another example, Víctor Jara's "Preguntas por Puerto Montt" (1969)—notably devoid of metaphor and speaking in a direct and accusatory tone, the poet-musician presents a stream-of-consciousness monologue decrying a March 6, 1969, government-sanctioned attack on unarmed peasant families in the Chilean port city of Puerto Montt. In the 1970 Chilean presidential campaign, an important *Nueva Canción* ensemble that had formed in the mid-1960s, Quilapayún, accompanied speakers for Salvador Allende's broad-based Popular Unity party, which had brought together workers, peasants, and students into a mass movement. A musical example of this remarkable spirit of unity is Jara's "Plegaria a un labrador" ("Public Prayer to a Worker"), which was composed for the first Festival of Chilean Song in 1969. Modeled on the Lord's Prayer, this impassioned call for worker solidarity emphasizes the line "Stand up and look at your hands."

. . . Levántate y mírate las manos,	Stand up and look at your hands,	Partial text from
Para crecer, estréchala a tu hermano,	Take your brother's hand, so you can grow,	**"PLEGARIA A UN LABRADOR"**
Juntos iremos unidos en la sangre,	We'll go together, united by blood,	
Hoy es el tiempo que puede ser mañana.	The future can begin today.	
Líbranos de aquel que nos domina en la miseria,	Deliver us from the master who keeps us in misery,	
Tráenos tu reino de justicia e igualdad . . .	Thy kingdom of justice and equality, come . . .	
Hágase por fin tu voluntad aquí en la tierra,	Thy will be done, at last, here on earth,	
Danos tu fuerza y tu valor al combatir	Give us the strength and the courage to struggle	

In 1973 the elected Marxist government of President Allende was overthrown in a bloody coup. Allende and some 2,800 others lost their lives, hundreds disappeared, and thousands were jailed. On September 18, 1973, a young man ushered Joan Jara into the Santiago city morgue, where she found the body of her husband, Víctor Jara, "his chest riddled with holes and a gaping wound in his abdomen. His hands seemed to be hanging from his arms at a strange angle as though his wrists were broken" (Jara 1984:243). The singer who had cried out in word and song on behalf of "him who died without knowing why his chest was riddled, fighting for the right to have a place to live" ("Preguntas por Puerto Montt"), the singer whose songs had so often lauded eloquently the hands of his people (in "El lazo," "Angelita Huenumán," and "Plegaria a un labrador"), had met his fate—in a stroke of terrifying irony—with his own chest riddled with holes, his own hands made lifeless.

Numerous *Nueva Canción* musicians were imprisoned or, like Inti Illimani, remained in exile, but to gain support for human rights in Chile they continued to spread the message of *Nueva Canción* in performances abroad. Within Chile, the movement went underground and was transformed into *Canto Nuevo.*

After the overthrow of Allende, the music of *Nueva Canción* was prohibited on the airwaves and removed from stores and destroyed. Certain prominent folkloric instruments associated with *Nueva Canción*, such as the *charango*, were also prohibited (Morris 1986:123). In this repressive political and cultural atmosphere, the metaphoric character we have discussed in the songs of Atahualpa Yupanqui, Víctor Jara, and Violeta Parra became exaggerated and intensified, in order to express thoughts that would have been censored if stated directly. For example, in "El joven titiritero" ("The Young Puppeteer") by Eduardo Peralta, a puppeteer's departure and hoped-for return served as a metaphor for exile and renewed hope.

The status of *Canto Nuevo* was precarious. The government would grant permission to perform a concert, but then abruptly revoke the permission; radio programs featuring its music were established, then eliminated; Jara cassettes were at one moment confiscated, sold openly in stores the next. As noted earlier with regard to Inti Illimani, after subsequent changes in political conditions, banished musicians were permitted to return to Chile.

Bolivian K'antu

CD 4:9

"Kutirimunapaq" ("So That We Can Return") (3:50). *K'antu* of Bolivia. Performed by Ruphay. *Jach'a Marka.* 1982. Ruphay. Discos Heriba SLP 2212. Heriba Ltda. La Paz, Bolivia.

Certain *Nueva Canción* performers such as Inti Illimani chose the *zampoña* (sam-*pon*-ya), or panpipes, among other traditional instruments, to symbolize their esteem for the native traditions of the Andes and neighboring regions. It is true that panpipes are widely known outside South America. Nevertheless, the depth of the panpipe tradition in South America is remarkable. Today, we can find a huge number of named varieties of panpipes among native peoples from Panama down to Peru, Bolivia, and Chile. In Peru and Bolivia, cultures dating back fifteen centuries knew and played panpipes of bamboo or clay.

Listen to "Kutirimunapaq" (koo-tee-ree-moo-*na*-pakh) as performed by Ruphay, a Bolivian ensemble. They are playing *k'antu* (k-*an*-tu), a type of ceremonial panpipe music from the altiplano, or high plateau of Peru-Bolivia. The word *k'antu* might be related to a widely known flower of Bolivia, the *kantuta*, or it might be derived from the Spanish word for song, *canto*. The Close Listening guide illustrates the formal structure of this Bolivian *k'antu*.

Close Listening

"KUTIRIMUNAPAQ" ("SO THAT WE CAN RETURN")

CD 4:9

COUNTER NUMBER	COMMENTARY
Introduction	
0:00	*Wankaras* (drums) and *ch'inisku* (triangle) only enter. Unmetered, gradually increasing tempo that tapers off.
1st full cycle—A section	
0:10	Full ensemble (multiple *zampoñas,wankaras; ch'inisku*).
0:26	Repeat. Characteristic rhythmic break just before cadence and start of repeat each time through.
B section	
0:37	Full ensemble Characteristic rhythmic break just before cadence.
0:53	Repeat.
1:06	Cadence, moves directly into C section.
C section	
1:07	Full ensemble.
1:12	Cadence (no break beforehand).
1:13	Immediate repeat.
1:19	Characteristic break at cadence, leading right back to beginning of A section and 2nd full cycle.
2nd full cycle—A section	
1:20	Full ensemble (multiple *zampoñas, wankaras, ch'inisku*).
1:33	Characteristic rhythmic break just before cadence.
1:34	Repeat.
B section	
1:47	Full ensemble.
2:01	Characteristic rhythmic break just before cadence.
2:02	Repeat.
2:16	Cadence moving directly into C section.

C section

2:16	Full ensemble.
2:21	Cadence (no rhythmic break beforehand) and immediate repeat.
2:27	Characteristic break at cadence, leading right back to beginning of A section and 3rd full cycle.

Third full cycle of A—C

2:29	A section.
2:55	B section.
3:25	C section.
3:31	Repeat.
3:38	Final cadence: *Wankaras* and *ch'inisku* play unmetered/accelerando motif similar to outset.

The entire piece is played three times. Sing some of the melody to get a feel for the rhythm and flow of this zampoña music. On a second hearing, the sound may seem richer to you than on the first; you hear a panpipe ensemble playing what seems to be the same melody at various pitch levels, one at an octave below the original pitch level, another a perfect fourth above that lower octave, or a perfect fifth below the original octave. See Transcriptions 9.1 and 9.2.

"Kutirimunapaq" (Quechua for, roughly, "So That We Can Return") is music of the Kallawaya people, who live on the eastern slope of the Bolivian Andes, north of Lake Titicaca, close to the Peruvian border. The Kallawaya *campesinos* (farmers, peasants) live at different altitudes in the Charazani Valley—from 9,000 to 16,000 feet above sea level. Those at the lower elevations speak Quechua and cultivate potatoes, barley, and beans; at the upper elevations they speak Aymara and keep llamas, alpacas, and sheep. The Inkas adopted Quechua as their official language and spread it with them throughout their empire (1200–1533 C.E.). Today, from 5.5 to 8 million Andeans in Bolivia, Peru, Ecuador, and Argentina speak Quechua (or Quichua), while a minority speak Aymara (Bastien 1978:xxi). "Kutirimunapaq" is a *k'antu* from the community of Niñokorin, at 11,000 feet.

The *k'antu* ensembles, for which the Charazani region is famous (Baumann 1985), each comprise twenty to thirty *zampoña*-playing dancers, who move in a circular pattern. Some of them simultaneously beat a large, double-headed drum called a *wankara*. The triangle (in Quechua, *ch'inisku*), which we hear on CD 4, Track 9, is often present as well.

The Kallawaya play the panpipes in their dry season, which lasts roughly from June to September; they play transverse flutes (played horizontally, like the Western silver flute) or duct flutes (played vertically, and constructed like a recorder) during the rainy season, which lasts from November to at least late February. The preference on the altiplano for duct flutes during the rainy season may be related to the belief that their clear sound attracts rain and prevents frost, both of which are necessary conditions for growing crops.

TRANSCRIPTION 9.1
One melody line of the
k'antu "Kutirimunapaq."

Da Capo

Our ensemble consists of *zampoñas* of different sizes but with the same basic construction, in terms of numbers of tubes. Each musical register is represented by one named pair of panpipes, consisting of an **ira** (*ee*-ra) set of pipes (considered in the Bolivian altiplano to embody the male principle, and serving as the leader) and an **arca** (*ar*-ka) set of pipes (considered to embody the female principle and serving as the follower). In our context, the *ira* set has six pipes and the *arca* set has seven; we may refer to this type as 6/7-tubed. The different-sized instruments play the same melody, which results in the rich musical fabric of parallel octaves, fifths, and fourths.

There are at least two especially interesting aspects of this music (see Transcription 9.2). One is the doubling of the melodic line; the other is the way a melody is produced. Doubling the melody at a fixed interval has occurred at other times, in other places. One was in Europe, during the Middle Ages. There, by the ninth century, one-line Christian liturgical chant was being accompanied either by one lower part at the octave below or by a lower part at the fourth or fifth below. Another alternative augmented the two-voice complex to three or four voices by doubling one or both lines at the octave. Thus, early medieval Europe had musical textures with parallel octaves, fourths, and fifths very similar in intervallic structure

TRANSCRIPTION 9.2
Ensemble notation of
"Kuturimunapaq."

(if not in rhythm) to what we hear in twentieth-century Bolivian *k'antu*. In twentieth-century Africa, songs in parallel fourths and fifths are found among groups that have the tradition of pentatonic, or five-pitch, songs, such as the Gogo people of Tanzania (a good example of a Gogo song in parallel fourths and fifths appears in Nketia 1974:163).

Many peoples have used, and continue to use, the performance practice of **hocketing:** The melody is dispersed among two or more voices or instruments;

when one sounds, the others do not. Performing music in hocket is a uniquely communal way of making music: You cannot play the entire melody yourself—you need one or more partners to do it with you. In Africa, the hocketing technique appears among instrumental traditions, in the flute parts of Ghanaian Kasena *jongo* dance music, in the *akadinda* xylophone music of the Baganda of Uganda, and in several flute and gourd-trumpet traditions elsewhere in eastern and southern Africa; for vocal traditions, hocketing can be heard in the singing of the San (Bushmen) of southern Africa (Koetting 1992:94–97; Kaemmer 1998:703, 705; Cooke 1998:601). Certain European music of the thirteenth and fourteenth centuries had several parts but used notes and rests in a way that effectively divided the melody line between two voice parts: as one sounded, the other was silent. A hiccuping effect was thus created (*hoquetus* is Latin for "hiccup" and the likely derivation of the term). Hocketing with panpipes appears closer in time and space to our modern Bolivian music. In Panama, the Kuna Indians play six-tubed *guli* panpipes. Each person holds one tube, with the melody distributed among all six players. The Kuna also play *gammu burui* panpipes. Each fourteen-tubed set is bound into two groups, or rafts, of seven tubes (two rafts each of four tubes and three tubes, held side by side), the melody distributed between the two seven-tubed players in hocketing technique (Smith 1984:156–59, 167–72).

As among the Kuna, in Bolivian *k'antu* the hocketing procedure is integral to the overall musical fabric. In fact, hocketing is actually required by the way these panpipes are constructed. Although altiplano panpipes can range from three to seventeen tubes, a widely used type is 6/7-tubed—that is, the "total" instrument has thirteen tubes, consisting of one line, or rank, of six tubes (the *ira*) and one rank of seven tubes (the *arca*), as we have seen. This type of panpipe may be tuned in e minor (or in another perspective, G Major), as shown in Figure 9.1.

The type of *zampoña* shown in this figure has made an accommodation to European-derived scales. Not all *zampoñas* of the altiplano are tuned in this

FIGURE 9.1

Example of *zampoña* tuning. Left: Seven-tubed *arca* rank. Right: Six-tubed *ira* rank.

FIGURE 9.2

Tuning of full thirteen-
tubed *zampoña*.

diatonic manner; many have different scales. This basic tuning is nonetheless widely found among both Quechua-speaking and Aymara-speaking peoples.

When the full instrument is combined (six- and seven-tubed ranks joined together or played by two people), we have a thirteen-tubed e minor scale, over the space of an octave and a half with subtonic below (D), or a thirteen-tubed G Major scale, going up to the tenth above and down to the perfect fourth below (D) (Figure 9.2).

As seen earlier in the Close Listening guide, the formal structure of this performance of "Kutirimunapaq" is ABC, each section being repeated, then the entire piece repeated twice, for a total of three times. This is a characteristic structure for the Bolivian *k'antu*, accommodating the continuous dancing that goes with the music making. Counting the number of different notes that sound in this particular *k'antu* we find that, within the octave, five notes predominate: C#, E, F#, G#, and B. Then, the C# and E come back in the upper octave. Note that C#, not E, serves as the tonic pitch in this case. There is one more note used (D#), but this comes in only at the end of sections A, B, and C—once each time, just prior to the final cadence, or stopping point, itself marked by a rhythmic "break" in "Kutirimunapaq."

This *k'antu* is primarily five-pitch, or pentatonic. Many traditional dance musics in the Andes region are similarly pentatonic, though certainly not all of them. "Kutirimunapaq" is strongly rhythmic, with the steady pound of the *wankara* supporting the beat. Andean dance music, from Bolivia up to Ecuador, has this powerful rhythmic cast, underscoring its dance function.

Hocketing panpipes, with rhythmic melodies played in parallel fifths and octaves and with strong, steady rhythm on a large drum, begin to distinguish this Bolivian altiplano stream of Latin American music. The evocation of Indigenous cultures such as this high-Andean one, through use of Andean instruments, begins to demarcate *Nueva Canción.* As we have seen, New Song is not only nostalgic but also politically committed and international. Above all, it speaks of and on behalf of the people—characteristically, the forgotten people. We now turn our attention north of Chile, Bolivia, and Peru to a nation of many other unsung (or less-sung) individuals and peoples, a country itself frequently overlooked in discussions of Latin America: Ecuador.

The Quichua of the Northern Andes of Ecuador

We can best appreciate the traditional nature of northern Ecuadorian Quichua music by knowing something of the traditional setting in which Quichua live. The musicians we will be listening to have traditionally lived in *comunas,* or small clusters of houses, on the slopes of Mount Cotacachi, one of several volcanoes in the Ecuadorian Andes. These *comunas* lie outside the town of Cotacachi, in Imbabura Province (see the map at the beginning of the chapter).

The Quichua spoken in Cotacachi-area *comunas* was spoken there four hundred years ago. Today in Ecuador more than one million people speak the language.

The agriculture and material culture of the Andes around Cotacachi are also traditional. In this rich green countryside dotted with tall eucalyptus, at 8,300 to 9,700 feet above sea level, maize has been the principal cultivated crop for hundreds of years. Quichua homes have typically had one room, often with a covered patio, both with dirt floor. Regional Quichua homes have been constructed this way for four hundred years. One such home is shown in Figure 9.3.

Styles of dress have also remained basically the same since the sixteenth century. Everyone covers his or her head to protect it from the intense heat and light of the near-vertical sun at midday (Cotacachi is almost precisely on the equator.). Women wear cloths, and men wear hats. Quichua women wear embroidered blouses, over which they drape shawls (in Quichua, *fachalina*). They secure their two skirts, one

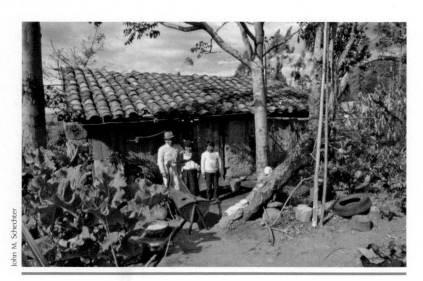

John M. Schechter

FIGURE 9.3

Home of Mama Ramona and Miguel Armando in the *comuna* of Tikulla, outside Cotacachi. May 1980. Today, homes made of concrete block are replacing the older type of dwelling.

FIGURE 9.4

Three generations of
Quichua men. May 1980.

John M. Schechter

blue and one white, with two woven belts: a wider, inner belt, called the *mama chumbi* (mother belt) and a narrower, outer belt, called the *wawa chumbi* (child belt). Designed in this region, these belts were traditionally woven on home back-strap looms by Quichua families in various *comunas*, and they usually carried the names of Imbabura towns. Men and boys have traditionally worn a white or blue shirt, white pants, and a dark *poncho*, though today in Imbabura you will see Quichua teenagers wearing English-language sweatshirts and jeans. Any large gathering of Quichua, such as for Saturday market or Palm Sunday procession, is still largely a sea of blue and white. In Figure 9.4, we see three generations within the same family. The grandfather wears traditional dress; his adult son retains the white sandals, white shirt, pants, and hat; his grandson wears Western-influenced clothes.

Among Cotacachi Quichua, a strong sense of community arises from a common regional dialect, a common dress, and common aspects of material culture. Quichua eat the same diet of beans and potatoes, grown in their own plots. They gather regularly for weekly markets, for periodic community work projects (*mingas*), and for fiestas—such as a child's wake or a wedding. We will discuss harp/vocal music at the Cotacachi-area child's wake later in this chapter. Further, I have examined the ubiquity of the festive child's wake in Latin America in other works (Schechter 1983, 1994a); you can also read of harp performance in the celebration of a Cotacachi-area Quichua wedding, held in October 1990, in Andrade Albuja and Schechter (2004).

In 1980 few Cotacachi Quichua owned vehicles; by 1990 a few community leaders possessed new pickup trucks. In any case, Quichua homes on Cotacachi's slopes are for the most part not located on roads but interspersed along a network of footpaths called *chaki ñanes* (*cha*-ki *nyan*-es). Without telephones, Quichua families have traditionally communicated only by foot, along *chaki ñanes;* these paths bear the weight of Quichua women carrying infants, brush, and food to and from market, and of Quichua men carrying potatoes, milled grain, or perhaps a harp (see Figure 9.5). For all Quichua, the way around the slopes on *chaki ñanes* is second nature.

John M. Schechter

FIGURE 9.5

Chaki ñan (Ecuadorian footpath). May 1980.

THE MUSICAL TRADITION: *SANJUÁN*

The common language, dress, material culture, and daily labor all find a musical echo in *sanjuán*. The term **sanjuán** (san-*hooan*) arose at least as early as 1860. At that time, it referred to either a type of song played at the festival of St. John (San Juan) the Baptist held in June or a type of dance performed at that festival.

Today, the instrument that Cotacachi Quichua often use to perform *sanjuán* is the harp without pedals, often referred to in English as the diatonic harp because it is usually tuned to one particular scale and cannot be changed quickly to another. Reflecting their other deep-rooted traditions, Quichua have been playing the harp in the Ecuadorian highlands for hundreds of years; in the eighteenth century, it was the most common instrument in the region

FIGURE 9.6

Harpist Raúl, playing his Imbabura harp. Ecuador, March 1980.

(Recio [1773] 1947:426). The harp's popularity in the Andes is not limited to Ecuador; recall that in the Peruvian highlands, it is so widespread among Quechua that it is considered a "native" instrument. Brought from Europe initially by several different groups of missionaries, especially the Jesuits, and even by the first conquistadors, the harp has been in Latin America for more than four hundred years.

The Imbabura harp, seen and heard here, is common only in Imbabura Province (Figure 9.6). It appears as an oddity among harpists in central highland Ecuador, where musicians play a larger instrument. The type of harp Raúl plays here is made of cedar and uses wooden nails. The sound emanates through three circular holes on

John M. Schechter

FIGURE 9.7

Schematic diagram show-
ing position of sound holes
in an Imbabura harp.

CD 4:10

"Muyu muyari warmigu"
("Please Return, Dear Woman")
(4:19). Performed by Efraín, harp;
Rafael, voice and *golpe*. Field
recording by John M. Schechter,
inside a schoolhouse in a
comuna on the slopes of
Mt. Cotacachi, October 13, 1990.

FIGURE 9.8

Rafael (tapping the *golpe*) and
Efraín (playing the Imbabura
harp), during the recording of
CD 4, Track 10. Mt. Cotacachi,
Ecuador, 1990.

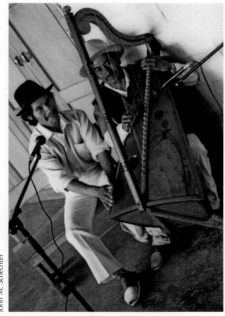

John M. Schechter

the top of the soundbox; they are consistently found
in the pattern shown in Figure 9.7, on either side of
the column, or pole, that connects the neck to the
soundbox.

Looking at Raúl's harp, you may think that the
instrument has an unusual shape, compared with
Western harps with which you may be familiar. The
Imbabura harp's column is straight but short, giving
the instrument a low "head," or top. Its soundbox is
distinctively arched, wide, and deep. On older harps
in this region, bull's-hoof glue was used. The tuning
pegs are made of iron or wood. The single line of strings is typically a combination
of gut, possibly nylon, and steel. The gut strings—used for the bass and middle
registers—used to be made by the Quichua themselves from the cut, washed,
dried, and twisted intestinal fibers of sheep, dogs, cats, or goats. Sometimes
musicians use nylon strings for the middle register, or range, of notes. The steel
strings, closest to the performer, play the treble register, in which the melody line
is articulated. Once again relying on their environment for necessary materials,
Quichua musicians may use the leg bone of the sheep (Quichua: *tullu*, "bone") to
turn the tuning pegs on the harp neck.

This Imbabura harp is a descendant of sixteenth- and seventeenth-century
Spanish harps, as shown by shared features of tuning, construction, configuration,
and stringing. The Imbabura harp has remained essentially unchanged in appearance
for one to two hundred years, and possibly longer (Schechter 1992).

Let us now look at the *sanjuán* "Muyu muyari warmigu" ("Please Return, Dear
Woman"), sometimes referred to as, "Chayamuyari warmigu" ("Come Here,
Indeed, Dear Woman") (CD 4, Track 10). This performance is by the highly
esteemed Cotacachi-area harpist, Efraín, together with one of his favored singers,
Rafael. Having worked with Efraín ten years earlier, in the environs of Cotacachi
(see Schechter 2002:405–11), I was pleased to renew our acquain-
tanceship in 1990. We met to plan the recording session, which
would be held in a classroom of the same primary school on
Cotacachi's slopes at which my wife and I had resided from
October 1979 through April 1980; this stereophonic recording of
"Muyu," along with other pieces for harp and voice, took place on
October 13, 1990.

Harpists play the higher, or treble strings (treble clef part) with
their stronger hand; the lower, or bass, strings (bass clef part) with
their weaker hand. Efraín, left-handed, plays treble with the left
hand, bass with the right hand (Figure 9.8).

In general, the form of "Muyu muyari warmigu" is typical of
Cotacachi Quichua *sanjuanes*. It is fundamentally a repetitive form,
in which one or two different phrases, typically contrasting in
register, are occasionally inserted into an otherwise similar phrase
pattern. In *sanjuán*, the main motive predominates; these are the
ones you hear the most, which I refer to as A phrases in "Muyu."
These are the melodies one identifies with a particular *sanjuán*. The
sanjuán phrase often lasts 8 beats, and the rhythm of the first half of
the phrase is often identical, or nearly identical, to the rhythm of the

second half; we can call this phrase structure, then, **isorhythmic**—of "equal rhythm," or the "same rhythm." Here, in "Muyu," the rhythm of the first half of the A phrase is Ta Ta Ta-Ta, Ta Ta Ta Ta; the rhythm of the second half of the phrase is exactly the same: Ta Ta Ta-Ta, Ta Ta Ta Ta. The Close Listening guide provides the full text of "Muyu" and illustrates the formal structure. *Sanjuanes* are most often in double-couplets: one two-line verse is stated, then immediately repeated; then, another double-couplet, or a harp interlude.

Close Listening

"MUYU MUYARI WARMIGU" ("PLEASE RETURN, DEAR WOMAN")

CD 4:10

COUNTER NUMBER	COMMENTARY	LYRICS	TRANSLATION
Introduction			
0:00	Harp plays seven A phrases, then two B phrases.		
1st double-couplet			
0:44	Vocal and harp.	*Muyu muyari warmigu*	Please return, dear woman
		Muyu muyari payagu.	Please return, dear "old lady."
		Muyu muyari warmigu	Please return, dear woman
		Muyu muyari payagu.	Please return, dear "old lady."
2nd double-couplet			
0:52	Vocal and harp. (Couplet repeats.)	*Kambaj shayashka puistuka Sisagullami viñashka.*	The place in which you've stood Just a dear flower has grown.
Instrumental Interlude			
1:01	Harp plays six A phrases, then two B phrases.		
1st double-couplet repeats			
1:37	Vocal and harp.		
2nd double-couplet repeats, modified			
1:45	Vocal and harp. (Couplet repeats.)	*Kambaj shayashka puistupi Sisagullami viñashka.*	The place in which you've stood Just a dear flower has grown.
Instrumental interlude			
1:54	Harp plays five A phrases, then two B phrases, then one A phrase.		

3rd double-couplet

| 2:30 | Vocal and harp. (Couplet repeats.) | *Llakiwanguichu warmigu Juyawanguichu warmigu?* | Will you be sad, to me, dear woman? Or will you be loving, to me, dear woman? |

2nd double-couplet repeats, modified

| 2:38 | Vocal and harp. (Couplet repeats.) | *Kambaj shayashka puistupi Sisagullami viñashka.* | The place in which you've stood Just a dear flower has grown. |

Instrumental interlude

| 2:47 | Harp plays two A phrases, then two B phrases, then six A phrases, then two B phrases. |

1st double-couplet repeats, modified

| 3:41 | Vocal and harp. (Couplet repeats.) | *Muyu muyari warmigu Muyu muyari urpigu.* | Please return, dear woman Please return, dear turtle dove. |

2nd double-couplet, modified

| 3:50 | Vocal and harp. (Couplet repeats.) | *Kambaj shayashka puistupi Sisagullami viñashka.* | The place in which you've stood Just a dear flower has grown. |

Instrumental ending

| 3:59 | Harp plays three A phrases leading to final chord. Words spoken at end by John Schechter: *"Diusílupagui, maistrugukuna; Alimi llujshirka; disílupa'i."* "Thank you, esteemed maestros; it came out well; thank you." |

As you can hear and can see in the guide, the A phrase predominates in this song. The consecutive A phrases (by harp alone and by harp and voice) are varied by two B phrases, in the harp. Most *sanjuanes* follow this general pattern, although perhaps less regularly, with A phrases predominating and sometimes without any B phrases at all. The A phrases are supported largely by E♭ Major, while concluding on its relative minor, c minor; in terms of key relationships, relative major and their own relative minor keys carry identical key signatures (here, three flats for E♭ Major and c minor) and the same basic collection of pitches; the relative minor key takes as its home-note the 6th scale degree of its relative major key (C̲ is the 6th degree of the E♭ Major scale). The B phrases are in A♭ Major, the subdominant key (IV) of the home-key of E♭ Major. In the previous edition (Schechter 2002:405–12), I discussed another *sanjuán* ("Cascarón") played on harp by Efraín (no vocals); the harmonic scheme was essentially the same as that for "Muyu." This scheme of harmony—notably the "bimodality" of a constant alternation between the major and its relative minor key—is characteristic of both northern Ecuadorian highland *sanjuán* and many other Andean traditional musics as well.

The isorhythm discussed earlier is a regular feature of northern highland Ecuadorian Quichua *sanjuanes.* Transcription 9.3 illustrates how regular these rhythmic features are. This collection gives you a dozen *sanjuanes* to learn and practice singing. All of these were recorded in Cotacachi comunas in 1979–1980; "Ilumán tiyu," "Cascarón," and "Chayamuyari warmiku" were also recorded in 1990. Note the 8-beat patterning and the equal rhythm halves; "Muyu muyari warmiku" (or, "Chayamuyari warmiku") is number six; Efraín played a slight variant of the melody you see transcribed here, but with identical isorhythmic phrasing, in our CD recording from October 1990. Also note that some combination of sixteenth-eighth-sixteenth and two eighths is characteristic of most *sanjuanes.* Thus, the careful listener can often identify a Quichua *sanjuán* by the presence of these rhythm kernels alone.

TRANSCRIPTION 9.3
Twelve Cotacachi Quichua *sanjuanes.*

* "NI.5" refers to the fifth sanjuán recorded in my fieldwork with the title not identified; "Ñ6‴" refers to the second variant of the sixth sanjuán I recorded by the Quichua blind harpist José Manuel Calapi, who was known in 1980 by his nickname, "Ñausa" (Quichua: blind).

It is always interesting to observe how oral tradition works, in traditional cultures. Here are three comparable segments of "Muyu" ("Chayamuyari"), all performed by regional Quichua musicians. The first was recorded on December 28, 1979, by the solo singer César, who was then twelve years old. The second was recorded on September 16, 1990, eleven years later, by the singer-guitarist Segundo "Galo" Maigua Pillajo, the composer of the *sanjuán* "Ilumán tiyu," which we will discuss next in this chapter. The third, our "Muyu," was performed about a month later, on October 13, 1990. All three performances were to roughly the same A phrase with which we are now familiar:

"Muyu": December 28, 1979	*Chayamuyari warmiku*	Come here, indeed, dear woman (or, wife)
	Chayamuyari warmiku,	Come here, indeed, dear woman,
	Chayamuyari warmiku	Come here, indeed, dear woman
	Chayamuyari warmiku,	Come here, indeed, dear woman,
	Kampak purishka llaktaka	The community you've walked
	Sumakllamari rikurin,	Appears just beautiful, indeed,
	Kampak purishka llaktaka	The community you've walked
	Sumakllamari rikurin,	Appears just beautiful, indeed,
"Muyu": September 16, 1990	*Kampak shayashka pushtuka*	The place in which you've stood
	Sumbrallamari rikurin,	Appears just shady, indeed,
	Kampak shayashka pushtuka	The place in which you've stood
	Sumbrallamari rikurin,	Appears just shady, indeed,
	Muyu muyari nigragu	Please return, dear dark woman
	Muyu muyari payagu,	Please return, dear "old lady,"
	Muyu muyari nigragu	Please return, dear dark woman
	Muyu muyari payagu,	Please return, dear "old lady,"
"Muyu": October 13, 1990	*Muyu muyari warmigu*	Please return, dear woman
	Muyu muyari payagu,	Please return, dear "old lady,"
	Muyu muyari warmigu	Please return, dear woman
	Muyu muyari payagu,	Please return, dear "old lady,"
	Kambaj shayashka puistuka	The place in which you've stood
	Sisagullami viñashka,	Just a dear flower has grown,
	Kambaj shayashka puistuka	The place in which you've stood
	Sisagullami viñashka,	Just a dear flower has grown,

We can see several things here. First, performers are constrained by an 8-syllable line: every line must be 8 syllables long. Elsewhere (Schechter 1996), I have addressed the issue of how Quichua performers of *sanjuán* operate under this oral-traditional principle, known as formulaic expression; most centrally, though, the pattern is that of Milman Parry's "formula," cited by Lord ([1960] 1978:4): "'a group of words which is regularly employed under the same metrical conditions to express a given essential idea.'" Second, each double-couplet equates to 8 quarter-note beats. The melody proceeds sequentially, the first 4 beats—corresponding to one 8-syllable line—winding down to the 5th scale-degree of the minor key, the last 4 beats continuing the twisting descent to take the next 8-syllable line down to the lower home-note of the key. We also note, as regards the lyrics, a kind of parallel meaning (semantic parallelism): for example, "Please return, dear woman," followed by "Please return, dear 'old lady.'" That is, a couplet like this one often has the two lines nearly identical, with only a small word-shift, in the second line; this also facilitates transmission via oral tradition, since the near-repetition of a line means one does have to remember so much. In the case of young César's version, he has actual identical lines in his first couplet.

This is also a love song; a major theme of all the lyrics is praise for one's beloved. Many traditional songs throughout Latin America speak to the beauty of, and general admiration for, the women of a man's home region (for a fuller discussion, see Schechter 1999a:4–7). Hence, in "Muyu" we read the following: "That place in which you've stood/walked—been, appears beautiful/shady/produces a flower."

Finally, we find that the verbs are interchangeable: Come here—(*Chayamuyari*)/ Return—(*Muyu muyari*). In short, we have in "Muyu" a carefully structured, entirely traditional package of oral tradition: It follows rather strict rules having to do with a consistent subject matter, particular syllabic constraints and verb interchangeability, with musical isorhythm in an 8-beat phrase, and with semantic parallelism in the text.

A CLASSIC *SANJUÁN*

David McAllester calls certain Navajo great ceremonial chants "classic" (2002:60). Similarly, we can point to at least one Imbabura Quichua *sanjuán* that qualifies as a classic in its highland region: "Ilumán tiyu."

Popular both in 1980 and still in 1990, the *sanjuán* "Ilumán tiyu" (ee-loo-*mahn tee*-yoo; "Man of Ilumán") was composed by Segundo "Galo" Maigua Pillajo, a Quichua composer-guitarist-singer of the Imbabura village of Ilumán. Galo Maigua's *sanjuán* compositions are often motivated by autobiographical forces. His fame among Imbabura Quichua is attested to by wide acknowledgment of his being the composer of highly popular *sanjuanes.* His fame is also apparent in the high level of local demand for his ensemble, Conjunto Ilumán, and their having produced a commercial cassette.

My fieldwork in 1990 in Imbabura brought to light the fact that *sanjuán* often takes on the nature of a ballad, even in instances where that fact is not immediately obvious. A *sanjuán* text typically expresses the essence of a large story, making the *sanjuán* a highly distilled ballad form, the synoptic character of the text being in keeping with the elliptical character of Andean poetry dating back to the Inkas (Schechter 1979:193). The ballad nature of "Ilumán tiyu"—the story behind the *sanjuán*—is not at all obvious. We will explore this enigma a bit later, but for now, listen to "Ilumán tiyu" (CD 4, Track 11). In the village of Ilumán, in the home of a local policeman, I recorded the composer, "Galo" Maigua, singing "Ilumán tiyu" and playing guitar together with his Conjunto Ilumán, on October 27, 1990 (Figure 9.9). The Close Listening guide provides the full text of "Ilumán tiyu" and illustrates the formal structure.

If **II** stands for the Introduction/Interlude, **AI** for the A phrase played by instruments, **AV** for the A phrase vocalized by the ensemble, and **B** for the B phrase, the formal structure of Galo Maigua's composition "Ilumán tiyu" is as follows:

CD 4:11

"Ilumán tiyu" ("Man from Ilumán") (3:17). Segundo "Galo" Maigua Pillajo. *Sanjuán* of Ecuador. Performed by "Galo," guitar and vocal, with the Quichua ensemble Conjunto Ilumán. Field recording by John Schechter. Ilumán, Imbabura, Ecuador. October 1990.

II / AI / II / AV / B / AI / II / AV / B / AI / II / AV / B / AI

Close Listening

"ILUMÁN TIYU" ("MAN FROM ILUMÁN")

CD 4:11

COUNTER NUMBER	COMMENTARY		LYRICS	TRANSLATION	FORM
Introduction					
0:00	Violin outlines home chord four times.				II
0:09	*Kenas* and violin play the principal melody of "Ilumán tiyu"—four A phrases.				AI
0:27	Violin outlines home chord four times.				II
Quichua language double-couplets					
0:36	Vocalists sing the two double-couplets to four A phrases. Violin plays in harmony.	A	*Ilumán tiyu cantanmi, Ilumán tiyu nijunmi.*	The man [not uncle] from Ilumán sings, The man from Ilumán is saying.	AV
		A	*Ilumán tiyu cantanmi, Ilumán tiyu nijunmi.*	The man from Ilumán sings, The man from Ilumán is saying.	
		A	*Sultira kashpa paya kashpa, ñuka tunupi bailapai.*	Being a young [unmarried] woman, [or an] old woman, Dance to my song.	
		A	*Sultira kashpa paya kashpa, ñuka tunupi bailapai.*	Being a young woman, old woman, Dance to my song.	
Interlude					
0:55	*Kenas* and violin play two B phrases.				B
1:04	Violin plays two A phrases.				AI
1:13	*Kenas* and violin play two A phrases.				(AI)
1:23	Violin outlines tonic chord, four times.				II
	Musician shouts, *"Kushi, kushiguta!"* ("Real happy!").				
The Spanish-language double-couplets					
1:32	Vocalists sing the two Spanish-language double-couplets to four A phrases. Violin plays in harmony.	A	*Este es el indio de Ilumán, El que canta (canto)* sanjuanito,*	This is the indígena of Ilumán, He who sings sanjuán,	AV

	A	*Este es el indio de Ilumán,* *El que canta (canto)** *sanjuanito,*	This is the indígena of Ilumán, He who sings sanjuán,
	A	*Para que bailen toditos,* *Para que bailen toditas.*	So that all men might dance, So that all women might dance.
	A	*Para que bailen toditos,* *Para que bailen toditas.*	So that all men might dance, So that all women might dance.

Interlude

1:50	Violin plays two B phrases.	B
2:00	*Kenas* and violin play the principal melody of "Ilumán tiyu"—four A phrases.	AI
2:18	Violin outlines home chord four times. ("¡*Ahora,tshhh!*")	II

Repeat Quichua language double-couplets

| 2:27 | Double-couplets sung to four A phrases, the violin playing in harmony. | AV |

Conclusion

2:46	*Kenas* and violin play two B phrases.	B
2:55	*Kenas* and violin play the principal melody of "Ilumán tiyu"-four A phrases.	AI

*Segundo "Galo" Maigua Pillajo sings *canto*. ["I sing"], referring to the fact that it is he who is the composer of the song, about whom its lyrics are centered. Lyrics used with permission of Galo Maigua.

The symmetries/balance here are prodigious: three vocal statements and three B statements; four Intro/Interludes and four instrumental statements; the consecutive pattern, AV-B-AI enunciated three times; the consecutive, overlapping larger pattern, II-AV-B-AI-II occurring twice—itself being framed by the II statements. In sum, a distinctive cohesiveness—strongly reinforced by the Ta-Ta, Ta Ta Ta Ta Ta Ta; Ta-Ta, Ta Ta Ta Ta Ta Ta 8-beat isorhythm and by the rising, then falling (archlike) melodic shape of the 8-beat A phrase.

What had never been comprehensible since my 1980 research, when I recorded numerous versions of "Ilumán tiyu" in the environs of Cotacachi, was the nature of the lyrics. When I was informed that Segundo "Galo" Maigua Pillajo was in fact the composer of this *sanjuán*, I tried, during a visit to his Ilumán home on September 30, 1990, to learn what might lie behind words that seem merely a statement that the man singing and speaking is an *indígena* from Ilumán.

FIGURE 9.9

Members of the Quichua ensemble Conjunto Ilumán, in the village of Ilumán, Imbabura Province, northern highland Ecuador. October 1990.

John M. Schechter

Galo Maigua described the tale behind the text. He told me that before he composed "Ilumán tiyu," he had become extremely ill with tuberculosis; the condition of his lungs had deteriorated, and he believed he was about to die. Although during his 1972–1973 wanderings through the *comunas* around Cotacachi he had sung the melody to a variety of words (Galo says he composes by first hearing a melody and later setting a text), he now determined that he would like everyone—be they young woman or old woman, for example—to dance to this, his song, after his death. In effect, "Ilumán tiyu" was ultimately texted as Galo's final statement of his identity to posterity: "I"—the man singing, speaking—am a man from Ilumán; remember me by remembering my music: "Dance to my song." In sum, what appeared to the uninformed listener to be innocuous words came, on greater understanding, to have profound import for a composer believing himself to be on his deathbed.

Spanish speakers will note that the intermingling of Spanish and Quichua words we spoke of early in this chapter appears prominently in this *sanjuán*. Moreover, the verse *Este es el indio de Ilumán, el que canta sanjuanito* is a rough translation of the first, critically important, verse; Galo Maigua commented to me that a major area radio station had prompted him to produce the parallel text in Spanish. Some of his other *sanjuanes*, such as "Antonio Mocho" and "Rusita Andranga," share the distilled-ballad character of "Ilumán tiyu." Both of these *sanjuanes*, along with "Ilumán tiyu," appear on the commercial cassette *Elenita Conde*, by Conjunto Ilumán; the cassette was mastered in Otavalo and mass-produced in Bogotá, Colombia, somewhat prior to 1990.

Efraín and Rafael, Segundo "Galo" Maigua Pillajo and his Conjunto Ilumán colleagues, and hundreds of other Quichua musicians in the Otavalo Valley, Imbabura Province, are not the only regional stakeholders in the genre that is northern Ecuadorian highland *sanjuán*. *Sanjuán* can also be heard in area mestizo households, and, a few hours up the Pan American highway toward the Colombia border, in African Ecuadorian gatherings. The lesson here is that a prominent regional music can trump racial and cultural barriers and establish itself firmly in a region, with different cultural signatures therein. Let us take a closer look at the musicians up the road, in Chota.

AFRICAN ECUADORIAN MUSIC OF THE CHOTA RIVER VALLEY

On October 27, 1979, I was fortunate to meet Germán Congo, the excellent lead guitarist of the ensemble Conjunto Rondador (the *rondador* is a single-rank panpipe of Ecuador) at one of their performances in Ibarra, the capital of Imbabura Province. Germán invited me to visit him and his musician-brothers in the Chota Valley. Some months later, on March 1, 1980, my friend Don Valerio, my wife Janis, and I journeyed to Chota. This was the first of several visits to Chota and Ibarra, in 1980 and again in 1990, in which my research focused on the musical artistry of the Congo brothers, their colleague Milton Tadeo, and fellow Chota musicians (Schechter 1994b).

When we think of Latin American regions that have large populations of African Americans, Ecuador does not usually come to mind. Yet as much as 25 percent of the country's population are African Ecuadorians. They are heavily concentrated in coastal Esmeraldas Province, which neighbors Imbabura Province. The first Africans arrived in Ecuador in the sixteenth century, after which Jesuit missionaries brought in large numbers of African slaves to work on plantations both on the coast and in the central highlands: Indigenous laborers were hard to find in some areas and unwilling to serve as slaves in others. The relatively small pocket of approximately fifteen thousand African Ecuadorians in the Chota Valley, comprising ten to fifteen small villages, has an uncertain origin. The most widely accepted view is that the African Ecuadorians of the Chota Valley are descended from slaves held by the Jesuits on their plantations in the highlands (Lipski 1987:157–58).

During the 1980s and 1990s, the best-known musicians in the Chota Valley were the guitarist-composer-singers Germán, Fabián, and Eleuterio Congo and their colleague Milton Tadeo. Twenty-seven years ago, they played mostly around their home village of Carpuela; by 1990 they were regional celebrities with regular weekend performances in local villages, on the coast, and in nearby Colombia. As of October 1990 they had recorded six long-playing records within seven years. The Congo brothers are the third generation of composer-performers in their family.

On October 21, 1990—more than ten years after I had first worked with them (March 1980), Fabián, Germán, and Eleuterio Congo, with Milton Tadeo and colleague Ermundo Mendes León (on *güiro*), performed "Me gusta la leche" (meh *goo*-sta la *leh*-cheh; "I Like Milk"), heard here on CD 4, Track 12. At this time, the full ensemble identified themselves as Grupo Ecuador de los Hermanos Congo y Milton Tadeo ("Ecuador Ensemble of the Congo Brothers and Milton Tadeo"). We made the stereo recording in a community house near Germán's home, close by the Imbabura Provincial capital, Ibarra. Germán played lead guitar (*requinto*); Fabián and Milton both played guitar and sang in duet; Eleuterio played the **bomba,** the Chota-area double-headed drum held between the knees and played with the hands; and Ermundo Mendes León played the *güiro*, a scraper (see Figures 9.10 and 9.11).

CD 4:12

"Me gusta la leche" ("I Like Milk") (2:31). Performed by Germán Congo, lead guitar (*requinto*); Fabián Congo and Milton Tadeo, vocals and guitars; Eleuterio Congo, *bomba*; Ermundo Mendes León, *güiro*. Field recording by John M. Schechter, outside Ibarra, Imbabura, Ecuador, October 21, 1990.

FIGURE 9.10

Grupo Ecuador de los Hermanos Congo y Milton Tadeo. Back row, left to right: Ermundo Mendes León plays the metal *guiro*; Germán Congo, *requinto*; Milton Tadeo, guitar; Fabián Congo, guitar. In front: Eleuterio Congo plays *bomba*. Imbabura, Ecuador, 1990.

John M. Schechter

FIGURE 9.11

Left to right: Eleuterio Congo, Milton Tadeo, Fabián Congo, John Schechter, Germán Congo, and Ermundo Mendes León. Outside the house of Germán Congo, Imbabura, Ecuador, 1990.

Courtesy of Germán Congo family.

In this *sanjuán*, we see the same 8-beat phrases and double-couplet structure of text that we saw in "Muyu muyari warmigu," a Quichua *sanjuán* that would in 1990 have been performed in the Otavalo Valley, a couple of hours down the highway from the Chota River Valley, site of the Congos' home village of Carpuela. However, despite the double-couplet construction and comparable tempo, of the music (one can easily dance Quichua *sanjuán* to "Me gusta la leche"), this is *not* Quichua *sanjuán*, though it is *sanjuán* (see the Close Listening guide).

Close Listening

"ME GUSTA LA LECHE" ("I LIKE MILK")

CD 4:12

COUNTER NUMBER	COMMENTARY	LYRICS	TRANSLATION
Introduction			
0:00	*Requinto* guitar plays introductory motive *a* (twice), then		
0:10	introductory motive *b* (twice), then		
0:20	introductory motive *c* (twice).		
	Each motive is eight quarter-note beats long.		
1st stanza (double-couplet)—A phrase			
0:29	Vocals on the A phrase, the principal melody of the *sanjuán*.	*Me gusta la leche, me gusta el café,* *Pero más me gusta lo que tiene Usted.* *Me gusta la leche, me gusta el café,* *Pero más me gusta lo que tiene Usted.*	I like milk, I like coffee, But I like what you have better. I like milk, I like coffee, But I like what you have better.
2nd stanza (double-couplet)—A phrase			
0:38	*Requinto* counterpoint added to vocal melody in A phrase (principal melody).	*Así negra linda de mi corazón,* *Cuando yo te veo, me muero de ilusión.* *Así negra linda de mi corazón,* *Cuando yo te veo, me muero de ilusión.*	So, beautiful black woman of my heart, When I see you, I'm filled with anticipation. So, beautiful black woman of my heart, When I see you, I'm filled with anticipation.
***Requinto* interlude**			
0:48	Lead guitar and ensemble. Lead plays *c* motive from introduction twice.		
3rd stanza (double-couplet)—A phrase			
0:58	*Requinto* counterpoint added to vocal melody in A phrase (principal melody).	*En esta cuaresma no me confesé* *Porque en viernes santo yo me enamoré.* *En esta cuaresma no me confesé* *Porque en viernes santo yo me enamoré.*	During this Lent I did not go to confession, Because, on Good Friday, I fell in love. During this Lent I did not go to confession, Because, on Good Friday, I fell in love.

2nd stanza repeat

1:08   Vocals with *requinto* counterpoint

Instrumental interlude

1:18   Ensemble plays two new B phrases.

1:27   Germán's *requinto* guitar repeats the introduction motives.

3rd stanza repeat

1:57   Vocals return with *requinto* counterpoint.

2nd stanza repeat

2:06   Vocals with *requinto* counterpoint.

***Requinto* interlude repeat**

2:16   Lead guitar and ensemble. Lead guitar plays *c* motive from introduction twice.

Final cadence

2:26   Ensemble with lead guitar playing melodic riff (in the minor home-key).
                Spoken at end by John Schechter: *Gracias.*

In the first place, we do not have clear phrase isorhythm: the second 4 beats are *not* identical here to the first 4 beats, as in Quichua *sanjuán.* Looking at the stanza 1 (beginning *Me gusta la leche* ...):

First 4 beats: 4 sixteenth notes/2 eighths/4 sixteenths/quarter
Second 4 beats: 4 sixteenth notes/sixteenth-eighth-sixteenth/eighth and
                   2 sixteenths/quarter

This is quite fascinating. In this musical genre "shared" between two neighboring cultures, Quichua and African Ecuadorian, there is a *suggestion* of isorhythm, in that beat 5 is the same as beat 1 (4 sixteenths), and beat 8 is the same as beat 4 (quarter note); the divergence comes with beats 6 and 7. Beat 6 is sixteenth-eighth-sixteenth. The sharp-eyed and sharp-eared among you will recall that this small rhythmic fragment—sixteenth-eighth-sixteenth—was a rhythmic marker for Quichua *sanjuán.* Here it is again, in neighboring African Ecuadorian *sanjuán.* Beat 7 (eighth and 2 sixteenths) is close to beat 3 (4 sixteenths) yet also different. Looking for a moment at stanza 3 (*En esta cuaresma* ...), the "noteworthy" beat 6 now gives us a syncopation, accenting the fourth sixteenth-note—a weak beat—thus providing increased rhythmic drive. Quichua *sanjuán* almost never, in my experience, utilizes such weak-beat accent and syncopation.

In the second place, we have the wonderful counterpoint (independent melody and rhythm) of Germán's lead guitar (*requinto*), which provides a remarkable texture, depth, and richness to the music—something Chota musicians often refer to as *dulzura,* or sweetness (Schechter 1994b:293).

"Me gusta la leche" is a rich musical expression of a border region: African Ecuadorian, close to a major Quichua cultural zone, within a Spanish-speaking nation. It therefore demonstrates hybrid traits: a genre (sanjuán) native to the neighboring Quichua Indigenous people, yet here borrowed and—with phrasing twists, rhythmic variance and nuance, and *requinto dulzura*—made unique to Chota.

The Andean Ensemble Phenomenon: Going Abroad

By 1990 the reputation of the Congo brothers and Milton Tadeo had caused them to travel throughout Ecuador and into Colombia, playing for substantial fees, and on television (Schechter 1994b:288). Segundo "Galo" Maigua and his Quichua colleagues have been to Europe to play. The case of Conjunto Ilumán in particular represents a now-broad phenomenon, both in the Andes and beyond: the itinerant Andean ensemble and the globalization of Andean musics. Other Ecuadorian ensembles focusing on Quichua or *Nueva Canción* musics have included ñanda Mañachi (Quichua: "lend me the way"; 1977, 1979, 1983); Conjunto Indígena "Peguche" (Spanish: "*indígena* ensemble from the village of Peguche [near Otavalo]"; 1977); and Jatari (Quichua: "Get up!"; 1978). The carefully and elaborately produced albums of ñanda Mañachi, in particular, are notably evocative of the Quichua music-culture of Imbabura.

In the Otavalo Valley of Imbabura, Quichua ensembles date back at least to the 1940s and 1950s and began to proliferate in the 1970s (Meisch 1997:200; see also Meisch 2002:133–34). Groups such as ñanda Mañachi and Conjunto Indígena "Peguche" emphasized in their album liner notes the central role of "music as an expression of indigenous values and its role in [the 1970s Indigenous Quichua] cultural resurgence" (Meisch 1997:201). The Otavalo Quichua musical-ensemble renaissance is evident from Lynn Meisch's listing of numerous long-playing records recorded from 1970 to 1986—nearly all of which were recorded in Ecuador and contained only Ecuadorian music (Ibid. 205–6).

In 1990, in this same broad, green valley, teenagers and young men were actively engaged in music making. In Imbabura, one radio station had an annual festival of musical ensembles, in which any and all area village ensembles could participate, each playing perhaps two songs on the radio. In July 1990 this village ensemble marathon featured enough groups to last twelve hours.

Music making provides an important means of socialization among Quichua youths who have long since ceased attending school and who find few community activities available to them, except for volleyball, which is pursued with a vengeance in the village plazas and *comunas* of Imbabura. You will hear Quichua teenagers rehearsing diligently on weekends at an ensemble member's home, performing a few traditional *sanjuanes* and, like their counterparts in the United States, often experimenting with their own compositions.

The 1990s witnessed an explosion of this music as Otavalenian musicians left their homeland to seek larger audiences throughout the world. Lynn Meisch (1997, 2002) has documented this phenomenon carefully and in detail. As she notes, "Otavalo music [performed by Quichua Indigenous musicians] has now become globalized, part of the world music beat influencing the music made by others, with Sanjuanitos seen as emblematic of Ecuadorian music" (1997:217). Motivated by potential economic rewards, many Imbabura Quichua ensemble members have, in effect, become **"transnational migrants"** (Ibid. 218) or "immigrants who develop and maintain multiple relationships—familial, economic, social, organizational, religious, and political—that span borders . . . [creating a] multiplicity of involvements . . . in both home and host societies" (Basch, Schiller, and Blanc 1994:7). Today's Quichua musicians are recording CDs, not LPs; those CDs are most often produced outside of Ecuador, and they include ample proportions of non-Ecuadorian as well as Ecuadorian Andean songs (Meisch 1997:253–55).

Not surprisingly, as the Bolivian ethnomusicologist Gilka Wara Céspedes says, "The Andean Sound is becoming a part of the sonic scene from Europe to Japan" (1993:53). Further, "Otavalo [Quichua] musicians are everywhere, playing in malls, on street corners, at music festivals, and in concert halls and clubs on six continents, and recording and selling their music at locales around the world" (Meisch 1997:243). Where Ecuadorian Andean *indígena* textile manufacturers have for some fifty years traveled the international byways, selling their home-woven ponchos, blankets, and scarves, today the entrepreneurial instinct remains intact but the product has changed: from bulky woolens to featherweight cassettes and CDs, delicate bamboo *zampoñas*, and *kenas*. As one Otavalenian musician, Héctor Lema, told Lynn Meisch in 1994, "'We have two ways to earn a living in whatever locale: music and the sales of *artesanías* [arts and crafts]'" (1997:187). Specifically, Otavalo Quichua ensembles have appeared at First Peoples powwows in Canada and the United States, in folk festivals in Poland and Washington, D.C., and on street corners, tourist thoroughfares, and subway stations in Quito, New York, San Francisco, Florence, Moscow, Montreal, Paris, Sevilla, Córdoba, and Madrid, among numerous other places (1997:243).

The United States unquestionably plays a vital role in this international Andean sonic scene. As of about thirteen years ago, Amauta, based in Seattle, comprised Chilean and Bolivian musicians playing traditional Andean instruments; they had appeared at the Seattle Northwest Regional Folklife Festival. Condor, out of Corvallis, Oregon, was an ensemble of five professional, college-educated musicians from Argentina, Peru, and Mexico; the group focused on traditional Andean musics. Andanzas (Spanish: "wanderings") performed music from a variety of Latin American and Caribbean traditions; this widely traveled, four-member ensemble included musicians from Argentina, Bolivia, and Mexico, as well as a classically trained U.S. harpist. Andesmanta (Quichua: "from the Andes"), an ensemble of Ecuadorian musicians playing traditional highland Ecuadorian musics—including *sanjuanes*—as well as other South American folk musics, had performed at Carnegie Hall and the Metropolitan Museum of Art. Among the most well-established of U.S.-based Andean groups is Sukay (Quechua: "to work furrows in straight lines," or, "to whistle musically"); this group formed originally in 1974, with some eight albums by 1994, along with performances at Lincoln Center and major folk music festivals (Ross 1994:19–24). (You can find a list of selected recordings by these and other Andean Ensembles in Ross 1994:27; for recordings of Ecuadorian Andean ensembles, see Meisch 1997:357–65.)

One of the cofounders of Sukay was the Swiss multi-instrumentalist and instrument craftsman Edmond Badoux. With the flautist-percussionist Francy Vidal (self-described as "an 8th-generation 'Californiana' with roots in Mexico and in Europe" (Vidal n.d.), he formed in 1985 the gifted California-based duo, Chaskinakuy (Quechua: "to give and receive, hand to hand, among many"). Chaskinakuy's husband-and-wife members, Edmond and Francy, characterize themselves as "dedicated revivalists" (Figure 9.12). The two musicians sing in

FIGURE 9.12

Duo Chaskinakuy. June 1992.

© Irene Young. Used by permission.

Quechua/Quichua and Spanish, and they play more than twenty-five native Andean instruments, some rarely heard outside their highland Andean contexts: Peruvian harp (Edmond even plays this instrument, on occasion, upside-down, in accordance with the Peruvian harp's unique processioning posture), pelican-bone flute, long straight trumpet, condor-feathered *zampoña*, and *pututu* (Quechua: "conch trumpet").

Chaskinakuy has appeared in concerts, festivals, university lecture series, and schools in eighteen U.S. states, in Canada, and in Switzerland. They have three times received the Multi-Cultural Grant from the California Arts Council and for six seasons were picked for the Council's Touring and Presenting Program. Chaskinakuy has three recordings on their own label: *A Flor de Tierra* (2002), *Cosecha* ([1991] 1993), and *Music of the Andes* (1988). They return frequently to the Andes to sustain their performance research into traditional village musics and festivals. Their renditions of Andean musics reflect the musicians' wonderful blend, when singing in duet, and their remarkably close attention to every stylistic detail appropriate to the particular regional music: harmonic underpinnings, melodic lines and inflections, vocal tone qualities, phrasing, and rhythmic accentuations. Now listen to Chaskinakuy's rendition of the Peruvian *wayno*, "Amor imposible" (CD 4, Track 13).

In this piece, you are listening to your second Latin American "harp-country genre"; earlier you heard Ecuadorian *sanjuán*, and now Peruvian *wayno*. As such, we can note four prominent similarities to the "Muyu muyari warmigu" *sanjuán* of Efraín and Rafael. First, we see the use of the harp—now as accompaniment to the lively South Andean *wayno*, then as accompaniment to its lively North Andean cousin, the *sanjuán*. Second, we hear the now-familiar Andean bimodality, the use of the minor and its relative major—here, b minor/D Major. Moreover, where the B statements of Efraín and Rafael's "Muyu" explored the region of the subdominant of the relative major (as did Efraín's other *sanjuán*, "Cascarón"; see Schechter 2002:411), similarly, Edmond and Francy's "Amor imposible" employs G Major, the subdominant of its relative major—D. Third, those with

CD 4:13

"Amor imposible" ("Impossible Love") (2:31). Traditional Peruvian *wayno*. Performed by Chaskinakuy. Edmond Badoux, harp; Francy Vidal, vocal and *golpe. Chaskinakuy. Music of the Andes: Cosecha.* CD engineered and mixed by Joe Hoffmann and remastered by Brian Walder at Hoffmann Studios. Occidental, California, 1993.

keen ears will remark that the rhythm is not beaten on a drum, but rather—as in "Muyu"—on the harp soundbox; this type of percussive *golpe*, or *cajoneo*, on the harp soundbox can be heard in several Latin American countries, including Peru. Fourth and last, we are cognizant of two distinctive rhythmic motifs. Those of Ecuadorian *sanjuán* revolve around sixteenth-eighth-sixteenth notes. In Peruvian *wayno* the *golpe* involves something close to an eighth and two sixteenths; this pattern, sometimes close to three triplets, is the near-invariant rhythmic signature of the *wayno*. (You can find a substantial discussion of the history, regional varieties, other musical traits, and poetic substance of the *wayno* in Romero 1999:388–89.)

Again, this performance of "Amor imposible" proves particularly compelling because Edmond captures the distinctive character of Peruvian harp-accompanimental style, and Francy grasps the distinctive melodic turns of phrase, characteristic portamento, and distinctly focused and clear vocal quality of the female Peruvian singer of *wayno*. The Close Listening guide provides the full text of "Amor imposible" and illustrates the formal structure of this Peruvian *wayno*.

Close Listening

"AMOR IMPOSIBLE" ("IMPOSSIBLE LOVE")

CD 4:13

COUNTER NUMBER	COMMENTARY	LYRICS	TRANSLATION
Introduction			
0:00	Harp enters.		
0:05	*Golpe* enters emphasizing long-short-short rhythmic pattern.		
1st stanza—A phrase			
0:13	Harp and *golpe* play main melody. Vocal style with distinctive phrasing and characteristic portamento of the *wayno*.	*Es imposible dejar de quererte,* *Es imposible dejar de amarte,* *Este cariño que yo a tí te tengo* *Es un cariño puro y verdadero.*	It's impossible to stop loving you, It's impossible to stop loving you, This affection that I have for you Is an affection pure and true.
1st stanza repeat—A phrase			
0:28	Harp and *golpe*.		
Harp interlude, "Arpita!"—A phrase			
0:43	Harp.		

2nd stanza—A phrase

0:58	Harp and *golpe* play main melody.	*¡Cómo quisiera que venga la muerte!* *¡Cómo quisiera morir en tus brazos!* *Quizás así podría olvidarte* *Porque, en mi vida, todo es imposible.*	How so, would I like death to come! How so, would I like to die in your arms! Perhaps that way, I could forget you Because, in my life, everything is impossible.

3rd stanza—A phrase

1:14	Harp and *golpe* play main melody.	*Ay, cruceñito, amorcito mío* *Este cariño te traigo y te digo* *Aunque mi cuerpo quede sepultado* *Queda mi nombre grabado en tu pecho.*	Ay, dear man from [Santa] Cruz, my dear love This affection I offer you and tell you of Even though my body might be buried My name remains engraved in your breast.

4th stanza—B phrase

1:29	Harp and *golpe* play contrasting melody.	*Dicen con la muerte* *Se llega a olvidar,* *Quizás en la tumba* *Más nos amamos.*	They say that, with death, One comes to forget, Perhaps in the grave We'll love one another more.

5th stanza—B phrase

1:37	Harp and *golpe* play contrasting melody.	*Si muero primero* *Yo allá te espero,* *Así para amarnos* *Eternamente.*	Should I die first, I'll wait for you, over there, In that way, to remain loving one another Eternally.

Harp interlude—CC′—DD′—EE′—EE′

1:46–1:56	Harp plays new C phrase twice.
1:57–2:06	Harp plays new D phrase twice.
2:07–2:27	Harp plays new E phrase four times.
2:28	Final cadence.

As you can see from the lyrics, "Amor imposible" offers one example of the poetic character of this genre: "Most *waynos* . . . are of an amorous nature. Despite the immense variety of *waynos*, many depict nostalgia for a lost love" (Romero 1999:389). The theme of nostalgia runs powerfully throughout songs that have emerged through the ages in Latin America (Schechter 1999a:2–7).

Each stanza is four lines long. The first three stanzas all have 11-syllable lines, whereas stanzas 4 and 5 have the syllable pattern 6-5-6-5.

The formal structure of the music of "Amor imposible," as laid out in the Close Listening guide, is as follows:

Intro-A-A-A-A-A-B-B-CC'-DD'-EE'-EE'

Raúl Romero (1999:388–90; 414–15) discusses the character and formal structure of the Peruvian *wayno*. One of the possible formal structures, he notes, is roughly AABB (Ibid. 414). What we hear in "Amor imposible" is an expansion, extrapolation, of that form: Much of the song is occupied with the A phrase—which correlates with the 11-syllable stanzas, with lesser emphasis being given to the B phrase—which correlates with the 6-5-6-5 stanzas. Then, Edmond's C phrase explores the subdominant key, which lasts into the D phrase; the concluding E phrase dwells on the 5th scale degree, prolonging the final arrival to the home-note, the 1st scale degree.

Finally, the *waynos* and *sanjuanes* of Andean ensembles—as well as *Nueva Canción* musics—have taken root in U.S. universities. For example, the University of Texas at Austin for some years maintained an Andean ensemble, among their other Latin American groups. This began in 1976 with the *Nueva Canción* ensemble Toqui Amaru (Mapuche and Quechua: "chief serpent"), founded by Renato Espinoza of Chile, with Guillermo Delgado-P. and Enrique Cuevas of Bolivia, Néstor Lugones of Argentina, and Alejandro Cardona of the United States. At the University of California, Santa Cruz, students have, since 1986, performed in intermediate and advanced Andean ensembles called Voces (Spanish: "voices") and Taki Ñan (Quichua: "song path"), respectively.

Taki Ñan, which recorded an in-house cassette in 1992 and an in-house CD in 1998, focuses on traditional Andean musics in Spanish and Quichua/Quechua, as well as on *Nueva Canción* musics. Starting out as a single, ten-student Latin American ensemble in 1986 that focused on Ecuadorian genres, Voces and Taki Ñan became independent of each other in 1991. Over the years, Taki Ñan has tended to follow two approaches: focusing its repertory or presenting a more varied program. When focusing in depth, during one particular quarter of study, the group would emphasize, for example, Colombian musics, Argentinean musics, Afro-South American musics; in fall 1992 they prepared six different field-recorded versions of "Ilumán tiyu." Taki Ñan has also presented programs with a variety of traditional and *Nueva Canción* musics. In nearly every one of these programs, from 1989 to the present, both Taki Ñan and Voces have performed South Andean *zampoña* musics—including the *k'antu* "Kutirimunapaq." Over these years Taki Ñan has benefited enormously from the musical and linguistic assistance of Guillermo Delgado-P., as well as from workshops offered by Chaskinakuy and by the Peruvian musician Héctor Zapana. (A full account of the evolution of the Taki Ñan ensemble—which is currently directed by one of its alumnae, Diana Nieves—appears in Schechter 2003.)

Aconcagua, at Florida State University, performs a variety of Andean musics and has been directed by an alumna of Taki Ñan. Viento, in Berkeley, California, is directed by Chaskinakuy and comprises Berkeley students and community members. Frequently performing at the La Peña Cultural Center in Berkeley, Viento focuses on traditional South Andean musics for *zampoña* and *tarqa* (wooden duct flute). Lydia Mills, another Taki Ñan alumna, directs Los Mapaches, an ensemble of some thirty-five to fifty schoolchildren from the Berkwood Hedge School in Berkeley, who perform Andean musics—on *zampoñas* and other instruments—locally, in concert; on July 24 and 25, 2007, members of Los Mapaches joined forces with a Bolivian young peoples' ensemble, Orquesta de Instrumentos Autóctonos, for two concerts, in La Paz, Bolivia.

Let us return now to the Andes of Imbabura, where the traditions of the Quichua of Cotacachi—the people, the language, the dress, the material culture, the character of *sanjuán* and the harp that plays it—have been preserved for hundreds of years. The uniqueness of many aspects of their expressive culture is ensured by *cada llajta*, the locally asserted special character of a northern Ecuadorian highland Quichua community's musical expressions, dialect, mortuary customs, or dress (note that this commitment/insistence on a uniqueness of local clothing and speech dates back to Inkaic times; see Mannheim 1991:50). Even so, the Cotacachi Quichua share some traits with other regions and cultures of Latin America. One of these is the wake ritual for a dead child. Let us look at *wawa velorio* to see how it accommodates *cada llajta* as well as broader beliefs and practices that transcend cultural and political boundaries.

Wawa Velorio

In Imbabura as elsewhere in Latin America, infants struggle to survive. In three consecutive months in 1979–1980 I witnessed three *wawa velorio* rituals on Cotacachi's slopes. I observed a fourth child's wake there in August 1990. The infant mortality rate in Ecuador continues to be quite high; deaths are caused in large part by intestinal and respiratory diseases. U.S. history has also seen high infant mortality rates: In the era of Puritan New England (1620s to 1720s), in Boston as many as three in ten people died in infancy. The death of young children in Ecuador and throughout Latin America is a daily tragedy, one that through its very frequency ironically serves to preserve dozens of unique regional traditions of genre, instrument, and dance.

Let us now join the harpist and his family to attend a *wawa velorio* on Mt. Cotacachi. After nightfall, Sergio, the harpist contracted to provide music for the wake (Figure 9.13), his younger brother and apprentice-harpist, César, and their family leave their Tikulla home for the home of the deceased. After more than an hour's uphill winding journey on *chaki ñanes*, with their father and *golpeador* Miguel Armando bearing the family harp, they arrive. At about 9:30 Sergio sits down with his harp next to the platform bearing the deceased infant. A few candles illuminate the casket and the home. After tuning, Sergio plays a strongly percussive music called *vacación*

FIGURE 9.13

Harpist Sergio. March 1980.

John M. Schechter

Vacación (1:23). Performed by Quichua harpist Sergio, at a child's wake. Field recording by John Schechter, ouside Cotacachi, Ecuador, February 1980.

(CD 4, Track 14). The all-night *wawa velorio*—the wake for the deceased Quichua child—has begun. The Close Listening guide provides the full accounting of *Vacación* and illustrates the formal structure of this Ecuadorian Quichua special child's-wake harp music.

Close Listening

VACACIÓN

CD 4:14

COUNTER NUMBER	COMMENTARY
0:00	Solo harp, without *golpeador* or singer. Harpist's right hand plays octaves, on the minor tonic pitch (scale degrees 1–8). (The remaining comments may be assumed to refer to the harpist's right hand.)
0:06	Begins open fifths, on scale degrees 3–7; also, with the perfect fourth, 4–7.
0:15	Repetition of scale degree 5.
0:18	Begin 2-eighths–quarter figure, emphasizing two open fifths a third apart, representing the tonic minor (1–5) and its relative major (3–7).
0:29	Outlines a repeated dyad of a minor seventh, with the lower pitch being the tonic note (1–7).
0:34	Tonic octaves, again.
0:37	Repeated 1–7 minor seventh dyad, again.
0:40	Repetition of scale degree 5, again.
0:43	Repetition of scale degree 3.
0:46	Repetition of scale degree 1.
0:48	Begin 2-eighths–quarter figure emphasizing 1–3, in the tonic minor key.
0:58	Repeated octaves on the minor tonic pitch, again.
1:04	Repeated 1–7 minor seventh dyad, again.
1:10	Repetition of scale degree 5, again.
1:13	2-eighths–quarter figure, again emphasizing the tonic minor (1–5) and its relative major (3–7).

Vacación (the same term is used for both the genre and the title itself) differs audibly from *sanjuán*. First, *vacación* does not require a *golpeador* but is performed by the harpist alone. Second, it is purely instrumental, not sung. Whereas *sanjuán* has a simple meter, *vacación* lacks the regular stresses that characterize a particular meter. *Vacación* is not built, like *sanjuán*, in 8-beat phrases but in long, descending cycles. *Sanjuán* is dance music; *vacación* is not. As we listen to *vacación* and follow the Close Listening guide, we can hear several things. First, there is the unmistakable overall percussiveness, emphasized by hammered quarter notes, in both hands. We also cannot escape the repetitiveness of individual melodic notes and note sequences. Conversation audible in the background reminds us that we are in a natural context, here in *wawa velorio*. Harmonically, we are impressed by the prominence of both treble octaves and minor sevenths. Moreover, the alternation of the tonic octaves (8-1) and open fifths (7-3) is one of Sergio's signature features, characterizing his harp style in general—including his playing of *sanjuanes* and extending even to the manner in which he tunes his harp (see Schechter 1992:112, 127, 130–31, 159–62). Sergio's *vacación* is decidedly cyclical, with each new cycle of gradually descending melody having its beginning at the upper tonic octave. Finally, the tonic minor key is reinforced in several ways: through the emphasis given in repeated 5th, 3rd, and 1st scale-degree pitches, one after the other—the defining triad of the key; through the repeated tonic octaves, 8-1; and through the repeated 1-3-1 pattern of 2 eighth notes and a quarter note, clearly demarcating the lower tonic pitch.

Sanjuán is performed throughout the night at *wawa velorio*, accompanying the dancing of family and guests. *Vacación*, however, is tied to two special ritual moments: the outset of the wake and whenever behavior centers on the deceased child. Harpists informed me that they play *vacación* at the beginning of the ritual in order to drive out the *demonio*, or devil, from beneath the platform supporting the deceased child. The second ritual moments include the late-evening adorning of the corpse and the closing of the casket at dawn.

Before playing *vacación*, after playing it, and periodically throughout the night, the harpist and his family are offered food and drink—bananas, homemade bread, barley gruel, maize gruel, stewed corn, and *trago* (cane alcohol). The consumption of *trago* or other alcoholic beverages is centrally important in ritual settings both in Cotacachi and throughout the Andes (Schechter 2002:417–18). In a *wawa velorio*, most of those present consume the drink. The man (never a woman) with the *trago* bottle and plastic cup goes around the room, offering a *copa* (cup) of *trago* to each man and woman: "*Ufyapai!*" ("Drink!"), he says; the one being offered the *copa* usually first asks him to drink—which he does—then accepts the offer him- or herself.

Until approximately midnight, Sergio performs mostly *sanjuanes*. By 10:30 P.M., he has played about five to ten *sanjuanes*, including perhaps "Muyu muyari warmigu" and "Ilumán tiyu." Occasionally, to keep the dancing going, he changes from one *sanjuán* to another without stopping. There is a distinctly regular and nearly metronomic sense of tempo about this father-son duo. Miguel Armando's *golpe* is solid and reliable, and Sergio's rhythm is strong and regular. Sergio's companions, Roberto and Gerónimo, sometimes serve as vocalists for the duo. One sings with Sergio. The voice-harp duo performs typically texted *sanjuanes*, including "Rusa María" and "Muyu." To enhance the *alegre* (happy) character of the festive ritual, the harpist likes to have near-constant chatter together with his music and *golpe*.

Around 10:30 P.M., perhaps in the middle of playing a *sanjuán*, Sergio suddenly stops and shifts into *vacación.* Now the child, in its casket, is removed from the platform where it has been prominently displayed and is placed on the floor for adorning and crowning. The infant is given usually to its mother, who mourns the loss of her baby with a lament. This sobbed music uses the principal notes of *vacación:* D-C-A (scale degrees 8-7-5 of d minor). A crown of flowers is put on the baby's head. Its waist and wrists are wrapped in ribbons, and bouquets of flowers are placed alongside the body in the casket. During this entire time, Sergio plays *vacación;* he stops only when the infant and its casket are again placed on the platform.

Although dancing to *sanjuán* was slow to start, by 1:30 A.M. everyone is dancing: with the air growing colder, at 9,000 feet, the music and the festive night are warming up. The godmother and the father might begin to dance, prompting Sergio to shout a pleased *"Achi mamaka kallarinka ña!"* ("The godmother will begin [to dance] now!"). Gerónimo shouts, *"Shinlli shinlli bailapankich' kumarigukuna!"* ("Dance really strongly, dear *comadres!"*). Sergio now hardly stops for small talk, immediately replenishing the musical warmth with one, then another *sanjuán*—maybe several strung together. He next begins to alternate *sanjuán* with *pareja*, a slightly faster music, also for dancing but usually without text.

Very late, at about 3:00 A.M., Sergio leaves the harp and asks his younger brother, César, to take over (Figure 9.14). With very few people still awake, César plays a string of short *sanjuanes*. There is no banter between César and his *golpeador*-father, as there had been between musicians of the same generation, such as Sergio and Gerónimo. This is *sanjuán* without reaction—functional dance music with little function, since no one is dancing.

By about 5:00 A.M., everyone is awake and shares a morning meal of boiled potatoes. Before sunrise (an hour later) Sergio again takes over the harp, tuning and perhaps playing a *pareja*. Suddenly, he shifts into *vacación* and the casket is

FIGURE 9.14

Harpist César. March 1980.

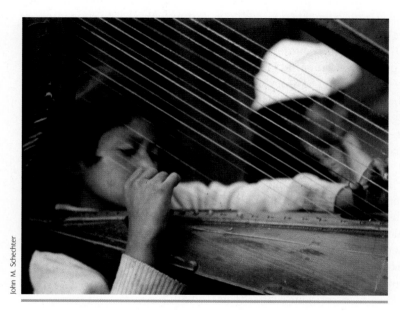

John M. Schechter

and heard, in the Cotacachi *comuna*, the child conspicuously displayed during the night, the seemingly "cued" lament, and the Quichua mother caressing her child on the patio of their home.

Indeed, in keeping with our understanding of the prescriptive nature of ritual, most accounts of Latin American (and Spanish) children's wakes share certain prominent behaviors, regardless of cultural group or country. The child is always conspicuous by his or her presence, in the same room in which family and friends dance to the favorite music of the region (*sanjuán* in highland Ecuador, *jota* in Mediterranean Spain): This is *cada llajta* in operation. The infant is not only present but raised: lying on the elevated platform, seated on the table, tied to a ladder placed atop the casket, suspended from the roof, or pushed back and forth between poles. Each of these ritual gestures symbolizes the transformation into an angel and entry into eternity. Similarly, the infant is washed and dressed in the finest clothing available and is bedecked in ribbons, flowers, and paper or cardboard wings. On the child's head sits a crown of real or artificial flowers, which is both ubiquitous (in Latin American and Spanish children's wakes) and ancient (the practice of crowning dead children dates back to the time of the ancient Greeks; see Schechter 1994a). The atmosphere of the wake is always festive, with dancing, food, and alcoholic beverages.

Many Spanish and Latin American visual and literary artists have depicted the child's wake in paintings, novels, short stories, plays, and poems; many of these portrayals, however, criticize what the native artists view as an indefensible diminution of a life, in making its extinction the pretext for merrymaking. Nevertheless, the Latin American child's wake is a deep-rooted ritual that embodies local cultural preferences in song types, dance types, instrument types. Whether or not local artists or outsiders approve of the *velorio del angelito*, the practice serves as a reliable stamp—designed by the culture itself—of that local culture at that point in time (Schechter 1994a).

The Career Dilemma of Don César Muquinche

We have seen how vital the harpist is in Quichua children's wakes in northern highland Cotacachi. The harpist is also quite visible in the central highlands, especially in Tungurahua Province. One talented artist, Don César Muquinche, is a harpist of Illampu, a village outside Ambato, in Tungurahua.

As you can see from Figure 9.16, Don César's harp is considerably larger than the Imbabura harps. It is modeled on the harps of Paraguay; these instruments are distinguished by their substantial size and by their neck shape—an inverted arch. The neck's tuning pegs are guitar-type mechanical tuning pegs, used also by the Paraguayans. The pattern of small, paired sound holes on either side of the column—holes that in fact come at the ends of (barely visible) painted S shapes—dates to Spanish harps of the seventeenth century.

An artist of national stature, Don César plays numerous musical genres, including *sanjuanito*, an adaptation of the Imbabura *sanjuán*. On CD 4, Track 16, we hear him playing an *albazo* called "Toro barroso" (Spanish for "Reddish Bull"). *Albazos* are well-known among Spanish speakers throughout the highlands and

CD 4:16

"*Toro barroso*" ("Reddish Bull") (3:32). *Albazo* of Ecuador. Performed by Don César Muquinche. Field recording by John Schechter, outside Ambato, Ecuador, 1980.

even throughout the country, heard on the radio and at public and private celebrations.

Don César's decision to take up the harp was complicated. His father, Don Francisco, had been a professional harpist. Attending his father's performances as a child, the son witnessed the physical suffering that this career brought with it. César initially decided he would apprentice as a hatmaker. But Don Francisco advised his son that whatever César chose to do, he should select something that would make him content and leave him with good memories. Ultimately these words led César back to music. His decision to be a musician also reflected Don César's great admiration and respect for his father—specifically for his father's ability to resist the temptations inherent in the harpist's career—and for his father's concern for him and his serious advice.

In fact, both father and son followed similar paths. Both had a strong business orientation. Don César speaks of Naranjo's harps and the services of Camilo Borja, Don Francisco, and himself as harpists as being "in some demand." Don César saw himself as being upwardly mobile; he disdained his own *indígena* roots. Yet both he and his father performed for both *indígena* and *blanco* (white) society, bridging this cultural gap as performers. Finally, both Don César and his father learned to play in ensemble as well as solo and to adapt to changing performance arenas, such as radio and television.

Both men appreciated playing as an art. They felt great pride in developing it both for their own self-esteem and for the satisfaction of their clients. Don César's highest compliment to artists or craftspeople was to call them "artists of quality."

In July 1980, after I had studied with him for several months, Don César Muquinche told me about the development of his artistic career. Let us look at the types of conflict he faced and how he finally resolved them, choosing harp music over hatmaking. Through his thoughts we can gain some insight into the reputation, the *fama*, of a harpist in Ecuador. I conducted the following interview of Don César Muquinche in Spanish and translated it into English (Schechter 1980).

FIGURE 9.16

Don César Muquinche, harpist of Illampu, Tungurahua Province, at his home outside Ambato, Ecuador. August 1980.

John M. Schechter

> I was born in 1920, here in Illampu [Tungurahua]. My father, Francisco, was planning to become a tailor—to make men's suits. Well, he heard Camilo Borja play—a man who lived just alongside us—and, on hearing him play the harp, my father paid attention. And he said, "I would like to learn harp from this man."
>
> My father then proposed to Borja that he teach him the harp. The man said yes and told him, "Let's make a deal: You make me trousers and I will give you harp lessons." My father told me that he had these lessons every day; he was very interested in learning quickly, taking advantage of the goodwill of the *maestro*.
>
> When Borja saw that my father was beginning to play the harp fairly well, the *maestro*, who was in great demand at that time, told him he needed to buy his own harp.... There was a man, Segundo Alejandro Naranjo, who made fine instruments—very special harps. They had a fantastic resonance....
>
> My father told me that the harps made by this man were instruments in some demand and of very fine quality; there was no danger that the glue might

loosen from the pieces. Even when the harp was hit hard, the wood would not dent or come loose, as might happen today with harps made of rough wood....

My father was in demand in various places—in fiestas, in *wawas muertos* [dead children, i.e., *velorio del angelito*, or *wawa velorio*].... And with the rhythm of this beating upon the harp, they [the father and his *golpeador*] put on a fine show, without the need of other instruments.

[At children's wakes] the *golpeador* had to stay right there, by the harpist. Then, there were other events—*matrimonio*, patron saint fiestas. Among [*indígenas*], the *matrimonio* lasts three or four days. And the harpist has to be there. Day and night.... It is the same in the fiestas—of devotion to some saint, for example. In the *wawas muertos*, some better-off people had it lasting some three days, but without doubt, one night and one day, for sure.... In gratitude for their having been well entertained, the people had to treat the *golpeador* and the harpist to some gifts, like *medianos*, as they call them here: a whole chicken, a rabbit, or a *cui*—a thing of great value.

Yes, they made a good ensemble. And ever since I could remember, my father was in great demand—as much among the *indígenas* as among the white people. He became an innovative, popular artist who liked to entertain. [He played for] the people of society—a governor, a subtreasurer, here or beyond—in Quito [the capital], in different places. My father was very much in demand, very important: an artist of quality. He traveled to Quito, through the entire country. He became a very well known artist ... a very distinguished artist, for every class of society.

The musicians might go to their engagements in a cart pulled by a horse. At times, they went on horseback, to Quito—carrying the harp, cushioned and secured with a scarf, or something else soft. There was a person who led the horses. [My father] told me about this.

Sometimes, traveling in this way was very trying. Finally my father said, "No, I won't travel like that. If we could go in those carriages ... then I would go. I think I have been treating myself badly." And the people [provided what he requested], as they seemed to want my father's services greatly. Many times he went to Riobamba [capital of Chimborazo Province, just south of Tungurahua Province], I recall.

When I began growing up, I sometimes accompanied him, to see how he was treated, or how he might have been suffering. I saw that my father, being responsible, did not get drunk at the fiestas; he was careful to fulfill his responsibilities honorably. And wherever he went, the people paid him well.... But it is sad that he had to suffer a lot [owing to the extremely long hours, the demands for continuous music, and the constant pressure to partake of alcohol with the guests] because the people never tired of enjoying themselves. So I felt bad for my father, and I said to him, "Now, father, when can I learn how to play, to help you?"

I lament the death of my father. But he left good memories, as an artist—very good memories. He died while still capable, surrounded by the profits of his labors. By contrast, [another] harpist of quality [whom I knew] died poor because he was quite a womanizer. They say he squandered all he had earned, drinking with women. He died, poor, leaving his children poor. By contrast, my father said, "I have to extract a good inheritance from this profession [of harpist]. If the upper-class people occupy me well, pay me well, if the *indígenas* also pay me well, why not plant crops? Why not use [the money] for land, in things that are to serve me for life?"

My father thought about this very conscientiously. He [bought land and] worked the fields two or three days each week; he did not attend to the fields any more than that because he was in great demand in this career of music. My mother worked the fields more.

Now that I was becoming a young man, I had to think about it. There were harpists who went around poorly dressed, barefoot, dirty; I looked, and realized that my father took very good care of himself. There were other harpists,

Cui: Quichua for "guinea pig." These are native to the Andes, and groups of them are kept in the house by many rural residents of highland Ecuador. Today they are raised, killed, and broiled, and used as gifts for fiestas or, as here, for the harpist and *golpeador.*

but awful ones. They got drunk and walked around looking like a mess—not even the instruments were well treated. And that's worse.

And so I said no, I do not want to be a harpist because they get very drunk. Of course, my father is fine, he takes care of me; but I see that most people put pressure on the harpist—they say, "Drink, *maestro*," with great fervor. "Drink." They put it into your mouth. I said to myself, "Not me . . . I won't dedicate myself to the harp." My father, when they asked him to drink, said, "Don't force me to. I must carry out my responsibilities and earn my money. After I have completed my commitment for which you have hired me, then I shall be delighted to drink. But I have to be responsible for my musical colleagues; they come with me, to earn a living. And since I made the contract, I have to charge the *patrón* who has contracted me and, in turn, pay my *compañeros*, in order to assure their accompaniment in the future. If I get drunk, I can't discharge either my contract or my agreement to pay my *compañeros*, who came along expecting me to pay them. Thus you are hurting me [by insisting that I drink and get drunk]." This retort worked very well.

Nevertheless, I still felt very suspect about being a harpist. I told my father that I did not wish to be a musician but rather a hatmaker. I liked seeing young women or men who appreciated a truly elegant hat. And there was a hatmaker of first quality, a man by the name of Segundo Villa Paredes, in Ambato [the provincial capital of Tungurahua]. I went there and learned all that the *maestro* had to teach—how to make hats. I was there some two years, while I was young. I think I was already hatmaking by the age of fifteen years. By the age of eighteen or twenty I was a [hatmaking] *maestro*.

I became independent and set up a workshop in Ambato. I worked for the "people of society," who liked my style of work. I had all the confidence of these people, and it went well for me. I had quite a nice workshop there in the city of Ambato.

When my father saw that I was a successful [hatmaking] *maestro*, he told me, "Son, I congratulate you. You have distinguished yourself, now, don't you see? Now, I am going to recommend to you that you take advantage, in your youth, of your profession. Of music, I have my fond memories. In the same way, I would recommend that you take advantage of, enjoy, your profession." I had to listen to my father, pay attention to him: He was making this recommendation for my own good.

Well, when I had become a very popular *maestro*, well esteemed and with plenty of work there in the city, guaranteeing me a good living, some people came to me on their own to ask that I teach them the craft of hatmaking. Others came so they might help me expedite my commitments to deliver the completed work. I accepted them as working assistants. I looked for those who already knew the craft. Others came and said, "*Maestro*, be so kind as to teach my son the profession." "Delighted," [I said,] and accepted them.

Soon I organized the work for those who had come to help and those who had come to learn, and I had some free time. Over there the people already knew—"You're the Muquinche—?" I said, "Yes." "Listen, and your father is a harpist of quality?" I said, "Yes." "And you don't know anything?" "I too know a little bit." "And why don't you let us hear it? Why don't you bring a harp here to your workshop and play for us? Let us hear what your style is like, or how you play."

I thought, "Perhaps, yes, I must have a harp—as recreation from work."

Since the people had requested me to play the harp for them, I had a harp made. I brought it to my workshop, and I began to play it. Every once in a while, as a rest, I would sit down and begin to play . . . [and] some people came, curious. "It sounds nice, it sounds—" this or that. "Play, *maestro*, play," they exhorted me. "Play the harp, *maestro*." "Play the harp." And I had to listen to them: "Fine, I'm delighted to. Sit down." I had them sit down in one spot, and I would do a small performance.

Meanwhile, some of the people continued talking with me: "Why not better dedicate yourself to the harp?" At times, to my good friends, I paid attention to this. But of some people, I thought, "These [people] are going to do me harm," because they said [as many had done to my father], "Look, *maestro*, you play beautifully; accept just one [drink]." I said, "No, I have my business—I have my workshop. I have this—how can I abandon my workshop?" When I put it this way, some withdrew their invitation; others continued asking me to play: "Play the harp, *maestro*." I said to myself, "Listen, this is bad; I am going to get hooked on this."

Well, as I was getting popular with my music, there came this man, I remember, from Radio Ambato, a man by the name of Villa Lobos, the manager of Radio Ambato. Juan Villa Lobos. Well, he said, "*Maestro*, can you do programs for Radio Ambato?"...I said, "Fine."

Well, then, I had to put attention into improving my art. And he said to me, "*Maestro*, would you be able to play together with other instruments, to make a nice *conjunto* [ensemble], with violins, *bandolín*, guitar, and flute?" I said, "Yes, sir, but only with the agreement that it is to be you who is in charge of getting these people together; if it is to be left to me to do this, then, no. I am busy." The man [did it], of course, since he liked the idea of organizing a *conjunto típico* ["typical" ensemble], as we called it.... A very nice ensemble was thus created, now along with the harp...[and] it was a great hit with the people—"Such-and-such *conjunto*, directed by..." They named me director of the ensemble.

We did the Radio Ambato programs Saturdays and Sundays—Saturdays in the afternoon and Sundays at midday. This was all the time, for some three years in a row. Every weekend.

This man Villa Lobos came to my hat workshop when I was about twenty-eight years old.... I was by then a harpist, no? By then, I had practiced my profession [of hatmaker] for some eight years. When I came into popularity [as a harpist], I was twenty-eight years old....

My father visited me and said, "César, you came to like the harp?" I said yes. He answered, "Very well, between the music and the hats, I think that you are going to become a rich man—for you are accumulating money." I confided in him that I did the same as he. With the monies that I earned—as much from the music as from the hats—I bought some small pieces of land....

Well, trying to maintain the workshop, trying to fulfill my commitments, I came home from work at any old hour—at dawn, practically exhausted, wasted. To get the work done, I had to dig in and work myself.

I became ill. A fever, a lung infection, or a typhoid fever. This illness was very strong.... It was in 1949. It was serious. I had to be hospitalized. Thank God, my hour had not yet arrived. I recuperated, my health restored. My father procured doctors to attend to me....

[One] doctor said, "You have to stop practicing one of your professions. If you continue at this rate, with the hats and the music, you won't do anything, neither the one nor the other. There is a danger that very easily you could drive yourself to complete exhaustion. Continue only with the music, or continue only with the hats." Of course I had to obey him. I said, "Very well. If I try to force it—the attention to the hats, and to the music, as well—I'll be treating myself very badly." I had to pay attention to the doctor.

And so I felt myself obliged to leave the profession of hatmaking.

Don César continues, discussing how his harp career continued to develop, to a substantial degree through his performances on radio—in Ambato, Guayaquil, Quito—as well as on television. He, too, was occasionally taken to play on horseback, in areas around Illampu, Don César himself occasionally carrying the harp on his shoulder. More typically, now, a car is sent for him and then returns him to his home—or, for performances at distant locations, he is sent the travel fare.

The Close Listening guide provides the full accounting of "Toro barroso" and illustrates the formal structure of this Ecuadorian *albazo*.

Close Listening

"TORO BARROSO" ("REDDISH BULL")

CD 4:16

COUNTER NUMBER	COMMENTARY
0:00	Solo harp, without *golpeador* or sung text.
	Introduction (Intro): f# minor arpeggio sequence (scale-degree numbers): 3-5-8, 3-5-8, 5-8-10; 3-5-8, 5-8-9, 11-10-8. This sequence is repeated. (Subsequently, in this song, 10 may replace 9 in the sequence.)
0:10	**A** section, harmonized largely in the relative major (A Major), though cadencing, ultimately, in the tonic minor, f# minor. The scale-degree numbers in A Major are 1-3-5, 1-3-5, 1-3-5-3; 1-3-5, 1-3-5, /7-2-1-/6. The sequence is repeated.
0:20	**B** section, harmonized initially in the relative major, only to cadence in the relative minor (f# minor). The scale-degree numbers in f# minor are 10-8, 8-7, 7-8-5; (8)(7)-5, 4-3, 3-4-1. The sequence is repeated.
0:30	**Intro**
0:39	**A**
0:49	**B**
0:59	**Intro**
1:09	**C** section, harmonized largely by D Major, the subdominant of the relative major, with ultimate cadence in A Major. The scale-degree numbers in A Major are 4-6-8, 4-6-8, 4-6-8-6; 4-6-8, 4-6-8, 5-6-5-3. The sequence is repeated.
1:18	**A**
1:27	**B**
1:37	**Intro**
1:47	**C**
1:56	**A**
2:05	**B**
2:15	**Intro**
2:25	**A**
2:35	**B**
2:44	**Intro**
2:54	**C**
3:03	**A**
3:13	**B**, extended, ending with a V-i cadence in f# minor.

Perhaps the most cohesive force in Don César Muquinche's interpretation of "Toro barroso" is balance. First, we feel an overall sense of balance in the phrasing of its melody. The Introduction has a subsequence of three phrases that concludes on scale-degree 10, followed by another three-phrase subsequence ending on 8 (the tonic pitch); then, this entire sequence is repeated. The A section absorbs the notion of three-phrase sequential patterning, the first subsequence ending on 3 of the relative major, the second subsequence moving to rest on 6 in that relative major—which is also 1 (the tonic pitch) in the relative minor (bimodality). The B section also is in three-phrase subsequences, the first cadencing on 5 in the relative minor, the second ending on the minor tonic pitch (1). The C section follows suit (three-phrase subsequences), the first going to 6 in the major (which is also 3 in that major's subdominant key), the second moving ultimately to 3 in the major.

The balance is also evident in this piece's formal structure and in its harmony. The overall form of [Intro A B] [Intro A B] (Intro C A B) (Intro C A B) [Intro A B] (Intro C A B) has the bracketed pattern appearing twice, followed by the parenthesized pattern twice, then the bracketed once and the parenthesized once. Harmonically, "Toro" is fully infused with, and firmly grounded on, the rich bimodality of its A Major and f# minor poles. Those with good memories will recall that both our "Muyu muyari warmigu" *sanjuán* and Chaskinakuy's "Amor imposible" *wayno* employed major/relative minor bimodality, as well as the major subdominant; so also here in "Toro" we find the relative major/relative minor/ subdominant of the major. The bimodality in these three expressions particularly reflects its prominence, in both Quechua/Quichua and mestizo musics throughout the Andean region.

Rhythmically, in the Introduction one feels particularly the lilt of a dancelike $\frac{6}{8}$ meter. In the A, B, and C sections, though, Don César accompanies the $\frac{6}{8}$ accents of the melody with bass-line movement that can be perceived in $\frac{3}{4}$ meter (he does this especially noticeably at certain moments in the C sections). Ultimately, Don César's "Toro" expresses its affinity with *sesquialtera* ($\frac{6}{8}$ simultaneous with $\frac{3}{4}$) musics found throughout Latin America (recall "El aparecido" for one example).

Without question, in Don César Muquinche we find a central highland Ecuadorian "artist of quality." His "Toro barroso" is imbued with a special grace and lightness, as he crafts a dancelike structure erected on firm structural posts. As suggested in Don César's autobiographical remarks and their epilogue, his was a distinguished performing career—following in his father's footsteps. As I have commented elsewhere, Don César Muquinche owned a huge repertoire of harp pieces: Over a four-month period of tape-recorded interviews/lessons with Don César, in 1980, he performed numerous examples of both Ecuadorian national folk music (*música nacional*)—whose genres included *pasillo, pasacalle, albazo* ("Toro"), *tonada*, and *aire típico*—and modifications/adaptations of Indigenous genres: *sanjuán, yaraví,* and *danzante.* He also "traveled" beyond Ecuador's borders, playing examples of Paraguayan *polca* and *galopa*, Peruvian *wayno*, Colombian *porro* and *cumbia*, Argentine tango, Peruvian *valse*, and Mexican *ranchera* (Schechter 1992:86–87). It was my privilege to have made the acquaintance of a musician such as Don César Muquinche, and it continues to be a privilege to share his artistry with you.

Afro-Peruvian Music: A Landó

The steel and flint of Don César Muquinche's harp in "Toro barroso" ignite a spark of local color and a smile of recognition in the mind and spirit of a highland Ecuadorian listener. Francy Vidal's and Edmond Badoux's "Amor imposible" rings with remarkably true character as a Peruvian *wayno*. The distinctive rhythm and contrapuntal *dulzura* of "Me gusta la leche" stamped the border music of African Ecuadorian *sanjuán*. The interpretations and reinterpretations of traditional South American musics continue—both abroad and on the continent itself.

One prominent instance of the reconstruction of an imagined music of the past occurs with today's Afro-Peruvian music. In the colonial era, Peru was a major nucleus of African slavery; a substantial segment of eighteenth-century Lima was black (Romero 1994:307). However, the concurrent disappearance of the African marimba and African drum types marked the diminution of African-related musical practice at that time. By the outset of the twentieth century, songs and choreographies of African origins were entering a clouded past (Ibid. 313–14). In 1940, blacks represented only about 0.47 percent of the population of Peru (Feldman 2003:156).

Contravening these demographic and cultural trends, a revival of Afro-Peruvian traditions took place. Raúl Romero, a Peruvian ethnomusicologist, summarizes the mid-twentieth-century revival movement as follows:

> The revival and reconstruction of ancient and almost forgotten "Afro-Peruvian" song-genres began in the late 1950s. Rather than originating in a popular spontaneous movement, this was initiated by local intellectuals interested in the revival and recognition of the contribution of blacks to Peruvian culture. The late historian José Durand (1935–1990), along with Nicomedes Santa Cruz (1925–1992) and his sister Victoria Santa Cruz (1992) were the main collectors, producers, and promoters of black performances during this period. (1994:314)

Heidi Feldman notes that there was originally a tie between a 1960s black Peruvian political movement (roughly simultaneous with the U.S. Civil Rights Movement) and the Afro-Peruvian musical revival; she claims that of late, though, the link to political agendas has been weakened, with Afro-Peruvian music making now serving primarily to divert tourists (2003:156–57). Among the genres and dance-plays considered Afro-Peruvian are the *landó*, the *son de los diablos*, the *festejo*, and the *ingá* (Romero 1994:318; see also Tompkins 1998, especially 496–98).

Let us study, then, an Afro-Peruvian *landó* (lan-*do*)—a reconstructed genre (Feldman 2003:156; Romero 1994:318). It was written by Daniel "Kiri" Escobar and performed in this rendition by the soloist Eva Ayllón. The recording "Azúcar de caña" (CD 4, Track 17) appears on *The Soul of Black Peru*, "the first recording of Afro-Peruvian music widely available in the United States" (Feldman 2003:157). The Close Listening guide provides the full text of "Azúcar de caña" (ah-*soo*-kar deh *kah*-nyah) and illustrates the formal structure of this Afro-Peruvian *landó*.

Here, we are impressed by the rhythmic subtleties of Eva Ayllón's singing, how she declaims the text so expressively, with a distinct sensuality: The song

CD 4:17

"Azúcar de caña" ("Sugar Cane") (4:20). Performed by Eva Ayllón and ensemble. *The Soul of Black Peru/El Alma del Perú Negro/Afro-Peruvian Classics.* 1995.

Close Listening

"AZÚCAR DE CAÑA" ("SUGAR CANE")

CD 4:17

COUNTER NUMBER	COMMENTARY	LYRICS	TRANSLATION
Introduction			
0:00	Ensemble with vocal solo.	*¡Aha! ¡Vamos temple! !Sí!*	Aha! Let's go in [musical] harmony! Yes!
0:02	Distinctive *quijada* sound.		
1st stanza			
0:10	Vocal solo: expressive singing style.	*Salgo de mañana, a tumbar la caña,*	I go out in the morning, to cut sugar cane,
		Salgo de mañana, a tumbar la caña,	I go out in the morning, to cut sugar cane,
		Lucero del alba siempre me acompaña.	The morning star always accompanies me.
		Lucero del alba siempre me acompaña.	The morning star always accompanies me.
2nd stanza			
0:31	Vocal solo.	*Machete en la mano, corazón de vino,*	Machete in hand, heart of wine,
		Machete en la mano, corazón de vino,	Machete in hand, heart of wine,
		El río, mi hermano, zafra mi destino.	The river, my brother, the sugar-cane harvest my destiny.
		El río, mi hermano, zafra mi destino.	The river, my brother, the sugar-cane harvest my destiny.
1st interlude			
0:52	Music reinforces relative minor key.	*Sale el sol tras la montaña,*	The sun rises behind the mountain,
		Sale el sol tras la montaña,	The sun rises behind the mountain,
		Sale el sol tras la montaña,	The sun rises behind the mountain,
1:06		*E, inundando todo el valle con aromas de la caña.*	And, flooding the whole valley with the aroma of the sugar cane.

2nd interlude

1:14	Relative minor key again reinforced.	*Esta noche en mi cabaña,* *Esta noche en mi cabaña,*	Tonight in my cabin, Tonight in my cabin,
1:27	One-line connector produces tonal instability and introduces text of vocal choral echo.	*Esta noche en mi cabaña,*	Tonight in my cabin,
		Voy a bailar coba coba con mi mochera,* esta saña.[†]	I'm going to dance body to body with my *mochera,** this dance.[†]

Choral echo with Ayllón interjections

1:32		*—con mi mo-chera,esta saña,*	—with my mochera, this dance,
		—con mi mo-chera, esta saña,	—with my mochera, this dance,
		—con mi mo-chera, esta saña,	—with my mochera, this dance,
		—con mi mo-chera— *("Je-ye, esta saña, señores;¡pata en el suelo!")*	—with my mochera— ("Yes, yes, this dance, folks; feet to the floor!")

Multipart chorus

1:42	Chorus with Eva Ayllón and male-voice interjections.	*Azúcar de caña,* *Sombrero de paja,* *Mula resongona,* *Juguito guarapo.* *Azúcar de caña,* *Sombrero de paja,* *Mula resongona,* *Juguito guarapo.* *("¡Toma! ¡De la negra! ¡Así! ¡Eso es!")*	Sugar cane, Straw hat, Whining mule, Sugar-cane liquor. Sugar cane, Straw hat, Whining mule, Sugar-cane liquor. ("Drink! My woman's! Like that! That's it!")

Vocal solo

2:03		*Azúcar, azúcar,* *Azúcar, azúcar,*	Sugar-, sugar-, Sugar-, sugar-,

Instrumental interlude

2:09	Transition to 3rd stanza.		

3rd stanza

2:14	Vocal solo.	*Roncan los trapiches, moliendo la caña,*	The sugar mills roar, grinding the sugar cane,
		Roncan los trapiches, moliendo la caña,	The sugar mills roar, grinding the sugar cane,
		Juguito guarapo, quémame el entraña.	Sugar-cane liquor, burn my innards.
		Juguito guarapo, quéma mis entrañas.	Sugar-cane liquor, burn my innards.
		("¡Rico!")	("Delicious!")

4th stanza

2:35	Vocal solo.	*Noche de la zafra,luna de cañero,*	Night of the sugar-cane harvest,moon of the sugar-cane worker,
		Noche de la zafra, luna de cañero,	Night of the sugar-cane harvest, moon of the sugar-cane worker,
		¿Cuándo será mío, mi valle, mochero?	When will my valley be mine, *mochero?*
		¿Cuándo será mío, mi valle, mochero?	When will my valley be mine, *mochero?*

Repeat from 1st interlude through multipart chorus and subsequent vocal solo

2:57–4:13   Vocal solo and call-and-response texture.

4:13   Reprise of multipart chorus, and fade out.

[*]*Mochera mochero:* woman/man from the Moche region of coastal Peru.

[†]*Saña* is also a coastal district, in the Peruvian provinces of Lambayeque and Chiclayo; it has been influenced by older Afro-Peruvian traditions (Casas Roque 1993:299–300; 331).

incorporates several terms of flirtation and eroticism. Barely acknowledged in the 1970s, Eva Ayllón by the mid-1980s was among the most esteemed of Afro-Peruvian singing artists (Martínez and Jarque 1995). We hear the distinctive buzz of the **quijada** (kee-*ha*-da)—a donkey, horse, or cow jawbone that is a traditional instrument dating back in Peru to the eighteenth century (for an eighteenth-century drawing, see Casas Roque 1993:308; see also Romero 1994:312–13). Also known as *carraca llanera* in the Plains of Colombia, this instrument is a struck idiophone; the animal's molars, when loosened by exposure to the elements, produce a clear dry crack when struck with the fist. In some ensembles of Colombia, the molars may be scraped with a stick. We also hear a sense of exchange between the solo vocalist Ayllón and a chorus; this resounds with the call-and-response texture that we typically associate with an African or African-derived music.

Then there are the lyrics. The entire piece resounds with the culture and ecology of its home region. First, the Moche culture (*mochera, mochero*) existed prior to the time of the Inkas, in northern coastal Peru; the *Muchik* (Moche) irrigation systems were taken up by the Inkas. One can still observe remnants of the Moche culture, both in the physical features of the inhabitants of this coastal zone and in their surnames and place-names (Casas Roque 1993:299). Today, in fact, in political and lexicographic efforts in the region, aided by the late distinguished anthropologist Richard P. Schaedel (d. 2005), one sees a remarkable revival of Moche culture under way (Delgado-P. and Schechter 2004:x). Second, "Azúcar de caña" oozes with the harvest, milling, aroma, and drink of the *caña*—sugar cane, grown in lowland areas. *Guarapo* is an alcoholic beverage made from the cane—a *licor* that can burn one's insides. *Trapiches*, or sugar mills, process the *caña*.

Trapiche and *caña* emerge in music not only along the Peruvian coast, but also to the north in Ecuador and Colombia. In an October 31, 1990, interview with Milton Tadeo and Ermundo Mendes León, these Chota Valley musicians told me that the *bomba*—a traditional, emblematic genre of Chota—had actually emanated from the *trapiche* (sugar-mill) culture of the older generations of Chota: Jesuit missionaries derived a degree of wealth, up to the eighteenth century in Ecuador, through several sugar plantations located near today's Carpuela, the Congo brothers' home village. Milton recounted to me one traditional *bomba* text that goes like this: "'A la culebra verde, negrita, no hagas caso, mete *caña* al trapiche, chupa y bota gabazo.' (Don't pay attention to the green snake, dear woman; put cane to the sugar mill, suck on it, and throw away the waste pulp.)" (Schechter 1994b:288–89; for a discussion of this version and a slightly different one, see Coba Andrade 1980:42. Coba Andrade provides a deeper discussion of this entire phenomenon.). Further north, in Colombia, we find a lively and raucous festive *bambuco* called "El Guaro." As William Gradante notes, "The terms *guaro* and *guarapo* refer to the sugary juice squeezed from sugar cane—in this case in its fermented, highly intoxicating, homemade form" (1999:341). This upbeat *sesquialtera* folk song, made famous in an interpretation by the renowned Colombian duo of Garzón y Collazos, speaks to the same joy of the *caña* that we have seen in Peru and Ecuador: "De la *caña* sale el *guaro*—¡Qué caramba!—Sí la *caña* es buena fruta. Si la *caña* se machaca—¡Qué caramba!—El *guaro* también se chupa...." [*Guaro* comes from sugar cane—Whew!—Sugar cane sure is great. If the cane is squeezed—Whew!—Then you can even drink it....] (Ibid. 347).

Despedida, or Farewell

In this chapter, we began with the comment that Latin America was a kaleidoscope of cultural patterns, and we explored the musical manifestation of several of these. We discovered the urgency of a *Nueva Canción* song of Víctor Jara, as interpreted by Inti Illimani; the power and impact of Bolivian *zampoña*-ensemble music-making; the isorhythm and thematic consistency of the

Ecuadorian Quichua *sanjuán* "Muyu muyari, warmigu"; the symmetries, balance, and autobiographical intent of "Galo" Maigua's "Ilumán tiyu"; the way neighboring Chota Valley musicians mold the *sanjuán* to certain of their own musical priorities of phrase, rhythm, and guitar-counterpoint; and the manner in which non-Andeans such as Edmond Badoux and Francy Vidal of Chaskinakuy, in the context of the globalization of Andean ensemble music, have captured exquisitely the musical essence of a Peruvian *wayno*—its instrument, formal structure, rhythm, and harp and vocal performance practices. We witnessed the poignant Ecuadorian highland Quichua ritual of *wawa velorio*—dancing at the wake of a child—and sought to understand the reasons for that untrammeled joy. We similarly came to comprehend the reasons that the son of a renowned central Ecuadorian harpist ultimately followed in his father's footsteps, despite the evident personal hazards found along that career path. Finally, we heard a suave Afro-Peruvian expression, highlighting local coastal *caña* life and culture.

In our *despedida*, or farewell, to Latin American music-culture, we can begin to appreciate the richness of ensemble and solo music making in Latin America. These *Nueva Canción* songs, *k'antus, sanjuanes, waynos, albazos,* and *landós* speak to strongly felt political concerns; deep-rooted musical forms of expression; detailed and attentive attempts, from afar, to capture the overall character of an Andean song-dance type; and dedicated efforts to recreate local musical style. From "El aparecido" and "Muyu," to "Amor imposible" and "Azúcar de caña," we have feasted on a substantial buffet, one that I hope will entice you to savor the many other pungent and satisfying flavors of Latin American music.

Book Companion Website

You will find tutorial quizzes, Internet links, and much more at the Book Companion Website for *Worlds of Music*, Fifth Edition, at
academic.cengage.com/music/titon/worlds_5

The Arab World

ANNE K. RASMUSSEN

This chapter introduces music of the Arab world. A vast collection of twenty-two countries, where Arabic is the official spoken and written language, the Arab world is home to a surprising diversity of peoples, including Jews, Christians, and Muslims. Furthermore, the people of the Arab world have been "on the move" both historically and in the present time. So, the music and the culture of the Arab world spreads out in a **diaspora:** Rather than being confined to a single geographic location, its people and their traditions are dispersed beyond the boundaries of the region. One aim of this chapter is to help you understand the routes of these musical traditions. Another aim is to share an appreciation of the historical and literary legacy of Arab music-culture. While modern and dynamic, Arab music today offers also a glimpse into the roots of some of the oldest ideas, philosophies, and theories about music.

Which aspects of music make it sound Arab, Chinese, African, or "like Chicago" to us? How does music paint a picture of people we have never met and places we have never been? Why *is* music so evocative? How does music transport the listener? In this chapter we go beyond a sonic snapshot of the Arab world. Like all good exercises in ethnomusicology, this chapter uses music as a window onto the culture, history, and ideas of a people. Opening this window, and your ears and eyes, to a selection of musical scenes from the Arab world should enrich and refine whatever knowledge you might already have of this region, and offer the possibility of further investigation. Through looking at several kinds of Arab music making, you will explore the inspirational influence of religion, the history of the region, relationships to Western musical practice and ideas, some wonderful celebrations, the musical roles and activities of men and women, and the importance of music in the Arab diaspora.

In short, like all of the chapters in *Worlds of Music,* this one presents a variety of regional musical styles and subcultures, yet the overarching theme of the chapter is music in diaspora—Arab music-culture as it exists throughout the world—where it thrives and where it is endangered—and the ability of music and musicians to create culture and connect communities through music.

"Arabia"

For centuries, the Western world has consumed fanciful images of a timeless "Arabia" though art, literature, film, and popular culture. Some of these images originate in the stories of *The Arabian Nights,* which are set in Persia and Mesopotamia (present day Iran and Iraq) as early as the seventh century C.E. The stories relate a variety of adventures on the **Silk Road,** an ancient network of trade that ran from China to Morocco (see Map 10.1). Versions of the stories were written in Arabic on papyrus (a kind of fibrous paper made from a plant of the same name and used by ancient Egyptians, Greeks, and Romans) and date to the ninth century. However, familiar tales such as "Aladdin and the Magic Lamp," "Ali Baba and the Forty Thieves," and "Sinbad the Sailor" have been rewritten and retold by a wide range of authors—from those living in different parts of Asia to the literati of nineteenth-century England (such as Robert Louis Stevenson) to teams of screenwriters at Disney and Dreamworks studios.

The reimagining of Arabia through art, literature, and music has produced wonderful images as well as misleading stereotypes. Every period of Western art music includes masterpieces inspired by the so-called Orient. During the Tin

Map 10.1
The Silk Road

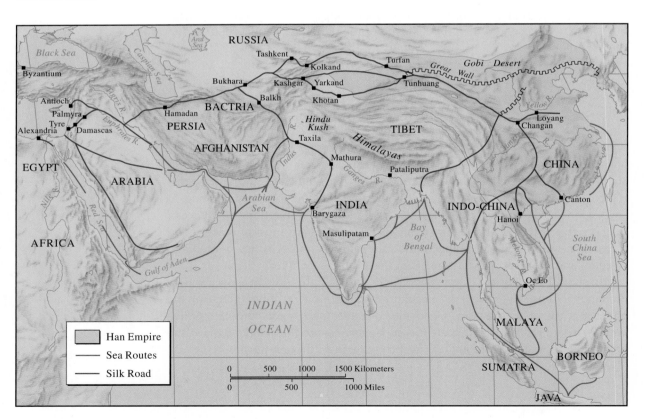

Pan Alley era of American popular music in the 1920s and 1930s, songs such as "Leena from Palesteena" or the "Sheik of Araby" were standard fare. In the 1950s and 1960s, the soundtracks of motion pictures such as *Casablanca* (set in Morocco with a musical score by Max Steiner) and *Laurence of Arabia* (which takes place in Turkey, Mesopotamia, and the Levant, with a score composed by Maurice Jarre) created the evocative soundscape of the unpredictable desert and the animated bazaar. This music became a springboard for later musical explorations heard in the soundtracks of James Bond and Indiana Jones films and of certain animated productions, such as *Aladdin* or *The Prince of Egypt,* marketed to children and their parents. The popular imagination regarding this vast area is also fueled by political history and current events, particularly today, with the news media's constant focus on the Middle East and the larger Arab world. Today, news reports about the Middle East are effectively situated in a land that is unfamiliar to most of us, with sound bites of the Call to Prayer or of celebrative folk song and drumming because, just like images and works of visual art, sounds and music can serve as powerful representations of people and places, whether real or imagined. But let us leave the imaginary world of Arabia behind and turn instead to the reality of Arab music and culture.

The Takht Ensemble

Listen to the excerpt of the performance of "Al-Shaghal" (pronounced ash-Sha-*ghal*, the gh is similar to the French "r" and the a of *ghal* is like that of "apple"). It was recorded live at a concert at Mount Holyoke College at the end of a weeklong summer workshop called the Arabic Music Retreat (CD 4, Track 18). The title translates roughly as "Obsession," referring to an obsession or preoccupation with the beloved, a common theme in Arabic-language poetry and literature. Even if you have never heard music like this in your life, you might enjoy it; but, then again, maybe not. By the end of this initial foray into the rich world of Arab music you should be able not only to understand and therefore enjoy it, but also to answer several questions about "Al-Shaghal." For example: What are the instruments involved? How do the musicians interact? What parts of the performance are composed? What is improvised? Why might the melodies sound slightly out of tune to someone accustomed to Western music? Why is the audience audibly excited about the performance? Who are the performers? Can we find more of their music on recordings? Why did this performance occur in Massachusetts and not in Cairo or Beirut?

CD 4:18

"Al-Shaghal" ("Obsession"), excerpt (2:48). Performed by A. J. Racy, Simon Shaheen, and the Arabic Music Retreat Ensemble. Field recording by Anne Rasmussen. South Hadley, Massachusetts, August 2001.

THE PERFORMERS AND THEIR INSTRUMENTS

The ensemble you hear is called a ***takht*** and comprises seven instrumentalists who play the most important instruments in Arab traditional music (see Figure 10.1). Simon Shaheen and his younger brother William both play the *'ud,* a short-necked, pear-shaped fretless lute, usually with eleven strings arranged in four double courses with a fifth single bass string. The Arab *'ud* is generally tuned in fourths (with a major third between the third and fourth course). Beginning with the lowest single string, the *'ud* is tuned C2, F2, A2, D3, G3, C4. Simon Shaheen is

FIGURE 10.1

The *takht* ensemble. From left to right, Nasim Dakwar (violin), William Shaheen (*'ud*), Simon Shaheen (*'ud*), A. J. Racy (*buzuq*), Jamal Sinou (*qanun*), Bassam Saba (*nay*), and Michel Mirhige (*riqq*).

Anne Rasmussen

a virtuoso performer on *'ud* and violin as well as a composer and ensemble leader who has produced numerous recordings, concerts, and festivals of traditional Arab and Middle Eastern Music. He is also known for his more fusion-oriented projects with musicians specializing in jazz and other world music traditions; in 1996 he founded the Arabic Music Retreat, an intensive summer music workshop.

A. J. Racy (Figure 10.2), an ethnomusicologist, composer, and performer based at the University of California, Los Angeles, plays the *buzuq,* a long-necked

FIGURE 10.2

A. J. Racy playing the *buzuq.*

Dan Neuman

lute with twenty-four movable frets, two sets of strings in triple courses C and G, and a single bass string tuned to C. You will see Racy's name cited frequently in this chapter because he is one of the most important scholars of Arab music. He is also the codirector of the Arabic Music Retreat.

Nasim Dakwar of Haifa, Israel, plays the violin, which is identical in construction to the Western violin or fiddle except that most Arab musicians tune the highest two strings down a whole step. Thus, rather than the Western tuning G3, D4, A4, and E5, the Arab violin is tuned G3, D4, G4, D5.

Bassam Saba of New York plays the *nay,* a reed flute that is blown obliquely at an angle. Jamal Sinou of Boston plays the *qanun,* a zither with seventy-five strings in triple courses with a series of small tuning levers that allow the strings to be retuned in the course of performance. Michel Mirhige, formerly one of the most important percussionists in Lebanon, now living in New York, plays the *riqq,* the Arab tambourine, also known as the *daff.*

MUSICAL TEXTURE

All of the musicians play virtually the same melody, a composition by the Egyptian musician Muhammad 'Abd al-Wahhab (d. 1991). But even though they play the same melody, they are not playing precisely in **unison** (together on the same pitches); they are free to add their own ornaments and nuances. Some instruments leave notes out, while others double them. The plucked stringed instruments, *'ud, buzuq,* and *qanun,* create a thicker, more sustained texture by employing evenly paced double or quadruple picking, or fast **tremolo** (fast strumming or picking up and down on a string). They also decorate their melodies with **grace note pickups** (playing the note above or below very quickly before landing on the main note) and **octave leaps** (jumping up or down an octave). The reed flute, or *nay,* and violin can sustain longer tones; can alter the timbre, or tone color, of those tones with bow, air pressure, or vibrato; and can slide between notes. Each instrument decorates the melody with **trills** (oscillations between two adjacent notes), **turns** (ornaments including a note above or below the main note), slides, and variations in the tone color characteristic of that instrument. The *qanun,* for example, can easily do a run of an octave or more. The *nay* can sustain pitches, bend them, and shift the tone color from the breathy tone that is characteristic of the instrument to a purer, more focused sound similar to that of the Western silver flute. The *'ud* can reinforce important tones by quickly playing the same note an octave lower. The musicological term for the texture produced by the *takht* is heterophony (see Chapter 1), something that occurs rarely in Western art and pop music but is easy to find in many other musics around the world. Heterophony is one of the most compelling aspects of playing and listening to Arab music, even though many Arab musicians rarely comment on this remarkable aspect of Arab performance practice, perhaps considering it one of the more unteachable aspects of performance.

RHYTHM

The *riqq,* a tambourine with an extremely sensitive skin head and heavy cymbals, is an instrument that alone can sound like an entire percussion section. The rhythmic pattern or *iqa'* played by Mirhige is made up of eight beats and is called *wahdah* (see Transcription 10.1).

Variation heard

TRANSCRIPTION 10.1
The rhythmic pattern or *iqa': Wahdah.*

First, listen for the difference between the low-sounding *dumm* (D) and the higher, drier-sounding *takk* (T). The name *wahdah* comes from the Arabic word *wahad,* or "one," because there is only one *dumm* to each 8-beat cycle. Second, notice that Mirhige can fill or sometimes simplify this repeating pattern with an almost infinite number of rhythms and variations. Third, when the ensemble is playing all together (during the refrains, for example), Mirhige plays on the head of the instrument but lets the jingles ring through slightly (at 0:05 and 2:10). Fourth, when the ensemble features a soloist within the group, he may choose to play only on the head of the instrument, still producing several variations but silencing the potentially clamorous jingles.

TRANSCRIPTION 10.2
Common Rhythmic
Patterns or *iqa'at.*

Transcription 10.2 presents a few other common rhythmic patterns in 4- or 8-beat rhythmic cycles. Try alternating back and forth between *maqsum, baladi, malfuf, sa'idi,* and *ayyub,* without varying the tempo. You can make the lower, resonant *dumm* and the higher, drier *takk* in several ways:

1. By cupping your hand slightly and slapping your notebook (*dumm*), and then, with the fingers straight out, striking your desk (*takk*)
2. By using a muffled clap (*dumm*) and the crisp sound of four fingers slapped on the bottom of the palm (*takk*)
3. By using a foot tap (*dumm*) and a slap on your lap (*takk*)
4. Simply by saying "*DUMM*" and "*takk*" at two different pitches

A good *riqq* player may incorporate all of these rhythms as he or she plays in a piece or accompanies an improvisation.

FORM, MELODY, AND IMPROVISATION

Now we will focus on the melody and form of "Al-Shaghal" (see the Close Listening guide). After an 8-measure melody, the ensemble plays a kind of melodic, rhythmic **ostinato** (repetitive pattern), during which each individual plays a solo *taqasim,* or improvisation. Prior to the excerpt on your CD, the violinist has already performed a solo. As we join the performance, it is Racy's turn to solo on the *buzuq.* The solid rhythmic and melodic ostinato provides the canvas upon which Racy paints his *taqasim.* Notice the way the rhythm of the *buzuq taqasim* has a regular pulse in some places but is nonmetrical or in free rhythm in others (see Chapter 1).

At times it seems as if Racy is in synchrony with the other musicians, but for the most part he seems to be doing his own thing. The juxtaposition of nonmetered rhythm and metrical rhythm, and the possibility of combining them, as we hear when Racy plays his relatively unmetered solo against the regular ostinato of the other musicians, is a distinctive feature of the music of the Arab world and the Middle East in general.

Close Listening

"AL-SHAGHAL" ("OBSESSION")

CD 4:18

COUNTER NUMBER	COMMENTARY: MUSICAL ACTION	COMMENTARY: PERFORMER–AUDIENCE INTERACTION
0:00	End of violin solo (*taqasim*)	Exclamation: "Allah" by either a musician or someone in the audience
0:05	8-measure refrain played by the whole ensemble or *takht*	Audience applause
0:14	Second phrase of 8-measure refrain (measures 5–8)	
0:23	Two measures of rhythmic/melodic ostinato played by the *'ud*	
0:28	Beginning of *buzuq taqasim* after the "*dumm*" or downbeat by the ensemble	
0:33	Silence: pause between phrases	Audience murmers: "Ahh"
0:37	Tiny idea or fragment	
0:39	Silence	
0:41	Longer phrase with repeated notes, emphasized notes, and **sequences** (musical ideas that are repeated a step higher or lower)	
0:58	*Qafla* or ending idea of the first "paragraph" of the improvisation	Complete silence
1:08	Paragraph 2 of the *taqasim*	
1:14	Melodic development, sequence, and another cadential phrase, or *qafla*	Vocal response by the audience members and other musicians

1:15–1:48	The *buzuq* continues the solo and concludes it with a *qafla* at 1:41 that is met with another vocal response by audience members and musicians. The *taqasim* ends as the main melody of the refrain is reintroduced at 1:48; some ensemble members join him subtly, with "fillers" and bits of the main melody.	Vocal response by the audience members and other musicians at 1:41
2:05	Descending run of notes by the *'ud* to lead the ensemble back into the repeat of the refrain melody.	
2:10	8-measure refrain repeated by ensemble	Huge audience applause
2:28	Beginning of *nay taqasim*	Exclamation of "Allah!" at the end of the first phrase of the *nay taqasim*

A *maqam* is a musical mode or scale, and there are several kinds described by name, as we will discuss further later in the chapter. "Al-Shaghal" is in *maqam Bayyati* (ba-*yeah*-tee) beginning on the note G (see Transcription 10.3). One might also hear *maqam Bayyati* beginning on the note D or A, for example.

TRANSCRIPTION 10.3
The scale of *maqam Bayyati.*

The second degree of the scale is a half-flat (indicated in this text with the sign ♭) also sometimes called a neutral interval or a quarter tone. The A♭ falls between the notes A♭ on the piano. Try humming along and then singing the scale of *maqam Bayyati.* If you have grown up in Europe or North America you have heard these kinds of intervals in popular and folk music, but if you have been trained as a pianist or in the tradition of Western classical music you may find this difficult to do. One way for someone new to this music to approach the quarter tone might be to first sing the A as an A natural: G A B♭ (just like the do re mi of a minor scale). Then return to the A and slide down ever so slightly to a note that creates some tension with that A natural but is not as low as the full A♭. The best way to get a sense of the intervals in *maqam Bayyati* is really to just sing along with this and other music that is in that *maqam* and match your voice to the pitches of the performers.

Listen again to the *buzuq taqasim* by Racy (CD 4, Track 18). Let us call the first section of the solo (0:28–1:05 on the recording) a "paragraph." We hear several phrases or sentences, separated by pauses, that emphasize the four notes of the bottom of the scale (G A♭ B♭ C) with particular emphasis on the 4th degree C, the 5th degree D, and the tonic (first or bottom) note, G. The second paragraph of the improvisation, beginning at 1:08, showcases the lower range of the instrument. This paragraph extends to about 1:41 on the recording. The final phrase features a purposeful ascent up the scale of *maqam Bayyati* and then descent down the steps of the scale with a few twists and turns at the bottom. This concluding musical statement or **cadential phrase** is called a *qafla* (pl. *qaflat*). See if you can notice the raised 6th degree (E♮) that Racy employs on the way down the scale. While this is an occasional note, it is very much a part of the character of this *maqam*, especially when it occurs as effectively as it does in this *qafla*.

TRANSCRIPTION 10.4
Key structures in the form of "Al-Shaghal."

After a couple of seconds during which we hear only the ostinato, the *buzuq* comes quietly back into the main melody of the composition (1:43). The rest of the musicians hang back, allowing the soloists's moment to continue, and do not join in until Racy reaches the repeat of the melody that has become a kind of recurring refrain (see Transcription 10.4). The dramatic descending run by the *'ud*, played by the virtuoso Simon Shaheen, brings the group back into the refrain definitively and all join in at this repeat of the melody (2:05). At this moment we might describe Shaheen's deviation from the ensemble **vamp** (rhythmic or melodic ostinato) more as polyphony (see Chapter 1) than heterophony because he is really creating a countermelody that becomes a "pickup" to the group's return. The descending *'ud* line underscores the end of Racy's solo and receives resounding approval from the audience.

TARAB

To many, this music sounds beautiful in and of itself, but the fact that you can hear the live audience in the background tells even the novice that this is an exciting event. Even after the first phrase of Racy's *taqasim* on the *buzuq*, we can hear the audience murmur acknowledgment. In fact, rather than remaining respectfully silent, this audience participates actively in the music making. Listen again to the juncture between Racy's solo and the group refrain (2:05 to the end of the excerpt). Following this refrain, we hear just the beginning of Basam Saba's *nay taqasim*.

This concert follows the parameters of performance, or the principles of a musical event, which are at first learned and later expected or even desired by the participants (see the performance model in Chapter 1). Active listeners, including the members of the ensemble themselves, might respond to the music with exclamations of "Oooh" and "Ahhh," and words like *Allah* (God), *Ya Salam* ("Oh, peace"), or *Ya 'Ayni* ("Oh, my eye"). With these exclamations, the audience encourages the musicians by making a statement that the music is moving and exciting. The musicians in turn respond to the audience's acclamations with more good music.

In this context, interaction between musicians and audience is at the same time a catalyst for and the result of *tarab,* which translates roughly as "ecstasy" or "enchantment." The concept of *tarab* gets to the very heart of Arab musical aesthetics. The term refers to a repertory of traditional compositions as well as to a style of performance that both embodies and invokes *tarab* (Racy 2002). (You will notice later in this chapter that the female and male singers Sana and Amer Khadaj are called *mutribah* and *mutrib,* literally "enchantress" and "enchanter"; both the terms derive from *tarab*). In "*tarab* culture," musicians and audiences expect performances to be inspired and inspiring (like the performance of "Amazing Grace" at the New Bethel Baptist Church, in Chapter 4). Listeners are expected to contribute to the overall atmosphere of an evening's music by offering complementary exclamations of encouragement to singers and instrumentalists alike. A performance without such participation would be considered lifeless, uninspired, and more like a concert of Western classical music, where the audience is expected to be silent while the music is playing and to applaud only after it is over.

During the performance of "Al-Shaghal," the conditions were ripe for *tarab*. And although the concert was in Massachusetts, rather than somewhere like

Cairo, Egypt, what made it an evening of Arab music (as opposed to an evening of New England music) was—along with the musicians, their repertory, and the instruments on which it was performed—the experiences and expectations the participants shared.

Of course, this performance represents but one aspect of Arab music. It has introduced us to the melodic and rhythmic building blocks of Arab music and to a discussion of Arab musical aesthetics. We move now to clarify a variety of categories and terminology surrounding the Middle East, the Arab world, and the Muslim world. As this chapter progresses, we will listen next to the Call to Prayer and discuss the important relationship among music, spirituality, and Islamic practice, a discussion that takes us to the historical writings of medieval Mesopotamia (modern-day Iraq). To complement this early history, we meet, through an interview, Rahim Alhaj, an Iraqi performer and composer who came to the United States as a refugee. As the chapter continues, a more extensive discussion of music and history brings us to the Western Arab world, or Maghrib, where we are introduced to Jewish Sephardic music, another tradition that has migrated repeatedly throughout its history. Next, we focus on women's communal music-making in North African wedding rituals, paying special attention to creativity and identity. We also consider the significance of poetry in Arab culture, the marriage of music and poetry, and the art of improvisation in both media. At the end of chapter you will read about the music of Israel and the Palestinian territories and will listen to musical performances that highlight the roots and routes of Arab music. And we will hear the music of another Jewish artist, Ofra Haza, the Yemeni-Israeli singer whose very "local" music went "global"; this is also our single performance from the area known as the Arab Gulf or the Arabian Peninsula.

Categories and Terminology: Middle East, Arab World, Muslim World

How do we define the geographic borders of a music-culture like this one? As musicians or students and scholars of music, we quickly realize that political boundaries, those we see on maps, are fickle when it comes to representing cultural practices. You may have noticed that, with the exception of Nasim Dakwar from Haifa, Israel, the rest of the performers were from Boston, New York, and Los Angeles. Although they were born outside North America, these musicians have spent the majority of their adult lives in the United States, home to a significant component of the Arab diaspora. Musicians and audiences of Arab heritage living outside the Arab world (the diaspora) have been involved not only in processes of adaptation and reaction—in which language, culture, and music change, are watered down, or disappear altogether—but also in exciting musical processes of continuous exchange, amalgamation, collaboration, and renewal. Investigating music-cultures beyond the borders of nation states is key to understanding the music of the world's peoples, particularly because music in its many media, from a children's song to an mp3 file, is imminently transportable.

In reading and hearing about the *Middle East*, the *Arab world*, and the *Muslim world* on an almost-daily basis in the press, we come to accept these terms without questioning them, even though, as commonly used, they are problematic. Unlike labels that define a continent (such as *Africa*) or a former colonial empire (such as *Latin America*), the *Middle East* and the *Arab world* describe regions that (1) cover more than one continent; (2) comprise a multitude of nations, languages, religions, and ethnic groups; and (3) are witness to a checkered colonial and contemporary political history. The *Muslim world* describes a population that lives in all four hemispheres of the globe.

The political boundaries of the Middle East encompass an area that runs from south of the Sudan in North Africa, through Israel, to the top of Turkey in southwestern Asia (sometimes called Asia Minor), and from Mauritania on the western coast of Africa through Afghanistan and Pakistan in southern Asia. The term *Middle East* is not indigenous; rather, European military strategists and map makers of past wars and colonial forays created the term. Nevertheless, it has become an acceptable label around the world, even among "Middle Easterners" themselves. The vast region of the Middle East encompasses three major cultural-linguistic areas: Turkish, Arab, and Persian. The major languages spoken in addition to Turkish, Arabic, and Persian (or Farsi) include Kurdish, Hebrew, Berber, Pashtu, Baluchi, Aramaic, and Armenian.

Although the term *Middle East* is European in origin, the *Arab world* is a concept developed in the 1950s by Egyptian President Gamal 'Abd al-Nassr. The Arab League, a voluntary organization of independent countries, includes twenty-two member nations where the majority speak Arabic. Beginning in northwest Africa, Arab-world countries include Mauritania, Morocco, Algeria, Tunisia, Libya, Egypt, Sudan, Djibouti, Somalia, Lebanon, Jordan, Syria, Iraq, Israel, and what are at this writing called the Palestinian territories of Israel. The Arabian Gulf, another distinct area of the Arab world, includes Saudi Arabia, Kuwait, Bahrain, Qatar, the United Arab Emirates, Oman, and Yemen. Although the Arabic language is dominant throughout this diverse Arab-world mosaic, dozens of local dialects and even separate languages (such as Kurdish, Berber, and Armenian) are spoken as well.

How can we consider the Middle East or the Arab world, with its undeniable diversity, a single music-culture? One prominent anthropologist of the Middle East, Dale Eickelman, writes: "It is the presence throughout the area of key cultural symbols and their variants and through shared historical circumstances that this region can justifiably be considered as a single socio-cultural area" (Eickelman 1989:9). In the domain of music, the key cultural symbols to which Eickelman refers include the theoretical building blocks of music, such as scales, rhythms, and forms; the material culture of music, including families of related instruments; the relationship of language, poetry, and storytelling to music; and musical aesthetics, or the power and beauty associated with making and experiencing music.

Religion and Music in the Arab World

Newcomers to this music and culture sometimes assume that all Arabs are Muslims (people of the Islamic religion) and that Arab music is therefore Muslim music. On the contrary, with the exception of music used in religious rituals, Arab music is part of a tradition shared by Jews, Christians, and Muslims. In fact, in spite of the emigration of significant communities of both Jews and Christians away from Arab lands, many historically prominent musicians were Jews and Christians, and the three religious communities share a long history of musical and cultural exchange that lives today in spite of mass exodus and political rupture. So, although the performance of much music can be correctly categorized as Arab music *and* Middle Eastern music, it is not necessarily Islamic, or Muslim, music.

The religion of Islam is prominent throughout the Arab world and the Middle East; however, only about 20 percent of the world's Muslims live in the Arab world, and the majority of Muslims live in South and Southeast Asia. In fact, Indonesia, Pakistan, India, and Bangladesh are the countries that have the largest Muslim populations. The Arab world is actually the birthplace of three monotheistic religions—Judaism, Christianity, and Islam—which, owing to their common roots, share many cultural attributes, from liturgical texts and stories, to traditions of religious chant, to philosophical ideas regarding mysticism. When viewed in terms of cultural practices, the three religions exhibit many similarities. For example, Judaism, Christianity, and Islam all have strong traditions of sung, religious chant perpetuated by ritual practices.

A CHANCE MEETING WITH SABRI MUDALLAL

On Christmas Day 1993, my husband and I flew to Damascus, Syria. After a couple of days in Damascus, we traveled to Aleppo by bus, checked into a modest hotel, and soon set out on foot to explore. It was cold and dreary, the streets nearly empty because tourism to the Arab world was suffering in the aftermath of the First Gulf War, which had exploded just three years earlier.

A man approached and fell into step with us. "May I help you?" he offered. "Do you need a place to stay?" We politely declined, but I did mention that I was a musician and a great admirer of the singer Sabri Mudallal, a man I knew to be from Aleppo. In a fulfillment of the old Arabic proverb "A chance meeting is worth a thousand appointments," our self-appointed guide, Hamid, soon had us sitting in the Great Mosque of Aleppo (the Zakariyya Mosque), on the edge of the old market, with Sabri Mudallal himself (1918–2006).

We had been taken through the sanctuary entrance and into a small room off the mosque's expansive courtyard. Here various callers (*muezzins*, [moo-ez-zeen] from the Arabic *mu'adhdhin* [moo-*ez*-zeen]) broadcast the Islamic Call to Prayer (from the Arabic **Adhan** [a-*zan*]) at five designated times each day. Sabri Mudallal's voice is well known as the "first muezzin" of the Great Mosque, where he called the noon prayer. Over the course of several days in Aleppo, he invited us to make several recordings, including the Call to Prayer. (See Chapter 11 on making field recordings.)

THE CALL TO PRAYER: *AZAN*

The entire text of the Call to Prayer is printed here. Note that each phrase is repeated except for the final phrase. Only about half of the call, through the fourth line, is heard on the recording.

The Call to Prayer		
	Allahu Akbar, Allahu Akbar	God is Great, God is Great
	Ashshadu an la ilaha illa Allah (x2)	I testify that there is no God but God (x2)
	Ashshadu anna Muhammad rasul	I testify that Muhammad is the prophet
	Allah (x2)	of God (x2)
	Hayya 'ala salah (x2)	Come to prayer (x2)
	Hayya 'ala falah (x2)	Come to salvation (x2)
	Il salah ghairu min al-noum	Prayer is better than sleep
		[for the morning call]

CD 4:19

Call to Prayer (*Azan*) (2:24). Performed by Sabri Mudallal. Field recording by Anne Rasmussen. Aleppo, Syria, 1994.

In Muslim communities throughout the world, the Call to Prayer is heard five times a day from every mosque. In many countries where Islam is prevalent, such as Indonesia, for example, such broadcasts—both prerecorded and live—are heard on radio and television, throughout neighborhoods large and small, in the city or in the countryside. Although most contemporary muezzins, like those at the Great Mosque, use a sound amplification system, the minarets of mosques were originally built so that those with beautiful, powerful voices could broadcast their call throughout the community.

The call to prayer is not considered music, but it *is* musical. As you listen to it (CD 4, Track 19), notice the way the phrases are separated by long pauses during which you can hear the sounds of the city. At the appointed times for the call (predawn, noon, midafternoon, dusk, and about an hour and a half after sunset), the soundscape of Aleppo, like that of may cities in the Muslim world, is a loose tapestry of *azans,* all of them starting just a few seconds or minutes apart, with each proceeding at its own pace. Listen for the way the *azan* progresses (see Transcription 10.5). Each phrase, when repeated, becomes longer and more ornamented. Listen also to the declamatory nature of Sheikh Mudallal's voice. This is no lyrical lullaby, but a *proclamation*. Finally, though the timbre or color of the voice might to a Western ear seem nasal or harsh, it is a model of beauty in this cultural context, a sound to which reciters throughout the Islamic world— even in Indonesia, South Africa, or Bosnia—might aspire. (See the Close Listening guide.)

Each phrase when repeated takes quite a bit longer than the first time: for example, 4 and 12 seconds for line 1 and its repetition; 8 and 13 seconds for line 2 and its repetition. The longest phrase on the recording is line 4 repeated, at 19 seconds. Try singing something for 19 seconds without taking a breath to see what a challenge it is! Two other aspects of this singing that make it so distinctive are (1) a nasal vocal timbre, called **ghunna** in Arabic, and (2) the way the muezzin holds or sustains vowelless consonants. Listen, for example, to the held "nnnnnnn" at 1:30 on the track. While these vocal techniques are undesirable to trained singers of Western classical music, nasalization and sustaining or "sitting on" consonants are a part of the sound of American country and western music, as well as many other American popular music styles (compare with

TRANSCRIPTION 10.5
Call to Prayer (*Azan*).

*Sequence: Pattern of 4 notes beginning on g, repeated 3 times, each time a step lower.

"Amazing Grace" as sung by John Sherfey and the congregation of the Fellowship Independent Baptist Church on CD 1, Track 23).

The vocal techniques cultivated in the performance of the *azan,* the recitation of the Islamic Qur'an, and the singing of religious songs are considered the hallmarks of excellent singing in other Arab contexts as well. Sabri Mudallal's call to prayer falls into a cultural category that is separate from music for

Close Listening

CALL TO PRAYER (*AZAN*)

CD 4:19

COUNTER NUMBER	COMMENTARY	ARABIC TRANSLITERATION	TRANSLATION
0:00	Line 1 presented with one note per syllable of text	*Allahu Akbar* *Allahu Akbar*	God is Great God is Great
0:04	Pause (ambient noise in the background)		
0:13	Line 1 repeated, with more long-held notes and ornaments or melisma (several notes for a single syllable)	*Allahu Akbar* *Allahu Akbar*	God is Great God is Great
0:25	Pause		
0:34	Line 2	*Ashshadu an la ilaha illa Allah*	I testify that there is no God but God
0:42	Pause		
0:50	Line 2 repeated, again with longer notes and more ornaments and melisma	*Ashshadu an la ilaha illa Allah*	
1:03	Pause		
1:13	Line 3	*Ashshadu anna Muhammad rasul Allah*	I testify that Muhammad is the prophet of God
1:21	Pause		
1:28	Line 3 repeated. Listen for the sequences, part of the reciter's approach to decorating the phrase.	*Ashshadu anna Muhammad rasul Allah* (listen for melisma on nnn)	I testify that Muhammad is the prophet of God
1:44	Pause		
1:52	Line 4 followed by silence	*Hayya 'ala salah*	Come to prayer
1:58	Pause		
2:05	Line 4 repeated	*Hayya 'ala salah*	Come to prayer

entertainment's sake, but his performance nevertheless exhibits several important aspects of Arab traditional music: the Arab mode called *maqam Rast* (this is also the mode we hear in Ayad al-Asadi's *'ud taqasim* on CD 4, Track 25), the construction and timing of his phrases, his enunciation, and the *qafla* or end of each phrase. In her ethnography of Egyptian reciters of the Qur'an, Kristina Nelson (1985) comments on the reciprocity of good singing and recitation. Just as reciters are recognized for their vocal and musical talent, a few singers are especially praised for sounding like reciters. When conducting research in Egypt for her book about Umm Kulthum, the most famous singer of the Arab world, Virginia Danielson (1997) was told time after time that Umm Kulthum was a good singer "because she could recite the Qur'an." Stories about Umm Kulthum's early training in the traditional religious school, and even a short scene from the feature-length film *Salama,* in which she recites a passage from the Qur'an, enhance her legendary reputation throughout the Muslim world in spite of the fact that she was a singer and actor and not a religious specialist.

It is understood that, for religious matters, devotional intent matters far more than musical talent. Nevertheless, the talented reciter (muezzin) is acknowledged by fans and connoisseurs alike. Even in small communities, the talented reciters will be recognized by their neighbors. In addition to their work as **ritual specialists** (those who specialize in facilitating others' experience of cultural traditions), people like Sabri Mudallal, who was also known for his performance of traditional vocal repertory, may live a life similar to that of a professional singer, with a busy schedule of performance engagements and lively concerts packed with admiring fans and students. We were treated to his singing one evening when he invited us to a gathering of muezzins (Figure 10.3). After following him through the labyrinthine alleyways of old Aleppo, we entered a chilly fortresslike

FIGURE 10.3

Muezzins of Aleppo.

Anne Rasmussen

space and then a warm inner chamber. The floor was covered with oriental carpets and the perimeter of the space was lined with benches and couches; a wood stove was the source of heat.

The singers, all of them muezzins and Qur'anic reciters, alternated between long solo introductions in free rhythm and metered and strophic songs with choral refrains that the whole group sang, enlivening the music by playing *daffs* (frame drums). The participants murmured or sometimes shouted their approval of a well-turned phrase. Sometimes they lifted their caps off their heads and waved them in the air, in a gesture of approval. Someone stoked the stove in the center of the room and rotated the *daffs,* so that the fire would warm them evenly. My husband and I were the only audience. The muezzins seemed to be singing for pleasure, although they may also have been rehearsing for more-public performance. Once the singing started, the music continued for two hours. There was no break, no pause for applause, no conversation, and no introductions—all behaviors that one might associate with either a performance or a rehearsal. Social activity occurred through the sharing of songs.

MUSIC AND ISLAM

The widespread notion that "Muslims do not approve of music" is problematic. Certainly, in the past and particularly today, some Muslim individuals and communities have condemned music and musicians in the name of religion. Sometimes thought of as "fanatic," "fundamentalist," "Islamist," "legalist," or just conservative, these groups, the most well-known of which today is the Afghani-based Taliban, use arguments they say are based on religious dogma to close theatres, destroy musical artifacts, and persecute musicians (Shiloah 1997). In truth, however, a wealth of musical genres and styles exist in Islamic communities throughout the world. At the most basic level, ritual speech, like the Call to Prayer, the verses of the Qur'an, and even group prayer are almost always intoned or chanted, rather than simply spoken. In more elaborate manifestations the performance of religious language can be remarkably musical. Furthermore, in certain social contexts such as public celebrations or family-based rites of passage, ritual language often occurs alongside religious singing, sometimes with instrumental accompaniment. As such, the performance of religious language—from prayer to many different kinds of song—constitutes a dense constellation of Islamic vocal arts and music.

Arabic language and music pervades the **umma,** or the global community of Muslims. Islamic texts are studied and ritually performed only in the Arabic language. The **Qur'an,** for example, is believed to be the word of God and, when recited, is done so according to a system of rules, called *tajwid* (taj-*weed*), that preserve the original manner of Arabic pronunciation in quite specific ways. Along with vedic chant of India, or the chanting of the Jewish **Torah** (teachings in the Hebrew Bible), *tajwid* and its application to the recited Qur'an constitute one of the world's most elegant systems of religious language performance, perpetuated today in virtually every continent on the globe.

In Indonesia, for example—which has the largest Muslim population in the world (about 200 million)—one can hear daily the Call to Prayer, the recited Qur'an, and a range of Islamic music. One of the distinctive aspects of Islam in Indonesia is the multitude of excellent reciters, both male and female, and the lively festivals and

Anne Rasmussen

FIGURE 10.4

Contestants Abdul Hamid and Isa Siswatika, both age twenty, in preparation for upcoming competition in Quranic recitation, Jakarta, Indonesia.

competitions (Figure 10.4) that celebrate Islamic arts and reward excellence in Qur'anic recitation, knowledge, interpretation, and calligraphy.

That the Arabic language is used in ritual performance throughout the Muslim world—from Indonesia to Pakistan; from South Africa to Bosnia to California—presents an interesting case for students of the music of the world's peoples who are trying to locate the "boundaries of culture." On the one hand, there is much across the Muslim world that is shared. At the same time, every country, region, culture, and community has developed its own local religious practices, as you have seen throughout this book in relation to other cultures. Within Indonesian Islam, for example, we can find a plethora of unique Islamic musics. We can also find a prevalence of women in public religious life, which might seem remarkable when compared with practice in other Muslim regions.

Music in History/Music as History

The Qur'an is not only essential for Muslim ritual, but it also provides an important source of guidance in matters of everyday life, including those that involve music. Alongside the Qur'an, people look to the **Hadith** (ha-*deeth*), the traditions of the prophet Muhammed that were preserved in the statements of his closest companions and eventually recorded in writing. Together, the Qur'an and the Hadith contain much information related to the attitudes toward and the practice of music during the dawn and development of Islam (the seventh and eighth centuries). These are the first in a rich library of early written sources on music history in the Arab world.

MUSICAL LIFE IN MEDIEVAL MESOPOTAMIA

Formerly called Mesopotamia (literally "the land between two rivers": the Tigris and the Euphrates), Iraq has long been recognized as the site of phenomenal human invention: the wheel, written cuneiform script, and ingenious architectural and agricultural techniques. Baghdad was for centuries a cosmopolitan city humming with intellectual activity and music. Cities such as Baghdad, as well as Aleppo and Damascus (now in Syria), served as cultural crossroads and mercantile centers characterized by a multicultural mix of peoples from Mesopotamia, Syria, Byzantium (Turkey), and Persia (Iran) (Racy 1984).

The medieval Arab world witnessed rich intellectual and scientific investiga- tion. During the ninth century, the translation into Arabic of the treatises of Plato, Pythagoras, Plotinus, and Aristotle took place at the *Bayt al-Hikmah* (House of Learning) under the patronage of the Abassid Kalif al Ma'mun. Works written between the ninth and thirteenth centuries in this environment considered the scientific nature of music—from its importance in the universe, to the measure- ment of pitch intervals, to the construction of musical instruments such as the *'ud.* Authors were preoccupied with the cosmological and metaphysical meanings of music (Racy 1984:9; Turner 1995), as well as with its applications for healing and therapy (Shiloah 1991). Arabic translations of Greek treatises became available in medieval Europe and greatly influenced the development of music there, where the ancient world's ideas about music and its relationship to both the mundane and the sublime caught on. The Latin concept of the *quadrivium,* which allied music with the study of mathematics, geometry, and astronomy, was directly influenced by Greek philosophies that were made known, in part, through the Arabic translations originating in Mesopotamia.

The ethnomusicologist George Sawa (1985, 1989) relates details of the musical life of Baghdad through the eyes of Abu al-Faraj al-Isbahani (d. 967 C.E.), an incredible journalist of the Abassid Era, 750–932 C.E., and the author of the *Kitab al-Agani (Book of Songs).* Written over the course of fifty years, al-Isbahani's twenty-four-volume work of ten thousand pages is a comprehensive musical ethnography. Al-Isbahani came from Baghdad's aristocracy and was conversant in numerous subjects, including the Qur'an, the Hadith, grammar, philology (linguis- tics), medicine, astrology, falconry, farriery (the art of the blacksmith), and even "the preparation of beverages." As a poet, he maintained a huge repertory of fables, anecdotes, biographies, and, of course, songs. Al-Isbahani's many anecdotes about music making reveal the complex position of music and musicians in medieval Baghdad. Although the aristocracy enjoyed music as both performers and listeners, they indulged in musical gatherings only in private circles, behind closed doors. Some people, in fact, considered music to be sinful and sacrilegious, and musicians to be of questionable character (compare the Chinese attitude, Chapter 8). Neverthe- less, musicians played an indispensable role as entertainers and companions, and their music was used for greeting and well wishing, in secular and religious situations, and to legitimate the position of rulers. One thousand years later, ideas about the positive and negative effects of music and musical professionalism, as well as the dangers of indulging in music, may still be encountered, not only in Arab culture, but also in our own (see, for example, Chapter 4).

INTERVIEW WITH RAHIM ALHAJ, MUSICIAN FROM BAGHDAD

Given Iraq's contemporary history, you may find it difficult to imagine Baghdad as a city bustling with cosmopolitanism, intellectual activity, and music. During the

Second Gulf War (begun in 2003), an Iraqi *'ud* player and composer, Rahim Alhaj (also known as Al Haj) came to visit my campus in January 2004. His concert was "standing room only"; in fact, more than one hundred people were turned away. Our curiosity to know and share something with "a real musician from Baghdad" was apparent. During Rahim's visit I kept a tape recorder running: in the car, at restaurants, and during his formal presentations. What follows is an edited version of his story. I have polished his English, which he humorously refers to as "a disaster"; but then Rahim reviewed the transcript to make sure I had not misinterpreted anything that he said. Because this was a very personal exchange, I refer to Mr. Alhaj as Rahim, as he does on his own website.

Many themes in Rahim's interview underscore aspects of music in the Arab world or of music and life in general.

- Like many musicians worldwide, Rahim attributes his discovery of the *'ud* to a teacher who took the time to mentor him.
- His father was not in favor of music as a profession.
- He describes his relationship with his instrument and with music as a love affair (see Figure 10.5).
- Even though he was "only a musician," he was persecuted for his politics. As is the case with many political refugees and emigrants, a family member went to extraordinary lengths and great expense so that Rahim could leave his homeland for a better life.
- One of the side effects of war can be cultural genocide; musicians can be disempowered, and entire traditions can be wiped out.
- As a newcomer to the United States, Rahim was an unknown whose life's work no longer had a context. (By now, however, he has been featured on National Public Radio and recorded as part of the Smithsonian Folkways collection.)

Little by little, owing to fortuitous circumstances and new friendships, Rahim began to build a life in the United States. His story exemplifies the dynamic nature

FIGURE 10.5

Rahim Alhaj.

Anne Rasmussen

of musicians and a music-culture that can survive the harshest of circumstances. Further, the story of any individual musician shows us again that, even though we can generalize about the music-culture of a nation, an ethnic group, a religious community, a town, a community, a band, or even a family, the trajectory of each and every person making music—and "people making music" includes musicians, patrons, audiences, dancers, producers—is unique.

I was born in Baghdad to a middle-class family. I was the only musician. I started playing the 'ud when I was nine. I was a little boy compared to the big 'ud. I was trying to find my way [just to hold the instrument]. But I watched my teacher and how he played with the instrument. So fortunately, or unfortunately, I could make some noise. Anyway, so he said, "You are a musician," and he gave me his instrument and he gave me some lessons, and I was . . . by myself . . . practicing all day. Then I found myself totally in love with the instrument. In fact, I couldn't sleep without it . . . sometimes I had to hold it and just sleep, until my father said, "He is insane!" My father was fighting with my mom a lot, because he didn't want me actually to be a musician. He wanted me to be a doctor. It is like this in America, [too]: parents don't like their children to be musicians. You know: "Go be a doctor!" "Money! A lot of money!" Anyway, the great thing was, my mom, she supported me a lot . . . she made me a musician. My first concert was when I was in elementary school.

And actually, because my father refused to let me study music unless I studied something else, I also studied Arabic literature to be a teacher. During that time, I entered my career as a professional musician. I graduated from the Conservatory of Baghdad under one of the greatest 'ud players in the world, Munir Bashir. And up until 1991 I was politically active against the regime [of Saddam Hussein]. I was against the Iran-Iraq War, and I was imprisoned [twice because of that].

Rahim was finally able to leave Iraq in 1991 with a false identity: a real passport that his mother had purchased for him.

In 1991 I had the chance to leave Iraq under false travel documents. My mom bribed a man. She bought me this Iraqi passport under another name, so I got the chance to leave from Iraq to Jordan, which cost one million *dinari,* which is like twenty thousand dollars. When I left Iraq, I had a bad experience—and this was the saddest moment in my whole life. At the border between Jordan and Syria they took my instrument from me because the Iraqi constitution does not allow a musician to take an instrument out of Iraq to another country unless you have permission from the minister of culture. If you have something [like a scheduled performance], then you are allowed to take an instrument with you. But because I was traveling under another name, I couldn't tell the soldier on the border, "I am Rahim Alhaj." This instrument was . . . it wasn't just an instrument, it was my life: my love, my wife, my mom, my life. And I let go of it.

Anyway, I stayed a while in Jordan, two or three years as a teacher, and then left for Syria where I stayed quite a while, five years or so until I came here with my wife, who I met in Syria, in March 2000. The United Nations granted me political asylum and arranged for me to come to the United States, and they choose New Mexico for me. Now I am here playing a lot of music, and composing, and doing some lectures.

Rahim provided some details about the process of resettlement in the United States. After being granted refugee status and placement in Albuquerque, New Mexico, his case was taken up by a local charity. Given a month's rent and some money for food, Rahim was on his own, with no friends and just a few phrases of English.

It's a funny story. After a month this guy came to me, and he said, "We found you a job." And I said, "Okay!" And he said, "McDonald's." And I said, "So which kind of institute is that? Is that teaching history, musicians, music . . . ?" Yeah, so I swear to God I asked him, "Is this Western music they teach or Eastern music?" And he said, "No. This is McDonald's." "I don't know what McDonald's is!" I said. And he said, "It's McDonald's. It's a restaurant." I told him, "What?! A restaurant? I'm not playing in a restaurant! I'm a concert musician!" And he said, "Well, you're not *going* to play there. Your job is dishwasher." I was astonished. I had no English, but I told him, "Do you know me? Have you read my résumé?"

Well, the Iraqi people are proud of two things in Iraq, basically. Not just because the first civilization started in Iraq; we are proud of music and art. But the time under Saddam was a long disaster for a lot of reasons. The music scene and environment in the Iran-Iraq War [was like this]: All of the songwriters and poets wrote songs about Saddam: how great he is, and how the [Iran-Iraq] War was justified. As a musician, if you are not against the government, you will continue as a musician. In Iraq, when you are a musician, you have a salary. You take money from the government that allows you to live. And then you don't need to go to bars and play. That's nice. So that's what happened with the music.

But it was *after* what happened during the Iran-Iraq War in Iraq under Saddam [that was really bad]. Unfortunately, as you know, after the First Gulf War, we had sanctions for fifteen years, and it had an undeniable impact on the Iraqi people. We lost two million kids as a consequence of sanctions [because there was a shortage of medicine and supplies]. And all the musicians, you know, composers and so forth, left Iraq. Music became more of a secondary thing, not a way to live. So all the musicians could not make a living in Iraq, so they left Iraq.

Amazingly, in Iraq at that time, half, if not most, of the National Iraq Symphony Orchestra played with two strings. The stringed instruments needed strings, but we couldn't buy them; it was not allowed to bring instruments or instrument supplies into Iraq. It was forbidden. It was like one of the 165 items that weren't allowed into Iraq. Yeah! So you have to function on two strings. You know, cello . . . two strings . . . violin, viola, whatever you have. So you have to figure out how to play the music with only two or maybe three strings.

The 'ud in Iraq is different from other Arab world traditions. It's not just associated with other instruments [as in the example of the *takht* ensemble heard on CD 4, Track 18]. No! The 'ud becomes a solo instrument. This is what I'm doing. And it's not just for entertaining. The new music for the 'ud as a solo instrument has a meaning: There are stories behind the music, not just something like a *taqasim* or improvisation [which is more abstract]. This is a different concept. You express *feelings*: compassion, love, and peace. We in Iraq have moved beyond the traditional forms. We are just a few, really, who are doing this kind of thing. My composition called "Helum" ("Dream") is about the desire we have to touch our dreams. The piece is actually based on a phone conversation with my nieces and nephews. Before my recent trip to Iraq, I asked them, "What are you, you know, *dreaming* right now?" They were in college, and they said, "Well, just to have a regular life." That's the dream: to have a regular life, to go to school, get an education, and start lives. And to have a safe, basic life, which includes clean water and electricity. Their dream is to have a life.

For example, when I came to the United States, I composed this piece: [Rahim plays the beginning of "Horses" (CD 4, Track 20; Transcription 10.6) for a group of students]. What does it remind you of? The rhythm. . . What does it remind you guys of? [A student guesses almost immediately: "Galloping?"] Galloping. The horses, right? Yeah, that's it! And so this is called "Horses." I composed this piece the third day I was in the United States. I was in the Albuquerque desert, and I found myself like a horse, able to run anywhere, you know, to touch my freedom. So I thought, how can I make horses? So I took [the idea of] galloping, and I composed this. That's totally, totally new in the music of the 'ud.

When one student asked Rahim about the various contexts for musical performance, he responded, "Well you wouldn't hear it in a mosque. This is not gospel music." But you would hear it in someone's house, or at a concert, or at a wedding or in a club where you would stay up late and where there would be dancing. Rahim also commented on the extent to which people in the current environment are setting new texts to familiar tunes.

Fortunately Rahim met someone who spoke Arabic and understood his predicament. She and some others supported his first concert and then another and another. As his career as an Arab musician in the United States became more established, he began to see his role as a cultural ambassador, something he speaks about passionately. Rahim told us about music during the regime of Saddam Hussein, who was ousted from power and captured in 2003, during the Second Gulf War, and subsequently executed in 2006.

The notes accompanying his CD *When the Soul is Settled* (2006) report that the conservatory he attended was "empty, burned, and silent" when he visited Iraq in 2004. When Rahim studied there, the curriculum included two years of Western art music, two years of Iraqi/Arab music, and then two years during which a student focused on a more specific area, such as composition or solo performance. He also described the importance of the 'ud in Iraq and of various musicians such as the teacher Sharif Muhi ud-Din Haydar (1892–1967), his students Munir Bashir and Jamil Bashir, who advanced a new style of virtuosic and Western-influenced 'ud playing that has been very popular among younger Iraqi musicians such as Rahim.

 CD 4:20

"Horses" (1:42). Rajim Alhaj. Performed by Rahim Alhaj. *Rahim Alhaj: Iraqi Music in a Time of War*. Live in concert, New York City, April 5, 2003. Voxlox 103.

TRANSCRIPTION 10.6
"Horses" by Rahim
Alhaj.

TRANSCRIPTION 10.6
(*continued*)

When I was back in Baghdad last February [2004] . . . and you know the situation is a disaster there . . . it's incredibly unbelievable. Anyway, one time in the morning I heard my niece singing a beautiful, beautiful . . . [Sings] . . . a beautiful song that's from the seventies. And then I listened carefully, and she put other words in. It's not the same words. I know it as a love song. And I said, "Do you know who composed this song?" And she says, "No, no, this is a religious song." I said, "No!" So what I found out [is that] in Iraq right now they transfer love songs that are already complete, and then they take the words out and put in other poems that talk about God, talk about Muhammad, whatever. This is a trend. I was astonished, because, you know, Iraqi people have become more conservative now, after sanctions and killings. This has all affected them very badly. You know when you became poor and hopeless you look to God and ask —"Save me." So that is what the Iraqi people do. I was astonished.

As Rahim introduced his compositions he juxtaposed the despair of his nieces and nephews—who hope for the basic privileges of clean water, electricity, and safety—and the destruction of a cultural practices—like playing music in a public venue or at a community wedding, or the freedom to walk down the street carrying an instrument—with the sensations of hope and freedom he felt when he began to establish his home in Albuquerque, New Mexico. Rahim summed up his philosophy, evident in his performances, his frequent interviews with the press, and his public presentations, as follows:

I believe, profoundly believe, that there is nothing called Western music and Eastern music. This is an illusion. There is one something that's called music. You listen to this or that kind of music because you were born here or there. That's the way I see it. Just music.

Based on his first feelings in Albuquerque, of being free like a wild horse, Rahim Alhaj's composition "Horses" is what we call *programmatic.* That is, all of his music is *about* something: galloping horses, lovers on the beach, destruction in Baghdad, or the dreams of his nieces and nephews; in concert, Rahim prefaces all of his performances with a story. The programmatic aspect of his style contrasts with the traditional music of Egypt and the Levant, which includes as its core a canon of pieces inherited from Ottoman Turkey. This Turko-Arabic music is often *abstract* and identified only by the name of the piece's form and its mode (*maqam*) or, in some cases, an impressionistic title, as in "Al-Shaghal" ("Obsession"). Although the newcomer to Arab music might find "Horses" quite similar to "Al-Shaghal," this performance differs from the Arab tradition exemplified by the latter, in the following ways:

- "Horses" is programmatic: There is a story behind the piece.
- It favors major and minor diatonic scales rather than Arab modes, which feature characteristic phrases and progressions and, in many cases, quarter tones.
- There is an emphasis on virtuosity over emotionality (*tarab*), which can be heard in fast passages, Western-style scalar runs, harmonics, and arpeggios.
- The use of harmonics and arpeggios requires the player to exploit the upper range of the instrument, something not heard in traditional *'ud* playing.
- The repetitive, sequential phrases combined with the use of arpeggios and sometimes chords suggests the application of Western harmonic progressions in ways that are uncommon in traditional Arab music. See the Close Listening guide for more.

Close Listening

"HORSES"

CD 4:20

COUNTER NUMBER	SECTION	COMMENTARY
0:00	Introduction (2 measures/8 beats)	3-note idea (or motive) repeated.
0:03	Introduction (2 measures/8 beats)	3-note idea repeated one octave lower.
0:06	More of the introduction; transition	3-note idea is repeated in various ways, with a transitional passage at the end.
0:17	Section A	Interplay between a bass line and repeated notes in the upper register of the instrument.
0:30	Section A repeated	

0:43	Section B Here the melody moves to the upper range of the scale and a descending pattern is heard twice: C to Bb C Bb, A Bb A, G A G— repeated at m. 24: C D C, Bb C Bb, A Bb A, G A G. At m. 29 a descending sequence leads into a dramatic octave-and-a-half-run at m. 31, down to the tonic note C—which then leads back into the melody. (The run begins on A and concludes on C in m. 31).	Last measure of this melody features a descending line into the lower register of the 'ud which leads in to the return of the A section.
1:04	1st melody (A) repeated	
1:18	2nd melody (B) repeated	

Another Iraqi 'ud soloist, Naseer Shamma, now based in Cairo, Egypt, is disseminating this virtuosic performance style by cultivating an entire school of 'ud soloists through his conservatory *Bayt al-'Ud* (House of the 'Ud) and through his own solo compositions, which are also programmatic rather than based on traditional forms. Although many subscribe to this flashy style, just as many would hear this music as vapid and "without *tarab*" because it exhibits fewer of the values of traditional Arab music that are rooted in folk and ritual musics (CD 4, Tracks 18, 19, 23, 24, and 25). By jumping from medieval Baghdad to the Baghdad of Rahim Alhaj, which he left in the year 2000, we skipped about ten centuries of Arab music history, so we now return to our thumbnail sketch of the rich history of Arab music.

THE OTTOMAN EMPIRE AND THE COLONIAL ERA

Up until the beginning of the nineteenth century, Arab world countries were subject to the cultural and colonial powers of the Ottoman Empire, which lasted from about 1326 to 1918. The Ottoman Turks created and left behind a musical legacy that still provides the basis for the "classical" tradition, particularly in the nearby Arab countries Syria, Lebanon, Jordan, Palestine, and Egypt. Their political power combined with their cultural achievements allowed the widespread distribution of many developments in musical form and style—in the theory and practice of musical modes and rhythms, in the art of improvisation (*taqasim*), in the adaptation of Western musical notation, and in the development of modern instruments. Thus, Turkish Ottoman music-culture greatly influenced music throughout the Maghrib and the Mashriq.

Following and overlapping the Ottoman rule, European colonialism of the eighteenth and nineteenth centuries extended well into the twentieth century— with certain North African countries not gaining independence from the French until 1956 (Morocco and Tunisia) and 1962 (Algeria). Colonialism influenced music in the Arab world as much as the Ottoman rule had. In fact, because foreign occupying powers (both Turkish and European) dominated large-scale government

FIGURE 10.6

Line drawing of Ghawazee dancers after and not from *The Manners and Customs of the Modern Egyptians*, showing musicians in the background playing the *rabab* (left) and *daff* (right).

in so many Arab-world countries, an official music of the court or government-sponsored musics never developed in most Arab countries. Rather, tradition remained on its own, to wax and wane according to circumstance.

The letters, journals, and reports of foreign visitors during the colonial era are documents invaluable for understanding the musical history of a particular culture. Although sometimes tinged with bias and misunderstanding, these documents include firsthand accounts of music making, the commentary of the locals, and sometimes even pictures and musical transcriptions. From 1798 to 1801, Napoleon Bonaparte dispatched an entire team of researchers to Egypt, among them M. Villoteau, whose *Description de L'Égypt* (1823) includes renderings of musical instruments and his account of musical life there. The prolific English researcher Edward Lane, who lived off and on among the Egyptians for more than ten years between the 1820s and 1840s, produced several important works that document his life among the Arabs. Most interesting for the ethnomusicologist is *The Manners and Customs of the Modern Egyptians,* a book that includes chapters on music, epic poetry, festivals, games, dance (Figure 10.6), funeral rites, and the practices of Muslims, Jews, and Coptic Christians (Lane [1908] 1963).

MUSIC THEORY IN THE COLONIAL ERA

Written documents about Arab music took on a new tone in the so-called modern period, beginning in 1780 (Marcus 1989). Arab music theorists of that time sought to codify musical practice by combining European theoretical categories with medieval Arab models based on the classification of *ajnas* (aj-*nass;* s. *jins*), or tetrachordal analysis. Although Arab music was a coherent system in practice, these theorists perceived a need to explain the musical modes (*maqams*), with their non-Western intervals, as a rational system and to theoretically streamline the many non-Western notes embedded in intervallic structure of the various Arab *maqams* (see Transcription 10.7). Prior to this time, notes like E$\natural$, or *sikah* in Arabic, were simply considered natural, regular notes, with their own names. Theorists at this time, however, presented the modes in terms of single-octave scales, each with eight tones (like the major and minor scales of Western music). The eight tones of each scale were chosen from a theoretical scale of twenty-four equidistant quarter tones contained within an octave, something that was as elegant as the twelve half-tone or half-step octave of equal-tempered Western music (C, C#, D, D#, E, F#, G, G#, A, A#, B. C).

Maqam Bayyati

Maqam Saba

Maqam Rast

Maqam Huzam

Maqam Nahawand

Maqam Kurd

Maqam Hijaz

Maqam Ajam

The tonic notes are relative; a *maqam* can start on any note. What is important is the intervallic structure of the *maqam*. *Maqams* are conceptualized as a combination of *ajnas*, usually a tetrachord or group of four notes, but sometimes a trichord (three notes) or a pentachord (five notes). The upper tetrachord of the *maqam* often exhibits variation; some common variations are indicated in parentheses.

TRANSCRIPTION 10.7
Several common Arab *maqams*.

In the Arabic language the new terminology—*nisf bémol* or *nisf dièse,* meaning "half-flat" or "half-sharp"—reflects a transition from thinking about these notes as "perfectly normal" to thinking about them as "special" or "different from" Western music, as if Western music were some sort of authoritative rule against which Arab music should be measured. The term itself was a combination of Arabic: *nisf* for "half" and the French *bémol* for "flat" and *dièse* for "sharp." Ironically, the attempts of Arab theorists to simplify and standardize intonation in terms of equal temperament did not affect practice definitively, particularly for singers and certain instrumentalists who have the option of fine-tuning, and many variations in intonation are absolutely intentional (Marcus 1992, 1993; Rasmussen 1997). Note that while equal temperament is the norm for students of the Western classical tradition, many popular musics and many of the musics introduced in this book, from African American work songs and blues, to Native

American singing, to the scales of the West Africa, to Javanese and Balinese *gamelan* traditions of Indonesia, intentionally employ notes that fall between the cracks of the equal-tempered scale.

THE TWENTIETH CENTURY

The twentieth century saw further attempts to collect Arab music and to codify repertory, musical forms, scales, and rhythms. Baron Rudolphe d'Erlanger, a French musicologist who settled in Tunesia, published several books that include not only the French translation of historical writings but also transcriptions of the music that he collected from throughout the region. D'Erlanger was a driving force behind the **Congress of Arab Music,** an event sponsored by the Egyptian Government in 1932 that assembled Arab theorists and performers along with European music scholars, such as Eric von Hornbostel, Béla Bartók, Curt Sachs, Paul Hindemith, and Robert Lachmann. A particularly exciting aspect of the congress was that they made more than 175 78-rpm recordings that captured the sounds of Arab music at the time. These recordings, which were thought to represent ancient traditions, were archived, and some of them have been reissued on compact disc. The seven committees of the congress recorded and codified various Arab music traditions. They also discussed and documented musical elements such as rhythm, modes, and musical instruments, and they described and debated such subjects as music history, manuscripts, education, recording, and general issues (Racy 1991:71). The conference was a snapshot of the points of convergence and divergence between Arab and Western approaches to the study and performance of music, many of which remain relevant today. The records of the conference and the historical writings of people like d'Erlanger also highlight the differences between the musical practices of the Mashriq and those of the Maghrib.

The Maghrib

North Africa is the area above the Sahara Desert, as opposed to sub-Saharan Africa, described in Chapter 3, and comprises the part of the Arab world called the **Maghrib** (also Maghreb)—literally "the place where the sun sets." In addition to Morocco, the Maghrib includes the countries Mauritania, Algeria, Tunisia, and Libya. Egypt and the Sudan, although technically in North Africa, are not considered part of the Maghrib but are in the **Mashriq** ("where the sun rises") as part of the eastern Arab world. The Maghrib became part of the Arab empire through the trade fostered by the trans-Saharan caravan routes, beginning in the eighth century. Along with the silks and spices of the Arabian Peninsula and Mesopotamia came the religion of Islam. Islamic ideas and practices took hold more firmly in the lowland and coastal cities and where urban trade centers flourished, as opposed to the Atlas Mountains where the people preserved their Berber language and culture and continue to do so today. This Arab, Islamic empire extended North into Europe into an area then referred to as Andalusia. Beginning in 711 and for about the next seven hundred years until the Spanish Inquisition in 1515, a diverse civilization developed in Andalusia, anchored by court centers in Granada, Córdoba, and Seville, that boasted a rich artistic life.

THE ANDALUSIAN LEGACY

European Christians and their mission to recapture the south culminated in the marriage of King Ferdinand II of Aragón and Queen Isabella I of Castile, along with the Spanish Inquisition that ensued in the first decades of the 1500s. The progressive reconquest or *Reconquista* of southern Europe resulted in the gradual exile of Muslims and Jews and a widespread diffusion of Andalusian peoples and cultures in three directions: southward throughout North Africa, westward to the Americas, and eastward throughout the Mediterranean and eastern Arab world. Although, as we have seen, the word *diaspora* is usually used to describe the modern diffusion of peoples, languages, and cultures throughout the world, the term can certainly be used to describe the diffusion of people and cultures that were forced to emigrate from southern Europe at the end of the 1400s.

The contemporary nations of Morocco, Algeria, and Tunisia developed further with the immigration of Jewish and Muslim Arabs who left Spain in a series of expulsions that culminated with the Spanish Inquisition of 1515 and continued to 1609. The art musics of the Andalusian cultural centers Córdoba, Granada, and Seville were transplanted to the new urban coastal centers of Algeria, Tunisia, Morocco, and to a lesser extent, Libya, where they developed further along the regional lines already established in the North African seaside cities of the Maghrib. The classical Andalusian musical traditions of the Maghrib, while related to those of Egypt and the Levant, have a distinct repertory and instrumentation and thus deserve their own musical study.

Outcasts of the Inquisition also migrated to the Americas by joining the aggressive and adventuresome teams of Spanish, Italian, and Portuguese explorers (such as Ponce de León and Christopher Columbus) who established colonial outposts in the New World. These explorers brought with them not only the stringed instruments originally derived from the Arab plucked lute and bowed fiddle (*'ud* and *rabab*), but also traditions of poetic dueling, as well as improvised rhymed sung poetry, which still survive in places such as New Mexico and Cuba (Blank 1987; Romero 1997, Wenders 1999). Another remnant in the Americas of our Andalusian heritage is the dish *Moros y Christianos,* the beans and rice that are a staple of Cuban and Caribbean cuisine. The brown beans (*Moros*) represent the Arab Muslims also known as Moors, and the white rice (*Christianos*), the European Christians.

Poetic traditions that developed in Arab Andalusia were also transplanted to the eastern Mediterranean and Mesopotamia when displaced Muslims and Jews migrated back to their ancestral homes or settled in new locales. For example, performances of sung poetry like the *zajal* and the *muwashshah* became popular among people of the Levant (Lebanon, Syria, Jordon, Palestine). This repertory is thought to evoke the glorious past and the golden age of Andalusia. People of the Jewish faith, called Sephardim or Sephardic Jews, from the term *Sephard,* which means Spain, have also preserved repertories of sung poetry in an early form of the Spanish language called Ladino, in enclaves that range from Istanbul and Izmir, Turkey, to Tetuán and Tangier in North Africa, to Buenos Aires, Argentina, in South America. These old musical repertories have taken on the musical techniques and styles of their new homelands or of multiple locations and, because often only texts survive, the music has sometimes been reinvented anew. Nevertheless, the Arab singing styles of Sephardic Jewish cantors (religious singers) who trace their roots to Andalusia can still be heard in communities as far away as South America.

Ramon Tasat is a living example of these kinds of multiple musical migrations. Born in Buenos Aires to a family of Sephardic Jewish origin, who migrated from Andalusia to Turkey and then to South America, Ramón learned songs in the Ladino language from his grandmother. Tasat is now an active cantor near Washington, D.C., who performs and teaches Ladino ballads, or romances, and religious songs. Listen to CD 4, Track 21, a dialogue between the Moorish Prince Abenamar and King Juan II of Castille, which describes the Alhambra, the splendid palace built in 1273 that served as the summer residence of the Moors of Grenada. Although there are many Jewish liturgical and paraliturgical songs with Ladino or Hebrew and Ladino texts, Sephardic Jews also consider ballads and narrative songs in Ladino as part of their Andalusian cultural legacy. The instrumentalists—Tasat on guitar; Tina Chancy, who plays bowed medieval and Mediterranean lutes, *rebec, vielle, kamenj,* and viol; and Scott Reiss, who specializes in recorders, flutes, percussion, and hammered dulcimer—draw from numerous related traditions, particularly the aesthetics, instruments, and techniques of European early music, to construct a musical reinterpretation of this thirteenth-century ballad for which no score or recording survives. (See the Close Listening guide and Transcription 10.8.)

CD 4:21

"Abenamar" (2:04). Performed by Ramon Tasat, vocal and guitar, with Tina Chauncy, viol, and Scott Reiss, flute and percussion. English translation by Ramón Tasat and Dwight F. Reynolds. From *Como la Rosa en la Güerta.* Recording produced by Roman Tasat. No date.

Close Listening

"ABENAMAR"

CD 4:21

COUNTER NUMBER	COMMENTARY	LADINO TEXT	TRANSLATION*
0:00	Solo voice.	Abenamar, Abenamar, / Moro de la morería / El día ke ut naciste, / Grandes sinyales había.	Abenamar, Abenamar / Moor of the Moorish quarter / The day that you were born, / Great signs appeared in the sky.
0:20	Bowed drone of the viol enters.		
0:21	Drone continues under the voice.	Estava la mar en calma, / La luna estava crecida, / Moro que en tal sinyo nace, / No deve dezir mentira.	The sea was calm, there / was a crescent moon, / A Moor born under such a sign, / Should not lie.
0:43	Double stops (2 notes bowed at once) or 3-note chords are played in support of the melody.	Yo no os la dire senyor / Aunque me kosta la vida. / Ke de chiko y de muchacho, / Mi padre me lo dezía.	"I will not lie to you, / Sir, Even if it costs my life. / As a child and as a young man, / My father told me this."
0:58	Flute joins in.	Ke mentiras no dijese, / ke era grande villanía. / Pregunta, pues el buen rey, / Ke la verdad te diría.	"That I should not tell lies, For / that is a great wickedness. / Ask, then, O good King, / For I will tell the truth."

1:16	Guitar joins in.	*Qué castillos son aquellos?*	"Which palaces are those
		Altos son y relican!	That stand tall and
			shimmering?"
		La Alhambra era senyor,	"That is the Alhambra, Sir,
		Palasyo de gran valía.	A palace of great value."
1:38	*Dumbek* (Middle Eastern		
	drum) enters and a lively,		
	metrical instrumental		
	version of the tune is played.		

*English translation by Ramón Tasat and Dwight F. Reynolds.

TRANSCRIPTION 10.8
"Abenamar."

TRANSCRIPTION 10.8
(*continued*)

na es - ta - va cre - ci - da, Mo - ro que en el tal sin - yo na - ce, No de-

ve de - zir men - ti - ra. Yo no os la di re, sen - jor,

a - un que me kos - ta la vi - da. Ke de chi - ko y de mu-

cha - cho, Mi pa - dre me lo de z1 a. Ke men-

TRANSCRIPTION 10.8
(*continued*)

TRANSCRIPTION 10.8
(*continued*)

INDEPENDENT MOROCCO

The sites and sounds of old Arab Andalusia, for example the splendid architecture of the Alhambra in Granada, or the sounds of the urban song genres **fado** in Portugal and **flamenco** in Spain, both thought to resonate with Arab-Andalusian influence, are now tourist attractions of the Iberian Peninsula. Just a ninety-minute boat ride across the Straits of Gilbraltar transports you from Europe and old Andalusia into the contemporary Arab world. Morocco gained independence from the French in 1956, so it is impossible *not* to notice the French presence in Morocco. Excellent baguette and espresso café can be procured along the grand boulevards of the cities and even in the small coffee shops of the Atlas Mountain roads where buses stop to collect passengers. French is learned in schools, and everyone in the cities speaks it, along with Arabic and Berber. Just as Moroccans exhibit the cultural influences of past colonial domination, France also benefits from its inextricable involvement with Arab North Africa. *Maghrebi* culture is one of France's most notable cultural features, from the wonderful couscous restaurants of Paris, to first-class literature and film, to the *Rai* North African pop music that has become a staple sound of commercially marketed World Music.

Owing in part to the proximity of Morocco to Europe, the country has been much more accessible to Westerners than, say, Syria in the eastern Arab world or Saudi Arabia in the Gulf. Following independence, the country became a magnet for counterculture musicians such as the jazz saxophonist Ornette Colman and the English rock group the Rolling Stones, as well as for writers who, like Brian

Gyson and Timothy Leary, visited and in some cases stayed (Schuyler 1993). Fifty years later, the accessibility and allure of North Africa still draws artists from the United States and Europe, such as Peter Gabriel (*The Last Temptation of Christ*), Sting ("Desert Rose"), and Jimmy Page and Robert Plant (*No Quarter* and their tour called "UnLedded," based on their former band's name, Led Zeppelin, which featured Middle Eastern musicians). Such musicians have helped introduce North African music and musicians to an international fan base. As World Music projects like this explode in all directions, it invites us to think about the implications of this kind of global exchange for musicians and audiences. The case studies in Chapter 2 represent another example of the global musical exchange that increasingly influences the commercial pop music world.

The Music of Celebration: Communal Music Making at a Wedding in Morocco

To provide a contrast to our focus up to this point on concert and ritual music and aesthetics, music in and as history, and the performances of male musicians, we next explore women's communal music making in the Maghrib. A few years ago, I traveled to Casablanca, Morocco, to attend my friend's wedding. My experience of that city and the multiday wedding festivities began with a visit to the public baths.

THE PUBLIC BATHS

The evening I arrived I learned that some of the groom's sisters were planning to go the next morning to the *hamam*, the traditional prenuptial communal bath. Jet-lagged or not, I was not going to miss an opportunity to visit a *hamam* in Casablanca. The sisters woke me around 6:00 A.M., all prepared with kits of soaps, towels, lotions, brushes, and natural, rough loofah sponges from the sea. We piled into a little car and drove down the wide boulevards in the modern part of the city that are modeled after the French *Nouvelle Ville* (New City). We arrived at a building in a modest neighborhood of Casablanca and entered a stone-walled area lit only by the natural light seeping in through cracks where the rock walls met the ceiling. The stone walls and floors glistened with moisture. We found mats to sit on and buckets of warm water. I had no implements, but one of the women gave me a rough cloth to slip over my hand, and I borrowed some soap. I sat next to my tub of water, splashing water all over, lathering and rinsing myself clean, listening to the conversation, a combination of Moroccan Arabic and French.

But my companions were still at only the earliest stages of their bathing ritual. We next went into a steam room with stone fountains and tubs, where one of the bath attendants started massaging me with a rough cloth. Although my new friends scrubbed their skin vigorously and at length with their loofah sponges, I cringed at the roughness of the massage. The experience was unquestionably physical, but not at all like the erotic depictions of the *hamam* by French Orientalist painters or colonial-era photographers; rather, it was intensely social. In Morocco, as elsewhere in the world, women socialize together when they can. They cook together, have their children together, and care for them and their extended families together. They sing together and play the frame drum called the *bendir*. My companions from Casablanca worked regular jobs, too, as teachers, flight attendants, and retail salespeople. That morning I learned about a kind of gender-specific socializing that also generates music, poetry, and performance specifically by and for women. The experience also helped prepare me for the particular role that the women, including me, would play in the wedding that would take place over the next few days.

THE WEDDING CELEBRATION

Two days after my trip to the *hamam* I awoke from a jet-lagged nap to the sounds of women serenading the bride with boisterous, cheering songs accompanied by their own playing of the *bendir*. My friend, the bride, sat immobile, her arms resting on towers of pillows, her legs propped up by an ottoman. Her skin had become a canvas for delicate curlicues of henna, a natural red dye used for staining the skin and hair in a widespread ritual of beautification practiced most prominently by women of the Middle East and South Asia (Figure 10.7). Many of the other women also had their hands dyed by the wedding attendant, who turned out to be the ritual specialist who would accompany us for the next two days. For most of the day and on into the evening the gathering of women drank mint tea, visited, and sang songs of passage and congratulations to the bride, accompanied by vigorous polyrhythmic playing of the *bendir*.

The **bendir** is a variation of the frame drum, an instrument found throughout the entire Middle East and virtually everywhere in the Islamic world. The instrument is held in one hand and supported with the other in a way that frees some of the fingers of each hand to strike the skin on various places, producing *dumms* and *takks* in a remarkable variety of timbres. Although a staple of the Middle East and Arab world, the construction of the Moroccan *bendir* also reflects the preferred aesthetics of both the Arab world and Africa. Two or three semitaut strings across the inside of the *bendir* actually touch the skin's surface and vibrate, acting as snares when the instrument is struck. To my ear, the snares (added also to other Moroccan drums) reflect the African aesthetic delight for "buzz" (also discussed in Chapters 3 and 4). Just like the metal plate with its rattling rings on the bridge of a Gambian *kora* (Knight 1984), or the bottle caps or shells sewn onto the perimeter of the large gourd resonator of the *mbira* of Zimbabwe (Turino 2001), the snares on a *bendir* add another timbral component to the *dumm* and *takk* of this Arab frame drum.

Playing frame drums is the provenance of women in Morocco and throughout much of the Middle East and even in much of central and southern Europe. Similar to the way the piano was once considered an acceptable "ladies' instrument" in the West, the frame drum is the one instrument that women of the Arab world have historically been allowed to play. Associated with healing, spirituality, and celebration, learning to play percussion may be as natural as learning to sing the songs that propel these social contexts. Veronica Doubleday, who has lived among Afghan women musicians, reports that even in the face of limitations, or perhaps even because of them, the women's

FIGURE 10.7

The henna party.

Anne Rasmussen

drumming that accompanies the singing, music, and dancing at weddings provides "a 'boiling hot' (*por jush*) atmosphere for the eventual consummation of marriage" (1999:117). Another aspect of Arab weddings that adds to the excitement and the ritual is the **zaffah,** a procession where the new couple is literally danced or paraded into the public space.

THE *ZAFFAH* WEDDING PROCESSION

The *zaffah* procession for my friend's wedding was splendid. The couple arrived by car at a rented hall already filled with guests. They were whisked out of the car and escorted up the steps to the blaring of trumpets and the beating of *bendirs*. We all fell into line and walked with the couple and the musicians around the room in a regal procession, which resumed several times that evening and through the night until sunrise. For each procession the bride and sometimes the groom wore different clothes, and each time they were announced musically by the ritual specialists hired for the occasion.

CD 4:22

Zaffah procession at a Casablanca wedding (1:39). Field recording by Anne Rasmussen. Casablanca, Morocco, June 1997.

FIGURE 10.8

Performers at a Casablanca wedding.

Anne Rasmussen

Three hired groups of musicians entertained us until about 8:00 in the morning. The first was a band of men who sat on a stage and performed Egyptian and North African urban pop, the music you might hear on the radio. The second group included four Berber women who sang and danced in a style unique to the Atlas Mountains, to the accompaniment of *bendir* and *rabab* (Figure 10.8). The men who played *bendir* and *rabab* at the beginning of the evening were also part of the third musical configuration, which animated the *zaffah* procession by playing huge tambourines called *mazhars* and long, straight, valveless trumpets called *nafirs,* which are rather unusual in the Arab world, where brass instruments of any kind are rare. (See Figure 10.9.) As you hear on CD 4, Track 22, both the *nafir* trumpets and the *mazhars* play a repeating ostinato pattern (see the Close Listening guide). In the context of performance, the focus of the overlapping patterns—which are organized into 6-beat units—can shift from two groups of three (**123456 123456 123456**—ONE two three FOUR five six) to three groups of two (**123456 123456 123456**—ONE two THREE four FIVE six). And during the night, as these various musics played on, the guests also clapped in patterns that alternated between a 2-beat rhythm (two groups of three) and a 3-beat rhythm (three groups of two). This aspect of polymeter, discussed at length in Chapter 3, is, like the snares on the *bendir,* an aspect of Arab *Maghrebi* music that is distinctly African.

The ways in which music is used to articulate, explore, or even teach identities serve as a fascinating aspect of ethnomusicological inquiry. (See the music-culture model from Chapter 1.) By featuring both the pop band, who played tunes from the Arabic-language hit parade on amplified instruments including electric keyboard, electric viola, electric guitar, trumpet, and drum set, and the Berber groups, who played traditional music on acoustic folk instruments, the groom's family seemed to be making a statement about both the richness of Moroccan culture and their multiple identities: urban and rural, Arab and Berber. Sometimes music and dance can encapsulate feelings

Anne Rasmussen

FIGURE 10.9

Zaffah procession at Casablanca wedding, with *nafir* trumpets in the rear and *mazhars* in the front.

Close Listening

ZAFFAH PROCESSION AT A CASABLANCA WEDDING

CD 4:22

COUNTER NUMBER	COMMENTARY
0:07	*Zagareet* (high-pitched, excited, trilling calls) by the women.
0:12	Percussion by *bendir.*
0:15	*Nafirs,* long trumpets, enter playing an ostinato pattern on a single tone; percussion continues.
0:55	Voices of the trumpeters heard in the background (here the music has a 3-beat feel).
1:19	Trumpet ostinato resumes with percussion.

about identity, about "who we are," with unmatched power. Weddings in any context are busy intersections of cultural performance where people from different generations, regions, and sometimes ethnic and religious groups articulate through enacted customs—prayers and poems, cuisine and costuming, and, of course, music and dance—one ideal of who they are.

WEDDING TRADITIONS OF THE EASTERN MEDITERRANEAN ARAB WORLD (THE LEVANT)

Dancing is certainly an important aspect of celebrations worldwide, but among Arab families, singing and poetry recitation are also communal and obligatory expressions of joy. Despite the presence of white dresses and tiered, sugar-frosted cakes with little plastic bride and groom dolls on top (wedding practices imported from the West), the traditions of the *zaffah* or of gender-specific performance contexts and repertoires for men and women have not been lost to modernity, either in the urban environments of the Arab world or among the Arab diaspora.

In Dearborn, Michigan, where we find the largest community of Arab people outside of the Arab World, Palestinian and Lebanese women call out, in a high-pitched declamatory voice, improvised verses to the bride and groom, or to their own family and friends, on any occasion when hospitality is celebrated (Rasmussen 1997). These little poems, half-sung, half-shouted, are generally punctuated with **zagareet,** the high-pitched trilling cries that proclaim excitement. The tradition that is preserved in Arab American communities today is consistent with practices in "the homeland"; in fact, wedding traditions such as these may be even healthier in the Arab diaspora then they are in their land of origin. Khadija Fayoumi, who is the mother of my cousin's husband, is an elderly woman from Raffa, a city on the far eastern tip of the Gaza Strip in Palestine. She told me about her role at Palestinian weddings. She explained that, before the first **intifadah** (Palestinian uprising against Israeli occupation)—before curfews, before security concerns, and before the rampant unemployment that renders marriage less frequent and much less extravagant today—when celebrations were still abundant, the neighborhood women always called on her for weddings. Not because she was a great singer, she clarified modestly, but because she knew all the songs! One evening she sang song after song for our family, drumming along on the bottom of a plastic bucket, giving us a taste of a special brand of Palestinian women's domestic music making (Personal communication, 1993, 2000).

Listen to the Palestinian Popular Arts Troupe *(Firkat El-Funoun Al-Sha'biyyah Al-Filastiniyyah),* also known as *El-Funoun* (The Arts), from the Palestinian territories (CD 4, Track 23). In this modern recasting of folk performance, we first hear the high-pitched, poetic cries of a woman who calls for blessings on the groom, who is, possibly, referred to as "the moon." (See the Close Listening guide.) Women respond with *zagareet.* A drum enters, and then we hear a male voice singing vocables (meaningless syllables) in free rhythm: "Ooof, ooof, ya bay"; another overlapping voice is heard toward the end of this sung melody. This is followed by a solo introduction by the **mijwiz,** a single-reed, double-piped folk clarinet, typical of the Levant (Syria, Lebanon, Jordan, and the Palestinian territories). The *mijwiz* drops out, and the *nay, buzuq,* and *qanun* play in call and response. The song proper begins with a man singing the beginning of each line of poetry and a group of women completing each line. The musical material, poetic form, and singing style draw on folk models, and the poetry contains metaphoric language that is as rich as any classical verse. A person, man or woman, who has been abandoned by his beloved, or a community whose friends have deserted them, in both cases usually without saying good-bye, are common themes of Arabic poetry and song. The images of hair flowing over the garments, weeping

CD 4:23

El-Funoun. "Initiation of Ecstasy" (2:08). Performed by *El-Funoun* (The Arts). From *Zaghareed: Music from the Palestinian Holy Land.* Sounds True STA MI09D. 1999.

eyes, sleepless nights, and the distraught lover who is left with images of his beloved's cheeks are well known. Later, the singer continues by touching on scenes of village life and the wedding celebration. For the troupe *El-Funoun*, the staged performance of traditional expressive culture, including poetry, music, ritual, and dance, is part of their mission to "revive regional folklore as a form of Palestinian identity" (*El-Funoun* 1999).

Close Listening

"INITIATION OF ECSTASY"

CD 4:23

COUNTER NUMBER	COMMENTARY	ARABIC TRANSLITERATION*	TRANSLATION
0:00	Female solo voice	*Aay yay yay* *Ya Rabb khalli bayya* *Aay yay yay* *Wa'tî wa'tî il-ghâli* *Aay yay yay* *Wa shufi-it-'amar fi darû* *Aay yay yay* *Ya rub kattir malû*	Aay, God keep his Father Aay, God give him the big gift Aay, I saw the moon in his house Aay, God increase his wealth
0:21	*Zagareet* by women		
0:25	Male solo(s)	Vocables	Oooh oooof ooof oooof ooof ya bay
0:36	Solo *mijwiz* with percussion		
0:56	*Nay, buzuq,* and *qanun* enter.		
1:18	Male solo with female chorus singing the second half of each line as a response; the response is underlined.	*Ya-bû-l-shhûr mrakhiyyîn* <u>*foug-l-hdûm*</u> *Min yowm frâqaq 'anni <u>ma shuft-l-hdûm</u>* *Min yowm-l-hajartûni tibki 'ayouni* <u>*'ala-l-firqa jan-antuni*</u> *w-il khad-i- 'ahh.*	You whose hair flows gracefully over your garments From the day you left me, sleep has evaded me From the day you deserted me, my eyes have wept incessantly The day you left me, you made me crazy, And, your beautiful cheeks are like buoys (bobbing about)
1:38	Instrumental interlude		
1:49	Singing in a nonmetrical improvisatory style	Vocables	We yeh ho ho yeh willa ya bye

*Underlined text is sung by a chorus of women's voices.

Poetry and Core Values of Bedouin Culture

Whether among women, among men, or in mixed company, poetry, like the formulaic folk verse adapted by *El-Funoun,* can serve as a medium for expressing intimate feelings such as love, desire, or shame, as well as controversial issues such as protest, frustration, or liberation, in ways that are culturally appropriate. The prevalence of poetry and of song illustrates the key position of language in Arab culture (see works by Racy 2002; Caton 1990; Abu-Lughod 1986). Poetry was recited or sung for centuries in pre-Islamic Arabia by poets, or **sha'irs** (sha-eer, a as in apple), who "developed a poetic heritage that, along with the Qur'an, was to become the wellspring for the new Arabic-Islamic civilizations" (Sells 1999:7). But poetry isn't just some archaic aspect of Arab culture, of interest only to historians and linguists. It is very much a part of contemporary culture. For example, Adonis (born Ali Ahman Said Asbar), whose poetry is published in newspapers and heard on radio and television, is a household name in much of the Arab world. And poetry continues to be relevant in the context of political conflict (Caton 1990). In January 2004, Stacy Gilbert, reporting from Irbil in Northern Iraq, quoted an elder tribesman in the city of Kirkuk: "The chief warned me that if I couldn't bring them blankets before the first snowfall, he would scold me with a bad verse. If I could help them however, he promised to honor me with a verse of unparalleled beauty" (Gilbert 2004). Being able to compose poetry "on the fly" has been part of Arab history for centuries and is characteristic of other cultures as well. We now turn our attention to one of the last living traditions of epic poetry, the *Sirat Bani Hilal,* which embodies some of the essential values and parables of the original nomadic Bedouin Arabs, which A. J. Racy has referred to as "the Bedouin ethos" (1996).

The transient nomadic desert tribes called **Bedouins** traditionally adapted to the harsh ecological conditions of their world by moving between water sources and grazing lands. Such was the culture of the nomads of the Arabian Peninsula before and during the dawn of Islam; the ways of the Bedouins are even inscribed in the Qur'an, which includes references to their daily life and social practice. Although people in the modern Arab world may not trace their own ancestry to Bedouin tribes, the ethos or distinctive characteristics of Bedouin life that are memorialized in song, dance, poetry, stories, and artifacts are key to Arab collective identity, both in the Arab world and in the diaspora. The idea of the Bedouin is attractive in part because of key Bedouin values and moral codes, which include bravery in battle, protection of the weak, hospitality toward the visitor, generosity to the poor, loyalty to the tribe, and fidelity (Racy 1996; also Eickelman 1989; Patai 1983).

SIRAT BANI HILAL

The *Sirat Bani Hilal* is one of the oldest continuously performed epic traditions in the world (Reynolds 1995). It has attracted the attention of both contemporary scholars and writers of the past, including the fourteenth-century Arab historian and sociologist Ibn Khaldun and the nineteenth-century English writer Edward Lane. The following sketch of the tradition and the performance excerpt that you hear on CD 4, Track 24, comes from the research and field recordings of Dwight Reynolds, a folklorist, ethnomusicologist, and specialist in Arab language and literature. In this epic tradition, stories are spoken and sung in rhymed verse by the *sha'ir*, a poet-singer who accompanies himself on the **rabab** (also *rabab*, *rababa*), a one- or two-stringed, spiked, skin-covered fiddle. The epic recounts the adventures of the Bedouin tribes of the Bani Hilal and the Bani Sulaim as they migrated, during the ninth century, from their original homelands in the Arabian Peninsula all the way to Algeria and Tunisia in North Africa. The tribes met their ultimate defeat at the hands of the Moroccan Almohad dynasty in the twelfth century and scattered throughout the North African desert.

CD 4:24

Sirat Bani Hilal, excerpt (3:44). Performed by Sheikh Taha. Field recording, transliteration, and translation by Dwight Reynolds. Al-Bakatush, Kafr al-Shaykh Province, Egypt, June 1–2, 1987.

The episodes, which are performed in a familiar yet flexible and spontaneous manner, memorialize four prototypical characters in Arab lore:

- Abu Zayd, the protagonist, possessing uncanny charm, intelligence, and wit, is responsible for outsmarting the many enemy camps and tribes that the Bani Hilal tribes meet on their migration across Arab lands.
- Dieb, the "blade of the tribe," is the fearsome warrior.
- Sultan Hasan is the level-headed wise man of the tribe, competent in all manner of Islamic Law and tribal protocol, but often ineffective.
- Al-Jazaiyah, the most beautiful woman in the world, known also for her strength and bravery, rides into battle with the rest of the men and defeats the enemy through her ability to outwit any opponent.

These characters are pitted against the ultimate enemy, al-Zanati Khaligah, the Berber ruler of Tunisia, a "villain beyond redemption who must be defeated at any cost" (Reynolds 1993:8).

In transcriptions of the epic, one exciting story follows another. The epic is also of interest to us for the *way* in which it is performed. A *rabab* poet (*sha'ir*) composes on the spot and can sing (and speak during certain sections) in rhymed verse in performances that last for hours, sometimes all night. Epic song and the poet-singer as a performer type are found in many parts of the world, and the oral technique of training and performance that they employ has been dubbed "formulaic composition."

THEORY OF FORMULAIC COMPOSITION

The theory of *formulaic composition* was developed by a Harvard University professor of Classics, Milman Parry (assisted by Albert Lord) and is based on the ground-breaking fieldwork they conducted in 1932 among poet-singers of Yugoslavia, where the performance of epic was also still a living tradition. These intrepid scholars came up with the idea that epic performance, remarkable for its form in rhymed verse and for its great length, was not the work of individual authors. They speculated that, rather than relying on written or memorized "scores," poets draw their improvisations from a storehouse of familiar ideas and poetic formulas. This was a revolutionary idea in the academic climate of the 1930s, when the prestige of literacy (the written word) eclipsed any consideration of "folklore" learned and perpetuated orally through memory and performance. Parry's theories were later tested and refined after his death by his colleague Albert Lord and published in the landmark study *The Singer of Tales* (1960). The theory of formulaic composition contributes to our understanding of the Greek epics the Iliad and the Odyssey and is useful for understanding how many contemporary musicians, such as blues or rap artists, work as well.

Dwight Reynolds lived among fourteen families of poet-singers in the Egyptian village of al-Bakatush (1989, 1991, 1995, 1996), where he tested the theory of formulaic composition. In the course of his fieldwork he was able to affirm that poets work orally, from memorized texts, to "manipulate a vast repertory of traditional phrases, half-lines, and whole verses and retell the stories at each performance using the rhetoric and style of epic poetry" (1996:109). His hypothesis was confirmed during a *sahra,* an evening event where men gather to hear the epic.

> On this night, in a moment of inspiration I asked Shaykh Taha not only if he would re-sing the passage we had just heard but, if he would do so on a different rhyme. He looked at me and squinted, a teacher looking at a precocious pupil: "What rhyme do you want?"
>
> We had just heard the passage on an "r" rhyme [ar], so I quickly ransacked my mind for a rhyme that was quite different but that I knew to be standard.
>
> "How about 'mîm'?" (i.e., any vowel plus the final letter m).
>
> Shaykh Taha put out his cigarette, picked up the *rabab* and asked, "From where?"
>
> "From where Abû Zayd finds the horse in the desert."
>
> With no preparation, and with apparently total ease, Shaykh Taha sang the passage again on the new rhyme. I was ecstatic.... Here was evidence for both the total fluidity of the traditional process of composition, and the virtuosity of the performing artist himself. (Reynolds 1996:107–8)

Listen again to CD 4, Track 24, a three-and-a-half minute excerpt from Reynolds's field recordings during which the poet Sheikh Taha begins by honoring Sheikhs Rizq, Sarhan, Zayyan, and Ghanim, who are the fathers of the main characters in the epic (see the Close Listening guide). Note that the end rhyme in the recorded performance is *iH.* His entire performance of approximately thirteen thousand verses lasted fifty-four hours! The performer's sung line and *rabab* accompaniment work together closely: The *rabab* underscores the vocal melody continuously and also provides a responsorial interlude between each phrase of text. Each phrase of text is a half-line of a full line of the epic poem. You will notice that the range of the melody is small—but the melody (of both *rabab* and voice) begins with a dynamic presentation of a specific mode, *maqam Huzam,* based on the tonic, E♮ (C D E♮ F G), with a change (or modulation) at to *maqam Bayyati* (D E♭ F G) at 1:17, and later the introduction to *maqam Saba* (D E♭ F G♭) just at the end of the excerpt. The sophisticated presentation and change of melodic mode underscores the text of the poetry deliberately; even in this short excerpt we can appreciate the phenomenal artistry of both the performer and the sung epic. Unlike the next example, where the instrument explores more than one octave, the range of the melody is small, encompassing not even an octave. Nevertheless a *jins,* which is three notes (a trichord), four notes (a tetrachord), or five notes (a pentachord), is enough to establish the intervallic character of the three *maqams* heard (*Huzam, Bayyati,* and *Saba*). (See Transcription 10.9.)

Close Listening

SIRAT BANI HILAL, EXCERPT

CD 4:24

COUNTER NUMBER	COMMENTARY	TRANSLITERATION/TRANSLATION*
0:00	Preperformance commentary by Sheikh Taha conveying blessings upon the Prophet Muhammad and honoring the fathers of the main characters.	
0:20	*Rabab* begins with two bow strokes on C below the "tonic" E♮ of *maqam Huzam* and then establishes the *maqam* with several phrases (at 22, 26, 29, 35, and 40 seconds).	
0:43	The sung melody of the first four phrases has a small range that oscillates between E♮ and G, usually dipping below the E♮ to the leading tone, D, just before the end of the phrase. The *rabab* follows the vocal line very closely and provides a short and slightly louder interlude after each phrase or half-line of poetry. The *rabab* response between each line reinforces the E♮ and dips below it to the C each time.	1a. *Anā 'abd man ya'shiq jamāl Muhammad* I am the servant of all who adore the beauty of Muhammad; 1b. *Tāhā llāzī yastāq lahu kull rāyiH* Taha, for whom every pilgrim yearns. 2a. *Isma' mā gāl Rizg is-sajī' ibnu Nāyil* Listen to what said Rizq, the Valiant, son of Nayil; 2b. *Dam'in jarā min muglit il-'ēn sāyiH* Tears from the orb of his eye did flow.
1:17	The *rabab* response begins like the previous responses but lands on the D, which is established as the tonic. This is a shift or modulation at to a *Bayyati* tetrachord (**D** E♮ F G).	
1:22	These phrases and the next lines of poetry are sung between the ambitus (range) of D E♮ F with the C heard as a leading tone to the D.	3a. *Ahēn min id-dunyā wi-d-dahr wi-z-zaman* "Ah! Ah! The World and Fate and Destiny!; 3b. *wi-kull mā shuftuh bi-l-'ēn rāyiH* All I have seen with my eyes shall disappear!"
1:36		4a. *Mā-mdahsh fi l-ayyām yōman yasirrinī* I do not praise among the days one which pleases me; 4b. *illā yijī 'ugbuh nakad wi-shahāyiH* But that its successor comes along, miserable and mean.

1:51	Here the vocal range expands slightly to encompass the range of a 4th, with a jump from D to G, a common gesture in *maqam Bayyati*. There is an audible emphasis on "casting the weapons at fate."	5a. *Yā bēn sālihnī kifā mā fa'alti bī* O Fate, make peace with me, 'tis enough what you've done to me; 5b. *irmeyt silāhī ilēk wi-bi-l-'uzr wādiH* I cast my weapons at thee, but my excuse is clear.
2:12	The ambitus of the vocal melody continues to encompass the interval of a 4th: D E♭ F G.	6a. *Mālī kitīr yā rijālī min ghēr zikrā* My wealth is great, O men, but [I am] without an heir; 6b. *mālin bilā zikrā ba'd il-'umr rāyiH* Wealth without an heir after a lifetime disappears.
2:29	The mention of Sarhan is spoken rather than sung. Singing resumes at the second half of the line (7b).	7a. *Anzur bi-'ēnī alāgī Sarhān izā rakab* I look out and catch sight of Sarhan when he rides; 7b. *tirkab wi-awlāduh umarā wi-falāyiH* His sons ride [with him], princes and prosperous.
2:46	Sung melody and *rabab* accompaniment touches and sustains the 4th degrees of the scale, G. This is a dramatic musical gesture that underscores the action of the poetry.	8a. *Anzur bi-'ēnī alāgī Zayyān izā rakab* I look out and catch sight of Zayyan when he rides; 8b. *tirkab wi-awlāduh tisidd al-matāriH* His sons ride [with him] and fill open spaces.
3:04	Melody focuses on the jump between the tonic and the 4th degree.	9a. *Anzur bi-'ēnī āh alāgī Ghānim izā rakab* I look out—Ah!—and catch sight of Ghanim when he rides; 9b. *tirkab wi-awlāduh wi-umarā falāyiH* And his sons ride with him and are princes, so prosperous.
3:23	Reference to *maqam Saba* with the introduction of G♭ and the oscillation between F and G♭. This suggests a modulation to *maqam Saba*: D E♭ F G♭. Again the sudden introduction of the F/G♭ motif underscores the melancholy evident in the lyric.	10a. *Wa-nā farīd il-gōm magsūr khātirī* But I am the last of my line, my spirit is broken, 10b. *gadēt zamānī mā shuft dā wād fāliH* I have spent my life and not seen a son, prosperous.

*Text translated and transliterated by Dwight Reynolds.

TRANSCRIPTION 10.9
Sirat Bani Hilal excerpt.

TRANSCRIPTION 10.9
(*continued*)

2:11–3:23 The poet-singer continues with lines 6a and b, 7a and b, 8a and b, and 9a and b. The vocal melody and supporting *rabab* emphasize the fourth degree and reiterate the tonic-to-fourth (D-G) relationship. The singer speaks some of the poetry and even shouts certain words for dramatic effect.

FORMULAIC COMPOSITION AND THE SOLO *TAQASIM*

The theory of formulaic composition is applicable not only to vocal arts—song, poetry, and storytelling—it is also a useful way to think about instrumental music. We will therefore return now to instrumental improvisation, or *taqasim* (ta-qa-*seem*), one of the most important building blocks of Arab and Middle Eastern music. Listen to the *taqasim* in the scale *maqam Rast* played on the *'ud* by Ayad al-Asadi (CD 4, Track 25). The musician you hear is Ayad al-Asadi, a very talented but modest young musician, then somewhere in his twenties.

CD 4:25

'Ud Taqasim in *Maqam Rast* (3:45). Performed by Ayad al-Asadi, *'ud.* Field recording by Anne Rasmussen. Nazareth, Israel, July 2000.

I recorded this performance in the al-Asadi home in Nazareth, Israel, during summer 2000, when I made a two-week trip to Israel and the Palestinian territories, the West Bank, and Gaza to explore the possibility of bringing a group of students to the area in order to study with Arab musicians there. I spent an evening with Ayad and his brother Bashir al-Asadi, who was a phenomenal violinist. Summoned by Soheil Radwan, a musical leader of Nazareth, they were presented to me as professional young musicians who would be excellent teachers for my students. Following the evening of music making with Mr. Radwan, the brothers invited me to their home the next day so I could meet their parents. The al-Asadi family warmly welcomed me, and that day we made many recordings, ate wonderful food, and discussed music and poetry. I described the project I was doing for this book and asked Ayad al-Asadi if I could record him. He, his father, and his brother were more than generous with their time, their hospitality, and their music.

Based in *maqam Rast*, Al-Asadi's *taqasim* features some of the same aspects of musical organization as did the *Azan* (Call to Prayer) analyzed earlier. We can also hear the way in which characteristic phrases of the *maqam* are introduced and emphasized, something that occurs in the music of the *sha'ir* Sheikh Taha. In the *'ud taqasim* musical statements, separated by pauses, become longer, more expansive in range, and more decorous as the improvisation continues. To understand the structure of an improvisation we can think about the way language works—although this may or may not be the way musicians think about it. Musical ideas are grouped together like words into phrases and phrases into sentences (see the Close Listening guide and Transcription 10.10). Phrases and sentences are organized into paragraphs. Phrases, sentences, and paragraphs all feature "concluding remarks" or cadential statements called *qaflat* (s. *qafla*), a technique that is essential to instrumental improvisation in Arab music. Unlike the cadences of Western classical or American popular music, both of which typically set up tension on a dominant chord and then resolve that tension with a move to the tonic, creating a real feeling of finality and stability, a *qafla* can sometimes just melt away, leaving the listener wanting more; on the other had a *qafla* can also create a real sense of arrival and dramatic conclusion. Appreciating the architecture of the nonmetrical *taqasim,* getting used to the intonation of the Arabic *maqam,* and sensing the significance of the *qafla* are all challenges for the new listener. In Arab music, a solo *taqasim* can occur as a prelude to a composition, in a space between composed passages of a performance, with an ensemble providing a rhythmic-melodic ostinato in the background, as in the first performance of Arab music we considered ("Al-Shaghal"), or as a performance in and of itself. What we have heard is just a little more than one-third of Ayad al-Asadi's ten-minute improvisation.

Close Listening

'UD TAQASIM IN MAQAM RAST

CD 4:25

COUNTER
NUMBER   COMMENTARY

1st paragraph

0:00–0:20   **1st sentence:** Al-Asadi introduces the tonic note, C, of *maqam Rast* (C D E♮ F G A B♮ C—you can also think of these notes as 1 2 3 4 5 6 7 8) by first ornamenting the tonic and then reinforcing it with a series of "drop notes" on the C an octave below. Before the end of the phrase, he introduces the four notes below and the four notes above the tonic. The final *qafla* may be thought of as the last four notes of this phrase; in numeric scale degrees this would be 3, 3 2 1. We can think of this statement as the 1st sentence.

0:22   **2nd sentence, 1st phrase:** Beginning on the note G four notes below the tonic, he runs up to the note F above the tonic and then runs back down to the lower G, pausing to emphasize the note D repeatedly. Short pause.

0:28   **2nd sentence; 2nd phrase:** He ascends to the upper G and establishes all of the notes of the bottom five notes (or pentachord) of the scale: C D E♮ F G in the ear, resting on the C, but then returning to the lower G for an inconclusive stopping point.

0:38–0:47   **2nd sentence; 3rd phrase:** He "touches" the A♭ above the G. When he returns to the A (very briefly) it is as A♯. He then descends to the C and concludes the paragraph with the *qafla* 3, 3 2 1. End of the first paragraph. A friend in the room murmurs "mmm" in response to the *qafla* and as feedback to the performer.

2nd paragraph

0:50   He establishes the note G, the 5th degree of the scale and second most important note of the *maqam;* refers quickly back to the tonic; and comes to a resting point on the G.

1:03–1:13   He explores the upper part of the scale from G to the high tonic note, C. There are three characteristic upper tetrachords in *maqam Rast.* At this point, listen for the A♭ and B natural—a *Hijaz* tetrachord (G A♭ B C—as opposed to A and B♮). This variation is expected in a *taqasim* in *maqam Rast.*

1:18   He pauses and emphasizes the note D, the second degree of the scale, reinforcing it with a drop note in the lower octave.

1:19   He runs to the G above the tonic to the G below the tonic.

1:26   He lands on the tonic, C, and reinforces it briefly.

1:27	A run down from the A♭ to the F, an expected phrase within a *Rast taqasim*. Soon after we hear the note B♭ within a phrase from the upper to the lower tonic, (8, 7, 6, 5, 4, 3, 2, 1). These gestures are musicals signals that say "this paragraph is ending soon."
1:38	Again the simple *qafla* 3, 3 2 1 closes the busy and decorated melody. As after the 1st paragraph, we hear humming from friends in the room as a response to the performer and his *taqasim*.

3rd paragraph

1:42–1:58	On to the 3rd paragraph and the continuation of the rest of the *taqasim* (less than half of which is heard in this recording). It begins with an elaborate introduction of the upper tonic note, reinforced by the lower tonic. This is an expected part of the *taqasim*, called *jawab* (literally "answer"), where the musician explores the upper octave of the *maqam* and introduces the expected tetrachordal variations of *maqam Rast* as well as modulations to other *maqams*. For example, beginning at 1:56 we hear a high E♭. This introduces *maqam Nahawand* on C (C D E♭) and, although the statement of E♭ is brief, it contrasts sharply with the E♮ of the *Rast* tetrachord C D E♮ F.
2:04	An arrival at the F and emphasis on this note with the phrase A♭ G F and pause at 2:08. But then an ascent back up to the upper-octave C using the upper *Rast* tetrachord G A B♮ C.
2:14–2:22	Restatement and emphasis of the upper tonic note C.
2:24	Passing modulation to *maqam Bayyati* (on the note G). Although the performer never comes to rest on the note G, he hints at this *maqam* with a fall from the upper E♭ to D C B♭ A♮ (the G may be implied in the ear of the listener).
2:33	Passing modulation to *maqam Hijaz* (on the note G): G A♭ B C.
2:39	The note B♭ "cancels out" the passing modulation to *maqam Hijaz*.
2:40	The playing becomes quieter and drier as the player dampens the strings, thus controlling their resonance and ringing. Reemphasis of the upper tonic note C.
2:55	As in the close of the 2nd paragraph, we hear several moves toward the *qafla* for this 3rd paragraph.
3:10	Listen for several sequences, or musical ideas, usually 3–5 notes that are repeated several times, each time a step lower. You can hear a descent (twice) to the G below the tonic, and ascent again to the upper tonic, C, and several sequences down the scale beginning at about 3:26 for the final *qafla* of this paragraph on C, which concludes at 3:36.
3:41	Beginning of the continuation of the *taqasim*, which goes on for 5 more minutes.

TRANSCRIPTION 10.10
Key phrases in Ayad
al-Asadi's 'ud taqasim.

Homeland and Diaspora: An Unexpected Reaction

We now return to the al-Asadi home. As mentioned earlier, I met Ayad and his brother Bahir, a fine violinist, through a man named Soheil Radwan, long recognized as an important figure in the Arab music scene in the Israeli city of Nazareth. They had invited me to meet with their father, Saud al-Asadi, an accomplished poet who specialized in various forms of vernacular sung Arabic poetry. The elder artist of the family, Saud al-Asadi, presented me with two published books of his poetry and also sang some traditional genres of Palestinian poetry called 'ataba and mijana. I gave the family a copy of the compact disc recording I produced in 1997 entitled *The Music of Arab Americans: A Retrospective Collection* (Rounder 1122). The recording is a kind of "greatest hits" of the Arab American community from about 1915 to 1955; all of the original performances were recorded on 78-rpm records so the production values and techniques are obviously out of date.

Saud al-Asadi's reaction to my CD was completely unexpected. He insisted we put it on and listen to it—all fourteen tracks—right away. He showed a deep interest in these archival performances and seemed to be captivated by some of them, particularly those of Palestinian musicians who had immigrated to the United States. Mr. al-Asadi went on to tell me that during the first half of the twentiety century, when people left Palestine for the United States, everyone assumed it was "just for money." He was completely astonished that these two musicians, originally singers for *Radyu al-Sharq al-Adna*, a radio station established by the British in Palestine, were never able to return to home to Palestine after what they thought, in 1947, would be just a six-month tour to the United States, because of the Arab-Israeli war and the establishment of the state of Israel in 1948. Their home and the radio station in Jerusalem were destroyed as a consequence of the war, so the musicians made a life in the United States. What struck Mr. al-Asadi even more profoundly was not their unsuspected exile but rather that his Palestinian countrymen had been perpetuating their culture, particularly their poetry and music, in places like Brooklyn, New York, and Dearborn, Michigan. He couldn't believe that this music had been living on in Arab American communities for more than half a century. This was all a complete revelation for him. As he listened to the music of these Arab immigrant musicians, Mr. al-Asadi was moved to tears.

Listen to CD 4, Track 26, which has just the first couple of phrases of "Lamma Ya Albi" ("When, O Heart of Mine"). It features the singer Sana Khadaj accompanied by Amer Khadaj, Jalil Azzouz, and Naim Karakand on violin and Muhammad al-Aqqad on *qanun*. This New York session was recorded by Farid Alam for his label, Alamphon, and the 78-rpm record circulated widely within the Arab American community during the 1940s and 1950s (Figure 10.10).

CD 4:26

"Lamma Ya Albi" ("When, O Heart of Mine"), excerpt (1:55). Sana Khadaj, vocal; Amer Khadaj, Jalil Azzouz, and Naim Karakand, violin; and Muhammad al-Aqqad, *qanun*. New York, NY. Alamphon 2096-1 and 2, c. 1949. Rereleased on *The Music of Arab Americans: A Retrospective Collection*. Produced by Anne Rasmussen. Rounder 1122. 1997.

Courtesy of Lila Kadaj.

FIGURE 10.10

Photograph of the original Alamphon paper sleeves for the 78-rpm recordings made by Sana Khadaj. The Arabic between the photographs translates as "The new records of the singing stars, the enchanting singer Sana and her husband, the enchanting singer Amer Khadaj."

In Chapter 1, you considered recordings as a part of the material culture of music (Table 1.1), and in the last chapter of this book, you will learn about commercial music as domain of music-culture. This recording, like thousands of non-English-language–based musics recorded by immigrant musicians on 78-rpm records, exemplifies the ways in which commercial, "disembodied" records can reflect the initiatives and needs of very localized communities. In a way similar to the independent labels of today, as well as music that is only shared on the Web, these records were made by and for the Arab community in the United States diaspora, a phenomenon that Saud al-Asadi, living in the homeland, could hardly believe. The song is preceded with the announcement *Istiwanat Alamphon, al mutribah Sana* ("Alamphon Records, the singer [literally, "enchantress"] Sana; see the Close Listening guide). Sana Khadaj, who was know for her aptitude for serious classical music, alternates between metrical, strophic verses and solo vocal lines in free rhythm where she demonstrates her range of vocal color and ornamentation. Although this "commercial" record may not be up to par in terms of today's production values, the quality of the recording is remarkably good considering the technology available in the 1940s. The lyrics exhibit typical themes of Arabic literature and poetry: love, longing, and nature.

"Lamma Ya Albi,"
Translation of full text

When, O heart of mine, your beloved returned
The moon came out early (without an appointment)
Our nights returned again, all of them joys
I forgot my pains and sorrows as my mind relaxed
How much, my spirit, have I stayed up with you, with passion like
    torture
And remained alone until the farewell appeared
Refrain
Why don't you tell me where you have been? You make me confused!
You whose beauty is in the antimony of the eye, come back and make me happy.

Close Listening

"LAMMA YA ALBI" ("WHEN, O HEART OF MINE"), EXCERPT

CD 4:26

COUNTER NUMBER	COMMENTARY	ARABIC TRANSLITERATION	TRANSLATION
0:00	Spoken introduction	*Istiwanat Alamphon, al mutribah Sana*	Alamphon Records, the singer, Sana
0:02	Instrumental introduction		
0:47	First vocal line, repeated; each half line complemented by deliberate "fillers" or *lawazim* by the *qanun*	*Lamma ya albi habībak 'ād Tili' il-'amar min ghayr mi'ād* (x2)	When, O heart of mine, your beloved returned The moon came out early (without an appointment)
1:19	Refrain	*Lamma ya albi, ya albi, ya albi, ya albi*	When, O heart of mine
1:28	Improvisatory vocal line by the singer in free meter with instrumentalists following along	*Ya... Ya... albi*	My heart...
1:46	Instrumental beginning of the next metrical section of the song		

From Diaspora to Globalization: Ofra Haza and World Beat

We have just considered a very specific example of Arab music in diaspora—immigrant musicians who recorded their own music on their own labels for their own community, and the way in which their recording deeply touched someone from their original homeland fifty years afterward. Now we end our exploration of Arab music with an example of a local musician whose music went global. Israel and the Palestinian territories are one of the most dynamic areas of the Middle East. This small area, about the size of the state of Connecticut, is home to Jews, Muslims, and Christians who differ in terms of ethnicity, socioeconomic class, and political orientation. Everyone there is affected by political histories that have dictated family trajectories for hundreds of years and that, today, keep decision making and daily mobility beyond the control of ordinary people. If we look at the performer Ofra Haza and her music as one window into the music and culture of the Middle East and Arab world, we quickly discover that our window is more like a dynamic prism that refracts various histories, trajectories, and interactions than a static tableau that presents a panoramic view. Jews lived in ancient Palestine well before the birth of Jesus Christ or the revelations of the Prophet Muhammad. A significant number of them immigrated to Yemen in the southern part of the Arabian Peninsula about two thousand years ago after the destruction of the first temple (586 B.C.E.). They lived in isolation for hundreds of years perpetuating a supposedly pure style of Jewish music and liturgy that was thought immune to foreign influence—a phenomenon I have called **marginal preservation** (Rasmussen 1997).

In 1948, the same year that Jalil Azouz and Sana and Amer Khadaj found themselves exiles on the streets of New York, Israel organized an exodus for Yemeni Jews known as "The Magic Carpet." Israelis sent planes to evacuate virtually the entire Jewish community (about fifty thousand) from Yemen to Israel. There are perhaps a couple of thousand Jews who remain in Yemen today, but for the most part the Yemeni Jewish community now resides in Israel. Ofra Haza (1957–2000) grew up in Israel performing community theatre. She was eventually awarded the Israeli equivalent of the Grammy award in 1980, 1981, and 1986 owing to the sales of her immensely popular records. After being picked up on the nascent mediascapes of international pop music, by the 1990s she was a strong player in a relatively new music/marketing category called World Beat or EthnoPop, something we now more often find under the ambiguous term World Music.

"Im Nin'alu" (CD 4, Track 27) is from the traditional collection of religious songs of the Yemenite Jews called the Divan and was written by a seventeenth-century poet, Rabbi Shalom Shabbezi. "The basic idea, expressed in the first two lines is that heaven is attentive even when men are not. The poem, which is filled with images from Jewish mysticism, alternates between Hebrew and Arabic" (Zahavi-Ely, personal communication, 2006). (The verse following the two you hear is in Arabic.) In addition to a quasi-Western–sounding chamber ensemble that includes oboe and violin, you can hear a brass tray and tin can, household items that acquired the function of percussion instruments during a time of musical repression in Yemen (see the Close Listening guide). Ofra Haza's recording of "Im Nin'alu" was sampled and remixed several times, notably for the title track to the film *Colors,* a movie directed by Robert Duvall, about African American gangs in Los Angeles. Ofra Haza's voice was later heard in households across North America when she became the voice of Yochoved, the mother of Moses, for the Dreamworks film *Prince of Egypt.*

CD 4:27

"Im Nin'alu" (2:24). Ofra Haza, vocal, with instrumentalists Iki Levy, Chaim Gispan, Eli Magen, Yigal Tuneh, Rima Kaminkowski, Yuval Kaminkowski, Israel Berkowitch, Yitchak Markowetzki, Israela Wisser, Abraham Rosenblatt, Elchanan Bregman, Abigail Erenheim, Meril Grinberg, Lesli Lishinski, and Ilan School Shlomo Shochat. From *Fifty Gates of Wisdom: Yemenite Songs.* Shanachie 64002. 1988. Track 1. Recorded at Triton Studios, Tel Aviv, Israel.

Concluding Remarks

We could just as well take this last performance as a point of departure for an investigation into the Arab world and, by extension, the Middle East. Using music as our point of entry, we could ask and answer questions regarding geography, history, and material culture. We could use the music as a way to explore issues of ethnicity and identity, aesthetics, gender, and spirituality. A consideration of this

"IM NIN'ALU"

CD 4:27

COUNTER NUMBER	COMMENTARY	HEBREW TEXT*	TRANSLATION*
0:00	Exposition of the Hebrew text in 6 phrases free meter	*Im nin'alu daltei n'divim* *Daltei marom lo nin'alu* *El Chai, mareimawam al kawruvim* *Kulawm b'rucho ya'alu* *El Chai*	Even when the doors of the generous ones (the wealthy) are locked, The doors of heaven will never be barred. Oh! Living God, up high above the cherubim They all go up through His spirit. Oh! Living God!
0:48	Verse 1 begins, 1st line of text	*Im nin'alu daltei n'divim* *Daltei marom lo nin'alu*	Even when the doors of the generous ones (the wealthy) are locked, The doors of heaven will never be barred.
0:55	Listen for percussion		
0:58	2nd line of text, same melody as 1st line	*El Chai, mareimawam al kawruvim* *Kulawm b'rucho ya'alu*	Oh! Living God, up high above the cherubim They all go up through His spirit.
1:04	Listen for percussion		
1:07	"B" part of melody (refrain)	*El Chai*	Oh! Living God!
1:16	Verse 2, similar in arrangement to verse 1	*Ki hem elai kis'o kawruvim* *Yodu sh'mei weihal'lu* *Chayet shelhem rotzeh washawvim* *Miyom b'ri'aw nichlawlu* *El Chai*	They are near to His throne They thank His name and praise (Him). Beasts who have been running back and forth Since the day the world was created, they have been crowned. Oh! Living God!
1:44	Instrumental rendition of the melody		
2:02	Return of the "B" section at verse 3	*El Chai*	Oh! Living God!

*The Hebrew text is a transliteration of Yemenite Hebrew as Ofra Haza sings it; the English translation was provided by Na'ama Zahavi-Ely.

music in its cultural context—whether in a Dreamworks film soundtrack or a concert in Massachusetts—would lead us to think about the function of music in the culture of diaspora and to investigate the biographies of individual musicians and audience members. This in turn would lead to a discussion of the roots of their individual musical worlds and the routes their musical paths have taken over time. This might bring us to the larger themes of diaspora, cultural genocide, and the political economy of music. Finally, we could try to figure out what the music means and to whom.

At the turn of the twenty-first century, the Middle East was known for its complex politics and rich natural resources. In the aftermath of the unparalleled events of September 11, 2001, and the Second Gulf War, which began in spring 2003 and is ongoing at this writing, many U.S. citizens are being forced to take a hard look at their ideas, attitudes, and knowledge about the Middle East and Arab world. In many parts of the Arab world, particularly Iraq and the Palestinian territories, grave security risks, rampant unemployment and economic strife, the loss of music patronage, and the dearth of the material culture of music from concert halls to blank tape to violin strings have taken their toll. Such everyday conditions make things like planning a wedding—or even walking down the street with an instrument to play music with a friend or take a music lesson—unthinkable. Nevertheless, music lives on as one of the most tenacious elements of culture. For centuries, Middle Eastern and Arab music have proven to be of great interest to musicians and audiences worldwide. Explorations of Middle Eastern history, culture, religion, and politics in the news media and cultural industries have never been more vigorous. The introduction to Arab music in this chapter comes with an invitation to learn more. Listen, read, and explore the Internet resources that make performers and performances throughout the Arab world available to you. Investigate the recordings and works listed in the references sections and discover the arts and culture of the Arab world by engaging with the people who create it throughout the world and in our own midst.

Book Companion Website

You will find tutorial quizzes, Internet links, and much more at the Book Companion Website for *Worlds of Music,* Fifth Edition, at **academic.cengage.com/music/titon/worlds_5**

Discovering and Documenting a World of Music

JEFF TODD TITON AND DAVID B. RECK

All of us are familiar with the tale of Dorothy and her adventures with the Tin Man, the Lion, and the Scarecrow in the fantastic land of Oz. But most of us have forgotten Dorothy's startling discovery once she got back to Kansas: Home was where her heart was, a fascinating world of people, family, neighbors, and friends, and of things that before her adventures she had overlooked. This is a familiar theme in literature the world over. The hero (representing us) travels to faraway places, sees and does fabulous things, meets incredible people, searches for marvelous treasures. But invariably the rainbow leads home; the pot of gold is buried in one's own backyard; the princess is none other than the girl next door.

Music in Our Own Backyards

In our explorations of the world's musics, we—as students and scholars alike—are fascinated by cultures and peoples greatly separated from us by place or time, in sound and style, or in ways of making and doing music. In a sense, for every one of us there is an Oz. But there is also a music-culture surrounding us, one that we see and hear only partially because it is too close to us, because we take it for granted, as fish do water. Our musical environment is held both within us—in our thoughts—and outside us—by other members of our community. It expands outwardly from us (and contracts into us) in a series of circles that may include family, ethnic groups, regional styles, geographic location, and cultural roots (Western Europe, Africa, Asia, and so on). It is available to us live or mechanically reproduced. It comes to us out of history (the classical masterworks, old-time fiddle tunes, bebop jazz) or from the here and now (the latest hit on the music charts or the avant-garde—the "new thing").

This chapter is all about gathering reliable information on today's music. We encourage you to seek out a nearby musical world, to observe it in person, to talk with the people involved in it, to document it with recordings and photographs, and to interpret the information in a project that will contribute to knowledge about today's musical activities. If this research project is part of a course, you should check with your instructor for specific directions. What follows is a general guide, based on the experience that we and our students have had with similar projects at our colleges and universities.

Selecting a subject for your research is the first step in the project. Songs and instrumental music serve a great many purposes and occur in a wide variety of contexts, from singing in the shower to the Metropolitan Opera, from the high school marching band to the rock festival, from the lullaby to the television commercial, and from music videos to computer music via the Internet. Whether trivial or profound, it is all meaningful. To help you select a subject, we will consider a few organizing principles: family, generation and gender, avocation/ leisure, religion, ethnicity, regionalism, nationalism, and commercialization. As you read through the following brief survey you will be led to or reminded of some subjects that interest you. Here we focus on North American examples, but if you are using this book elsewhere you should apply these (and perhaps other) organizing principles to examples from your own music-culture. Later we will give you some specific suggestions on how to move from a subject to a topic, and how best to proceed from there to gather the information.

FAMILY

As is true of all cultures, most North Americans first hear music in family life (Figure 11.1). Much of that music comes from the CD player, radio, television, or computer. People often say that the kind of music they heard before they were old enough to have their own albums strongly influenced them. Families also usually provide some live music. Many mothers and grandmothers sing lullabies, for example. Sometimes lullabies are the only songs in a foreign language that North American children with strong ethnic backgrounds hear, since people (particularly grandparents) often fall back on old, familiar languages for intimate songs.

In short, most North Americans have an early layer of songs learned in childhood in a family setting. Often they are just songs for entertaining children, with no deep cultural message to impart. What they do teach are the musical tastes of the particular group, whether rural Quebecois, California suburban, Illinois heartland,

FIGURE 11.1

A sharecropper family sings hymns in front of their home. Hale County, Alabama, 1936.

Walker Evans. Courtesy of the Library of Congress.

Appalachian, or New York inner-city. Children then work in harmony with (or work against) this basic musical background as a part of growing up and finding their identity. As they grow up, if they are attracted to making music, they will be able to listen to a great many different kinds of music, inside and outside of their families and communities. By the time they are adult musicians they may have multiple musical identities as a result of choices they made along the way. While growing up in Maine, Erica Brown (Figure 11.12) learned Franco-American music from her family and community; later she took classical violin lessons. Now a singer and fiddler at age twenty-two, she performs Franco-American music of New England at ethnic festivals; she also serves as the leader of a bluegrass band playing music associated with the southern Appalachian mountains.

GENERATION AND GENDER

Much North American music-making is organized along age-group or generational lines. Schools, church classes, scouting groups, children's sidewalk games, college singing groups, and many other musical situations include people of about the same age. Songs learned by these groups may stay with them as they grow older.

Even so, the amount of generational mixing in North American musical life has grown under the influence of television and recordings. For example, much of the music thought to belong only to the young in the 1960s, such as Beatles' music, appealed to older generations as well. And today's youngsters like their parents' music better than their parents liked that of their own parents. In ethnic musics, too, young people have taken to learning traditional songs from their grandmothers instead of laughing at the old folks' songs as they might have one or two generations ago.

There are fewer gender differences regarding music today than there used to be. Just as women now take up sports like race-car driving and become professional jockeys, so more women play instruments, such as the drums and saxophone, that used to be largely limited to men (Figure 11.2). A whole genre that used to be exclusively male—barbershop quartet singing—now has a parallel female style, exhibited by such groups as the Sweet Adelines. One women's bluegrass group called themselves the All Girl Boys, while a new generation of bluegrass stars includes Alison Krauss, Rhonda Vincent and Laurie Lewis. But gender differences remain important as many of today's musical groups, like other North American social groups, are organized along gender lines.

LEISURE

Music as a recreational leisure activity is an important part of North American life. For example, one barbershop quartet program listed the wives of the singers as "Thursday Night Widows"—perhaps one reason for the formation of women's quartets. Many North Americans feel the need for a strong group pastime, and of course some of this impulse is channeled into musical organizations. A local American Legion Post or an ethnic group such as the Polish Falcons may have a band; here the music-making affirms group solidarity. Fielding a band for the local parade or festival brings the group visibility and pride. Individual members may find performing in a fife-and-drum corps or the Governor's Footguard Band (to use Connecticut examples) a satisfying way to spend leisure time. Black youngsters in high school and college form extracurricular, informal hip-hop or gospel groups;

FIGURE 11.2

"The boys in the band."
Grove Lake Concert Band,
a brass band from Oregon,
1911. Photographer
unknown.

sometimes these groups become semiprofessional or even fully professional. Most high schools and colleges can boast a few rock bands and possibly even a jazz group, as well as cocktail pianists, folk-singing guitarists, and chamber music ensembles.

The computer has facilitated music-making as a leisure hobby. Using their instruments with sampling and software such as Apple's GarageBand, composers can put together and arrange songs and instrumental compositions, then record a final version with the computer supplying the instrumental accompaniment. Amateur and professional composers and musicians can access websites where they collaborate to produce layered arrangements of musical compositions (see Chapter 1).

RELIGION

Religion is one of the better-documented areas of North American musical life. Scholars know about music's role in many religious movements, ranging from the eighteenth-century Moravians through the revival movements of the nineteenth century and the founding of sects such as the Mormons or Pentecostals. Much has been written about the appropriateness of certain types of music-making in religious settings, such as organ playing in the Jewish synagogue or the introduction of folk and jazz elements to church services. Scholarly study focuses on the Negro spiritual, while the tent-revival preacher, the snake handler, and the old-time churches also receive attention (see Figure 11.3). But the musical activities of contemporary, mainline middle-class churches, synagogues, and mosques offer equal interest, though few people study them. The songs of new religious movements, such as small meditation groups based on Christian or Eastern religious thinking, also deserve attention. These groups need to encourage solidarity and teach their message, but they have no traditional music. Often they change the words of well-known songs as a way of starting, just

Jeff Todd Titon

FIGURE 11.3

Music almost always accompanies formal rites of passage, such as this old-time baptism. Eastern Kentucky. 1990.

as Martin Luther changed the words of German drinking songs 450 years ago to create a body of sacred songs we know as Protestant chorales. The new groups may also work hard on developing an "inner music" of their members, through which the believer reaches the desired state of tranquility.

ETHNICITY

Ethnicity is the oldest consideration in the study of the North American music-culture in the sense that the United States is usually regarded as a nation of immigrants. It is also one of the newest considerations because of the interest in ethnic identity, diversity, and multiculturalism, a trend that has gathered force since the late 1960s (Figure 11.4).

Jeff Todd Titon

FIGURE 11.4

Alan Shavarsh Bardezbanian plays 'ud with his Middle Eastern ensemble. National Folk Festival, Bangor, Maine, 2003.

Throughout North America, ethnicity has played a major role in musical history. Whether in the dialect and songs of the French Acadians in New Brunswick, the heroic *corrido* ballads sung along the Rio Grande by Mexican Americans, the retelling of the story of hard-hearted Barbara Allen by British-American ballad singers, or the singing of a Yiddish lullaby in a Brooklyn tenement, North Americans have built and maintained ethnic boundaries through music. Music's function as a sign of group solidarity and common ancestry is nowhere clearer than in the variety of songs, dances, and instrumental tunes that characterize the North American ethnic mosaic. Students in the United States whose parents or grandparents stopped publicly singing Old World songs on their way to becoming "one-hundred-percent Americans" have become enthusiastic about joining ethnic music groups or studying their group's heritage. Other parents and grandparents, of course, never stopped singing their native songs.

North American ethnic music has always involved transcontinental exchange. On the one hand, Greek Americans are influenced by new developments in popular music in Athens, while on the other, Polish American records find great favor among farmers in far-off mountain villages in Poland. American jazz and country music have spread around the world, from Holland to Russia and Japan. A complicated interplay goes on between black music in the United States and the Caribbean (Figure 11.5). A single song may embody layer upon layer of musical travel. Reggae developed in Jamaica, where it represented a blend of Afro-Caribbean and black U.S. soul music. This already complicated style came to America from England, where pop groups repackaged it and exported it, and the cycle continues: Reggae is now popular in most parts of Africa, and in the Tatra Mountains in Poland, where we might not expect it (see Chapter 5), it has fused with traditional village music.

In today's world, family- and community-based musics have become markers of ethnic identity and an older way of life. At the same time, they are packaged,

FIGURE 11.5

One of Boston's Caribbean steel-drum bands performs at a women's prison, 1979.

Jeff Todd Titon

bought, and sold in the marketplace; this encourages originality and virtuosity, qualities that may not have been important in the musics' traditional contexts.

REGIONALISM

Regionalism in North America is thought to have declined with the spread of the interstate highway system, chains of fast-food restaurants, and the spread of television, all of which began in the 1950s. But just as ethnic groups never really dissolved into the so-called melting pot, so ways of life still differ according to region, by speech, food, music, and so forth. Regionalism crops up in the names of styles, such as the Chicago blues sound, the Detroit "Motown" soul sound, or even within ethnic styles, as in the distinction between a Chicago and an East Coast polka. The crisp bowing, downbeat accents, and up-tempo performance of a fiddle tune in the Northeast (Figure 11.6) bears little resemblance to the same tune's performance in the Southwest, with its smooth bowing and more-relaxed beat. The same hymn tune shows considerable variation even within the same denomination in different parts of the country. One Indiana Primitive Baptist was overheard to comment on the slow, highly decorated tunes of her Primitive Baptist neighbors to the Southeast: "They take ten minutes just to get through 'Amazing Grace!'"

Like ethnicity, regionalism is coming back into fashion. There are now so many local festivals that event listings can be found on the Internet. Some locales host mock battles, which are fought again and again for throngs of tourists to appropriate live or recorded music. One highly visible regional music performance is the singing of "My Old Kentucky Home" at the May running of the Kentucky

Jack Delano. Courtesy of the Library of Congress.

FIGURE 11.6

Fiddler Ed Larkin,
Tunbridge, Vermont, 1941.

Derby. In a recent year 150 thousand spectators joined in, and millions of television viewers were on hand to link the song and event to the region of its origin.

In summary, even if it sometimes seems the result of shrewd marketing to promote local cultures, regional musical diversity has not yet given way to a one-size-fits-all music. North America is still too large and diverse to turn all music into brand names or to have the entire population respond equally to all music, and the search for revival or for novelty continues.

NATIONALISM

As a colony that declared its independence and fought a war to preserve it, the United States long ago began seeking ways to establish a national musical identity. Popular national sentiment was evoked by the frequent performance of patriotic songs, as when John Philip Sousa's band and its imitators played flag-waving tunes on the bandstand for Sunday promenaders, and schoolchildren knew all the verses of the national anthem. After declining throughout the twentieth century, this tradition found fresh life in the new millennium with the singing of "God Bless America" on various occasions to evoke solidarity in the face of the destruction of the World Trade Center towers in New York City on 9/11.

Perhaps our most obvious repertory of national music consists of Christmas songs such as "Jingle Bells," "White Christmas," and "Rudolph the Red-Nosed Reindeer." During the holiday season, it is almost impossible to escape them. The curmudgeon who shoos away carolers from his front yard is said to lack the Christmas spirit, and he soon gains a neighborhood reputation as a Scrooge. Other examples include patriotic songs learned in public school, such as "The Star-Spangled Banner," "America the Beautiful," and "My Country 'tis of Thee." "Take Me Out to the Ballgame" and "God Bless America" represent songs that began life in musical theatre or on recordings but that have now become part of the national repertory.

COMMODIFIED MUSIC

While amateurs still make most of the music in North American culture, paid professionals supply much of it as well. It is remarkable that this complex culture carries musical events that are also typical of non- or preindustrial societies. Though some genres, such as the funeral lament, have largely disappeared in the United States, rituals that mark a change of life, such as weddings and initiations (bar mitzvahs, debutante parties, senior proms), still demand solemnization by music. A wedding may take place in a park with an ice-cream truck, balloons, and jeans instead of in a formal church setting, yet music remains indispensable even if it consists of pop tunes instead of an official wedding march. Elegant yacht clubs tend to schedule dances during full-moon evenings, continuing a practice of certain ancient cultures.

A great deal of the commodified music North Americans come into daily contact with may be described as "disembodied"—that is, the listener does not feel the physical presence of the performer and many times cannot even see the original musical situation (as in Figure 11.7). Some of this music can be partially controlled by the listener who selects recordings from his or her collection to suit a

John Collier. Courtesy of the Library of Congress.

FIGURE 11.7

Dancing to records on a jukebox. West Virginia, 1942.

mood. Although the listener can imagine an original musical situation—a concert or recording studio—there is no possibility of interaction with the performers, and the music is the same each time it is heard. Indeed, much of this music is never performed "live" in concert or recording studio at all; rather, it is generated partly in live performance and partly by engineers and musicians who add tracks in a recording studio or by means of a computer.

One of the most significant recent developments in commodified music is the rise of mp3 technology and the distribution of music in this format over the Internet. Musicians who think that the music industry takes too much of the profits from album sales have been able to market their recordings directly to consumers via the World Wide Web. Consumers flock to websites where they can download music, often for free.

Ethnomusicologists pay close attention to how people use music in their daily lives. Many young people today have become active consumers who not only select music but engineer and package it for themselves and their friends. Mix tapes—tracks selected from CDs and sequenced to cassettes (later CDs) given to friends—were popular in the last decades of the twentieth century. One model for this kind of musical activity was the "Deadhead," who recorded and traded tapes of live Grateful Dead concerts. Long before the Deadheads, jazz buffs were recording after-hours jam sessions and trading the results. Today, the person who downloads music from the Internet, edits it, and sequences the music on an iPod plays quite an active role in choosing music to suit a lifestyle. Music-making on the computer does not require singing or playing a traditional instrument; instead, the computer becomes both the instrument and the recording studio.

Public background music is another kind of commodified music heard in daily life. There is no logical connection between buying groceries and hearing piped music in a supermarket or shopping mall. In offices and factories, the employer may choose to have background music that is manufactured and programmed to increase worker productivity. This of course represents a particularly powerful type of unrequested music. Some do not even notice it.

This brief survey of music-making organized around family, generation and gender, leisure, religion, ethnicity, regionalism, nationalism, and commodified music should help you select a subject for your project: a nearby musical world that you're interested in, have access to, and can gather information about.

Doing Musical Ethnography

Your aim in discovering and documenting a world of music is a **musical ethnography**—a written representation, description, and interpretation of some aspect of a music-culture. The **subject** of your musical ethnography is the aspect of the music-culture that is being represented; the **topic** of your musical ethnography enables your analysis and interpretation of your subject. Approaching a music-culture for the first time, you may feel overwhelmed, but if you use Table 1.1 (p. 19) to organize your thinking about what you see and hear, you will see how you might go about gathering information on specific aspects of it so that you may write on a particular topic within the music-culture. Your writing may be accompanied by photographs, recordings, or even videotapes that you make while documenting the music-culture.

The music in the repertory can be recorded for later study and analysis. Much of social organization and material culture can be observed. By listening to musicians talk with each other, and by talking to them, you can begin to understand their ideas about music; through interviews you can learn more about those ideas, the repertory, musical activities, and material culture. (After all, conversations and interviews formed the basis for the musicians' life histories in this book.) But discovering and documenting a world of music is not like examining an amoeba under a microscope. People will differ in how they behave, what they believe, and what they say to you. Different people will sing "the same tune" differently. Under these conditions, accurately representing and interpreting a music-culture, even a single aspect of it, in a musical ethnography is a complex and subtle undertaking. It is probably not something you will have done before.

SELECTING A SUBJECT: SOME PRACTICAL SUGGESTIONS

It is obvious that your project requires you to collect, understand, and organize information about music in order to present it. It differs from the usual school research paper in that it focuses on a musical situation that you seek out directly from people rather than from books in a library. In ethnomusicology, as in anthropology and folklore, this in-person witnessing, observing, questioning, tape recording, photographing, and in some cases performing is called **fieldwork**. Fieldwork is research "in the field" rather than the laboratory or library. Of course, library research is often quite helpful as part of this endeavor. You might find background information on your topic in the library and by searching on the Internet; and you should not overlook the opportunity to do so. But most of your project takes you into the field, where you will obtain your most valuable and original information.

Collecting, understanding, and organizing information about music are, of course, interrelated. You will begin with certain insights about the information you collect. As you organize it, you will gain new insights. After you organize it, you will be able to describe it and move toward an interpretation of it.

You can approach the choice of a research subject in different ways. First, you might try to chart the music you hear daily:

1. Keep a log or journal of all the music you hear over three or four days or a week. Note the context, style, and purpose of the music. Calculate how much of your day is spent with music of some sort.
2. Record, videotape, or simply describe in words several television commercials that employ music. Note the style of the music and the image it attempts to project. How is the music integrated into the message of the advertisement? Is it successful? Offensive? Both?
3. Map the uses of music in various movies or television shows as you watch them. For contrast, select a daytime serial and a crime-fighting show, or a situation comedy and a popular dramatic series, for example.
4. Survey the uses of background music in local stores. Interview salespeople, managers, owners, customers (always obtaining their permission). See what they say about music and sales.
5. Survey the music that you listen to on the Internet. On what occasions do you seek out music there? What is your relationship to this music and how does it compare with your relationship to other music in your daily life? Is there a group of people interested in the same music you are? If so, does this group get together, over the Internet, to discuss this music? What kind of a community does this constitute?

A second approach is to examine the music in your own background. Explore your memory of songs and music. Note how your religious and ethnic heritage influenced the music you heard and your current musical interests. How has your musical taste changed as you have grown older? Survey the contents of your CD collection or your preferences in listening to music on the radio, television, or the Internet. You can ask your friends and family the same questions.

A third approach is to explore music in your community—your school community or your hometown. There you can interview people, listen to musical performances, possibly take part in them yourself, and gather quite a lot of information. Here are several possible subject headings:

Ethnic groups
Piano teachers
Private instrumental instruction (music stores, private lessons in the home)
Choir directors
Church organists, pianists, and so on
School music (elementary, junior high, high school)
Music stores
Musical instrument makers
Background music in public places
The club scene (bars, coffeehouses, restaurants, clubs)
Musical organizations (community choral groups, bands, barbershop
    quartets, and so forth)

Part-time (weekend) musicians
Professional or semiprofessional bands (rock, pop, jazz, rhythm and blues,
     country, gospel, and so forth)
Chamber music groups
Parades and music
Disc jockeys
Symphony orchestras

A fourth approach narrows the subject and concentrates on an individual musician's life, opinions, and music. Often we focus our attention on the musical superstars, but in the process we forget the many fine and sensitive musicians, many of them amateurs, who live in our communities. Senior citizens, teachers, owners of record or music stores, or tradespeople like the local barber, school custodian, or factory worker have sometimes had rich musical experiences as professional or part-time musicians. To search out such people is not always easy. Try the musicians' union, ethnic organizations, word of mouth, school or college music teachers, radio station disc jockeys, the clergy, club owners, newspaper columnists and feature story writers, or even local police stations and fire departments. Musicians can be approached directly at fairs, contests, festivals, concerts, and dances (Figure 11.8). Many colleges and universities have foreign-student associations that include amateur musicians, and they can tell you about others in the area. Ethnic specialty restaurants and grocery stores provide another resource.

The musical world that surrounds you is so diverse that you may feel swamped, unable to focus your energy. But when it finally comes down to deciding on a subject for your project, two guiding principles will help you: *Choose something you are interested in, and choose something you have access to.* Succeeding will be hard if you are not curious about the music you examine, and you must be close to it in order to look at it carefully. Many students find it helpful to discuss their proposed subjects with the instructor and other students, in class if time allows.

FIGURE 11.8

Nathan, Chris, and Robin Sockalexis, Penobscot Nation, Old Town, Maine, singing and drumming. Bangor, Maine, 2003.

COLLECTING INFORMATION

Once you have chosen a subject, your next move is to immerse yourself in the musical situation, consider what aspects of it interest you, and select a topic. Then you need to plan how to collect information—what questions to ask when you talk to the musicians or others involved, what performances to record, and so forth. Almost always you will need time and flexibility to revise your plans as you collect the information you need. For that reason you should get started as early in the term as possible. Most people will be happy to tell you about their involvement with music as long as you show them you really are interested.

GAINING ENTRY

Musical activities usually have a public (performance) side and a private (rehearsal) side. The performance is the tip of the iceberg; you will want to understand what lies beneath, and that is best learned by talking to the people involved. If you must approach a stranger, you may want to arrange an introduction, either by a mutual friend or by a person in authority. If, for example, you want to talk with musicians in an ethnic organization, it is wise to approach the president of the organization and seek his or her advice first. This not only allows you to get good information but also to share your plans with the president, who needs to know what is going on in the group. In other situations it is best to let the people in authority know what you intend to do, and why, but to avoid having them introduce you, particularly if their authority is legal only and they do not belong to the same ethnic group as the people whose music you will be studying.

The first contact is especially important, because the way you present yourself establishes your identity and role. That is one reason why you must take the time to be honest with yourself and others about your interest in their music and the purpose of your project. If you are a college student, you may find yourself being assigned the role of the expert. But this is a role to avoid. Tell the people who give you information that they are the experts and that you are the student who wants to learn from them—that otherwise you would not seek their help. Let them know that you hope they will be willing to let you talk with them, observe them, and, if appropriate, participate in the music.

PARTICIPATION AND OBSERVATION

Doing research in the field requires a basic plan of action. Which people should you talk with? Which performances should you witness? Should you go to rehearsals? What about a visit to a recording studio? If you are studying a music teacher, should you watch a private lesson? Should the teacher teach you? Will you take photographs? Videotape? What kind of recording equipment can you get? Who will pay for it? You have probably been thinking about these and many similar questions. One more that you should pay attention to at this time regards your personal relationship to the people whose music you will study. Should you act as an observer—as a detached, objective reporter? Or should you, in addition to observing, also participate in the musical activity if you can?

Participating as well as observing can be useful (and quite enjoyable). You hope to learn the music from the inside. Rather than hanging around the edges of the action, depending on others to explain all the rules, you will come to know some of the musical belief system intuitively.

But participating has its drawbacks. The problem with being a participant-observer is that you sometimes come to know too much. It is like not knowing the forest for the trees: The closer you are to a situation, the less of an overall view you have, and in order to address your project to an outside reader, you will need to imagine yourself as an outsider, too. We tend to filter out the regularities of our lives. If every time we met a stranger we had to stop and think about whether our culture says we should shake hands, rub noses, or bow, we would be in constant panic; if we had to think hard whether red means stop or go, driving would be impossible. This filtering process means that we take the most basic aspects of a situation for granted. So if you are participating as well as observing, you must make a special effort to be an outsider and take nothing for granted. This dual perspective, the view of the participant-observer, is not difficult to maintain while you are learning how to participate in the musical situation. In fact, when you are learning, the dual perspective is forced on you. The trouble is that after you have learned, you can forget what it was like to be an outside observer. Therefore it is very important to keep a record of your changing perspective as you move from outsider to participant. This record should be written in your field notes or spoken into your tape recorder as your perspective changes.

In fact, you may already be a full participant in the music-culture you intend to study. Writing a musical ethnography about a music-culture in which you have been involved for some time may seem quite appealing. Although this kind of research appears easy, it is not. Your knowledge usually is too specialized for general readers. Further, the issues that matter to you as a member of the music-culture may not interest anyone outside the music-culture very much, and if that is so, your musical ethnography will find a limited audience. You may feel that because of the depth of your knowledge, you do not need to interview any other members of the music-culture, but this is not so. Other participants' perspectives will differ from yours, and although you may favor your own, in a musical ethnography they are all important. You may also, without even realizing it, express a particular point of view as if it is a generally accepted truth rather than a bias coming from inside the music-culture.

What if you work as an observer only and forego participation? There are some advantages to doing so. It saves time. You can put all your energy into watching and trying to understand how what people tell you is going on matches what you can actually see and hear going on. You can follow both sides of "what I say" and "what I do" more easily when you are merely observing as opposed to participating. On the other hand, you do not achieve objectivity by keeping yourself out of the action. Your very presence as an observer alters the musical situation, particularly if you are photographing or tape-recording. In many situations, you will actually cause less interference if you participate rather than intrude as a neutral and unresponsive observer. If you are studying dance music, it is a good idea to dance (Figure 11.9).

SELECTING A TOPIC

After you have narrowed your subject, you face the next step, which is one of the most difficult: selecting a good *topic* to write about. In most undergraduate writing projects, students work on assigned topics. But for this project you are being asked to generate your own topic. A topic is not the same as a subject. A subject may be a music culture, a musical scene, a musician, or a group of musicians. A topic is your subject viewed from a particular perspective, and with a thematic question in mind. By themselves, subjects cover too much ground. Topics focus your attention on specific questions that will (1) help you organize the information you collect and (2) lead you from documentation to interpretation. For example, "the Jewish cantor" is a subject, something to investigate. "Musical education of Jewish cantors in New York City" is a topic. The cantor is viewed from a thematic perspective: education. You want to understand what the education of a cantor consists of and what the results are. Putting this into a thematic question, you ask "What is the musical education of cantors in New York City?" Another example of a subject is "the Outlaws, a local country music

Russell Lee. Courtesy of the Library of Congress.

FIGURE 11.9

Fiddler and guitarist at a fiesta. Taos, New Mexico, 1940.

band." A topic turned into a thematic question that involves the band might be "How is gender a factor in the music of the Outlaws, a local country music band?" Here the focus is on the band members' attitudes, interactions, lyrics, social scene, and so forth, as they relate to gender. This topic is in itself too large and would have to be refined further, narrowed down, perhaps to "What role does gender play in the social scene that surrounds the Outlaws, a local country music band?" The social scene would include the members of the band, their activities, and their interactions with the music industry and their audience.

The process of refining a topic is gradual and involves a lot of thought. To begin, go back to Chapter 1 and use the music-culture model to select aspects of your subject that interest you. Do you want to focus on conceptions of music, activities involving music, repertories, or material culture? Of course, these aspects are interrelated, and ignoring any of them completely will be difficult; nevertheless, concentrating most of your attention on one of them will help you select a topic you can manage. It will also give you some initial ideas to think about as you gather your information. While doing field research you will find that some areas of your topic yield better information than others. As you assess the results of your research-in-progress you should be able to refine and refocus your topic to take advantage of the good information you have gathered. As you do so, you may have to deemphasize, or possibly even discard, other aspects of your topic that you have found difficult to research.

Your instructor can help you move from a subject to a topic. Many teachers ask students to begin their field research early in the term and to make a short written proposal in which they describe their subject and, if they have done enough fieldwork to this point, their topic. Instructor feedback at this point can save you a lot of time later. As we have suggested, students at first often choose topics that are too broad, given the limitations on their time and the instructor's guidelines for the paper's length. Another common problem is a topic that is too vague. Interpretation—figuring out what your documentation means—always goes in the direction of answering increasingly specific questions about your topic. If you have decided to focus on one band's repertory, a thematic question like "What is the repertory of the Accidental Tourists, a campus rock band?" should be made more precise with questions like "How does the band choose, learn, arrange, and maintain songs for their repertory?" A series of questions like this can help you focus your observations and interviews. In this case, you would want to ask the band members these questions and to attend some rehearsals and see how the band chooses, learns, and arranges their songs. After starting field research, working with your thematic question to generate a series of more precise, related questions will help you, in that you can organize your project around those questions. When you write your project up, the answers to those questions, and how the answers relate to each other, will lead you to an overall interpretation of the topic and the main point you want to make.

For example, you may be interested in bluegrass music and find a local group of bluegrass musicians who allow you to observe one of their rehearsals. Or possibly you go to a bluegrass festival and observe the jam sessions in and around the RVs and tents on the site. You may become interested in how bluegrass harmony works. "What are the principles of bluegrass harmony?" is your thematic question. As you do your fieldwork observation and interviewing, you will find that you can ask more-specific questions. You would hear the musicians use terms for the different harmony parts, like "lead" and "tenor" and "baritone," and you could observe, hear, and ask about the role of each part and how the parts relate to the whole. Alternatively, you may become interested in the etiquette of the jam sessions. What is the purpose of these elaborate social arrangements, and how does jam session etiquette promote social and musical harmony as well as minimize conflict? What are the rules of jam session etiquette? In both cases you have proceeded from a subject (bluegrass) to a topic (bluegrass harmony or bluegrass jam sessions) and you have narrowed down and further sharpened those topics through questions that will lead you from documentation to interpretation of those aspects of the music-culture.

In other words, gathering information is not simply a matter of recording it all as a sponge soaks up water. You will want to be selective in what you document, because after documentation you will need to interpret your material. In the bluegrass rehearsals you will pay particular attention to the way the musicians work out the harmonies, and when you interview them you will ask them about that. If your topic involves jam session etiquette, you will focus on that rather than on other aspects of bluegrass.

To take another extended example, suppose that your subject is music on the school radio station, and your topic has to do with the radio station's attitude toward women's hip-hop groups. Your topic will be rephrased as a thematic question: "What is the station's attitude toward women's hip-hop groups?" To find out, you listen carefully to the station over a period of time. You decide to interview some of the people who work at the station, and you try to figure out a way to approach your topic during these interviews. One deejay might play a lot of women's music on a particular show, and you might find out something about this deejay's attitude by asking. As you gather information, you try to estimate how well theory is put into practice—the station people say they are in favor of women's music, but you find that overall they do not play very much of it. You wonder why. Do the station people think the audience does not want to hear it? What does the audience want to hear, how do they know, and should they play what the audience wants to hear, anyway?

Questions that arise during the course of your research can help you to select the kind of documentation that you will do—whether, for example, to survey the recordings in the radio station's library or to interview members of the listening audience—and help you to focus your interpretation so that by the end of your project you will have some answers to your questions. You will not merely be gathering material but also focusing that material on a topic; the heart of your project is your own interpretation of the material in light of the topic you have chosen. In our example about women's hip-hop on campus radio, perhaps the station does not express a coherent attitude toward this music at all. Perhaps you find that female deejays have a different attitude than male deejays do. The answers to your questions should lead you to your main point, or the thesis of your interpretation. One thesis might be "On the campus radio station, male deejays ignore women's hip-hop, while many female deejays are very much aware of it, play it, and expect their listeners to enjoy it." If your fieldwork led you to a different conclusion, your thesis might be something like, "On the campus radio station, male deejays feel obligated to play women's hip-hop, and they do, but without much knowledge or understanding of it. Female deejays play women's hip-hop because it represents a point of view they understand and sympathize with, but they also realize they can't overdo it because they don't want women as their main audience." Or maybe they do: Maybe there is one show that does. Such a narrow topic might be the best of all, as you discovered after learning about this particular deejay and show. This very narrow focus would have the advantage of specificity— you would not feel like you were generalizing about the station all the time, then making exceptions for different points of view. But this narrow topic would fall into place only after you had done a good deal of fieldwork.

LIBRARY AND INTERNET RESEARCH

Depending on the topic you have selected, you may want to search the Internet at this point to see if anyone has published information on your topic. Wikipedia is often helpful on music topics. Do not neglect your library's collection either. It might be useful to spend a couple of hours in the library stacks, looking at books on the shelves and opening any on your subject, for finding everything you need in the electronic card catalog can be challenging. One reference work that you may find useful is *American Musical Traditions*, edited by Jeff Todd Titon and Bob Carlin (Titon and Carlin 2001).

If your library subscribes to *Ethnomusicology*, the journal of the Society for Ethnomusicology, you will find in each of its three yearly issues an invaluable guide to published research in the "Current Bibliography, Discography and Filmography" section. The most recent years' entries are available on the Society for Ethnomusicology's website: http://www.indiana.edu/~ethmusic/. Another useful resource is *Ethnomusicology On Line*, at http://research.umbc.edu/efhm/eol.html.

The American Folklife Center, at the Library of Congress, and the Smithsonian Institution's Center for Folklife and Heritage, both of which have extensive collections of recorded sound, can be accessed on the Internet via the following addresses:

http://www.loc.gov/folklife/
http://www.folklife.si.edu/

You may find some of the following additional periodicals helpful:

American Music
Asian Music
Black Music Research Journal
The Black Perspective in Music
Bluegrass Unlimited
Journal of American Folklore
Journal of Country Music
Journal of Jazz Studies
Journal of Popular Culture
Journal of Popular Music and Society
Latin American Music Review
Living Blues
Music Educators' Journal
The Old-Time Herald
Popular Music
Southern Exposure
Western Folklore
World of Music
Yearbook of the International Council for Traditional Music

If your library subscribes to JSTOR or other electronic databases with articles from scholarly journals, you should search for your subject and topic there. Look also in the reference section of your library or on the Internet for such bibliographies as the Music Index and RILM, as well as specialized bibliographies and reference works. There may even be discographies (a list of musicians, titles, record numbers, places, and dates) of recordings in music in the area you are researching. For example, Richard Spottswood's *Ethnic Music on Records: A Discography of Ethnic Recordings Produced in the United States, 1893 to 1942* is a five-volume work that lists 78-rpm recordings made during that period (Spottswood 1990). If your research topic involves a U.S. ethnic music, then this could be a valuable resource for you. Music and photographs on the Internet can also be helpful in your research (Figure 11.10). The

FIGURE 11.10

Corozal, Puerto Rico. Orchestra furnishing music for dancing at a tenant purchase celebration, 1941. Two men, one with guitar and one with *cuatro*, and a boy with maracas.

Jack Delano. Courtesy of the Library of Congress.

bibliographies will point you toward books and articles on your subject. The reference librarian can help you find these. Many of these music-related bibliographies and discographies are now available electronically. Some are on the Internet and others are available on CD-ROM.

The Internet has become a vast resource for information about music. Try searching for keywords that surround your topic. You will probably have to refine your search greatly in order to make it efficient. Also realize that some of the information you find on people's websites, such as their opinions about music, does not carry the authority of a scholarly book. Nevertheless, some of these specialized sites offer a good deal of useful information that you might not be able to find in books; amateur research has contributed significantly to certain areas of music, such as discographical information.

The Internet is particularly good for gathering groups of people together to discuss a subject of common interest and share insights. For example, numerous bluegrass websites reflect how bluegrass fans think and talk about their music. A bluegrass list (discussion group) called Bluegrass-L is open to subscribers and might even be a good place to do research. Other interest groups involving music abound on the Internet. Look in the newsgroups listed under Rec.Music. Several discussion lists focus on musics in India, for example; there is an Arab music list, and so forth. Of course, the Internet also offers a great deal of music, now available in mp3 and other audio formats, as well as in streaming audio and video.

Another good reason for visiting the library early in your project is that you may find a reference to a promising article or book that you will need to request on interlibrary loan. But avoid the temptation to read everything that might somehow be relevant. The Internet can also take up a lot more time than it should, and its information is not always scholarly or reliable. Remember that you will gather most of your information directly by observing a music-culture in action and by speaking with people who participate in the music-culture. Library and Internet research merely provides background information, and sometimes it cannot even do that—your subject may not have received attention yet, or the little that has been written may not be useful. But if research on your topic has been published, learning about it will help you undertake a better project. Further, the people whose music you are studying often can suggest good books and articles for you to read, saving you time in your search.

ETHICS

Doing fieldwork involves important ethical considerations. The people you photograph, record, and interview have ethical rights to their musical performances and their images. Most colleges and universities have a policy designed to prevent people from being harmed by research. Be sure to find out from your instructor if your project is bound by your institution's human subjects research policy and whether you need to get it reviewed and approved by your institution. Also be sure to discuss the ethics of the project with your teacher before you begin and, if things change, as you proceed.

Whether your project is part of a course or not, think carefully about the impact of what you propose to do. *Always* ask permission of the people involved. Besides ethical rights, people have legal rights to privacy and to how they look, what they say, and what they sing, even after you have recorded it. Be honest with yourself and with the people you study about your interest in their music and the purposes of your project. Tell them right from the start that you are interested in researching and documenting their music. If you like their music, say so. If the project is something for you to learn from, say so. Explain what will happen to the project after you finish it. Is it all right with them if you keep the photographs and tapes you make? Would they like a copy of the project? (If so, make one at your expense.) Is it all right if the project is deposited in the college or university archive? Most archives have a form that the people (yourself included) will sign, indicating that you are donating the project to the archive and that it will be used only for research purposes. If this project is not merely a contribution to knowledge but also to your career (as a student or otherwise), admit it and realize that you have a stake in its outcome. Ask the people whose music you are studying why they are cooperating with you and what they hope to achieve from the project, and bear that in mind throughout. *Never* observe, interview, make recordings, or take photographs without their knowledge and permission.

Today many ethnomusicologists believe that simply going into a musical situation and documenting it is not enough. The fieldworker must give something back to the people who have been generous with their thoughts, music, and time. In some cultures, people expect money and should be paid. Fieldworkers sometimes act not simply as reporters, or analysts, but also as cultural and musical advocates, doing whatever they can to help the music they are studying to flourish. Not all ethnomusicologists work in colleges and universities. Some in the United States work for arts councils, humanities councils, and other public agencies where they are expected to identify, document, and present family and community-based arts to the public. Some work for government or nongovernment agencies that formulate cultural policy. Many taxpayers believe that if the government supports the fine arts, it should also support folk and ethnic arts. In fact, most European governments do more than the United States and Canada to preserve and promote their folk and ethnic music. Ethnomusicologists hear a similar kind of commercial popular music throughout the world, and many conclude that local musics—of which there are a great variety—are endangered. It is to humankind's advantage to have many different kinds of music, they believe. For that reason, they think advocacy and support are necessary in the face of all the forces that would make music sound alike the world over. This argument may at first seem remote to your project, but not when you think about your own involvement with the people and music you are studying.

FIELD GEAR: NOTEBOOK, RECORDER, CAMERA

The perfect fieldworker has all-seeing eyes, all-hearing ears, and total recall. Because none of us is so well equipped, you must rely on written notes, recordings, and photographs that you make in the field. You may also be able to use a video camcorder. These documents serve two purposes: They enable you to reexamine your field experiences when you write up your project, and they may be included in the final form your project takes because they are accurate records of performances, interviews, and observations. On the other hand, field equipment presents certain difficulties: It costs money, you need to know how to work it properly, and you may have to resist the temptation to spend much of your time fiddling with your gear when you should be watching, thinking, and listening instead.

Fifty years ago, fieldworkers relied primarily on note-taking, and today it is still necessary. No matter how sophisticated your gear is, you should carry a small pocket notebook. It will be useful for writing down names and addresses, directions, observations, and thoughts while in the field. In the days before sound recording, music was taken by dictation in notebooks. While this is still possible, it is not advisable except when performances are very brief and you have the required dictation skills. Dictating a song puts the performer in an unnatural context and changes the performance. However, notebooks are especially useful for preserving information learned in interviews, particularly if a recording machine is unavailable or awkward in the interview situation. In addition, you should try to write down your detailed impressions of the overall field situation: (1) your plans, questions, any difficulties you meet with; (2) as complete a description as possible of the musical situation itself, including the setting, the performers, the audience, and the musical event from start to finish; and (3) your reactions and responses to the field experience. Your field notebook becomes a journal (and in some instances also a diary) that you address to yourself for use when you write up your project. As such, writing in it daily is useful.

Most university music departments and many university libraries now loan inexpensive portable recorders to students for use in fieldwork projects. Whether you use a recorder, and if so what type it is (microcassette, portable cassette, minidisc, CD, DAT, flash, and so forth), largely depends on the nature of your project and your instructor's expectations. Although they may be adequate for some interview situations, microcassette recorders do not record music well enough for documentation purposes. The inexpensive, portable, full-sized cassette tape recorders are well suited to recording speech (interviews, for example). Although they come with built-in microphones, the sound quality can be improved dramatically if you use an inexpensive external microphone plugged into the recorder's microphone input jack. So equipped, a portable cassette tape recorder may be adequate for recording music. Of course you need to be thoroughly familiar with its operation—*before* you go into the field—in order to make accurate recordings. But the portable cassette recorder is mechanically simple, and anyone can learn to operate it in just a few minutes. Digital minidisc, DAT, and flash card recorders can make higher quality recordings. One thing to remember about cassette tape is that it does not age well. The useful life of a cassette tape may be as short as ten years, while a DAT or videotape may not last longer than five, depending on storage conditions. Digitized and stored on a hard drive, CD-R, or DVD, an analog tape recording can have a longer archival life. Original digital recordings can be directly uploaded into a computer.

The best way for beginners to improve the sound of a recording is to place the microphone in a good spot. If the sound is soft or moderate and it comes from a small area (a solo singer, a lesson on a musical instrument, or an interview, for example), place the microphone close to the sounds and in the middle of them. If the sounds are loud and spread out (a rock band or a symphony orchestra, for example), search out "the best seat in the house" and place or hold the microphone there. Make a practice recording for a few seconds and play it back immediately to check microphone placement and to make certain the equipment is working properly (Figure 11.11). Take along spare batteries and blank tapes.

If properly used, even the simplest cameras take adequate pictures of musical performances. A picture may not be worth a thousand words, but it goes a long way toward capturing the human impact of a musical event. A consumer-grade digital camera is especially useful because it allows you to see the photograph

James T. Koetting

FIGURE 11.11

A chief checks the quality of a recording of his musicians. Kasena-Nankani Traditional Area, Ghana.

immediately and correct mistakes (such as standing too far from the action) at once. Digital pictures have another advantage: You can give copies easily to the people you photograph. But an older SLR film camera with interchangeable lenses is a better value and can produce better pictures, particularly under difficult lighting conditions.

Using a video camcorder to document a musical event offers the advantage of sound combined with a moving picture. It may allow you to focus selectively on certain aspects of the musical event, such as dancers or particular musicians, so that they can be seen as well as heard in action. Video accompanying your project should be edited down to a manageable size, and it should reveal those aspects of the music-culture that are related directly to your topic. Video formats are changing rapidly, while the quality available at a particular price point keeps improving.

Americans are in love with technology, even technology to get away from technology (backpacking equipment, for example). If you already know a lot about recording and photography, and you own or can borrow high-quality equipment, by all means use it. Some of the photographs in this book and the accompanying recordings were made by the authors using professional equipment; after all, fieldwork is a part of our profession. But the more sophisticated our equipment is, the more difficult it is to use it to its full potential. Consider the true story of a photographer who went to a rock music festival and brought only his pocket camera. In the photographer's pit in front of the stage, he had maneuvered himself into the best position and was standing there taking pictures when a professional nudged him, saying, "Get out of here with that little toy!" The pro stood there with cameras hanging from his neck and shoulders, covering his body like baby opossums. "Well," said the amateur, yielding his position with a smile, "I guess if you need all of that equipment, you need to stand in the best spot, too!"

INTERVIEWING

Interviews with people whose music you are studying can help you get basic information and feedback on your own ideas. Ethnomusicologists used to call such people *informants* but today they are often called *consultants*. Be careful not to put words in your consultants' mouths and impose your ideas. The first step in understanding a world of music is to understand it as much as possible in your consultants' own terms. Later you can bring your own perspective to bear on the musical situation. Remember that much of their knowledge is intuitive; you will have to draw it out by asking questions. Observe the relationships among the musicians in the music-culture you are documenting and interpreting (Figure 11.12). This will help you formulate questions for interviews.

Come into an interview with a list of questions, but be prepared to let the talk flow in the direction your consultant takes it. In his 1957 preface to *Primitive Man as Philosopher*, Paul Radin distinguished between two procedures for obtaining information: question-and-answer and "letting the native philosopher expound his ideas with as few interruptions as possible" ([1927] 1957). Your consultants may not be philosophers, but they should be given the chance to say what they mean. Some people are by nature talkative, but others need to be put at ease. Let the person know in advance what sorts of questions you will be asking, what kind of information you need, and why.

FIGURE 11.12

Erica Brown performs the traditional Franco-American music of her family and community with her teacher, Don Roy. She is also the leader of a bluegrass band. American Folk Festival, Bangor, Maine, 2005.

Often you will get important information in casual conversations rather than formal interviews; be ready to write down the information in your field notebook. For example, you may be able to gather information informally by listening to conversations that musicians have in the normal course of their music-making activities. Some people are by nature silent and guarded; despite your best intentions, they will not really open up to you. If you encounter that sort of person, respect his or her wishes and keep the interview brief.

Beginning fieldworkers commonly make two mistakes when doing interviews. First, they worry too much about the tape recorder, and their nervousness can carry over to the person they interview. But if you have already gotten the person's consent to be interviewed, then getting permission to tape the interview should not be hard. One fieldworker always carries her tape recorder and camera so they are visible from the moment she enters the door. Then she nonchalantly sets the tape recorder down in a prominent spot and ignores it, letting the person being interviewed understand that the tape recorder is a natural and normal part of the interview. Still ignoring the recorder, she starts off with the small talk that usually begins such a visit. Eventually the other person says something like, "Oh, I see you're going to tape-record this." "Sure," she says steadily. "I brought along this tape recorder just to make sure I get down everything you say. I can always edit out any mistakes, and you can always change your mind. This is just to help me understand you better the first time." She says that once they have agreed to be interviewed, nobody has ever refused her tape recorder. But she adds that if anyone told her to keep the recorder shut off, she would certainly do so.

A second problem is that beginning fieldworkers often ask leading questions. A *leading question* is one that suggests or implies (that is, it leads or points to) one particular answer. Leading questions make the information obtained unreliable. In other words, it is not clear whether the person being interviewed is expressing his or her own thoughts or just being agreeable and giving the answer the consultant thinks the interviewer wants. In addition, leading questions usually result in short, uninteresting answers. Study this first dialogue to see how *not* to interview:

FIELDWORKER 1:   Did you get your first flute when you were a girl?

CONSULTANT: Yeah.

FIELDWORKER 1:   What was the name of your teacher?

CONSULTANT: Ah, I studied with Janice Sullivan.

FIELDWORKER 1:   When was that?

CONSULTANT: In college.

FIELDWORKER 1:   I'll bet you hated the flute when you first started. I can remember hating my first piano lessons.

CONSULTANT: Yeah.

The trouble here is that the consultant gives the kinds of answers she thinks are expected of her. She is just agreeing and not necessarily telling the fieldworker what she thinks. She is not even giving the conversation much thought. The fieldworker has asked the wrong kind of questions. Now look what happens when another fieldworker questions the same person.

FIELDWORKER 2:   Can you remember when you got your first flute?

CONSULTANT: Yeah.

FIELDWORKER 2:   Could you tell me about it?

CONSULTANT: Sure. My first flute—well, I don't know if this counts, but I fell in love with the flute when I was in grade school, and I remember going down to a music store and trying one out while my father looked on, but I couldn't make a sound, you know!

FIELDWORKER 2:   Sure.

CONSULTANT: So I was really disappointed, but then I remember learning to play the recorder in, I think it was third grade, and I really loved that, but I didn't stick with it. Then in college I said to myself, I'm going to take music lessons and I'm going to learn the flute.

FIELDWORKER 2:   Tell me about that.

CONSULTANT: Well, I had this great teacher, Janice Sullivan, and first she taught me how to get a sound out of it. I was really frustrated at first, but after a while I got the hang of it, and she would always tell me to think of the beautiful sounds I knew a flute could make. I used to think a flute could make a sound like water, like the wind. Well, not exactly, but sort of. And then Mrs. Sullivan let me borrow a tape of *shakuhachi* music—you know, the Japanese flute?— and I heard different kinds of water, different kinds of wind! I knew then that I would play the flute for the rest of my life.

Compare the two fieldworkers' questions: "Did you get your first flute when you were a girl?" is a leading question because it leads to the answer, "Yes, I got my first flute when I was a girl." What is more, fieldworker 1 implies that most people get their first flutes when they are girls, so the consultant probably thinks she should answer yes. By contrast, the question of fieldworker 2—"Can you remember when you got your first flute?"—is open-ended and invites reflection, perhaps a story. When the consultant says "Yeah," fieldworker 2 asks for a story and gets a much better—and different—answer than fieldworker 1. Go over the rest of the first interview, see how fieldworker 1 injects her opinions into the dialogue ("I'll bet you hated the flute when you first started") and fails to draw out the consultant's real feelings about her lessons, whereas fieldworker 2 establishes better rapport, is a better listener, asks nondirective questions, and gets much fuller and truer answers.

If your project concentrates on a single consultant, you may want to obtain his or her life story (Titon 1980). For this purpose you truly need a recorder to get the story accurately. Because the way your consultants view their lives can be as important as the factual information they give, you should try to get the life story in their own words as much as possible. This means refraining from questions that direct the story as you think it should go. What matters is how your consultant wants it to go. Come back later, in another interview, to draw out specific facts and fill in gaps by direct questioning. In the initial interview, begin by explaining that you would like your consultant to tell you about his or her life as a musician (or whatever is appropriate—composer, disc jockey, and so forth) from the beginning until now. Once begun, allow plenty of time for silences to let your consultant gather thoughts. If he or she looks up at you expectantly, nod your head in agreement and repeat what has just been said to show that you understand it. Resist any impulse to ask direct questions. Write them down instead, and say you will come back to ask questions later—for now you want the story to continue.

Not everyone will be able to tell you his or her musical autobiography, but if you are fortunate enough to find someone who can, it may turn out to be the most important part of your project. On the other hand, if your consultant's life story is a necessary part of your project, but you cannot obtain it except by direct and frequent questioning, you should certainly ask the questions. If you get good answers, the result will be your consultant's life history, a collaborative biography rather than an autobiography.

Interviews, then, with the people whose music you are studying (and perhaps with their audience) help you obtain factual information and test your ideas. They also help you begin to comprehend the musical situation from their point of view: their beliefs, their intentions, their training, their feelings, their evaluations of musical performance, and their understanding of what they are doing—what it is all about. Ultimately, because this is your project, you will combine their ideas with your own interpretations when you write the project up using the information you have collected.

OTHER MEANS OF COLLECTING INFORMATION

Another technique, often used in social science research, is the questionnaire. Although its role in studying music is limited, and it should never be substituted for interviewing, a questionnaire can help you map out the general nature of a situation before moving into a specific subarea to focus on. For example, to begin exploring the meaning of pop songs in students' lives, you may want to circulate a questionnaire to uncover the eventual sample you will study intensively. Questionnaires are most at home in studies of musical attitudes. To find out how shoppers react to supermarket background music, it would be hard to set up interviews but easy, if the store manager agrees, to distribute a questionnaire.

Aside from questionnaires, which seek out information, you might find information already gathered: autobiographical manuscripts, diaries, photos, and recordings made by consultants for themselves. Clubs, fraternities, schools, churches, and various organizations often store away old materials that shed light on musical activities. At concerts, the programs handed out may be rich in information, ranging from descriptions of the music to the type of advertisers that support the concerts. Membership lists and patrons' lists may be included as well.

Newspapers are enormously helpful. Hardly a day passes without journalistic commentary on the musical environment, in news stories, reviews, and advertisements. Feature stories provide up-to-date information on current concerts, trends, and musical attitudes, both local and national, while advertising can furnish insights into the ideals of the U.S. musical world projected by the media, ideals that influence most of us one way or another.

FINISHING THE PROJECT

As you do all the hard work of organizing and collecting information, always think ahead to what you will do with it. As you go along, return to the list of questions you formulated in relation to your topic—the questions you wanted to ask about the musical situation. You also will have formulated more questions during your fieldwork and other research. These questions and the information you have gathered are related, and they offer a natural organization for your project around your main idea, the answer to the question posed by your topic. Remember that the point of your project is to document some aspect of a nearby music-culture and to interpret it based on the topic you have chosen. More-specific advice on how to write it up and what form to present it in will be available from your instructor. He or she may ask you to write a preliminary proposal describing your subject and a topic phrased as a thematic question; then, after you have been immersed in your fieldwork for a week or two, you may need to write a final proposal describing both your subject and your refined topic. Feedback on these proposals, from your instructor and, possibly, from other students, will be helpful; they may know some things that will help your field research go better, or they may have some good suggestions for questions to ask of the music-culture you are documenting and interpreting.

If you need to clear up research questions, check back with your consultants. As you interview, collect information, and think about the musical situation you study, new questions always will occur to you. It is no different when you write up your project; you will probably find it helpful to get back in touch with your consultants and ask a few final questions. Thus, unlike some term papers, a fieldwork project is built up and accomplished gradually over at least several weeks' time, not quickly at the end of the term.

You are not the only one affected by your finished project. Your work reflects other people's feelings and, on occasion, their social position. Be clear in what you say about the people you worked with. Confidentiality may be important; if people asked you not to use their names or repeat what they said to you, respect their wishes. As is customary in many anthropological works, you may decide to change names of people or places to make certain no one is identified who does not want to be. Imagine the problems created for the member of a band who criticizes the leader if word gets back to the group, or for a school music teacher if he criticizes the school board to you in private and you quote him.

The authors of this book intend, as the Preface put it, that our readers experience "what it is like to be an ethnomusicologist puzzling out his or her way toward understanding an unfamiliar music." A good field project inevitably provides just that experience and makes an original contribution to knowledge. Valuable and enjoyable in and of itself, discovery, documentation, and interpretation of a world of music takes on added significance, because even the smallest project illuminates our understanding of music as human expression.

Book Companion Website

You will find tutorial quizzes, Internet links, and much more at the Book Companion Website for *Worlds of Music,* Fifth Edition, at **academic.cengage.com/music/titon/worlds_5**

References

Chapter 1 – The Music-Culture as a World of Music

REFERENCES

Blacking, John. 1973. *How Musical Is Man?* Seattle: Univ. of Washington Press.
Feld, Steven. 1990. *Sound and Sentiment: Birds, Weeping, Poetics and Song in Kaluili Expression.* 2nd ed. Philadelphia: Univ. of Pennsylvania Press.
Krause, Bernie. 2002. *Wild Soundscapes.* Berkeley, CA: Wilderness Press.
Merriam, Alan P. 1964. *The Anthropology of Music.* Evanston, IL: Northwestern Univ. Press.
Olajubu, Chief Oludare. 1978. "Yoruba Verbal Artists and Their Work." *Journal of American Folklore* 91:675–90.
Pantaleoni, Hewitt. 1985. *On the Nature of Music.* Oneonta, NY: Wellkin Books.
Sachs, Nahoma. 1975. "Music and Meaning: Musical Symbolism in a Macedonian Village." Ph.D. diss., Princeton Univ.
Schafer, R. Murray. 1980. *The Tuning of the World: Toward a Theory of Soundscape Design.* Philadelphia: Univ. of Pennsylvania Press.
Titon, Jeff Todd. 1988. *Powerhouse for God: Speech, Chant, and Song in an Appalachian Baptist Church.* Austin: Univ. of Texas Press.
———, ed. 1992. *Worlds of Music.* 2nd ed. New York: Schirmer Books.

ADDITIONAL READING

Barz, Gregory, and Timothy J. Cooley. 1997. *Shadows in the Field.* New York: Oxford Univ. Press.
Bohlman, Philip. 2002. *World Music: A Very Short Introduction.* New York: Oxford Univ. Press.
Crafts, Susan D., Daniel Cavicchi, Charles Keil, and the Music in Daily Life Project, 1993. *My Music.* Hanover, NH: Univ. Press of New England.
Myers, Helen, ed. 1992. *Ethnomusicology: An Introduction.* New York: Norton.
———. 1993. *Ethnomusicology: Historical and Regional Studies.* New York: Norton.
Nettl, Bruno. 1995. *Heartland Excursions: Ethnomusicological Reflections on Schools of Music.* Urbana: Univ. of Illinois Press.
———. 2005. *The Study of Ethnomusicology.* Urbana: Univ. of Illinois Press.
Reck, David. 1997. *Music of the Whole Earth.* New York: Da Capo.

Chapter 2 – North America/Native America

REFERENCES

Begay, Danny Whitefeather, Cindy Yazzie, and Roger McCabe. *My Beautiful Land.* Phoenix, AZ: Canyon Records ARP-6078.

Burch, Sharon. 1989. *Yazzie Girl.* Phoenix, AZ: Canyon Records CR534. Cassette.

Farella, John R. 1984. *The Main Stalk: A Synthesis of Navajo Philosophy.* Tucson: Univ. of Arizona Press.

Faris, James C. 1990. *The Nightway: A History and a History of Documentation of a Navajo Ceremonial.* Albuquerque: Univ. of New Mexico Press.

Fenton, William. 1942. *Songs from the Iroquois Longhouse.* Washington, DC: Smithsonian Institution Publication 369.

———. n.d. *Songs from the Iroquois Longhouse.* Library of Congress AFS L6.

Frisbie, Charlotte J., and David P. McAllester. 1978. *Navajo Blessingway Singer: Frank Mitchell, 1881–1967.* Tucson: Univ. of Arizona Press.

Griffin-Pierce, Trudy. 1992. *Earth Is My Mother, Sky Is My Father: Space, Time, and Astronomy in Navajo Sandpainting.* Albuquerque: Univ. of New Mexico Press.

Haile, Berard. 1938. *Origin Legend of the Navajo Enemy Way.* New Haven, CT: Yale Univ. Press.

———. 1947. *Prayerstick Cutting in a Five Night Ceremonial of the Male Branch of Shootingway.* Chicago: Univ. of Chicago Press.

Kluckhohn, Clyde, and Dorothea Leighton. 1938. *The Navajo.* Cambridge, MA: Harvard Univ. Press.

Kluckhohn, Clyde, and Leland C. Wyman. 1940. *An Introduction to Navajo Chant Practice.* Menasha, WI: Memoirs of the American Anthropological Association, no. 53.

Matthews, Washington. 1894. "Songs of Sequence of the Navajos." *Journal of American Folk-Lore* 7:185–94.

McAllester, David P. 1949. *Peyote Music.* New York: Viking Fund Publications in Antropology, no. 13.

———. 1954. *Enemy Way Music.* Papers of the Peabody Museum of Archaeology and Ethnology, vol. 41, no. 5. Cambridge, MA: Harvard Univ. Press.

———. 1994. "The Music of R. Carlos Nakai." In *To the Four Corners: A Festschrift in Honor of Rose Brandel,* edited by Ellen C. Leichtman. Warren, MI: Harmonie Park Press.

McNeley, James K. 1981. *Holy Wind in Navajo Philosophy.* Tucson: Univ. of Arizona Press.

Nakai, R. Carlos. 1985. *Cycles: Native American Flute Music.* Phoenix, AZ: Canyon Records Productions CR614-C. Cassette.

———. 1994. *Ancestral Voices.* Phoenix, AZ: Canyon Records CR-7010. CD, cassette.

Reichard, Gladys A. 1928. *Social Life of the Navajo Indians.* New York: Columbia Univ. Press.

———. 1950. *Navajo Religion.* New York: Bollingen Foundation.

Sachs, Curt. 1962. *The Wellsprings of Music.* The Hague: Martinus Nijhof.

Smythe, Willie. 1989. "Songs of Indian Territory." In *Songs of Indian Territory: Native American Music Traditions of Oklahoma.* Oklahoma City, OK: Center for the American Indian.

Williams, Arliene Nofchissey. 1989. *Encircle . . . in the Arms of His Love.* Composed and performed by Arliene Nofchissey Williams, featuring flutist John Rainer, Jr. Blanding, UT: Proud Earth Productions PE-90. Cassette.

Witherspoon, Gary. 1977. *Language and Art in the Navajo Universe.* Ann Arbor: Univ. of Michigan Press.

Witmer, Robert. 1973. "Recent Change in the Musical Culture of the Blood Indians of Alberta, Canada." *Yearbook for Inter-American Musical Research* 9:64–94.

Wyman, Leland C. 1983. *Southwest Indian Drypainting.* Albuquerque: Univ. of New Mexico Press.

ADDITIONAL READING

Bailey, Garrick, and Roberta Glenn Bailey. 1986. *A History of the Navajos: The Reservation Years.* Santa Fe, NM: School of American Research Press.

Deloria, Vine, Jr. 1969. *Custer Died for Your Sins: An Indian Manifesto.* London: Collier-Macmillan.

Gill, Sam D. 1981. *Sacred Words: A Study of Navajo Religion and Prayer.* Westport, CT: Greenwood Press.

Goodman, James B. 1986. *The Navajo Atlas: Environments, Resources, People, and the History of the Diné Bikeyah.* Norman: Univ. of Oklahoma Press.

Hadley, Linda. 1986. *Hózhǫ́ǫ́jí Hané (Blessingway)*. Rough Rock, AZ: Rough Rock Demonstration School. [In English and Navajo]

McAllester, David and Susan. 1980. *Hogans: Navajo Houses and House Songs*. Wesleyan, CT: Wesleyan Univ. Press.

McCullough-Brabson, Ellen, and Marilyn Help. 2001. *We'll Be in Your Mountains, We'll Be in Your Songs: A Navajo Woman Sings*. Albuquerque: Univ. of New Mexico Press.

Nakai, R. Carlos, James Demars, David P. McAllester, and Ken Light. 1997. *The Art of the Native American Flute*. Pacific, MO: Mel Bay Publications.

ADDITIONAL LISTENING

Anilth, Wilson, and Hanson Ashley. 1981. *Navajo Peyote Ceremonial Songs*. Vol. 1. Taos, NM: Indian House 1541. LP.

Boulton, Laura. 1992. *Navajo Songs*. Recorded by Laura Boulton in 1933 and 1940. Annotated by Charlotte Frisbie and David McAllester. Washington, DC: Smithsonian/Folkways, SF 40403. CD, cassette.

Burton, Bryan. 1993. *Moving Within the Circle: Contemporary Native American Music and Dance*. Danbury, CT: World Music Press. WMP 012. Cassette.

The Chinle Galileans. n.d. *Navajo Country Gospel*. Larry Emerson, Jerry Tom, Roland Dixon, Donnie Tsosie, Lee Begaye, Emerson Luther. Chinle, AZ: LPS 9039. LP.

DeMars, James. 1991. *Spirit Horses, Concerto for Native American Flute and Chamber Orchestra*. Composed for and performed by R. Carlos Nakai. Phoenix, AZ: Canyon Records Productions CR-7014. CD, cassette.

The Fenders. 1966. *Second Time Roun'*. Thoreau, NM. LP. recording. Patrick Hutchinson made a careful study of "Folsom Prison Blues," noting interesting textual and rhythmic elisions and complications not found in the original Johnny Cash recording. These are similar to alterations noted by Robert Witmer in popular music performed by Blood Indians in Canada (1973:79–83).

Rhodes, Willard. 1949. *Music of the Sioux and the Navajo*. Washington, DC: Smithsonian/Folkways 4401. LP. With 6-page pamphlet.

———, ed. n.d. *Navajo: Folk Music of the United States*. Washington, DC: Library of Congress, Division of Music, Archive of American Folk Song AFS L41.

———. n.d. *Puget Sound: Folk Music of the United States*. Washington, DC: Library of Congress, Division of Music, Archive of American Folk Song AAFS L34. With 36-page booklet on Northwest Coast culture (Erna Gunther) and music (Willard Rhodes).

Smith Family Gospel Singers. 1987. *Touching Jesus*. Vol. 2. Phoenix, AZ: Canyon Records 620. Cassette.

Songs from the Navajo Nation. n.d. Recorded by Kay Bennet (Kaibah). Gallup, NM: K. C. Bennet (producer). LP.

Williams, Arliene Nofchissey. 1989. *Encircle . . . in the Arms of His Love*. Composed and performed by Arliene Nofchissey Williams, featuring flutist John Rainer, Jr. Blanding, UT: Proud Earth Productions PE-90. Cassette.

———. *Proud Earth*. n.d. Performed by Chief Dan George, Arliene Nofchissey Williams, Rick Brosseau. Provo, UT: Salt City Records SC-60. LP.

MAJOR SOURCES FOR RECORDINGS

Canyon Records Productions, 3131 W. Clarendon Ave. Phoenix, AZ 85017-4513; (800) 268-1141. http://www.canyonrecords.com

This is the main distributor of Native-American recordings. It not only stocks the large inventory under its own label but also keeps in print many of the recordings of smaller distributors, some of which might otherwise have gone out of business. It carries recordings of traditional music and also newer genres such as Indian rock, gospel, and country and western.

Indian House, Box 472, Taos, NM 87571; (505) 776-2953. http://www.indianhouse.com

This company specializes in traditional Indian music and typically devotes an entire recording to one genre such as Taos Round Dance songs or Navajo Yeibichai songs. The abundant examples and the excellent notes make these recordings valuable for scholars as well as other interested listeners.

Library of Congress. Archive of Folk Culture, Motion Picture, Broadcast, and Recorded Sound Division, Library of Congress, Washington, DC 20540; (202) 707-7833. http://www.loc.gov/folklife/rec.html

This collection includes the Willard Rhodes recordings of Native-American music: excellent recordings and notes from all across the country.

Smithsonian/Folkways. The Folkways Collection, Smithsonian Institution, Washington, DC 20560; (202) 287-3262. http://www.folkways.si.edu/index.html

The inventory of the Ethnic Folkways Records and Service Corp., formerly of New York City, has been preserved at the Smithsonian Institution and new recordings on a joint label are being produced. Their holdings include many early recordings of Native American music.

INTERNET RESOURCES

Omaha Indian Music, a website maintained by the Library of Congress, featuring music from the 1890s and 1980s http://lcweb2.loc.gov/ammem/omhhtml/omhhome.html

Index of Native American Musical Resources on the Internet http://www.hanksville.org/NAresources/indices/NAmusic.html

Directory of sites on Native American music, languages, powwows, art http://www.georgiejessup.com/links3.htm

Native American music and arts: organizations and individuals http://www.nativeculturelinks.com/music.html

Native American Radio has five streams playing Native American music twenty-four hours a day. They have one of the largest online archives of digitized Native American music in the world. Search for music by Artist, Album, Label, or Song Title. http://www.nativeradio.com/

Chapter 3 – Africa/Ewe, Mande, Dagbamba, Shona, BaAka

REFERENCES

Amoaku, W. Komla. 1985. "Toward a Definition of Traditional African Music: A Look at the Ewe of Ghana." In *More Than Drumming*, edited by Irene Jackson, 31–40. Westport, CT: Greenwood Press.

Appiah, Anthony. 1992. *In My Father's House*. Cambridge, MA: Harvard Univ. Press.

Arom, Simha. 1987. *Centrafrique: Anthologie de la Musique des Pygmees Aka*. Ocora CD559012 13.

———. 1991. *African Polyphony and Polyrhythm*. Cambridge: Cambridge Univ. Press.

Asante, Molefi. 1987. *The Afrocentric Idea*. Philadelphia: Temple Univ. Press.

Bebey, Francis. 1975. *African Music: A People's Art*. Translated by Josephine Bennet. New York: Lawrence Hill.

Bender, Wolfgang. 1991. *Sweet Mother: Modern African Music*. Chicago: Univ. of Chicago Press.

Berliner, Paul. 1993. *The Soul of Mbira*. Rev. ed. Berkeley: Univ. of California Press.

Bohannan, Paul, and Phillip Curtin. 1995. *Africa and Africans*. 4th ed. Prospect Heights, IL: Waveland Press.

Breasted, J. H. 1906. *Ancient Records of Egypt*. Chicago: Univ. of Chicago Press.

Charry, Eric. 1994. "West African Harps." *Journal of the American Musical Instrument Society* 20:5–53.

———. 2000. *Mande Music: Traditional and Modern Music of the Maninka and Mandinka of Western Africa*. Chicago: Univ. of Chicago Press.

Chernoff, John. 1979. *African Rhythm and African Sensibility*. Chicago: Univ. of Chicago Press.

Davidson, Basil. 1991. *African Civilization Revisited: From Antiquity to Modern Times*. Trenton, NJ: Africa Word Press.

Davis, Art. 1994. "Midawo Gideon Foli Alorwoyie: The Life and Music of a West African Drummer." M.A. thesis, Univ. of Illinois–Urbana-Champaign.

DeVale, Sue Carole. 1989. "African Harps: Construction, Decoration, and Sound." In *Sounding Forms: African Musical Instruments*, edited by Marie-Therese Brincard, 53–61. New York: American Federation of Arts.

Dieterlen, Germaine. 1957. "The Mande Creation Myth." In *Peoples and Cultures of Africa*, edited by Eliot Skinner. Garden City, NY: Doubleday.

Djedje, Jacqueline. 1978. "The One-String Fiddle in West Africa." Ph.D. diss., Univ. of California–Los Angeles.

Eyre, Banning. 1988. "New Sounds from Africa." *Guitar Player* (October): 80–88.

———. 1991. "On the Road with Thomas Mapfumo." *The Beat* 10(6): 48–53, 78.

Fiawo, D. K. 1959. "The Influence of the Contemporary Social Changes on the Magico-Religious Concepts and Organization of the Southern Ewe-Speaking People of Ghana." Ph.D. diss., Univ. of Edinburgh.

Frye, Peter. 1976. *Spirits of Protest.* Cambridge: Cambridge Univ. Press.

Innes, Gordon. 1976. *Kaabu and Fuladu: Historical Narratives of the Gambian Mandinka.* London: School of Oriental and African Studies, Univ. of London.

Jackson, Bruce. 1972. *Wake up Dead Man: Afro-American Worksongs from Texas Prisons.* Cambridge, MA: Harvard Univ. Press.

Jones, A. M. 1959. *Studies in African Music.* London: Oxford Univ. Press.

Kisliuk, Michelle. 1991. "Confronting the Quintessential: Singing, Dancing, and Everyday Life Among the Biaka Pygmies (Central African Republic)." Ph.D. diss., New York Univ.

———. 1998. *"Seize the Dance!": BaAka Music Life and the Ethnography of Performance.* New York: Oxford Univ. Press.

Knight, Roderic. 1971. "Towards a Notation and Tablature for the Kora." *African Music* 5(1): 23–36.

———. 1972. "Kora Manding: Mandinka Music of the Gambia." Sound recording and booklet. Tucson, AZ: Ethnodisc ER 12102.

———. 1984. "Music in Africa: The Manding Contexts." In Gerard Behague, ed., *Performance Practice.* Westport, CT: Greenwood Press.

Koetting, James. 1992. "Africa/Ghana." In *Worlds of Music.* 2nd ed. New York: Schirmer.

Kubik, Gerhard. 1962. "The Phenomenon of Inherent Rhythms in East and Central African Instrumental Music." *African Music* 3(1): 33–42.

Ladzekpo, Kobla. 1971. "The Social Mechanics of Good Music: A Description of Dance Clubs Among the Anlo Ewe-Speaking People of Ghana." *African Music* 5(1):6–22.

Lan, David. 1985. *Guns and Rain.* Berkeley: Univ. of California Press.

Laye, Camara. 1983. *The Guardian of the Word.* Translated by James Kirby. New York: Vintage Books.

Locke, David. 1978. "The Music of *Atsiagbekor*." Ph.D. diss., Wesleyan Univ.

———. 1982. "Principles of Offbeat Timing and Cross-Rhythm in Southern Eve Dance Drumming." *Ethnomusicology* 26(2): 217–46.

———. 1983. "*Atsiagbekor*: The Polyrhythmic Texture." *Sonus* 4(1): 16–38.

———. 1988. *Drum Gahu.* Tempe, AZ: White Cliffs Media.

———. 1990. *Drum Damba.* Tempe, AZ: White Cliffs Media.

———. 1992. *Kpegisu: A War Drum of the Ewe.* Tempe, AZ: White Cliffs Media.

Mallows, A. J. 1967. *An Introduction to the History of Central Africa.* London: Oxford Univ. Press.

Maraire, Dumisani. 1971. *The Mbira Music of Rhodesia.* Booklet and record. Seattle: Univ. of Washington Press.

Miller, Christopher. 1990. *Theories of Africans.* Chicago: Univ. of Chicago Press.

Mphahlele, Ezekiel. 1962. *The African Image.* London: Faber and Faber.

Nketia, J. H. Kwabena. 1964. *Continuity of Traditional Instruction.* Legon, Ghana: Institute of African Studies.

Nukunya, G. K. 1969. *Kinship and Marriage Among the Anlo Ewe.* London: Athlone Press.

Quinn, Charlotte. 1972. *Mandingo Kingdoms of the Senegambia.* Evanston, IL: Northwestern Univ. Press.

Saad, Elias. 1983. *Social History of Timbuktu: The Role of Muslim Scholars and Notables.* Cambridge: Cambridge Univ. Press.

Senghor, Leopold Sedar. 1967. *The Foundations of "Africanite" or "Negritude" and "Arabite."* Translated by Mercer Cook. Paris: Presence Africaine.

Skinner, Eliot, ed. 1973. *Peoples and Cultures of Africa.* Garden City, NY: Doubleday.

Thompson, Robert F. 1973. "An Aesthetic of the Cool." *African Arts* 7(1): 40–43, 64–67, 89.

Tracey, Andrew. 1970. *How to Play the Mbira (Dza Vadzimu).* Roodepoort, Transvaal: International Library of African Music.

Turnbull, Colin. 1961. *The Forest People.* New York: Simon & Schuster.

———. 1983. *The Mbuti Pygmies: Change and Adaptation.* New York: Holt, Rinehart, & Winston.

Waterman, Christopher. 1990. "Our Tradition Is a Modern Tradition." *Ethnomusicology* 34(3): 367–80.

Zantzinger, Gei. n.d. "Mbira: Mbira dza Vadzimu: Religion at the Family Level." Film. Available from University Museum, Univ. of Pennsylvania.

ADDITIONAL READING

Agawu, Kofi. 1995. *African Music: A Northern Ewe Perspective.* Cambridge: Cambridge Univ. Press.

Berliner, Paul. 2006. "Grasping Shona Musical Works: A Case Study of Mbira Music." In *Art from Start to Finish,* edited by Howard S. Becker, Robert R. Faulkner, and Barbara Kirshenblatt-Gimblett, 126–34. Chicago: Univ. of Chicago Press.

Brincard, Marie-Therese, ed. 1989. *Sounding Forms: African Musical Instruments.* New York: American Federation of Arts.
Collins, John. 1992. *West African Pop Roots.* Philadelphia: Temple Univ. Press.
Jackson, Irene, ed. 1985. *More Than Drumming.* Westport, CT: Greenwood Press.
Knight, Roderic. 1991. "Music out of Africa: Mande Jaliya in Paris." *World of Music* 33(1): 52–69.
Nketia, J. H. Kwabena. 1974. *The Music of Africa.* New York: Norton.
Nzewi, Meki. 1991. *Musical Practice and Creativity.* Bayreuth, Germany: IWALEWA-Haus, Univ. of Bayreuth.
Stone, Ruth. 2000. *Garland Handbook of African Music.* New York: Garland.

ADDITIONAL LISTENING

Berliner, Paul. 1995. *Zimbabwe: The Soul of Mbira.* Nonesuch Explorer Series 9 72054-2.
Chernoff, John. 1990. *Master Drummers of Dagbon.* Vol. 2. Rounder CD 5406.
Knight, Roderic. 1996. *Gambie. L'Art de la kora: Jali Nyama Suso.* Ocora C580027 (rerelease of 1972 OCR 70).
Locke, David. n.d. *Drum Gahu: Good-Time Drumming from the Ewe People of Ghana and Togo.* White Cliffs Media WCM 9494.
Lunna, Abubakari. 1996. *Drum Damba featuring Abubakari Lunna, a Master Drummer of Dagbon.* White Cliffs Media WCM 9508.

ADDITIONAL VIEWING

Knight, Roderic. 2006. *Mande Music and Dance.* Lyrichord UPC 744457200124. DVD.
Konkombe: Nigerian Music. n.d. Produced and directed by Jeremy Marre. Harcourt Films.
The Language You Cry In. 1998. Directed and produced by Alvaro Toepke and Angel Serrano. Inko Producciones. San Francisco: California Newsreel.
Mbira Dza Vadzimu Urban and Rural Ceremonies with Hakurotwi Mude. 1978. Devault, PA: Constant Spring Productions.
Music and Culture of West Africa: The Straus Expedition. 2002. Gloria J. Gibson and Daniel B. Reed. Indianapolis: Indiana Univ. Press. CD-ROM.
A Performance of Kpegisu by the Wodome-Akatsi Kpegisu Habobo. 1990. Produced by David Locke. Boston: Educational Media Center, Tufts Univ.
Rhythm of Resistance: The Black Music of South Africa. 1988. Directed by Chris Austin and Jeremy Marre. Produced by Jeremy Marre. Harcourt Films/Shanachie Records.

INTERNET RESOURCES

African Music Encyclopedia http://www.africanmusic.org
African Music on RootsWorld http://www.rootsworld.com/rw/africa.html
Afropop Worldwide http://www.afropop.org
allAfrica.com: Music: Newsfeed source for news and reports on music in Africa http://allafrica.com/music/
Cora Connection http://www.coraconnection.com/
The International Library of African Music http://www.ilam.ru.ac.za
Stern's Music http://www.sternsmusic.com/
Yahoo! Groups: african_music; mailing list established in 1995 http://groups.yahoo.com/group/african_music/

Chapter 4 – North America/Black America

REFERENCES

Brooks, Cleanth, R. W. B. Lewis, and Robert Penn Warren. 1973. *American Literature: The Makers and the Making.* 2 vols. New York: St. Martin's Press.
Brunoghe, Yannick, ed. 1964. *Big Bill Blues.* New York: Oak.
Cantwell, Robert. 1984. *Bluegrass Breakdown.* Urbana: Univ. of Illinois Press.
Charters, Samuel. 1977. *The Legacy of the Blues.* New York: Da Capo.
Davis, Angela Y. 1999. *Blues Legacies and Black Feminism.* New York: Vintage Books.
Eliot, T. S. [1920] 1964. "Hamlet and His Problems." In *The Sacred Wood.* Reprint, New York: Barnes & Noble.

Evans, David. 1971. "Booker White." In *Nothing But the Blues*, edited by Mike Leadbetter. London: Hanover Books.

Fishel, John. 1981. "Magic Sam and the Ann Arbor Blues Festival." Liner notes to *Magic Sam Live*. Delmark DL-645/646.

Forte, Dan. 1991. "Otis Rush." In *Blues Guitar*, edited by Jas Obrecht, pp. 156–62. San Francisco: GPI Books.

Gordon, Robert. 2002. *Can't Be Satisfied: The Life and Times of Muddy Waters*. Boston: Little, Brown.

Grazian, David. 2003. *Blue Chicago: The Search for Authenticity in Urban Blues Clubs*. Chicago: Univ. of Chicago Press.

Groom, Bob. 1971. *The Blues Revival*. London: Studio Vista.

Gussow, Adam. 2002. *Seems Like Murder Here: Southern Violence and the Blues Tradition*. Chicago: Univ. of Chicago Press.

Herzhaft, Gerard. 1992. *Encyclopedia of the Blues*. Fayetteville: Univ. of Arkansas Press.

Jackson, Bruce. 1972. *Wake up Dead Man: Afro-American Worksongs from Texas State Prisons*. Cambridge, MA: Harvard Univ. Press.

Johnson, Charles S. [1934] 1966. *Shadow of the Plantation*. Reprint, Chicago: Univ. of Chicago Press.

Lomax, Alan. 1976. Brochure notes to *Negro Prison Songs from the Mississippi State Penitentiary*. Reissue of Tradition LP 1020 (see "Additional Listening"). Vogue Records VJD 515.

Lucas, William ("Lazy Bill"). 1974. *Lazy Bill Lucas*. Philo LP 1007.

McLeod, Norma, and Marcia Herndon. 1981. *Music as Culture*. 2nd ed. Darby, PA: Norwood Editions.

Obrecht, Jas. 2000. "Otis Rush." In *Rollin' and Tumblin': The Postwar Blues Guitarists*, edited by Jas Obrecht. San Francisco: Miller Freeman.

Oliver, Paul. 1965. *Conversation with the Blues*. London: Cassell.

———. 1998. *The Story of the Blues*. Boston: Northeastern Univ. Press.

Rowe, Mike. 1979. *Chicago Breakdown*. New York: Da Capo.

Santelli, Robert, and Holly George-Warren. 2002. *American Roots Music*. New York: Abrams.

Seeger, Charles. 1977. *Studies in Musicology, 1935–1975*. Berkeley: Univ. of California Press.

Segrest, James, and Mark Hoffman. 2004. *Moanin' at Midnight: The Life and Times of Howlin' Wolf*. New York: Pantheon.

Shurman, Dick. 1981. "Magic Sam: An Overview." Liner notes to *Magic Sam Live*. Delmark DL-645/646.

Tedlock, Dennis. 1977. "Toward an Oral Poetics." *New Literary History* 8, pp. 507–19.

Titon, Jeff Todd. 1969. "Calling All Cows: Lazy Bill Lucas" *Blues Unlimited*, no. 60, pp. 10–11; no. 61, pp. 9–10; no. 62, pp. 11–12; no. 63, pp. 9–10.

———. 1971. "Ethnomusicology of Downhome Blues Phonograph Records, 1926–1930." Ph.D. diss., Univ. of Minnesota.

———. 1974a. Brochure notes to *Lazy Bill Lucas*. North Ferrisburg, VT: Philo Records 1007.

———, ed. 1974b. *From Blues to Pop: The Autobiography of Leonard "Baby Doo" Caston*. Los Angeles: John Edwards Memorial Foundation.

———. 1994. *Early Downhome Blues: A Musical and Cultural Analysis*. 2nd ed. Chapel Hill: Univ. of North Carolina Press.

———. 2002. "Labels: Identifying Categories of Blues and Gospel." In Allan Moore, ed., *The Cambridge Companion to Blues and Gospel Music*. Cambridge: Cambridge Univ. Press.

Wilson, Al. 1966. "Robert Pete Williams: His Life and Music." *Little Sandy Review* 2, no. 1.

ADDITIONAL READING

Evans, David. 1982. *Big Road Blues*. Berkeley: Univ. of California Press.

Finn, Julio. 1992. *The Bluesman*. New York: Interlink.

Floyd, Samuel A. 1995. *The Power of Black Music*. New York: Oxford Univ. Press.

Franz, Steve. 1996. "The Life and Music of Magic Sam." *Living Blues*, no. 125, pp. 33–44.

Grissom, Mary Alle. [1930] 1969. *The Negro Sings a New Heaven*. Reprint, New York: Dover Books.

King, B. B., with Dave Ritz. 1996. *Blues All Around Me: The Autobiography of B. B. King*. New York: Avon.

Palmer, Robert. 1981. *Deep Blues*. New York: Viking Press.

Salvatore, Nick. 2005. *Singing in a Strange Land*. New York: Little, Brown. Biography of Rev. C. L. Franklin.

Taft, Michael. 2006. *The Blues Lyric Formula*. New York: Routledge.

Titon, Jeff Todd. 1990. *Downhome Blues Lyrics*. 2nd ed. Urbana: Univ. of Illinois Press. Anthology of post–World War II lyrics.

Tracy, Steven, ed. 1999. *Write Me a Few of Your Lines: A Blues Reader*. Amherst: Univ. of Massachusetts Press.

ADDITIONAL LISTENING

The Blues. 2003. 13-series radio program produced for Public Radio International by Robert Santelli and Ben Manilla to celebrate the Year of the Blues. Listen to all programs online at http://www.yearoftheblues.org/radio/index.asp.

Alan Lomax Collection. Prison Songs, Vol. 1: Murderous Home. Rounder 1714.

B. B. King Live at the Regal. Beat Goes On 235.

Bessie Smith: Chattanooga Gal. Properbox 78.

Blind Blake: All the Published Sides. JSP Records 7714.

Blues in the Mississippi Night. Rounder 1860.

Charley Patton: Complete Recordings. JSP 7702.

Chicago Blues: The Chance Era. Charly 146. (Lazy Bill Lucas.)

The Essential Gospel Sampler. Columbia Legacy 57163.

Fred McDowell: First Recordings. Rounder 1718.

Johnny Shines: Traditional Delta Blues. Biograph 121.

Magic Sam Live. Delmark DE 645.

Muddy Waters: His Best, 1947–1955. MCA/Chess 9370

Negro Blues and Hollers. Rounder 1501.

Negro Religious Songs and Services. Rounder 1514.

Otis Rush: Ain't Enough Comin' In. Mercury CD 314518769-2.

Rev. C. L. Franklin: Legendary Sermons. MCA Universal Special Products 21145.

Robert Johnson: King of the Delta Blues. Columbia Legacy 65211.

Roots 'n' Blues: The Retrospective. Columbia C4K 47911.

T-Bone Walker: The Original Source. Properbox 38.

Menhaden fishermen's worksongs preserved by the Northern Neck Chantey Singers may be heard on the Internet at http://www.npr.org/templates/story/story.php?storyId=6605894&ft=1&f=1021

ADDITIONAL VIEWING

Note that live performances by many of the blues singers mentioned in this chapter may be found on YouTube. Search under the singer's name, such as Otis Rush, Johnny Shines, Fred McDowell, Big Bill Broonzy, Magic Sam, and so forth.

The Blues Accordin' to Lightnin' Hopkins. 1979. DVD, 31 min. Color. Directed by Les Blank. El Cerrito, CA: Flower Films. http://www.lesblank.com

Bukka White and Son House. 2000. Yazoo DVD, 60 min. Black and white. Riveting performances of Mississippi Delta blues.

Otis Rush: Mastering Chicago Blues Guitar. (c. 1993). VHS videotape, 90 min. Color. Pound Ridge, NY: Hot Licks Productions. Instruction and some footage of Rush's fine playing.

The Road to Memphis. 2003. Directed by Richard Pearce, written by Robert Gordon. One of seven films in the series *Martin Scorcese Presents the Blues.* PBS Videos. http://www.pbs.org/theblues/index.html. Features B. B. King and Bobby Rush.

A Singing Stream. 1987. Online video, 57 min. Color. Directed by Tom Davenport. Delaplane, VA: Davenport Films. http://www.folkstreams.net. African American religious music.

Wild Women Don't Have the Blues. 1989. VHS videotape, 58 min. Color. Directed by Christine Dall. San Francisco: California Newsreel. A documentary on women blues singers.

INTERNET RESOURCES

Blues Bibliographic Database: Compiled by Görgen Antonsson http://bluesnet.hub.org/gorgen/

Blues-L: Listserver discussion group http://www.blues.net/blues-FAQ.html

Blues World: Essays, with links to organizations, magazines, discographies, auctions http://www.bluesworld.com/

Pre–World War 2 blues lyrics concordance, by Michael Taft http://www.dylan61.se/taft.htm

Chapter 5 – Europe/Central and Southeastern Regions

REFERENCES

Anderson, Benedict. 1991. *Imagined Communities: Reflections on the Origin and Spread of Nationalism.* Rev. ed. London: Verso.

Armistead, Samuel G. 1979. "Judeo-Spanish and Pan-European Balladry." *Jahrbuch fuur Volksliedforschung* 24: 127–38.

Austerlitz, Paul. 2000. "Birch-Bark Horns and Jazz in the National Imagination: The Finnish Folk Music Vogue in Historical Perspective." *Ethnomusicology* 44(2): 183–213.

Bohlman, Philip V. 2000a. "East-West: The Ancient Modernity of Jewish Music." *East European Meetings in Ethnomusicology* 7: 67–90.

———. 2000b. "Jewish Music in Europe." In *Europe: The Garland Encyclopedia of World Music*. Vol. 8, 248–69. New York: Garland.

———. 2004. *The Music of European Nationalism: Cultural Identity and Modern History*. Santa Barbara, CA: ABC-CLIO.

Buchanan, Dona. 1996. "Wedding Music, Social Identity, and the Bulgarian Political Transition." In *Retuning Culture: Music and Change in Eastern Europe,* edited by M. Slobin. Durham, NC: Duke Univ. Press.

Chybiński, Adolf. [1923] 1961. *O polskiej muzyce ludowej: Wybór prac etnograficznych*. Edited by Ludwik Bielawski. Kraków: Polskie Wydawnictwo Muzyczne.

Cooley, Timothy J. 1999. "Folk Festival as Modern Ritual in the Polish Tatra Mountains." *World of Music* 41(3): 31–55.

———. 2001. "Repulsion to Ritual: Interpreting Folk Festivals in the Polish Tatras." *Ethnologies* 23(1): 233–53.

———. 2005. *Making Music in the Polish Tatras: Tourists, Ethnographers, and Mountain Musicians*. Bloomington: Indiana Univ. Press.

Czekanowska, Anna. 1990. *Polish Folk Music: Slavonic Heritage, Polish Tradition, Contemporary Trends*. Cambridge: Cambridge Univ. Press.

Davies, Norman. 1996. *Europe: A History*. Oxford: Oxford Univ. Press

Erlmann, Veit. 1996. "The Aesthetics of the Global Imagination: Reflections on World Music in the 1990s." *Public Culture* 8(3): 467–87.

Feld, Steven. 2001. "A Sweet Lullaby for World Music." In *Globalization*, edited by Arjun Appadurai, 189–216. Durham, NC: Duke Univ. Press.

Frolova-Walker, Marina. 1998. "'National in Form, Socialist in Content': Musical Nation-Building in the Soviet Republics." *Journal of the American Musicological Society* 51(2): 331–71.

Gellner, Ernest. 1997. *Nationalism*. New York: New York Univ. Press.

Hall, Derek R., ed. 1991. *Tourism and Economic Development in Eastern Europe and the Soviet Union*. London: Belhaven Press.

Hobsbawm, Eric J. 1990. *Nations and Nationalism Since 1780: Programme, Myth, Reality*. Cambridge: Cambridge Univ. Press.

Hobsbawm, Eric J., and Terence Ranger, eds. 1983. *The Invention of Tradition*. Cambridge: Cambridge Univ. Press.

Hutchinson, John, and Anthony D. Smith, eds. 1994. *Nationalism*. Oxford: Oxford Univ. Press.

Marshall, Robert, and Robin A. Leaver. 2001. "Choral: 5. Luther's Melodies." *New Grove Dictionary of Music and Musicians,* Vol. 5, edited by S. Sadie and J. Tyrrell, 738–39. London: Macmillan.

McKim, LindaJo H. 1993. *The Presbyterian Hymnal Companion*. Louisville, KY: Westminster/John Knox Press.

Pasternak, Velvel, ed. 1994. *The International Jewish Songbook*. Cedarhurst, NY: Tara.

Petrović, Ankica. 2000. "Bosnia-Hercegovina." In *Europe: The Garland Encyclopedia of World Music*. Vol. 8, 962–71. New York: Garland.

Pettan, Svanibor. 1998. *Music, Politics, and War: Views from Croatia*. Zagreb: Institute of Ethnology and Folklore Research.

Plastino, Goffredo. 2001. *Tambores del Bajo Aragón*. PRAMES Aragón LCD D.L.Z 635-2001.

———. 2003. "Fifteen Fragments on My (Field)work." *British Journal of Ethnomusicology* 12(1): 97–112.

Rice, Timothy. 1994. *May It Fill Your Soul: Experiencing Bulgarian Music*. Chicago: Univ. of Chicago Press.

———. 2000. "The Music of Europe: Unity and Diversity." In *Europe: The Garland Encyclopedia of World Music*. Vol. 8, 2–15. New York: Garland.

———. 2004. *Music in Bulgaria: Experiencing Music, Expressing Culture*. New York: Oxford Univ. Press.

Rubin, Ruth. 1979. *Voices of a People: The Story of Yiddish Folksong*. Philadelphia: Jewish Publication Society of America.

Schulenberg, David. 2000. "History of European Art Music." In *Europe: The Garland Encyclopedia of World Music*. Vol. 8, 68–87. New York: Garland.

Slobin, Mark. 2002. "Bosnia and Central/Southeastern Europe: Music and Musicians in Transition." In *Worlds of Music: An Introduction to the Music of the World's Peoples*, 4th ed., edited by Jeff Todd Titon, 211–41. New York: Schirmer.

Smith, Anthony D. 1998. *Nationalism and Modernism*. London: Routledge.

Taylor, Timothy D. 1997. *Global Pop: World Musics, World Markets.* New York: Routledge.

Titon, Jeff Todd, and Bob Carlin, eds. 2002. *American Musical Traditions.* Vol. 4: *European American Music.* New York: Schirmer.

White, George W. 2000. *Nationalism and Territory: Constructing Group Identity in Southeastern Europe.* Lanham, MD: Rowman & Littlefield.

Wrazen, Louise. 1988. "The *Góralski* of the Polish Highlanders: Old World Musical Tradition from a New World Perspective." Ph.D. dissertation, Univ. of Toronto.

———. 1991. "Traditional Music Performance Among *Górale* in Canada." *Ethnomusicology* 35(2): 173–93.

———. 2007. "Relocating the Tatras: Place and Music in *Górale* Identity and Imagination." *Ethnomusicology* 51(2): 185–204.

ADDITIONAL READING

Bartók, Béla. 1981. *The Hungarian Folk Song.* Edited by Benjamin Suchoff. Translated by M. D. Calvocoressi. Annotated by Zoltán Kodály. Albany: State Univ. of New York Press.

Buchanan, Donna. 2005. *Performing Democracy.* Chicago: Univ. of Chicago Press.

Cartner, Holly. 1991. *Destroying Ethnic Identity: The Gypsies in Romania.* New York: Helsinki Watch.

Kligman, Gail. 1988. *The Wedding of the Dead.* Chicago: Univ. of Chicago Press.

Ling, Jan. 1997. *A History of European Folk Music.* Rochester, NY: Univ. of Rochester Press. [First published in Swedish by Akademiförlaget, 1988]

Nettl, Bruno. 1973. *Folk and Traditional Music of the Western Continents.* 2nd ed. Englewood Cliffs, NJ: Prentice Hall.

Rasmussen, Ljerka V. 2002. *Newly Composed Folk Music of Yugoslavia.* New York: Routledge.

Rice, Timothy, James Porter, and Chris Goertzen, eds. 2000. *Europe: The Garland Encyclopedia of World Music.* Vol. 8, 962–71. New York: Garland.

Slobin, Mark, ed. 1996. *Retuning Culture: Music and Change in Eastern Europe.* Durham, NC: Duke Univ. Press.

Sugarman, Jane C. 1997. *Engendering Song: Singing and Subjectivity at Prespa Albanian Weddings.* Chicago: Univ. of Chicago Press.

ADDITIONAL LISTENING

Kapela Staszka Maśniaka. 1997. *Muzyka Kościelisk.* Folk CD 009.

Márta Sebastyén and Ókrös Ensemble. 1993. *Transylvanian Portraits: Hungarian Village Music from Transylvania.* Koch 3-4004-2H1.

Márta Sebastyén, Alexander Balanescu, and Muzsikás. 1999. *The Bartók Album.* Rykodisc/ Hannibal HNCD 1439.

Plastino, Goffredo. 2001. *Tambores del Bajo Aragón.* PRAMES Aragón LCD D.L.Z 635-2001.

Trebunie-Tutki. 2000. *Folk Karnawał.* Folk CD-029.

Twinkle Brothers & Tutki. 1992. *Twinkle Inna Polish Stylee: Higher Heights.* Twinkle Music. http://www.twinklemusic.com

Various Artists. 1990. *Polish Folk Music: Songs and Music from Various Regions.* Polskie Nagrania Muza PNCD 048.

Various Artists. 1993. *Bosnia: Echoes from an Endangered World.* Smithsonian Folkways Recordings SFW40407.

Various Artists. n.d. *Bring it all Home.* Kamahuk kcd-1. http://www.kamahuk.net

ADDITIONAL VIEWING

Ashkenaz: The Music of the Jews from Eastern Europe. 1993. Created and directed by Tzipora H. Jochsberger. Written and directed by Asher Tlalim. Teaneck, NJ: Ergo Media; Jerusalem: Israel Music Heritage Project.

A compilation of Jewish music from Eastern Europe, including Yiddish folksongs, the liturgical music of the synagogue, and Klezmer and Yiddish theater tunes. The film also features rare archival footage of Jewish life in Eastern Europe as it existed prior to World War II, providing an understanding of the environment from which the music grew.

The JVC Smithsonian Folkways Video Anthology of Music and Dance of Europe. c. 1996. Directed by Kunihiko Nakagawa. Japan: JVC, Victor Company of Japan. Barre, VT: Distributed by

Multicultural Media. These videos are mixed in quality and in their supporting documentation, but at least the section on Bulgaria is useful. They were filmed during the communist period but do not feature professional folklore groups. The booklet notes are helpful.

The Popovich Brothers of South Chicago. 1977. Directed by Jill Godmilow. Distributed by Balkan Arts Center. This video is a dated but moving portrayal of a family of musicians who for decades provided music for the Serbian American community in and around Chicago.

The Romany Trail. c. 1992. Directed and produced by Jeremy Marre. Harcourt Films. Newton, NJ: Distributed by Shanachie Records. 2 videos. Part of the *Beats of the Heart* series. Part 1 is a search for the "lost" gypsy tribes of Egypt and traces their route into Spain. Part 2 first goes to India to find what are believed to be the original gypsy families whose descendants migrated across the Middle East to Africa and Europe, then it goes to Eastern Europe, among the oppressed gypsy communities of then-Communist Europe. See the essay on these films in the *Beats of the Heart* booklet.

Chapter 6 – India/South India

REFERENCES

The Beatles. 1966. *Revolver.* Parlophone CDP 7 464412. CD.

Chandra, Sheila. 1991. *Silk.* Shanachie 64035. CD.

———. 1993. *Weaving My Ancestor's Voices.* Caroline CAROL 2322-2. CD.

Iyer, Vijay. 2005. *Reimagining.* Savoy Jazz SVY 17475. CD.

Panjabi MC (Rajinder Rai). 2003. *Panjabi MC Beware.* Sequence SEQ 8015-2.

Raman, Susheela. 2001. *Salt Rain.* Narada B00005BJIG. CD.

Shankar, Ravi. 1978. *East Greets East.* Deutsche Grammophon 2531-381.

———. n.d. *West Meets East* (with Yehudi Menuhin) *I–III.* Angel S-36418, S-36026, SQ-37200.

DVD TAMIL MOVIES

Note: The acquisition of recommended Tamil movies on DVD is essential for understanding the pop music sections of this chapter and should be purchased in advance (under $20 each). All DVDs have song tracks listed separately on their menus. Make sure to ask for movies with English subtitles. The recommended Tamil movies are: *Bombay, Dum Dum Dum* (sometimes spelled with double m's), *Kadalan, Mudalvan,* and *Thillana Mohanambal.* An excellent Hindi film is *Kal Ho Na Ho* about Indians living in New York. To order via the Internet:

In the United States: http://www.AnyTamil.com

In the United Kingdom: http://www.ayngaran.com (e-mail: sales@ayngaran.com)

ADDITIONAL READING AND VIEWING

Brown, Robert E. 1971. "India's Music." In *Readings in Ethnomusicology,* edited by David P. McAllester, 192–329. New York: Johnson Reprint.

Kumar, Kanthimathi, and Jean Stackhouse. 1988. *Classical Music of South India: Karnatic Tradition in Western Notation.* Stuyvesant, NY: Pendragon Press. Beginning lessons and simple songs with free translations of song texts.

Mohan, Anuradha. 1994. "Ilaiyaraja: Composer as Phenomenon in Tamil Film Culture." M.A. thesis, Wesleyan Univ.

Reck, David. 1985. "Beatles Orientalis: Influences from Asia in a Popular Song Tradition." *Asian Music* 16(1): 83–149.

Shankar, Ravi. 1968. *My Music, My Life.* New York: Simon & Schuster.

Wade, Bonnie. 1988. *Music of India: The Classical Traditions.* Riverdale, MD: Riverdale.

ADDITIONAL LISTENING: CARNATIC MUSIC

Annotated Website

The website http://www.medieval.org/music/world/carnatic/cblsup.html has an annotated list of CDs, plus relevant information on South Indian (Carnatic) music, composers, performers, and music styles. In particular, you might want to look for the following CDs.

An Anthology of South Indian Classical Music. Ocora 5900001/2/3/4. Four CDs.

Gopinath, Kadri. *A Tribute to Adolphe Sax.* Oriental 230/231. [saxophone]
Iyer, Semmangudi Srinivasa. *The Doyen of Carnatic Music.* Oriental 140. [vocal]
Jayaraman, Lalgudi J. *Violin Virtuoso: Lalgudi J. Jayaraman.* Oriental AAMS-125.
Krishnan, T. N. *The Vibrant Violin of "Sangita Kalanidhi."* Oriental 140.
Mahalingam, T. R. ("Mali"). *Divine Sounds of the Bamboo Flute.* Oriental 183/184. Two CDs.
Moulana, Sheik Chinna. *Nadhasvaram.* Wergo SM-1507. [nagasvaram]
Music for Bharata Natyam. Oriental 176. [South Indian dance music]
Narayanaswamy, K. V. *Guru Padam.* Koel 063. [vocal]
Padmanabhan, Rajeswari. *Surabi. SonicSoul Acoustics.* [veena; no number; released in 1998].
Ramani, N. *Lotus Signatures.* MOW CDT-141. [flute]
Ranganayaki Rajagopalan. *Makar 029.* [veena]
Sankaran, Trichy. *The Language of Rhythm.* MOW 150. [mridangam]
Subbulakshmi, M. S. *M. S. Subbulakshmi: Live at Carnegie Hall.* EMI India 147808/809. Two CDs. [vocal]
———. *M. S. Subbulakshmi: Radio Recitals.* EMI India CDNF 147764/65. Two CDs. [vocal]
Viswanathan, T. *Classical Flute of South India.* JVC VIGG-5453.

OTHER RECORDINGS

Ilaiyaraja. n.d. *How to Name It.* Oriental Records ORI/AAMS CD-115. CD.
McLaughlin, John. n.d. *Best of Mahavishnu.* Columbia PCT-36394.
———. n.d. *Shakti.* Columbia Jazz Contemporary Masters CK-46868. CD.
Shankar, Ravi. 1971. *Concerto for Sitar and Orchestra.* Angel SPD 36806.
———. n.d. Ragamala: *Concerto for Sitar and Orchestra No. 2.* Angel DS 37935.

ADDITIONAL LISTENING: HINDUSTHANI MUSIC

Compiled by Peter Row, New England Conservatory of Music *Ajoy Chakrabarty, Vocal, Raga Bageshri—Malkauns (Vol 2).* Ajoy Chakrabarty (*khyal*) with Samar Saha (*tabla*) and Sultan Khan (*sarangi*): *ragas* Bageshri and Malkauns. Navras Records: NRCD 0011.
Buddhadev Das Gupta—Nayak ki Kanra. Buddhadev Das Gupta (*sarod*) with Anand Gopal Bandopadhyay (*tabla*): *raga* Nayak ki Kanra. Raga Records: RAGA 210.
Chant Dhrupad—Nasir Zahiruddin Dagar et Nasir Faiyazuddin Dagar. Nasir Zahiruddin Dagar and Nasir Faiyazuddin Dagar (*dhrupad*) with Laxmi Narain Pawar (*pakhawaj* drum): *ragas* Bageshri and Bhatiyar. Ethnic: B 6159.
Gathering Rain Clouds. Vishwa Mohan Bhatt (*mohan vina*) with Sikhvinder Singh Namdhari (*tabla*): *ragas* Miya ki Malhar and Gavati. Water Lily Acoustics: WLA-ES-22-CD.
Great Masters of the Rudra-Veena. Ustad Zia Mohiuddin Dagar (*rudra veena*) with Manik Munde (*pakhawaj* drum): *ragas* Pancham Kosh and Malkauns. Auvidis: A 6131.
Kanhra. Hariprasad Chaurasia (flute) with Sabir Khan (*tabla*): *raga* Kaunsi Kanhra. Nimbus Records: NI 5182.
Lakshmi Shankar: The Hours and the Seasons. Lakshmi Shankar (*khyal* and *bhajan*) with Sadanand Naimpalli (*tabla*): *ragas* Ahir Bhairav, Dhani, Khafi and Bhajans in *ragas* Megh and Bhairavi. Ocora: C 581615.
Lalita. Ustad Imrat Khan (*surbahar*): *rag* Lalit (*alap, jor,* and *jhala*). Water Lily Acoustics: ASIN B000002VYH.
Padmabhushan Nikhil Banerjee—Sitar Recital. Nikhil Banerjee (*sitar*) with Kanai Dutt (*tabla*) and Swapan Choudhury (*tabla*): *ragas* Komal Rishabh Asavari, Jaunpuri, Mand and Dhun (Baul folk song). EMI: CDNF 150043.
Rag Kaunsi Todi, Desh, and Bhatiali Dhun. Sagarika: Cat No. S-500-01-4.
Ravi Shankar in Celebration—Classical Sitar. Ravi Shankar (*sitar*) with Chatur Lal (*tabla*), Kumar Bose (*tabla*), Anoushka Shankar (*sitar*), Zakir Hussain (*tabla*), Alla Rakha (*tabla*) and Kanai Dutt (*tabla*): *ragas* Charu Keshi, Bhatiyar, Adarini, Marwa, and Dhun Kafi. Angel: 7243 5 55578-2.
Sitar Recital Selection, Shahid Parvez. Shahid Parvez (*sitar*) with Bikram Ghosh (*tabla*): *ragas* Bilaskhani Todi, Desh, and Bhatiali Dhun. Sagarika: Cat. No. S-500-01-4.
Ustad Ali Akbar Khan, Pandit Nikhil Banerjee: Rag Manj Khammaj, Rag Misra Mand. Ali Akbar Khan (*sarod*), Nikhil Banerjee (*sitar*) with Mahapurush Misra (*tabla*): *ragas* Manj Khammaj and Misra Mand. Alam Madina Music Productions: AMMP CD 9405.
Ustad Ali Akbar Khan, Signature Series: Vol. 1: Three Ragas. Ali Akbar Khan (*sarod*) with Mahapurush Misra (*tabla*): *ragas* Chandranandan, Gauri Manjari, and Jogiya Kalingra. Alam Madina Music Productions: AMMP CD 9001.

Ustad Amjad Ali Khan (Compilation). Amjad Ali Khan (*sarod*) with Samta Prasad, Chandra Mohan, and Shafaat Ahmed Khan (*tabla*): *ragas* Sughrai Kanada, Bihag, and Tilak Kamod. Gramophone Company of India: CDNF 150209.

Ustad Vilayat Khan—Sitar. Vilayat Khan (*sitar*) with Akram Khan (*tabla*): *raga* Jaijaivanti. India Archive Music: CD 1010.

Veena Sahasrabuddhe, A Morning Raga. Bhoopal Todi. Veena Sahasrabuddhe (*khyal*) with Sanjay Deshpande (*tabla*): *raga* Bhoopal Todi. Navras Records: NRCD 0031.

MAJOR SOURCES FOR RECORDINGS

Music of the World (MOW label). P.O. Box 3620, Chapel Hill, NC 27515; (888) 264-6689; http://www.musicoftheworld.com/

Oriental Records. P.O. Box 387, Williston Park, NY 11596; http://www.orientalrecords.com

Raag Music. Los Angeles, CA; (310) 479-5225; http://www.raaga.com

SonicSoul Acoustics. 15183 Dane Lane, Portland, OR 97229; (503) 531-0270; http://members.tripod.com/~kartha1/index.html or use a search engine

Chapter 7 – Asia/Music of Indonesia

REFERENCES

Becker, Judith. 1979. "Time and Tune in Java." In *The Imagination of Reality: Essays in Southeast Asian Coherence Systems,* edited by A. L. Becker and Aram A. Yengoyan, 197–210. Norwood, NJ: Ablex.

———. 1980. *Traditional Music in Modern Java: Gamelan in a Changing Society.* Honolulu: Univ. of Hawaii Press.

———. 1981. "Hindu-Buddhist Time in Javanese Gamelan Music." In *The Study of Time,* 4, edited by J. F. Fraser. New York: Springer-Verlag.

———. 1988. "Earth, Fire, Sakti, and the Javanese Gamelan." *Ethnomusicology* 32(3): 385–91.

Frederick, William. 1982. "Rhoma Irama and the Dangdut Style: Aspects of Contemporary Indonesian Popular Culture." *Indonesia* 34:103–30.

Hatch, Martin. 1989. "Popular Music in Indonesia (1983)." In *World Music, Politics and Social Change,* edited by Simon Frith. Manchester, England: Manchester Univ. Press.

Hoffman, Stanley B. 1978. "Epistemology and Music: a Javanese Example." *Ethnomusicology* 22(1): 69–88.

Hood, Mantle. 1954. *The Nuclear Theme as a Determinant of Patet in Javanese Music.* Groningen, The Netherlands: J. B. Wolters.

Keeler, Ward. 1987. *Javanese Shadows, Javanese Selves.* Princeton, NJ: Princeton Univ. Press.

Kunst, Jaap. 1973. *Music in Java: Its History, Its Theory, and Its Technique.* Edited by Ernst Heins. 3rd ed. 2 vols. The Hague: Martinus Nijhoff.

Surjodiningrat, Wasisto, P. J. Sudarjana, and Adhi Susanto. 1972. *Tone Measurements of Outstanding Javanese Gamelans in Jogjakarta and Surakarta.* Yogyakarta: Gadjah Mada Univ. Press.

Tenzer, Michael. 2000. *Gamelan Gong Kebyar: The Art of Twentieth-Century Balinese Music.* Chicago: Univ. of Chicago Press.

ADDITIONAL READING

On Music

Bakan, Michael B. 1999. *Music of Death and New Creation: Experiences in the World of Balinese Gamelan Beleganjur.* Chicago: Univ. of Chicago Press.

Becker, Judith, and Alan Feinstein, eds. 1984, 1987, 1988. *Karawitan: Source Readings In Javanese Gamelan and Vocal Music.* 3 vols. Ann Arbor: Univ. of Michigan Center for South and Southeast Asian Studies.

Brinner, Benjamin. 2008. *Music of Central Java: Experiencing Music, Expressing Culture.* New York: Oxford Univ. Press.

Herbst, Edward. 1997. *Voices in Bali: Energies and Perceptions in Vocal Music and Dance Theater.* Hanover, NH: Univ. Press of New England, Wesleyan Univ. Press.

Hood, Mantle, and Hardja Susilo. 1967. *Music of the Venerable Dark Cloud: Introduction, Commentary, and Analysis.* Los Angeles: Univ. of California Press.

Kartomi, Margaret. 1980. "Musical Strata in Java, Bali, and Sumatra." In *Musics of Many Cultures,* edited by Elizabeth May, 111–33. Berkeley: Univ. of California Press.

Lindsay, Jennifer. 1992. *Javanese Gamelan: Traditional Orchestra of Indonesia.* 2nd ed. New York: Oxford Univ. Press.

Manuel, Peter. 1988. *Popular Musics of the Non-Western World: An Introductory Survey.* New York: Oxford Univ. Press. (See especially pp. 205–20.)

McPhee, Colin. 1966. *Music in Bali.* New Haven, CT: Yale Univ. Press.

Perlman, Marc. 2004. *Unplayed Melodies: Javanese Gamelan and the Genesis of Music Theory.* Berkeley: Univ. of California Press.

Simon, Artur. 1984. "Functional Changes in Batak Traditional Music and Its Role in Modern Indonesian Society." *Asian Music* 15(2): 58–66.

Sumarsam. 1995. *Gamelan: Cultural Interaction and Musical Development in Central Java.* Chicago: Univ. of Chicago Press.

Sutton, R. Anderson. 1987. "Identity and Individuality in an Ensemble Tradition: The Female Vocalist in Java." In *Women and Music in Cross-Cultural Perspective,* edited by Ellen Koskoff, 113–30. Westport, CT: Greenwood Press. Reprint, Urbana: Univ. of Illinois Press, 1989.

———. 1993. *Variation in Central Javanese Gamelan Music.* DeKalb, IL: Center for Southeast Asian Studies, Northern Illinois Univ.

Tenzer, Michael. 1991. *Balinese Music.* Berkeley, CA: Periplus.

Vetter, Roger. 1981. "Flexibility in the Performance Practice of Central Javanese Music." *Ethnomusicology* 25(2): 199–214.

On Indonesia

Anderson, Benedict R. O'G. 1965. *Mythology and the Tolerance of the Javanese.* Ithaca, NY: Cornell Modern Indonesia Project.

Becker, A. L. 1979. "Text Building, Epistemology, and Aesthetics in Javanese Shadow Theater." In *The Imagination of Reality: Essays in Southeast Asian Coherence Systems,* edited by A. L. Becker and Aram A. Yengoyan, 211–43. Norwood, NJ: Ablex.

Geertz, Clifford. 1960. *The Religion of Java.* New York: Free Press.

Holt, Claire. 1967. *Art in Indonesia: Continuities and Change.* Ithaca, NY: Cornell Univ. Press.

Ricklefs, Merle C. 2001. *A History of Modern Indonesia since c. 1200.* 3rd ed. Stanford, CA: Stanford Univ. Press.

ADDITIONAL LISTENING

Java (including West Java and Jakarta)

Bedhaya Duradasih, Court Music of Kraton Surakarta II. King Record, World Music Library, KICC 5193.

Betawi and Sundanese Music of the North Coast of Java: Topeng Betawi, Tanjidor, Ajeng. Music of Indonesia, 5. Smithsonian Folkways SFW CD 40421.

Chamber Music of Central Java. King Record, World Music Library, KICC 5152.

Court Music of Kraton Surakarta. King Record, World Music Library, KICC 5151.

The Gamelan of Cirebon. King Record, World Music Library KICC 5130.

Indonesian Popular Music: Kroncong, Dangdut, & Langgam Jawa. Music of Indonesia, 2. Smithsonian Folkways SF 40056.

Java: Langen Mandra Wanara, Opéra de Danuredjo VII. Ocora CD C559014/15.

Java: Palais Royal de Yogyakarta. Volume 4: La musique de concert. Ocora (Radio France) C 560087.

Javanese Court Gamelan. Elektra/Nonesuch Explorer Series 972044-2.

Klenengan Session of Solonese Gamelan I. King Record, World Music Library, KICC 5185.

Langendriyan, Music of Mangkunegaran Solo II. King Record, World Music Library, KICC 5194.

Music from the Outskirts of Jakarta: Gambang Kromong. Music of Indonesia, 3. Smithsonian Folkways SF 40057.

The Music of K. R. T. Wasitodiningrat. CMP Records CD 3007.

Music of Mangkunegaran Solo I. King Record, World Music Library, KICC 5184.

Shadow Music of Java. Rounder CD 5060.

Songs Before Dawn: Gandrung Banyuwangi. Music of Indonesia, 1. Smithsonian Folkways SF 40055.

The Sultan's Pleasure, Javanese Gamelan and Vocal Music from the Palace of Yogyakarta. Music of the World CDT-116.

Bali

Bali: Court Music and Banjar Music (*Musique de cour et musique de banjar*). Réédition Auvidis, Unesco collection, Musiques et musicians D 8059.

Bali: Gamelan and Kecak. Elektra Nonesuch Explorer Series CD 979204-4.

Bali: Les Grands Gong Kebyar des Anneés Soixante. Ocora, Harmonia Mundi, C 560057–C 560058. 2 CDs.

Gamelan Gong Gede of Batur Temple. World Music Library, King Records KICC 5153.

Gamelan Gong Kebyar, Bali. Elektra Nonesuch CD 79280-2.

The Gamelan Music of Bali. World Music Library, King Records KICC 5126.

Gamelan Semar Pegulingan "Gunung Jati," Br. Teges Kanginan. World Music Library, King Records KICC 5180.

Gender Wayang of Sukawati Village. World Music Library, King Records KICC 5156.

Golden Rain: Gong Kebyar of Gunung Sari, Bali. Elektra Nonesuch CD 79219-2.

Kecak Ganda Sari. Kecak from Bali. Bridge BCD 9019.

Music in Bali. World Music Library, King Records KICC 5127.

Music of the Gamelan Gong Kebyar, Bali. Vital Records 401-2. 2 discs.

Other Indonesian Islands

Batak of North Sumatra. New Albion Records NA 046 CD.

Gongs and Vocal Music from Sumatra. Music of Indonesia, 12. Smithsonian Folkways SFW C 40428.

Indonesian Guitars. Music of Indonesia, 20. Smithsonian Folkways SFW CD 40447.

Kalimantan: Dayak Ritual and Festival Music. Music of Indonesia, 17. Smithsonian Folkways SFW C 40444.

Kalimantan Strings. Music of Indonesia, 13. Smithsonian Folkways SFW CD 40429.

Lombok, Kalimantan, Banyumas: Little-known Forms of Gamelan and Wayang. Music of Indonesia, 14. Smithsonian Folkways SFW CD 40441.

Melayu Music of Sumatra and the Riau Islands. Music of Indonesia, 11. Smithsonian Folkways SFW CD 40427.

Music from the Forests of Riau and Mentawai. Music of Indonesia, 7. Smithsonian Folkways SFW CD 40423.

Music from the Southeast: Sumbawa, Sumba, Timor. Music of Indonesia, 16. Smithsonian Folkways SFW CD 40443.

Music of Biak, Irian Jaya. Music of Indonesia, 10. Smithsonian Folkways SFW CD 40426.

Music of Madura. Ode Record Company CD ODE 1381.

Music of Maluku: Halmahera, Buru, Kei. Music of Indonesia, 19. Smithsonian Folkways SFW CD 40446.

Music of Nias and North Sumatra: Hoho, Gendang Karo, Gondang Toba. Music of Indonesia, 4. Smithsonian Folkways SF CD 40429.

Night Music of West Sumatra. Music of Indonesia, 6. Smithsonian Folkways SFW CD 40422.

Sulawesi: Festivals, Funerals, and Work. Music of Indonesia, 18. Smithsonian Folkways SF CD 40445.

Sulawesi Strings. Music of Indonesia, 15. Smithsonian Folkways SFW CD 40442.

Vocal and Instrumental Music from East and Central Flores. Music of Indonesia, 8. Smithsonian Folkways SFW CD 40424.

Vocal Music from Central and West Flores. Music of Indonesia, 9. Smithsonian Folkways SFW CD 40425.

ADDITIONAL VIEWING

Karya: Video Portraits of Four Indonesian Composers. 1992. Videocassette. Produced and Directed by Jody Diamond. Distributed by American Gamelan Institute, Box 5036, Hanover, NH 03755. Balinese, Javanese, and Batak composers talk about their recent work.

The JVC Video Anthology of World Music and Dance. 1990. Thirty videocassettes plus guide. Edited by Fujii Tomoaki, with assistant editors Omori Yasuhiro and Sakurai Tetsuo, in collaboration with the National Museum of Ethnology (Osaka). Produced by Ichikawa Katsumori. Directed by Nakagawa Kunihiko and Ichihashi Yuji. Victor Company of Japan, Ltd., in collaboration with Smithsonian Folkways Recordings. Distributed by Rounder Records, Cambridge, MA 02140.

- Volume 9 contains footage of Javanese shadow puppetry (poor quality), along with studio footage of Balinese *kecak* ("monkey chant") and Sundanese music (recorded in Japan).
- Volume 10 contains a variety of Balinese examples, recorded in Bali, mostly employing a *gamelan semar pegulingan* (even for contexts in which this ensemble is not appropriate).

Bali

Bali Beyond the Postcard. 1991. Videorecording and 16mm. Produced and directed by Nancy Dine, Peggy Stern, and David Dawkins. Distributed by Filmakers Library, 124 East 40th Street, New York, NY 10016; and by "Outside in July," 59 Barrow Street, New York, NY 10014. *Gamelan* and dance in four generations of a Balinese family.

Compressed Version of a "Gambuh" (Dance Drama) in Batuan. 1981. 16 mm. Produced by T. Seebass and G. van der Weijden. Distributed by Institut für den Wissenschaftlichen Film, Göttingen, Germany. Performance of *gambuh,* "classical" Balinese dance drama.

Releasing the Spirits: A Village Cremation in Bali. [1981] 1991. Videocassette. Directed by Patsy Asch, Linda Connor, et al. Distributed by Documentary Educational Resources, Watertown, MA. Cremation rituals in a central Balinese village.

Shadowmaster. 1980. Videocassette and 16 mm. Directed by Larry Reed. Distributed by Larry Reed Productions, 18 Chattanooga Street, San Francisco, CA 94114. Fiction film about the social and artistic life of a shadow puppeteer in Bali.

Java

Bird of Passage. 1986. 16 mm. Directed by Fons Grasveld. Distributed by Netherlands Film Institute, Postbus 515, 1200 AM Hilversum, The Netherlands. Javanese traditions in Java, Suriname, and the Netherlands.

The Dancer and the Dance. (1990?). Videocassette and 16 mm. Produced by Felicia Hughes-Freeland. Distributed by Film Officer, Royal Anthropological Institute, 50 Fitzroy Street, London, England W1P 5HS. Javanese court dance in its current social context.

Traditional Dances of Indonesia, Dances of Jogjakarta, Central Java: Langen Mandra Wanara. 1990. Videocassette from 16mm film made in 1975. Directed and produced by William Heick. Distributed by University of California Extension Media Center, 2176 Shattuck Ave., Berkeley, CA 94704. Dance-opera presenting episode from the Ramayana.

Traditional Dances of Indonesia, Dances of Surakarta, Central Java: Srimpi Anglir Mendung. 1990. Videocassette from 16mm film made in 1975. Directed and produced by William Heick. Distributed by University of California Extension Media Center, 2176 Shattuck Ave., Berkeley, CA 94704. Refined female court dance. (Ten additional videorecordings from the same distributor present additional dances from Java, Bali, and West Sumatra.)

North Sumatra

Karo-Batak (Indonesien, Nordsumatra)—Gendang-Musik "mari-mari" und "patam-patam." 1994. 16 mm. Directed by Artur Simon. Distributed by Institut für den Wissenschaftlichen Film, Göttingen, Germany. Ceremonial music performed by *gendang keteng-keteng* ensemble.

Karo-Batak (Indonesien, Nordsumatra)—Tänze anlässlich einter Haarwaschzeremonie in Kuta Mbelin. 1994. 16 mm. Directed by Franz Simon and Artur Simon. Distributed by Institut für den Wissenschaftlichen Film, Göttingen, Germany. Dances associated with the hair-washing ceremony of Kuta Mbelin, North Sumatra. (Fourteen additional films from the same distributor cover performing arts of Karo and other Batak groups in North Sumatra and of Kayan-Dayak groups in West Kalimantan [Borneo].)

INTERNET RESOURCES

American Gamelan Institute http://www.gamelan.org
Home page with links to archived materials, musical examples, and other information pertaining to traditional and contemporary *gamelan* music—Javanese, Balinese, Sundanese, and experimental/international.

Central Javanese Gamelan http://www.medieval.org/music/world/java.html
Introductory essay, followed by descriptions of some Central Javanese *gamelan* CDs.

Dewa 19 http://dewa19.com
In Indonesian; official website of rock group Dewa 19, with links to various Indonesian music sites, mostly pop.

Gamelan Hawaii http://remus.shidler.hawaii.edu/gamelan/home.htm
> University of Hawaii *gamelan* website; includes link to useful introductory article "Towards an Appreciation of Javanese *Gamelan*," by Hardja Susilo.

Gamelan Kyahi Telaga Madu, University of Michigan http://www.si.umich.edu/CHICO/gamelan/gamelanVT2.html
> Background information on central Javanese *gamelan*, with focus on the *gamelan* set at the University of Michigan.

The Gamelans of the Kraton Yogyakarta http://www.grinnell.edu/courses/mus/gamelans/index.html
> Exquisite photos, sound excerpts, and thorough commentary, covering the many palace *gamelan* ensembles and their cultural contexts, by Roger Vetter.

Gendhing Jawa http://www.calarts.edu/~drummond/gendhing.html
> Thorough set of Javanese *gamelan* pieces in cipher notation, organized by tuning system and *pathet*, neatly and clearly presented.

Indonesian Music http://trumpet.sdsu.edu/M151/Indonesian_Music1a.html
> General introductory material on Javanese and Balinese *gamelan* music.

National Geographic World Music: Indonesian Pop http://worldmusic.nationalgeographic.com/worldmusic/view/page.basic/country/content.country/indonesia_10
> Coverage of a small number of Indonesia's most enduring pop stars.

Krakatau http://www.krakatau.net
> In English; official website of Indonesian fusion group Krakatau, led by Dwiki Dharmawan.

Music > Indonesia > Yahoo! Directory http://dir.yahoo.com/Entertainment/Music/By_Region/Countries/Indonesia/Complete_List
> Links to various Indonesian music sites, informational as well as commercial.

Northern Illinois University SEASite, Arts and Culture http://www.seasite.niu.edu/Indonesian/Budaya_Bangsa
> Discussion of Javanese *gamelan* and shadow puppetry, nicely illustrated.

Tembang http://www.tembang/com/
> Links to various kinds of music in Indonesia, mostly pop.

Top 10 Lagu Indonesia http://musik.karebosi.com/
> Audio files of current Indonesian pop hits, updated regularly.

UK Gamelan Information http://www.gamelan.org.uk/links.htm
> Comprehensive site with information on *gamelan* for students and for people traveling in Indonesia, description of instruments, annotated discography, links to various *gamelan* sites, including *gamelan* groups in Europe and the United States, as well as the United Kingdom.

Yamaha Music Indonesia http://www.reference.com/browse/wiki/Music_of_Indonesia
> Brief descriptions and definitions of a wide variety of Indonesian musical genres from various islands and cultural groups.

Chapter 8 – East Asia/China, Taiwan, Singapore, Overseas Chinese

REFERENCES

DeWoskin, Kenneth. 1982. *A Song for One or Two: Music and the Concept of Art in Early China.* Ann Arbor: Univ. of Michigan.

Jones, Andrew. 2001. *Yellow Music: Media Culture and Colonial Modernity in the Jazz Age.* Durham, NC: Duke Univ. Press.

JSCP. 2003. *Beautiful Energy.* Guangzhou: JSCP. [DVD]

Liang Mingyue. 1985. *Music of the Billion: An Introduction to Chinese Musical Culture.* Berlin: Heinrichshofen.

Lomax, Alan. 1968. *Folk Song Style and Culture.* Washington, DC: American Association for the Advancement of Science.

Mayuan. 2005. http://gsh.taiwanschoolnet.org/gsh2005/3679/index.htm [website, with music tracks and photographs, by Bunun school children featuring the Mayuan Presbyterian Church Choir]. Accessed July 8, 2005.

Schimmelpenninck, Antoinet. 1997. *Chinese Folk Songs and Folk Singers: Shan'ge Traditions in Southern Jiangsu.* Leiden: CHIME Foundation.

Shanghai. 2005. http://shanghaisoup.com/zhouxuan/zhouxuan.html [site with numerous mp3s of Zhou's songs]. Accessed July 28, 2005.

So, Jenny, ed. 2000. *Music in the Age of Confucius.* Washington, DC: Freer Gallery of Art and Arthur M. Sackler Gallery.

Stock, Jonathan P. J. 1996. *Musical Creativity in Twentieth-Century China: Abing, His Music, and Its Changing Meanings.* Rochester, NY: Univ. of Rochester Press.

———. 2004. "Interface at the Peripheries: Western Impact on Other Musics." In *Cambridge History of Twentieth-Century Music,* edited by Anthony Pople and Nicholas Cook, 18–39. Cambridge: Cambridge Univ. Press.

Tang, Hera. 2005. "Twentieth-Century Chinese Oratorios and Cantatas in Hong Kong: An Investigation of Musical and Cultural Contexts." M.Phil. Dissertation, Univ. of Sheffield.

Watson, Rubie S. 1996. "Chinese Bridal Laments: The Claims of a Dutiful Daughter." In *Harmony and Counterpoint: Ritual Music in Chinese Context,* edited by Bell Yung, Evelyn S. Rawski, and Rubie S. Watson, 107–29. Stanford, CA: Stanford Univ. Press.

Yung, Bell. 2002. "Instruments: Qin." In *Garland Encyclopedia of World Music: East Asia,* edited by Robert C. Provine, Yosihiko Tokumaru, and J. Lawrence Witzleben, 157–65. New York: Routledge.

ADDITIONAL READING

Always check standard reference sources, like the *New Grove Dictionary of Music and Musicians,* and the *Garland Encyclopedia of World Music,* both available online.

Adshead, S. A. M. 2000. *China in World History.* 3rd ed. London: Palgrave.

Baranovitch, Nimrod. 2003. *China's New Voices: Popular Music, Ethnicity, Gender, and Politics, 1978–1997.* Berkeley: Univ. of California Press.

Bender, Mark. 2003. *Plum and Bamboo: China's Suzhou Cantefable Tradition.* Urbana: Univ. of Illinois Press.

Benson, Carlton. 1996. "From Teahouse to Radio: Storytelling and the Commercialization of Culture in 1930s Shanghai." Ph.D. dissertation, Univ. of California–Berkeley.

Han Kuo-Huang. 1978. "The Chinese Concept of Program Music." *Asian Music* 10 (1): 17–38.

———. 1979. "The Modern Chinese Orchestra." *Asian Music* 11 (1): 1–43.

Jones, Stephen. 1995. *Folk Music of China: Living Instrumental Traditions.* Oxford, England: Clarendon Press.

Lum, Casey Man Kong. 1996. *In Search of a Voice: Karaoke and the Construction of Identity in Chinese America.* Mahwah, NJ: Erlbaum.

Mackerras, Colin P. 1972. *The Rise of the Peking Opera 1770–1870: Social Aspects of the Theatre in Manchu China.* Oxford: Oxford Univ. Press.

Mittler, Barbara. 2003. "Cultural Revolution Model Works and the Politics of Modernization in China: An Analysis of *Taking Tiger Mountain by Strategy.*" *World of Music* 45 (2): 53–81.

Rees, Helen. 2000. *Echoes of History: Naxi Music in Modern China.* New York: Oxford Univ. Press.

———, ed. forthcoming. *Lives in Chinese Music.* Urbana: Univ. of Illinois Press.

Riddle, Ronald. 1983. *Flying Dragons, Flowing Streams: Music in the Life of San Francisco's Chinese.* Westport, CT: Greenwood Press.

Stock, Jonathan P. J. 1995. "Reconsidering the Past: Zhou Xuan and the Rehabilitation of Early Twentieth-Century Popular Music." *Asian Music* 26 (2): 119–35.

———. 2003. *Huju: Traditional Opera in Modern Shanghai.* Oxford, England: Oxford Univ. Press.

Tan, Hwee-San. 2002. "Saving the Soul in Red China: Music and Ideology in the *Gongde* Ritual of Merit in Fujian." *British Journal of Ethnomusicology* 11 (2): 119–40.

Thrasher, Alan R. 1985. "The Melodic Structure of Jiangnan Sizhu." *Ethnomusicology* 29:237–63.

———. 2000. *Chinese Musical Instruments.* Oxford: Oxford Univ. Press.

van Gulik, Robert. 1940. *The Lore of the Lute: An Essay in Ch'in Ideology.* Tokyo: Sophia Univ.

Wichmann, Elizabeth. 1991. *Listening to Theatre: The Aural Dimension of Beijing Opera.* Honolulu: Univ. of Hawaii Press.

Witzleben, J. Lawrence. 1995. *"Silk and Bamboo" Music in Shanghai: The Jiangnan Sizhu Instrumental Ensemble Tradition.* Kent, OH: Kent State Univ. Press.

———. 1999. "Cantopop and Mandapop in Pre-Postcolonial Hong Kong: Identity Negotiation in the Performances of Anita Mui Yim-Fong." *Popular Music* 18 (2): 241–58.

Wong, Isabel K. F. 1984. "*Geming gequ:* Songs for the Education of the Masses." In *Popular Chinese Literature and Performing Arts in the People's Republic of China 1949–1979,* edited by Bonnie S. McDougall, 112–43. Berkeley: Univ. of California Press.

Yung, Bell. 1989. *Cantonese Opera: Performance as Creative Process.* Cambridge: Cambridge Univ. Press, 1989.

———, ed. 1997. *Celestial Airs of Antiquity: Music of the Seven-String Zither of China.* Madison, WI: A-R Editions.

Yung, Bell, Evelyn S. Rawski, and Rubie S. Watson, eds. 1996. *Harmony and Counterpoint: Ritual Music in the Chinese Context.* Stanford, CA: Stanford Univ. Press.

ADDITIONAL LISTENING

Anthology of World Music: China. 1998. Cambridge, MA: Rounder Records CD 5150.

Chine: Fanbai. Chant liturgique bouddhique. Hymnes aux Trois Joyaux. 1997. Ocora Radio France C560109.

Chine: Le pêcheur et le bûcheron: Le qin, cithara des lettrés. 2007. VDE-Gallo CD-1214.

The Music of the Aborigines on Taiwan Island Vol. 1: The Songs of the Bunun Tribe. 1992. Taipei: Wind Records.

Songs of the Land in China: Labor Songs and Love Songs. 1996. Taipei: Wind Records.

Yangguan san die: Parting at Yangguan. 2002. Berlin: Wergo.

INTERNET RESOURCES

Rock singer Cui Jian http://www.cuijian.com/ENGLISH/Pages/main_interface.html

Tomb of Marquis Yi of Zeng http://depts.washington.edu/chinaciv/archae/2marmain.htm

Wesleyan University's Virtual Instruments Museum http://learningobjects.wesleyan.edu/vim/cgi-bin/instrument.cgi?id=19 [online recording of an *erhu*]

Chinese Christian music http://www.redbeanmusic.com/ [mostly Chinese-language site]

John Thompson's site on the *qin* http://www.silkqin.com/

Folk musician Abing http://www.shef.ac.uk/music/staff/js/AbPref.html

Twelve Girls Band http://www.12girls.org/english/

Chapter 9 – Latin America/Chile, Bolivia, Ecuador, Peru

REFERENCES

Abbad y Lasierra, Fray Iñigo. 1788. *Historia geográfica, civil y política de la Isla de S. Juan Bautista de Puerto Rico.* Madrid: Imprenta de Don Antonio de Espinosa.

Acevedo, Claudio, and Rodolfo Norambuena, José Seves, Rodrigo Torres, and Mauricio Valdebenito. [1996?]. *Víctor Jara: obra musical completa: Textos partes I y II, Rodrigo Torres.* Santiago, Chile: Fundación Víctor Jara.

Andrade Albuja, Enrique, and John M. Schechter. 2004. "'*Kunan punlla rimagrinchi…*': Wit and Didactics in the Quichua Rhetorical Style of Señor Enrique Andrade Albuja, Husbandman-Ethnographer of Cotacachi, Imbabura [Ecuador]." *In Quechua Verbal Artistry: The Inscription of Andean Voices/Arte Expresivo Quechua: La Inscripción de Voces Andinas,* edited by Guillermo Delgado-P. and John M. Schechter, 311–36. Bonn: Bonner Amerikanistische Studien (BAS, Volume 38); Aachen: Shaker Verlag.

Basch, Linda, Nina Glick Schiller, and Christina Szanton Blanc. 1994. *Nations Unbound: Transnational Projects, Postcolonial Predicaments and Deterritorialized Nation-States.* Langhome, PA: Gordon and Breach Science Publishers.

Bastien, Joseph W. 1978. *Mountain of the Condor: Metaphor and Ritual in an Andean Ayllu.* St. Paul, MN: West. American Ethnological Society Monograph 64.

Baumann, Max Peter. 1985. "The Kantu Ensemble of the Kallawaya at Charazani (Bolivia)." *Yearbook for Traditional Music* 17:146–66.

Boilès, Charles L. 1978. *Man, Magic, and Musical Occasions.* Columbus, OH: Collegiate.

Carrasco Pirard, Eduardo. 1982. "The Nueva Canción in Latin America." *International Social Science Journal* 94 (34:4): 599–623.

Casas Roque, Leonidas. 1993. "Fiestas, danzas y música de la costa de Lambayeque." In *Música, danzas y máscaras en los Andes,* edited by Raúl R. Romero, 299–337. Lima: Pontificia Universidad Católica del Perú, Instituto Riva-Agüero.

Céspedes, Gilka Wara. 1993. "Huayño, Saya, and Chuntunqui: Bolivian Identity in the Music of 'Los Kjarkas.'" *Revista de Música Latinoamericana/Latin American Music Review* 14(1): 52–101.

Chaskinakuy. 1988. *Music of the Andes.* Cassette. Edmond Badoux and Francy Vidal. Penngrove, CA. http://www.chaskinakuy.com/recording.htm

———. [1991] 1993. *Music of the Andes: Cosecha.* Produced by Edmond Badoux and Francy Vidal. 1991: Cassette. Also recorded at Hoffmann Studios, Occidental, CA, 1993: CD. All arrangements are by Chaskinakuy. http://www.chaskinakuy.com/recording.htm

————. 2002. *Chaskinakuy: A Flor de Tierra. Music from the Andes of Peru, Bolivia and Ecuador.* Edmond Badoux and Francy Vidal, with Daniel Zamalloa. Recorded at Hoffmann Studios, Occidental, CA. http://www.chaskinakuy.com/recording.htm

Coba Andrade, Carlos Alberto G. 1980. *Literatura popular Afroecuatoriana.* Serie: Cultura Popular. Otavalo, Ecuador: Instituto Otavaleño de Antropología.

Conjunto Ilumán. n.d. (pre-1990). *Elenita Conde.* Ensemble directed by Segundo "Galo" Maigua Pillajo of Ilumán, Ecuador. Cassette.

Conjunto Indígena "Peguche" [Ecuador]. 1977. *Folklore de mi tierra.* Orion 330-0063. Industria Fonográfica Ecuatoriana (IFESA). Guayaquil, Ecuador. Distributed by Emporio Musical S.A., Guayaquil and Psje. Amador, Quito.

Cooke, Peter. 1998. "East Africa: An Introduction." In *Africa: The Garland Encyclopedia of World Music,* vol. 1, edited by Ruth M. Stone, 598–609. New York: Garland.

Davillier, Le Baron [Jean] Ch[arles]. 1874. *L'Espagne.* Illustrated by G. Doré. Paris: Hachette.

Delgado-P., Guillermo, and John M. Schechter, eds. 2004. *Quechua Verbal Artistry: The Inscription of Andean Voices/Arte Expresivo Quechua: La Inscripción de Voces Andinas.* Bonn: Bonner Amerikanistische Studien (BAS, Volume 38); Aachen: Shaker Verlag.

Feldman, Heidi. 2003. "The International Soul of Black Peru." In *Musical Cultures of Latin America: Global Effects, Past and Present: UCLA Selected Reports XI,* edited by Steven Loza, 155–61. Los Angeles: Univ. of California, Los Angeles Department of Ethnomusicology and Systematic Musicology.

González, Juan Pablo. 1989. "'Inti-Illimani' and the Artistic Treatment of Folklore." *Revista de Música Latinoamericana/Latin American Music Review* 10(2): 267–86.

Gradante, William J. 1999. "Chapter Seven: Andean Colombia." In *Music in Latin American Culture: Regional Traditions,* edited by John M. Schechter, 302–82. New York: Schirmer.

Jara, Joan. 1984. *An Unfinished Song: The Life of Víctor Jara.* New York: Ticknor and Fields.

Jatari. 1978. *Jatari!! 4. Fadisa.* Fábrica de Discos S.A. Quito, Ecuador. 710129.

Kaemmer, John E. 1998. "Southern Africa: An Introduction." In *Africa: The Garland Encyclopedia of World Music,* vol. 1, edited by Ruth M. Stone, 700–21. New York: Garland.

Koetting, James T. 1992. "Three: Africa/Ghana." In *Worlds of Music: An Introduction to the Music of the World's Peoples,* 2nd ed., edited by Jeff Todd Titon, 67–105. New York: Schirmer.

Levy, Lisa, producer and narrator. 1988. *Violeta Madre.* Four-part series on the life and work of Violeta Parra. 2 cassettes. Olympia, WA: KAOS-FM, Evergreen State College.

Lipski, John M. 1987. "The Chota Valley: Afro-Hispanic Language in Highland Ecuador." *Latin American Research Review* 22(1): 155–70.

Lord, Albert. [1960] 1978. *The Singer of Tales.* New York: Atheneum; reprinted by arrangement with Harvard Univ. Press. First edition 1960.

Malinowski, Bronislaw. [1925] 1954. "Magic, Science, and Religion." In *Magic, Science, and Religion and Other Essays.* Garden City, NY: Anchor.

Mannheim, Bruce. 1991. *The Language of the Inka Since the European Invasion.* Austin: Univ. of Texas Press.

Manz, Beatriz. 2005. "A Journey Toward Simplicity." In *Berkeley Review of Latin American Studies.* Berkeley: Center for Latin American Studies, Univ. of California, Winter, 25–28.

Martínez, Gregorio, and Fietta Jarque. 1995. Liner notes to *The Soul of Black Peru/Afro-Peruvian Classics/El Alma del Perú Negro.* Compiled by David Byrne and Yale Evelev. Warner Bros Records Inc. 9 45878-4. Cassette.

McAllester, David P. 2002. "Chapter 2: North America/Native America." In *Worlds of Music: An Introduction to the Music of the World's Peoples,* 4th ed., edited by Jeff Todd Titon, 35–85. Belmont, CA: Schirmer.

McDowell, John H. 1972. "The Mexican *Corrido:* Formula and Theme in a Ballad Tradition." *Journal of American Folklore* 85:205–20.

Meisch, Lynn A. 1997. "Traditional Communities, Transnational Lives: Coping with Globalization in Otavalo, Ecuador." Ph.D. dissertation, Stanford Univ.

————. 2002. *Andean Entrepreneurs: Otavalo Merchants and Musicians in the Global Arena.* Austin: Univ. of Texas Press.

Moreno Chá, Ercilia. 1999. "Chapter Six: Music in the Southern Cone: Chile, Argentina, and Uruguay." In *Music in Latin American Culture: Regional Traditions,* edited by John M. Schechter, 236–301. New York: Schirmer.

Morris, Nancy. 1986. "*Canto porque es necesario cantar:* The New Song Movement in Chile, 1973–1983." *Latin American Research Review* 21(2): 117–36.

Ñanda Mañachi. 1977. *Ñanda mañachi 1 (Préstame el camino).* Jean Chopin Thermes, producer. Llaquiclla. IFESA (Industria Fonográfica Ecuatoriana S.A.) 339-0501. Guayaquil, Ecuador. Recorded in Ibarra, Ecuador.

————. 1979. *Ñanda mañachi 2 (Préstame el camino).* Jean Chopin Thermes, producer. Llaquiclla. IFESA (Industria Fonográfica Ecuatoriana S.A.) 339-0502. Guayaquil, Ecuador. Recorded in Ibarra, Ecuador.

————. 1983. *Ñanda mañachi/Boliviamanta: Préstame el camino desde Bolivia. Música quichua del equinoccio Andino. Churay, Churay!* Llaquiclla. Fediscos. Guayaquil, Ecuador. Onix L.P. 59003.

Nandorfy, Martha. 2003. "The Right to Live in Peace: Freedom and Social Justice in the Songs of Violeta Parra and Víctor Jara." In *Rebel Musics: Human Rights, Resistant Sounds, and the Politics of Music Making,* edited by Daniel Fischlin and Ajay Heble, 172–209. Montreal: Black Rose Books.

Nketia, J. H. Kwabena. 1974. *The Music of Africa.* New York: Norton.

Paredes, Américo. 1958. *"With His Pistol in His Hand": A Border Ballad and Its Hero.* Austin: Univ. of Texas Press.

————. 1976. *A Texas-Mexican Cancionero: Folksongs of the Lower Border.* Urbana: Univ. of Illinois Press.

Recio, P. Bernardo. [1773] 1947. *Compendiosa relación de la cristiandad (en el reino) de Quito.* Madrid: Consejo Superior de Investigaciones Científicas, Instituto Santo Toribio de Mogrovejo.

Romero, Raúl R. 1994. "Black Music and Identity in Peru: Reconstruction and Revival of Afro-Peruvian Musical Traditions." In *Music and Black Ethnicity: The Caribbean and South America,* edited by Gerard H. Béhague, 307–30. Coral Gables, FL: Univ. of Miami North-South Center.

————. 1999. "Chapter Eight: Andean Peru." In *Music in Latin American Culture: Regional Traditions,* edited by John M. Schechter, 383–423. New York: Schirmer.

Ross, Joe. 1994. "Music of the Andes." *Acoustic Musician Magazine* (June): 18–27.

Schechter, John M. 1979. "The Inca—*Cantar Histórico:* A Lexico-Historical Elaboration on Two Cultural Themes." *Ethnomusicology* 23(2): 191–204.

————. 1980. Interview with César Muquinche. Illampu, Tungurahua Province, Ecuador, July 12.

————. 1983. "*Corona y Baile*: Music in the Child's Wake of Ecuador and Hispanic South America, Past and Present." *Revista de Música Latinoamericana/Latin American Music Review* 4(1): 1–80.

————. 1992. *The Indispensable Harp: Historical Development, Modern Roles, Configurations, and Performance Practices in Ecuador and Latin America.* Kent, OH: Kent State Univ. Press.

————. 1994a. "Divergent Perspectives on the *velorio del angelito*: Ritual Imagery, Artistic Condemnation, and Ethnographic Value." *Journal of Ritual Studies* 8(2): 43–84.

————. 1994b. "Los Hermanos Congo y Milton Tadeo Ten Years Later: Evolution of an African-Ecuadorian Tradition of the Valle del Chota, Highland Ecuador." In *Music and Black Ethnicity: The Caribbean and South America,* edited by Gerard H. Béhague, 285–305. Coral Gables, FL: Univ. of Miami North-South Center/Transaction.

————. 1996. "Tradition and Dynamism in Ecuadorian Andean Quichua *Sanjuán:* Macrocosm in Formulaic Expression, Microcosm in Ritual Absorption." In *Cosmología y música en los Andes,* edited by Max Peter Baumann, 247–67. Frankfurt am Main: Vervuert; Madrid: Iberoamericana.

————. 1999a. "Chapter One: Themes in Latin American Music Culture." In *Music in Latin American Culture: Regional Traditions,* edited by John M. Schechter, 1–33. New York: Schirmer.

————. 1999b. "Chapter Nine: Beyond Region: Transnational and Transcultural Traditions." In *Music in Latin American Culture: Regional Traditions,* edited by John M. Schechter, 424–57. New York: Schirmer.

————. 2002. "Chapter 9: Latin America/Ecuador." In *Worlds of Music: An Introduction to the Music of the World's Peoples,* 4th ed., edited by Jeff Todd Titon, 385–446. Belmont, CA: Schirmer.

————. 2003. "Chapter 25: Taki Ñan: South American Affinity Interculture in Santa Cruz, California." In *Musical Cultures of Latin America: Global Effects, Past and Present: UCLA Selected Reports XI,* edited by Steven Loza, 271–84. Los Angeles: Univ. of California, Los Angeles Department of Ethnomusicology and Systematic Musicology.

Smith, Sandra. 1984. "Panpipes for Power, Panpipes for Play: The Social Management of Cultural Expression in Kuna Society." Ph.D. dissertation, Univ. of California–Berkeley.

Sonnichsen, Philip. 1975. Liner notes to *Una historia de la música de la frontera: Texas-Mexican Border Music,* vol. 2, *Corridos,* part 1, *1930–1934.* Edited by Chris Strachwitz. Folklyric Records LP 9004.

Tompkins, William David. 1998. "Afro-Peruvian Traditions." In *The Garland Encyclopedia of World Music, Volume 2: South America, Mexico, Central America, and the Caribbean,* edited by Dale A. Olsen and Daniel E. Sheehy, 491–502. New York: Garland.

Univ. of Iowa. 2003, March 7. http://www.news-releases.uiowa.edu/2003/march/030703inti-illimani.html (Arts Center Relations, 300 Plaza Centre One, Suite 351, Iowa City, IA 52242-2500).

Vidal, Francy. n.d. "Biography." http://www.chaskinakuy.com/biography.htm

ADDITIONAL READING

Aretz, Isabel. 1980. *Síntesis de la etnomúsica en América Latina.* Caracas, Venezuela: Monte Ávila editores.

———. 1991. *Historia de la etnomusicología en América Latina (Desde la época precolombina hasta nuestros días).* Caracas: Ediciones FUNDEF—CONAC—OEA.

Baumann, Max Peter, recopilado y editado. 1983. *Soqta Chunka Qheshwa Takis Bolivia Llajtamanta: Sesenta canciones del Quechua Boliviano.* Cochabamba, Bolivia: Centro Pedagógico y Cultural de Portales.

Béhague, Gérard. 1990. "Latin American Folk Music." In *Folk and Traditional Music of the Western Continents,* 3rd ed., edited by Bruno Nettl; revised and edited by Valerie Woodring Goertzen, 185–228. Englewood Cliffs, NJ: Prentice Hall.

———, ed. 1994. *Music and Black Ethnicity: The Caribbean and South America.* Coral Gables, FL: Univ. of Miami North-South Center/Transaction.

Cavour, Ernesto. c. 1974. *La zampoña, aerófono boliviano: Método audiovisual.* La Paz(?), Bolivia: Ediciones Tatu.

Den Otter, Elisabeth. 1985. *Music and Dance of Indians and Mestizos in an Andean Valley of Peru.* Delft, The Netherlands: Eburon.

Dicks, Ted, ed. 1976. *Víctor Jara: His Life and Songs.* London: Elm Tree.

Fairley, Jan. 1985. "Annotated Bibliography of Latin-American Popular Music with Particular Reference to Chile and to Nueva Canción." In *Popular Music, vol. 5, Continuity and Change,* 305–56. Cambridge: Cambridge Univ. Press.

Harrison, Regina. 1989. *Signs, Songs, and Memory in the Andes: Translating Quechua Language and Culture.* Austin: Univ. of Texas Press.

Holzmann, Rodolfo. 1986. *Q'ero, pueblo y música.* Lima: Patronato Popular y Porvenir Pro Música Clásica.

Hurtado Suárez, Wilfredo. 1995. *Chicha peruana: Música de los nuevos migrantes.* [Lima, Perú?]: Grupo de Investigaciones Económicas ECO.

List, George. 1983. *Music and Poetry in a Colombian Village: A Tri-Cultural Heritage.* Bloomington: Indiana Univ. Press.

Mendoza, Zoila S. 2000. *Shaping Society Through Dance: Mestizo Ritual Performance in the Peruvian Andes.* Chicago Studies in Ethnomusicology. Chicago: Univ. of Chicago Press.

Moreno Andrade, Segundo Luis. 1930. "La música en el Ecuador." In *El Ecuador en cien años de independencia, 1830–1930,* vol. 2, edited by J. Gonzalo Orellana. Quito: Imprenta de la Escuela de Artes y Oficios.

Obando, Segundo. 1988. *Tradiciones de Imbabura.* 3rd ed. Quito: Abya-Yala.

Olsen, Dale A. 1980. "Folk Music of South America: A Musical Mosaic." In *Musics of Many Cultures: An Introduction,* edited by E. May, 386–425. Berkeley: Univ. of California Press.

———. 1986–1987. "The Peruvian Folk Harp Tradition: Determinants of Style." *Folk Harp Journal* 53:48–54; 54:41–58; 55:55–59; 56:57–60.

———. 1996. *Music of the Warao of Venezuela: Song People of the Rain Forest.* Gainesville: Univ. Press of Florida.

Olsen, Dale A., and Daniel E. Sheehy, eds. 1998. *South America, Mexico, Central America, and the Caribbean.* Vol. 2 of *The Garland Encyclopedia of World Music.* New York: Garland Reference Library of the Humanities, vol. 1193.

Parra, Violeta. 1970. *Décimas: Autobiografía en versos chilenos.* Santiago de Chile: Ediciones Nueva Universidad, Universidad Católica de Chile, Editorial Pomaire.

Roel Pineda, Josafat. 1959. "El Wayno del Cuzco." *Folklore Americano* 6–7:129–246.

Romero, Raúl, ed. 1993. *Música, danzas y máscaras en los Andes.* Lima: Pontificia Universidad Católica del Perú: Instituto Riva-Agüero.

Schechter, John M. 1982. "Music in a Northern Ecuadorian Highland Locus: Diatonic Harp, Genres, Harpists, and Their Ritual Junction in the Quechua Child's Wake." 3 vols. Ph.D. dissertation, Univ. of Texas.

———. 1987. "Quechua *Sanjuán* in Northern Highland Ecuador: Harp Music as Structural Metaphor on *Purina.*" *Journal of Latin American Lore* 13(1): 27–46.

———, ed. 1999. *Music in Latin American Culture: Regional Traditions.* New York: Schirmer.

Seeger, Anthony. 1987. *Why Suyá Sing: A Musical Anthropology of an Amazonian People.* Cambridge, England: Cambridge Univ. Press.

Slater, Peter Gregg. 1977. *Children in the New England Mind in Death and in Life.* Hamden, CT: Archon Books/Shoe String Press.

Turino, Thomas. 1993. *Moving Away from Silence: Music of the Peruvian Altiplano and the Experience of Urban Migration.* Chicago: Univ. of Chicago Press.

Turino, Thomas, and James Lea, eds. 2004. *Identity and the Arts in Diaspora Communities.* Detroit Monographs in Musicology/Studies in Music, No. 40. Warren, MI: Harmonie Park Press.

Valencia Chacón, Américo. 1989. *El siku o zampoña: Perspectivas de un legado musical preincaico y sus aplicaciones en el desarrollo de la música peruana/The Altiplano Bipolar Siku: Study and Projection of Peruvian Panpipe Orchestras.* Ed. Bilingue (Bilingual ed.). Lima: Centro de Investigación y Desarrollo de la Música Peruana: Artex Editores.

ADDITIONAL LISTENING

Afro-Hispanic Music from Western Colombia and Ecuador. 1967. Recorded and edited by Norman E. Whitten, Jr. Folkways FE 4376.

El cancionero noble de Colombia. 1962. Recorded by Joaquín Piñeros Corpas. Bogotá: Ministerio de Educación-Editorial Antares-Fontón. 3 discs, 36 pp. text.

Cantan Garzón y Collazos [Colombia]. n.d. (pre-1970). Industria Electro-Sonora, Medellín, Colombia: Sonolux LP 12-104/IES-1.

Clásicas de la canción paraguaya: Alfredo Rolando Ortiz, arpa. n.d. (pre-1980). Quito, Ecuador: Industrias Famoso LDF-1015.

The Inca Harp: Laments and Dances of the Tawantinsuyu, the Inca Empire [Peru]. 1982. Recorded by Ronald Wright. Lyrichord LLST 7359.

Indian Music of Mexico. 1952, 1962. Recorded by Henrietta Yurchenko. Ethnic Folkways Library FE-4413. 4 pp. notes by Gordon F. Ekholm and Henrietta Yurchenko.

Mountain Music of Peru. 1966. Recorded by John Cohen. Folkways FE 4539.

Mushuc huaira huacamujun: Conjunto indígena "Peguche" [Ecuador]. Runa Causay. 1979. IFESA (Industria Fonográfica Ecuatoriana S.A.). 339-0651. Guayaquil, Ecuador.

Music of the Jívaro of Ecuador. 1972. Recorded and edited by Michael J. Harner. Ethnic Folkways Library FE 4386.

Música andina de Bolivia. 1980. Recorded with commmentary by Max Peter Baumann. Lauro Records LPLI/S-062. 36 pp. booklet.

Música folklórica de Venezuela. n.d. (post-1968). Recorded by Isabel Aretz, Luis Felipe Ramón y Rivera, and Álvaro Fernaud. International Folk Music Council, Anthologie de la Musique Populaire. Ocora OCR 78.

Perou: Julio Benavente Diaz: "Le charango du Cuzco." 1985. Recorded by Rafael Parejo and Regina Baldini. Ocora. Musiques traditionnelles vivantes. Sacem 558 647.

Pre-Columbian Instruments: Aerophone [Mexico]. 1972. Produced by Lilian Mendelssohn, with Pablo Castellanos. Played by Jorge Daher. Ethnic Folkways Library FE 4177.

Traditional Music of Peru 1: Festivals of Cusco. 1995. Annotated by Gisela Cánepa-Koch. Series compiled and edited by Raúl R. Romero, director of the Archives of Traditional Andean Music, Lima, Peru. Smithsonian Folkways SF 40466. 25-page booklet.

Traditional Music of Peru 2: The Mantaro Valley. 1995. Produced in collaboration with the Archives of Traditional Andean Music. Series compiled and edited by Raúl R. Romero, director of the Archives of Traditional Andean Music, Lima, Peru. Smithsonian Folkways SF 40467. 21-page booklet.

Traditional Music of Peru 3: Cajamarca and the Colca Valley. 1996. Series compiled and edited by Raúl R. Romero, Archives of Traditional Andean Music of the Riva-Agüero Institute of the Catholic University of Peru, Lima, Peru. Smithsonian Folkways SF 40468. 25-page booklet.

Traditional Music of Peru 4: Lambayeque. 1996. Series compiled and edited by Raúl R. Romero, Archives of Traditional Andean Music of the Riva-Agüero Institute of the Catholic University of Peru, Lima, Peru. Smithsonian Folkways SF 40469. 25-page booklet.

ADDITIONAL VIEWING

Ayala, Fernando, and Héctor Olivera, directors. 1972. *Argentinísima I.* In Spanish, without subtitles. Featured performers: Atahualpa Yupanqui, Ariel Ramírez, Los Chalchaleros,

Mercedes Sosa, and Astor Piazzolla. Media Home Entertainment, Inc., 510 W. 6th St., Suite 1032, Los Angeles, CA 90014.

———. 1976. *El canto cuenta su historia.* In Spanish, without subtitles. Film/video. Featured performers: Cayetano Daglio, Ángel Villoldo, Francisco Canaro, Carlos Gardel, Rosita Quiroga, Ignacio Corsini, Ada Falcón, Agustín Magaldi and Pedro Noda, Marta de los Ríos, Margarita Palacios, Eduardo Falú, Los Cantores de Quilla Huasi, Jorge Oafrune, Amelita Baltar, and Hermanos Abalos. Condor Video (A Heron International Company), c/o Jason Films, 2825 Wilcrest, Suite 670, Houston, TX 77042. Aries Cinematográfica, Argentina.

Benson-Gyles, Anna, producer. 1980. *The Incas.* Odyssey Series. Narrated by Tony Kahn. Michael Ambrosino, executive producer. For Odyssey: Marian White, producer; David Berenson, editor. Coproduction of British Broadcasting Corporation (BBC) and Public Broadcasting Associates, Inc., Boston, MA. Incas/Odyssey Series/Box 1000, Boston, MA 02118. PBS Video, 1320 Braddock Pl., Alexandria, VA 22314.

Cohen, John, director. 1979. *Q'eros: The Shape of Survival.* 53 min. 16mm film/video. Color. Berkeley: Univ. of California, Extension Center for Media and Independent Learning, 2000 Center St., 4th Floor, Berkeley, CA 94704.

———. 1984. *Mountain Music of Peru.* 16mm film/video, 60 min. Color. Berkeley: Univ. of California, Extension Center for Media and Independent Learning, 2000 Center St., 4th Floor, Berkeley, CA 94704.

Cross, Stephen, director. 1977. *Disappearing World: Umbanda: The Problem Solver.* In English and in Portuguese with English subtitles. Peter Fry, narrator. Brian Moser, series editor. Public Media Video, 5547 N. Ravenswood Ave., Chicago, IL 60640-1199. Granada Colour Production, Granada UK.

Dibb, Michael, director. 1985. *What's Cuba Playing At? (¿Qué se toca en Cuba?).* 72 min. In Spanish, with subtitles. BBC TV Production, in association with Cuban Television. Center for Cuban Studies, 124 W. 23rd St., New York, NY 10011.

Hernández, Amalia, director. 1989. *Folklórico: Ballet Folklórico de México.* In Spanish, without subtitles. Featured performers: Ballet Folklórico de México. Madera Cinevideo, 525 E. Yosemite Ave., Madera, CA 93638.

Rivera, Pedro A., and Susan Zeig, directors. 1989. *Plena Is Work, Plena Is Song.* 16mm film/video. Cinema Guild, Inc.: 1697 Broadway, Suite 506, New York, NY 10019-5904.

Schaeffer, Nancy. 1995. "Directory of Latin American Films and Videos: Music, Dance, Mask, and Ritual." *Revista de Música Latinoamericana/Latin American Music Review* 16(2): 221–41.

Summa, John, and John Travers, coproducers and codirectors. Forthcoming, c. January 2008. *The Power of Their Song: The Untold Story of Latin America's New Song Movement.* 90-minute documentary film. New Cinema Films. Depicts the lives and music of the first generation of *Nueva Canción* musicians, including Víctor Jara. http://www.newsongfilmproject.org

INTERNET RESOURCES

Chaskinakuy http://www.chaskinakuy.com http://www.chaskinakuy.com/recording.htm http://www.chaskinakuy.com/biography.htm

Chapter Author, John M. Schechter http://arts.ucsc.edu/faculty/schechter/

Florida State University School of Music Center for Music of the Americas
http://www.music.fsu.edu/ctr-americas.htm
The Center for Music of the Americas was established in 1985 to create and enhance understanding among the peoples of North, South, and Central America and the Caribbean through music and its related arts and folkways. It forms an integral part of the Florida State University School of Music. The center oversees numerous world music performance groups, within the School of Music, and it seeks to support any and all activities related to music in the Americas. The center is closely related to the disciplines of Ethnomusicology, Historical Musicology, and Multicultural Music Education.

Latin American Music Center, Indiana University School of Music
http://www.music.indiana.edu/som/lamc/
A major research center for the study of Latin American music. This website includes a link to "Online Resources."

LAMC-L: Academic Discussion of Latin American Music
http://www.music.indiana.edu/som/lamc/edusearch/lamc-l/
At the Latin American Music Center, Indiana University School of Music. LAMC-L is an e-mail discussion list and file server for the Latin American Music Center at the School of Music, Indiana University, Bloomington. This list provides subscribers with an avenue for exchanging news about work-in-progress; for posing questions of general interest about Latin American music; for announcing conferences, festivals, concerts, recordings, and

publications; and for engaging in the serious discussion of issues pertaining to Latin American music.

Latin American Music Review/Revista de Música Latinoamericana
  http://www.utexas.edu/utpress/journals/jlamr.html
  This journal, published by University of Texas Press, explores the historical, ethnographic, and sociocultural dimensions of Latin American music in Latin American social groups, including the Puerto Rican, Mexican, Cuban, and Portuguese populations in the United States. Articles are written in English, Spanish, or Portuguese.

New Song Film Project http://www.newsongfilmproject.org

Revista Musical Chilena
  http://www.scielo.cl/scielo.php?script=sci_serial&pid=0716-2790&lng=en&nrm=iso
  Published by the Universidad de Chile, Facultad de Artes. One of the major musicology/ethnomusicology journals published in Latin America.

Chapter 10 – The Arab World

REFERENCES

Abu-Lughod, Lila. 1986. *Veiled Sentiments: Honor and Poetry in a Bedouin Society.* Berkeley: Univ. of California Press.

Alhaj, Rahim. 2006. *When the Soul is Settled: Music of Iraq.* Smithsonian Folkways SFW 40533.

Blank, Les. 1987. *Cuba: Routes of Rhythm.* Flower Films. Volume 1 (of 3). Videotape.

Caton, Steven C. 1990. *On the Peaks of Yemen I Summon: Poetry as Cultural Practice in a North Yemeni Tribe.* Berkeley: Univ. of California Press.

Danielson, Virginia. 1997. *The Voice of Egypt: Umm Kulthûm, Arabic Song, and Egyptian Society in the Twentieth Century.* Chicago and Cairo: Univ. of Chicago Press, American Univ. in Cairo Press.

Doubleday, Veronica. 1999. "The Frame Drum in the Middle East: Women, Musical Instruments and Power." *Ethnomusicology* 43(1): 101–34.

Eickelman, Dale F. 1989. *The Middle East: An Anthropological Approach.* Upper Saddle River, NJ: Prentice Hall.

El-Funoun. 1999. *Zaghareed: Music from the Palestinian Holy Land.* Sounds True STA M109D.

Gilbert, Stacy. 2004. *NPR Morning Edition.* January 22.

Knight, Roderic. 1984. "Music in Africa: The Manding Contexts." In *Performance Practice,* edited by Gerard Béhague, 53–90. Westport, CT: Greenwood Press.

Lane, Edward W. [1908] 1963. *The Manners and Customs of the Modern Egyptians.* London: Everyman's Library.

Lord, Albert. 1960. *The Singer of Tales.* Cambridge, MA: Harvard Univ. Press.

Marcus, Scott L. 1989. "Arab Music Theory in the Modern Period." Ph.D. dissertation, Univ. of California–Los Angeles.

———. 1992. "Modulation in Arab Music: Documenting Oral Concepts, Performance Rules and Strategies." *Ethnomusicology* 36 (2): 171–95.

———. 1993. "The Interface Between Theory and Practice: Intonation in Arab Music." *Asian Music* 24 (2): 39–58.

Nelson, Kristina. 1985. *The Art of Reciting the Qur'an.* Austin: Univ. of Texas Press.

Patai, Raphael. 1983. *The Arab Mind.* Rev. ed. New York: Scribner.

Racy, A. J. 1984. "Arab Music—An Overview." In *Maqam: Music of the Islamic World and its Influences,* edited by Robert Browning, 9–13. New York: Alternative Museum.

———. 1991. "Historical Worldviews of Early Ethnomusicologists: An East-West Encounter in Cairo, 1932." In *Ethnomusicology and Modern Music History,* edited by Stephen Blum, Philip V. Bohlman, and Daniel M. Neuman, 68–94. Urbana: Univ. of Illinois Press.

———. 1996. "Heroes, Lovers, and Poet-Singers: The Bedouin Ethos in the Music of the Arab Near East. *Journal of American Folklore* 109 (434): 404–24.

———. 2002. *Making Music in the Arab World: The Culture and Artistry of Tarab.* Oxford: Oxford Univ. Press.

Rasmussen, Anne. K. 1997. "Theory and Practice at the 'Arabic Org': Digital Technology in Contemporary Arab Music Performance." *Popular Music* 15 (3): 345–65.

Reynolds, Dwight F. 1989. "Tradition Replacing Tradition in Egyptian Epic Singing: The Creation of a Commercial Image." *Pacific Review of Ethnomusicology* 5:1–14.

————. 1991. "The Interplay of Genres in Oral Epic Performance: Differentially Marked Discourse in a Northern Egyptian Tradition." In *The Ballad and Oral Literature,* edited by Joseph Harris, 292–317. Cambridge, MA: Harvard Univ. Press.

————. 1993. *Sirat Bani Hilal: A Guide to the Epic and Its Performance.* Dearborn, MI: Arab American Community Center for Economic and Social Services.

————. 1995. *Heroic Poets, Poetic Heroes: The Ethnography of Performance in an Arabic Oral Epic Tradition.* Ithaca, NY: Cornell Univ. Press.

————. 1996. "Crossing and Recrossing the Line and Other Moments of Understanding." In *The World Observed: Reflections on the Fieldwork Process,* edited by Bruce Jackson and Edward D. Ives, 100–117. Urbana: Univ. of Illinois Press.

Romero, Brenda. 1997. "Cultural Interaction in New Mexico as Illustrated in the Matachines Dance." In *Musics of Multicultural America: A Study of Twelve Musical Communities,* edited by Kip Lornell and Anne K. Rasmussen, 155–86. New York: Schirmer.

Sawa, George D. 1985. "The Status and Roles of the Secular Musicians in the *Kitab al-Aghani* (Book of Songs), of Abu al-Faraj al-Isbahani (d. 356 A.H./967 A.D.)" *Asian Music* 17 (1): 69–82.

————. 1989. *Music Performance in the Early 'Abbasid Era 132–320 A.H./ 750–932 A.D.* Toronto: Pontifical Institute of Mediaeval Studies.

Sells, Michael A. 1999. *Approaching the Qur'an: The Early Revelations.* Ashland, OR: White Cloud Press.

Shiloah, Amnon. 1991. "Musical Modes and the Medical Dimension: The Arabic Sources (c.900–c.1600)." In *Metaphor: A Musical Dimension,* edited by Jamie C. Kassler. Sydney: Currency Press.

————. 1997. "Music and Religion in Islam." *Acta Musicologica* 69 (July–December): 143–55.

Turino, Thomas. 2001. "Chapter 7: The Music of Sub-Saharan Africa." In *Excursions in World Music,* 3rd ed., edited by Bruno Nettl, Charles Capwell, Philip V. Bohlman, Isabel K. K. Wong, and Thomas Turino, 227–54. Upper Saddle River, NJ: Prentice Hall.

Turner, Howard R. 1995. *Science in Medieval Islam: An Illustrated Introduction.* Austin: Univ. of Texas Press.

Villoteau, M. 1823. *Description de L'égypt: De l'état Actuel de L'Art Musicale en égypt.* Vol. 14, 2nd ed. Paris: Imprimerie de C.L.F. Panckoucke.

Wenders, Wim. 1999. *Buena Vista Social Club.* A film by Wim Wenders. Road Movies production. Produced by Ulrich Felsberg and Deepak Nayar. Santa Monica, CA: Artisan Entertainment.

ADDITIONAL READING

The Garland Encyclopedia of World Music. Volume 6: The Middle East. 2002. Edited by Virginia Danielson, Scott Marcus, and Dwight Reynolds, with Alexander J. Fisher. New York: Routledge. The first source to turn to for further information on the Middle East, this encyclopedia is a collection of the best and most concise work of most of the major scholars in the area of Middle Eastern music. The volume also includes extensive bibliographic references and the comprehensive "A Guide to Recordings of Middle Eastern Music."

Ahmed, Leila. 1992. *Women and Gender in Islam.* New Haven, CT: Yale Univ. Press.

Berliner, Paul. 1993. *The Soul of Mbira.* Rev. ed. Berkeley: Univ. of California Press.

Bowen, Donna Lee, and Evelyn A. Early. 1993. *Everyday Life in the Muslim Middle East.* Bloomington: Indiana Univ. Press.

Browning, Robert, ed. 1984. *Maqam: Music of the Islamic World and its Influences.* New York: Alternative Museum.

Danielson, Virginia. 1992. "Artists and Entrepreneurs: Female Singers in Cairo During the 1920s." In *Women in Middle Eastern History: Shifting Boundaries in Sex and Gender,* edited by Nikki R. Keddie and Beth Baron. New Haven, CT: Yale Univ. Press.

Davis, Ruth. 2004. *Ma'luf: Reflections on the Arab Andalusian Music of Tunesia.* Scarecrow Press.

Doubleday, Veronica. 1990. *Three Women of Herat.* Austin: Univ. of Texas Press.

Farmer, Henry George. 1929. *A History of Arabian Music to the XIIIth Century.* London: Lyzac and Co.

Feldman, Walter. 1996. *Music of the Ottoman Court.* Intercultural Music Studies, 10. Berlin: International Institute for Traditional Music.

Kulthum, Umm. 1967. "Umm Kulthum: Famed Egyptian Singer (1910–1975)." In *Middle Eastern Muslim Women Speak,* edited by Elizabeth Fernea and B.Q. Bezirgan. Austin: Univ. of Texas Press.

Marcus, Scott L. 2006. *Music in the Middle East: Experiencing Music, Expressing Culture.* Global Music Series. Bonnie C. Wade and Patricia Shehan Campbell, General Editors. Oxford: Oxford Univ. Press.

Nelson, Kristina. 1982. "Reciter and Listener: Some Factors Shaping the Mujawwad Style of Qur'anic Reciting." *Ethnomusicology* 26(1): 41–7.

Racy, A. J. 1983. "Music in Nineteenth-Century Egypt: An Historical Sketch." *Selected Reports in Ethnomusicology* 4:157–79.

———. 1988. "Sound and Society: The *Takht* Music of Early-Twentieth Century Cairo." *Selected Reports in Ethnomusicology* 7:157–79.

———. 1991. "Creativity and Ambience: An Ecstatic Feedback Model from Arab Music." *World of Music* 33(3): 7–28.

Rasmussen, Anne. K. 1991a. "'An Evening in the Orient': The Middle Eastern Nightclub in America." *Asian Music* 23(2): 63–88.

———. 1991b. "Individuality and Social Change in the Music of Arab Americans." Ph.D. dissertation, Univ. of California–Los Angeles.

———. 1995. "The Celebration of Community and Culture Through Music and Dance at Three Arab-American Weddings." *Michigan Folklife Annual* 1996: 40–50.

Regev, Motti, and Edwin Seroussi. 2004. *Popular Music and National Culture in Israel.* Berkeley: Univ. of California Press.

Said, Edward W. 1979. *Orientalism.* New Work: Vintage Books.

Schade-Poulsen, Marc. 1999. *Men and Popular Music in Algeria: The Social Significance of Rai.* Austin: Univ. of Texas Press.

Schuyler, Philip. 1978. "Moroccan Andalusian Music." *World of Music* 20 (1): 33–44.

———. 1984. "Moroccan Andalusian Music." In *Maqam: Music of the Islamic World and Its Influences,* edited by Robert Browning, 14–17. New York: Alternative Museum.

———. 1993. "A Folk Revival in Morocco." In *Everyday Life in the Muslim Middle East,* edited by Donnal Lee Bowen and Evelyn A. Early, 287–93. Bloomington: Indiana Univ. Press.

Shaheen, Jack G. 1984. *The TV Arab.* Bowling Green, OH: Bowling Green State Univ. Popular Press.

Touma, Habib Hassan. 1996. *The Music of the Arabs.* Expanded ed., translated by Laurie Schwartz. Portland, OR: Amadeus Press.

Van Nieuwkerk, Karen. 1995. *A Trade Like Any Other: Female Singers and Dancers in Egypt.* Austin: Univ. of Texas Press.

ADDITIONAL LISTENING

Alhaj, Rahim. 2003. *Rahim Alhaj: Iraqi Music in a Time of War.* (Live in concert, New York City April 5, 2003). Voxlox. Original compositions.

———. 2006. *When the Soul is Settled: Music of Iraq.* With notes by D.A. Sonneborn. Smithsonian Folkways SFW 40533.

Bashir, Munir. n.d. *The Stockholm Recordings.* VDL 688. Original music by the Iraqi master of the *'ud.*

———. n.d. *Masters of Oud: Munir Bashir and Omar Bashir.* BR 001. Original music by the Iraqi master of the *'ud* with his son.

Congrès du Caire. 1988. *Muhammad al Qubbanji, Dawud Hosni, Muhammad Ghanim, . . .* 2 CDs made from historical recordings in the occasion of Cairo Congress in 1932. Including a special booklet. Edition Bibliogeque Nationale-L'institute du Monde Arabe. Paris. APN 88-9, 10.

Jones, Brian. 1971. *Brian Jones Presents the Pipes of Pan at Joujouka.* LP. New York, NY: Rolling Stones Records. COC 49100. Rereleased by Phillips. 1995. CD. Recording from 1968, of musicians from the Moroccan village of Jahjoukah, produced by Brian Jones, former member of The Rolling Stones.

El-Funoun. n.d. *Zaghareed: Music from the Palestinian Holy Land.* Sounds True STA M109D. Folkloric troupe presents creative renditions of musical folk traditions.

Ensemble Morkos. 2000. *Cedre: Arabo-Andalusian Muwashshah.* L'empreinte Digitale. ED 13067. Traditional music from Arab-Andalusian tradition. Instrumental compositions and improvisations and *vocal muwshshahat* performed by Lebanese ensemble.

Fakhri, Sabah, and Wadi al Safi. 2000. *Two Tenors and Qantara: Historical Live Recording of Arabic Masters.* Ark 21. Live concert recording of two fine singers from Syria and Lebanon accompanied by excellent ensemble led by Simon Shaheen.

Gabriel, Peter. 1989. *Passion: Music for the Last Temptation of Christ.* Geffen Records. Soundtrack for film of the same title. Music chosen and arranged based on creative imagination of music during the time of Jesus Christ.

The Musicians of the Nile (*Les Musiciens du Nil*). 2001. *Mizmar Baladi.* Ocora C582006. Music in the style of epic traditions described in this chapter, as well as other Egyptian folk music.

Racy, A. J. 1997. *Mystical Legacies.* Lyrichord Discs LLCT 7437. Original compositions and improvisations and traditional music interpreted by Racy performing on 'ud, buzuq, and nay with Soheil Kaspar, percussion.

Racy, A. J., and Simon Shaheen. 1993. *Taqasim: The Art of Improvisation in Arabic Music.* Lyrichord Discs LLCT 7374. Racy and Shaheen perform in traditional Arab style of improvisation on 'ud, buzuq, and violin.

Shaheen, Simon. 2002. *Turath: Master Works of the Middle East.* CMP Recordings 3006. Shaheen and traditional ensemble perform canon of Turkish/Arab repertory.

Sting. 1999. *Brand New Day.* Interscope Records. This CD features the Algerian singer Cheb Mami for the song "Desert Rose," which was hailed as an unprecedented collaboration.

Tasat, Ramon. n.d. *Como la Rosa en la Güerta.* CD produced by Ramon Tasat. Collection of Sephardic ballads and paraliturgical songs primarily in Ladino language with texts and translations; accompanied by Tina Chauncy and Scott Reiss.

Various Artists. 1997. *The Music of Arab Americans: A Retrospective Collection.* Rounder 1122. Collection of the most important artists from within the Arab American community between 1915 and 1955. Informative notes and photographs in booklet.

ADDITIONAL VIEWING

100% Arabica. 1997. Feature film, 85 min. Directed by Mahmoud Zemmouri. Coproduced by Fennec Productions, Les Films de la Toison d'Or, and Incoprom. Screenplay by Mahmoud Zemmouri. Music by Mohamed Maghni. New York: ArtMattan Productions.

A Little for My Heart a Little for My God. 1993. Documentary film, 60 min. Directed by Brita Landoff. Produced by Lindberg and Landorg Film HB. New York: Filmmaker's Library.

The Master Musicians of Jahjouka. 1983. Videocassette. A. J. Racy, Narrator. Long Beach, CA: Mendizza and Associates Mendiza Films.

Sallamah. 1943. Feature film. Starring Umm Kulthum and Anway Wajd. Lyrics by Bayram al-Tunsi. Music by Zakariya Ahmad. Ave 44 Arabian Video Entertainment.

Silences of the Palace (Samt al-Qusur). 1994. Feature film, 127 min. Written and directed by Moufida Tlatil. Produced by Ahmed Baha Eddine Attia and Richard Magnien. Music by Anouar Brahem. Produced by Mat Films and Cinétéléfims. Magfilms coproduction. Bethesda, MD: Capitol Home Video.

Wedding in Galilee (Hatunah B'Galil). 1987. Feature film, 113 min. Directed by Michel Khleifi. Original screenplay by Michel Khleifi. New York: Kino on Video.

A Wife for My Son. 1990s. Feature film, 93 min. Directed by Ali Ghanem. Produced by Mohammed Tahar Harhoura. Script by Françoise Penzer. Seattle WA: Arab Film Distribution.

INTERNET RESOURCES

Here are just a few websites of the performers and related traditions mentioned in the chapter. All of these sites have been reliable for several years; however, I encourage you to explore Internet and YouTube sites frequently; new sites and resources emerge as others disappear.

El-Funoun http://www.el-funoun.org/

In Their Own Voices http://henriettayurchenco.com/ITOV/ITOV1.html
Henrietta Yurchenco's website leads to the table of contents of her book *In their Own Voices: Women in Judeo-Hispanic Song and Story* and to the lyrics of the songs described and to audio files of performances.

Jewish Devotional and Liturgical Poetry http://www.piyut.org.il/english/

Maqam http://www.maqam.com

Maqam World http://www.maqamworld.com/index.html
Extensive, multitiered website featuring information and demonstration of musical modes, rhythms, and forms.

NPR: "In Baghdad, a Rare Musical Performance" http://www.npr.org/templates/story/story.php?storyId=11202774
Report by Jamie Tarabay, *Morning Edition,* National Public Radio, June 20, 2007.

Simon Shaheen and Arabic Music Retreat http://www.simonshaheen.com/

A. J. Racy http://www.ethnomusic.ucla.edu/people/racy.htm

Rahim Alhaj http://www.rahimalhaj.com/

Naseer Shamma http://www.naseershamma.com/

Silk Road http://www.silkroadproject.org/silkroad/map.html
Al Jadid: A Review and Record of Arab Culture and Arts http://www.aljadid.com/music/
The Store: Rap and Hip-Hop http://www.freethep.com/tunage.htm
    Compilation of Palestinian and other rap/hip-hop in the Arab diaspora.

Chapter 11 – Discovering and Documenting a World of Music

REFERENCES

Radin, Paul. [1927] 1957. Preface to *Primitive Man as Philosopher*. New York: Dover.

Spottswood, Richard. 1990. *Ethnic Music on Records: A Discography of Ethnic Recordings Produced in the United States, 1893 to 1942*. 5 *vols*. Urbana: Univ. of Illinois Press.

Titon, Jeff Todd. 1980. "The Life Story." *Journal of American Folklore* 93: 276–92.

Titon, Jeff Todd, and Bob Carlin, eds. 2001. *American Musical Traditions*. New York: Gale Research.

ADDITIONAL READING

Barz, Gregory F., and Timothy J. Cooley. 1997. *Shadows in the Field: New Perspectives for Fieldwork in Ethnomusicology*. New York: Oxford Univ. Press.

Emerson, Robert M., Rachel I. Fretz, and Linda L. Shaw. 1995. *Writing Ethnographic Fieldnotes*. Chicago: University of Chicago Press.

Ethnomusicology 36(2). 1992. [Special issue on fieldwork in the public interest]

Golde, Peggy, ed. 1986. *Women in the Field: Anthropological Experiences*. 2nd ed. Berkeley: Univ. of California Press.

Ives, Edward D. 1980. *The Tape-Recorded Interview: A Manual for Fieldworkers in Folklore and Oral History*. Knoxville: Univ. of Tennessee Press.

Jackson, Bruce. 1987. *Fieldwork*. Urbana: Univ. of Illinois Press.

Lornell, Kip, and Anne K. Rasmussen. 1997. *Musics of Multicultural America*. New York: Schirmer Books.

Sanjek, Roger, ed. 1990. *Fieldnotes: The Makings of Anthropology*. Ithaca, NY: Cornell Univ. Press.

Spradley, James P. 1972. *The Cultural Experience: Ethnography in Complex Society*. Chicago: Science Research Associates. Contains sample student ethnographies.

Van Maanen, John. 1988. *Tales of the Field: On Writing Ethnography*. Chicago: Univ. of Chicago Press.

Wolcott, Harry F. 2005. *The Art of Fieldwork*. 2nd ed. Walnut Creek, CA: Alta Mira Press.

Credits

This page constitutes an extension of the copyright page. We have made every effort to trace the ownership of all copyrighted material and to secure permission from copyright holders. In the event of any question arising as to the use of any material, we will be pleased to make the necessary corrections in future printings. Thanks are due to the following authors, publishers, and agents for permission to use the material indicated.

Chapter 2. 39: With permission of Canyon Records. **43:** With permission of William N. Fenton. **43:** With permission of William N. Fenton. **55:** With permission of Albert Sanoval, Jr. and Ray Winne. **55:** With permission of Albert Sanoval Jr. and Ray Winne. **57:** Text, Navajo Sway song, David P. McAllester, Enemy Way Music, pp. 29, 37. Papers of the Peabody Museum of Archaeology and Ethnology, vol. 41, no. 3. Copyright © 1954 by the President and Fellows of Harvard College. **58:** Text, Navajo Sway song, David P. McAllester, Enemy Way Music, pp. 29, 37. Papers of the Peabody Museum of Archaeology and Ethnology, vol. 41, no. 3. Copyright © 1954 by the President and Fellows of Harvard College. **58:** Text, Navajo Sway song, David P. McAllester, Enemy Way Music, pp. 29, 37. Papers of the Peabody Museum of Archaeology and Ethnology, vol. 41, no. 3. Copyright © 1954 by the President and Fellows of Harvard College. **66:** All excerpts reprinted with permission from Frisbie & McAllester, 1978. **72:** Transcription by David P. McAllester from field recording by Willard Rhodes. **76:** With permission of Roland Dixon. **77:** With permission of Ruth Roessel. Translation by Ruth Rossel for David McAllester. **78:** "Los Angeles Sweetheart" by Danny Whitefeather Begay, from My Beautiful Land (ARP-6078). Courtesy Canyon Records. **79:** "Mother Earth" from Yazzie Girl (CR-534) by Sharon Burch. (P) © 1989 Sharon Burch. Courtesy Canyon Records. **80:** "Proud Earth" by Arliene Mofchissey Williams. With permission of Arliene Nofchissey Williams.

Chapter 3. Text translation, "Nyarai" by Thomas Mapfumo, courtesy of Information Office, Zimbabwe High Commission, London. **141:** Arom 1991:305. Used with permission.

Chapter 4. "From Dark Till Dawn," words and music by John Shines, © Uncle Doris Music, ASCAP. Used by permission. "You Don't Love Me" (3:35). Willie Cobbs. Performed by Magic Sam (Sam Maghett), vocal and guitar; Sam Lay, drums; unknown bass player. Field recording by Jeff Todd Titon. Ann Arbor, Michigan, August, 1969. Used by permission of the artists and the copyright holder, Embassy Music Corp., BMI. © 1974 by William Lucas and Jeff Todd Titon. A fuller version accompanies Titon 1974b. **166:** Lomax 1976. © Alan Lomax. Used by permission. **167:** Collected by Alan Lomax; transcribed by Mieczyslaw Kolinski. From Courlander 1963. Reprinted courtesy of Columbia University Press. **185:** Words and music by William Lucas. Used by permission. **194:** "Dog Me Around," by Howlin' Wolf (Chester Burnett). Copyright © 1974, Modern Music Publishing Co., Inc. Used by permission. **194:** "Kokomo Blues" by Fred

McDowell, © 1996 Tradition Music/BMI, administered by BUG. All Rights Reserved. Used by permission. **203:** Words and music by Otis Rush, © 1994 Otis Rush Music, administered by BUG. Used by permission.

Chapter 5. "Sisters, Hold on to Your Chastity" reprinted by permission of Mirjana Lausevic. "Zuta Baba" by Zabei Babe, Bison Publications. Reprinted by permission. Going to the Village/Krzesany Po Dwa from TWINKLE INNA POLISH STYLEE—HIGHER HEIGHTS. Reprinted by permission of Twinkle Records. Oyfn Pripetshok, created in Kerr Hall, UCSB. Used by permission of Katherine Meizel, Lillie Gordon and Ralph Lowi. **224:** Words and music by Himzo Polovina. © Himzo Polovina. Used by permission of Edmir Polovina. **235:** Words and music by Dino Merlin. Used by permission of the artist.

Chapter 7. "Begadang II" by Rhoma Irama. Used by permission. "Distorti" by Dhani Ahmad Manaf. Used by permission.

Chapter 8. Qi cun lian ("Seven-inch Lotus"). Tindei jaan mei ("Praise from Heaven and Earth"). Chorping Chang and Gabriel Chi. Performed by Cherith Baptist Church. Field recording by Hera Tang. Hong Kong, China, 2005. Used by permission of Hera Tang. Yundao ge ("Weeding Song"). Traditional Jiangsu folksong. Performed by Jin Wenyin. Field recording to Antoinet Schimmelpennick and Frank Kouwenhoven. Qiandai, China, 1987. CHINESE FOLK SONGS AND FOLK SINGERS: Shan'ge Traditions in Southern Jiangsu, Leidin, 1997. Used by permission of Antoinet Schimmelpennick.

Chapter 9. 389: Words and music by Victor Jara. Copyright © 1976 Mighty Oak Music Ltd., London, England. TRO-Essex Music International, Inc. controls all publication right for the U.S.A. and Canada. Used by permission. **423:** n/a

Chapter 10. 481: Performed by A. J. Racy, Simon Shaheen, and the Arabic Music Retreat Ensemble. Used by permission of the artists. **496:** Music by Rahim Alhaj. Used by permission of the artist. **504:** English translation by Ramón Tasat and Dwight F. Reynolds. **519:** Transliteration and English translation by Dwight F. Reynolds. **528, 529:** Used by permission of the Khadaj family.

Index

Note: Glossary terms appear in boldface print in this Index. You can find their definitions on the pages indicated.

"Abenamar" (Andalusian), 504–509
Abing, 358–363
Absolute pitch, 374
Activities, involving music, 23–26
Additive meters, 220–221
Adi tala (Indian), **280,** 286, 291
Adonis, 516
Adzokpi, **95,** 96
Adzo songs, **95,** 107–108
Aesthetics, of music, **20**
Affect, in music-culture model, **15**
Affinity groups, 17
African-American music, 415
    blues music, 165–202
    Christian worship and hymns, 145–156
    play, music of, 164–203
    worksong, 156–164
African-Ecuadorian music, 443–447
African Music: A People's Art (Bebey), 87
African music and culture
    African-American music and, 149
    African-Ecuadorian music, 443–447
    Agbekor, 89–110
    BaAka people, 134–143
    blues, influence on, 175–176
    chimurenga music, 131–134
    cross-cultural misunderstanding, 87
    Dagbamba people, 119
    Ewe people, 89–91
    history of, 85–86
    humanism of, 143
    intercultural identity of, 83–84
    "Lambango" (Mande), 110
    "Makala" (BaAka), 136–142
    Mali, 110–111
    Mande people, 110–123

    Mbira, 123–131
    music-culture, 85–87
    "Nhemamusasa" (Shona), 123–131
    North American music, influence on, 145
    Nyarai ("Be Ashamed," Chimurenga), 131–134
    Postal workers' melody, 2, 6–8, 9, 84–89
    Shona people, 123–124
    Taliya, 110–123
Afro-Peruvian music, 466–470
Agbekor, 10, **89**–110, 199
Agbeli, Godwin, 94, 98
Ahmad Band, 347, 350–352
"Ain't Enough Comin' In" (Blues, by Rush), 199–201
Ajinas, 500
Akami, 142
Alam, Farid, 527
Alapana, 283, 291, **292**–293, 296
al-Asadi, Ayad and Bashir, 523, 527
al-Asadi, Saud, 527
Albazo (Ecuadorian), 459, 463
Alcohol and alcoholic beverages, 455
Alegría, Fernando, 422
Alhaj, Rahim, 483, 492–499
al-Haj, Rahim, 24
Ali, Salif, 256
al-Isbahani, Abu al-Faraj, 492
Allende, Salvador, 423–424
All Girl Boys (group), 535
Allison, Luther, 11, 191
allmusic.com, 27
Alorwoyie, Midawo Gideon Foli, 92, 93, 102
Alpana, 9
"Al-Shaghal," 475, 478–480
al-Wahhab, Muhammad 'Abd, 476
Amauta (ensemble), 448
"Amazing Grace" (hymn), 147–150

591

American Folklife Center (Library of Congress), 550
American music. *See* African-American music; Native American music
American Musical Traditions (Titon and Carlin, ed.), 549
"A Mighty Fortress," 213, 218, 219, 224
"Amor Imposible" (Peru), 449–451
Ancestor worship, 356
Andal, 290
Andalusia, 502–509
Andean ensembles, 447–453
Anderson, Benedict, 210
Andesmanta (ensemble), 448
"Angelita Huenumán" (Jara), 423–424
Aniruddha, K.S.R., 278
Ann Arbor Blues Festival, 191, 192
Anya Agbekor Society of Accra, 94
Apprenticeships, 28, 289–290
The Apu Trilogy (film, Ray), 272
Arab music, 9–12, 472–532
    Bedouin culture, 516–526
    categories and terminology, 483–484
    form, melody, and improvisation, 478–482
    as history, 491–502
    Maghrib, 502–510
    Moroccon wedding music, 510–515
    religion and, 484–491
    rhythm, 477–478
    takht ensemble, 475–483
    tarab, 482–483
    in 20th century, 502
Arab stereotypes, 474–475
Arca, 427
Archives, 552
Argentina, 417
Arifin, Zainal, 349
Armando, Miguel, 431, 453, 455
Armstrong, Louis, 12
Arom, Simha, 135
Aryans, 268
Asymmetrical meter, 221–222
Atamuga, 92
Atmaka, Pak, 333
Atsiabekor, 92
Atsiawo, 92, 95
Atsimevu, 96
Audiences, in music-culture model, 15, 16
Axatse, of *Agbekor,* 96, **99,** 100
Ayllón, Eva, 466
Ayyar, Pulaiyur Doraismy, 293
Azan. See Call to Prayer
Azim, Erica Kundizora, 127–128
"Azúcar de cana" (Peru), 466–469
Azzouz, Jalil, 527

BaAka people, 2, 134–143
Babemou, **136**
Bach, Johann Sebastian, 12

Background music, public, 541–542
Badoux, Edmond, 448–449, 452, 471
Baghdad, 492–493
Bagpipes, 12, 220, 247
Bali and Balinese music, 300, **338**–341
Balkan jazz (Balkanski dzhaz), 256–259
Ballads (Chinese), 390–392
Balungan melody, 315–316, 319–320, 326
BaMbuti Code, 142
Bandic, Azra, 227
Banjo, 191
Bannister, James, 173
Baquiné, 458
Bardezbanian, Alan Shavarsh, 537
Bashir, Munir, 494
Basy, 215, 234
Batak people, 341–342
The Beatles, 296
Bebey, Francis, 87
Becker, Judith, 315
Bedhaya (Javanese), **309**
Bedhaya (Javanese), **311**
Bedhug, 306, 307
Bedouin music, 516–526
    formulaic composition, 517–522
    Sirat Bani Hilal, 516–517
Begadang II (Indonesian), 345–346
Begay, Danny Whitefeather, 76
Beiguan ensemble, **379**–384, 403
Beijing opera (Jingju), 384–390
Bells, 97–98, 138
Bendir, 10, **511**
Bennett, Kay (Kaibah), 76
Benson, Carlton, 390
Beratha, Wayan, 339
Berry, Chuck, 191
Bhajan, **276**
Bhangra, 296
Bharata natyam, **278**
Bimo, 350
Bimodality, 436, 465
Biophony, 2
Bird songs, music and, 6
Birimintingo, **114**
Black American music
    blues music, 165–202
    Christian worship and hymns, 145–156, 149–156
    play, music of, 164–203
    worksong, 156–164
Blackwell, Scrapper, 171
Blake, Blind, 13
Blessingway ceremony, 65–67
Blind Blake, 190
Bluegrass, 27
Blue Rhythm, Lazy Bill and the (band), 172, 178
Blues Boy. See King, Riley B. B. (Blues Boy)

Blues music, 165–202
　"Ain't Enough Comin' In" (Rush), 199–201
　autobiography and, 169–174
　bands, racial integration of, 191–192
　composing, 177–178
　"Dog Me Around" (Howlin' Wolf), 187
　downhome or "early" blues, 188
　form and structure of, 13
　"From Dark Till Dawn" (Shines), 195
　in Great Britain, 191
　"I Need $100" (One-String Sam), 181–184,
　　186
　and jazz compared, 165
　"Kokomo Blues" (McDowell), 188, 189–190
　learning, 174–180
　Mississippi Delta blues, 190
　"Poor Boy Blues" (Lucas), 166–169, 176
　popular music, influence on, 191–192
　rhythm of, 175–176, 183
　roots music, 202–203
　"She Got Me Walkin'" (Lucas), 179–180
　social context and meaning of, 185–188
　social status and, 24
　society, cultural effect on, 185–188
　structure, rhythm, and scales of, 174–176
　truth and feeling in, 166–169
　urban blues, 191
　yesterday's blues, 189–199
The Blues Rockers (group), 178
Bolivia and Bolivian music, 424–431
Bomba, **415,** 443–447, 470
Bonangs, 304, **305,** 307, 309
Bongky, 350
Borja, Camilo, 460
Bosnia and Bosnian music, 9, 227
Bosnia and Herzegovina, 259
Bradshaw, Tiny, 191
"Bridal Chorus" (Wagner), 208
Bridal laments, 366
Bridge harp, 113
British colonization of India, 270–271
Bronze, for gamelan instruments, 308
Broonzy, Big Bill, 172
Brown, Charles, 191
Brown, Erica, 535, 555
Brown, James, 192
Bubaran, **312**–321
Buck, Joshua, 41
Buddhism, 338, 356–357
Buddhist music industry, 403
Buford, George *Mojo,* 173
Bunun people, 404–405
Burch, Sharon, 77
Burnett, Chester *Howlin' Wolf,* 179, 187, 190, 191,
　192, 193
Butterfield, Paul, 191
Buzuq (lute), **476,** 477, 480–481

Cada Ilajita, 453, 459
Cadential phrase, 481
Cajoneo, 450
Calhoun, Walker, Mr. and Mrs., 20
Call-and-response, 41, 103
Call of the Yei, 48
Call to Prayer, 212, 214, 485–490
Cantonese music, 399
Canto nuevo, 424
Cantopop, 409
Cao Man, 388
Cardona, Alejandro, 452
Carlin, Bob, 549
Carnatic music, 11
Carraca llanera, 469
Carter, Henrietta McKee, 7
"Cascarón" (sanjuán, Ecuador), 436
Cash, Johnny, 49
Caston, Leonard *Baby Doo,* 158–159, 194
Catholicism, 211, 213, 422–423, 457–458
Celempung, 304–**305,** 305, 307
Center for Folklife and Heritage (Smithsonian
　Institution), 550
Ceremonial music. *See* Rituals and ritual music
Ceremonial practitioner (Navajo), 62–68
César (harpist), 453, 456
Céspedes, Gilka Wara, 448
Chaki ñanes, 432
Chaminuka, **127**
Chance Records, 178
Chancy, Tina, 504
Chandra, Sheila, 297
Chanting, 151–155
Chapu tala (Indian), 286
Charango, 417, 424
Charles, Ray, 191
Charulata (film, Ray), 272
Chaskinakuy (ensemble), 448–449, 452
Cheng Yanqiu, 384
Chen Yang, 399
Cheung, Jacky, 409
Chi, Joseph, 406
Chicago
　blues in, 179, **191,** 192, 193, 196, 203
　Polish music in, 251, 252
Childhood, songs learned in, 534–535
Children, wake for, 422, 453–459
Chile and Chilean music, 417–424
　social change and, 423–424
Chimurenga music, **131**–134
China and Chinese music, 27–28, 353–414
　Abing, 358–363
　Cultural Revolution, 389
　dynasties of China, 356
　erhu solos, 399–400
　folk songs, 366–373
　genres of, 364–366

China and Chinese music (*continued*)
  guoyue ("national music"), 398–399
  instrumental ensemble traditions, 374–384
  Jiangnan *sizhu* music, **13**
  Mandarin pronunciation, 357–358
  opera and ballad traditions, 384–392
  piano solos, 401–403
  popular music, 408–414
  qin, 10, 20
  religious traditions, 403–408
  social realist movement, 401
  solo instrumental traditions, 393–403
  wedding laments, 23
  yin and yang, 19
Chinese Rural Scenes in 24 Solar Terms, 401
Chinle Galileans, 73
Chorales, 213
Chords, 12, 226
  in blues music, 177
  pitch and, 224
Chota River Valley, 443
Christianity, 211, 213, 405, 536–537
Christmas songs, 540
Chuning, 126
Chybinski, Adolf, 247
Cine music, 273
Circle Dance (Shizhané'é), 53–56
Civil Rights Movement, 165
Clapton, Eric, 189, 191, 201
Classical music, 12, 17, 229
Cliché, 175
"Clinging to a Saving Hand" (Navajo), 74–75
Cobbs, Willie, 197
Coda, 36, 37
Coe, Steve, 297
Collins, Albert, 165
Colors (film), 530
Commodified music, 540–542
Communism, 21–22
community, in music-culture model, **16**–17, 17, 142–143
  digital recorders, computers, and multi-media
    programs and, 18
  effect of, on performance, 17
Composition, 27
Computers
  community music history, 18
  music composition and, 22
Concerts. *See also* Performances
  of Javanese music, 309
  karnataka sangeeta of South India, 281–282
  of *kriti,* 293–294
Condor (ensemble), 448
Confidentiality, in ethnography, 559
Confucianism, 356
Congo, Eleuterio, 443, 444
Congo, Fabián, 443, 444
Congo, Germán, 443, 444
Congress of Arab Music, 502

Conjunto Ilumán (ensemble), 439, 442, 447
Conjunto Indígena Peguche (ensemble), 447
Conjunto Rondador ensemble, 443
Contexts, for music, 20–22
Cooley, Timothy, 11
Copyright issues, 25–26
Corea, Chick, 347
Corrido tradition, **421**
Costumes, 38
Cotacachi Quichua. *See* Quichua culture and music
Count Basie's Orchestra, 191
Counterpoint, 420
Country and western music, 13, 27, 49
The Court of the Phoenix, 6
Cowhorn rattle, 41–45
Crayton, Pee Wee, 191
Creole, 251
Crouching Dragon, Hidden Tiger (film), 392
Cueca (Chile), 419, 421
Cuevas, Enrique, 452
Cui Jian, 411
Culture
  diversity in cultural practices, 209
  music and, **2**–4 (*See also* Music-culture)
Cycles (album, by Nakai), 80

Daff, 476
Dagbamba people and their music, 119
Dai Xiaolian, 393
Dakwar, Nasim, 476
Dances and dance music
  Afro-Peruvian, 466
  Agbekor, 89–110
  Balinese, 339–341
  bedhaya (Javanese), 309, 311
  Bolivian, 430
  Circle Dance (Shizhané'é), 53–56
  Dance song (Navajo), 57
  Enemyway (Navajo), 56–59
  góralski (po góralsku), 238–245
  Grass Dance (Sioux), 36–37
  Javanese, to *gamelan* music, 308–311
  jongo (Ghana), 429
  jota, 457
  "Krzesana," 243, 244, 254
  "Makala" (BaAka), 136–142
  Ndáá' (Navajo), 53
  "Nightway" (Navajo), 45–48
  polka, 252, 254
  Praise Name Dances, of Dagbamba people, 119–120
  ruchenitsa, 220–221, 222–223, 256
  sanjuánes (Ecuador), **433,** 456
  Shizhané'é (Navajo Circle song), 53–56
  Sioux Grass Dance, 33–39
  Skip Dance song (Navajo), 75
  South India, 278
  srimpi (Javanese), 309–310
  "Yeibichai" (Navajo), 45–48

Dangdut, 345–347
Danielson, Virginia, 489
Daoism, 353
Da pu, 396
Darsono, Yoyon, 349
Databases, 550
Davillier, Jean Charles, 457
Davis, Sammy, Jr., 15
Deacons' devotional, 151
Deaths. *See* Funerals; Wakes
Delgado-P., Guillermo, 452
Delta blues, 190
d'Erlanger, Rudolphe, 502
Devi Niye Tunai (Shivan), 279–281
Devo (band), 28
Dewa 19 (band), 350
Deze, 125
Dhani, 350
Dharmawan, Dwiki, 347
Diaspora, 473, 503
Diatonic harp, 433
Diddley, Bo, 180
Diddly-bow, 29, **180**–185
Digital recorders, 18
Dikshitar, Muttsvamy, 278
Diné (Navajo), 51
"Distorsi" (Ahmad Band), 350–352
Distribution, of music, 25
Divan, 530
Dixon, Willie, 201
Dizi (flute), **376,** 377
"Dog Me Around" (blues, by Howlin' Wolf),
    187
Donkilo, **115**
Donkor, Freeman, 100
Do-re-mi (solfege) scale, 11
Doubleday, Veronica, 511
Douglass, Frederick, 158
Downhome blues, 188
Dranes, Earl, 172
Drobne, 239
Drones, 12, 283
Drum language, 101–102
Drums and drumming. *See also* Percussion
    in *Agbekor,* 92, 96–102
    Balinese, 339–341
    bendir, 511
    of Dagbamba people, 119–120, 121–123
    in *gendhings* (Javanese), 316–321
    Holy Week snare and bass performances in Spain,
        213
    in Indian music, 283, 287–288
    Javanese, 306
    lunga (Dagbamba), 119–123, 121–123
    mora, 287
    mridangam, 9, 283, 287–288, 289
    Native American, 35
    in Navajo music, 56, 70–73

tani avartanum, 295
    wankara, 426
    water drum (Navajo), 70–73
    "Wilujeng" (Javanese), 324–327
Dub, 252, 254
Dulzura, 446
Duple meter, 216, 218
Durand, José, 466

Early blues, 188
East Asia/China, 353–414
East Greets East (album, by Shankar), 296
Eboka, of Mabo, **136**–138
Ecological worlds, of music, 30–32
Ecuador and Ecuadorian music, 431–437
    African-Ecuadorian music, 443–447
    Andean sound in, 447–453
    ensembles in, 447–453
    "Ilumán tiyu" (sanjuán), 437, 439, 440
    Imbabura harp, 433–435
    map of, 416
    Quichua life and culture, 415, 417, 431–447
    sanjuán, 433–439
    "Toro barroso" (albazo), 459
    vacación, 454–455
Efraín (harpist), 13, 434, 442
Eickelman, Dale, 484
Ekimi, 142
"El aparecido" (Jaro), 418–419
Electronics and music, 29–30
El-Funoun, 514–515, 516
"El Guaro" (Colombia), 470
"El lazo" (Chile), 422–424
Emphasis, 10
Enemyway ceremony (Navajo), 53, **56**–59
"Engel kalyanam" (Indian), 274–276
Enlightenment, 214
Ensembles. *See also* Orchestras
    Agbekor, 96–97
    gamelan, 302–307
    in Hindu music, 282–284
Equipment, for field research, 552–554
Erhu, 358, 376, 398, **399**–400
Espinoza, Renato, 452
Ethics, ethnography and, 551–552
Ethnicity, music and, 22, 537–539
*Ethnic Music on Records: A Discography of Ethnic Recordings
    Produced in the United States 1893–1942*
    (Spottswood), 550
Ethnography. *See* **Musical ethnography**
Ethnomusicology, 18, 24, 541. *See also* Musical
    ethnography
    music and identity principle, 209, 262
Ethnomusicology (journal), 549
Ethnomusicology On Line, 549
EthnoPop, 530
European American music-culture, 8

Europe (Central and Southeastern regions), 205–263
  harmony in music of, 225–229
  nationalism and nation-states, 214–215
  pitches, scales and melody, 224–225
  Podhale case study, 230–251
  regional music case studies, 251–261
  religion and society, 211–214
  rhythm and meter in music of, 215–223
  social and political organization, 210–215
  village music festivals, 250–251
  wedding processionals, 105–109
"Ever So Lonely/Eyes/Ocean" (Chandra), 297
Ewe people, 89–91. See also Agbekor
Eyre, Banning, 132

Fado (Portugal), 509
Falsetto, 33
Families, music and, 534–535
Farewell My Concubine (film), 384
Fayoumi, Khadija, 514
Feldman, Heidi, 466
Fellowship Independence Baptist Church, Stanley,
    Virginia, 149
The Fenders, 13, 50
Feng Menglong, 372
Fenton, William N., 41
Festival Night Canzonetta, 400
Festivals, 251
Fiddles, rebab (Javanese), 304, 306, 307
Field holler, 158–159
Fieldwork, 542, 545–554
Fishel, John, 197
Flamenco (Spain), 509
Flutes. See also Pipes
  Indian, 9, 283
  Javanese, 306
  Navajo, 80–81
  suling, 307
Foku songu, 27
Folk music, 229
  Chilean, 417–424
  Chinese marriage lament tradition, 366
  festivals, 21–22
  "Lady Mengjang" (China), 367–369
  sesquialtera, 470
  Shan'ge (China), 369–373
"Folsom Prison Blues" (Fenders), 13, 49
Forest people. See BaAka people
The Forest People (Turnbull), 135
Form, of music, 13, 14–15
  Agbekor, 108
  blues music, 174–180
  gendhings, 312
  kora music, 113–118
  Makala (BaAka), 137–138
  Postal workers' melody, 88
  sanjuánes (Ecuador), 434–437

Formulaic composition, 517–526
Franklin, Aretha, 154, 192
Franklin, Rev. C. L., 154
Free rhythm, 9, 107–108
"From Dark Till Dawn" (Johnny Shines), 194, 195
Fujarka, 248
"Full Moon and Blooming Flowers" (China), 409, 410
Funerals, 91, 123. See also Wakes
Fusion, 251–252, 254, 260, 295

"Gadasjot" (Iroquois), 41–43
Gaida, 220
Gambangs, 301, 304, 305, 307, 338
Gambia River, 111
Gamelans, 302–303
  Balinese, 338
  construction of, 308
  gamelan gong kebyar (Balinese), 339, 340
  identity of, 308
  instrumentation of, 303–307
  performance contexts, 20, 308–311
  performing your own, 321
  polyphonic harmony in, 12
  popular music and, 347–349
  scales of, 11
  shadow puppetry and, 334–338
Gamma burui, 429
Gandhi, Mahatma, 271
Ganga songs (Bosnia and Herzegovina), 9, 227, 259–260,
    262
Gankogui, of Agbekor, 96, 97, 100
GarageBand software, 25
Garzón y Collazos, 470
"Gatutkaca Sungging" (Nartosabdho), 333
Gendang keteng-keteng, 342, 343–344
Gender, and music genres, 535
Gender roles. See also Women
  blues music and, 177–178
  in Hindu music, 290
  in music-culture, 24–25, 535
Gendérs, 304, 305, 307, 338
Gendhings, 311–321
Generations, music and, 535
Genres, 26–27
George, Chief Dan, 77
George-Warren, Holly, 202
Gérong, 306
Ghana, 2, 6–8, 82, 93. See also Ewe people
Ghatam, 283, 287
Ghina, 5
Ghostway ceremony, 67–68
Ghunna, 486
Gibson, Simeon, 41
Gift song (Navajo), 58
Gilbert, Stacy, 516
Ginda, 136
Ginting, Tukang, 342

Globalization, and musical practices, 251
Global music, 252
Golpe, 450
Golpeador, 455
Gong ageng, 304, 307
Gongan, 312
Gongche notational system, **380**
Gongs
    Balinese, 338
    construction of, 308
    Javanese, **302**–305
Górale, **232,** 238
Górale kapela, 234, 235
Górale nuta, 232
Góralski (po góralsku), **238**–245
Government
    Chilean, 423–424
    Communist control of music, 21–22
Grace note pickups, 477
Gradante, William, 470
Grant, Norman, 255
Grass Dance (Sioux), 33–39
Great Britain, 191
Greater Twin Cities Blues Music Society, 174
"Great Waves Washing the Sands" (China),
    359–361, 398
Gregorian Chant, 8
"Gregorio Cortez," 421
Griots, **18**
Grove Lake Concert Band, 536
Grupo Ecuador de los Hermanos Congo y Milton Tadeo,
    443, 444
Gudulka, **220**
Guevara, Ernesto Che, 420
Guitars, 177, 417
Guli, 429
Gung, alep, 407–408
Gung-gong, **119**
Gunka, 27
Guoyue ("national music"), **398**–399
Guqin solos, **393**–399
Guruh Gypsy (album), 348
Gurukula apprenticeship, **289**
Guy, Buddy, 165, 189, 190, 192, 202,
    203
Guzheng, 377

Hadith, 491
Hamam, 510–511
Hamengku Buwana X, Sultan of Java, 301
Han Chinese, 353, 355
Handel, George Frederick, 217–218, 262
Handy, W. C., 189
Harmonic rhythm, 226
Harmony, 4, **12**–13, 225–229
    European contribution to, 225–229
    pitch and, 224–225

Harps
    in Ecuadorian music, 433–443
    kora, 113
Harris, Corrie, 192
Harris, Wynonie, 191
Harrison, George, 296
Hart, Alvin Youngblood, 192
Haza, Ofra, 483, 529–530
"Heráclio Bernal," 421
Hera Tang, 405
Heterophonic harmony, 12, 477
Hinduism, 269, 271, 338
    lyrics and mythology of, 281
Hindusthani (northern) music, 278
Hip-hop, 18, 25
History, in music-culture model, 15, 17
Hobby, music as, 535–536
Hocketing, 428, 430–431
Hocketing panpipes, 421
Hoffman, Stanley, 315
Homophonic harmony, 13
Hong Kong, 357, 405–406, 409
Hood, Mantle, 323
Hoogan (Navajo), 52
Hooker, John Lee, 165, 193
Hopkins, Lightnin', 193
Horn, Paul, 296
Horon (freeborn), **112**
"Horses" (Alhaj), 496–499
Hosho, **125,** 129, 130
House, Eddie *Son,* 168, 193, 203
Howlin' Wolf. *See* Burnett, Chester *Howlin' Wolf*
Hsin, Winnie, 411
Hua Yanjun. See Abing
Hudson, Little, 172
Hungary and Hungarian music, 458
Huro, **127**
Hurt, Mississippi John, 13, 193
Hussain, Zakir, 272, 295
Hybrid music, 251
Hymns, 74–76, **147**–156

Iambic pentameter, 9
Identity, music and, 209
Ilaiyaraja, 276, 297–298
"Ilumán tiyu," 452
"Ilumán tiyu" (sanjuán, Ecuador), 12, 437, 439, 440,
    452, 455
Imagined communities, 210, 215
Imbabura harp, 433–435, 434–436
"I Met Bach at My House" (Ilaiyaraja), 298
"Im Nin'alu," 530, 531
Improvisation. *See also* Taqasim music
    in Indian music, **281,** 287
    niraval, 295
    Polish music and, 16
    prayers, chanted, 151–155
    rules of, 16

India and Indian music, 265–298
   Aryans, 268
   bhajan, 276
   British colonization, 270–271
   cine music, 273
   classical music, 277–278
   classic and medieval periods, 268–269
   drums and drumming, 287–288
   ensembles in, 282–284
   Hinduism and, 269, 271
   history, culture, and politics, 267–272
   improvisation in, 287
   independence and modern period, 271–272
   Indus Valley, 267–268
   karnataka sangeeta of South India, 277–288
   kriti of South India, 293–294
   map of, 264
   Moghuls, 269–270
   northern *vs.* southern, 278
   popular music, 273–276, 295–298
   ragas scales, 3, 11
   religious music, 276
   rhythm of, 9–10
   Sarasiruha (kriti), 291–294
   sounds of, 277–281
   texture of, 282–284
   types of music in, 273–276
   wedding music, 274–276
   western influences on, 295–298
   women and, 290
Indonesia and Indonesian music, 299–352
   Bali and Balinese music, 338–341
   Begadang II, 345–346
   culture of, 299–301, 345–352
   dangdut, 345–347
   Distorsi (Ahmad Band), 350–352
   Java and Javanese music, 301–338
   map of, 300
   Muslims and, 490–491
   popular music, 345–352
   protest music, 350–352
   Sumatran music, 341–344
   western influences on, 347–349
Indus Valley civilization, 267–268
"I Need $100" (One-String Sam), 181–184, 186
"Initiation of Ecstasy" (Palestine), 515
Inkas, 426, 439
Inmates, 160–163
Instruments, 29–30
Instruments, making
   cowhorn rattle, 41–45
   diddly-bow, 180–185
   water drum (Navajo), 70–73
Internet, 25, 540
Intervals, 12
Interviewing, in ethnography, 554–557
Intifadah, **514**
Inti Illimani, 418–421, 424

iPods, 20
Ira, **427**
Irama, Rhoma, **345**–347, 352
Irama level, 321
Iraq, 491–492
Iroquois drum, 72
Iroquois Quiver Dance, 41
Islam and Islamic music, 111, 211–212, 214, 490–491. *See also* Arab music
Isorhythmic phrase structure, **435,** 446
Iyer, Karaikudi Sambasiva, 289
Iyer, Vijay, 296

Jackson, Bruce, 161
Jacobs, Little Walter, 172
Jacobs, Russell, 5
Jalolu (jali), **110,** 111, 112, 113, 114
James, Elmore, 192
James, Skip, 193
Jánosík, Juraj, 255
Japanese music, 12
Jara, Joan, 417, 424
Jara, Victor, 417–421, 424
Jarre, Maurice, 475
Jatari (ensemble), 447
Java and Javanese music, **301**–338
   Balinese music *vs.,* 338–339
   culture of, 301–302
   gamelan and its performance, 302–311
   gendhing performance, 312–321
   instruments of, 303–307
   Kembang Pacar, 312–321
   Lasem, 334–338
   scales of, 11, 303
   Udan Mas, 321–322
   Wilujeng, 322, 324–327
Jazz music
   Balkanski dzhaz (Balkan jazz), 256–259
   and blues compared, 165
   fusion, 347–349
   Indonesian, 347–349
   polyphony of, 12
Jefferson, Blind Lemon, 171
Jewish music. *See also* Arab music
   Sephardim, 503
   Yemenite religious songs, 530
Jiangnan sizhu music, 13, **376**–379
Jianzipu, **396**
Jingju (Beijing opera), **384**–390, 399
Jins, 518
Jin Wenyin, 369–372, 373
"Joaquín Murieta," 421
John Paul II, Pope, 423
Johnson, Robert, 192, 193, 195, 196
Jones, A. M., 96
Jones, Curtis, 171
Jongo dance music, **429**
Jong (slave descendants), **112**

Joropo (Venezuelan), 421
Jota, 457, 459
Journals, published, for research, 550
"Joyous Festival of Lunar New Year's Day" (China), 401–402
"Joy to the World" (hymn), 11, 217–219, 224–226, 262
JSTOR, 550
Judah, Dub, 255
Judaism, 211, 212–213

Kadaj, Sana and Amer, 482
Kaganu, of *Agbekor,* 96, **99**–100, 100, 101
Kahluli culture, New Guinea, 6
Kalidasa, 269
Kallawaya people, 426
Kalpana svaras, 294–295
Kanjira, **283**
K'antu, **424,** 426, 430
Kapela, **239**
Karakand, Naim, 527
Karnataka sangeeta of South India, 9, **277**–288
Kaval, **220**
Kawindro, Pak, 312
Keb' Mo', 192
Kebyar (Balinese), **339**
Kejawín, 301
"Kembang Pacar" (Javanese), **312**–321
Kempul, **304,** 307
Kempyang, **304,** 307
Kendhangs, **304, 306,** 307
Kenong, **304,** 307
Keroncong, 330
Keteng-keteng, 342, 343
Kethroprak, 331
Kethuk, **304,** 307
Khadaj, Amer, 527
Khadaj, Sana, 527, 528
Khaldun, Ibn, 517
Khanda tala (Indian), **286**–287
Kidi, of *Agbekor,* 96, **100**
King, Albert, 192
King, Freddy, 192
King, Riley B. B. (Blues Boy), 165, 191, 192, 193, 202, 203
Kisliuk, Michelle, 134, 139–141
Kleszcz, Wlodzimierz, 255
Klezmer, 212
Kloboto, of *Agbekor,* 96, 100, **101**
Knight, Roderic, 110, 115
Koetting, James, 7, 84
"Kokomo Blues" (McDowell), 188, 189–190
Konkong, **113**
Kora, **113**–115, 511
Korean soap operas, 409
"Kosalina Arini" (Balinese), 339–341
Kpegisu, **95**
Krakatau, 347, 348, 348, 349
Krause, Bernie, 2

Krauss, Allison, 535
Kriti **(composition), 293**–294
Krupa, Stanislaw, 206
Krzeptowski-Sabala, Jan, 206
Krzesana, 243, 244, 245, 254
Krzesane, 239
"Krzesany Po Dwa" ("Going to the Village"), 252, 253–254
Kudeketera, **127**
Kulcapi, 343
Kulthum, Umm, 489
Kuma, **113**
Kumbengo, **114**
Kunaka, John, 127
Kuna people, 429
Kunst, Jaap, 323
"Kurdzhaliiska Ruchenica," 257, 258
Kushaura, **127,** 128, 130
Kusuma, Sri Handaya, 333
"Kutiramunapaq" (Bolivian), 424–431, 452
Kutsinhira, **127,** 129, 130
Kuyateh, Mariatu, 110, 115, 118
Kyai Kanyut Mésem, 303, 309

"Lady Mengjiang" (China), 367–369
Lambango (Mande), 110, 113, 115–118
"Lamma Ya Albi," 527, 528–529
Lanaiditsa, 39, 41
Landó, 466–470
Lane, Edward, 500, 517
Language
    codes, 194
    of *kora* music, 115
    Mandarin, 357–358
    music and, 5
    Navajo, 55
    Quichua, 415, 417
"La plegaria a un labrador" (Chilean), 423
Larkin, Ed, 539
"Lasem" (Javanese), 334–338
Latin America. *See* Ecuador and Ecuadorian music
Lau, Andy, 409
Laurence of Arabia (film), 475
Lauseviç, Mirjana, 260
Lazy Bill Lucas Blues Band, 166
Learning. *See* Transmission, of music-culture
Led Zeppelin, 201
Left Beaver Old Regular Baptist Church, Kentucky, 5
Lennon, John, 297
León, Ermundo Mendes, 444, 470
Levant, 514–515
Lewis, Laurie, 535
Liang Mingyue, 398
Liao Shengjing, 398, 401
Library, for ethnography, 549–551
"Li Chun: Xinnian Jiajie" (China), 401–402
Life history, in ethnography, 554–557

Lightning Deity (Navajo), 49
Li Jinhui, 409
Lining out, 148
Li Shiji, 384
Listening skills, 1
Little Rock Baptist Church, 151
Liu Tianhua, 400
Logogenic music, 35
Lohengrin (Wagner), 208
Lomax, Alan, 160–162, 164, 399
"The Long Walk" (Navajo, by Roessel), 76
Lord, Albert, 517
"Los Angeles Sweetheart" (Navajo, by Begay), 76–77
Los Mapaches, 453
"Love You To" (Beatles), 296
Lowisz, Boguslawa, 236
Lucas, *Lazy* Bill, 166, 169–174, 178–179, 191, 192
Luckin, Mevla, 227
Lugones, Néstor, 452
Lullabies, 534
Lunga, **119,** 123
Lunna, Abubakari, 121–123, 143
Lunsi, of Dagbamba people, 119
Lutes, 343, 358, 359, 376, 475–476
Luther, Martin, 218, 219, 225, 537
Lü Wencheng, 399

Mabo, **136**–138
Mabon, Willie, 172
Macedonia and Macedonian music, 4
Maghett, *Magic Sam,* 193, 196–199, 202
Maghrib, 502–510
    Andalusian legacy, 503–509
    independent Morocco, 509–510
Magical Match (album), 348
"Magic Carpet, The," 530
Magic Sam. *See* Maghett, *Magic Sam*
Magic Sam Live (Sam Maghett), 197
Mahabharata (Indian epic), 269, **311**
Mahanthappa, Rudresh, 296
Mahonyera, **127**
Major scale, 11, 224, 229, 420
"Makala" (BaAka), 134, 136–142
Mali, 110–111
Mali, Umayalpuram, 277
Manaf, Dhani Ahmad, 350
Mandarin Chinese, 355, 357–358
Mande people, 110–123
Mangkuk, 343
Mangkunegaran Palace, 303, 309
Manners and Customs of the Modern Egyptians, 500
Mapfumo, Thomas, 131–134
Maqam, 16, **480,** 518
Maqam Bayyati, **480**
Maqam Rast, 489
Maraire, Dumisani, 127
Marginal preservation, 530

Margolin, Bob, 191
Marquis Yi, 374
Martha Graham Dance Company, 80
Mashriq, 502
Mason, Lowell, 217
Mass media, 30, 540–542
Material culture, of music, 20, **29**–30
Mawu, 90
Mayall, John, 191
"Maybelline" (Berry), 191
Mbira, **123**–131, 511
Mbira dzavaddzimu, **125,** 126
McCabe, Roger, 76
McDowell, Fred, 188, 189–190
McGraw, Tim, 49
Meenakshi Temple, 279
"Me Gusta La Leche" (Ecuador), 445–446
Meisch, Lynn, 447–448
Melakarta *ragas,* 284–286
Melody and melodies. *See also* Songs and singing
    of *Agbekor,* 104–106
    "Amazing Grace" (hymn), 147–150
    "Cascarón" (*sanjuán,* Ecuador), 436
    "Clinging to a Saving Hand" (Navajo), 75
    components of, 10–12
    field holler, 158–159
    in *gendhings* (Javanese), 315–316
    Grass Dance (Sioux), 36–37
    Hindu music *vs.* piano, 280, 281
    of Indian music, 280–281, 283
    kushaura, 131
    "Kutiramunapaq" (Bolivian), 427
    of "Makala" (BaAka), 138–141
    "Michael, Row the Boat Ashore," 159–160
    "Nag Biegu" (Dagbamba), 119–120
    "Nhemamusasa" (Shona), 130–131
    Peyote song (Navajo), 70
    "Poor Boy Blues" (Lucas), 175, 176
    Postal workers' melody, 88
    prayer, chanted, 151–155
    Quiver Dance (Iroquois), 43
    "Rosie" (American worksong), 161–164
    sanjuánes (Ecuador), 434–435, 437
    scales and organization of, **10**–12
    sermon, chanted, 151–155
    Shizhané'é Navajo Circle song, 53–56
    vacación (Ecuador), 454–455
    Yeibichai (Navajo), 45–48
    Zuni lullaby, 39
Memory, in music-culture model, 15, 17
Menuhin, Yehudi, 296
Messiah, 217–218
Metaphor, 420
Meter, 8–10, 98–101
    additive, 220
    asymmetrical, 221–222
    duple, 216, 218
    triple, 216, 218

Metrical rhythm, 8
"Michael, Row the Boat Ashore,"
159–160
Middle East, 483–484. *See also* Arab music
Miernicki, Zdzislaw, 236
Mijwiz, **514**
Mills, Lydia, 453
Minor scale, 224, 225, 229, 420
Minyo scale, 27
Mirabai, 290
Mirhige, Michel, 476
Misra tala (Indian), **286**
"Miss Hi-Fi," 173
Mississippi Delta blues, 190
Mississippi State Penitentiary, 160–164
Mistreatment, theme of Blues music,
186, **187,** 188
Mitchell, Frank, 62–68, 143
Moche culture (Peru), 470
Mode, and scale compared, 386
Model, of music-culture, 15, 16–18
Modes, of *ragas* (Indian), 282
Moghuls, 269–270
Mó.kóndi, 138
Mo.mbénzélé, 138
Monophonic harmony, **12**
Monsoon (band), 297
Mó.nzóli, 138
Mora, **287**
Morganfield, McKinley *Muddy Waters,* 165, 189,
191, 192, 193
Moroccan bendir, 10
Moroccan wedding music, 510–515
Morocco, 509–510
Morsang, **283**
"Mother Earth" (Navajo, by Burch), 77, 78
Mountain music, 227
Mountain residents, cultural practices of,
231–232
Mountainway ceremony (Navajo), 59–62
Movement, music and, 28–29, 149. *See also* Dances and
dance music
Movies and musicals, in India, 273
Mozi, 375
mp3, 541, 551
Mridangam, 9, 277, 279, **283,** 289, 290
Mróz, Stanslaw, 247
Mudallal, Sabri, 485, 489
Muddah, **111**
Muddy Waters. *See* Morganfield, McKinley *Muddy
Waters*
Muezzins, **485**
Mugabe, Robert, 133
Mui, Anita, 409
Multiculturalism, 537–539
Multimedia programs, 18
Muquinche, Don César, 24, 459–466
Murle, Priya, 278
Musasa, 127

Music
activities involving, 19
of Africa, 85–89, 143–144
of BaAka people, 134–143, 142
in churches, 150–155
commodified, 540–542
as commodity, 25
contexts of, 20–22
cultural ideas of music, 18
culture and, 2–4
definition of, 4, 6, 16
dynamic nature of, 30–31
of Ecuador, 457
ethnicity and, 537–539
ethnicity in, 22
ethnographic study of, 542–559
in the family, 534–535
four components of, 18–30
generations and, 535
history of, 22–23
as a hobby, 535–536
as human behavior, 229
ideas and, 18–23
of India, 267–272
of Indonesia, 299–301, 345–352
language and, 5
logogenic, 35
of Mande people, 112–113, 116–117
material culture and, 29–30
model of, 15, 16–18
nationalism and, 540
Navajo, 49–53
nonmusic, 6
oral *vs.* written, 28
organization of sounds in, 10–12
pathogenic, 35
patronage of, 21–22
Quichua, 431–432, 433–439
regionalism of, 539–540
religion and, 536–537
religion in, 18–20
social change, Nueva Canción and, 423–424
structure of, 8–14
subcultures of, 23
and understanding music, 4–8
Musical analysis, 16
Musical ethnography, 541, **542–559**
collecting information, 545
ethics and, 551–552
field gear, 552–554
gaining entry, 545
interviewing, 554–557
library and Internet research, 549–551
music and identity, 209
participation and observation, 545–546
questionnaires, 557–558
recording, 553–554
subject selection, 542–544
topic selection, 546–549

Music-culture, 2, 3–8
  activities involving music, 23–26
  as adaptive resource, 142–143
  and aesthetics, 20
  affinity groups, 17
  commonalities in, 5
  European American, 8
  four components of, 18–30
  music as human resource, 31
  performance model, 18
  subcultures within, 3
  transmission of, 60
Music distribution, 25–26
Music industry, 25, 541. *See also* Mass media
Music of Arab Americans: A Retrospective Collection, 527
Musiqa, 5
Muslims and Muslim music, 110–111, 211–212, 484.
    See also Arab music
Musselwhite, Charlie, 191
Muwashshah, **503**
"Muyu," 438
"Muyu Muyari Warmigu" (Ecuador), 435–436,
    455
Muzika (instrumental music), 4
Muzyka Podhala, 232–238, 246–250, 262
Muzyka Podhala
  ozwodna genre, 235
  pasterska genre, **233,** 237
  reggae and, 252–256
  wierchowa genre, **234,** 237
My Beautiful Land (album, by Begay, Yazzie, and
    McCabe), 76
My Bondage and My Freedom (Douglass), 158
Mystical Mist (album), 348
Mysticism, 485

Nagasvaram, **272,** 273, 276
Nag Biegu (Dagbamba people), 119–120
Nakai, R. Carlos, 80
Nandorfy, Martha, 423
Nartosabdho, Ki, 330–334
Nasalization, 486
Natai raga, **292,** 293
Nationalism, music and, 540
Native American Church, 68–71
Native American music, 33–81. *See also* Ecuador and
    Ecuadorian music; Navajo music and culture
  flute revival in, 80–81
  form and structure of, 41
  Grass Dance (Sioux), 33–39
  powwows, 38
  Quiver Dance (Iroquois), 41–43
  Zuni lullaby, 39–41
"Navajo Inn" (Tsoisdia), 75
Navajo music and culture, 45–80
  Blessingway ceremony, 65–67
  ceremonial practitioner, 62–68

  composers of, 76–77
  Enemyway ceremony, 56–59
  flute revival in, 80–81
  form and structure of, 13, 61
  Ghostway ceremony, 67–68
  life and culture, 49–53, 62–68
  "Los Angeles Sweetheart" (Begay), 76–77
  "Mother Earth" (Burch), 77, 78
  Mountainway ceremony, 59–62
  Native American Church, 68–71
  "Navajo Inn" (Tsoisdia), 75
  Ndáá' music, 53
  new, 76–77
  Nightway ceremonial, 45–48
  with orchestral accompaniment, 77–80
  "Origins" (Nakai), 80
  performance contexts, 21
  Peyote song, 70
  pronunciation of language, 55
  "Proud Earth" (by Williams), 77, 79
  Shootingway, 61–62
  Skip song, 75
  Sway song, 56–57
  "The Long Walk" (Roessel), 76
  traditional popular music, 53
  women in, 56–57
  Yeibichai songs, 10, 45–48
Nay (flute), **476**
Ndáá' Dance music (Navajo), 53
Nelson, David P., 279
Nelson, Kristina, 489
Neshev, Neshko, 256
Nevaquaya, *Doc Tate,* 80
New Bethel Baptist Church, Detroit, 147
Ngbôl·, 138
"Nhemamusasa" (Shona), 123, 125, 127–131
Nieves, Diana, 452
Nigeria, 27
Nightchant ballet, 80
Niraval, **295**
Nisf bémol, 501
Nisf dièse, 501
Nketia, J. H. K., 93
Nonmetrical music, 9–10
North America and its music, 145–203. *See also* Western
    music, influence of
  African-American music, 145–203
  the blues, 165–202
  country and western, 49
  Iroquois Quiver Dance, 41–43
  map of, 34
  Navajo, 45–80
  Sioux Grass Dance, 33–39
  worship, music of, 145–156
  Zuni lullaby, 39–41
Northern Neck Chantey singers, 159
North Sumatra, 341–344
Notation, of music, 213

Nueva Canción, 417–424, 422
Nuta, 232, 234, 237
Nyamalo, 112
"Nyarai" ("Be Ashamed," Chimurenga), 131–134
Nyu myushiku, 27

Obrecht, Jas, 202
Octave leaps, 477
Oden, St. Louis Jimmy, 174–175, 178
Odum, Howard, 189
"Oifn Pripetshik" (Yiddish), 213, 216–217, 224, 225
One-String Sam, 181–184, 186
Opera (Chinese), 384–392
Oral literature, 166
Orchestras, 35. *See also* Ensembles
    Count Basie's Orchestra, 191
    in Navajo music, 77–80
Organologists, 113
Origins (Navajo, by Nakai), 80
Oriki (Nigerian praise songs), 27
Ornamentation, 38, 284–285
Orquesta de Instrumentos Autóctonos, 453
Orthodoxy, 211
Oscher, Paul, 191
Ostinato, 113, **215,** 234, 241, 478
Ottoman Empire, 499–500
Ownership, of music, 18–19
Ozwodna, **235,** 237, 238, 239
"Ozwodna," 236–238, 239

Page, Jimmy, 201
Palestinian Popular Arts Troupe, 514
Panpipes, 424, 426–429, 443
Pantaleoni, Hewitt, 8
Papasov, Ivo, 256–259, 262
Parra, Violeta, 420, 421–423, 424
Parry, Milman, 438, 517
"Pasibutbut" ("Prayer for a Rich Millet Harvest") (China), 404
Pasibutbut singing, 404
Pasterska, **233,** 237
Pathet, 322–324
Pathogenic music, 35
Patriotic songs, 540
Patronage, of music, 21–22, 112
Patton, Charley, 190
Pay, 350
Pélog scale, **11,** 303, 312
Pentatonic songs, 368, 403, 414, 428
Peralta, Eduardo, 424
Percussion. *See also* Drums and drumming
    African music, 85, 89
    in Agbekor, 96–102
    in Balinese music, 339–341
    gambang-kromong, 301
    gamelan, 302–309
    in *gendhings* (Javanese), 312
    Javanese instruments, 303–307

Performance model, 14, 18
Performances. *See also* Concerts
    of *Agbekor,* 93–96
    "Amazing Grace" (hymn), 149–150
    of blues music, 197
    community effect on, 17
    contexts of music and, 20–22
    elements of, **15–16**
    of *gamelan* music, 308–311
    gendhings (Javanese), 312–321
    Internet performances, 17
    of Javanese music, 308–311
    of *karnataka sangeeta,* 277
    of *kora,* 113–118
    "Makala" (BaAka), 137–142
    of *mbira,* 126–127
    music-culture and, 17
    in music-culture model, 15–16
    of *sanjuán,* 433
    of shadow puppetry, 334–338
Persian liguistic area, 484
Peru. *See* Afro-Peruvian music
Pesindhín, 306
Pesni (songs), 4
Peyote Church, 68–71
Peyote song (Navajo), 70
Piano
    melody of notes, 280, 281
    solos, Chinese, 401–403
Pickup, 218
Pillajo, Segundo *Galo* Maigua, 438, 439, 441, 442, 447
Pipa, **358,** 359, 366, 376, 390
Pipes. *See also* Flutes
    bagpipes, 12
    flutes, 9, 80–81, 283, 306
    nagasvaram, 273, 276
    panpipes, 424, 426–429, 443
Pitch, 10, 224–225, 374
    of African-American music, 149
    in *gendhings* (Javanese), 312, 315
    in *pathet* (Javanese), 323
    tuning *gamelan* instruments and, 308
Pitch skeleton, 386
Plains Sun Dance, 72
Play, music of, 164–203
Podhale (Poland), **205**
    case study, 230–251
    dance music (*góralski*), 238–245
    free rhythm, 215
    influence of mountains on cultural practices, 231–232
    muzyka Podhala genres, 232–238
    people and music in, 232
Po dwa, 244
Po góralsku, **238**–245, 245
Poland
    improvisational music in, 16
    wedding celebration, 205–207

Polka, 252, 254
Polymeter, 10
Polyphonic harmony, **12,** 139–142, 142, 209, 227, 229
Polyphony, 209
Polyrhythm. *See also* **Rhythms**
    in African music, **9**
    in Agbekor, 97–98, 103
    in blues music, 175
    of kora music, 128–130
    of "Makala" (BaAka), 138–141
"Poor Boy Blues" (Lucas), 167, 176
Pop berat, 27, 348
Pop music, global, 252
Pops, 27
Popular music, 229
    in China, 408–414
    cine music, of India, 273
    of Indonesia, 345–352
    influence of blues on, 191–192
    in Japan, 27
    music-culture and, 4–8
    rock music, 350–352
    soul music, 192
    Sundanese music, 347–349
Postal workers' melody, 2, 6–8, 9, 84–89, 88
Powwows, 38
"Praise from Heaven and Earth," 406–407
Praise Name Dances, of Dagbamba people, 119–120
Praise songs, 27
Preaching, 152–155
"Preguntas por Puerto Montt" (Jara), 423
Preservation, of traditional music, 22, 31
Primitive Man as Philosopher (Radin), 555
Primitive savagery, 136
Prisons, 160–164
Privacy issues, in research, 551
Programmatic music, 498
Protestant choral music, 213
Protest music, 350–352, 423–424
Protest songs, 421–422
"Proud Earth" (Navajo, by Williams), 77, 79
Public background music, 541–542
Public domain, 26
Pulsation, in Agbekor, 98–101
Punctuation patterns, in Javanese music, 314–315
Punjis, **273**
Puppetry (shadow puppetry), 302, 309–311, 322–323, 328, 332–338
Puranas of Hinduism, 269
Pututu, 449
Pygmies, 135
Pytace, 205–206, 208

Qafla, **16,** 481
Qaflat, 523
Qanun (zither), **476,** 477

Qin, 10, 20, 366, **393,** 395–398
Qin Ch'in, 28
Qin (guqin) solos, **393**–399
Qingyi, **384**
Quadrivium concept, 492
¿Que dirá el Santo Padre? (Chilean), 422
Questionnaires, in ethnography, 557–558
Quichua culture and music, 21, 415, **417,** 430, 431–447
Quijada (Peru), **469**
Quilapayún, 423
Quiver Dance (Iroquois), 41–43
Qur'an, 490, 491

Rabab, 517
Racy, A. J., 476, 478, 516
Radin, Paul, 555
Radwan, Soheil, 523, 527
Rafael, 434, 442
Ragam-tanam-pallavi, 289
Ragas **(Indian),** 11, **284**–287
    improvisation in, 295
    keeravani raga scale, 279
    melakarta, 284–286
    natai, 292, 293
    origin of word, 284
    scales, 3
Raghavan, Ramnad V., 9
Raghupathy, Sudharani, 278
Rahayu, Tudi, 349
Rahman, A. R., 273, 276
Rai, 509
Rajagopalan, Ranganayaki, 289–290, 294
Rakha, Alla, 296
Ramadhan, Andra, 350
Raman, Susheela, 295–296
Ramayana (Indian epic), 269, **311**
Ramé, 309
Ramgopal, Sukanya, 290
Rampal, Jean-Pierre, 296
Ranchera (Mexico), 421
Ranganathan, T., 279
Rao, V. Raja, 290, 291, 295
Raos, Condhong, 333
Rasmussen, Anne, 4
Rattles
    cowhorn, 41–45
    hosho, 125, 129, 130
    in Navajo music, 70
    peyote, 70
Raúl (Ecuadorian harpist), 433
Raul (harpist), 433
Ray, Satyajit, 272
Rebab, 304, **306,** 307, 338
Red Devils trio, 172
Redding, Otis, 192
Reed, Jimmy, 191
Reggae, 538
    muzyka Podhala and, 252–256

Regionalism, of music, 539–540
Reiss, Scott, 504
Relative pitch, 374
"Releasing the Horse into Pasture" (China), 372–373
Religion
    Arab religions, and music, 484–491
    of BaAka people, 135–136
    of Bali, 338
    of Batak people, 341–342
    black Christian worship, 149–156
    Buddhism, 338
    Catholicism, 422–423, 457–458
    children's wakes, 457–459
    Christianity, music in, 536–537
    effect of, on music, 212
    of Ewe people, 90–91
    Hinduism of India, 271
    hymns, 74–76, **147**–156
    literacy and, 213
    of Mali, 110–111
    of Mande people, 110–111, 113
    Mormon influence, on music, 77, 80
    music and, 536–537
    in music-culture, 18–20
    music of India and, 276
    Native American Church, 68–71
    in Navajo music, 56–59, 68–71
    prayers, chanted, 151–155
    preaching and sermons, chanted, 151–155
    of Shona people, 124
    social qualities of organized, 213–214
    society and, 211–214
    wawa velorio and, 457
    worship, music of, 145–156
Repertory, 19, **26**–29
Research. *See* Musical ethnography
Revolver (album, by Beatles), 296
Reynolds, Dwight, 517, 518
Rhythms, 8–10. *See also* **Polyrhythm**
    in blues music, 175–176, 183, 199
    cliché, 175
    in Indian music, 286–287
    in Javanese music, 312, 332
    in *karnataka sangeeta,* 9
    metrical, 8
    of Postal workers' melody, 6–8, 9, 88
    in *sanjuán,* 434–437
    triplet, 175
Riddles, in Javanese music, 328
Riddle songs, 368, 370
Ring-shout, 349
Riqq, 476, **477**
Rituals and ritual music
    Agbekor, 95–96
    Enemyway ceremony (Navajo), 56–59
    Mountainway ceremony (Navajo), 59–62
    of Native American Church, 74–76
    "Nhemamusasa" (Shona), 131

    Nightway (Navajo), 45–48
    performance contexts, 21–22
    religion and, 536–537
    Shootingway (Navajo), 61–62
    wawa velorio, 453–459
Ritual specialists, 489
Rockabilly, 27
Rock 'n Roll music
    British rock 'n roll, 191
    in China, 411
    Indonesian, 350–352
    influence of blues on, 191
Rodgers, Jimmy, 190
Roessel, Ruth, 76
Rolling Stones, 191
Roman Catholicism, 209, 211, 213, 422–423, 457–458
Romantic philosophy, 214
Romero, Raúl, 452, 466
Rondador (panpipe), 443
Roots music, 202–203
"Rosie" (American worksong), 161–164
Ross, Diana, 191
Roy, Don, 555
Ruan (lute), 376
Rubato, 237
Ruchenitsa, **220,** 222–223, 256
Rudiana, Adhe, 349
Rupaka tala **(Indian), 286**
Ruphay, 424
Rush, Otis, 199–202
Rushdie, Salman, 272
Rushing, Jimmy, 191

Sa, 224
Saba, Basam, 476, 482
Sachs, Curt, 35
Sachs, Nahoma, 4
Sahra, 517
Sainte-Marie, Buffy, 77
Salima, 119
Salinas, Horacio, 421
Saljive pjesme (joking songs), 260
Salsa, 415
Sanjuánes (Ecuador), 421, **433**–443, 453–456, 457
Santa Cruz, Nicomedes, 466
Santa Cruz, Victoria, 466
Santelli, Robert, 202
Sanxian, 390
Sarajevo, 259
"Sarasiruha" (kriti), 291–294
Saron demung, 305
Sarons, 304, **305,** 307, 309, 338
Sastrapustaka, Pak, 312
Sastry, Syama, 278
Sataro, **115**
Sauta tuning, 114
Sawa, George, 492

Scale systems, 10–12, 229, 420. *See also* Modes
  of *Agbekor,* 104
  in Balinese music, 338–339
  of blues music, 176–177
  of Ecuadorian music, 434–436
  for *Imbabura* harp, 434–436
  in Javanese music, 11, 303
  keeravani raga scale, 279
  major scale, 11, **224**
  maqam, 480
  mbira, 130
  melakarta, 284–285
  minor scale, 224
  and mode compared, 386
  pélog scale, 11
  Postal workers' melody, 88
  sléndro scale, 11
  solfege (do-re-mi) scale, 10–12
Schaedel, Richard P., 470
Schafer, R. Murray, 1
Schimmelpenninck, Antoinet, 370
"Scholar Qian: Yanda Looks in the Mirror" (Chinese), 390–391
Seeger, Charles, 165
Sephardim, 503
Sergio (harpist), 453, 457
Sermons, 152–155
Sesquialtera, **419,** 470
"Seven-Inch Lotus" (China), 380–383
Shabbezi, Shalom, 530
Shadow puppetry
  gamelan music and, 309–311, 334–338
  Javanese, 322–323, 328, 332–338
  wayang kulit, 302, 309–311
Shaheen, Simon, 475, 482
Shaheen, William, 475
Sha'ir, 517
Shamma, Naseer, 499
Shan'ge (Chinese folk songs), **369**–373
Shankar, L., 295
Shankar, Ravi, 272, 296
Shankar, Uday, 296
Sharecropping, 170, 185
Sheng (mouth organ), 376
Sheridan, Art, 172, 178
Shines, Johnny, 193–196
Shizhané'é Navajo Circle song, 54–55
Shona people, 123–124
"Shufflendang-Shufflending," 349
Shurman, Dick, 197
Singapore, 355
Sinou, Jamal, 476
Sioux Grass Dance, 33–39
Sirat Bani Hilal, 516–517
"Sister, Hold Your Chastity" (Bosnia and Herzegovina), 9, 227, 228
Sitar, **296**
Siter, **306,** 307

Sithole, Jonah, 132
Sivan, Papanasan, 279
Siyem, **304,** 307
Sizhu music, 13, 376–379
Skaini, 233, 237
Skalni, 249
Skip song (Navajo), 75
Slamet, Pak, 333
Slavery, 112, 148, 156–164
Sléndro scale, **11**
Slenthem, 304, **305,** 307
Slides, **477**
Slokam, **289**
Smith, Bessie, 145, 171, 190
Smith, Martin, 297
Smithsonian Institution's Center for Folklife and Heritage, 550
Social organization
  African-American music, 149
  blues, social status and, 185–188
  community, in music-culture model, 16–17
  of Mande people, 112–113
  music-culture and, 24–26
Sockalexis, Nathan, Chris, and Robin, 544
Soedarsono, R. M., 312
Software, 25
Solfege (do-re-mi) scale, 10–12, 224
Sollukattu, 9, **287**
Son (Cuba), 421
"Song of Happiness" (China), 377–378
Songs and singing. *See also* Melody and melodies
  in *Agbekor,* 102–106
  with *gamelan,* 327–330
  Javanese, 327–330
  yeibichai (Navajo), 45–48
  Zuni lullaby, 39–41
Soul music, **192**
Soul of Black Peru, 466
Sounds, as music, 4–8
Soundscape, 1–2, 2
Space, in music-culture model, 14, 17
Spike harp, **113**
Srimpi (Javanese), **309**–310
Sri Wandowo, 331
Sruti (drone), **283**–284
St. Mark's Baptist Church, Minneapolis, 154
Steelbands, 24, 538
Steiner, Max, 475
Stovepipe, Daddy, 171
Strophic songs, **368**
Structure, of music. *See* Form, of music
Style, **26**
Styrczula-Maßniak family, 240
Subbiah, Aruna, 278
Subcultures, of music-culture, 23
Subhani, Kaleeshabi Mahaboob, 290
Subramanyam, L., 295
Sudan, 110–111

Suhardi, 322
Sukarno Putra, Guruh, 348
Sukay (ensemble), 448
Sula, **112**
Suling, 304, **306,** 307, 338
Sumatran music, 341–344
Sun Dance (Plains Indians), 72
Sundanese music, 347–349
Sundarajan, Krishnaveni, 278
Suona, 382
Supremes, Diana Ross and, 191
Suso, Kekuta, 110, 115
Suzhou Tanci, 390–392
Svara, **281**
Sway song (Navajo), 56–57
Sweet Adelines (group), 535
Sykes, Roosevelt, 193
Syncretism, 251
Synthesis, 251–252
Szymanowski, Karol, 247

Tadeo, Milton, 443, 444, 470
Taiwan, 355, 403–404, 409
Tajwid, **490**
Takht ensemble, **475**–483
　　form, melody, and improvisation, 478–482
　　musical texture, 476–477
　　performers and instruments of, 475–476
　　rhythm, 477–478
　　tarab, 482–483
Taki -Ñan (ensemble), 452
Tala (time-cycle), in Indian music, 280, **286,** 287–288
Tale of the Western Chamber, The (Chinese), 393
Taliya, 110–123
Tambura, 282
Tanam, 291, **293**
Tanci, 390–393
Tango, 24
Taoism, 353
Taqasim music, 16, **478,** 523–526
Tarab, 482–483
Tasat, Ramon, 504
Tassa-beat soca, 296
Tatarovic, Emsija, 227
Tatra Mountains (Poland), 205, 208. *See also* Podhale (Poland)
Teaching. *See* Transmission, of music-culture
Technology, and global music exchange, 251
Tempo, 98–101
Tenzer, Michael, 339
Texts, 27
　　"Abenamar," 504–505
　　of Agbekor, 98, 102–103
　　"Ain't Enough Comin' In" (Rush), 200–201
　　"Amazing Grace" (hymn), 147–150
　　"Amor imposible" *(wayno),* 450–451
　　"Begadang II" (Indonesian), 346

Call of the Yei (Navajo), 48
Call to Prayer, 486
"Clinging to a Saving Hand" (Navajo), 75
of Dagbamba music, 120
"Devi Niye Tunai" (Sivan), 279–280
"Distorsi," 350–352
"Dog Me Around" (Blues, by Howlin' Wolf), 187
Enemyway Dance song (Navajo), 57
Enemyway Gift song (Navajo), 58
"Engal Kalyanam" (Indian), 274–275
field holler, 158–159
"From Dark Till Dawn" (Shines), 195
Grass Dance (Sioux), 37
"Ilumán tiyu" *(sanjuán,* Ecuador), 437
"Kokomo Blues" (McDowell), 188, 189–190
"Krzesany Po Dwa," 253
"Lambango" (Mande), 116–117
"Lamma Ya Albi," 528
"La plegaria a un labrador" (Chilean), 423
"Los Angeles Sweetheart" (Navajo, by Begay), 76–77
"Makala" (BaAka), 140–141
"Michael, Row the Boat Ashore," 159–160
"Mother Earth" (Navajo, by Burch), 78
Navajo prayer, 60
"Nhemamusasa" (Shona), 131
"Nyarai" ("Be Ashamed," Chimurenga), 133–134
"Ozwodna," 236–237
"Pasterska," 233
Peyote song (Navajo), 70
"Poor Boy Blues" (Lucas), 167, 176
"Praise from Heaven and Earth," 407
prayer, chanted, 151–155
"Proud Earth" (Navajo, by Williams), 79
"¿Que dirá el Santo Padre?" (Chilean), 422
"Rosie" (American worksong), 161–164
"Sarasiruha" (kriti), 293–294
sermon, chanted, 152–153
"She Got Me Walkin'" (Lucas), 179–180
Shizhané'é Navajo Circle song, 54–55
Shootingway (Navajo), 61
"Sister, Hold Your Chastity," 228
Sway song (Navajo), 57
"The Long Walk" (Navajo, by Roessel), 76
"Žuta Baba," 261
"Wierchowa," 234
"Wilujeng" (Javanese), 328
Yeibichai (Navajo), 46–47
Zuni lullaby, 39
Texture, 12
　　of Indian music, 282–284
　　of "Makala" (BaAka), 137–138
　　Postal workers' melody, 88
Third Wife Teaches Her Son, 384–388
Thoreau, Henry David, 1, 2
"Three Variations on Yang Pass" (China), 394–395, 396
Timbre, 10
　　of African-American music, 149
　　of "Makala" (BaAka), 138

Time, in music-culture model, 14, 17
Time-feel. *See* Meter
Tin Pan Alley, 408, 474–475
Titon, Jeff Todd, 549
"Tomorrow Never Knows" (Beatles), 297
Tonality, Postal workers' melody, 88
Tone languages, 356
Toqui Amaru, 452
Torah, 490
Toro barroso (albazo), 459
"Toro Barroso" (Ecuador), 464
Totodzi, of Agbekor, 96, 100, **101**
Trago, 455
Training. *See* Transmission, of music-culture
Transmission, of music-culture, 27–28, 60
    African music and culture, 87
    of Agbekor, 93–94
    by jalolu, 112–113
    of Lunsi drumming, 121–123
    of Navajo music, 65–68
Transnational migrants, 448
Trawick, Rev. George, 153
Trebunia-Tutka, Krzysztof, 240, 246–250, 262
Trebunia-Tutka family, 240, 246–250, 252, 255
Tremolo, 199, 477
Trills, 477
Triple meter, 216, 218
Trzy a ros, 243
Tsihuahjinne, Andy, 56
Tsoisdia, Lena, 75
Tucker, Sophie, 190
Tuning
    of *gamelan* instruments, 308
    of Imbabura harp, 434
    of *zampoña,* 429–430
Tupan, 220
Turkish region, 484
Turnbull, Colin, 135, 139, 142
Turner, Joe, 191
Turns, 477
Twelve Girls Band, 413, 414
Twinkle Brothers, 249, 252, 255
Twinkle Inna Polish Stylee: Higher Heights, 255
Tyagaraja, 278–279

'Ud, 492, **495**
"Udan Mas" (Javanese), 321–322
'Ud (lute), 475, 477
Umoljani, Bosnia, 259
University of Ghana, 2, 7
Upanishads of Hinduism, 268
Urban blues, 191
Utami, Trie, 347, 349

"Vacación" (Quichua), 454–456
Vamp, 482
Varnam (etude), 289

Vasudevan, Shobha, 279
Vaughn, Stevie Ray, 192, 201
Veblen, Thorstein, 375
Vedas, of Hinduism, **268**
Veena, **290,** 291
Velorio del angelito, 457
Venezuela and Venezuelan music, 421, 458
Vidal, Francy, 448–449, 471
Vienna Symphony, 24
Viento, 452
Villa Lobos, Juan, 463
Villa Paredes, Segundo, 462
Villoteau, M., 500
Violins, in Indian music, 283
Viswanathan, T., 9
Vocables, 33, 46, 127
Vocal ornamentation, 212
Voces, 452
Volume, 10
Vulolo, **95**
Vutsotsoe, 95

Wagner, Richard, 208
Wakes, 21, 422. *See also* Funerals
    Agbekor in, 95
    wawa velorio, 453–459
Walden (Thoreau), 2
Walker, Aaron *T-Bone,* 172, 191, 193, 202
Waltz, 216
Wang Tingting, 396, 397
Wang Wei, 393
Wankara, 426
Warrior's Stomp Dance Song, 41
Warshawsky, Mark, 225
War songs and dances
    Agbekor, 92, 102–103
    Enemyway (Navajo), 56–59
    Kpegisu, 95
    Nhemamusasa (Shona), 131
Water drum (Navajo), 70–73
Watts, Isaac, 262
Wawa velorio, 453–459, 471
Wayang kulit, 302, 309–311
Wayang orang, 299, 331, 332
Wayno, 421, 449, **450–451**
Weddings
    in Hinduism, 274–276
    Levant, 514–515
    music, 205–209
    Polish processions, 205–207
    Zaffah processions, 512–513
"Weeding Song" (China), 370, 371
"Weidao" ("Scent"), 411
Western music, influence of
    on Indian music, 295–298
    on Indonesian music, 347–349
"What'd I Say" (Charles), 191

Wheatstraw, Peetie, 171
White, Booker, 177, 193
"Wierchowa," **234**–235, 237
Williams, Arliene Nofchissey, 77, 79
Williams, Big Joe, 171, 193
Williams, Joseph *Jo Jo,* 173
Williams, Robert Pete, 177
Williamson, James "Homesick," 172, 178, 179
Williamson, John Lee *Sonny Boy,* 171, 172, 196
Wilujeng (Javanese), 322, 324–327
Winter, Johnny, 11, 191
Wirya, Pak, 333
Wombie, Lun-Naa, 121
Women. *See also* Gender roles
   in Agbekor, 95
   Chinese gender relations, 413
   communal music in Morocco, 510–512
   in Grass Dance (Sioux), 38–39
   in kora music, 115
   in Navajo music and culture, 56–57, 63
   in traditionally male music genres, 535
Wong, Faye, 409
Worksong, 7, 22, 84–85, **156**–164
Worldbeat, 252, 255, 260, 529–530
World music, 252
Worship, music of, 145–156
Wrazen, Louise, 251

Xiao, 377
Xibei feng, 409
Yaji, 395

Yangqin, 376
Yan Hua, 409
Yazzie, Cindy, 76
Yazzie Girl (Yazzie), 77
Yeibichai songs, 10, 45–48

Yellow Earth (film), 372
Yin and yang, 19
Ying Shangneng, 399
Yodeling, 127
Yómbé, 138
Yoruba culture, 26
Young, Johnny, 172
Yueji, 375
Yue shu, 399
Yunakov, Yuri, 256–259, 262
Yung, Bell, 397
Yupanqui, Atahualpa, 420, 424

Zabe i Babe, 260
Zaffah wedding procession, **512**–513, 514
Zagareet, 514
Zajal, 503
Zampoña, 424, 427–429, **429**–430, 449
Zapana, Héctor, 452
Zawinul, Joe, 347
Zen Buddhism. *See* Buddhism
Ze stary, 244, 245
Zhang Jianting, 390–392
Zhao Yue, 372–373
Zheng, 377
Zhou Xuan, 408–409, 411
Zielona, 239, 244, 245
"Zielona," 239
Zimbabwe, 133
Zithers, 377
   celempung (Javanese), 304–305, 305, 307
   qin (*guqin*) solos, 393–399
Zlóbcoki, 247, 248
Zulfiqar, Elfik, 349
Zuni lullaby, 39–41
"Zuta Baba," 260, 261
"Zywot Janicka Zbójnika," 249